# INDIANA SOURCE BOOK

## Material from
## THE HOOSIER GENEALOGIST, 1989—1990

### Volume Seven
### with index

### Compiled by
### Ruth Dorrel

© Indiana Historical Society
Indianapolis
1994

**Library of Congress Cataloging-in-Publication Data**
(Revised for volume 7)

Indiana source book.

Vol. 5 compiled by Rebah Fraustein; v. 6 — compiled by Ruth Dorrel.
Vols. 2-3: Published by Family History Section, Indiana Historical Society;
v. 5 — published by Indiana Historical Society.
Include indexes.
Contents: v. 1. Genealogical material from the Hoosier genealogist,
1961-1966 — v. 2. Genealogical material from the Hoosier genealogist,
1967-1972 — [etc.] — v. 7. Material from the Hoosier genealogist, 1989-1990.
1. Registers of births, etc. — Indiana. 2. Indiana — Genealogy. I. Heiss,
Willard C. II. Fraustein, Rebah Morgan. III. Dorrel, Ruth. IV. Indiana Historical Society. Family History Section. VI. Hoosier genealogist.
F525.I55                    929'.3772                    82-109870

The paper used in this publication meets the minimum requirements of
American National Standard for Information Sciences — Permanence of Paper
for Printed Library Materials, ANSI Z39.48-1984.

ISBN 0-87195-108-8

## PREFACE

In 1989 *The Hoosier Genealogist* changed in format and size. During the first twenty-eight years, the pages were 8½″ × 11″, the number of pages varied from four to twenty. The information in these twenty-eight volumes of *The Hoosier Genealogist* was printed in the first six volumes of *Indiana Source Books*. In 1989, the number of pages included in the magazine was increased; therefore *Source Book VII* includes material from only two years of the magazine.

Not included in this volume are queries, meeting announcements, book reviews, and lists of added ancestors of the Society of Indiana Pioneers. The latter will be published in book form in the future.

The encouragement of the entire staff of the Publications Division is acknowledged. Kathy Breen, George Hanlin, and Shirley McCord were actively involved in the production of this volume. Connie McBirney of the Education Division helped prepare the index.

# CONTENTS

# THE FORT WAYNE NORMAL SCHOOL YEARBOOKS
Compiled by Ruth Dorrel

In 1867 the Fort Wayne Normal School began training teachers for the Fort Wayne, Indiana Public Schools. During its early years the school occupied the first floor of the Fort Wayne High School. The school was suspended in 1886, was begun again in 1894, and reestablished in 1897 to continue until 1922. The first yearbook of the school was published in 1917; the second and last yearbook in 1922. Copies of these yearbooks were discovered at a garage sale recently and loaned to *The Hoosier Genealogist*. Photocopies of the entire yearbooks are available at the Allen County Public Library and the Indiana Division, Indiana State Library. Of special interest to family historians in the 1917 yearbook is the list of graduates, by year, with married names and current addresses. This list is reproduced below. It is assumed that a "d." following a name indicates the person is deceased.

## GRADUATES OF FORT WAYNE TRAINING SCHOOL
### Class of 1868.

| | | |
|---|---|---|
| Armstrong, Harriet M.[1] | | |
| Crumley, Amanda S., d. | Mrs. Chas. Blaisdell | |
| Jones, Martha A. | Mrs. Jay Moderwell | City |
| Jones, Helen M. | Mrs. Helen M. Soule | Crestline, O. |
| Knapp, Abba M., d. | | |
| Sharp, Abbie J. | Mrs. Frank Morton | San Francisco |
| Schaeffer, Susan E. | | |
| Wilson, Sarah H., d. | ----[2] | Chicago, Ill. |
| Stevens, Mary E., d. | Mrs. Edgar[3] | |

### Class of 1869.

| | | |
|---|---|---|
| Cochrane, Margaret S. | | City |
| Lynn, Adelia | Mrs. S.C. Lumbard | City |
| Mahurin, Malvina R. | Mrs. W.H. McQuiston[4] | Auburn, Ind. |
| Pierce, Robina L. | Mrs. Robina Orvis | City |
| Snively, Jennie, d. | ----[5] | |
| Smith, Sarah E.[1] | Mrs. P.D.[6] Smyser | City |
| Tower, Margaret A. | | City |

### Class of 1870.

| | | |
|---|---|---|
| Butler, Louisa[7] J., d. | | |
| Drake, Leonora[8] I.[1] | Mrs. Roger Butterfield | Grand Rapids, Mich. |
| Dykes, Agnes, d. | | |
| Eckels, Emma E., d. | | |
| Hamilton, Frank[1] | | Atlantic City |
| Metheany, Clara A. | | Lima, Ohio |
| Sinclair, Orlinda S., d. | | |
| Strong, Josephine | | City |

## Class of 1871.

| | | |
|---|---|---|
| Clark, Frances S., d. | Mrs. James Humphrey | |
| Embry, Ella N. | Mrs. Ella Wilding | City |
| Evans, Elizabeth M. | | California |
| Gay, Bessie | | |
| Imrie, Elizabeth I. | | |
| Jones, Mary E., d. | | |
| McLain, Zerniah[9] E., d. | | |
| O'Connor, Agnes J.[1] | Mrs. Chas. Taylor | South Bend, Ind. |
| Phelps, Clara, d. | | |
| Pierce, Alise[10] S., d. | Mrs. Henry Orbison | |
| Rupert, Emma | Mrs. Wallace Dawson | Los Angeles, Calif. |
| Spore, Belle, d. | | |

## Class of 1872.

| | | |
|---|---|---|
| Bennett, Rosa[1] | | |
| Hassler, Fannie S. | Mrs. James Turner | City[11] |
| Hassler, Fannie S. | Mrs. James Humphrey | |
| Humphrey, Mary A., d. | | |
| McPhail,[12] Margaret M. | Prin. Bloomingdale School | City |
| Remmel, Ada E. | Mrs. G.E. Benson | Fort Leyden, N.Y. |
| Requa, Florence, d. | Mrs. King | |
| Robertson, Deborah | Mrs. MacMacken | Florida |
| Soloman, Carrie | Mrs. John Ross | Leavenworth, Kas. |

## Class of 1873.

| | | |
|---|---|---|
| O'Connor, Cornelia F. | Mrs. John Orff | City |
| Payne, Anna M.[1] | | |
| Rowan, Mary E. | Mrs. J.B. Harper | City |
| Sinclair, Susan S., d. | Mrs. W.A. Bohn | |
| Wood, Jennie | Mrs. F.T. Benoy | City[13] |

## Class of 1874.

| | | |
|---|---|---|
| Abel, Mary A. | Prin S. Wayne School | City |
| Davis, Annie M. | Mrs. Chas. W. Bixby | Wilkes-Barre, Pa. |
| Embry, Virginia N., d.[14] | Mrs. A. Warriner | |
| Hewes, Margaret A.,[15] d. | Mrs. John Pieper | |
| Kauffman, Matilda L.[1] | Mrs. Wm. Hartseiff[16] | |
| Howey, Susan | Mrs. C.W. Squires | Emporia, Kas. |

## Class of 1875.

| | | |
|---|---|---|
| Fairbank, Ellen A. | | |
| Harrison, Edith, d. | Mrs. D. Worthington | City |
| McKeag, Ellen | Teacher | City |
| Orff, Mary Ella | Teacher | City |
| Kinnaird, Annie A., d. | Mrs. M.A. Tower | |

2

| | | |
|---|---|---|
| Mathers, Caroline | | |
| Nones, Celestine | Mrs. C.N. Biewand | City |
| Hall, Lida | | |

## Class of 1876.

| | | |
|---|---|---|
| Bowen, Clara A., d. | | |
| Cannan, Agnes, d. | | |
| Leonard, Hattie M. | Mrs. W.W. Wright | Fort Dodge, Ia. |
| Lewis, Marietta M. | | |
| Markey, Flora A., d. | Mrs. Jesse Kunse | |
| McKean, Sarah E.[1] | Mrs. J.J. Insley | Crawfordsville, Ind. |
| Schell, Mary M. | Mrs. Mary Henderson | City |
| Stanley, Emma | Teacher | City |

## Class of 1877.

| | | |
|---|---|---|
| Armstrong, Emma[17] | Prin. Washington School | City[18] |
| Beals, Ida D. | Mrs. Bush | Calif. |
| Bowman, Jane E. | Teacher | City |
| Carll, Sarah, d. | | |
| Conklin, Caroline E. | Mrs. J. Marsh | Toledo, Ohio |
| McDonald, M.E. Belle | Mrs. Holiday | Cleveland, Ohio |
| Schlatter, Caroline | Mrs. Longacre | Lindsey,[19] Calif. |
| Woolsey, Martha | Mrs. Frank Poole | City |

## Class of 1878.

| | | |
|---|---|---|
| Babcock, Ellen M. | Mrs. Lapp | ----[20] |
| Burkholder, Zilla M., d. | | ----[21] |
| Freeman, Catherine | Mrs. Harvey McCracken | Louisville, Ky. |
| Humphrey, Jessie L., d. | | |
| Myersen, Esther | Mrs. Getz | St. Louis, Mo. |
| Newell, Agnes[22] | Mrs. J.E.K. France | City |
| Schlatter, Emmeline | Mrs. John Payne[23] | City |
| Wade, Margaret A., d. | | City |
| Adams, Ida E. | | City[18] |
| Brenton, Marion[24] H. | Teacher | ----[43] |
| Cochrane, Agnes J. | | City |
| Freeman, Mary E. | | Louisville, Ky. |
| Harter, Mary C., d. | Mrs. Mary Winch | |
| Housh, Frank M. | | |
| Mellinger, Lizzie | Mrs. Myron Aken | Fort Collins, Colo. |
| Potter, Mary E., d. | Mrs. Cook | |

## Class of 1879.

| | | |
|---|---|---|
| Hedges, Sarah L., d. | Mrs. Miller | |
| Nill, Lillie D., d. | | |
| Orff, Julia E., d. | | |
| Orr, Flora E. | Mrs. Chas. Bash | City |

| | | |
|---|---|---|
| Reitze, Augusta G., d. | | |
| Wolfort, Martha E. | Prin. Franklin School[25] | City |
| Henseil, L. Adelia, d. | | |
| Irwin, Mary E. | | Lafayette, Ind. |
| McNair, Cassie | Mrs. Geo. Clark | City |
| Rowe, Clara, d. | | |
| Snider, Mary Alma | Mrs. Jas. Smith | Pasidena,[26] Cal. |
| Straugh, Jesse[27] L. | | City |

### Class of 1880.

| | | |
|---|---|---|
| Conklin, Frances L., d. | | |
| Dick, Mary Emma[1] | Teacher | City |
| Gould, Lucy Candace | Mrs. Thos. Pickard | Lagrange, Ind.[28] |
| Larrabee, Mary Emma, d. | Teacher[29] | City |
| McFee, Elizabeth J.[1] | Mrs. James McKay | City |
| Sutermeister, Louise M. | Mrs. Delap | Kansas City, Mo. |
| Williams, Addie Helene | Teacher | City |
| Stophlet, Agnes Hannah | Mrs. Agnes Ogden | City[18] |

### Class of 1881.

| | | |
|---|---|---|
| Barnett, Nancy K.[22] | Mrs. W.B. Beamer | Los Angeles, Cal. |
| Boyd, Georgiana[30] | Mrs. W.E. Lipsett | City |
| Diggins, Cora A. | Mrs. M.S. Mahurin | City |
| Fronefield, Edith E.[1] | | City |
| Hormsher, Minnie F. | | Denver, Colo. |
| Jacobson, Addie | Mrs. Max Fisher | City |
| Ross, Adellia[31] V. | Mrs. Wolcott | Rome City, Ind. |
| Wiley, Lulu J., d. | Mrs. Andrew Wallace | |

### Class of 1882.

| | | |
|---|---|---|
| Collins, Elizabeth | ----[32] | ----[33] |
| French, Lillian D.[1] | Mrs. L.F. Stouder, Teacher | City |
| Goshorn, Laura | Mrs. A.J. Detzer | City |
| Habecker, Alice M.[1] | Principal Hanna School | City |
| Hamilton, Emma L. | | Brooklyn, N.Y. |
| Holman, Martha B. | Mrs. E.L. White | Atlantic City |
| Orr, Kate C. | Mrs. A.L. Johns | City |
| Sidle, Gracie[34] E. | Mrs. W.D. Miner | City |
| Wells, Harriet M. | | City |

### Class of 1883.

| | | |
|---|---|---|
| Abel, Jennie M. | Mrs. D.H. Caldwell | City |
| Brewster, Edith M. | Mrs. Jno. McKean | City[35] |
| Chaplin, Alice B. | Mrs. R.A. Curtis | Fountain City, Ind. |
| Cothrell, Edith M. | Mrs. C.J. Lose | City |
| Dick, Annie B. | Nurse | Boston, Mass. |

4

| McClure, Mary E. | Mrs. Jno. Abercrombie | City |
| Sidle, Minnie A. | Mrs. C.W. Weaver | City |
| Farmon,[36] Mary Alice | Mrs. A.M. Baxter | City |
| Van Alstine, Lettie Anna | Mrs. W.W. Barnett | |

**Class of 1884.**

| Clay, Virginia Adelme | Mrs. H. Wolf | Columbus, Ohio |
| Colerick, Margaret M. | Librarian | City |
| Hemel,[37] Vermilla F. | Mrs. Geo. Carll | Kansas City, Kas. |
| Kinniard, Emma F. | Mrs. F. Olds | Los Angeles, Cal. |
| Lehr, Kittie J., d. | Mrs. Herbert Tigar | ----[38] |
| Newell, Minnie E., d. | Mrs. Chas. Cross | |
| Rank,[39] Louise | Mrs. H. Reichart | Ann Arbor, Mich. |
| Schrader, Carrie B., d. | Mrs. Gesaman | |
| Trenam, Anna M. | Teacher | City |
| Taylor, Nellie | Mrs. J.M. Stouder | City |
| Brown, Jane E.[1] | | |

**Class of 1885.**

| Bowen, Lillie | Mrs. J.B. Wagner | City |
| Bowman, Prudence L. | Mrs. H.W. Clark | Fairport, Iowa |
| Ersig, Edith E. | Mrs. E. Williamson, | |
| | Teacher | City |
| Goshorn, Maggie L. | | City |
| Jones, Harriet, d. | Mrs. McKracken | ----[40] |
| Knight, Matilda E., d. | Mrs. Norton | |
| Lumbard, Effie | Teacher | City |
| Neireiter, Ada A. | Mrs. Wm. Meyers | Chicago, Ill. |
| Ransom, Nellie Philura, d. | Mrs. R. Van Fleet | |
| Rosenthal, Hattie | Mrs. Benj. Brunswick | Chicago, Ill. |
| Ross, Katie A. | Mrs. F.C. Tolan | City |
| Smith, Lucy Caroline, d. | | |

**Class of 1886.**

| Beaber, Lillie B. | School Principal[41] | Tabriz, Persia |
| Boles, Luella C., d. | Mrs. Chas. Tanier | |
| Chapin, Elizabeth E. | Teacher | City |
| Dennison, Georgia L. | Mrs. F. Kimmons | Bowling Green, O. |
| Gaskins, Emma F. | Mrs. Clarence Cook | City |
| Hayden, Grace G. | Mrs. A.L. Randall | City |
| Keegan, Abbie C. | | City |
| Miles, Lydia C. | Mrs. Chas. A. Doswell | City |

**Class of 1898.**

| Akers, Carrie[42] | ----[32] | City |
| Clark, Anna | | ----[43] |

5

| Crosby, Mabel | ----[32] | City |
| Haberkorn, Augusta[44] | Teacher | City |
| Haberkorn, Emma[45] | Teacher | City |
| Haines, Myrtle, d. | | |
| Hauck, Carrie | Mrs. E.V. Emrick | City |
| Hebert, Elizabeth[1] | Mrs. E.J. Jefferies | City |
| Hormel, Augusta | Mrs. T. Kucher | City |
| Lansdown,[46] Agnes | | Yakamo, Wash. |
| Markey, Georgene | | City |
| Sauer, Emma | Teacher | City |
| You, Jennie[47] | | Tonapah, Nev. |
| Wortman, Gertrude[47] | | City |

## Class of 1899.

| Arnold, Minnie[45] | Mrs. Albert Powell | Monessen, Pa.[43] |
| Bledsoe, Bessie E. | ----[32] | Seattle, Wash. |
| Evans, Zella[48] | Mrs. Robert Gillis | Hammond, Ind. |
| Gregg, Zella[49] | Mrs. Geo. Heckman | Los Angeles, Cal. |
| Hatch, Mabel[44] | Teacher | City |
| Huestis, Bertha[50] | | Seattle, Wash. |
| Jones, Anna[51] | Mrs. Fred Sutton | Hoquiam, Wash. |
| Lund, Julia,[51] d. | | |
| Reitze, Helen[45] | Mrs. Ben F. Heaton | City |
| Seaton, Mary[52] | Teacher[53] | City |
| Sinclair, Anna | Teacher | City |
| Tennant, Leah[6] | Mrs. W.E. Stout | Chicago, Ill. |
| Walters, Lora[52] | Teacher | City |
| Webb, A. Marion[54] | Librarian | City |
| Williams, Gladys[23] | Teacher[55] | City |
| Wolf, Louise M. | Supervisor of German[32] | City |

## Class of 1900.

| Cunningham, Margaret | Teacher | City |
| Foster, Sara[56] | Teacher | City |
| Koons, Ida[50] | Teacher | City |
| Ortman, Lillian | Teacher[57] | City |
| Sauer, Martha[58] | Mrs. E. Zucker | Beecher, Ill. |
| Tinkham, ----[34] | | City |
| Warner, May J. | Mrs. Peter Goda | City[59] |
| Wiebke, Bertha | Mrs. Bruce Havens | ----[60] |

## Class of 1902.

| Benoy, Grace[61] | Teacher | City[13] |
| Blystone, Morning | | City |
| Brimmer, Mary | Teacher | City |
| Clemens, Penelope | Mrs. Peter Epple | |

| Eckels, Lola[62] | Teacher | City |
| Fissel, Gertrude | Teacher | City |
| Liggett, Blanche | Teacher | Gary, Ind. |
| Parham, Edna | Mrs. E.L. Feustel | City |

### Class of 1903.

| Buch,[63] Eva Leah, d. | | |
| Burdette, Ada Reifel[64] | Teacher | City |
| Fee, Georgia Lura | Mrs. S.B. Rohrer | Newton, Kas.[43] |
| Fitch, Alice May | Mrs. Judd Overmeyer | St. Louis, Mo. |
| Geake, Susan Lurah | Mrs. S.F.[61] Hirsh | City |
| Higgins, Adah Louisa | Mrs. E.[65] Allfree | Chicago, Ill. |
| Holland, Gertrude O. | Teacher[66] | City |
| Mooney, Jennie[67] J. | Teacher | City |
| Stockbridge, Mary W. | Mrs. Ray Grosjean | City |
| Tennant, Mabelle[68] C. | Mrs. Ray Adams | New York |

### Class of 1904.

| Baker, Marion, d. | Mrs. Orville Rinehart[52] | |
| Biddle, Anna | Mrs. W.W. Scherer | Wash, D.C.[69] |
| Davis, Georgia L. | Mrs. Will Thompson | City |
| DeVilbiss, Laurinda M. | Teacher | City |
| Dochterman, Erma | Teacher | City |
| Eiter, Mae Marguerite | Mrs. Fred Barr | Bluffton, Ind.[70] |
| Foster, Edith Josephine | ----[71] | City |
| Hopkins, Zona | | Washington, D.C. |
| Littlejohn, Agnes T. | Mrs. Frank Bright | City |
| Mohahan, Bernadette | Teacher | City |
| Owen, Clara Eaton | Mrs. Chas. Stop | Midland, Pa.[72] |
| Robinson, Orpha A. | Mrs. Bert Woods | Gill, Colo. |
| Stockbridge, Alathea | Teacher | City |
| Warner, Emma Clara | Teacher | City |
| Warner, Georgia Mae | Mrs. William Brown | City |

### Class of 1905.

| Banning, Florida | Mrs. Chas. Hart | City[18] |
| Brown, Jeanette | Mrs. Robt. Kell | Huntertown, Ind.[43] |
| Callahan, Winifred | Teacher | City[18] |
| Greene, Francisca[45] | Mrs. W.V. Ford[73] | Heightstown, N.J.[38] |
| Hale, Desdamona[61] | Teacher[74] | City |
| Helmer, Estella K.[17] | Mrs. Roger Frisby | Chicago, Ill. |
| Muller, Mary K. | Teacher[75] | City |
| Sauer, Adele P. | Teacher[75] | City |
| Scheumann, Emma | Teacher | City |
| Schmidt, Clara C. | Teacher | City |
| Staub, Helen Burd | Mrs. Hugh Dare | Marion, Ind.[76] |

7

## Class of 1906.

| | | |
|---|---|---|
| Banning, Corinna[77] | Mrs. W.H. Warrington | City |
| Bechtol, Mabel Ethel | Teacher | City |
| Blackburn, Blanche, d. | | |
| Davis, Julia Florence | Mrs. F.W. Woodbridge | Tacoma,[78] Wash. |
| Gaskill, Maud May | Teacher | City |
| Irwin, Grace C. | Teacher[79] | City |
| Saylor, Margaret | Teacher | City[20] |
| Valentine, Minnie Ethel[1] | Mrs. M.W. Bartmass[80] | Wilkensburg, Pa. |
| Zook, Gertrude Amanda | Teacher | City |

## Class of 1907.

| | | |
|---|---|---|
| Foster, Lillian K. | Teacher | City |
| Garrity, Alice Mary | Teacher | City |
| Jackson, Bessie | ---- | ----[81] |
| Kiefer, Emma Emillie | Teacher | City |
| McMillan, Grace M. | Teacher | City |
| Parry, Jessie Tirzah | Teacher[75] | City |
| Zucker, Marie Louise | Teacher | City |

## Class of 1908.

| | | |
|---|---|---|
| Ehrman, Mary[51] | | City |
| Foley, Celia | | City |
| Gallmeier, Anna M. | Mrs. E. Luecke | Cornelius, Ore.[82] |
| Hart, Bertha | Mrs. A.[83] H. Schaaf | City |
| Heyman, Anna | Teacher | City |
| Holland, Mabel K. | Teacher[75] | City |
| Ingham, Helen A. | Mrs. Ernest D. Gray[32] | City |
| Maxwell, Ina | Teacher | City[84] |
| Monahan, Edith | | City[85] |
| Sheridan, Carroll, d. | | |
| Thompson, Millie | Teacher | City |
| Williamson, Vera[17] | ---- | City[86] |

## Class of 1909.

| | | |
|---|---|---|
| Affleck, Vita S. | Teacher | City[87] |
| Buck, Clara | Mrs. Joe O'Mara[88] | City |
| Doty, Mary Carolyn | Mrs. Whiting Alden | Calgary, Can.[89] |
| Havens, Nellie[52] | Teacher | Milwaukee, Wis. |
| Matsch, Emma Maria | Teacher[90] | City |
| Nelson, Esther Pearl | Mrs. H.K. Chambers | City |
| O'Rourke, Elizabeth[17] | Teacher | City |
| Rohyans, Mildred C. | Open Air School[91] | City |
| Shully,[92] Ethel B. | | Milwaukee, Wis. |

## Class of 1910.

| | | |
|---|---|---|
| Blackburn, Helen[45] | Teacher | City |
| Brannan, Grace[45] | Teacher | City |

8

| Ellenwood, Clara | Teacher[93] | City |
|---|---|---|
| Hinton, Verna C. | ----[94] | City |
| Kampe, Frieda[51] | Teacher | City |
| Kennelly, Mary C. | Mrs. Elmer Jockyll | City |
| Ross, Laura E. | Teacher | Jeannette,[95] Pa. |
| Stecker, Edith J. | ----[96] | City |
| Weaver, Helen E. | Teacher[97] | City |
| Weseman, Olga K. | Mrs. Phil Fiess | Rockham, S.D. |
| Becker, Adeline[98] C. | Mrs. R. Ritchie | Indianapolis, Ind. |

### Class of 1911.

| Beman, Catherine[99] | Teacher | City |
|---|---|---|
| Cleary, Julia G.[1] | Teacher | City |
| Glass, Anna M. | Mrs. Hulburt | Colton,[100] Calif. |
| Hartle, Katherine L. | Teacher | City |
| Hugenard, Edna M. | ---- | Terre Haute, Ind.[101] |
| O'Laughlin, Florence M. | Teacher | City |
| Puddy, Lois E. | Teacher[102] | City |
| Stouder, Alice[51] | Mrs. Warren Sweet | City |
| Wilson, Belle[52] | Mrs. R.C. Howder | Belfast, N.Y. |

### Class of 1912.

| Baade, Corinna[17] | Teacher | City |
|---|---|---|
| Bohne, Gertrude[17] | Teacher | City |
| Comparet, Irene | Mrs. Carl Getz | City |
| Miller, Lola C. | Teacher | City |
| McMullen, Marie C. | Teacher | City |
| Noll, Irene M. | Teacher[103] | City |
| Reese, Paula C. | Mrs. Walter Edwards | Chicago, Ill. |
| [Travers, Larene] | ---- | ----[104] |

### Class of 1913.

| Christiansen, Grace[1] | Mrs. Geo. Tuck | City |
|---|---|---|
| Clark, Helen | Teacher | South Bend, Ind. |
| Jacobs, Esther[45] | Teacher | City |
| Josse, Elsie | Mrs. C.J. Chandler | City[105] |
| Lakey, G. | Mrs. B.H. Kaufman | Lawrenceburg, Ind. |
| Miller, Hazel[106] | Teacher | City |
| Shust, Gladys[107] | Teacher | City |
| Sirit, Rachel[17] | Teacher | City |
| Thomas, Alice C. | Teacher | City |

### Class of 1914.

| Axt, Bertha K. | Teacher | City |
|---|---|---|
| Bower, Janet C. | Teacher | City[108] |
| Fortrede,[109] Lorena | Teacher | City |
| Havens, Chloe J. | Teacher | City[110] |

| | | |
|---|---|---|
| Stump, Florence A. | Mrs. M.W. Emrich[111] | City |
| Thompson, Vesta O. | Teacher | City |
| Tower, Bertha | Teacher | City |
| Travers, Josephine E. | Teacher | City |

## Class of 1915.

| | | |
|---|---|---|
| Anderton, Delight G. | Teacher[112] | City |
| Becker, Gladys C.[86] | Teacher | City |
| Behler, Marcella G. | Teacher | City |
| Doyle, Ellen M. | Teacher[Mrs [113]Ben- ninghoff] | City |
| Ehle, Helen A. | Teacher | City |
| Feiertag, Luella M. | Teacher[71] | City |
| Gross, Loraine C. | Teacher[114] | City |
| Gruber, Leonard[115] | Teacher | City |
| Keeran, Edith L.[51] | Teacher | City |
| Kimble, Miriam G. | ----[116] | City[13] |
| Lepper, Irene E. | Teacher[117] | City |
| Lloyd, Jessie | Teacher | City[118] |
| Stolte, Susanna | Teacher | City[119] |
| Mackwitz, Vera C. | Teacher | City |
| Rowe, Bessie W. | Teacher[120] | City |
| Monroe, Marie L. | Mrs. ---- Martin | City[121] |
| Phipps, Esther[122] | Teacher | City |
| Stewart, Zillah M. | Teacher | City |

## Class of 1916.

| | | |
|---|---|---|
| Bates, Mabel C. | Teacher | City |
| Bauer, Blanche | Teacher | City[122] |
| Bauer, Georgia | Teacher | City |
| Blondoit, Clara[48] | Teacher | City |
| Cleary, Bessie V. | Teacher | City |
| Comparet, Irma | Teacher | City |
| Eckhardt, Dorothy | Teacher | City[124] |
| Greider, Hattie | Teacher | City[125] |
| Gross, Gertrude[43] | Teacher | City |
| Honeck, Lydia[126] | Teacher | City |
| Logue, Ruth[44] | Teacher | City |
| McGuire, Marie | Teacher[127] | City |
| Oren, Helen | Teacher | City[128] |
| Tapp, Erna[23] | | City |
| Thompson, Helen | Teacher | City[129] |
| Trisch, Helen | Teacher[130] | City |
| Withers, Vivian[126] | Teacher | City |
| Zent, Mary E. | Teacher | City |
| Zucker, Gertrude | Teacher | City |

## Class of 1917.

| | | |
|---|---|---|
| Bryant, Indra[45] | ----[32] | ----[43] |
| Lakey, Omah | ----[132] | ----[43] |
| Polhamus, Helen J. | ----[32] | ----[43] |
| Rohyans, Helen M. | ----[32] | ----[43] |
| Schultheiss, Ruth E. | ----[32] | ----[43] |
| Stover, Carol[133] | ----[32] | ----[43] |
| Sullivan, Verna[44] | ----[32] | ----[43] |
| Umbach, Hilda[17] | | ----[43] |
| Young, Mary A. | ----[32] | ----[43] |

Apparently the only other yearbook published was in 1922, the last year the school existed. A list of graduates is included, divided into two parts: 1867-1886, and 1897-1922. Following are the changes found in comparing the lists in the two yearbooks.

1. Deceased.
2. Mrs. Edgar.
3. Not Mrs. Edgar.
4. McQueston.
5. Critic Teacher.
6. Middle initial O.
7. Louise.
8. Leonoora.
9. Zeremiah.
10. Alice.
11. Des Moines, Iowa.
12. MacPhail.
13. California.
14. N. Virginia; Not listed as deceased in 1922.
15. Middle initial J.
16. Hartsuff.
17. Middle initial L.
18. Chicago, Illinois.
19. Lindsley.
20. Los Angeles, California.
21. Kansas.
22. Not listed in 1922.
23. Middle initial H.
24. Marian.
25. Mrs. V.C. McFarland.
26. Pasadena.
27. Straughan, Jessie.
28. LaGrange, Illinois.
29. Larrabie; Mrs. B. Lyman.

30. Georgianna.
31. Adelia.
32. Teacher.
33. St. Paul, Minnesota.
34. Grace.
35. Washington, D.C.
36. Tarmon.
37. Hamil.
38. New York City.
39. Rauh.
40. Dallas, Texas.
41. Principal Girls' Presbyterian School.
42. Middle initial I.
43. City.
44. Middle initial A.
45. Middle initial M.
46. Landsdown.
47. Middle initial G.
48. Middle initial K.
49. Stella M.
50. Middle initial S.
51. Middle initial C.
52. Middle initial B.
53. Principal, Hamilton School.
54. Marion A.
55. Principal, Franklin School.
56. Sarah M.
57. Mrs. R.H. McClure.
58. Middle initial J.
59. Pitcairn, Pennsylvania.
60. Harrisburg, Pennsylvania.
61. Middle initial P.
62. Middle name May.
63. Buck.
64. Burdett, Adah R.
65. Edwin.
66. Mrs. L.D. Nordstrum.
67. Jane.
68. Maybelle.
69. Indianapolis, Indiana.
70. Margaret; Celina, Ohio.
71. Musician.
72. Stoup; Norwalk, Ohio.
73. U.W. Word.

74. Assistant Principal, Normal Training School.
75. Normal Training School.
76. Texas.
77. Carina C.
78. Seattle.
79. Mrs. Curtis Coverdale.
80. Mrs. C. Wilkinson.
81. Middle initial E; Teacher; City.
82. Winfield, Kansas.
83. Albert.
84. Middle initial M.; Mrs. L.E. Goble; Columbia City, Indiana.
85. J. Edith; New York City.
86. Mrs. H.P. Williams; Detroit, Michigan.
87. Veta; Pasadena, California.
88. Middle initial C.; O'Meara.
89. Mabel, Oregon.
90. Mrs. William Marvel.
91. Mrs. Frank E. Swift.
92. Scully.
93. Clare; Mrs. Charles F. Hess.
94. Verma; Mrs. Christian Luecke.
95. Art Publication Society; Philadelphia.
96. Mrs. Willis Hite.
97. Mrs. H.F. Zimmerman.
98. Adaline.
99. C. Irene.
100. Hurlburt; Cotton.
101. Huguenard; Sister Edna Marie; Chicago, Illinois.
102. Mrs. Ralph Campbell.
103. Mrs. Fred Pothoff.
104. Middle initial I; Mrs. D.P. McDonald.
105. Middle initial L.; Jackson, Michigan.
106. R. Hazel.
107. Schust; Middle initial A.
108. Oil City, Pennsylvania.
109. Fortriede.
110. Mrs. T.E. Thomas; Muncie, Indiana.
111. Emrick.
112. Mrs. W.B. Rice.
113. Howard.
114. Mrs. Edward Young.
115. Lenore M.
116. Mrs. A.T. Sweetland.
117. Mrs. E.C. Moellering.

118. Mrs. Howard Gooley; Racine, Wisconsin.
119. Susanne; Hawaii.
120. Besse; Mrs. Fred Wagner.
121. Middle initial I; D.E. Martin; Marion, Indiana.
122. Middle initial V.
123. Middle initial M.; Mrs. James Knowlton; Grand Rapids, Michigan.
124. Dorothea; Mrs. L. Meyer; Decatur, Indiana.
125. Middle initial B.; Mrs. E.J. Merton; Akron, Ohio.
126. Middle initial E.
127. Middle initial L.; Mrs. Herbert W. Kocks.
128. Middle initial K.;Mrs. G.B. Prill; Lima, Ohio.
129. Middle initial A.; Columbus, Ohio.
130. Middle initial L.; Mrs. Fremont Herring.
131. Cuyahoga Falls, Ohio.
132. Mrs. Ralph Virts.
133. Carolyn V.

### Graduates 1918-1922.

It is assumed that graduates listed in the alphabetical listing in the 1922 yearbook who were not listed in the 1917 book graduated between 1918 and 1922. They are listed below.

| Beahler, Marie | Teacher | City |
|---|---|---|
| Bill, Naomi A. | Teacher | City |
| Bresnahan, Marie P. | Teacher | City |
| Brown, Bernice M. | Teacher | City |
| Bryson, Helen L. | Teacher | City |
| Cherry, Marion S. | Teacher | City |
| Curtis, Annadale E. | Mrs. Albert Mason | City |
| Daley, Catherine R. | Teacher | City |
| Daseler, Edna M. | Teacher | City |
| Dinklage, Katherine M. | Teacher | City |
| Ferguson, Margaret D. | Teacher | City |
| Gailey, Mildred E. | Teacher | City |
| Gerard, Floris E. | Mrs. Ed Keefer | Andrews, Indiana |
| Glover, Beatrice E. | Teacher | City |
| Goldberger, Rose | Teacher | City |
| Gumpper, Adah K. | Teacher | City |
| Haller, Mary R. | Teacher | City |
| Johnson, Eveleen | Teacher | City |
| Johnson, Irene | Teacher | City |
| Jopp, Ethel M. | Teacher | City |
| Keegan, Helen | Teacher | City |

| | | |
|---|---|---|
| Kell, Carolyn | Teacher | City |
| Kinnaird, Virginia | Teacher | City |
| Kuttner, Helen M. | Teacher | City |
| Logue, Esther I. | Mrs. Willard Enslen | City |
| Lowery, A. Elizabeth | Teacher | City |
| McComb, Lydia B. | Teacher | City |
| McMullen, Marie | Teacher | City |
| McLaughlin, Catherine M. | Teacher | City |
| Miller, Alice E. | Teacher | City |
| Miller, Esther M. | Teacher | City |
| Morris, Wilhelmina S. | Teacher | Roanoke, Virginia |
| Morrison, Lucille M. | Teacher | City |
| O'Connell, Charlotte R. | Teacher | City |
| Oren, Hazel E. | Teacher | City |
| Phipps, Laura E. | Teacher | City |
| Pohlmeyer, Helen L. | Teacher | City |
| Rabus, Alice M. | Mrs. Howard K. Abbott | Reading, Michigan |
| Reehling, Ruth H. | Mrs. Florenz Gumpper | City |
| Roebel, Helen R. | Teacher | City |
| Rogier, Elizabeth L. | Teacher | City |
| Saviers, Dorothy E. | Teacher | City |
| Scott, Margaret A. | Teacher | City |
| Sherbody, Estella | Teacher | City |
| Stolte, Emma M.M. | Teacher | City |
| Ulmer, Unafred | Teacher | City |
| Weaver, Mildred A. Mrs. Edward Haller | | City |
| Welch, Nina E. | Mrs. M.W. Bartness | Wilkensburg, Pa. |
| Zent, Mary E. | Teacher | City |

# DEATHS FROM THE CASS COUNTY TIMES

DIED at the Potawattomie Mills on the 23rd ult. Mrs. Shields, consort of Wm. Shields, aged 33 years. Mrs. Shields was universally respected in life and her death has caused a breach in the little society of which she was a member (being a sister of Mr. J. Lindsey) which can never be repaired.

On the 30th ultimo, at the Potawattomie Mills, in this County, Mrs. Mary Lindsey, consort of John Lindsey, aged 35 years. (March 31, 1832, p. 3)

OBITUARY. Died--On Saturday the 16th inst. between the hours of 9 and 10 A.M. Elizabeth S. infant daughter of Hon. John Tipton, aged 18 months. (June 23, 1832, p. 3)

OBITUARY. DEPARTED This life on the 18th ult. after a lingering illness of several months, MRS. NANCY SMITH of this town, aged 44 years and 4 days, she has long been a professor of religion, and she is no doubt enjoying the fruits of her labours with her redeemer. During the confinement of the deceased, she murmured not at her sufferings, great as they were she was perfectly reconciled to the will of that great Being who so wisely and justly deals out Death to every mortal, that, if it was His will to call her from here below, she was fully willing and prepared to go. The deceased was remarkable for her calm and even temper; her aid in time of need will ever be missed in the circle of those who knew her, she has left several children and numerous friends and acquaintances to lament her untimely exit. (April 4, 1833, p. 2)

OBITUARY. Died in this town on the 4th inst. Caroline infant daughter of Dr. H. Todd, of this place. (May 9, 1833, p. 2)

DIED--On Monday the 27th inst. at Miamisport, after a short illness, WILLIAM MORRIS, eldest son son of Dr. J.T. LISTON, aged 2 years 7 months and 27 days. (May 30, 1833, p. 2)

OBITUARY. Died on the 8th inst. at his residence in this vicinity Henry Murrell. He was an industrious and enterprising citizen. He has left a small family to lament his untimely exit. (September 12, 1833, p. 3)

OBITUARY. Departed this life on the 23rd inst., in the vicinity of this town, at the residence of Judge Edwards, Mrs. Margaret M'Corkle. She died in the 77th year of her age, and has left a great number of friends and relations to mourn her untimely exit. (October 31, 1833, p. 3)

ACCIDENT--Louis Godfroy, a brother of the Chief of the Miami tribe of Indians, was thrown off his horse at the Treaty Ground, on Wednesday evening the 30th ult. and his head coming in contact with a log, which so fractured his scull, as to cause his immediate death. (November 7, 1833, p. 2)

OBITUARY. Died on the 2nd inst. in this place MALINDA infant daughter of Mr. A. Flanigan. (December 5, 1833, p. 3)

# CLARK COUNTY, INDIANA
## ABSTRACTS OF WILLS AND EXECUTORS' RECORDS
### 1801-1817*
Compiled by Dorothy Riker

The following abstracts of wills and executors' records were originally printed in the *Indiana Magazine of History* in 1939 and 1940. In 1969, the Genealogy Section of the Indiana Historical Society reprinted them in combination with Clark County marriage records, 1807-1824. That publication has long been out-of-print. When the Society published in 1979, *Genealogical Sources; Reprinted from The Genealogy Section, Indiana Magazine of History*, also compiled by Miss Riker, these records were not included. Since the membership of the Indiana Historical Society has increased since 1940, and many new and younger members have not had access to previous printings, the Publications Committee of the Family History Section recommended that these records be made available to our current readers.

## WILL BOOK A
### 1801-1817

**FAIT**, Henry. Administrators, Henry, George, and Margaret FAIT, appointed 18 July 1801. Bond, $7000. Securities: Thomas DOWNS, William GOODWIN, Peter STACY. p. 1.

**STOOTSMAN**, Joseph. Administrator, widow Rachel STOOTSMAN, appointed 31 August 1802. Bond, $1200. Securities: Jacob STOOTSMAN, Sr., Samuel STOOTSMAN. p. 3.

**TULEY**, Charles P. Administrator, Captain George WOOD, appointed 29 September 1802, at request of widow, Betsy TULEY. Bond, $1000. Securities: George HUCKLEBERRY, Sr., Peter McDONALD. p. 4.

**MARTIN**, James. Administrator, John McCLINTICK, appointed 25 April 1804. Bond, $800. Securities: Joseph BARTHOLOMEW, James STEWART. Appraisement of personal property and bill of sale, pp. 5, 178-79.

**BRADFORD**, William. Will dated 4 May 1804; probated 8 August 1804. Heirs: wife, Susannah BRADFORD. Executors: Susannah BRADFORD, Davis FLOYD. Witnesses: Job GUEST, William HAWTHORN, Steven HARMON. pp. 6-7.

**STOOTSMAN**, John. Administrator, Daniel STOOTSMAN, appointed December 17, 1804. Bond, $800. Securities: Jacob and David STOOTSMAN. p. 8.

**SMITH**, William. Will dated 31 January 1804; probated 18 February 1805. Heirs: wife, Patsey SMITH, and sons, Peter, John, and James. Executor: Joseph BARTHOLOMEW. Witnesses: Samuel GWATHMEY, William PRATHER, George WOOD, Peter SMITH. pp. 9-10.

**McGUIRE**, William. Will dated 4 October 1805; probated 26 October 1805. Heirs: wife, Elizabeth McGUIRE, and children (not named with the exception of a daughter Martha). Executors: Elizabeth McGUIRE and James N. WOOD. Witnesses: James and Nancy McCOY. pp. 11-13.

**DORSEY**, Bales. Will dated 19 June 1806; probated 2 September 1806. Heirs: children, Thomas, Betsey, Margaret, Richard, Ely, Susanna, Bales, George, Mark. Executors: George WOOD and James DAVIS. Witnesses: John DOUTHITT, John FERGUSON, Hugh KELLEY. pp. 14-15.

**ANDERSON**, James. Inventory and appraisement of personal estate made by John POTTORFF and Nicholas HARMON, 23 December 1806. Filed January 1807. pp. 16-17.

**MOORE**, Robert K. Will dated 20 April 1806; probated July Term, 1807. Heirs: wife, Catharine (PRINCE) MOORE, James SNEED, of Jefferson County, Kentucky [relationship not indicated]. Executors: James SNEED, Cuthbert BULLITT, Thomas PRATHER, of Kentucky. No witnesses given, but will was proved by Thomas T. DAVIS, Worden POPE, Marston G. CLARK, Willis W. GOODWIN, John THOMPSON, Samuel GWATHMEY. pp. 17-18.

**KELLY**, Samuel. Will dated 7 November 1806; probated July Term, 1807. Heirs: brother, John KELLY, in trust for heirs not named. Executor: William McMEAN. Witnesses: William LOCKHARD (or LOCKART), Joseph POUND, James STOUT. p. 19.

**SCOTT**, James, Sr. Died 9 September 1807. Nuncupative will of 4 September 1807; probated October Term, 1807. Heirs: wife, Charlotte. Witnesses: Isaac HOLMAN, Bazil R. PRATHER. p. 20.

**JONES**, George. Will dated 13 August 1806; probated 9 January 1808. Heirs: wife, Jane JONES; stepdaughter, Polly ARCHER; sister, Polly JONES. Executors: Samuel GWATHMEY, Davis FLOYD. Witnesses: Susanne FLOYD, Polly L. FLOYD, Davis FLOYD. Will proved by Davis FLOYD, Robert A. NEW, Gabriel I. JOHNSTON. pp. 21-22.

**WILSON**, James. Will dated 20 March 1806; probated 7 March 1808. Heirs: sons, George and John; daughter, Jane. Executor: Samuel KAUFMAN. Witnesses: Aquilla ROGERS, Andrew SPEARS, Mary KAUFMAN. pp. 23-24.

**ROBERTSON**, James.[1] Will dated 9 December 1780; filed September Term, 1808. Heir: Philip BARBOUR, of Natchez, Tennessee. Executor: Philip BARBOUR. Witnesses: Thomas POLLOCK, John ALLEN, Joseph ROTUNGE (?). Will produced by Philip BARBOUR, Jr., and proved by George Rogers CLARK, Davis FLOYD, James N. WOOD. Protested by John BERRY, William FERGUSON, Jesse TURPIN. pp. 23-32.

**PERDUN**, Margaret. Will dated 27 September 1808; probated 25 October 1808. Heirs: grandchildren, Sarah and Elizabeth RIGHTHOUSE. No executor named. Witnesses: Sarah FOUTS, Abraham VANVEL (?), John VANVEL (?), Mary HACKET. pp. 33-34.

**McKLANE** (or **McCLEAN**), Bernard. Administrator, Josn VAWTER, appointed 1 December 1809. Bond $400. Securities: Willis W. GOODWIN, Robert A. NEW. p. 34. Appraisement of personal property and bill of sale. pp. 44-51.

**COOMBS**, William. Will dated 9 April 1810; codicil added 10 April; probated May Term, 1810. Heirs: wife, Nancy COOMBS; children, John, Jesse, William, Margaret. Executors: Thomas CARR, Nancy COOMBS. Witnesses: James McCOY, William REED, Elisha CARR. Appriasement of personal property and bill of sale. pp. 35-36, 114-19.

**HAY**, John. Will dated 24 October 1810; probated 5 November 1810. Heirs: wife, Nancy HAY; children, Andrew, Anne,[2] Milton, Nancy, Harry, Warefield, Julia, and Campbell. Executors: Nancy HAY, John McCLUNG, James SCOTT. Witnesses: B. WOOD, John T. CHUNN, John DENNY. p. 37.

**GUEST**, Bazel. Will dated 28 December 1810; probated 4 March 1811. Heirs: wife, Rachel GUEST, and daughter Anne. Executor: Rachel GUEST. Witnesses: Richard MOSLEY, Elizabeth CREW. pp. 38-39.

**McCANN**, Moses. Will and codicil dated 4 March 1811; probated 20 March 1811. Heir: son, Thomas. Executor: James N. WOOD. Witnesses: John K. GRAHAM, Joseph STROUD, John CONNER. Appraisement of personal property and bill of sale filed 15 June 1812. pp. 39-41, 57-71.

**BOLDORSON** (?), Andrew. Will dated — November 1811; probated 30 November 1811. Heirs: children, Betsy, Henry, Polly, Sally, John, Fany (or Lang?), Daniel, Thomas, David, Peter, Eve. Executors: John MILLER, Isaac HOLMAN. Witnesses: Peter ETTER, Gaspar POPE. pp. 42-43.

**HUTCHINGS** (or **HUTCHENS**), Joseph. Administrator, son Stephen, appointed 31 March 1812. Bond, not given. Securities: Charles BULLOCK, Davis FLOYD. p. 51. Appraisement of personal property presented 8 June 1812. pp. 64-67.

**MALOTT**, Joseph. Died 25 March 1812. Nuncupative will of that date presented 8 April 1812 by John DAILY and James Davis. Heir: wife [name not given, but probably Catherine as she purchased a number of items of the estate]. Administrator, father-in-law, Philip DAILY. Securities: James DAVIS and Jacob DAILY. Appraisement of personal property and bill of sale returned 18 and 26 April 1812. pp. 52-53, 72-76.

**SHAKE**, George. Appraisement of personal property by Patrick WELCH, Davis FLOYD, Joseph POUND, made 19 April 1811. pp. 54-58.

**BARNABY**, Mathew. Administrator, Robert BARNABY, appointed 14 May 1812. Bond, $400. Securities: John FERGUSON, James McCAMPBELL. pp. 58-59.

**CLENDENON** (or **CLENDENNING**?), Thomas. Administrator, widow Elenor, appointed 13 June 1812. Bond, $300. Securities: James ALEXANDER, Isaac WATKINS. p. 59.

**ROBY**, Townley.   Administrators, widow Rebecca and William ELLIS, appointed 10 July 1812. Bond, $600. Securities: Henry BOTTORFF, Abraham EPLER. p. 62.

**HOLLIS**, Sarah.   Administrator, Willis W. GOODWIN, appointed 22 September 1812. Bond, $500. Securities: John DOUTHITT, James ZENOR. p. 63.

**BLOOM**, Peter.   Appraisement of personal property made 19 October 1808 by John THOMPSON and Robert A. NEW. Bill of sale, 1 November 1808. pp. 77-80.

**DOMONT**, Barbara.   Will dated 6 October 1802; probated 13 June 1812. Heirs: son Jesse and granddaughters, Lane (Jane) and Sarah BOWMAN, daughters of Aaron BOWMAN. Executor: Aaron BOWMAN, son-in-law. pp. 81-82.

**WARD**, Richard.   Administrator, brother, John WARD, appointed 27 March 1813. Bond, $100. Securities: James SWENEY   (or SEVENEY?), David SMITH. p. 83.

**SUMMERS**, James.   Administrator, brother-in-law, John B. PITTMAN, appointed 19 April 1813. Bond, $160. Securities: John GIBSON, George BRATTON. pp. 83-84.

**KELLEY**, Cornelius.   Administrator, Elias KELLEY, appointed 3 May 1813. Bond, $80. Securities: John FERGUSON, James KELLEY. pp. 84-85.

**HUTCHESON**, John.   Administrator, Thomas Hutcheson, appointed 3 May 1813. Bond, $120. Securities: John FERGUSON, William P. MEREDITH. p. 85.

**GIBSON**, Thomas.   Administrator, John GIBSON, appointed 7 May 1813. Bond, $100. Securities: Alexander BUCKNER, William P. MEREDITH. p. 86.

**GOODWIN**, George.   Administrator, William GOODWIN, appointed 7 May 1813. Bond, $300. Securities: John FERGUSON, James CURRY. p. 87.

**FISLER**, William.   Administrator, John FISLER, appointed 11 May 1813. Bond, $200. Securities: John FERGUSON, George ROSS. p. 88.

**WARNOCK**, Joseph.   Administrator, Michael WARNOCK, appointed 17 May 1813. Bond, $200. Securities: James McCAMPBELL, John FERGUSON. pp. 88-89.

**JONES**, Henry.   Administrator, widow May, appointed 20 May 1813. Bond, $250. Securities: Robert BREEZE, Sr., Joseph JOHNSTON. pp. 89-90.

**SIGMAN**, Barnett.   Administrator, John ELDRIDGE, appointed 25 September 1813. Bond, $500. Securities: James SCOTT, John FERGUSON. p. 90.

**McCOY**, William.   Will dated 9 July 1813; probated 7 October 1813. Heirs: wife, Elizabeth; children, James, Isaac,[3] John, Royce, Mrs. Sarah PAYNE, Mrs. Lydia LITTLE (or LITTELL?). Executor: James LEMON. Witnesses: James LEMON, Jesse COOMBS, Royce McCOY. LEMON withdrew as executor on 7 October and the court appointed James McCOY and the widow, Elizabeth McCOY, as administrators. pp. 91-92, 105-08.

**ALEXANDER**, James. Administrators, widow Elizabeth and Samuel STEWART, appointed 20 October 1813. Bond, $500. Securities: James SCOTT, James BIGGER, pp. 92-93. Appraisement of personal property. pp. 150-52.

**COSNER**, John. Administrator, father, Henry COSNER, appointed 25 November 1813. Bond, $200. Securities: John WEATHERS, John FERGUSON. p. 93.

**STEWART**, James. Administrator, Merchant STEWART, appointed 14 February 1814. Bond, $500. Securities: Samuel REYNOLDS, George ROSS. p. 94.

**MOSLEY**, Richard. Administrator, Andrew FAIT, appointed 29 April 1814. Bond, $300. Securities: James LEMON and [name omitted]. p. 95.

**MILLER**, David. Administrators, widow, Elizabeth MILLER and David FANISIN, appointed 5 May 1814. Bond, $500. Securities: David IRWIN, John FERGUSON. p. 96.

**BOWMAN**, John. Administrator, Leonard BOWMAN, appointed 27 May 1814. Bond, $400. Securities: Andrew GELWICK, John FERGUSON. p. 97.

**HARTLEY**, Jonathan. Administrator, William HARTLEY, appointed 4 June 1814. Bond, $100. Securities: Henry HUCKLEBERRY, William N. GRIFFITH. p. 98.

**McCANNON**, James. Administrator, James DRUMMOND, appointed 3 September 1814. Bond, $300. Securities: William FERGUSON, John WORK, Jr. pp. 98-99.

**MARSH**, Elias. Administrators, Samuel and Robert MARSH, appointed 11 October 1814. Bond, $2000. Securities: James ANDERSON, Elkin MARSH. p. 99.

**SAGE**, James. Administrator, Abraham EPLER, appointed 24 October 1814. Bond, $1200. Securities: Charles BEGGS, John FERGUSON. pp. 100-01.

**SUMNER**, William B. Administrator, widow, Ann SUMNER, appointed 1 November 1814. Bond, $1200. Securities: Alexander BUCKNER, James SCOTT. p. 101.

**HUFFMAN**, Peter. Will dated 30 August 1810; probated 1 July 1813. Heirs: wife, Catherine; children, Benjamin, Rachel (Mrs. Henry COLLINS), Isaac, John, Mary, Winifred, Ann, Catherine, Rebecca. Executors: Catherine HUFFMAN, son, Isaac HUFFMAN. Witnesses: Moses COOK, John R. CLARK, Nancy COOK. pp. 101-02.

**DOWDEN**, Thomas. Will dated 13 July 1812; probated 12 October 1812. Heirs: wife, Nancy DOWDEN; son, Zephaniah. Executor: Nancy DOWDEN. Witnesses: James FERGUSON, William DOWDEN, Georme SUMMERS. p. 103.

**PARKS**, Andrew. Will dated 21 July 1812; probated 23 November 1812. Heirs: wife, Margaret PARKS; children, John, Sarah. Executor: Margaret

PARKS. Witnesses: John and Sarah PARKS, John NEWLAND, John W. COFFEY, John SUTTON. pp. 104-05.

**NUGENT**, Willoughby. Will dated 13 January 1812; probated 14 October 1812. Heirs: wife (name not given); children, Elender ADKINS, John Ross, Ignatius, Benedick, Levi Augustus, David; grandchildren, William MAY, Polly NUGENT. Executors: James McCOY, Levi Augustus NUGENT. Witnesses: David CROCE, John MONTGOMERY. pp. 108-09.

**HUCKLEBERRY**, George. Will dated 29 September 1806; probated 9 January 1813. Heirs: wife, Barbara; children, Henry, Jacob, John, Martin, Susanna, George, David, Abraham, Elizabeth. Witnesses: John H. BOLD-WIN, Peter McDONALD, Joseph SHAW. pp. 110-11.

**STEWART**, James. Will dated 4 April 1810; probated 22 March 1813. Heirs: wife [name not given]; children, Stephen, Isaac, Merchant, David, Elizabeth, Rebecca; Sarah FLEEHART (relationship not indicated). Witnesses: William GOODWIN, William AKIN, Amos H. GOODWIN. pp. 112-13.

**STUTSMAN** (or **STOOTSMAN**), Jacob. Will dated 7 August 1810; probated 28 December 1813. Heirs: children, Mary, Jacob, David, Samuel, Daniel; Philip WARMAN and Thomas HUTCHESON (possibly sons-in-law). Executor: son, Daniel. Witnesses: Christian PARKEY, Graham ANDERSON. pp. 113-14.

**PEARCY**, Blake. Administrator, Thomas PILE, appointed 17 January 1815. Bond, $400. Securities: Thomas WEATHERS, William FERGUSON. p. 120.

**FAIT**, George. Administrator, Andrew FAIT, appointed 27 March 1815. Bond, $200. Securities: John LEMON, Henry L. MINOR. pp. 120-21.

**SMITH**, Mary. Administrator, Peter SMITH, appointed 23 May 1815. Bond, $2000. Securities: Alexander BUCKNER, Henry L. MINOR. Inventory of estate made June 1815. pp. 121, 141.

**HERROD**, James. Administrator, mother, Sarah HERROD, appointed 19 July 1815. Bond, $250. Securities: George NEWLAND, William P. MEREDITH. p. 122.

**OWENS**, Hervey. Administrator, John OWENS, appointed 22 July 1815. Bond, $700. Securities: William P. MEREDITH, James McCAMPBELL. pp. 122-23.

**SEVENEY**, Thomas. Administrator, Mordecai SEVENEY, appointed 1 August 1815. Bond, $300. Securities: James McCAMPBELL, David VANCE. p. 123.

**HAWN**, Conrad. Administrator, David SPANGER, appointed 10 August 1815. Bond, $1000. Securities: John DOUTHITT, James McCAMPBELL. Appraisement of personal property and bill of sale. pp. 124, 144-49.

**ROBISON**, William. Administrator, widow, Martha ROBISON, appointed 2 October 1815. Bond, $400. Securities: James SEATON (?), Joseph ROBERTS. p. 125.

**BOWMAN**, Joseph. Will (no date). Administrator, William BOWMAN, appointed 26 February 1816. Bond, $12000. Securities: John DOUTHITT, John WEATHERS. Heirs: brothers and sisters, not named except for sister, THOMPSON; James FISLER; Sally STEED. Negro woman named Delphey to serve his sister for six years and then be liberated. pp. 126, 133-35.

**REED**, William. Will and codocil dated 28 March 1814; probated 4 May 1814. Heirs: wife, Sarah REED; children, names not given except for eldest son, Joseph. Executors: Sarah REED, Joel COOMBS. Witnesses: William HERROD, James FORDYCE, Robert WEIR. pp. 126-28.

**BROWN**, John. Will dated 28 February 1814; probated 8 June 1814. Heirs: wife, Polly BROWN; children, names not given except for son, Samuel. Executors: Isaac LAMB, Polly BROWN. Witnesses: William TEMPLE, Reuben RUCKER. pp. 128-29.

**ROBY**, Leonard. Will dated 8 June 1815; probated 2 August 1815. Heirs: wife, Lucy ROBY; children, names not given except for daughter Betsy and son Henry. Executors: Henry ROBY, John MILLER. Witnesses: Henry BOTTORFF, Abraham EPLER, John KELLEY. pp. 130-31. Appraisement of personal propery and bill of sale. pp. 142-44.

**PILE**, Richard. Administrator, widow, Rebecca PILE, appointed 26 March 1816. Bond, $800. Securities: James LEMON, Samuel MERRIWETHER. pp. 131-32.

**McCANN**, Thomas. Administrator, Jonathan LEWIS, appointed 10 April 1816. Bond, $1000. Securities: Richard ASTON, William P. MEREDITH. pp. 132, 135.

**KELLEY**, Thomas Ferguson. Administrator, John KELLEY, appointed 19 April 1816. Bond, $100. Securities: James LEMON, Samuel PRATHER. p. 133.

**BOWMAN**, Mary. Will dated 6 June 1814; probated 26 March 1816. Heirs: sister, Elizabeth THOMPSON, and on her death to her children, Susan and Samuel. Executor: Samuel GWATHMEY. Witnesses: Roderick GRIFFITH, Basel PRATHER. pp. 136-37.

**PROVINE**, Mary. Will dated 26 August 1815; probated 4 September 1815, in Jefferson County, Indiana. Heirs: children, William, Alexander, Ann HENDERSON, Polly McCLINTICK, Rebekah McCLINTICK; three grandchildren of deceased daughter, Sarah HARRIS. Saddle to negro woman Judy with request that no steps to be taken to bring Judy and her children into bondage. Executors: son, William, John TELFORD. Witnesses: William DUNN, John MAXWELL. Bill of sale. pp. 137-38, 168.

**PROVINE**, William. Will dated 11 October 1816 [1815]; probated 6 November 1815. Heirs: wife, Polly PROVINE; children [names not given]. Executor: Polly PROVINE. Witnesses: William GULICK, Joseph REESE, John TELFORD. Appraisement of personal property and bill of sale, 21 and 23 December 1815. pp. 139-40, 169-75.

**TRUEBLOOD**, Benjamin. Appraisal of personal property made 26 October 1815, by Jonah TRUEBLOOD and Joseph ALLEN. p. 140. [No appointment of administrator found.]

**RENARD**, Francis P.   Died 3 March 1815. Appraisal of personal property and bill of sale, 22 July 1815. pp. 149-52. [No appointment of administrator found.]

**DAUGHERTY**, William.   Administrators, widow, Susannah DAUGHERTY and James MAGILL, appointed 23 May 1816. Bond, $300. pp. 152-53, 155-56.

**ALDRIDGE**, Christopher.   Administrator, Andrew GELWICK, appointed 22 May 1816. Bond, $300. Securities: James LEMON, James PILE. p. 135.

**KEEP** (or **REEP**), Henry.   Administrator, John HAWN, appointed 11 June 1816. Bond $400. Appraisement of personal property and bill of sale, 2 August 1816. pp. 154, 165-67.

**SMITH**, Catharine.   Administrator, Joseph BARTHOLOMEW, appointed 19 July 1816. Securities: Henry L. MINOR, Isaac SHELBY. p. 155.

**ARMSTRONG**, John.   Administrator, widow, Tabitha ARMSTRONG and Henry MORTON, Jr., appointed 2 August 1816. Bond, $1200. Securities: William PLASKET and Andrew P. HAY. Appraisement of personal property made 12 September 1816. pp. 157, 182-88.

**BARNABY**, Mathew.   Administrator, Wallace SULLENDER, appointed 16 August 1816. Bond, $100. Securities: James N. WOOD and Joseph CARR. p. 156.

**RUSSELL**, Burr C.   Will dated 14 June 1816; probated 5 September 1816. Heirs: wife [name not given]; two children, one of whom was named Harrison. Executors: Charles JOHNSON, George RUSSELL. Witnesses: John RUSSEL, Elizabeth RUSSEL. Appraisement of personal property and bill of sale. pp. 159, 179-82.

**DAUGHTERY**, James. Administrator, Andrew GELWICK, appointed 3 September 1816. Bond, $400. Securities: David BLOOM, John WEATHERS. p. 160.

**RICKER**(?), Wentworth.   Administrator, Ebenezer SERLES (SEARLES?), appointed 30 September 1816. Bond, $200. Securities: Jesse HAMILTON, John CHEW. p. 161.

**ABORN**, Henry.   Administrator, widow Abby R. ABORN, appointed 1 October 1816. Bond, $200. Securities: Benjamin SPRALL, John FERGUSON. pp. 162, 175-77.

**SUMMERS**, David.   Administrator, George SUMMERS, appointed 24 October 1816. Bond, $400. Securities: Evan SHELBY, James SCOTT. Appraisement of personal property and bill of sale. pp. 163, 189-93.

**WILSON**, Alexander.   Administrators, John and Thomas WILSON, appointed 4 November 1816. Bond, $20000. Securities: Samuel MERIWETHER, William BOWMAN. p. 164.

**PEARSALL**, Jeremiah. Will dated 3 December 1816; probated 6 January 1817. Heirs: brother, John PEARSALL; stepdaughter, Nancy. Executors: John PEARSAL, Gasper POPE. Witnesses: William ROBERTS, Thomas TAYLOR, Richard ASTON. pp. 193-95.

**HARMON**, Samuel. Administrator, Samuel PACKWOOD, appointed 20 January 1817. Bond, $80. Securities: John McKINLEY, Frederick GORE. p. 195.

**McKINLEY**, William. Administrator John McKINLEY, appointed 20 January 1817. Bond, $300. Securities: Samuel PACKWOOD, Frederick GORE. p. 196.

**HAMILTON**, Archibald. Administrator, William HAMILTON, appointed 21 January 1817. Bond, $25. Securities: John CASS, George BRADFORD. p. 197.

**MUNDEN** (or **MOUDON?**), Elisha. Administrator, widow Nancy MUNDEN, appointed 21 January 1817. Bond, $50. Securities: Joshua W. REDMAN, John REED. p. 197.

**BOYER**, Frederick. Administrator, Christopher BOYER, appointed 21 January 1817. Bond, $200. Securities: John BOYER, Isaac SHELBY. p. 198.

**SUMMERS**, Jesse C. Administrator, Isaac SHELBY, appointed 21 January 1817. Bond, $30. Securities: Joshua W. REDMAN, John CARR. p. 199.

**CARR**, William. Administrator, Isaac SHELBY, appointed 21 January 1817. Bond, $25. Securities: Joshua W. REDMAN, John CARR. p. 199.

**FRAZIER**, John. Administrator, Isaac SHELBY, appointed 22 January 1817. Bond, $14. Securities: John WEATHERS, Alexander BUCKNER. p. 199.

**SMITH**, Stephen (late of Philadelphia). Will [not dated or date given for probation]. Heirs: aunt, Deborah ALDEN; sisters, Min BARCTON (?) and Phebe SPEAKMAN. [no executor and no witnesses] p. 200.

**SEVENEY**, James. Administrator, William FERGUSON, appointed 19 May 1817. Bond, $1000. Securities: George P. MEREDITH, George ROSS. p. 201.

**GRIFFITH**, Roderick. Administrator, Daniel FETTERS (or FETTER), appointed 7 June 1817. Bond, $6000. Securities: John DOUTHITT, Evan SHELBY. p. 202.

**SLOCUM**, Cornelius. Administrator, Zebulon LEAVENWORTH, appointed 22 August 1817. Bond, $400. Securities: Stephen RAMSEY, Christley SWARTS. p. 203.

**PHELPS**, Joseph. Administrator, Zebulon LEAVENWORTH, appointed 22 August 1817. Securities: Stephen RAMSEY, Christley SWARTS. pp. 203-04.

**LOWELL**, Jacob. Administrator, Mrs. Sarah LOWELL, appointed 9 September 1817. Bond, $800. Securities: Enathan (Johnathan?) JENNINGS, James LEMON. p. 205.

**ALLEN**, Samuel.  Administrator, Joshua THOMPSON, appointed 29 September 1817. Bond, $300. Securities: Joseph CARR, Evan SHELBY. p. 206.

*Compiled from microfilm copies of Clark County, Indiana, Will Record A, 1801-1817, made for the Historical Records Survey, Works Progress Administration, in 1936, and deposited in the Archives Division of the Indiana State Library. [Now in the Genealogy Division, Indiana State Library].

1. Robertson had been allotted 2,156 acres of land in Clark's Grant for his services as lieutenant in George Rogers Clark's army. The will was certified in French on 17 June 1782, by Carlos de Grand Pre, commandant of the Spanish Province of New Orleans.  Further proceedings are to be found in Clark County Will Record B, 1817-33, pp. 79-84. The Official Plat of Clark's Grant, made by William Clark, 1789-1810, shows that P. Barbour, Jr. was granted a deed to Robertson's land on 27 November 1809.

2. Anne (or Ann) Hay was married to Jonathan Jennings on 8 August 1811. Clark County Marriage Records, Vol. A, 7.

3. This is the Isaac McCoy who became a missionary to the Indians. The father, William McCoy, had been a pastor of the Silver Creek Baptist Church in Clark County.

# RECORD OF THE 14 MILE CHURCH
Transcribed by Madonna Snyder

William H. McCoy in his pamphlet, *History of the Oldest Baptist Church in Indiana organized at Charlestown, Ind. 1798*, published in 1880, proclaims the 14 Mile Church as the oldest Baptist church in Indiana.  The church, located near Charlestown in what is now Clark County, was organized in 1798 with four members in what was then Knox County, Northwest Territory.  The first meeting was February 16, 1799; the first building was approved in 1804, after the name was changed to Silver Creek church ca. 1803.  Madonna Snyder, a student at IUPUI, has transcribed the first few pages of one of two handwritten volumes located in the Indiana Division of the Indiana State Library.  These volumes were given to the library by William M. McCoy.  Volume 1 covers the years 1798 through 1806.  Volume 2 includes 1807 through 1837.  The pages reproduced here are at the beginning of the records, and are basically an index or abstract of the rest of the book.  The original book, covering 1798 until 1802 has not been found.  Apparently this copy was made in 1802 and continued. Records are reproduced as written.

The 14 Mile Church--Book;
Made Febuary. 1802;
Taken Exactly from the old Book.
With Some Beneficial Additions.
A List of the Members Names:

[Members Constituted]

 1. John Fislar.
 2. Sophia Fislar;
 3. John Pettet;
 4. Cateren Pettet;
 5. James Abbet
 6. Margaret Abbet.
 7. Stephen Shipman; Dismist
 8. Sarah Huff
 9. William Coombs
10. John Dunlap;
11. Jemima Dunlap;
12. Elizabeth Shipman;
13. Mary McCafferty.
14. Margaret Shipman. Dismist
15. Thomas Barry
16. Fanny Needum;
17.     Owens; Dead.
18. Mary Shipman; Dismist.
19. Nancy Carr.   [John]
20. Elisha Carr
21. Nella Stewart   [Lewis]
22. Issabella Harison,   [MC]
23. Sarah Royse,
24. Jean Coovert
25. Sarah Needles, Dismist.
26. James M.Coy,
27. Hesekiah Applegate
28. Rachel Coombs,
29. Lette Harrod;
30. Cateren Newland.
31. William Harrod, Excl.
32. William Coombs, Jun.
33. George Newland; Excl.
34. Hannah Coombs
35. Hannah Barry;
36. James Stewart

37. Nancy M.Coy
38. William Goodwin,
39. David Stuart
40. Thomas Downs.
41. Mary Hucklebery   Dead
42. Sally McDannall'd
43. Mary Goodwin
44. Pricilla Downs
45. James Curry. Exc.
46. Rachel Whorrall
47. Nelly Applegate
48. Rebeckah Stuart   exc
49. Mary Parks
50. John Royse
51. Phillip Hart
52. Margaret Slider
53. Amelia Parks
54. Susana Heart
55. Nicholas Carter
56. Sarah Harris--Dismist
57. Archibald Harris Excluded
    rest. Dismist
58. Gincy M.Coy
59. Gincy Biggs
60. Spencer Collins
61. Cater'n Collins
62. James Stott
63. Phebe Stott
64. Rebeckah Saffers
65. John Peyton
66. Charlotte Peyton
67. Isaac M.Coy
68. Ann Coombs
69. Jesse Tuel
70. Elizabeth McGuire
71. John Saffer

Index

Deacons. The prebetery Came Feb. 14th. Bro Abbet is ordained Bro Fislar Ordained ~~an elder~~ a deacon Bro Harrod ~~Mrs Sman Sist Newland Elders~~ Rec'd by Relation Wm Coombs by Exp.

March the 13th 1802 Bro Petet Desires to be relas'd George Newland Recd. by Relat Elizabeth Soverns Recantation Hanna Barry Recd. by Exp. Meeting house Laid Over 3. Elders Chosen Ferage to be paid A Pastur Chosen Communion Season in June A Code of Orders adopted

April the 12th 1802 Bro Pettet is released from the Office of a Deacon Church Meeting to be held at Bro. Coombs Sen half the time Sister Mc.Cofferty Cited to Next Meeting

May the 8th 1802 Sist. M.Cafferty Cited a 2nd time Bro Carr Chosen Deacon Members apointed to talk to the Members omiting Baptism Concerning the Elements for Communion Sally M.Dannal Recd by Exp

June the 12th 1801 Bro Goodwin Receiv'd by Letter David Stuart by Experience Bro Downs Receiv'd by Letter Mary Huckleberry by Experience Concerning Washing of feet. a Report Made Concerning Baptism Recei'd a Letter from Cinowths Run Another Letter Wrote to bros. Harrison Exc Mary M.Cafferty Secluded Members to be Secluded publickly.

July the 10th 1802 a Collection of one Dollar Receiv'd Sister Goodwin by Letter Receiv'd Pricilla Downs by Expr Receiv'd James Curry by Experience An alteration Made Concerning Excluding of Members & adopted as an order.

August the 7th 1802 a Distress in the Church with Bro Abbet Deposition to be taken the assistance of three Churches to Call'd in the Case of Bro. Abbet. The Association Letter to be Wrote And presented Messengers appointed to Carry it. A Letter Wrote to the sist. Churches approv'd of Collection to be made to print association Minutes

August 12th 1802 A Call Meeting. Bro Abbet Confesses his fault & is forgiven And he is satisfied with the proceding agreed that he preach as formerly, the letters not to be send to Sist Churches

September the 11th 1802. Bro Harrod is Griev'd with Bro abbet & no Reconciliation gain'd A Committee appointed to Settle it The Associaciation Letter approv'd of The Case of Elisa Soverns laid over Collection Referd Concerning a Union 2 Dismist by Letter

Oct. the 9th 1802 The Committee Make Report A Grievance Bro Fislar has got Reconcil'd Distress Laid over Elizabeth Soverns Bro' Abbet Releast from being pastor a Collection

November 13th 1802 Complaint by Bro Abbet Laid in Complaint Laid in by Sister huff & proov'd A Sister Cited to Next Meeting

December the 11th 1802. the Refference atended to The Church is Griev'd wt Sister abbet Complaint by Sister Huff & proov'd Bro abbet is silens'd & secluded

January the 8th 1803 A Committee appointed to Talk to Jas Curry & hesi Applegate for non atendance a petition to be sent for a preacher Jas Abbet Makes a Request Not Granted a Grievenace Laid in fellowship Denied

A Committee appointed to Settle it

Febuary the 12th 1803   The Committe Make Report   Jas Curry Cited to Meeting   Bro Applegate admonished   The Commitee Make Report   Margaret abbet Secluded   a Committe appointed

March the 12th 1803   Brother Curry appear'd & Makes Concession if forgiven Brethren Make Report   two sisters Requested to aten't   Committe appointed to talk to Pettet   Margt Abbet to be Read out by Declaration   about baptism Bro Jas Abbet Declaration

April the 9th 1803   The Committee Make Report   John Pettet to be Cited by Letter   a Transgressor forgiv'n   Rachel Worrall Receiv'd by Experience Meeting slated at Wm Coombs Sen

May the 7th 1803   The Refference is Continued   A Meeting House to be build by superscription

May the 29th 1803   Receiv'd by Experience Nelly Applegate & Rebeckah Stuart

June the 11th 1803   The Refference Continued   A Committee appointed Receiv'd Mary Parks John Royce & Phillip Hart by Experience   a Request sent to 18 Mile Creek Church   a committee appointed.

July the 9th 1803   John Pettet is secluded   two Ministers to atend us alternately a Committees Report   Trustees appointed   A Request Made & Laid over The first Order altered   The 9th Order disanuled   A request sent for a Minister

August the 13th 1803.   Bro Harrods Request not granted   a letter to be wrote to association & Messenger appointed   A Motion Made & fails   a Communion Season to be in November   A Bond to be Drawd

September the 19th 1803.   A Collection made of 50.c.   The Association Letter approvd of   Recei'd Margaret Slider by Experience   a Collection to be made   An answer from plumb creek Church on Sunday   Receiv'd Amelia Parks by Expr

October the 8th 1803   A Collection Made   Susanah heart Receivd by Experience.

November 12th 1803.   a Motion to be not recorded   a request made & referd

December the 10th 1803   Bro. Harrods Request is not Granted

January the 7th 1804   a brother has Transgress't & is Cited,   The ferages 5d. 25c.   the Members subscribe 5d. 62 1/2c.   Bro Carr to see it paid   & to Contract for this Year; Communion season Appointed.

February the 11th 1804   a tresspas forgiven.

March the 10th 1804   No Business Upon Docket

April the 7th 1804   No Business upon Docket

May the 12th 1804   Archibald Harris presented his Letter, but not Receiv'd Motioned that Depositions be taken answered in the Negative.

June the 9th 1804   a grieveance is Laid in to the Church by Hannah Coombs but is setled, With some Difficulty

July the 7th 1804   Messengers appointed to the Association.   three Citation sent

August the 11th 1804. a Committee apointed a Collection made. Nicolas Coster receivd by Letter the association Letter approv'd of

September the 8th 1804 A Committes report an Excuse taken Sarah Harris Receid by Letter A committee Appointed

October the 13th 1804 A Committee report Bro. Curry Cited Archibald Harris receiv'd by Letter a Request made an answer referd

November the 10th 1804 A Brother Excluded a request Laid over

December the 8th 1804 the refference Continued Gincy M.Coy rece'd by Letter the meeting House to be Compleated & a bill of Cost Laid in.

January the 12th 1805. a bill Laid over a member Laid under Censure & Cited to attend

Febuary the 9th 1805 a Bill of Cost recei'd of 2d. 50c A sum subscribd of 5d. 62 2/3c. of which 1.50 Cash a member Continued under Censure

March the 9th 1805 A members Case Continued a Query Answerd A bill of 6d. 25c. Laid in & 3d. of sd. bill paid

April the 13th 1805 A member Excluded two members appointed as Contractors.

May the 11th 1805. A request made, & answered in the Negative

June the 8th 1805 Receiv'd Jincy Biggs by Letter

July the 13th 1805 The association Letter to be wrote And Messengers appointed a members makes Concessions but not receiv'd

August 10th 1805 Spencer & Caty Collins by Letter receiv;d The Association Letter approvd of Archibald Harris restord Archibald & Sarah Harris get their Letters of Dismission It is Deemd nessary to send mony for the print the minutes

September The 7th 1805 A Request made & Laid over

October the 12th 1805 A request Granted

November the 9th 1805 Meeting to Be opened at 11 o.Clock.

December the 7th 1805 A Grieveance Laid in, & requested to be taken up by Isaac M.Coy against Bro Newland the Grieveance considered & a Committee appointed The Business Laid Over.

January the 11th 1806 The Church Deem a member Guilt of an Error. But waits till next meeting for a Hearing

February the 8th 1806 the refference still Continued & adjournd.

March the 8th 1806. Bro Newland will not Hear the Church. But the Church think proper to Lay it over Receivd Jas Stott. Phebe Stott. & Rebekah Saffers By Letter & adjourned

April the 12th 1806 Bro Newland Secluded A Letter Objected to, by Bro. Harrod Christiana M.Coy Receiv'd by Letter two members Considered guilty of Disorder their Case Referd

# FLOYD COUNTY MARRIAGES
## 1819-29

Floyd County, Indiana was formed by statute 2 January 1819; effective 1 February 1819; from parts of Clark and Harrison counties. Again on 10 January 1823, another part of Harrison County was added to Floyd County. A portion of vacant territory was added to Floyd County 5 January 1828.

The first marriage license issued in Floyd County was on 9 March 1819. Transcriptions, copies, and indexes of various marriage records are available in the Genealogy Division of the Indiana State Library. They are:

DAR, First marriage book . . . 1819-1845.

Slevin, Ruth M., . . . Marriages, 1837-1845.

WPA, Index to marriage records, 1845-1920.

WPA, Index to supplemental records, marriage transcripts, 1880-1895.

A microfilm of Floyd County marriage books, 1819-1853; 1885-1891, is available in the Genealogy Division. The CRIMP program has refilmed these records.

*The Hoosier Genealogist* has at its goal to publish all pre-1850 marriages in Indiana. Scattered counties and scattered dates have appeared in previous issues. To reach the goal, a subgoal has been set to first publish those marriages in the state before 1830.

Book 1, Floyd County Marriages is a small book, the pages are unlined, which causes difficulties when trying to decipher various items entered. Date of license, date of recording, man's name, woman's name, by whom married, and certificate of marriage are the columns used. In the following transcription, the spellings used in the initial entry are those in the man's and woman's name columns. Any deviations from that spelling in the certificate of marriage are place in brackets immediately below. The first date is the date the license was issued; the second date is the date the marriage was performed, if it is listed.

Page 1

Christopher Bruner-Catherine Groves
9 March 1819   11 March 1819

Peter Stoy-Mary E. Wicks
15 March 1819   14 March 1819

Henry Searles-Mary McFall
1 April 1819   8 April 1819

Joshua Cutter-Martha Canada
9 April 1819   no return

Mason Vermillion-Marcey Anderson
24 April 1819   no return

Beverly M. Morgan-Harriet Taylor
28 April 1819   no return

Isaac Byles-Catherine Evilsizer
5 May 1819   7 May 1819

Joseph W. Green-Louisa Ann Burrrows
22 May 1819   24 May 1819

Aaron Karnes-Sally Shearer
28 May 1819   31 May 1819

page 2

Richard Lewis-Julia Ann May
1 June 1819  23 June 1819
Henry Atkins-Nancy Chew
16 June 1819 16 July 1819
Thomas Oliver-Patsy Kennedy
17 June 1819  17 June 1819
Robert Slythe-Clarissa Hancock
19 June 1819  20 June 1819
Elias Lemon-Mary Sands
19 June 1819  19 June 1819

page 3

Obediah Wilson-Charlotte Reed
24 June 1819  24 June 1819
William Smith-Margaret Edwards
1 July 1819  4 July 1819
James Lenox-Mary Blunk
17 July 1819  24 July 1819
Harvey Scribner-Nancy P. Anderson
24 July 1819  25 July 1819
William Craven-Elender Bridgewater
27 July 1819  27 July 1829
Francls Lang-Nancy Kennedy
27 July 1819  not dated
David Holms-Elizabeth Stoker
7 August 1819  7 August 1819

page 4

Charles Burton-Mecca Purkins
   [Mekey Perkins]
7 August 1819  12 August 1819
Arthur Curtis-Amy Gallimore
9 August 1819-12 August 1819
John Leatherman-Mary Penny
25 August 1819  26 August 1819
Otho Williams-Anna McNew
4 September 1819  4 September 1819
John Irvin-Elizabeth Tayllor
   [Irwin]      [Taeller]
22 September 1819  23 September 1819
Joseph Brindley-Eliza Townley
23 September 1819  23 September 1819
Briant Tannen-Rachael Pearson
23 September 1819  24 September 1819

page 5

Asahel Clapp-Mary L. Scribner
30 September 1819  30 September 1819
Wyatt P. Tuley-Huldah West
16 October 1819  17 October 1819
Alpha Haskinds-Nancy Monroe
16 October 1819  16 October 1819
Peter Carmicle-Jane McCulloch
18 October 1819  21 October 1819
James Roberts-Abigail Fassett
20 October 1819  20 October 1819
Thomas Edwards-Elizabeth Hickman
29 October 1819  2 November 1819
Charles Woodruff-Ann Childs
2 November 1819  2 November 1819
Casper Shibe-Mary Hutton
6 November 1819  7 November 1819

page 6

Janson B. Nicholls-Rebecca Jones
6 November 1819  8 November 1819
Stephen K. Gillchrees-Mary Smith
13 November 1819  14 November 1819
John Jackson-Mary Applegate
18 November 1819  18 November 1819
Elisha Bowman-Caty Ann Miller
23 November 1819  25 November 1819
Joseph Williams-Malinda Hatfield
11 December 1819  11 December 1819
William Roberts-Sarah Chids
   [Childs]
14 December 1819  14 December 1819
William S. Field-Susan Dodge
24 December 1819  no return

page 7

James Dempster-Mary Beach
15 January 1820  no return
Isaac Sproatt-Mary Ann Fossette
1 February 1820  1 February 1820
Hugh McCulloch-Sarah Guest
5 February 1820  8 February 1820
Frederick Smith-Elizabeth McClennon
   [McClelland]

19 February 1820   21 February 1820
Mordecai M. Childs-Anna Kendall
February 1820   29 February 1820
Calvin Graves-Susan McFarlin
29 February 1820   no return
John Reymer-Delilah Miles
29 April 1820   29 April 1820
Joseph Cannon-Elizabeth Lucky
16 May 1820   16 May 1820

page 8
James Davis-Sarah Hutchinson
20 May 1820   22 May 1820
Walter W. Winchester-Mary Lucky
27 Mary 1820   28 May 1820
Peleg Underwood-Hannah Guest
31 May 1820   4 June 1820
Seth M. Levinworth-Esther Matheson
16 June 1820   16 June 1820
Francis Ransom-Sarah Allen
17 June 1820   no return
John Grosshart-Catharine Cottingham
19 June 1820   23 June 1820

page 9
David Paddoc-Phebe Scott
20 June 1820   no return
Amos C. Martin-Patsey Wilson
5 July 1820   9 July 1820
James Devenish-Mary Guest
15 July 1820   20 July 1820
Jacob Miller-Elizabeth Deal
7 September 1820   no return
James Besse-Mary Turner
16 September 1820   17 September 1820
John Bell-Sarah Keenan
23 September 1820   no return
Cooper Jourdon-Jane Branham
27 September 1820   no return

page 10
Richard Yarbrough-Miriam Lamb
16 October 1820   no return
Stephen T. Hughes-Abigail S. Cooper
23 October 1820   no return

Leverett Harman-Eleanor Hawkins
4 November 1820   no return
George Cooper-Matilda Gallion
9 November 1820   9 November 1820
James Niel-Margaret Newman
18 November 1820   18 November 1820
Lathrop Elderkin-Martha Elliott
27 November 1820   no return
Tilman Clark-Jane Lewis
    [Tilghman]
27 November 1820   27 November 1820
Ebenezer Baldwin-Elizabeth Hess
7 December 1820   7 December 1820

page 11
Thomas Allen-Nancy Brown
2 December 1820   no return
John Welsh-Maria Mowser
12 December 1820   20 December 1820
Thomas Aborn-Susannah Biggs
13 December 1820   15 December 1820
Allen Kendall-Asenith Huff
19 December 1820   undated
filed 15 November 1823
William Beeler-Elizabeth Brown
21 December 1820   22 December 1820
William M. Bruce-Catherine Bowman
23 December 1820   undated
William Kennedy-Sarah Beach
30 December 1820   1 January 1821

page 12
Francis Lang-Charlotte Walker
January 1821   11 January 1821
William C. Tucker-Rachel Merryfield
22 February 1821   22 February 1821
Zephaniah H. Smith-Nancy Redman
27 February 1821   28 February 1821
Charles Steele-Emeline Anderson
26 March 1821   26 March 1821
Mason C. Fitch-Anna Maria Paxson
29 March 1821   31 March 1821
Burk Huffman-Mary Miller
11 April 1821   12 April 1821

page 13
John H. Lemon-Charlotte Johnson
1 May 1821   1 May 1821
Samuel Brown-Lavina Akers
5 May 1821   10 May 1821
Peter T. Yaw-Sally Smith
28 May 1821   28 May 1821
Adam Smith-Elizabeth Kallahan
9 June 1821   no return
Benjamin Schoonover-Wilebur Wood
25 June 1821   27 June 1821
Robert Poore-Eliza Monday
28 June 1821   28 June 1821
William Wood-Lavise Schoonover
7 July 1821   8 July 1821

page 14
Joseph Vail-Sarah Garritson
24 July 1821   26 July 1821
Barnabas Thompson-Elizabeth Sandusky
10 August 1821   10 August 1821
John Bloor-Jane Black
16 August 1821   16 August 1821
Charles Wheeler-Matilda Faucett
16 August 1821   13 August 1821
Isaac Miller-Mary Hallowell
16 August 1821   16 August 1821
James Wright-Mary White
20 August 1821   21 August 1821
Jesse Mitchum-Violet Mitchum
25 August 1821   25 August 1821

page 15
David H. Baldwin-Margaret Chinweth
31 August 1821   2 September 1821
Henry French, Jr.-Sarah Mize
3 September 1821   5 September 1821
Thomas McLean-Mary Smith
8 September 1821   no return
Daniel Bailey-Sarah Fosett
12 September 1821   no return
Josiah Lamb-Mary Atkins
15 September 1821   15 September 1821
Josiah Winters-Harriet Westbey
27 September 1821   no return

Isaiah Lamb-Sally Smith
28 September 1821   30 September 1821
John Fowler-Hannan McCutchan
1 October 1821   4 October 1821
Francis F. Harrison-Maria Mallett
1 October 1821   1 October 1821

page 16
James Foster-Nancy Jones
26 October 1821   26 October 1821
Aaron Hey-Eliza Fowler
5 November 1821   no return
Miles Dillinger-Nancy Hickman
3 November 1821   no return
David Wilcox-Elizabeth Callahan
10 November 1821   no return
William Daniels-Caroline Wicks
15 November 1821   no return
John Hackett-Anna O'Bryan
21 November 1821   21 November 1821
Isaac Dewitt-Nancy Mize
6 December 1821   18 December 1821

page 17
Charles Paxson-Mary C. Woodruff
15 December 1821   15 December 1821
Epaphras Jones-Mary Ann Silliman
25 January 1822   25 January 1822
Asahel Clapp-Elizabeth Scribner
31 January 1822   no return
William Bentley-Jane McDowell
6 February 1822   10 February 1822
Wiley Crowder-Anna Williams
7 February 1822   7 February 1822
Samuel Angel-Mary Moffett
10 February 1822   10 February 1822
Benjamin Malone-Nancy Clark
14 February 1822   14 February 1822

page 17a
Francis Lang-Catula Burns
26 February 1822   28 February 1822
Lemuel Robins-Cinthia Lopp
26 February 1822   no return

35

Lewis Young-Margaret Sproull
10 March 1822   no return
Henry Sigler-Experience Kendall
12 March 1822   12 March 1822
Libbens Fhisbee-Martha Matthews
19 March 1822   no return
Thomas Smith-Margaret Black
27 March 1822   28 March 1822
Richard Fowler-Docey Miller
10 April 1822   14 April 1822

page 17b
Nicholas Holston-Mary Young
23 April 1822   23 April 1822
Adam Youmans-Delilah Cummings
24 April 1822   24 April 1822
Isaac S. Ashton-Sophia Childs
25 April 1822 no return
James Burke-Sarah Beach
27 April 1822   no return
Douglass Richey-Mary Smith
6 May 1822   no return
Fulton McCutchan-Rose Hey
13 May 1822   no return
William Williams-Harriet Booker
17 May 1822   20 May 1822

page 18
Elijah Brock-Eleanor Rose
20 May 1822   20 May 1822
James Wright-Elizabeth Smith
3 July 1822   3 July 1822
Jacob Anthony-Sarah Ann Marsh
12 July 1822   undated
George Mosar-Maria Creswell
12 July 1822   14 July 1822
Wyatt P. Tuley-Jane Warner
7 August 1822   7 August 1822
Eli Sigler-Rhoda Hurley
10 August 1822   11 August 1822
Joshua Wilson-Mary Dahman
19 August 1822   20 August 1822
Aaron H. Forceman-Caroline Deoing
20 August 1822   22 August 1822

page 19
Abel M. Sergeant,Jr.-Sarah Edwards
24 August 1822   25 August 1822
Joseph V. Wells-Mary Frederick
13 November 1822   14 November 1822
John Brown-Catherine Meeter
   [Caty]
13 October 1822   30 October 1822
John Straw-Maria Beeler
21 November 1822   22 November 1822
Francis Very-Elizabeth French
23 November 1822   23 November 1822
Dunbar Bell-Kizziah Smith
26 November 1822   28 November 1822
Ralph P. Richards-Amelia Sturges
10 December 1822   10 December 1822

page 20
Richard Redfield, Jr.-Elizabeth B.
   Meriwether
25 January 1823   2 February 1823
Austin Mudd-Lucinda White
25 January 1823   25 January 1823
John Nicholson-Abigail Roberts
30 January 1823   30 January 1823
James Reynolds-Charity Carter
3 February 1823   no return
Isaac Brooks-Ann McCleary
5 February 1823   5 February 1823
John Brown-Jane Monahan
11 February 1823   11 February 1823
David Meriwether-Sarah Leonard
24 February 1823   27 February 1823
William Langwell-Rebecca Tucker
6 March 1820   6 March 1820
Thomas Conner-Eliza Harris
6 March 1823   6 March 1823
Isaac Jackson-Henrietta Wicks
13 March 1823   13 March 1823

page 21
George Schwartz-Sarah Brown
28 March 1823   29 March 1823

John Nett-Elizabeth Lyman
3 April 1823   3 April 1823
John A. Spalding-Eliza M. West
9 April 1823   9 April 1823
James Mitchell-Nancy Leedy
9 April 1823   undated
Joseph Walden-Elizabeth Long
12 April 1823   15 April 1823
Edward Pennington-Mary Sigler
14 April 1823   14 April 1823
John K. Graham-Mary Huff
16 April 1823   16 April 1823
Daniel Keller-Zerniah Starr
2 May 1823   no date
William S. Campbell-Martha Hey
7 May 1823   2 December 1823

page 22
David Walker-Anna Marietta Hedden
16 May 1823   18 May 1823
Presley Clark-Caroline Hendelider
28 May 1823   28 May 1823
Jonathan Slythe-Elizabeth McCullough
4 June 1823   5 June 1823
Jacob Horner-Mary L. Miller
9 June 1823   undated
Jesse Aston-Elizabeth Graham
15 June 1823   15 June 1823
John Shackleton Bottomly-Susan Chew
19 June 1823   19 June 1823
Oliver Holmes-Elizabeth Shirley
23 June 1823   2 December 1823
Alexander Evans-Jane McKinly
30 June 1823   no return
Thomas Wright-Elizabeth Burton
16 July 1823   20 July 1823
Michael Frederick-Esther Wright
29 July 1823   29 July 1823
Isaiah Hammack-Ruth Erwin
29 July 1823   31 July 1823

page 23
Anthony Livers-Nancy Hanger
5 September 1823   no return

Allen Webster-Eleanor Clark
6 September 1823   11 September 1823
Liles Carter-Dicey Wilson
8 September 1823   8 September 1823
Martin Waltz-Susan Williams
16 September 1823   18 September 1823
Ephraim Jackson-Elizabeth Harmon
20 September 1823   23 September 1823
Henry Rodgers-Laura Crawford
26 September 1823   29 September 1823
William Stewart-Margaret Alexander
29 September 1823   29 September 1823
Alpheus B. Rowley-Achsah Gordon
6 October 1823   6 October 1823

page 24
Benjamin Lamb-Charlotte Atkins
11 October 1823   16 October 1823
Richard Sable-Nancy Gatewood
16 October 1823   undated
Martin Akers-Mary Clark
18 October 1823   23 October 1823
Joseph Potter-Barbara Utz
29 October 1823   29 October 1823
Peter Ross-Elizabeth Goin
5 November 1823   6 November 1823
James Guffey-Sarah Scantlan
14 November 1823   16 November 1823
Joel Cox-Mary Groves
21 November 1823   23 November 1823
William Lamb-Anna Hickman
22 November 1823   no return

page 25
David Byerly-Anna Taylor
25 November 1823   27 November 1823
Nathan Taylor-Susan Potter
11 December 1823   12 December 1823
John Johnson-Hannah Hale
17 December 1823   undated
Allen Shepherd-Elizabeth Dickens
4 February 1824   undated
James R. Shields-Hannah Woodruff
10 February 1824   10 February 1824

Isaac Murphy-Magdalena Evilsizer
9 March 1824  no return
James W. Shaw-Mary Burton
10 March 1824  22 March 1824
James Gragg-Anna Theresa Miller
17 March 1824  25 March 1824
Joseph Decker-Sarah Decker
23 March 1824  23 March 1824
William Drysdale-Sarah Beers
29 March 1824  3 April 1824
Richard McCaig-Elizabeth Kearnes
13 April 1824  no return

page 26
Jesse Wilson-Jane Eddins
20 May 1824  1 June 1824
James Baker-Lyncha Rust
22 May 1824  no return
Abraham Pilkinton-Indiana Skinner
7 June 1824  7 June 1824
James Hickman-Elizabeth Kirk
7 June 1824  17 June 1824
John Humm-Jane Adams
15 June 1824  15 June 1824
John Crook-Elizabeth Brown
16 June 1824  16 June 1824
James R. Nance-Nancy Chamberlain
16 June 1826  21 June 1824
Solomon Hamar-Sally Gregory
14 July 1824  29 July 1824
James Hillyer-Catharine Silliman
20 July 1824  20 July 1824
George Willett-Nancy Hancock
  [Willet]
26 July 1824  26 July 1824

page 27
Elijah C. Boilean-Anna Pennington
2 August 1824  2 August 1824
Josiah Given-Elizabeth Leedy
3 August 1824  5 August 1824
Aaron H. Forceman-Sarah Garritson
7 August 1824  7 August 1824

Isaac Elliott-Delilah Walker
  [Eliot]
23 August 1824  26 August 1824
William Stewart-Elizabeth Drysdale
23 August 1824  28 August 1824
Joshua Akers-Phebe Miller
4 September 1824  5 September 1824
Jacob Millen-Sarah Taylor
8 September 1824  undated
William Butler-Elizabeth Wilson
8 September  no return
Thomas Prothero-Elizabeth Bristow
13 September 1824  30 September 1824
Thomas W. McNeff-Sarah M. Smith
13 September 1824  no return
William Bridges-Margaret Forsyth
16 September 1824  16 September 1824

page 28
Joseph Southerland-Sally Ingram
29 September 1824  30 September 1824
Henry Edwards-Sarah Palmer
2 October 1824-11 October 1824
William Dollens-Nancy Lang
7 October 1824  10 October 1824
John Steelman-Elizabeth Smith
9 October 1824  11 October 1824
George Wheeler-Catharine Scysloaff
  [Sycloaff]
11 October 1824  14 October 1824
James McKenan-Elizabeth Snapp
14 October 1824  14 October 1824
John P. Allen-Mary Crowder
20 October 1824  21 October 1824
David Sillings-Nancy Crowders
  [Crowder]
23 October 1824  23 October 1824
Hiram Ransom-Ovanda Redfield
27 November 1824  1 December 1824

page 29
Chase C. Dockham-Patience Wearle
18 November 1824  18 November 1824
Edward Taylor-Elvira Barker
5 December 1824  5 December 1824

Nathan Bedleicome-Elizabeth Rodgers
[Bedlicome]
6 December 1824   7 December 1824
Cornelius L. Blair-Mary Ann Lamb
6 December 1824   15 December 1824
Nicholas Holston-Theny Perkins Dillinger
14 December 1824   15 December 1824
James Davis-Sarah Malone
18 December 1824   18 December 1824
John Barnett-Nancy Weaver
23 December 1824   27 December 1824
Joseph Thackwray-Ann Smith
27 December 1824   27 December 1824
Craven Henry-Eliza Smiley
27 December 1824   27 December 1824
Isaiah Townsend-Nancy Roberts
30 December 1824   30 December 1824

page 30
James Hand-Deborah Cochran
31 December 1824   31 December 1824
Thomas Lamb-Nancy Minick
1 January 1825   6 January 1825
John Huffstutter-Isabella Kapely
15 January 1825   no return
Alonzo S. Kellogg-Octava Smith
27 January 1825   30 January 1825
Jacob Kyzer-Sarah Self
29 January 1825   30 January 1825
Preston F. Tuley-Mary C. Paxson
12 February 1824   13 February 1824
William Shindler-Elizabeth Bradshaw
17 February 1824   no return
Somers B. Gilman-Maria Roche
17 February 1825   no return
Henry Bastion-Elizabeth Adams
23 February 1825   no return
Joseph Lamb-Nancy Baird
9 March 1825   10 March 1825

page 31
Samuel Dougherty-Elizabeth Lewis
11 March 1825   no return
William Brent-Ruth Vandyke
15 March 1825   15 March 1825

William Stark-Rebecca Ragsdale
29 March 1825   undated
Jeremiah Prather-Maria Merrick
30 March 1825   31 March 1825
Hezekiah Morris-Anna Penney
30 March 1825   31 March 1825
Grayson B. Taylor-Catharine Rice
7 April 1825   no return
James Robinson-Mary Harden
3 May 1825   no return
Enoch Hickman-Mary Hickman
4 May 1825   5 May 1825

page 32
John Williams-Hannah Lewis
11 May 1825   no return
Robert Fenwick-Elizabeth Smith
13 May 1825   15 May 1825
Godfrey Ragsdale-Ann Clements
16 May 1825   no return
Henry B. Shields-Joanna K. Day
1 June 1825   2 June 1825
Humphrey Shepherd-Eliza McCuatchan
10 June 1825   16 June 1825
James Slider-Louisa Howard
22 June 1825   23 June 1825
David H. Williams-Eliza Bowman
25 June 1825   26 June 1825

page 33
Robert Gowing-Elizabeth Sinclair
20 July 1825   20 July 1825
Henry Sigler-Elizabeth Miller
23 July 1825   24 July 1825
Drury Norton-Nancy Johnson
25 July 1825   31 July 1825
Richard Hayden-Cassandra Wearham
27 July 1825   27 July 1825
Henry Sigler, Jr.-Rebecca Akers
29 July 1825   no return
William Remick-Elizabeth Weaver
6 August 1825   6 August 1825
Hiram L. Miller-Rebecca Wells
10 August 1825   11 August 1825

page 34
Edward Applegate-Prudence Kepler
20 August 1825   20 August 1825
Joel Leek-Susanna Langdon
31 August 1825   1 September 1825
William Miller-Catharine Kindall
   [Kindell]
2 September 1825   4 September 1825
Hezekiah Beeler-Maria Warner
4 September 1825   5 September 1825
Benjamin R. Edwards-Catherine Ann
Marsh
10 September 1825   10 September 1825
Samuel Harris-Daphney Martin
14 September 1825   15 September 1825
Levi Lang-Elizabeth Lamb
14 September 1825   15 September 1825
John Martin-Jane Carmikle
15 October 1825   no return

page 35
Thomas Rouse-Jane Johnson
19 October 1825   no return
Adam Smith-Experience Garritson
20 October 1825   20 October 1825
William Brown-Elizabeth Maxcey Taylor
2 November 1825   3 November 1825
Henson Thomas-Nancy Wright
3 November 1825   3 November 1825
John Moore-Mary Roberts
17 November 1825   18 November 1825
Absalem Overby-Malinda Sillings
1 December 1825   1 December 1825
John Sanderson-Elizabeth Grigsby
1 December 1825   1 December 1825
William Seal-Sophia Stonebrake
1 December 1825   2 December 1825
Robert McCallend-Cynthia Haymore
7 December 1825   undated

page 36
John Schwartz-Susanna Friedley
   [Susannah]
10 December 1825   11 December 1825

Benjamin Godfrey-Hannah Gurthside
10 December 1825   11 December 1825
John Peyton-Emily Sproatt
22 December 1825   22 December 1825
Nicholas Dilinger-Margaret Mayall
26 December 1825   27 December 1825
Asa Smith, Jr.-Mary Ann Ferguson
28 December 1825   29 December 1825
John W. Ellis-M.A. Logan
29 December 1825   undated
Russell Robinson-Elizabeth Ferguson
29 November 1825   1 December 1825
James Conner-Roxanna R. Holley
9 January 1826   11 January 1826

page 37
Stephen Edwards-Elizabeth Penny
11 January 1826   12 January 1826
Prentice Latham Lamb-Sarah McCartney
12 January 1826   undated
William Tucker-Lydia Cottingham
25 January 1826   26 January 1826
John Spencer-Perthany Baxter
   [Perthaney]
26 January 1826   26 January 1826
Silas Kearnes-Elizabeth McLoghlin
   [Catharine]
4 February 1826   9 February 1826
Roderick Gates-Sally Hickman
7 February 1826   7 February 1826
John W. Tuley-Phebe Woodruff
9 February 1826   9 February 1826
Jacob Smith-Sarah Ann Ostrander
10 February 1826   12 February 1826

page 38
David Byerly, Jr.-Elizabeth Byerly
25 February 1826   26 February 1826
Ira W. Gunn-Elsey K. Beach
7 March 1826
Andrew McCafferty-Sarah Chew
14 March 1826   14 March 1826
Robert Hill-Susan Lewis
31 March 1826   31 March 1826

James Brown-Eunice Reasor
8 April 1826   14 April 1826
Henry Lewis-Ruth Smith
8 April 1826   14 April 1826
William Crowder-Elizabeth F. Overby
12 April 1826   19 April 1826
William Riddle-Elizabeth Brown
13 May 1826   no return
James Kennedy-Susan Miller
   [Keneday]
3 June 1826   4 June 1826

page 39
William Nutall-Charlotte Afflick
12 June 1826   12 June 1826
William J. Rance-Elizabeth Lefollett
23 June 1826   no return
Reuben J. Palmer-Margaret Landers
29 June 1826   30 June 1826
Samuel Lefavore-Fanny Dustin
13 July 1826   13 July 1826
Matthew M. Byrn-Margaret Chew
14 July 1826   undated
Daniel W. Voshall-Sarah Roberts
20 July 1826   21 July 1821
Joseph Atkins-Nancy Lamb
2 August 1836   3 August 1826
Preston Taylor-Nancy Glass Gunn
4 August 1826   12 August 1826
Patrick Byrn-Alice Byrn
   [Byrne]         [Byrne]
23 August 1826   23 August 1826
James Howard-Elizabeth Cannon
23 August 1826   23 August 1826
Rufus Edwards-Jane Eliza Rose
12 August 1826   no date

page 40
John Huffstutter-Nancy Burford
29 August 1826   31 August 1826
John Ellison-Rebecca Boots
30 August 1826   31 August 1826
George McKinney-Amanda Parker
31 August 1826   31 August 1826

James Eddins-Rebecca Lincas
4 September 1826   undated
Jefferson Engleman-Susannah Baker
5 September 1826   undated
Pierce Chamberlain-Thirza Overby
8 September 1826   15 October 1826
Thomas Goodwin-Margaret Snider
12 September 1826   18 September 1826
James Hancock-Nancy M. Nance
   [Mary]
16 September 1826   17 September 1826
James Duncan-Sarah Brand
16 September 1826   16 September 1826

page 41
Matthew Hansleman-Elizabeth Filmy
no date   21 September 1826
Samuel Thompson-Eliza Ann Campbell
   [Tomson]
7 October 1826   8 October 1826
Leonard S. Leach-Maria Hey
13 October 1826   no return
Benjamin F. Berry-Polly W. Green
24 October 1826   no return
William McLoghlin-Lydia Boyles
25 October 1826   26 October 1826
Chauncy P. Smith-Maria Hoke
9 November 1826   12 November 1826
William Brown-Julia Ann Kellogg
9 November 1826   undated
Frederick A. Varon-Maria Eddins
   [Veron]
15 November 1826   16 November 1826

page 42
John Doan-Susan Lamb
23 November 1826   23 November 1826
John S. Livingston-Anina Aston
   [Nanina]
9 December 1826   10 December 1826
Jacob Smith-Sarah Flickner
20 December 1826   21 December 1826
Joseph Garritson-Tacey Taylor
23 December 1826   28 December 1826

David Wolf-Polly Utz
25 December 1826  no return
William Cronk, Jr.-Rebecca Berkshire
26 December 1826  28 December 1826
Richard Harris-Mahala Mitchum
28 December 1826  no return
Isaac Bowman-Mary Bailey
   January 1827  11 January 1827
Benjamin Terrill-Dolly Briscoe
15 January 1826  no return

page 43
Stansberry Lang-Elizabeth Edwards
18 January 1827  18 January 1827
George Breedlove-Catharine Miller
30 January 1827  30 January 1827
Jacob Schnetz-Mary Goforth
8 February 1827  8 February 1827
George Armstrong-Chalista C. West
10 February 1827  10 February 1827
Leaven E. Hall-Elizabeth C. Reed
16 February 1827  18 February 1827
John McConkey-Frances Roberts
22 February 1827  1 March 1827
Samuel Potter-Nancy Burger
26 February 1827  no return
George W. Douglass-Vicey Bell
26 February 1827  no return

page 44
James Beam-Sarah Ann Burks
10 March 1827  31 March 1827
Andrew Ingram-Mary Gwinn
19 March 1827  undated
James Magall-Eliza Stuart
   [Steward]
24 March 1827  24 March 1827
Thomas Dargin-Rebecca Lucky
10 April 1827  10 April 1827
Thomas Thomas-Mary Martin
11 April 1827  12 April 1827
Benjamin Case-Mary Stuart
14 April 1827  15 April 1827
William Dye-Elizabeth Wells
23 April 1827  3 May 1827

Henry A. Moore-Sophia Steelman
24 April 1827  undated
Robert Benson-Melinda Sampson
28 April 1827  29 April 1827

page 45
William McKenzie-Mary Kane
28 April 1827  undated
Ephraim Collins-Margaret Young
3 May 1827  3 May 1827
William B. Breedlove-Frances Paulson
   [Poulson]
10 May 1827  12 May 1827
Francis Hutchinson-Libia Hand
11 May 1827  11 May 1827
Chain Miles Ashby-Jane D. Fletcher
19 June 1827  18 June 1827
William Anderson-Phebe Hedrick
26 June 1827  26 June 1827
Gamaliel Garritson-Jane Minich
7 July 1827  10 July 1827
Benjamin Akers-Margaret Smith
9 July 1827  10 June 1827
David Schwartz-Nancy Butler
13 July 1827  13 July 1827

page 46
Edward Brown, Jr.-Rachel Warnr
21 July 1827  no return
John Payton-Christena Sears
23 July 1827  25 July 1827
Absalom C. Ashbrook-Sarah Payton
24 July 1827  25 July 1827
William Cooper-Nancy Bliss
26 July 1827  28 July 1827
Alfred Sigler-Esther Ann Goff
28 July 1827  28 July 1827
David Pitman-Catharine Edleman
6 August 1827  no return
Giles Johnson-Elizabeth Stewart
9 August 1827  undated
Mark Phillips-Nancy P. Jenkins
10 August 1827  10 August 1827
Hardin Roberts-Jane Evans
13 August 1827  5 May 1827

page 47
James Tyler-Mahala Potter
12 August 1827 no return
Morgan Kennedy-Susan Roberts
[Kenneday]
25 August 1827 26 August 1827
John L. Gay-Louisa Taylor
26 August 1827 26 August 1827
William S. Woolley-Catharine Hunt
28 August 1827 28 August 1827
Charles Boyles-Rachel Paulson
4 September 1827 6 September 1827
Joseph Adams-Mary Nevill
4 September 1827 25 October 1827
Thomas Morgan-Harriet H. Buckman
24 September 1827 no return
John Angel-Rebecca Aplin
7 October 1827 27 October 1827
Benjamin Conner-Rebecca An Stewart
[Ann]
7 October 1827 7 October 1827
John Wilson-Patsey Wilson
13 October 1827 13 October 1827
Amelek Nicking-Betsy Friday
16 October 1827 16 October 1827
Augustus Turner-Martha Guest
17 October 1827 18 October 1827
Samuel C. Smith-Catherine Cline
18 October 1827 18 October 1827
Louis Brevet-Justine Emily Flotron
18 October 1827 18 October 1827
Joseph Miller-Tabitha Karnes
20 October 1827 21 October 1827
John Landers-Elizabeth Bowman
23 October 1827 undated
Runion Ellis-Margaret Fox
27 October 1827 27 October 1827

page 49
Vincent Sero-Mary Betts
27 October 1827 no return
Hiram S. Roberts-Matilda Reed
27 October 1827 28 October 1827
Samuel Swick-Susanna Shields
31 October 1827 no return

John Plaess-Anna Barbara Flock
2 November 1827 no return
Samuel Tomlin-Nancy Mayall
10 November 1827 11 November 1827
Thomas Roberts-Harriet Marsh
18 November 1827 18 November 1827
Joshua Wiley-Sarah Loyd
[Lloyd]
28 November 1827 29 November 1827
John Stucker-Didama Wood
3 December 1827 6 December 1827

page 50
Adam Smith-Mary Deal
13 December 1827 14 December 1827
Henry Edwards-Mary Crook
19 December 1827 no return
Jacob Smith-Elizabeth Bateman
22 December 1827 27 December 1827
John Walker-Margaret Fletcher
24 December 1827 25 December 1827
Mosias Nance, Jr.-Catharine Chamberlain
9 January 1828 10 January 1828
Lloyd White-Lydia Ann Shannon
[Loyd]
14 January 1828 15 January 1828
Samuel Bolin-Elizabeth Hutchinson
17 January 1828 17 January 1828
Lawson Very-Eliza Garritson
18 January 1828 no return

page 51
Matthew Ready-Marthy Leedy
21 January 1828 no return
James W. Stewart-Julia Ann Adams
21 January 1828 22 January 1828
George R. Love-Susan Edson
2 February 1828 3 February 1828
Moses Nickens-Milley Parker
[Nekin] [Milly]
7 February 1828 7 February 1828
Stephen Irwin-Fanny Walker
9 February 1828 no return
Benjamin Anderson-Elizabeth Washburn
12 February 1828 19 February 1828

Archibald Myers-Lucinda Dillinger
6 March 1828   9 March 1828
John Cronk-Sarah Crook
11 March 1828   13 March 1828
John Mahuren-Elizabeth Ferrell
[Ferrel]
11 March 1828   13 March 1828
Anthony Dennis-Mary Ann H. Conklin
11 March 1828   23 March 1828

page 52
John McLoghlin-Sarah Case
21 March 1828-23 March 1828
Abraham Miller-Calista Warren
22 March 1828   no return
William P. Thomasson-Charlotte Leonard
25 March 1828   25 March 1828
John Fox-Elizabeth Mosar
25 March 1828   undated
George Kepley-Catharine Sears
[Katharine]
7 April 1828   7 April 1828
Samuel Clark-Nancy Miller
10 April 1828   20 April 1828
Absalom Barnaby-Mary Ellis
12 April 1828   no return
Jacob Hand-Sarah Graves
26 April 1828   27 April 1828
William Crook-Delilah Creswell
5 May 1828   no return
Peter Smith-Sarah Akers
5 May 1828   8 May 1828

page 53
John Shirley-Fanny Minich
7 May 1828   8 May 1828
Charles S. Hurd-Nancy Buley
9 May 1818   9 May 1828
Samuel M. Osbourne-Cynthia Ann Stewart
14 May 1828   15 May 1828
Henry Shoemaker-Ellen Crane
20 May 1828   22 May 1828
James Shoemaker-Melinda Crane
20 May 1828   22 May 1828

Samuel Harris-Druzilla Livers
29 May 1828   29 May 1828
Jacob Sears-Nancy Ann Lagle
3 June 1828   5 June 1828
Shadrach Silling-Martha Potter
21 June 1828   no return
Wilson Ryan-Rebecca Taylor
2 July 1828   no return
Joseph Claibourne-Zelia C. Marsh
10 July 1828   10 July 1828

page 54
Morgan Smith-Mary Pectol
13 July 1828   17 July 1828
Christopher Samuel-Juliet M. Talbot
18 July 1828   18 July 1828
Alexander Courtney-Naomi Smith
26 July 1828   July 1828
James Stucker-Sarah Cronk
26 July 1828   27 July 1828
George Crook-Susan Butler
4 August 1828   17 August 1828
Isaac Tailor-Sarah English
[Taylor]
4 August 1828   August 1828
Joseph Johnson-Catharine Cronk
12 August 1828   undated
William Armstrong-Mahala Chenoweth
14 August 1828   undated
William Speaks-Mary Lapping
14 August 1824   undated
Jacob Fred-Harriet Harris
[Hannah]
14 August 1828   14 August 1828

page 55
John Stonebreaker-Harriet Compton
22 August 1828 no return
Samuel B. Walls-Nancy Thompson
22 August 1828   23 August 1828
Joseph A. Ashby-Elizabeth Clark
1 September 1828   2 September 1828
Charles Woodruff-Ruth Collins
4 September 1828   no return

Edmund Watkins-Anna Childs
6 September 1828   7 September 1828
Joseph Ingram-Dinidy Ingram
8 September 1828   10 September 1828
Reuben C. Buckman-Christena Brock
22 September 1828   no return
Gideon Atkins-Sarah Lamb
3 October 1828   7 October 1828
Samuel B. Alderson-Marinda Swope
26 September 1828   26 September 1828
James Beman-Pharaba Tucker
29 September 1828   undated
William Walden-Sarah Garner
8 October 1828   9 October 1828

page 56
Josiah LaRue-Mary Castleman
13 October 1828   13 October 1828
Joel H. Shields-Nancy McKown
14 October 1828   23 December 1828
Robert Ranking-Maria Taylor
15 October 2828   16 October 1828
James Duggins-Sarah Crane
17 October 1828   no return
George Pectol-Sarah Reasor
20 October 1828   2 November 1828
Samuel Johnson-Elizabeth Crane
20 October 1828   no return
John Ross-Eliza Livers
28 October 1828   29 October 1828
Daniel G. Hamblen-Jane Bagley
28 October 1828   no return
John Watson-Eliza Israel
6 November 1828   8 November 1828
John Perry-Sarah Schwartz
12 November 1828   13 November 1828

page 57
Barney B. Porter-Katharine Higgs
25 November 1828   27 November 1828
Jeremiah Barstow-Eleanora Peace
  Collett
26 November 1828   26 November 1828
Joshua Churchill-Eleanor Johnson
28 November 1828   no return

Samuel Carrol-Mary Thornburg
6 December 1828   8 December 1828
John F. Lemon-Mary Winchester
7 December 1828   7 December 1828
Cincinnatus F. Fontaine-Eliza Brindley
15 December 1828   15 December 1828
Andrew Cottingham-Margaret Grant
17 December 1828   18 December 1828
Daniel Mayall-Elizaabeth Aston
25 December 1828   25 December 1828

page 58
Andrew Conklin-Elizabeth Woodfill
17 January 1829   20 January 1829
Gasway Elliot-Elizabeth Flemming
  [Fleming]
17 January 1829   18 January 1829
Thomas Bowers-Eliza Ann Green
19 January 1829   20 January 1829
Joseph Underwood-Harriet E. Rickards
  [Elizabeth]
24 January 1829   25 January 1829
Joseph G. Montgomery-Almira Buckman
7 February 1829   8 February 1828
Edmund Goin-Charlotte Brown
7 February 1829   no return
Mitchell Ingram-Mary Lagle
10 February 1829   12 February 1829
Parnenas B. Huffe-Elizabeth Allison
25 February 1829   25 February 1829
Benjamin VanHorn-Amy Jackson
28 February 1829   1 March 1829

page 59
William Black-Harriet Clark
4 March 1829   5 March 1829
Philip Cook-Mahalna Evans
7 March 1829   8 March 1829
Henry Schoolcraft-Matilda Fontain
10 March 1829   10 March 1829
Isaac Edwards-Nancy Hickman
19 March 1829   19 March 1829
John Gresham-Susanna Nance
23 March 1829   no return

William English-Elizabeth Jones
24 March 1829  24 March 1829
Bennett Watson-Margaret Pierson
1 April 1829  1 April 1829
Nathaniel W. Parker-Elizabeth Baird
4 April 1829  5 April 1829
Charles K. Redman-Julia Ann McClintick
7 April 1829  8 April 1829

page 60
Alexexander S. Burnett-Eliza Gamble
16 April 1829  16 April 1829
George Clark, Jr.-Sally Blair
20 April 1829  23 April 1829
John Cox-Ann Bell Newhouse
26 April 1829  26 April 1829
Edmund Goin-Charlotte Brown
26 April 1829-30 April 1829
Charles S. Tuley-Susan Adams
12 May 1829  12 May 1829
William P. Williams-Sarah Lamb
13 May 1829  14 May 1829
John Hickman-Dicey Waring
13 May 1829  21 May 1829
Xavier Shies-Magdalena Warner
15 May 1829  no return
John Fulton-Susan Hill
15 May 1829  15 May 1829

page 61
Joseph Kirk-Rachel Oatman
23 May 1829  24 May 1829
McKinney L. Johnston-Lavinia Kendall
23 May 1829  undated
Joseph Ferguson-Amy Coates
  [Coats]
5 June 1829  5 June 1829
Levi McDougal-Elizabeth Sanders
13 June 1829  14 June 1829
Joseph A. Moffett-Mildred Jones
27 June 1829  undated
Ransom Hamon-Louisa Green
1 July 1829  undated

Harrison Kearnes-Eliza Plew
1 July 1829  2 July 1829
John Cummins-Ann Crabster
2 July 1829  2 July 1829

page 62
John Campbell-Mary Ann Ragans
6 July 1829  6 July 1829
Isaac Robertson-Harriet Mitcham
8 July 1829  undated
James H. Edmondson-Caroline M. Saltkeld
9 July 1829  undated
George W. Vreland-Roxanna Parker
12 July 1829  12 July 1829
William B. Swain-Jane Teston
17 July 1829  17 July 1829
John Deal-Mary Barker
18 July 1829  no return
Oliver Cassell-Rachel Baird
18 July 1829  undated
John Babtiste-Nancy Lane
  [Baptiste]
20 July 1820  21 July 1829
John Crawford-Mahala Hutchinson
4 August 1829  11 August 1829

page 63
Isaac McKown-Lydia Lamb
8 August 1829  13 January 1829
Jefferson Conner-Jane V. Daniels
11 August 1829  11 August 1829
Benjamin B. Watson-Hetty M. Watson
8 August 1829  9 August 1829
John Findley-Delilah Smith
15 August 1829  16 August 1829
Isaac Park-Mary Miller
13 August 1829  no return
Stith M. Otwell-Mary B. Day
18 August 1829  18 August 1829
John Hedrick-Anna Waltz
19 August 1829  20 August 1829

page 64

Elijah Campbell-Nancy Mitchum
22 August 1829  22 August 1829
Solomon Byerly-Barzilla Martin
25 August 1829  27 August 1829
Mastin Fendley-Winney Mitcham
14 September 1829  undated
John S. Doughten-Adell Jane Armstrong
19 September 1829  19 September 1829
Sheldon Stanley-Susan McDonald
22 September undated
Joseph Fleming-Mary Arnold
24 September 1829  24 September 1829
Jacob Poe-Indiana Boston
28 September 1829  28 September 1829

page 65

William Furguson-Elizabeth Hatfield
28 September 1829  28 September 1829
John Smith-Martha Creswell
5 October 1829  8 October 1829
James Bates-Eleanor McCulloch
12 October 1829  12 October 1829
Alexander Hockiday-Eliza Baird
17 October 1829  22 October 1829
Samuel Laferty-Tabitha Wilcox
19 October 1829  19 October 1829
Electious Athon-Caroline Harris
20 October 1829  20 October 1829
Edward Edson-Millicent Steelman
22 October 1829  undated
James Davis-Mary Goldsmith
24 October 1829  25 October 1829

page 66

Joseph Hull-Mary Burton
2 November 1829  2 November 1829
Jesse Boston-Mary Ann McNabb
[J.]
5 November 1829  5 November 1829
Thomas Smith-Mary Demine
5 November 1829  5 November 1829
Mathew Gunn-Susan Lafollett
9 November 1829  no return

Francis McHarry-Lucinda Leedy
12 November 1829  no return
John Miller-Alicia White
128 November 1829  no return
Thomas Burns-Ann Eliza Callan
19 November 1829  20 November 1829
Henry Aninger-Katharine Rule
23 November 1829  23 November 1829
Thomas Stephens-Elizabeth Roberts
29 November 1829  no return

page 67

James McCutchan-Susannah McHurin
1 December 1829  undated
Jacob Harris-Rachel Jane Tucker
3 December 1829  3 December 1829
Daniel W. Norris-Mary W. Daniel
7 December 1829  7 December 1829
Nelson Mitcham-Juda Carpenter
8 December 1829  undated
Silas Odam-Mary Garner
8 December 1829  no return
George G. Lane-Mary Ann Puckett
12 December 1829  undated
Hardy Johnson-Thirza Mullikin
15 December 1829  undated
William Wells-Mary Ann Akin
22 December 1829  24 December 1829
Joel Dyer-Catherine Pedigoe
25 December 1829  25 December 1829

page 68

Josiah Curtis-Julia Ann Martin
26 December 1829  undated
George Smith-Mary Ann Akers
26 December 1829  29 December 1829
Calvin Hollis-Priscilla Hand
29 December 1829  undated
Benjamin Adams, Jr.-Mary Ann Armstrong
30 December 1829  undated

# FRANKLIN COUNTY MARRIAGES
## 6 April 1824 - 31 December 1829

Franklin County, Indiana was formed from parts of Jefferson, Clark, and Dearborn Counties. In 1818, the formation of Fayette County reduced Franklin County's area. The boundaries were again changed in 1820 making provision for the New Purchase, adding some territory. A part of Franklin County was taken when Union County was formed in 1821. More territory was detached in 1826 and added to Union and Fayette counties.

Several transcriptions, compilations, and indexes of Franklin County marriages are available in the Genealogy Divison of the Indiana State Library. They are:

DAR Twin Forks Chapter (Brookville), Marriage records . . . 1811 to 1825, transcribed by Mrs. Roscoe C. O'Byrne. 1944. 186 pp. Arranged by the order the marriages occurred.

Microfilm records of Franklin County marriages, 1811-1890. Filmed in 1936, these records have miscellaneous indexes interspersed.

O'Byrne, Estella, [Marriage records . . . 1811 to 1820] 3 pts.

WPA, Index to marriage records Franklin County, 1850 to 1920. 2 v. 1941. An alphabetic list of books 6 through 16. Birth dates of applicants are usually given for books 14 through 16.

WPA, Index to marriage transcript record, 1882-1920. Gives parents' names, applicant's sex, color, age at next birthday, date of marriage (but not to whom!). Includes Supplemental index to Marriage Transcript Record, 1882-1890. This supplement actually only includes the two years 1884 and 1885.

Marriages, 1811 to March 1824 were published in *THG* in vol. 13, no. 3, (1973).

Names for brides and grooms are given as spelled in license application. Spelling variations used in the return are enclosed in brackets []; variations in the various indexes are enclosed in braces ().

| PAGE | GROOM | BRIDE | DATE LICENSE | DATE MARRIAGE |
|------|-------|-------|--------------|---------------|
| 66 | Samuel Harris | Mary Sparks | 5 Apr 1824 | 6 Apr 1824 |
| | Jacob Dennelsbeck | Mary Rusing | 7 Apr 1824 | 8 Apr 1824 |
| | Thomas Murphey | Mary Rudman | 12 Apr 1824 | |
| | William Odeor [Oldeor] | Mary Henderson | 9 Apr 1824 | 11 Apr 1824 |
| | William McCafferty | Edy Osborn | 20 Apr 1824 | |
| | Joseph Remy | Byes Nickols | 21 Apr 1824 | 22 Apr 1824 |

| PAGE | GROOM | BRIDE | DATE LICENSE | DATE MARRIAGE |
|---|---|---|---|---|
| 67 | Samuel Wilson | Diana Martin | 4 May 1824 | 6 May 1824 |
| | William Harris | Rebecah Short | 12 May 1824 | |
| | John Carter | Hanah Quick | 20 May 1824 | |
| | Benjamin J. Flint | Elizabeth White | 25 May 1824 | 29 May 1824 |
| | Matthew Hughes | Jane Logan | 26 May 1824 | 27 May 1824 |
| | Jewell Dodge | Elizabeth Clifton | 8 Jun 1824 | 10 Jun 1824 |
| 68 | John Pritchard | Erreley Hubart | 15 Jun 1824 | 17 Jun 1824 |
| | James P. Wilson | Elizabeth Cones (widow) | 23 Jun 1824 | 1 Jul 1824 |
| | James Baily | Elizabeth Johnson | 23 Jun 1824 | |
| | Benjamin Seely | Juliane Anna Lott | 8 Jul 1824 | 8 Jul 1824 |
| | Peter H. Rudman | Catharine Henry | 10 Jul 1824 | |
| 69 | Robert Hobbs | Rachel Alley | 21 Jul 1824 | 22 Jul 1824 |
| | Harris Owen | Susan Maker | 22 Jul 1824 | 22 Jul 1824 |
| | John Alsmon [Allsman] | Elizabeth Crewensbury | 23 Jul 1824 | 25 Jul 1824 |
| | Jacob Broadwell, Jr. | Mary Magdalene Capp | 29 Jul 1824 | 29 Jul 1824 |
| | Hugh Howard | Mary Lewis | 2 Aug 1824 | |
| | George Wilson | Mary Ann Hughell [Hudgell] | 2 Aug 1824 | 3 Aug 1824 |
| 70 | Stephen Hall | Mary Ann Turpen | 5 Aug 1824 | 5 Aug 1824 |
| | John Todd | Elizabeth Lacky | 7 Aug 1824 | 12 Aug 1824 |
| | Ebenzer Grist | Elizabeth Belk | 16 Aug 1824 | 19 Aug 1824 |
| | Henry S. Thorn | Polly Bouram | 17 Aug 1824 | 19 Aug 1824 |
| | George Brooks | Ruth Ramey | 20 Aug 1824 | 22 Aug 1824 |
| | James Doty | Mary Manwaring | 28 Aug 1824 | 2 Sep 1824 |
| | John Hendrickson | Miranda Goble | 31 Aug 1824 | 2 Sep 1824 |
| 71 | John McQuoid | Mary Rouze [Rouse] | 1 Sep 1824 | 22 Sep 1824 |
| | Hugh M. Bail | Mary Coy (widow) | 3 Sep 1824 | 5 Sep 1824 |
| | Thomas Arnett | Mary Morrow | 3 Sep 1824 | |
| | James Rariden | Mary H. Test | 5 Sep 1824 | 5 Sep 1824 |
| | John Harwood | Eliza Carel [Carrel] | 13 Sep 1824 | 13 Sep 1824 |
| 72 | Stewart Morrison | Delilah Remy | 20 Sep 1824 | 20 Sep 1824 |
| | William Smith | Jane Moody | 27 Sep 1824 | 30 Sep 1824 |
| | Samuel Blair | Elizabeth Fauch | 28 Sep 1824 | 28 Sep 1824 |
| | John Cooly | Hannah Gant | 9 Oct 1824 | 14 Oct 1824 |
| [Book Number 3] | | | | |
| 1 | John Bake | Jane Telfer | 27 Oct 1824 | 28 Oct 1824 |
| | James Heap | Easter Rudman Esther A. | 30 Oct 1824 | |
| 2 | Nathan Smith | Sophia Seely | 4 Nov 1824 | 4 Nov 1824 |
| | Oliver P. Thirston | Maria Flint | 8 Nov 1824 | 11 Nov 1824 |
| 3 | Malachi Clark | Rachel George | 10 Nov 1824 | 11 Nov 1824 |
| | David Wallace | Esther F. Test | 10 Nov 1824 | 10 Nov 1824 |

| PAGE | GROOM | BRIDE | DATE LICENSE | DATE MARRIAGE |
|------|-------|-------|--------------|---------------|
| 4 | Benjamin Snowden | Elizabeth Deakins [Dakins] | 21 Nov 1824 | 22 Nov 1824 |
|  | Emery Scotton | Mary S. Slaughter | 22 Nov 1824 | 26 Nov 1824 |
| 5 | Ramey S. Cloud | Hannah Sater | 2 Dec 1824 | |
|  | John Shultz Shutz | Maria Crawford | 7 Dec 1824 | 9 Dec 1824 |
| 6 | William Barnes Banes | Rosanna Serles (widow) Seiles | 11 Dec 1824 | 13 Dec 1824 |
|  | Edmund Moore | Elizabeth Higgs | 20 Dec 1824 | 23 Dec 1824 |
| 7 | James Kerr | Margaret Grist | 20 Dec 1824 | 23 Dec 1824 |
|  | Isaac N. Phipps | Julia Ann Cully | 21 Dec 1824 | |
| 8 | Isaac Bush | Margaret Adair | 22 Dec 1824 | 22 Dec 1824 |
|  | Samuel Thirston | Rebeccah Mash [Marsh] | 27 Dec 1824 | 30 Dec 1824 |
| 9 | Thomas Lough | Elizabeth Linch | 3 Jan 1825 | |
|  | Richard D. Andrews | Mary Blades | 5 Jan 1825 | 9 Jan 1825 |
| 10 | James Hancock | Rachel Stansbury | 8 Jan 1825 | 13 Jan 1825 |
|  | John A. Newland Nelson | Mary Ann Scott | 10 Jan 1825 | 14 Jan 1825 |
| 11 | David Lewis | Nancy George | 11 Jan 1825 | 13 Jan 1825 |
|  | David McKnight | Catharine Smally | 15 Jan 1825 | 20 Jan 1825 |
| 12 | John Colwell, Jr. [Coldwell] | Harriett Laing [Lane] | 20 Jan 1825 | 20 Jan 1825 |
|  | Stephen Kidwell | Mariah George | 20 Jan 1825 | 3 Feb 1825 |
| 13 | John Montgomery | Mary Padon | 27 Jan 1825 | 27 Jan 1825 |
|  | Francis E. Winship | Ann L. Phillips | 28 Jan 1825 | 29 Jan 1825 |
| 14 | William Vanzant | Mariah Simonson | 2 Feb 1825 | |
|  | William F. Ferguson | Salome Snow | 15 Feb 1825 | |
| 15 | Samuel W. Harper | Elizabeth Wildridge | 15 Feb 1825 | 17 Feb 1825 |
|  | Stephen Marsh (of Hamilton Co, OH) | Sarah Pursel | 17 Feb 1825 | 17 Feb 1825 |
| 16 | Francis C. Downin Dawnin | Hannah Davis | 21 Feb 1825 | |
|  | John Hughes | Mary W. Ogden | 7 Mar 1825 | 9 Mar 1825 |
| 17 | Urban Edgerton | Elizabeth Boots | 24 Mar 1825 | 31 Mar 1825 |
|  | John Weir | Elizabeth Hunt | 25 Mar 1825 | 8 Mar [sic] 1825 |
| 18 | Joseph Thackrey [Thackry] | Mary Dubois | 4 Apr 1825 | 7 Apr 1825 |
|  | Moses Abernathey [Abbernathey] | Jenny Hanna | 5 Apr 1825 | 7 Apr 1825 |
| 19 | William Davis | Mary Cathers | 7 Apr 1825 | 9 Apr 1825 |
|  | Moses P. Lamb | Margaret Russell | 9 Apr 1825 | |
| 20 | James Karr | Hesther Doty | 9 Apr 1825 | 10 Apr 1825 |
|  | Robert Morris | Amy Jones | 11 Apr 1825 | |

| PAGE | GROOM | BRIDE | DATE LICENSE | DATE MARRIAGE |
|------|-------|-------|--------------|---------------|
| 21 | Russell Hayselton (of Butler Co, OH) | Nancy Perry | 12 Apr 1825 | 14 Apr 1825 |
|  | Joseph Watkins | Ann Boutcher | 20 Apr 1825 | 21 Apr 1825 |
| 22 | Francis Kelley | Kisiah Austin | 30 Apr 1825 | 2 May 1825 |
|  | William Sims | Fear Sturdevant | 30 Apr 1825 | 1 May 1825 |
| 23 | Richard Loudenback [Louderback] (Lauden) | Rebecah Hawk | 10 May 1825 | 12 May 1825 |
|  | John Smith | Jeruse Brannen | 10 May 1825 | 15 May 1825 |
| 24 | Moses Obrien | Eliza Hinkson | 19 May 1825 | 19 May 1825 |
|  | John Stephenson | Lavenia Ross | 13 Jun 1825 | 14 Jun 1825 |
| 25 | James Alley | Ann Alley | 2 Jul 1825 | |
|  | John Wilson | Nancy Fay | 12 Jul 1825 | 14 Jul 1825 |
| 26 | Joab Stout | Amanda Rarden | 22 Jul 1825 | 24 Jul 1825 |
|  | Court V. Skilman | Mary T. Frazee | 1 Aug 1825 | 4 Aug 1825 |
| 27 | David L. Portlock | Sarah Scott | 1 Aug 1825 | 4 Aug 1825 |
|  | Andrew Jackson | Jane Golding | 1 Aug 1825 | 4 Aug 1825 |
| 28 | Anderson Jackson | Elizabeth Dolson | 3 Aug 1825 | 4 Aug 1825 |
|  | James S. Powers | Maria Sturdavant (Sturdevant) | 4 Aug 1825 | |
| 29 | Anthony Bissel | Sally Welch | 5 Aug 1825 | 15 Aug 1825 |
|  | James K. Anderson | Margaret Johnson (widow) | 4 Aug 1825 | 11 Aug 1825 |
| 30 | John C. Johnston | Madline Wheaton | 12 Aug 1825 | 14 Aug 1825 |
|  | John Flemming [Fleming] | Mary Lyons | 13 Aug 1825 | 14 Aug 1825 |
| 31 | Richard Freeman [Hulbart] | Tamsey Habbard | 30 Aug 1825 | 30 Aug 1825 |
|  | James Moody | Elizabeth Dixson | 6 Sep 1825 | |
| 32 | Edward Bransford | Milly Strainge [Strange] | 8 Sep 1825 | 8 Sep 1825 |
|  | Jacob Murphy | Elizabeth Flint | 9 Sep 1825 | 11 Sep 1825 |
| 33 | Cyrus Sackett | Nancy Jeffers | 14 Sep 1825 | 15 Sep 1825 |
|  | Samuel Barber | Elizabeth Neff | 14 Sep 1825 | 15 Sep 1825 |
| 34 | J.N. Hanna | Martha Richee Knight | 17 Sep 1825 | 18 Sep 1825 |
|  | Stephen Doty (of Ohio) | Rebeccah Bake | 22 Sep 1825 | 29 Sep 1825 |
| 35 | David Waggoner | Margaret Springer [Peggy] | 23 Sep 1825 | 29 Sep 1825 |
|  | Jesse Bennett (Bennet) | Lydia Oakes | 4 Oct 1825 | 4 Oct 1825 |
| 36 | Jeremiah Dare | Emley Brookbank | 10 Oct 1825 | 13 Oct 1825 |
|  | Robert Galbreath | Rebeca Margeson | 14 Oct 1825 | 22 Oct 1825 |
| 37 | Daniel Churchill (Churchhill) | Nancy Street | 15 Oct 1825 | 20 Oct 1825 |
|  | George W. Dolly | Catharine Clayton | 17 Oct 1825 | 17 Oct 1825 |
| 38 | Thomas Portteus | Jane Mitchell | 22 Oct 1825 | 17 Nov 1825 |

| PAGE | GROOM | BRIDE | DATE LICENSE | DATE MARRIAGE |
|------|-------|-------|--------------|---------------|
|      | Samuel Davis | Bárbary Miller | 5 Nov 1825 | 10 Nov 1825 |
| 39 | Beriann H. Larue | Mariann Nye | 7 Nov 1825 | |
|    | John Wilson | Polly Jones | 9 Nov 1825 | 12 Nov 1825 |
| 40 | James Miller | Anna Capper | 12 Nov 1825 | 13 Nov 1825 |
|    | James Blackburn | Nappy Sparks | 24 Nov 1825 | 1 Dec 1825 |
| 41 | Isaac Burkholder | Nancy Clover | 27 Nov 1825 | |
|    | Chancy Stevens | Mahalla Bartlow | 5 Dec 1825 | 5 Dec 1825 |
| 42 | Lewis Shideler (of Ohio) | Mary Bake | 5 Dec 1825 | 11 Dec 1825 |
|    | Sameul Eikenbury (of Ohio) | Martha Crawford | 5 Dec 1825 | 8 Dec 1825 |
| 43 | Noah R. Hobbs | Asby Christan Alley | 7 Dec 1825 | 15 Dec 1825 |
|    | Sylvester Golding | Getty Hutchens | 13 Dec 1825 | |
| 44 | Mark Fowler | Rebecca Russell | 10 Dec 1825 | 11 Dec 1825 |
|    | Kelom Abernathy | Hannah Loper | 19 Dec 1825 | 22 Dec 1825 |
| 45 | Christopher Welch | Sarah Abraham | 19 Dec 1825 | |
|    | James M. Stevens | Mariah Backhouse | 21 Dec 1825 | 25 Dec 1825 |
| 46 | Jonathan Smith | Catharine Stafford | 28 Dec 1825 | |
|    | Nathaniel Tucker | Anna Rockafellar | 28 Dec 1825 | 5 Jan 1826 |
| 47 | Thomas Whenden | Mary Lacky | 28 Dec 1825 | |
|    | Robert White | Nancy Reeds | 29 Dec 1825 | 29 Dec 1825 |
| 48 | William Price | Cynthia Randel | 30 Dec 1825 | 3 Jan 1826 |
|    | Isaac Updyke | Jerusha Tharp | 30 Dec 1825 | 1 Jan 1826 |
| 49 | Martin Williams | Isabel White | 3 Jan 1826 | 5 Jan 1826 |
|    | Thomas Dewyre | Nancy Hansel [Hensly] (Hansley) | 17 Jan 1826 | 19 Jan 1826 |
| 50 | Albert Dare | Jane White | 19 Jan 1826 | 22 Jan 1826 |
|    | Abishar Stubbs | Polly Risk | 21 Jan 1826 | 26 Jan 1826 |
| 51 | Samuel Ray | Ann Morris | 27 Jan 1826 | 8 Feb 1826 |
|    | Samuel Montgomery | Mary Pursel [Percel] | 11 Feb 1826 | 12 Feb 1826 |
| 52 | John Cowen | Martha Miles | 11 Feb 1826 | |
|    | Simon Fry (Sigler) | Elizabeth Siglar | 13 Feb 1826 | 14 Feb 1826 |
| 53 | Samuel Patterson | Nancy Davis | 14 Feb 1826 | |
|    | Peter F. Newland | Susan Hanna | 20 Feb 1826 | 23 Feb 1826 |
| 54 | Redden Osborn | Mary Dare | 21 Feb 1826 | 23 Feb 1826 |
|    | David C. Templeton | Matilda Baxter [Backster] | 4 Mar 1826 | 4 Mar 1826 |
| 55 | John Thirston | Rebecca Thirston | 7 Mar 1826 | 9 Mar 1826 |
|    | William Casto (of Bulter Co, OH) | Indiann Devall | 7 Mar 1826 | 10 Mar 1826 |
| 56 | Joseph Adams | Nancy Scott | 8 Mar 1826 | 9 Mar 1826 |
|    | Samuel D. Abbercrombie | Loretta Larue | 8 Mar 1826 | 9 Mar 1826 |
| 57 | Spencer Wiley | Nancy Deweese | 14 Mar 1826 | 14 Mar 1826 |

| PAGE | GROOM | BRIDE | DATE LICENSE | DATE MARRIAGE |
|------|-------|-------|--------------|---------------|
|  | David Patterson | Mary Evans | 18 Mar 1826 | 19 Mar 1826 |
| 58 | Daniel Goodwin | Judiah Goodwin | 22 Mar 1826 | 23 Mar 1826 |
|  | Willis Prewit (Prewitt) | Catharine Ann Woodworth | 31 Mar 1826 | 2 Apr 1826 |
| 59 | Alexander Davidson | Mary Prewit | 31 Mar 1826 | |
|  | William Montogemry | Mary Cooksey (Cook) | 1 Apr 1826 | 6 Apr 1826 |
| 60 | David Portteus | Jane Abbercrombie | 10 Apr 1826 | 13 Apr 1826 |
|  | Charles Newkirk | Margaret Milholland | 10 Apr 1826 | 11 Apr 1826 |
| 61 | Elijah Mesner | Emily Posey | 27 Apr 1826 | 4 May 1826 |
|  | George H. Robbinson (Robinson) | Mary Simpson | 11 May 1826 | 11 May 1826 |
| 62 | Berien Reynolds | Catherine Halsey | 18 May 1826 | 20 May 1826 |
|  | Henry Petree | Mary Snowden | 20 May 1826 | 21 Jun 1826 |
| 63 | Josiah Maul | Martha Morris | 30 May 1826 | 31 May 1826 |
|  | James Dickey | Elenor Shaw | 17 Jun 1826 | 18 Jun 1826 |
| 64 | John L. Dexter | Hannah Smith (widow) | 20 Jun 1826 | 20 Jun 1826 |
|  | Abraham Newkirk | Helen Hurst | 21 Jun 1826 | 22 Jun 1826 |
| 65 | Elihu Alley | Catharine Carr | 26 Jun 1826 | 29 Jun 1826 |
|  | Isaac Fuller | Elizabeth Cherry | 28 Jun 1826 | 15 Jul 1826 |
| 66 | Peace Maker | Jane Ross | 1 Jul 1826 | 1 Jul 1826 |
|  | Samuel Ross | Candias Maker | 3 Jul 1826 | 3 Jul 1826 |
| 67 | Moses Rarden | Mary Cason [Carson] | 13 Jul 1826 | 13 Jul 1826 |
|  | Joseph Weston | Lydia Crist | 17 Jul 1826 | 17 Jul 1826 |
| 68 | Galoway Finley | Harriet Ward | 22 Jul 1826 | 27 Jul 1826 |
|  | Esom B. Thomas | Elizabeth Young | 7 Aug 1826 | 17 Aug 1826 |
| 69 | William Cooksey | Rebecca Ann Debarris | 8 Aug 1826 | 13 Aug 1826 |
|  | Christopher Warmsley (Wamsley) | Charrity Gulick | 17 Aug 1826 | 20 Aug 1826 |
| 70 | Henry Debaun | Lufamey Chance | 28 Aug 1826 | 30 Aug 1826 |
|  | Titus H. Hinman | Emily Jeter | 9 Sep 1826 | 10 Sep 1826 |
| 71 | Highland Jacobs | Susanna Duglass [Douglass] (Douglas) | 9 Sep 1826 | 10 Sep 1826 |
|  | Martin Clark | Margaret Mewhinney | 12 Sep 1826 | 14 Sep 1826 |
| 72 | William Shultz | Elizabeth Tilfer | 18 Sep 1826 | 21 Sep 1826 |
|  | John Lemmon | Jane B. Crocker | 20 Sep 1826 | |
| 73 | Calvin Moor [Moore] | Elenor Longacre | 20 Sep 1826 | 21 Sep 1826 |
|  | Solomon Tyner | Mary Longacre | 20 Sep 1826 | 21 Sep 1826 |
| 74 | James Davis | Hannah Sanders | 21 Sep 1826 | 21 Sep 1826 |
|  | David M. Anthony | Elizabeth Lemon | 27 Sep 1826 | |
| 75 | William Carson | Sarah Ann Mitchell | 28 Sep 1829 | |
|  | Joseph Wallace (of Butler Co, OH) | Jane Simmons | 30 Sep 1826 | 11 Oct 1826 |
| 76 | John Smally (Smalley) | Sophia Hergerreader | 4 Oct 1826 | 13 Oct 1826 |
|  | Jeremiah Barkhurst | Anna Manwarring | 16 Oct 1826 | 19 Oct 1826 |

| PAGE | GROOM | BRIDE | DATE LICENSE | DATE MARRIAGE |
|---|---|---|---|---|
| 77 | William Jackson (Jackman) | Mary Stafford | 4 Oct 1826 | 5 Oct 1826 |
| | George Ridle [Riddle] | Julian Hughell | 14 Oct 1826 | 15 Oct 1826 |
| 78 | John C. Holstead | Annis Martin | 16 Oct 1826 | 18 Oct 1826 |
| | Ralph Coalscott (Colescott) | Ruth Updyke | 17 Oct 1826 | 17 Oct 1826 |
| 79 | David Benton | Thankful McCaine [McClaine] | 17 Oct 1826 | 17 Oct 1826 |
| | Abraham Larue | Rebecca Rockafellar | 20 Oct 1826 | |
| 80 | Jared G. Johnson | Anna Quick | 20 Oct 1826 | 22 Oct 1826 |
| | George Hoagland | Mary Vanzant | 21 Oct 1826 | |
| 81 | Abraham Coleman | Nancy Ladley | 24 Oct 1826 | 25 Oct 1826 |
| | David McCow | Jane Shearry | 26 Oct 1826 | 26 Oct 1826 |
| 82 | Robert Hazeltine | Mahala Shaw | 30 Oct 1826 | |
| | Samuel Fredd | Sarah Spradlin | 30 Oct 1826 | 2 Nov 1826 |
| 83 | Daniel Pursel [Pursell] | Mary St. John | 1 Nov 1826 | 2 Nov 1826 |
| | William Tryon | Mary McClure | 15 Nov 1826 | 19 Nov 1826 |
| 84 | Robert Hamilton | Nancy Owsley | 20 Nov 1826 | 23 Nov 1826 |
| | William Rhine | Phebe Cade | 21 Nov 1826 | |
| 85 | Francis Vargason | Lucinda Petty | 22 Nov 1826 | 22 Nov 1826 |
| | Richard Fox | Jane C. Williams | 25 Nov 1826 | 26 Nov 1826 |
| 86 | William McClure | Minerva Flint | 4 Dec 1826 | 7 Dec 1826 |
| | Benjamin Rucker (Rocker) | Sarah George | 5 Dec 1826 | 7 Dec 1826 |
| 87 | Nathan Overman | Ellen Wheeler | 8 Dec 1826 | 9 Dec 1826 |
| | Annanais Luddington | Polly Cook | 9 Dec 1826 | |
| 88 | Daniel Taylor | Rebecca Allen | 20 Dec 1826 | 24 Dec 1826 |
| | J.O. St. John | Jame Harvey | 20 Dec 1826 | 21 Dec 1826 |
| 89 | Harvey Blackledge | Selinda Gorden (Gordon) | 25 Dec 1826 | 28 Dec 1826 |
| | William Reed | Sarah Brouhard (Broadhead) | 25 Dec 1826 | 28 Dec 1826 |
| 90 | George Adams | Honour Atherton | 25 Dec 1826 | 25 Dec 1826 |
| | Lambert Larowe | Sarah Andrew | 27 Dec 1826 | 28 Dec 1826 |
| 91 | Minah Simonson (Simpson) | Catharine Hazel | 2 Jan 1827 | |
| | Joseph Thomas | Charlotte Simmons | 6 Jan 1827 | 11 Jan 1827 |
| 92 | David F. Cooley | Letes Petty | 8 Jan 1827 | |
| | Abram [Abraham] Hyler | Mather Whitney | 15 Jan 1827 | 16 Jan 1827 |
| 93 | John Leman | Ellen Skinner | 13 Jan 1827 | 15 Jan 1827 |
| | Constantine Ladd | Elizabeth McWhorter | 15 Jan 1827 | 18 Jan 1827 |
| 94 | Thomas Hawkins | Sally Morris | 16 Jan 1827 | 16 Jan 1827 |

| PAGE | GROOM | BRIDE | DATE LICENSE | DATE MARRIAGE |
|---|---|---|---|---|
|  | Absolem H. Blackburn | Hily Thomas | 26 Jan 1827 |  |
| 95 | Hiram Hamilton (of Butler Co, OH) | Isabella Bartlow | 30 Jan 1827 | 11 Feb 1827 |
|  | James Patterson | Harriet Warman | 30 Jan 1827 |  |
| 96 | William Wright | Rebecca Reed | 13 Feb 1827 | 15 Feb 1827 |
|  | Hiram Pond | Hanah Davis | 19 Feb 1827 | 22 Feb 1827 |
| 97 | Samuel Allen | Olive Howe | 20 Feb 1827 | 22 Feb 1827 |
|  | John J. Loper | Ann Miller | 21 Feb 1827 | 22 Feb 1827 |
| 98 | David Flack | Mary Harris | 26 Feb 1827 |  |
|  | Joseph Stansbury | Juliet Marshall | 27 Feb 1827 | 1 Mar 1827 |
| 99 | Rasumen R. Kelly | Olive White | 27 Feb 1827 | 1 Mar 1827 |
|  | Hiram Fay | Polly Cooksy [Cooksee] (Cooksey) | 27 Feb 1827 | 8 Mar 1827 |
| 100 | Hamilton Shaw | Mariah Price | 7 Mar 1827 | 8 Mar 1827 |
|  | David Logan | Mariah Hughes | 7 Mar 1827 | 8 Mar 1827 |
| 101 | James Collett [Collet] | Nancy Jones | 12 Mar 1827 | 15 Mar 1827 |
|  | Philip Rhinehart | Anna Low [Lowe] | 13 Mar 1827 | 15 Mar 1827 |
| 102 | William Hallowvill (Hallowell) | Nancy Jacobs | 19 Mar 1827 |  |
|  | Alexander Johnston | Jane Powers | 21 Mar 1827 | 24 Mar 1827 |
| 103 | Benjamin Seals (Seal) | Sally Gregg | 22 Mar 1827 | 29 Mar 1827 |
|  | Jeremiah Lindville | Eunice [Unis] Quick | 28 Mar 1827 | 11 Apr 1827 |
| 104 | Robert N. Taylor | Polly Shaffer | 31 Mar 1827 | 31 Mar 1827 |
|  | Thomas Cummins | Lucinda Cummins | 7 Apr 1827 | 12 Apr 1827 |
| 105 | John Spradlin | Elizabeth Whartoner [Fortner] (Whatener) | 25 Apr 1827 | 29 Apr 1827 |
|  | Moses Maxwell | Abigail Rigg | 27 Apr 1827 |  |
| 106 | George B. Holland | Rebecca French | 2 May 1827 | 2 May 1827 |
|  | William Price | Margaret Hyatt | 10 May 1827 | 10 May 1827 |
| 107 | Nathaniel Lee | Catharine Blackburn | 10 May 1827 |  |
|  | Elias Stubbs | Elizabeth Updegraff | 11 May 1827 | 15 May 1827 |
| 108 | Stephen Coffin (Coffey) (of Dearborn Co) | Susannah Allison | 21 May 1827 | 22 May 1827 |
|  | Absolem Parvis | Elizabeth Kennedy [Elisabeth] | 19 May 1827 | 24 May 1827 |
| 109 | Elisha Williams | Elizabeth McCarty (widow) | 2 Jun 1827 | 3 Jun 1827 |
|  | Benjamin H. Newkirk | Hancy Hurst | 4 Jun 1827 | 7 Jun 1827 |
| 110 | Peter McDaniel | Hannah Buffenton | 4 Jun 1827 | 4 Jun 1827 |
|  | Eli Atkinson | Margaret Cooper [Margret] | 13 Jun 1827 | 14 Jun 1827 |

| PAGE | GROOM | BRIDE | DATE LICENSE | DATE MARRIAGE |
|------|-------|-------|--------------|---------------|
| 111 | Cummins Gardner [John] | Elizabeth Wynn [Winn] | 22 Jun 1827 | 3 Oct 1827 |
|  | James Rogers | Mary Prewit | 2 Jul 1827 | 2 Jul 1827 |
| 112 | Jacob Henning | Polly Bills | 4 Jul 1827 | 2 Jul 1827 |
|  | Solomon Franklin | Biddy Turner | 15 Jul 1827 |  |
| 113 | Samuel Dearmond [John] | Jerusia Shaw | 16 Jul 1827 | 21 Sep 1827 |
|  | William Jones | Mary Williams | 17 Jul 1827 | 17 Jul 1827 |
| 114 | Thomas Mostetler | Charlotte Morris | 21 Jul 1827 |  |
|  | Caleb Seal | Sarah Saunders [Sanders] | 13 Aug 1827 | 23 Aug 1827 |
| 115 | Joseph B. Reed [Joseph Smith] | Clarinda Baldwin | 16 Aug 1827 | 16 Aug 1837 |
|  | Cornelius Bartelow [Bartlow] | Betsey Dunn | 21 Aug 1827 | 23 Aug 1827 |
| 116 | Peter Bake (of Union Co) | Tabbitha Phenice [Tabitha Phenis] | 30 Aug 1827 | 2 Sep 1827 |
|  | James Welsh | Polly Gooschorn (Gushorn) | 1 Sep 1827 | 1 Sep 1827 |
| 117 | Michael C. Snell | Ann Deliaferis | 6 Sep 1827 | 6 Sep 1827 |
|  | William Ferguson | Elizebeth Himes (Hinds) | 20 Sep 1827 | 20 Sep 1827 |
| 118 | James Campbell | Elizabeth Davis | 21 Sep 1827 | 21 Sep 1827 |
|  | John Barrackman | Sarah Shepherd (Sheppard) | 25 Sep 1827 | 27 Sep 1827 |
| 119 | Josiah P. Halstead | Rebecca Wilson | 27 Sep 1827 | 29 Sep 1827 |
|  | Frances Holland | Margaret Slaughter | 4 Oct 1827 | 11 Oct 1827 |
| 120 | William Lynn | Kesiah McWhorter | 15 Oct 1827 [sic] | 18 Oct 1827 |
|  | Levi Scott | Sarah Hasley [Hasly] | 21 Oct 1827 | 22 Oct 1827 |
| 121 | Daniel Moore (of Fayette Co) | Mary Shearwood | 22 Oct 1827 | 25 Oct 1827 |
|  | James Roseberry | Mary Ward | 27 Oct 1827 | 1 Nov 1827 |
| 122 | William Wamsley [Warmsley] | Anna Jones | 5 Nov 1827 | 8 Nov 1827 |
|  | Levan McFarland, Sr. | Mary Nichols | 13 Nov 1827 | 13 Nov 1827 |
| 123 | McKinney Jackson | Jedidah Lyons (Lines) | 14 Nov 1827 | 15 Nov 1827 |
|  | Valentine Mowery (Mowrey) | Nancy Eggans (Eggens) | 17 Nov 1827 | 20 Nov 1827 |
| 124 | Stephen Hart | Lois Ryckman | 21 Nov 1827 | 22 Nov 1827 |
|  | Isaac Colly | Fanna Alley | 30 Nov 1827 | 2 Dec 1827 |
| 125 | Elijah Barwick | Catharine Gayness | 5 Dec 1827 | 6 Dec 1827 |
|  | David Blazer (Blazier) | Emily Even [Ervin] | 11 Dec 1827 | 13 Dec 1827 |

| PAGE | GROOM | BRIDE | DATE LICENSE | DATE MARRIAGE |
|------|-------|-------|--------------|---------------|
| 126 | Thomas Winscott | Nancy Herndon | 12 Dec 1827 | 13 Dec 1827 |
| | Allen Baxter | Mariah Underwood | 13 Dec 1827 | 13 Dec 1827 |
| 127 | John H. Fauset | Jane Chance | 20 Dec 1827 | 27 Dec 1827 |
| | William Davis | Elizabeth Huddleston (widow) [Hudleston] | 22 Dec 1827 | 25 Dec 1827 |
| 128 | William Pain | Celia Lewis | 26 Dec 1827 | |
| | George Gwinnup (of Rush Co) | Sarah Stewart | 29 Dec 1827 | 29 Dec 1827 |
| 129 | Martin W. Morris | Ann Rarden [Rariden] | 31 Dec 1827 | 1 Jan 1828 |
| | Hiram Banks | Neoma Barwick | 2 Jan 1828 | 2 Jan 1828 |
| 130 | James R. Allbach (Albach) | Sophronia Snow | 5 Jan 1828 | 8 Jan 1828 |
| | Nathan Shumaker | Margaret O'Kain | 5 Jan 1828 | 23 Feb 1828 |
| 131 | William S. Hammond | Catharine Hansel | 9 Jan 1828 | 10 Jan 1828 |
| | Thomas C. Crosley | Emily Spencer | 9 Jan 1828 | 10 Jan 1828 |
| 132 | Thomas W. Smith | Mary Gant | 11 Jan 1828 | 11 Jan 1828 |
| | Thomas F. Smith | Pethena Hughell | 11 Jan 1828 | 15 Jan 1828 |
| 133 | Ranna Pering [Perring] | Maria Gregg | 12 Jan 1828 | 13 Jan 1828 |
| | John Petree | Mary Fisher | 16 Jan 1828 | 18 Jan 1828 |
| 134 | Vincent Wainright | Charlotte Spencer | 24 Jan 1828 | 31 Jan 1828 |
| | Benjamin Abrahams | Elizabeth Hawkins | 26 Jan 1828 | 7 Feb 1828 |
| 135 | John Hansel | Rozannah White | 28 Jan 1828 | 31 Jan 1828 |
| | Thomas Cooper | Elizabeth Brison | 28 Jan 1828 | 29 Jan 1828 |
| 136 | Hiram George | Ann Fitchpattrick (Fitchpatrick) | 5 Feb 1828 | 7 Feb 1828 |
| | Isaac Cox | Nancy Myres (Meyers) | 7 Feb 1828 | 8 Feb 1828 |
| 137 | Job Scott | Lorean Wallace | 9 Feb 1828 | 10 Feb 1828 |
| | Benjamin Griner | Patsy McGinnis | 12 Feb 1828 | 28 Feb 1828 |
| 138 | Joseph Evens (J J) [Evans] | Bediah Turner | 12 Feb 1828 | 14 Feb 1828 |
| | Hugh Hastings | Margaret Elgin | 13 Feb 1828 | 14 Feb 1828 |
| 139 | William Allsmon | Mary Morgan | 13 Feb 1828 | 14 Feb 1828 |
| | Luther Henman [Hainman] | Margaret Hoaglin [Hoagland] | 13 Feb 1828 | 21 Feb 1828 |
| 140 | Abel Bell | Susanna Miller [Susannah] | 15 Feb 1828 | 17 Feb 1828 |
| | John Bertenshaw (Bentenshaw) | Esther Hall | 18 Feb 1828 | 19 Feb 1828 |
| 141 | James Jones | Margaret Cotton | 18 Feb 1828 | 21 Feb 1828 |
| | Cyrus Quick | Hannah Clayton | 25 Feb 1828 | 28 Feb 1828 |
| 142 | William Stewart | Jemima Fisher [Jemimah] | 1 Mar 1828 | 1 Mar 1828 |
| | Felix Stubbs | Abbigail Arnold | 4 Mar 1828 | 8 Mar 1828 |
| 143 | Benjamin W. Remy | Abigail Henman | 15 Mar 1828 | 16 Mar 1828 |
| | James Shank | Amanda Case | 19 Mar 1828 | 23 Mar 1828 |

| PAGE | GROOM | BRIDE | DATE LICENSE | DATE MARRIAGE |
|---|---|---|---|---|
| 144 | Gilbert Gentry | Elizabeth Hall | 20 Mar 1828 | |
| | Daniel Cooms | Mary Smith | 26 Mar 1828 | |
| 145 | John Kuhns [Ruhns] | Epilespy Johnson (Johnston) | 28 Mar 1828 | 29 Mar 1828 |
| | Rufus Haymond | Caroline W. Northrup [Northrop] | 8 Apr 1828 | 8 Apr 1828 |
| 146 | David Moore | Sally Price | 8 Apr 1828 | 10 Apr 1828 |
| | James Phylbay | Judah Barlow | 11 Apr 1828 | |
| 147 | Jacob Fosher | Catharine Bradburn | 24 Apr 1828 | 24 Apr 1828 |
| | Moses Hornady | Maria Jones | 28 Apr 1828 | 29 Apr 1828 |
| 148 | James Loller | Matilda Blades | 29 Apr 1828 | 29 Apr 1828 |
| | Nathaniel Bell | Mary Jackson | 10 May 1828 | 11 May 1828 |
| 149 | William McManoman | Isabella Linn [Lynn] | 20 May 1828 | 22 May 1828 |
| | Joel Tucker | Anna Fix | 20 May 1828 | 29 May 1828 |
| 150 | Spencer Gill | Rebeccah McKee [Rebecca] | 24 May 1828 | 24 May 1828 |
| | Hugh Roach | Dorcas Johnson | 7 Jun 1828 | 9 Jun 1828 |
| 151 | William Hatfield | Margret Ewing | 9 Jun 1828 | 12 Jun 1828 |
| | Charles Thacker | Mary Luke | 15 Jun 1828 | 19 Jun 1828 |
| 152 | Jonathan Shaw | Susan Stafford | 21 Mar 1828 [sic] | 22 Jun 1828 |
| | Leven Henderson | Phebe Hannah | 5 Jul 1828 | 6 Jul 1828 |
| 153 | Benjamin Updyke | Lydia Ann Williams | 12 Jul 1828 | 13 Jul 1828 |
| | Masterson Clark | Mahala Harris | 12 Jul 1828 | 31 Jul 1828 |
| 154 | John Scott | Nancy George | 1 Aug 1828 | 2 Aug 1828 |
| | William Cook | Catharine Haymon [Haymond] | 14 Aug 1828 | 14 Aug 1828 |
| 155 | John Simpson | Mariah Bastion [Maria Baston] | 15 Aug 1828 | 16 Aug 1828 |
| | Absolem Armstrong | Mary Clark | 20 Aug 1828 | 21 Aug 1828 |
| 156 | Micajah Lewis Anthony | Anna Hansel | 25 Aug 1828 | |
| | James Slaughter | Susan Hutchen | 25 Aug 1828 | 25 Aug 1828 |
| 157 | Thomas Miller | Sally Rouk | 2 Sep 1828 | 4 Sep 1828 |
| | Warren Pond | Lucinda McClure | 3 Sep 1828 | 2 Apr 1829 [returned] |
| 158 | Abisha Stubbs [Stubs] | Mary Richardson | 5 Sep 1828 | 7 Sep 1828 |
| | Otheniel Reed | Abigail White | 8 Sep 1828 | 9 Sep 1828 |
| 159 | Alexander Wood | Elizabeth Templeton | 9 Sep 1828 | 9 Sep 1828 |
| | Jonathan E. Armstrong | Pruella Moody | 9 Sep 1828 | 11 Sep 1828 |
| 160 | Abner Leonard | Sally Owl | 11 Sep 1828 | 11 Sep 1828 |
| | John Powell | Lydia Collett | 11 Sep 1828 | 13 Sep 1828 |
| 161 | Abel Webb | Elizabeth Kelsey | 15 Sep 1828 | 25 Sep 1828 |
| | George W. Wallace | Nancy P. Ogden | 17 Sep 1828 | 18 Sep 1828 |

| PAGE | GROOM | BRIDE | DATE LICENSE | DATE MARRIAGE |
|------|-------|-------|--------------|---------------|
| 162 | Alexander W. Russell | Catharine Noble | 17 Sep 1828 | 17 Sep 1828 |
| | George Hawkins | Margret Frakes | 24 Sep 1828 | 24 Sep 1828 |
| 163 | Joseph Whitney | Olive Tyler | 26 Sep 1828 | 28 Sep 1828 |
| | William Wilson | Abagail Holsey [Halstead] (Halsey) | 29 Sep 1828 | 29 Sep 1829 |
| 164 | Joseph Alexander | Ann Reed | 1 Oct 1828 | 2 Oct 1828 |
| | Samuel Brees (Breese) | Elizabeth Crist | 4 Oct 1828 | 5 Oct 1828 |
| 165 | John Lynn | Nancy Gant | 4 Oct 1828 | |
| | Robert Stevenson [Stephenson] | Abagail Harding | 4 Oct 1828 | 25 Dec 1828 |
| 166 | Thomas Smith | Mahala Millus [Millis] | 7 Oct 1828 | 10 Oct 1828 |
| | George Lynn | Mary Mahaffy | 11 Oct 1828 | 11 Oct 1828 |
| 167 | Thomas Stringer | Harriet Fuller | 13 Oct 1828 | |
| | Nathaniel Davis | Eliza Marklin | 13 Oct 1828 | 16 Oct 1828 |
| 168 | Moses Craig | Matilda Ann Gillespie | 14 Oct 1828 | |
| | Kinzea Turner | Tamer Huff | 16 Oct 1828 | 19 Oct 1828 |
| 169 | Edward Davis | Cidney Newman | 20 Oct 1828 | 21 Oct 1828 |
| | Thomas Swiggett | Ann Swift | 28 Oct 1828 | 30 Oct 1828 |
| 170 | Oliver Simpson | Lavina Faucett | 3 Nov 1828 | 6 Nov 1828 |
| | James P. Wilson | Lucretia Oakes | 3 Nov 1828 | 13 Nov 1828 |
| 171 | Elijah Smalley | Mary Ann Blue (Blew) | 2 Nov 1828 | 6 Nov 1828 |
| | Alva Benton | Margret Winslow | 4 Nov 1828 | 6 Nov 1828 |
| 172 | James Malson | Drusilla Blackburn | 5 Nov 1828 | 6 Nov 1828 |
| | Daniel Morgan | Hannah Foster | 6 Nov 1828 | 6 Nov 1828 |
| 173 | Jabez L. Winship [Julian] | Julia Ann Woodworth | 15 Nov 1828 | 15 Nov 1828 |
| | William T. Beeks | Elvira A. Johnson | 15 Nov 1828 | 17 Nov 1828 |
| 174 | William Osborn [Osbon] | Milley Osborn [Osbon] | 19 Nov 1828 | 20 Nov 1828 |
| | William Pruett | Elizabeth Davison | 26 Nov 1828 | 27 Nov 1828 |
| 175 | Abraham Conrey | Rachel Larowe (Larue) | 3 Dec 1828 | 4 Dec 1828 |
| | Ralph Wildridge | Elizabeth Bilby | 5 Dec 1828 | 11 Dec 1828 |
| 175A | Elias Phillis | Elizabeth Halstead | 13 Dec 1828 | |
| | John Stansbury [Stanbury] | Ruth Hubble [Hubbel] | 14 Dec 1828 | 18 Dec 1828 |
| 175B | Matthias Luse (Luce) | Malinda Bartelow (Bartlow) | 17 Dec 1828 | 18 Dec 1828 |
| | David Colyer | Sarah George | 18 Dec 1828 | 25 Dec 1828 |
| 176 | John Hobbs | Jane Alley | 22 Dec 1828 | 28 Dec 1828 |
| | John Spencer | Mary Dunn | 24 Dec 1828 | 1 Jan 1829 |
| 177 | Waren [Warren] Lyman | Elcy Shepherd | 25 Dec 1828 | 25 Dec 1828 |
| | Hugh Finley | Jane Austen | 26 Dec 1828 | 28 Dec 1828 |

| PAGE | GROOM | BRIDE | DATE LICENSE | DATE MARRIAGE |
|------|-------|-------|--------------|---------------|
| 178 | Andrew McGahey | Elizabeth Manan | 30 Dec 1828 | 1 Jan 1829 |
| | James Cox | Mary Hulick | 7 Jan 1829 | 8 Jan 1829 |
| 179 | Samuel Pruett | Volley Moore | 13 Jan 1829 | 3 Oct 1829 |
| | John Morely (Marsley) | Mary Hares (Harris) | 17 Jan 1829 | 18 Jan 1829 |
| 180 | Ezekiel Thomas | Jemima [Gemima] Webb | 17 Jan 1829 | 22 Jan 1829 |
| | Eleazer Rose | Rebecca Elwell | 26 Jan 1829 | 3 Feb 1829 |
| 181 | Philip Mason [Phillip] | Maria [Mariah] Carson | 27 Jan 1829 | 29 Jan 1829 |
| | John Elden [Eldon] | Isabella Wynn | 28 Jan 1829 | 29 Jan 1829 |
| 182 | Daniel Smith | Nancy Hartman | 4 Feb 1829 | 5 Feb 1829 |
| | Joshua Parvis | Ann Mariah Lamarr [Lamar] | 7 Feb 1829 | 7 Feb 1829 |
| 183 | Hosea Alley | Senca Halsey | 11 Feb 1829 | 19 Feb 1829 |
| | John Green | Leah Chambers | 14 Feb 1829 | 15 Feb 1829 |
| 184 | Alexander Roseberry | Aly [Ally] Johnston | 16 Feb 1829 | 26 Feb 1829 |
| | Williams Evans | Mary Milor | 26 Feb 1829 | 27 Feb 1829 |
| 185 | Thomas H. Black | Mary Ann Norvelle [Norvell] | 3 Mar 1829 | 15 Mar 1829 |
| | John Ryburn | Nancy Nelson | 4 Mar 1829 | 5 Mar 1829 |
| 186 | Israel Carson | Sarah Ann Wise | 17 Mar 1829 | 19 Mar 1829 |
| | Edmund Huff | Nancy Harris | 19 Mar 1829 | 19 Mar 1829 |
| 187 | Hugh Morrow | Violet Johnson | 23 Mar 1829 | 23 Mar 1829 |
| | John Hudson | Elizabeth Richie | 24 Mar 1829 | |
| 188 | Seth E. Barwick | Eliza Jane Dorrell | 25 Mar 1829 | |
| | John Clark | Isabella Major | 28 Mar 1829 | 29 Mar 1829 |
| 189 | John Bowne (Bown) [Brown] | Elsey Gulley | 28 Mar 1829 | 28 Mar 1829 |
| | William Weston | Eliza Jane Hires (Hiers) | 30 Mar 1829 | 2 Apr 1829 |
| 190 | Wm Carter | Mary Adams | 1 Apr 1829 | 9 Apr 1829 |
| | Philip Sweetser | Rebecca Maria Noble | 2 Apr 1829 | 2 Apr 1829 |
| 191 | Abner Lewis | Margret Hamilton | 4 Apr 1829 | 5 Apr 1829 |
| | David Kilgore | Charity Sizelove | 7 Apr 1829 | |
| 192 | David Slaughter | Nancy Clemants (Clements) | 7 Apr 1829 | 9 Apr 1829 |
| | James Abrams | Sarah Hawkins | 14 Apr 1829 | 16 Apr 1829 |
| 193 | Abner Jones | Polly Simpson | 18 Apr 1829 | 23 Apr 1829 |
| | William Freeman | Ruth Lee | 6 May 1829 | 7 May 1829 |
| 194 | Joseph Smart | Margaret Yaw | 6 May 1829 | 7 May 1829 |
| | John S. Powers | Jane McCarty | 7 May 1829 | 7 May 1829 |
| 195 | William W. Carmichael | Mary Larue | 16 May 1829 | |
| | John Burk | Hariet Tucker | 20 May 1829 | 21 May 1829 |

| PAGE | GROOM | BRIDE | DATE LICENSE | DATE MARRIAGE |
|------|-------|-------|--------------|---------------|
| 196 | James Lackey | Mitilda Curry | 25 May 1829 | 28 May 1829 |
| | Isaac Thurston | Margret [Margaret] Lee | 25 May 1829 | 28 May 1829 |
| 197 | Nathan Vanhorn | Elizabeth Russell | 26 May 1829 | 28 May 1829 |
| | George W. Hammond | Mary Foster | 30 May 1829 | 31 May 1829 |
| 198 | Parry Wason | Jane Johnston | 6 Jun 1829 | 6 Jun 1829 |
| | Anderson McCoy | Charity Record | 2 Jul 1829 | 6 Jul 1829 |
| 199 | Andrew White | Delila Lines | 4 Jul 1829 | 4 Jul 1829 |
| | John Holloville (Hollowell) | Catharine Sizelove | 11 Jul 1829 | |
| 200 | Eli Havens | Maria Wilson | 14 Jul 1829 | 14 Jul 1829 |
| | Edward White | Sarah White | 21 Jul 1829 | 26 Jul 1829 |
| 201 | John Lockwood | Rachel Whitelock | 25 Jul 1829 | 26 Jul 1829 |
| | George Daniel | Jane Dale | 29 Jul 1829 | 30 Jul 1829 |
| 202 | David Alley | Rebecca Jones | 1 Aug 1829 | |
| | Charles Wise | Sally Simpson | 3 Aug 1829 | 6 Aug 1829 |
| 203 | Henry Wright | Mary Riburn | 4 Aug 1829 | 5 Aug 1829 |
| | Bazel Reed | Catharine Flood | 13 Aug 1829 | 15 Aug 1829 |
| 204 | John Camebridge (Cambridge) | Matilda Malson | 19 Aug 1829 | 20 Aug 1829 |
| | Samuel Alley | Nancy Bunyard | 26 Aug 1829 | 27 Aug 1829 |
| 205 | John Russell | Martha Seal | 5 Sep 1829 | 10 Sep 1829 |
| | William W. Carson | Maria Magdalene Voorhees | 8 Sep 1829 | 10 Sep 1829 |
| 206 | Lewis M. Clark | Mary Pond (Bond) | 15 Sep 1829 | 17 Sep 1829 |
| | Joseph Patterson | Loisa [Lousia] Foster | 19 Sep 1829 | 20 Sep 1829 |
| 207 | Joseph Sizelove | Grace Boutcher | 22 Sep 1829 | |
| | Allurad Chamberlain | Clarissa Slack | 28 Sep 1829 | 28 Sep 1829 |
| 208 | Charles Fausset (Faussett) | Elizabeth Ann Sanders | 29 Sep 1829 | 1 Oct 1829 |
| | William Crist | Catharine Deford | 29 Sep 1829 | 29 Sep 1829 |
| 209 | John T. Remy | Nancy Jones | 30 Sep 1829 | 1 Oct 1829 |
| | James B. Bunyard | Eliza O'Neal | 1 Oct 1829 | 4 Oct 1829 |
| 210 | Francis Malson | Elizabeth Camebridge (Cambridge) | 8 Oct 1829 | 9 Oct 1829 |
| | Amos Sparks | Murcy Harper | 10 Oct 1829 | 15 Oct 1829 |
| 211 | John Stringer | Mary Jones | 13 Oct 1829 | 15 Oct 1829 |
| | Eli Luark | Anna Sharewood (Sherwood) | 14 Oct 1829 | 15 Oct 1829 |
| 212 | Greenbury Steel | Fanna Kingery [Fanny Kinggery] | 24 Oct 1829 | 25 Oct 1829 |
| | William Golding | Elizabeth Neely | 26 Oct 1829 | 26 Oct 1829 |
| 213 | Albin Newton | Sarah Jackson | 7 Nov 1829 | |
| | Hiram Williams | Martha Jane Peticrew | 11 Nov 1829 | 12 Nov 1829 |

| PAGE | GROOM | BRIDE | DATE LICENSE | DATE MARRIAGE |
|------|-------|-------|--------------|---------------|
| 214 | Amos Martin | Salley [Sally] Vincent | 18 Nov 1829 | 19 Nov 1829 |
| | Thomas W. Smart | Elizabeth Shaw | 27 Nov 1829 | 17 Nov 1829 [sic] |
| 215 | James Ferguson | Esther Gibson | 3 Dec 1829 | 5 Dec 1829 |
| | Haynes Haseltine [Hazleton] | Mary Luse | 7 Dec 1829 | 10 Dec 1829 |
| 216 | Joseph Williams | Susan Henderson | 14 Dec 1829 | 17 Dec 1829 |
| | Joel Tuttle | Susannah Hart | 18 Dec 1829 | Dec 1829 |
| 217 | James Weston | Margret Nelson [Margaret] | 19 Dec 1829 | 24 Dec 1829 |
| | Isaac Master | Patsey Drake | 22 Dec 1829 | 24 Dec 1829 |
| 218 | James C. Gant | Joycey Alley | 23 Dec 1829 | 27 Dec 1829 |
| | Prince Jenkins | Joanah Eliza Ervin | 24 Dec 1829 | 31 Dec 1829 |
| 219 | Ezekiel L. Hanna (of Marion Co) | Nancy Todd | 28 Dec 1829 | 31 Oct 1829 [sic] |
| | Thomas C. Whitelock | Leah Jones | 30 Dec 1829 | 31 Dec 1829 |

## ADDITIONAL INFORMATION FROM *THE FRANKLIN DEPOSITORY*

October 30, 1826.  Married David Benton, age 56 of Ohio, to Mrs. Thankful McCaine of Indiana, age 25, on October 17, 1826.

December 4, 1826.  Married Ralph Coalscott, late of Maryland, age 60, to Mrs. Ruth Updyke, October 17, 1826.  She was his fifth bride, he her third husband.

April 26, 1828.  I Forbid all persons of trusting or harboring my wife Maria on my account for I will not pay no debts of her contracting after this date.  Ranna Paring. April 8th A.D. 1828.

November 19, 1828.  Married William T. Beeks to Elvira A. Johnson, November 16, 1828.

# SOME GIBSON COUNTY CEMETERIES

Copied by Irene Keith, Helen Marie Taylor and Alvetta Wallace

Gibson County was formed in 1813 from Knox County. From that time until 1852 when the present boundaries were fixed, Gibson County's area and boundaries changed eleven times. Work is in progress copying cemeteries in this county. The following transcriptions were done in 1985. A list of transcriptions of other Gibson County cemeteries available in the Indiana Division, Indiana State Library has been added.

## MEADE CEMETERY

Meade Cemetery is located northeast of Francisco, Center Township, Gibson County, Indiana on present day 725E, 2.1 miles north of State Road 64.

Row 1

Massie, Jeremiah  b 4-28-1841  d 2-20-1881
    Thomas  b 10-16-1872  d 3-13-1888


Row 2

Taylor, John B.  4-20-1815  d 1-30-1839
Wallace, Nancy w/o J.T.  d 9-16-1845  age ca. 27 yr.
Woolsey, Sarah A. d/o G. & J.J.  b 7-21-185?  d 3-25-1856
Annise, Sopha w/o W.J.  d 3-8-1873  29 y 5 m
Annis, Everett A.  b 9-1-1895  d 1-4-1964  Pvt Co. C 103 Inf WWI PH
White, Gladys Brucine  b 5-14-1927  d 8-14-1927
Annis, Luther  1875-1975
    Nancy E.  1880-1964
McCune, Sarrah  1781-1855  74 yr.
Gears, George  b 6-11-1863  d 11-16-1945  Father
    Mary A.  b 2-14-1863  d 4-25-1939  Mother
Gears, Rosco s/o Geo. & Mary A.  b 8-26-1898  d 1-19-1908
Gears, Infant of G.W. & M.A.  b 9-13-1884  d 9-20-1884
Gears, Infant of G.W. & M.A.  b 5-9-1893
Annis, Bertha  b 12-22-1895  d 1-7-1941
Annis, Charles  1863-1943  Father
    Necy  1873-1948  Mother
Camp, Rosa E.  b 4-16-1900 d
    Cecil A.  2-21-1894  d 12-22-1975  US Army WWI  married 12-23-1934
Farmer, Basil L.  b 7-30-1899  d 1-13-1968
    Lawa M.  d/o Charles & Necy  d

**63**

Row 4

Mans, Henry   b 7-25-1831
    Elizabeth   b 12-1-1887   d 4-25-1904
Mans, Infant s/o H & E
Malone, Nicklas   s/o A.J. & L.A.   b 9-28-1839   d 12-2-1853
Malone, Smith Miller   b 9-9-1857   d 9-3-1858   11 m 24 d
Malone, A.J.   d 3-5-1869   54 y 2 m 7 d
Malone, Lydia   b 10-27-1820   d 4-10-1863
Annis, John W.   s/o G. & M.   d 8-31-1881   23 y 2 m 4 d
Annis, Idie   b 7-26-1870   d 7-29-187?
Hill, Amy
Annise, George   b 1828   d 9-?-1903
    Phoebe   b 1831   d 1898
Anniss, Martha   1860-1930
Tooley, Vonnetta F.   b 10-2-1914   d 12-16-1941
Tooley, Cora   1891-1975


Row 5

Farmer, Louvicey   b 8-29-1808   d 6-16-1879
Farmer, Berbilla   d/o Louvicey   b 2-9-1825   d 5-3-1862
Farmer, Jesse   s/o E.S. & ?   d 8-26-1870   2 m 20 d
Malone, Logan   s/o J. & L.A.   b 9-23-1846   d 12-14-1846
Malone, Infant   s/o A.J. & A.   b & d 7-17-1867
Vickers, Windfield C.   s/o H.C. & M. Ann b 10-5-1852   d 11-3-1852
Vickers, Marinda Ann w/o H.G.   d 5-25-1873
Vickers, Wilber   s/o H.C. & M
Vickers, Mary L.   s/o H.C. & M. Ann b 1-4-1856   d 9-17-1856
Woolsey, Celia   d 12-10-1818   63 y 10 m 6 d
Coleman, Sarah Jane   b 2-8-1837   d 5-5-1840
Thompson, Clark   b 4-27-1844   d 5-12-1863


Row 6

Yager, Elenor   w/o Jeremiah V.   d 11-20-1849   30 y 2 m 3 d
Yager, Jasper   s/o J.V. & C.   d 8-4-1871   16 y 4 m 6 d
Gudgel, Lucy F.   d/o A. & E.   b 6-26-1850   d 5-18-1851
Gudgel, Martha   d/o A. & E.   b 7-11-?
Witherspoon, Violet Ann   granddaughter of Ollie Lance & Joan b 5-5-1866
    d 11-3-1877
Duke, John W.   b 12-5-1840   d 7-10-1876   35 y 7 m 5 d
Duke, Emma E.   d/o J.W. & Nancy A.   b 1-23-1869   d 2-8-1903
Duke, William P.   s/o J.W. & N.A.   d 11-22-1875   12 y 30 d
Osborne, Charles   1847-1921   186th Regt N.J. Infantry Co I
    Ruth his wife   1834-1924

Row 7

Pearson, William   1832-1854
Pearson, Nancy   1824-1897
     Hiram A.   1825-1863   Cook Co K 58th Ind. Inf.
     parents of Lucy Stapleron
Simpson, Mary J.   w/o W. and d/o Olley & J Lang d 2-3-188[1?]   40 y 1 m 3 d
Simpson, W.J.   1847-1923
Lange, Joanna   w/o Olley L.   b 4-3-1813   d 3-9-1891
Madden, Mary A.   1870-1949
     Charles P.   1851-1916
Madden, Palmer   s/o Mr. & Mrs. Chas. P.   b 4-3-1896   d 11-15-1896
Ayers, Anna L.   1868-1938
     David E.   b 1870 d
Ayers, Della A.   1870-1960
Hall, Olive M.   b. 4-25-1945   d 11-6-1952
Hall, Beverly   b 1-2-1955   d 12-21-1955
Hall, Lillian M.   b 4-19-1925   d 5-14-1962
Hall, Mable O.   b 6-27-1908   d 9-15-1981   Mother


Row 8

Lange, John W.   b 12-16-1842   d 9-12-1892   Co. B   58th Ind. Vol.
Johnson, Clark   1856-1946
Farmer, Fred S.   b 4-16-1874   d 4-10-1910


Row 9

Barber, Infant   d/o A.L. & M.A.   d 5-7-1882   21 d
Meade, Mary A.   d/o John S. & Minerva   b 5-22-1860   d 3-2-1899
Witherspoon, Namie Lucelia   d/o J.T. & E.A.   d 4-19-1885   1 y 2 m 20 d
Lange, Harry A.   1871-1920   Father
Trible, Mariah E. Lange   1874-1955   Mother
Lange, Infant   1892-1892


Row 10

Aydelotte, Walter R.   s/o S.P. & N.A.   d 8-11-1879   2 m 28 d
Aydelotte, Cynthia A.   w/o James R.   d 12-6-1883   57 y 27 d
Monroe, Pearl   1881-1886
Monroe, Frederick K.   1846-1915
     Amelia A.   1852-1932
McKedy, George   s/o R.S. & R.H.   b 11-20-1889   d 12-28-1889
Farmer, Ezekial S.   Co. A. Ind, Cav.
Farmer, Rosa B.   w/o E.S.   2-18-1847   d 5-2-1902
Farmer, Wm. Fleming   s/o E.S. & R.B.   b 4-30-1880   d 8-1-1898
Farmer, Oliver   1882-1920

Row 11

McKedy, Infant   d/o J.N. & M.A.   b 6-14-1882
      Infant   d/o J.N. & M.A.   b 3-27-1878
McKedy, Mary   w/o J.N.   b 2-10-1853   d 12-30-1897
McKedy, Daniel S.   s/o J. & M.   b ?-?-1891   d ?-?-1899
Farmer, Percy F.   s/o C.C. & W.P.   b 12-7-1900   d 1-4-1901
Farmer, Charles C.   1868-1951
Farmer, Pearl   1874-1921
Burns, R. Hobart   b 10-3-1896   d 8-13-1964
      Maude   b 7-23-1893   d

Row 12

Field, Malethie A.   b 12-5-1854   d
      Harrison E.   b 8-24-1848   d 6-28-1893
Field, James W.   s/o R. & M.E.   d 2-2-1885   5 y 2 m 22 d
Field, Infant   s/o R & M.E.   b 11-10-1879
Field, Carlie   s/o R. & M.E.   d 4 y 2 m 4 d
Field, Mattie E.   d/o R. & M.E.   d 10-24-1883   3 m 3 d
Nunley, Thomas H.   s/o E. & A.   d 2-18-1879   20 y 27 d
Pearson, William A.   d 4-21-1885   52 y 8 m 7 d   Co. H. 17 Ind.
Wilhite, Ardella   d/o W.W. & M.E.   d 9-28-1876   1 y 8 d
Abbott, Mary E. Dent   w/o Robert N.   b 3-1-1884   d 11-29-1906
Burns, Rosella   1874-1954
      Joshua   1877-1942
Father

Row 13

H.R.F.
M.A.R.
Wilhite, Twin babies of C & S.F.   b & d 5-15-1869
Roberts, Margaret A.   b 1-2-1824   d 2-22-1879   55 y 1 m 21 d
Trippett, Ruth A.   w/o Joseph D.   d 4-20-1874   24 y 9 m 15 d
Johnson, Carl D.   s/o R.S. & M.L.   d 9-6-1877   ? 6 m 26 d
Johnson, David   b 7-30-1791   d 3-6-1875

Row 14

Hill, James   b 7-22-1824 CO. Rowan, N.N.   d 11-27-1871
Hill, Nancy Gibbons   b 3-9-1824   d 4-28-1900
Lewis, Mary E.   1852-1938
Lewis, Infant of S.M. & M.E.   d 9-17-1873   17 d
Snyder, Infant   1-13-1909
Snyder, Ida B.   1887-1962
      George W.   1885-1965

Hayman, Moses 1850-1939
Hayman, Julia b 12-19-1858 d 1-19-1945

Row 15

Hughes, Infant d/o I.H. & M.E. b & d 11-18-1888
Hughes, Mary E. 1868-1938
Hughes, Isaac 1865-1952
Helsley, Franklin R. b 6-19-1846 d 10-13-1908
    Eliza J. his wife b 11-22-1848 d 12-12-1904
Henderson, Lora L. d/o J. & Lyda E. 5-3-1885 d 11-8-1886
Jinkins, Ann w/o Charles b 1816 d 2-10-1900
Jinkins, Rachel A. b 7-2-1851 d 4-24-1904
Ayers, Loda w/o Clarence b 1-2-1878 d 8-11-1911
Parker, Alfred b 2-15-1879 d 7-21-1907

Row 16

Ellis, H.C. 1863-1922
Ellis, Sallie A. b 1863 d
Annis, Effa A. Beasley w/o John W. b 8-16-1855 d 5-29-1956 Mother
    John W. b 6-20-1881 d 1-4-1935
Infant
Mabel
King, Sarah A w/o C.M. b 3-13-1866 d 12-19-1903 37 y 9 m 6 d
King, Emma F. w/o C.M. b 11-29-1878 d 9-17-1902 25 y 9 m 28 d
    Eathel d/o C.M. & E. b 5-24-1895 d 1-18-1896
    Jessie b 9-23-1898 1-13-1899 4 m 7 d
Father
King, John S. b 11-19-1800
Julian, Arena J. w/o J.J. b 5-9-1866 d 6-20-1897
Helsey, Herchel s/o D.S. & H.J. b 2-16-1905 d 7-13-1906
Gears, Mary Ola d/o Omer & Ethel b 2-27-1912 d 3-14-1912
Gears, John Omer 1851-1954
    Answorth E. b 1913 d
DeBoard, Ernest E. s/o C.E. & D.J. b 11-8-1912 d 1-6-1916
DeBoard, Charles E b 3-9-1885 d 5-12-1913
Ward, ?erry, Infant d 11-9-193?
Ashby, Tate 1867-1937

Row 17

Annise, Mary J. w/o George A. b 9-11-1877 d 1-29-1895
Messersmith, Mitchel 1846-1926
    Laura E. his wife 1852-1923
Messersmith, Margaret Z. d/o Michael & Laura b 8-3-1887 d 4-14-1915

Messersmith, Minerva K.  b 9-11-1896   d 9-25-1899
Messersmith, Arthur W.   d 9-15-1891   9 y 3 m 9 d
    Grant Earl  d 10-17-1889   31 y

Julian, Goocie E.   d/o J.J. & R.J.
Infant
King, Infant  d/o A.M. & C.   b & d 7-2-1904
King, Allen M.   1873-1942
    Clara  1878-1955
Wilhite, Carl W.   b 2-8-1877   d 7-20-1937
Wilhite, N. Mary   9-7-1876   d 3-18-1969
Wilhite, Infant  b 1-27-1902   d 1-31-1902
Wilhite, Sidney H.   1908-1958   Father
Gears, Attress J.   b 12-18-1908   d 6-29-1965   Ind. Sgt. Co B 818 Engr Avn
    WWII


Row 18

Abbott, Pricilla  b 3-7-1832   d 4-5-1904
Gears, Rhoda J.   b 1-31-1839   d 9-3-1895
Gears, George E.   s/o John & M.E.   b 9-22-1886   d 10-6-1890
Gears, John   1860-1933
Gears, Lizzie   1860-1935
Brown, Infant  d/o O.H. & M.B.   b 12-9-1891   d 12-10-1891
Allburn, Lucy P.   w/o John  b 5-8-1880   d 2-14-1911
Holton, Jacob S.   1848-1901   Father
Thomas, Rosetta   1870-1947
    Oliver  1871-1951
Shafer, Margaret J.   d/o S. & S.E.   b 10-30-1885   d 8-8-1896
Massey, William J.   b 9-5-1862   d 1-14-1914
    Florah H. his wife  b 3-14-1870   d 5-15-1910


ALBRIGHT CEMETERY
Albright Cemetery is located on Road 700S about two miles east of Mackey, Barton Township, Gibson County, Indiana, next to the Townsley Cemetery.


Row 1

Fischer, Georg  s/o Georg and Maria  b 9-12-1868   d 7-14-1869
    Maria  d/o Georg and Maria  b 8-21-1867   d 7-12-1868
Fischer, Maria, nee Hoffa w/o Georg  b 12-10-1843   d 12-16-1876
Fischer, Jacob  s/o J.G. & M.   b 12-7-1879   d 6-18-1880
Fischer, Daniel J.   s/o J. & Ursilla  b 9-4-1886   d 3-16-1887
Kohlmeyer, M. Dorothea w/o Rev. C.L.   d March ? 1880   age 36 years
Fischer, Johannes W.   s/o J. & M.   b 11-3-1898   d 2-7-1899
Fischer, Mary C.   1873-1937
    John  1869-1957

Fischer, Anna Marie  d/o William & M.M.  b 12-25-1908  d 10-18-1915
Fischer, Infant  s/o Wm. & M.M.  b 10-31-1915  d 11-1-1915
Fischer, Martha M.  w/o Wm.  b. 3-13-1885  d 11-19-1915
Fischer, Clara A.  w/o Wm.  b 3-22-1890  d 10-24-1918
Fischer, Eli C.  1906-1937
Hemmer, Augustus  s/o H.F. & L.C.  b 9-30-1885  d 9-3-1887
    Daniel S.  s/o H.F. & L.C.  b 1-20-1881  d 9-5-1887
Hemmer, Heney F.  b 11-8-1849  d 6-9-1928
    Louise C. his wife  b 4-20-1852  d 7-13-1910
Hemmer, Albert E.  b 8-16-1890  d 1-1-1916
Sibras, ----  d 1-14-1889  35 y 25 d
Sibras, Mary  d 7-30-1890  69 y
Siebras, Wm. M.  b 8-4-1842  d 1-8-1900
Jamieson, Gardner  b 1-1-1855  d 9-28-1908
Jamieson, Louise D. Siebrase  1862-1930
Wheaton, Charles  1881-1970
    Flora C.  1883-1949
Ireland, Dunice M.  1885-1927  Mother
Ireland, Edwin  1915-1970  Son


Row 2

Fischer, Anna  d/o J.G. & U.  b 10-3-1887  d 1-5-1891
Geiger, Mary  b 3-11-1826  d 11-4-1915
Fischer, J. George  b 8-9-1843  d 1-5-1923
    Ursila, his wife  b 7-12-1845  d 5-19-1917
Schmiedt, Caroline, consort of Carl  b 11-24-1824  d 11-25-1874
Fischer, Elmer G.  1911-1963  Pvt 1987th Service Command
Fischer, William  1882-1969
    Lena  1881-1953
Fischer, Mathew J.  1904-1946
Fischer, Anna Maria  b 1-7-1799  d 10-6-1875
Blumle, Loius  b 8-30-1834  d 10-7-1877
Bonnal[?], Rosa  b 9-23-1867  d 4-11-1892
Hemmer, Sarah E.  1879-1957
Hemmer, Amanda  1892-1972
Hemmer, Lawrence  b 1897  d
Siebrase, Fred  s/o Wm. & Louise
Siebrase, Infant  s/o Wm. & Louise
Koerner, John G.  1843-1894  Pvt Co. H 136 Ind Inf.
    Caroline, his wife  1846-1896
    Josephene, their daughter  1880-1895
May, Infant  s/o Irvin & Louella  1950
May, Irvin O.  b 11-20-1928  d
    Louella V.  b 11-24-1926  d 10-8-1982

Row 3

Kohlmeier, Louis  1835-1917  Father
   Henrietta  1851-1923  Mother
Kohlmeier, Sarah  consort of S. Jndh  b 9-1-1874  d 12-10-1897
Hassheider, Matilda L. w/of J.H.  b 5-2-1857  d 12-19-1888
Wilmsmeir, Maria  w/o Heinrich  d 9-22-1874  71 y 3 m
Kohlmeier, Maria,  nee Stunkel  w/o C.  b 11-25-1847  d 11-17-1870
Sampley, Adelia, nee Kohlmeyer  1885-1973
Kohlmeyer, Charles  b 10-7-1844  d 11-14-1907
   Wilhelmina, his wife  b 7-24-1846  d 8-7-1937
Kohlmeier, Freiderich  b 3-7-1800  d 12-7-1871
   Friderike, his consort  b 2-2-1794  d 11-29-1880
Kohlmeyer, infant  s/o C. & M  2-27-1882
Kohlmeier, Maria M.A.  d/o C. & M.  b 6-26-1880  d ?-?-1880
Kohlmeier, Martha S.C.  d/o C. & M.  b 9-29-1877
Voelkel, Frederich C.L.  s/o F. & M.M.  b 5-2-1890  d 7-24-1890
Battram, Sarah, born Luhring  w/o L. F. Battram  b 10-16-1851
Battram, Louis F.  d 6-26-1887  38 y 7 m 26 d
Luehring, Ellen L.  d/o D. & W.  d 10-1-1890  22 y 2 m 11 d
Luehring, Diderich  b 4-21-1815  d 5-14-1906  91 y 23 d
   Minna  w/o Diderich  b 8-4-1826  d 11-18-1896  70 y 3 m 9 d
Graper, August D.  1859-1945
   Alvina L.  1860-1935
Graper, Maude  1893-1984
Kohlmeier, Fred L.  1850-1921.
Kohlmeier, Susanna  1856-1923
Kohlmeier, Clarence F.  1889-1974
Simpson, Milton A.  1851-1935
   Lizzie D.  1862-1944
Lemme, Clinton Edward  1887-1979
   Alma May  1886-1969  married 6-12-1912
Graper, Susan Kaye  1945-1976
Miller, Mary M.  1858-1929
Miller, Perry A.  1859-1940


Row 4

Kohlmeier, Elias  s/o L. & H.  b 187?  d ?-1878?
Grossman, ---tena  d/o C. & ?R.  b 12-21-1883  d 2-25-?
P. Schau?
Kohlmeier, Christian  b 5-30-1838  d 6-2-1901
Kohlmeier, Margaretha  w/o Christian  b 10-8-1841  d 12-27-1898
Kohlmeier, Emory F.  1877-1933
   Daisy M.  1879-1974
Kohlmeier, Virgil L.  1881-1953
Wheaton, our precious baby, Peter Winston  5-26-1984

Row 5

Stunkel, Fridrich   b 6-4-1809   d 5-25-1888
Stunkel, Sarah L.   b 12-12-1869   d 7-15-1897
Sundemeier, Heinrich   s/o A.H. & Mina   b 1-4-1884   d 1-6-1884
Meier, Rubert F.   b 8-6-1909   d 12-31-1984
     Aliene   b 10-23-1912   d 8-29-1980
Meyer, Herbert L.   b 9-1-1888   d 4-21-1968   Ind. Pvt. 299 Aero Svc Sq WWI
     Leona A.   1893-1976
     David F.   b 1926   d
Meier, Joseph H.   1877-1952   Father
     Matilda   1879-1964   Mother
Meyer, Daniel H.   1863-1938
Meyer, Frederick   b 3-3-1833   d 11-19-1910
     Christine, his wife   b 9-29-1841   d 11-13-1930
Volker, Infant of J. & L.   b & d 12-9-1880
Volker, Roy J.   s/o J. & L.   b ?-3-1889   d 9-22-1890
     Alma N.C.   d/o J. & L.   b 2-16-1885   d 6-4-1890
Kohlmeyer, Anna Bartels   d Nov. 1887
Kohlmeyer, Emma   w/o F.C.   b 9-4-1865   d 1-6-1891
Kohlmeyer, Fred C.   b 5-3-1864   d 2-13-1893
Smith, Mildred H. Kohlmeier   1910-1957
Kohlmeier, Lucy L.   b 1883 d
Kohlmeier, Edward D.   1880-1971
Kohlmeyer, Conrad C.   b 2-20-1860   d 7-30-1909
     Carrie C. his wife   b 9-18-1870   d 9-6-1941
Kohlmeier, Benjamin F.   1889-1946


Row 6

Kallenbach, Emma M.   b 8-16-1884   d 2-13-1904
Bowman, David C.   b 8-10-1919   d 11-13-1980   S.Sgt. U.S. Army WWII
     Mabel C.   b 1920   d
Meier, Infant   b 9-3-1882   d 9-5-1882
Haley, Virgil J.   1904-1970
     Daisy L.   b 1908   d
Rea, Emory Lee b 11-18-1946   d 2-4-1969   Indiana Ap. 4 Co. B 60 Inf 9 Inf
     Div.   Vietnam BSM & 2 OLC AM & OLC ARCOM & OLC-PH
Rea, Naomi Lee, nee Kohlmeier   b 1909   d
McCullough, Roger E. "Doc"   b 5-22-1924   d 6-4-1973   Twc 5 U.S. Army
     WWII


Row 7

Eastwood, Louie   b 11-4-1888   d 3-20-1979   Pvt U.S. Army WWI
     Minnie   b 3-19-1889   d 2-12-1963
Meier, Henry C.   1849-1924

Myer, Mary, w/o Henry  b 6-8-1857  d 10-10-1895
Tepe, Matilda  1870-1871
Tepe, Henry  1867-1880
Tepe, Emil  1860-1881
Tepe, Frank H.  1827-1904
    Maria  1835-1883
Eisberg, Freddie W.  s/o W. & M  b 3-13-1888  d 11-9-1888
Eisberg, Infant  s/o Wm. & Mary  b & d ?-?-1893
Eisberg, Marie L.  w/o W.  b 2-11-1854  d 7-27-1900
Eisberg, William F.  b 11-17-1845  d 9-13-1920
May, Matilda  d/o C. & M.  b 10-10-1879  d 10-16-1879
May, Infant  s/o C. & M.  b 8-14-1892  d 9-1-1892  Twins
    Infant  s/o C. & M.  b 8-14-1892  d 9-1-1892
May, Martha  w/o Charles  b 3-7-1855  d 2-4-1904
May, Charles  b 3-22-1845  d 2-10-1906
May, William C.  1883-1960
    Mary Eva  1885-1942
May, William J.  d 3-2-1890  1 y 2 m 9 d
    Emma  d 1-7-1891  7d
May, Willie  s/o Wm. & H.  b 1-4-1892  d 1-23-1892
May, Freddie W.  s/o Wm. & H  b 2-16-1884  d 12-6-1894
May, William  b 3-29-1851  d 7-15-1896
May, Hannah  b 4-17-1854  d 2-11-1920
Kohlmeier, Christine  w/o Ludwig  b 3-12-1816  d 12-20-1894
Halwes, Henry  1881-1947
    Adelia  1880-1958
Seltzer, Jacob  b 4-17-1869  d 3-15-1943  Father
    Victoria  b 2-3-1878  d 10-31-1957  Mother
Kilpatrick, Alma  1886-1938
Kilpatrick, Marlin  1887-1951
Kilpatrick, Louedythe  b 1912  d
Kilpatrick, Arvel  1909-1974
Parker, Amelia M. Fischer  b 6-16-1902  d 6-25-1963
Parker, Carl Dennis  b 2-25-1901  d 12-22-1980  married 4-7-1934


Row 8

Meier, Elmer  s/o H. & Mary  b 8-20-1904  d 8-12-1906
Meier, Eddie F.  s/o H. & Mary  b 8-20-1893  d 10-12-1898
Myer, Matilda  d/o H.M.  b 8-14-1895  d 10-29-1895
Meier, Friedrich  s/o G. & M.  b 4-4-1884  d 6-12-1884
Hassheider, Infant of J. & N.
Eisberg, John F.  b 3-30-1881  d 8-26-1881
Hassheider, Emma L.  d/o J. & M.  b 1-20-1880  d 1-4-1883
Hessheider, ----  b 10-11-1881  d 1-12-1883
Eisberg, Lydia M.  d/o William & Mary  b 1-7-1886  d 8-6-1887

May, Robert Lee   b 8-25-1927
    Katherine V.   b 2-4-1922
May, Victor   b 1-31-1895   d 4-26-1968   Indiana Pvt Co F 117 Engrs WWI
    Ruth N.   1899-1978
May, Eli C.   b 8-14-1892   d 9-16-1973   Indiana Pvt U.S. Army WWI
    Elfrieda   b 1-16-1897   d 1-21-1982
Stunkel, Louis   d 12-8-1897   age 79 y
May, Roy W.   b 3-6-1897   d 9-2-1955
Baker, William   1876-1953
    Sarah H.   1886-1958
May Edward H.   b 2-6-1878   d 2-11-1941
Nolting, Emma   b 9-16-1891   d 7-28-1910
Infant son   b 7-19-1910   d 8-6-1910


Row 9

Tepe, Louis   1865-1912
    Mary   1875-1958
Dassell, Sophia   w/o G.A.   b 9-5-1881   d 12-6-1901
Christopher, L. Ora   s/o H. & L.   b 7-2-1878   d 10-28-1896
Fossler, John   b 1-12-1872   d 12-1-1908
Fossler, William V.   1907-1966
Fossler, Hannah   b 11-29-1874   d 7-6-1957
Prignitz, Fred   b 1-23-1846   d 4-28-1941
    Mary C. his wife   b 8-22-1856   d 8-9-1908
Fritz, Ernest H.   1884-1956
    Bessie M.   1897-1970
Schoonover, Clarence R.   1891-1979
    Eva E.   1894-1970
Busing, Sarah M.   1875-1944
Busing, Frank C.   1869-1943
Fischer, Pearl L.   1898-1973
Fischer, Edward G.   1896-1974
Fritz, Ermel L.   1919-1977
    Mary K.   b 1926   d


Row 10

Holtsgrafe, William, Sr.   Father
Holtsgrafe, Eliza   Mother
Holtsgraph, Henry W.   Son   1886-1943
Holtsgrafe, William, Jr.   Son   1879-1945
Holtsgrafe, Carrie   Daughter
Strickland, Albert Eugean   b 3-21-1919   d 9-9-1920
Schoonover, Richard K.   b 3-4-1916   d 8-4-1975
    Eula Mae   b 2-4-1985   d

73

Busing, Brett C.  b. 1965  d 6-22-1985
Busing, Infant  s/o Charles & Judy  5-2-1963
Busing, Infant  s/o Charles & Judy  6-17 to 6-18-1962
Busing, Maria  1906-1945
Busing, Herbert F.  1897-1950


Row 11

Weiberle, Ernest  b 9-20-1841  d 9-3-1929
    Caroline  b 1-29-1842  d 2-4-1907
Skelton, Festus  1889-1960
    Malinda  1893-1979
Skelton, Charlie  b 11-18-1894  d 1-20-1965


Row 12

Strickland, Thelma Geraldine  d/o L.J. & Alice B.  b 5-2-1919  d 1-6-1922
Kohlmeier, Raymond H. s/o H.F. & Tiney  1-21 to 11-3-1919
Melcher, Agnes Lain  1906-1976
Melcher, John F.F.  1899-1899
Melcher, Otto F.F.  1900-1900
Melcher, Hilda H.M.  1901-1901
Melcher, John H.  1871-1958  Father
    Matilda L.  1872-1955  Mother
Salat, Clarence  1907-1944
Salat, Marie  1869-1959  Mother
Salat, Elmer J.  b 2-17-1897  d 5-25-1925  Private First Class U.S. Med. Dept.
Salat, John  1866-1936
Weiberle, Albert C.  s/o H.E. & A.M.  b 5-12-1909  d 8-9-1909


Row 13

Bertram, Emma d/o Ed. L. & Ella  b 3-4-1900  d 3-21-1900
Bertram, Elmer E.  s/o Edward & Ella b 11-4-1920  d 12-6-1920
Bertram, Edward L.  b 6-21-1871  d 10-31-1946  son of William & Minnie
    Bertram
    Ella  b 3-30-1877  d 10-8-1950  daughter of Charles & Martha May
Meier, Otto H.  1907-1973
    Erma E.  1912-1981
Fischer, Matilda  1883-1974
    George  1873-1958
Fischer, Lydia M.  d/o George & M.  b 12-5-1901  d 7-1-1904
Brogan, Robert U. in memory of our baby  2-28-1927
Skelton, Vaughn Wade  b 3-26-1934  d 7-14-1971  Indiana SK3 US Coast
    Guard Korea
    Charlotte C.  b 12-31-1934  d        married 10-1-1955

Row 14

Skelton, William N.   1890-1967
    Flora   1892-1978

Row 15

Parker, Tommy Scott   s/o Glen & Phyllis   b 5-28-1967   d 7-16-1967
White, Alfred E.   1906-1984
    Lena C.   1899-1981
Doan, Jerry L.   b 5-21-1918   d
    Bernice   b 3-18-1921   d 1-9-1982   married 3-11-1939
Doan, Jerry R.   b 1-16-1943   d 7-28-1984
    Linda D.   b 4-16-1945   d          married 10-9-1970

## TOWNSLEY CEMETERY

Townsley Cemetery is located on Road 700E about two miles east of Mackey, Barton Township, Gibson County, Indiana.

Section 1, Row 1
Mentzel, Mary E. "Aunt"   b 2-7-1899   d 11-3-1892
Miller, Earl E.   b 1937
    Lavona M.   b 1932         married 11-21-1958

Row 2

Donohoo, Paul O.   b 8-22-1919   d 5-28-1973
    Thelma E.   b 3-19-1922   d
Stillwell, Charles E.   b 7-18-1915   d
    Mildred K.   b 5-19-1920   d
    Our children:   C. Darvin, Jerry D., Jo Anne, Russell L.
Richardson, Burch   b 10-4-1875   d 9-23-1977   P.F.C. U.S. Army WWII
    Hazel M.   b 7-20-1900   d
Richardson, Floyd B.   b 12-20-1921   d 9-5-1979   P.F.C. WWII
Doerner, Beverly O.   b 1-30-1912   d 9-5-972   Pvt U.S. Army WWII
    Audrey L.   b 2-8-1916   d
Strickland, Karl   b 9-18-1911   d
    Lillian M.   b 9-6-1917   d        married 9-6-1939

Row 3

Stillwell, Oscar   b 1892   d 1982
    Ethel   b 1892   d 1974
Russell, Charles L.   b 8-19-1918   d 3-27-1984   Cpl U.S. Army WWII
    Clara E.   b 8-9-1928   d
    Our children:   Linda S., Terry W., Billy J.

Row 4

Wilson, Loris LeRoy   b 11-23-1902   d 3-30-1982
    Minnie Adeline   b 9-12-1906   d 2-2-1982


Section 2, Row 1

Peed, John S.   b 1887   d 1974
Doener, George S.   b 8-23-1904   d 5-5-1982
Doener, Louis W.   b 1-29-1912   d 12-20-1971   Indiana Tec 3 Co C 2 Armed Div
    WWII
Doener, Fred E.   b 1876   d 1965   father
    Ing Adeline   b 1882   d 1961   mother
    Virginia M.   b 1921   d 1981   daughter
Miller, Gilbert   b 1884   d 1961
    Maud   b 1884   d 1961
Miller, George A.   b 1912   d 1973
Miller, Harry G.   b 1910   d 1981
    Margaret L.   b 1912   d 1984
Ingrum, Clem E.   b 1884   d 1964
    Rose P.   b 1885   d 1966
Kohlmeir, Eli C.   b 4-1-1898   d 5-6-1966
    Amelia A.   b 11-23-1904   d           married 12-22-1923
Strickland, Earl   b 10-1-1913   d
    Ethel   b 3-30-1914   d           married 12-16-1933
Strickland, Larry W.   b 1951   d 1985   son of Earl and Ethel Strickland
Townsley, James Russell   b 1-17-1891   d 9-17-1975
    Dora Margaret   b 7-9-1891   d 3-4-1977


Row 3

Barnard, Diane Lynne   d/o Harden, Jr. & Shirley   b 8-8-1961   d 8-21-1962
Barnard, Marlana Marie   Infant d/o Harden Jr. & Shirley   7-14-1966
Sunderman, Irvin A.   b 12-13-1909   d 4-20-1983   Dad
Sunderman, Henry L.   b 1869   d 1948
    Carrie   b 1871   d 1954
Miller, Edward E.   b 1906   d           Father
    Hermena   b 1908   d           Mother
Voelkel, Edward C.   b 1899   d
Voelkel, Frederick   b 1861   d 1952
    Minnie M.   b 1862   d 1943
Voelkel, Oscar   b 1894   d 1977
    Helen   b 1908   d 1981
Chapman, Russell   b 1924   d
    Chrystal J.   b 1926   d 1961
Chapman, Elaine Turnbloom   b 1-29-1944   d 1-18-1984
Chapman, Michael Ray   s/o Russell & Jean Chapman   b 1950   d 1950

Ashby, Ronald Dean   s/o Earl & Tommie   b 1951   d 1954
Higginbottom, Mayme Mary F.   b 1875   d 1957
Strickland, Larry Lynn   s/o Marvin & Irma   8-28-29-1947
Adkins, Donald Ray   s/o Raymond & Lucy   8-17-1936
Kallenbach, Simon   b 1856   d 1947   Father
    A. Bertha   b 1864   d 1934   Mother
Kallenbach, Thomas Edward   b 1885 d 1954
Kohlmeier, John F.   b 1876   d 1950
Kohlmeir, Alvin S.   b 10-27-1894   d 10-9-1967   Ind. Pvt. U.S. Army WWI
Kohlmeier, Emma   b 1889   d 1967
Breckwinkle, Frank   b 1878   d 1951
    Carrie   b 1882   d 1941
Strickland, William E.   b 1886   d 1964
    Alice M.   b 1887   d 1948
Beadles, Marie C.   b 1-28-1908   d 9-23-1975
Fossler, Ben G.   b 1898   d 1969
    Minnie M.   b 1900   d 1963
Weiberle, Henry E.   b 1870   d 1953   Father
    Alice M.   b 1883   d 1972   Mother
Weiberle, Alma   b 1-21-1911   d 2-19-1980
Beatty, James Edgar   b 1967   d 1954
    Lora Princess   b 1877   d 1965


Section 3, Row 1

Fischer, Irvin   b 1921   d 1922
Fischer, Otto E.   b 1915   d 1936
Fritz, Minnie (Aunt)   b 1877   d 1947
Fischer, Adam   b 1884   d 1956
    Louisa M.   b 1882   d 1954
Kohlmeier, Harry   b 1890   d 1959
    Piney   b 1892   d 1975
Kohlmeier, Louie M.   s/o H.F. & Piney   b 1928   d 1930
Smith, Setta Weiberle   b 1898   d 1981
Weiberle, Christian C.   b 1872   d 1955
    Ellen F.   b 1872   d 1936
Weiberle, Paul E.   b 1896   d 1979
Oliver, O. Delmar   b 1880 d 1951
Oliver, Chester D.   b 1910   d 1929
Oliver, Matilda S.   b 1869   d 1944
Stelloh, William H.   b 11-26-1862   d 5-24-1905
Stelloh, Raymond   b 7-29-1901   d 11-22-1906
Maikranz, Arthur Wm.   b 3-6-1900   d 10-26-1934   Son
    Sophia L.   b 1-10-1870   d 11-1-1968
Taylor, William Edward   b 10-25-1898   d 3-9-1975
    Helen Ruth   b 10-12-1912   d 11-1-1983   married 11-27-1952

Reid, Caroline W.   b 12-4-1897   d 7-5-1942   Wife
Maikranz, Odelia   b 9-29-1902   d
Maikranz, Arnold G.   b 1909   d 1972
Lamey, Henry   b 1881   d 1951
    Bessie   b 1888   d 1968
Baker, Joseph   b 1876   d 1974
    Della May   b 1880   d 1963
Wheaton, Warren   b 5-2-1915   d
    Mavis   b 3-10-1915   d


Row 2

Fischer, Albert G.   b 1909   d 1969
    Georgia C.   b 1908   d
Burnikel, John G.   b 1885   d 1964
    Clara C.   b 1892   d 1966
Burnikel, George   b 1881   d 1960


## GIBSON COUNTRY CEMETERY LISTINGS

Genealogy Division, Indiana State Library.

Cox, Carroll O., *Gibson County, Indiana cemetery records.*   1967. [Includes Archer, Clark, Fitzgerald, Maple Hill, Mauck, Maumee, Odd Fellows-Hazleton, Odd Fellows-Princeton, Old Schoolhouse, Phillips, Presbyterian, Patoka, Shiloh, and Warnock.]

Greubel, Lela, *West Salem (or Stunkel) cemetery* [Johnson Twp.].

Indiana Historical Society, Committee on Pioneer Cemeteries and Churches (Ella C. Wheatley, compiler), *Cemetery records in Gibson county, Indiana, 1941-42.* [Includes Oakland City Baptist Church, Hargrove, Montgomery, Oakland City.]

McGregor, Killpatrick and Morris cemeteries, Gibson county, Indiana. From: The *Tri State Packet* of the Tri State Genealogical Society, v. 8, no. 2, Dec. 1984.

Stone, Jane L., *Gudgel graveyard . . . Gibson County, Indiana.*   1972.

Turman, Robert Emerson, *Cemetery records of Southern Indiana: . . .* 1977. [Includes Antioch Church, Benson Family, Bethel or "David Smith," Blythe's Chapel (Methodist), Clark, Emerson Family, Johnson Family, Marvel Family, Mauck Family, Maumee, Mount Moriah, Mounts Family, Owensville, Powell Private, Thompson Family, Walnut Hill, Williams (old), Williams Private, and Wilson Family.]

[Woods, Robert M.], *Marsh Creek Cemetery, Gibson County, Indiana.* 1975.

# GIBSON COUNTY OLD SETTLERS

*The Princeton Democrat*, May 13, 1882, p. 1 printed an article headlined "Old Settlers" from which the following was extracted.

## THE SMITHS

Major James Smith, born in Virginia, removed with his father's family to Kentucky and in 1818 to this county . . . . death occured November, 1885, in his 82nd year of age. Served on Gen. Harrison's staff at the battle of Tippecanoe. Took over as Capt. when Jacob Warrick was killed. Delegate to State Constitutional Convention. Was first Commissioner of the Seminary, School township. Survivors: son, Thomas, died a few years hence, leaving widow and son.

## BASIL BROWN

. . . took out first license to keep a tavern in 1817, at the southwest corner of the public square Married Mary Warrick, sister of Jacob Warrick. Moved to Indianapolis and died there, January, 1849; his wife died in August of the same year at age of 77.

## SAMUEL A STEWART

. . . came to county in 1823, at age 20. Married Lucinda Howe. Minister, County collector, Judge. Died May, 1849 in 52nd year, his wife died a few days since at an advanced age.

## ROBERT MILBURN

. . . born in western part of Virginia; came to Gibson county via Kentucky in 1803. In 1812 married Miss Nancy Archer. Was a hatter in Princeton, and then a miller. Died December, 1847 in his 62nd year, leaving several children.

## CALVIN MINNIS

Came to Gibson county with his family in 1811. Wife Polly died in 1853 in her 75th year, he died at a greater age.

## ELISHA STRICKLAND, SEN.

Came to Gibson county in 1807. Fought in Tippecanoe campaign. Died 1853 at age 85. Father of eleven children, all married; left 106 grandchildren, 110 great grandchildren.

## JOHNSON FAMILY

John and Sarah Johnson came from Virginia in 1798 to Kentucky, hence to Gibson county in 1803. Parents of seven children: Rebecca, Betsy, Mary, Hannah, Jacob, David, John.

Jacob enlisted in Col. Hargrove's rangers in 1813. He first married a Stewart, then a daughter of John Skelton. Two children by first marriage: James Johnson of Mt. Carmel, and Mrs. McFetridge; children by second marriage: John, Jackson(now deceased), Mrs. Fairchild, Mrs. Cray, Lydia and David.

## WILLIAM CLARK

Moved west with his father in 1807, arrived Gibson county, 1807. Enlisted in war in 1815. Is now 81 years old.

## THOMAS ARCHER

Came from South Carolina to Gibson county in 1808. Son, John died in 1866, aged 62.

## JOSHUA DUNCAN

Was mong the first settlers of Gibson county; enlisted 1812, died September, 1861, age 65. Children: Mrs. A.C. McDonald of Princeton, and James Duncan.

## JOHN HINEMAN

Born in Pennsylvania, 1778; went to Kentucky, then to Gibson county in 1803. Died in 1863 at age 85, leaving a widow age 80.

## THE MILBURNS

Came to Gibson county from Virginia. [served with] Harrison. Died in 1859 at age 76. Four children: Felix, now deceased; Irene Rose, Sarah Arbuthnot and Garry Milbourn. David Milbourn died in 1861, age 72. Sally Cammick moved to Alabama; Jonathan to Texas, William was killed.

## PETER SIMPSON

Came to Gibson county with wife and children in 1812; settled on land now owned by Pressley Garrett. Survivor: Richard Simpson, now in his 80th year.

# GRANT COUNTY VOTERS 1844-66

John Selch of the Newspaper Section, Indiana Division, Indiana State Library discovered lists of voters in early Grant County IN in columns titled "Early Residents of Grant County" in the *Marion Daily Chronicle* in 1911-12.

October 24, 1911, p. 6.

At an election held in the home of James Hicks in Washington township in April of 1844, the following persons appeared and voted:

Redden Chance, Samuel Macnary, Alfred Bocock, James Hicks, Dennis Daily, Isaac Moore, Frame Love, Martin Gingery, William Jackson, Jacob Line, L. Bradford, William Daily, William Jackson, Daniel Bradford, S.H. Woolman, Wesley Allen, George Conn, James Thompson, Job Curtiss, Benjamin Woolman, Jacob Jackson, Thomas Campbell, Jesse Marsh, Ephriam Marsh, Samuel Williams, John Hummell, George Hobaugh, Enoch Marsh, Isaac Marsh, Jacob Whistler, Ben Marsh, Alfred Curtiss, Solomon Daily, Amer Allen, John H. Hobaugh and Van D. Hobaugh.

At an election held in the District No. 7 school house of Monroe township on the first Monday in April, 1847, the following persons appeared and voted:

James Haines, William H. Harrison, Robert Marshall, W.H. Crandall, Jacob Goodykoontz, Joel W. Long, Daniel Newport, Elias McKinney, Stephen Studyvin, Jacob Goodykoontz, Joel W. Long, Simon Goodykoontz, Thomas Craycraft, Griffin Jackson, Charles Coal, Raul Roberts, Andrew Patterson, Joseph Mills, Green B. Jacks, William A. Mitchel, G.W. Kessinger, James W. Farr, John Stout, John Shooly, Shadract Thornburg, James Wickersham, George W. Leonard, Dvid Henderson, Henry Smith, David Wall, S.A. Swift, Levi Lundy, Abner Wickersham, George Strange, Benjamin Schooly, M. Stotlar and G.W. Hults.

At an election held at the home of William Lougin in Van Buren township on the first Monday in April, 1848, the following persons appeared and voted.

Mills Whinnery, Soloman Fry, Samuel Pulley, William Kirkpatrick, Samuel Malcom, Jacob Stroup, Thompson H. Farr, Michael Roush, Warren Walters, Noah Cloud, Hiram Fry, D. Stranboner, Thomas C. Cloud, William Boxell, Joseph Boxell, Stephen H. Neisivaner, Henry Shainhuber, Henderson Tippey, Cyrus Crainford, Elier Long, Harrison Long, Willard Bevard, James Douglas, George W. Camplen, William Long, John Boxell, George H.D. Road, William Malcom, Joseph Malcom, Furgeson Malcom, Louis Lounders, John Dugan and Ezekiah Zinc.

January 25, 1912, p. 4

At an election at the house of school district No. 7, in Monroe township on the 7th day of November, 1848, for the purpose of electing twelve electors for the state of Indiana at which election the following persons appeared and voted:

Thomas Smith, Daniel G. Keever, Samuel Patterson, Daniel H. Hillman, John Patterson, William Roberts, David H. Crawford, William McKinney, Simon Goodykoontz, John Stout, Ambrose Hoffman, Charles Atkinson, Daniel Dwiggins, Lewis C. Beckford, Isaac Truax, John R. Palmer, Phillip Cole, Phineas Roberts, George C. Hatfield, Charles Pilcher, Silas Parke, Stephen Studyvin, Absolon Thomason, Daniel Newport, Campbell Parker, Joseph H. Hillman, Benjamin Hillman, Samuel R. Thompson, Griffith Jackson, Shedrick Thornburg, George W. Hults, David Oliver, Emanuel Cariger, George Strange, Isaac Hatfield, Benjamin Bird, Levi Lundy, Andrew Paterson, James Bird, Sr., Israel Phillips, William Roberts, Nathan Haines, James Lundy, John Zimmerman, Charles Cole, Mark Gage, Green Jacks, Michael B. Roberts, John Carll, Earl Potter, Robert P. Fornshell, S.A. Swift, George W. Kepsinger, Joseph Mills, Henry Gage, Lawrence W. Nelson, James Smith, George Lugar, Elias W. McKinney, George Stout, Matthew Nelson, John Oliver, James Wickersham, John Schooley, Jacob Goodykoontz, James Gillespie, A.B. Goodykoontz, Robert Marshall, Joel W. Long, John Lugar, David Wall, Thomas Beckford, George W. Leonard, Noah Pearce, Abner Wickersham, James M. Wilson, James Wilson, Henry Smith Bargil Shoemaker, Edmund Brown, Benjamin Schooley, Robert B. Brown, Matthias Stotlar, Rufus Walden, Israel Jenkins, Lysander Noe.

December 20, 1911, p. 9, and January 10, 1912, p. 9.

The poll book for an election held at the home of James Highley in Richland township the first Monday in August, 1850, at which Isaac Baldwin was inspector, Robert Mansfield and Abner Newman were judges and Joseph Wood and Membrance Blue were clerks, the following names appear.

James S. Foster, Thomas Reno, William Foster, Nathan Prickett, John Hains, John Powel, Matthias Copler, William N. Webster, John Loring, Jacob A. Galer, Allison Fieldz, James Highley, Samuel Nelson, John Frees, Zachariah Key, Thomas I. Keener, John Spears, Daniel Hartman, Charles Parker, John Hague, T.A. Surle, Michael France, T.C.P. Lawson, Silas Braffett, Isaac Renbarger, James Sinclair, E.J. Fisher, Daniel Stanley, A.T. Newman, George Peterson, Stephen Seward, James Turner, Joseph Wood, Samuel Clanin, Simon Bash, John P. Sinclair, Abram Simson, John Bash, James Lewis, Thomson Clanin, John Copic, James Tyler, Frederick Michael, Thomas Lewis, John Hiegley, William Duff, Robert Pixler, John W. Rhea, John Hubert, Abram Pixler, John Dunn, Clark Highley, David Goodrich, Samuel Stair, Joseph Cole,John Dayley, Christian Pence, Joseph Rollins, M.H. Maple, Benjamin Cline, Martin Pence, Darias Pence, Jacob Clester, Samuel Green, Alen B. Downs, Clabourn Wright, David Fisher, Daniel Fisher, Jonathan Fisher, John Shackelford, Isaac Flook, Membrance Blue, Jacob Druck, William W. Lane, J.T. Shackelford, Jacob Malsbery, T.I. Lewis, Gabriel Rees, Jacob Myer, Joseph Slagle, Abraham Crane, Jeremiah Strickler, George Strickler, John Druck, Thomas Clester, Harrison H. Powel, Robert Mansfield, I. Baldwin, Sabuel H. Logan, John Braffet, Isaiah Blue, David Warrenburg, Thomas Wood, James Alexander, Charles Stewart, Samuel Gelison, Michael Burk, James Mayne, Samuel Mayne, Shadrick Lawson, Elihu Stewart, Samuel Rose, Elmus Flemming,

James Higley, sr., David Clester, Job Clevenger, I.M. Shackelford, Lewis Pence.

December 15, 1911, p. 10.

On a poll book of an election held at the home of Jesse Winslow in Union township, Grant county, the first Monday in August, 1850, the following names appear:

David Baldwin, Otto Selby, Charles John, Sr., Enos McCormick, Jonathan F. Reader, Thomas D. Duling, Amaziah Beeson, Elijah Myres, G.W. Bowers, Edmund Duling, Timothy Kelly, Alfred Kelly, Seely Hollcroft, David Lucas, Jacob Hinkley, Lewis Harrison, Aaron Kennedy, George Mason, Green Duke, J.H. Wilson, Stephen Brewer, Sr., Henry Winslow, Joseph Jones, Hugh W. Winslow, Martin Simons, John Frank Boner, Elijah Lucas, Isaac Thomas, Thomas Reynolds, Charles Stanfield, Lewis Morman, James Young, Nelson Thomas, George W. Simons, Wm. Payne, Perry Evans, Wm. Fear, Wm. H.H. Reader, Samuel V. Stanfield, Isaac Stanfield, Jalez Moore, George W. Crist, Abram Heavilin, Jonathan Richardson, John J. Heavilin, John Lee, George Nose, Milton Winslow, James S. Wilson, Isaac Davidson, Stephen Brewer, Sr., Esom Leach, Joseph Power, Moses Quincy, Perry J. Morgan, John L. McCormick, Charles Beeson, Sebborn G. Knight, Jepe Winslow, Henry Simons, Peter S. Cook, Elijah Ward, Charles Wright, Francis T. Ward, Charles A. Johnson, Wm. Leach, Morgan Pain, Thomas Estle, Henry Furry, James Dille, Daniel T. Lindsey, John Leach, John Brewer, Abraham Carpenter, Abraham Myers, Joseph Hollingsworth, Joseph Corn, Daniel D. Ward, Morgan L. Pain, John Whitson, B.F. Furnish, John Minton, Edmond Leach.

November 23, 1911, p. 6.

An election was held in the school house of district No. 7, Monroe township, Grant county, the first Tuesday in 1852, at which time the following persons appeared and voted:

David Hodgson, George Phillips, Cephas Atkinson, James Hults, James Haines, Smith Skiner, Abner Holloway, James Bird, Geo. W. Hults, Nathan Haines, Levi Lundy, Benjamin Bird, Samuel Hodgson, James Wickershall, Daniel Achor, Simon Timberman, James Smith, Milton Davis, Axom Gray, John Lugar, John Zimmerman, Joseph Ballinger, George W. Leonard, Abram Roads, Curtis Paterson, Shadrack Thornburg, Isiah Miller, Charles Niccum, Joshua Pitcher, Barney Lugar, James Ballinger, John Patterson, John Jacks, Green B. Jacks, Benjamin Schooley, John Palmer, John Adamson, Nelson Hays, Isaac Ballinger, Hezekiah Mills, Mattws Nelson, Simon Goodykoontz, Jesse Livengood, Robert Wright, John Stout, Absolem Thomason, Henry Gage, Henry Smith, Robert Marshall, Abram Goodykoontz, Charles Atkinson, David Oliver, Jacob Goodykoontz, William Phipps, George Lugar, Isaac C. Farr.

November 27, 1911, p. 4.

At an election held in Fairmount township, Grant county, in April, 1852, the following persons appeared and voted:

Jonathan Richardson, Joseph Hill, Peter Havens, David Smithson, Charles Stanfield, P. Mott, James Symons, Jacob Hinkley, Carter Hastings, Robert

Davidson, John Heneld, Nathan Morris, Thomas Powel, John Benbow, Henry Winslow, Aaron Hauffman, Jesse Dillon, Hart Hauffman, William Wellington, Moses Benbow, Henry J. Reel, Mahlon Cook, John Philips, Jesse Winslow, Joshua Foster, Thomas Newby, William Hall, William Hunley, Isaac Stanfield, Andrew Buller, Henry Orsburn, Benjamin Havens, Isaac H. Johnson, William Fear, Joshua Mercer, Amos Freestone, John Bradford, Isaac Roberts, Peter Rich, Nixon Rush, Joseph W. Baldwin, John Willson, Mincher Cox, John Moor, Robert Corder, Lewis C. Bradford, David Pemberton, Nathan Vinson, William Cox, Micajah Willson, Jesse W. Winslow, John Patterson, Philip Patterson, Charles A. Johnson, Irdel Rush, Isah Pemberton, Thomas Baldwin, Charles Johnson, James Lytle, Joseph Hollingsworth, James Camack, Jose Brooks, James Johnson, Elijah Herrel, Richa Baldwin, Simon Kauffman, Albert Dillon, Thos. Harvey, John Lewis, William Passons, Eli Neil, William Winslow, Martin Bates, Milton Winslow, Ezra Foster, Isaac Thomas, Phineas Henley, Chas. A. Johnson, Nixon Winslow, John I. Bull, John Seal, James A. Wright, David T. Lindsay, Jesse Harvey, James Turner, John Quinn, Jonathan Baldwin, James Williams, Zachariah Freestone, Thomas Harvey, Morris Pain, John Henley, Nathan D. Willson, Seth Winslow, Thomas Knight, Thomas Winslow, George Lewis, William Pierce, Henry Level, Jesse Wilson.

November 29, 1911, p. 4.

At an election begun and held at the school house in Franklin township, Grant county, the first Tuesday in April, 1852, the following persons appeared and voted:

Charles Scott, Jobe Mills, John M. Marshall, John F. Himelwright, William Scott, James Wroie, Jemma Lloid, Lerama Lloid, Harper Lloid, Benjamin Wroe, Nathan Small, Benjamin Glistener, John J. Streete, John Wood, Reuben Modlin, Lemuel Johnson, John Thomas, Jabez Small, Martin Compton, Henry Babb, John Sheoles, George Role, Thomas Branson, Amos Small, Joshua Marshile, Daniel Slouterbeck, Adam Fantzler, William Lucas, John Patterson, Pleasant P. Poe, Orten Overholtz, John J. Poe, Patrck. J. Poe, Croomes Branson, David Kelley, Jackson Nance, William Baley, William Streete, Robert Mercer, Umphary Lloid, Joseph Martin, William L. Martin, Thomas Willcuts, Alfred Hogget, Samuel W. Patterson, John Morgain, Thomas Tysor, Gabriel P. Poe, Joseph Brown, Jabez Heely, Joseph B. Kerlin, Josiah Small, Jr., John Willents.

January 30, 1912, p. 6

At an election held at the town of Jonesboro, in Mill township, Grant county, Indiana, on the second Tuesday of October, 1852, for the purpose of electing one governor, one lieutenant governor, one secretary of state, one auditor, one treasurer, one reporter of supreme court, one clerk of supreme court, one superintendent of common schools, four supreme judges, one representative to congress, one circuit judge, one circuit prosecutor, one judge of common pleas, one prosecuting attorney of common pleas, one senator, one representative, one clerk, one recorder, one treasurer, one sheriff, two commissioners, one surveyor, one coroner, and one assessor. The following persons appeared and voted to wit:

Samuel Cole, Samuel Price, William Benbow, George Ambrose, James Collins, William Coate, Alexander Douglass, Allen Coate, Andrew Murray, Alexander Jordan, David Jay, Hudson Stewart, Joseph Jay, Morris Fankboner, Samuel Hughes, Jacob McCormick, Robert Wilson, Benjamin Johnson, Joseph R. Anderson, Wm. Roberts, James Ruley, Gasaway Farver, Enos Hallingsworth, Joshua Cannon, Peter Horsman, Jacob Kepler, B.P. Wallace, Rolbert Wiley, Jesse Benbow, James H. Douglass, Benoni Hill, Phineas Hillman, Robert Broaderick, Nathan Wright, Wm. Crilley, Rolbert Ellis, Jared Hiatt, Samuel W. Viess, John B. Ruley, John Troxell, John Pemberton, Silas Cook, T.H. Conner, John Wilson, Moses Mark, Henry Cochran, Henry C. Adkins, Samuel Marshall, George Carter, John Brushwell, Elihu Presnall, Samuel Russell, Elijah Thomas, John Entsminger, Preston Morris, Denny Jay, Wm. Viess, S.S. Thorne, Jas. Havens, Edward Moore, Jacob Fanning, Joseph Robberts, David Hutchins, John Coppoch, Aaron Hill, Henry Shugart, Wm. Perry, David Adamson, Andrew L. Perry, John Moorman, Timothy Kelly, John Parsons, John Shugart, Samuel Malcum, George Smith, Isaac Jackson, Daniel Thomas, Gabriel Keeton, Noah Harris, Dilton Modlin, Obidiah Harris, Bennett B. Coleman, Hiram Jackson, H. Baldwin, Pearson Horier, Jobe Jackson, John Ritter, Jas. Nelson, Joseph Small, Alfred Kelly, Nathan Coggeshall, Reuben Small, Mahlon Wines, Jonathan Rucker, Denny Jay, Jr. Alfred Hodson, Pearson Hester, Sr., Blasey Seiter, John A. Meek, Eli Smuck, William Hodson, John Stroup, James Ricks, Thomas Baldwin, D.W. Jones, Abraham Pressnell, Amos Thomas, Josiah Small, Geo. Broadrick, John Shugart, Joseph Morrow, Caleb Townsend, Wm. Jeffrey, Samuel Ladd, Lindsey Baldwin, John Adamson, A.F. Jones, David W. Swisher, Jonathan Coggeshall, John W. Parks, Wm. Raush, Jacob Candy, John Malcum, Levi Price, Zenas Jessup, Mark Davis, John Enstminger, Wm. Cochran, A.J. Ruley, Albert States, Obidiah Jones, Isaac Roush, John Crowel, Wm. Howell, Thomas Harris, Joseph Adamson, Wm. Sullivan, John L. Bradbury, Samuel C. Minie, Henry Burson, Elijah Thomas, Ezekial McCoy, Samuel C. Moore, Jordan Eleman, Wm. W. Ellman, James Allen, John Allen, John Horner, Sr., Jesse Mote, James Roberts, Jacob McCoy, George Felton, Robert McNealy, Wilson Hosier, Michael Ritter, Henley Thomas, Andrew Wooton, Jones Moreland, James Clark, Lancaster Bell, John Russell, Aaron Shideler, Jethro Barnard, Wm. F. Hallingsworth, Thomas Beckford, Joseph Hiatt, George H. Fankboner, E.P. Jones, Samuel Jay, Wm. Renaker, John Mason, Anthony Swisher, John Smith, George Shugart, Thomas C. Beall, Abira Baldwin, John S. Wise, Daniel Hiatt, Alexander Oren, Dillon Baldwin, Daniel Hollingsworth, Reason Ross, S.V. Standfield, Larkin Brooks, Elijah Godfrey, Milton Thomas, Moses Hollingsworth, James Hollingsworth, Joseph Johnson, Solomon Knight, Thomas Coleman, Evan Benbow, Daniel Coleman, Lewis Woody, wm. Cox, Rufus Dolman, David Shafer, Wm. Ballard, Henry Carter, Daniel Zeek, John Dolman, David Entsminger, L.D. Pierce, John Baldwin, Michael Mason, Alfred Norton, John Harris, Isaac Anderson, W.F. Spence, F.A. Moore, Mahlon Neal, Wm. Hiatt, Jr., Wilson Hiatt, Elihu Hiatt, Jonathan Jessup, Thomas Nelson, James W. Moore, Wm. Jessup, James Lacey.

November 17, 1911, p. 3.

At an election held in Center township, Grant county, November 29, 1852, the following persons appeared and voted:

Frederick Ellzroth, Wm. B. Cubberly, John P — -, B.W. Buley, Geo. W. Hendricks, Daniel B. Barley, A.R. Barley, C.W. Ward, O. Free, J. Horton, Alfred Horton, Lewis Williams, James Stout, C.W. Hill, R.B. Jones, Jesse Bridges, J.D. Howard, H.P. Weeks, Joshua Mackey, Lemuel Lumer, Tucs. J. McDowell, M.L. Marsh, Jas. P. McDowell, Joseph Scott, John Carll, Esq, H.F. Wallace, Isaac Wonderly, Jas. Brownlee, Stephen Hall, Sr., Lesh H. Campbell, Joseph Rodgers, Alexander Buckhanar, J.W. Harlin, Frederick Love, Amaziah Pilcher, David Shunk, Joseph Lomax, Samuel McClure, Augustus Claudius, Edward Guenin, Samuel Whistler, J.B. Stephens, James Morrison, Isaac Hall, Jacob Whisler, Geo. W. Webster, Andrew Diltz, Sr., Abram Yont, David Morris, Lewis Conner, Sr., David Hill, Aaron C. Swayzee, Samuel Clifford, John M. Lanney, Aaron H. Moore, Joseph Pierson, J.W. Brown, A.W. Reed, James White, Henry Norman, David R. Barley, Samuel Miller, Stephen Foster, C.S. Boots, Levi Reed, George Swope, O.A.P. Carey, Mathey Smith, Samuel Campbell, Lewis Lenkins, Levi Horton, Wm. Lomax, Abell Lomax, Samuel Beaty, John Willcats, Simon Goldthalt, J. Jackson, J.H. Jones, L.J. Neal, Reuben Small, George Bowman, Pleasant Foster, George Hollman, James A. Webb, Henry Barley, John Bowman, Nelson Conner, Baily Pierson, E.C. Overman, Thomas Bodle, Thomas Sailors, Moses Bradford, Wm. Gilpin, Jonathan Smith, B. Middleton, Thomas Williams, Lewis Conner, Jr., John Gray, David J. Fowler, William S. Lenfesty, John Dunn, Jr. J. H. Fowler, Isaac Lucas, George W. Jones, W.H. Webster, David Weaver, Elias Baldwin, Jacob Ring, D.E. Horton, Benj. Killey, Humphrey Q. Collins, Joel Overman, Noah Thomas, S.D. Ayres, Jacob Fentrel, Abraham Ricks, Stephen Overman, E. Hendricks, Esq., B. Martin, John Smith, Wm, Stover, Daniel Welsh, Lemon Waldron, John N. Turner, Wm. J. Smith, Jr., Wm. J. Smith, Sr., Wm. Middleton, John Hartsook, Noah Romine, George Webb, Henry Whisler, Jacob Whistler, Sr., Thomas Bretsford, W.G. Brandon, Nathan Compton, Scarlett M. Reynolds, Thos. Pyatt, John Pyatt, Eugene Norton, George Price, John W. Baily, James A. Stretch, David W. Fowler, John L. Thompson, Martin Griffin, Wm. Harens, John Pierce, Elisha Cast, Jesse Bogue, Young Shaws, Martin Nelson, Clark Willcuts, William Howell, J. Small, John Swartz, William Gray, George N. Winchell, P.S. McKinney, Jas. Hillman, H. J. Lenox, Simeon Thomas, Bellefield Jenkins, John Draper, J. Overman, Daniel Dwiggins, Joshua Draper, John Ledford, F.J. Leas, E.C. Hill, Hardin Cooper, B. Wall, Lemuel Nelson, Daniel Leas, W. Catum, Eli Lamb, W. Nelson, William Hutchinson, J. Emery, Jonas Wolf, Jacob Mick, G.W. Barley, Samuel Barley, John Brownlee, Daniel H. Barley, Wm. Price, David Devoe, Stephen Nelson, James Tharp, Robert Griffin, Thos. E. Carll, James Nelson, John Bix, John Ballinger, Chrisian Frederick, Ephriam Gahn, James M. Britter, David Burnworth, J. Gabriel, John D. Marshall, Eli Carll, Mathew Tyolor, Daniel Edwards, William C. Miles, Samuel Blinn, Seth Burson, Philip Shira, Alfred Stephens, William Smith, Thomas Peak, Thomas Murphy, Noah Draper, Michael Fentrel, Moses Adamson, Wm. Laylor, Jonathan Pierson, Joseph Hullinger, Daniel Malott, Samuel Burson, David Heavalon, Wm. Hullinger,

Henry Pierce, Daniel Powell, Andrew Heavalow, Peter Beshore, James Heavalow, Oliver Love, L. Foster, Isaac Parker, Henry Burson, John Conner, Jonathan Ellis, Bassil Foster, John Howe, William Grimes, J.P. Dillon, Constantine Smith, John W. Flinn, John W. Moore, John Overman, John Sutton, Levi Lines, W.D. Thompson, D.H. Martin, Levi Holeman, J. Sparks, David Horton,Idell Jackson, Joseph Work, Joseph Rodman, Edmond Lamb, Enos Johnson, Thomas Malott, Benjamin Knight, Caleb Morris, Jesse D. Morris, John Jackson, Wm. Black, Robert Beaty, Richard Jones, Andrew Diltry, Jr. Jonathan Burson, Richard Price, Arthur Norton, Jacob Spencer, Samuel Kiser, William Greff, Sr., A.J. Harlin, Oliver Goldthiat, Esq., William Darby, Wm. Jones, John Petty, John Yager, Isaac Vandevanter, Samuel Horton, Peter Michael, Adam Barley, John Hodge, Andrew Patterson, J. Simons, Joseph Vandevanter, William Nelson, Eli Thomas, Joseph Vanvactor, John Brady, William Harlin, Walter Lovin, Jonah Welsh, Thomas J. Marks, Gideon Small, J.F. Powell, G.H. Wickersham, Daniel Hopkins, Spence Brinkley, Eliza Hocket, John Colter, Joseph Allen, John W. Doods, Daniel Zeller, Henry H. Zeller, Scott Freeman, Wm. Thomas, Hiram Pearson, John Burson, Joab Robberts, Robert Malott, Benjamin Small, Edward Howe, Henry Made, James Sweetser, George W. Smith, Jeremiah Harsey, W.J. Foster, C.W. Head, John W. Wallace, Joseph Sample, Thomas Gregg, Wm. P. Walton, George White, Henry Murry, Sampson Reeves, M. Burk, J.F. Hall, Joab Right, Thos C. Moore, Thos. Helm, Allen Jay, David Lamb, Daniel Hockett, Edward Bird, Jeremiah Thomas, Elihu Small, Nimrod Lewis.

November 24, 1911, p. 5.

At an election held at the home of Isaac Deavis in Green township, Grant county, Indiana, the first Tuesday in November,1852, the following persons appeared and voted:

Strawther Yoll, Jonathan Kelley, Syrus A. Suan, Wm. Kever, Briton Larue, Shedrac Chittwood, Wm. P. Thrasher, Wm. M. Cain, Wm. W. Athen, Harrison Cremer, Samuel Swan, Amon W. Black, Peter Note, Levi Hiatt, Samuel Kelley, Wm. Kirtley, Geo. W. Little, Daniel Wintworth, AlbertLittle, John McCoy, Wm. G. Luallen, Garrett Ribolt, Geo. Hizer, Wm. Perry, Frederick Layne, Sr., Elisha Ogle, John A. Banion, Oliver Flener, Wm. Kunningham, Jesse Green, David Kilgore, John Roberts, Aaron Mawler, John A.J. Weir, Isaac Reavis, John J. Stephens, Henry Huff, Stephen Marsh, Elihu Moon, Spencer Spell, Virgil Hale, Wm. Kox, Andrew Miller, Wm. Wintworth, John Hammer, Levi Toll, Seth Mawler, John M. Cain, Jeremiah Hammer, Thomas Young, Henry Foster, Joseph Saine, Theopholus Smith, Irvin Green, Owen Hartley, Stephen B. Marsh.

November 17, 1911, p. 6.

At an election held in the house of G.H.D. Road in Van Buren township, Grant county, November 20, 1852, the following persons appeared and voted.

Joseph Cloud, Samuel Malcom, Patrick Stinebraner, Thos. C. Cloud, Wm. Long, T.G. Elwood, Lot Rea, James Douglas, Lewis Landers, John Lee, Sen, Ezra Rhodes, Noah Cloud, James Cloud, Wm. Bevard, Truman Lonsbury, Nathan Lonsberry, David Bevard, Samuel Young, John Boxell, Washington

Lamma, Peter Moritz, James Powell, Joseph W. Lee, Elihu Endsley, T.H. Farr, Wm. Cloud, Samuel Pulley, John Lee, Henry Shinhulser, Joseph Hunter, Jacob Palmer, William Malcom, Joseph Whinnery, Samuel Pulley, Wm. Terrill, David Welsh, Cyrus Crawford, Amos May, James Conwell, Stephen Corey, William Thorp, John Huff, Sen., Milton Camblin, Lewis Powell, Benjamin Wine, Joseph D. Corey, B. Matheny, Solomon Fry, John Boxell, Jr., William Hays, Daniel Creviston, Michael Doyle, John Miller, Elijah Lyons, Wm. M. Evans, Wm. Bole, Isaac Swisher, Jonathan Camblin, G.H.D. Road, R. Alexander, Harrison Long, John Duckwall, A. Endsly, E.E. Camdin, G.W. Camblin, G.W. McFadden, John Endsly, Lewis Lee, Wm. Boxell, Isaac Anderson, Abram Moler, David L. Camblin, William D. Corey, George Gardner, Nathan Thompson, Henry Douglas, William Lamma, Isaiah Lamma, John Huff, Jr., Hiram Huff, John Dugan, David Heckard, S. Humbarger, R.B. Boxell, Joseph Carson, Samuel Logan, Lot Green, Joseph Boxell, Thomas Boxell, Thomas Logan, Mills Whinnery, John Green, Michael Roush.

December 1, 1911, p. 3.

At an election held at Center school house, Washington township, Grant county, the first Tuesday in November, 1852, the following persons appeared and voted:

Ephraim Conn, James Hicks, John Secust, L.D. Marsh, Samuel Gilpin, Asbury Steele, William Cox, Robert Simpson, William Glaze, Anthony King, John Carr, W.H. Ellis, George Wabaugh, George Bradford, Sr., Geo. W. Habough, Ezra Conn, Wm. R. Jackson, Jacob Coon, Jacob Rich, George Wine, John W. Sibole, Davidson Culbertson, Casper Daily, Lewis Elliott, Saunders Allen, John King, John B. Hanaker, Enoch W. Moore, Henry Prickett, Wm. F. Lenfesty, Isaac Wiant, Elijah Cox, Alexander Campbell, Joseph Stibole, Harrison Harley, Carey Prickett, Adolpha Prickett, Jacob Wispler, David Williams, Stephen Conn, Elwen Harley, Wm. H. Hummel, Samuel Gearing, Levi Hummel, James Carr, Albert Westfall, Robert M. White, Joseph Bradford, Thomas Campbell, B.A. Madden, Samuel Brown, Jackson Hummel, George Conn, Smiley Smith, John Ellis, Isaac Boader, James Philips, Warren Conner, Dennis Daily, Samuel McNary, Samuel Hawkins, Jonathan Bevard, Samuel Pulley, Isaac Marsh, Benjamin Bond, Adam Pulley, Martin Gingery, Benjamin Marks, Oliver Ganes, Augustus Johnson, Andrew Ebert, Easton M. Line, Frame Love, Joseph Marsh, Samuel Woolman, John R. Hobaugh, Lewis G. Rice, Benjamin Marsh, George W. Wine, Jesse Moore, John Hummel, Jacob Line, Micajah Watkins, William Williams, Christopher Leass, Calvin R. McRae, Maurice Howard, Bailis D. Helm, James M. Helm, Wesley Allen, Peter Bowman, Michael Coon, James F. Carter, Wm. R. Bradford, Moses Bond, Henry J. Calentine, James Love, Burr Woolman, Noah Ream, Thomas Westfall, Joel Daniel Bradford, Wm. Chance, David Hillsamer, Reddin Chance, Francis Helm, Abraham Calintine, Wm. Watson, John McLean, William Howard, Andrew Yont, William Pulley, Robert Watson, Levi Carter, Edmund Gains, Job Curtis, Jacob Secrist, William S. King, Thomas Watson, Van D. Hobaugh, Robert H. Lenfesty, Elias Eviston, Hamilton Batkin, Alexander Lucas, Jefferson A. Hamaker, Eli Bootz, Henry R. Cretzinger, Allen Edwards, Franklin Thompson, John Beatman, Jackson, Benjamin Gains,

Frederick P. Lucas, Jonathan T. King, John Mays, James Thompson, Abraham Bish, Thos. Lenfesty, Elisha Marks, Benjamin Hamaker, James Dillon, James Holman, Daniel Gray, Richard W. Dicken, George Streib, Jacob Streib, Jr., Jacob Streib, Sr., Fielding Sidrez, Daniel Shank, Enoch Marsh, John Snider, Franklin Weaver, John Smith, Patterson Moore, John Hamaker, Ezra Porter.

November 15, 1911, p. 4

An election was held in Green township the first Monday in April, 1857, at which the following freeholders appeared and voted:

Hugh Hamilton, T.B. Loer, O.H. Loer, Jarred Rybolt, David Kilgore, James Minor, William Pary, Samuel Kelley, William Addington, John Fos. J. Stillwell, Joseph Hammer, Davie E. Loer, George Morine, Jefferson A. Morine, Daniel Matchet, J. Parson, George Miser, J. Eakins, Jonathan Kilgore, David Medley, Thomas Morine, J.A. Ware, William A. Bagwell, Samuel A. Swan, John A. Ware, Morrison Creamer, E.B. Watters, Jsack Rybolt, David Mannah, Grant Mane, Cyrus A. Swan, E.B. Williams, W.P. Thrasher, John McLain, Henry Foster, Spencer Spell, Jesse Green, John Wimmer, Samuel Wilson, Samuel Rush, Abel Mosman, John Galbreth, John Gossom, David Lair, Valentine Fritz, David Fritts.

November 14, 1911, p. 4.

At an election began and held in the town of Jalapa, Pleasant township, Grant county on the first Monday in April, 1857, the following persons, being freeholders in the township, appeared and voted:

Lemon Owings, Hudson Lowring, T.A. Shupe, Hesakiah Beeson, L.P. Clark, A.J. Heltner, D.C. Baldwin, John Dunn, Nathan Dawson, D.R. Seeger, Isaac Benson, Moses Harter, Wm. Miese, Wm. Ward, J.D. Scott, Nathaniel Cooper, G.W. Renberger, Isaac Hamilton, A.W. Miller, L.D. Jacobs, Isiah Owings, Elias Miller, J.J. Warrick, Levi Cravins, Samuel Harter, Jas. Jerls, J.H. Collins, John Raypholty, John Fields, Anthony Raypholtz, Wm. Lawring, Isaac Renberger, J.W. Rogers, Nathan Pricket, Joseph Wingon, G.W. McClure, Hyram Bennaker, Solomon Harter, Michael Rennaker, Peter Quilen, C.W.M. Smith, Abraham Slover, Platt Sutton, E.S. Cox, Edmond Winters, Joseph Swope, Jeremiah Sulivan, Jefferson Pugh, J.H. Protsman, Wm. Rennaker, Jacob Bechtel, Abraham Long, Wm. Foster, Daniel Cain, John Spear, Charles Renberger, D.A. White, Wm. Hail, Russel Field, Azor Bagley, Charles Lemon, James Renberger, L.W. Shannon, Conrad Wolfe, Jacob Daily, W. Williamson, Joseph Cravins, Robert McClure, Elias Bagly, J.B. Campbell, David McClure, Robert Bromfield, Garrison Dawson, S.C. Julian, J.T. Simpson, J.W. Grindle, George Egbert, J.A. Smith, Wm. Voris, Shedrich Lawson, John Rennaker, Wm. Young, Reuben Young, Jacob Speelman, Jacob Grindle, Luther Wiles, Laughlin O'Neal, Wm. Baird, Sr., James Six, Ephraim Collins, Wm. R. Webster, Michael Frantz, Harrison Berk, John Slover, J.M. Wagner, Moses Baldwin, Westly Hugh, J.H. Bain, Wm. Dawson, Samuel Williams, John Prickett, David Arthurholtz, Jackson Prickett, Henry L. Renberger, C.L. Swafford, J.F. Shannon, Samuel Rennaker, John Fox, Richard Speelman, Corbin Jackson, Joel Emrich, Harrison Hudson, S.M. Sherman, Henry Murphy, Charles Campbell, Wm. V. Hollman, Alexander Dunn, J.W.

Summons, Nicholas Eltzroth, E.E. Massey, S.R. Serls, John Dawson, Elias Graghill, Harrison Lawrence, O.P. Notingham, James Rennaker, Frederick Strawsberg, Henry Herld, Thomas Baxter, Joel Inks, F.M. Swafford, G.W. White, Stephen Snyder, Isaac Johnson.

November 15, 1911, p. 4.

At an election began and held in the usual place of holding elections in Sims township on the first Monday in April, 1857, the following persons appeared and voted:

Robert M. Pope, Samuel Jumper, Daniel Landis, Joseph Hutinger, William Miller, Vinton Miller, James Corder, Elias B. Burns, John M. Cook, Stephen Jones, Charles Martin, Samuel Grindle, Mathew Taylor, John P. St.Clair, David Burnworth, Robert Johnson, David Stewart, George Martin, W.B. Wetherow, Joseph T. Parton, Joshua Buraker, Nelson McGuire, Geo. W. Smith, Ewan Beece, Jacob Friermood, George Friermood, George W. Ammon, James B. Mark, A.S. Miller, Benjamin Moor, S.D. Barngrover, John Gilpin, David Pence, William Fox, Oliver McGuire, John Myer, Abraham Martin, Norton G. Barngrower, Ephraim Blonhan, Paul Miller, James M. Allen, Francis Smith, Jr., Stephen Norton, John Martin, Theadrick Johnson, Oliver Lillard, George Smith, Isaac Genter, James Gilpin, Aaron Penington, A. Newton, William Burton, James Penington, William Wolary, Stephen Mayden.


At an election held in the town of Van Buren on the first Monday in April, 1857, the following persons appeared and voted:

Michael Roush, Mills Whinnery, H. Barns, Lewis Fry, Milton Camblin, F. Malcom, Didrick Stinebruner, John Murphy, B. Mathena, G.W. Gardner, Thomas Carson, Jackson Malcom, A. Welch, S. Vanderdiu, G.H.D. Road, H. Webb, A.J. Miller, T.G. Elwood, David Welch, Enoch Camblin, Samuel Malcom, Hiram Huff, William Malcom, John Stroup, John Brower, H. Long, John Duckwall, E.C. Grice, G.W. Chriswell, Oliver Jones, William Terrill, A. Willson, Jonas Paxton, Solomon Fry, J. Dugan, Cyrus Crawford, Joseph Cloud, Lewis Landers, Michael Doyle, James Cloud, G.W. McFadden, John Huff, William Cloud.


November 16, 1911, p. 8.

At an election begun and held at Center school house in Washington township the first Monday in April, 1857, the following persons appeared and voted:

F.J. Lucas, Tom Cox, Ephraim Conn, Jacob Streib, George Streib, Joseph Bond, Franklin Thompson, James Thompson, David Horton, Jacob Cochran, Carey Prickett, Daniel Gray, Jesse Cranston, Nelson Turner, John Jackson, David Hillsamer, George Conn, S.R. Line, John Woodward, A.J. Hamaker, Albert Westfall, Woodson Woolman, Joel Jackson, Jacob Feighner, Caspar Bradford, Wm. Shatzer, Jacob Iine, Jacob Wistler, Oliver Ganes, Wm. Daily, L.D. Marsh, Daniel Shank, Wm. R. Bradford, Isaac Marsh, Jacob Rich, James Noble, John Rich, Christopher Sears, A.B. Riggle, James Marsh, Wm. Williams, George Ganes, W.H. Ellis, John Beekman, Davidson Culbertson, James Dillon, Josiah Otiss, Wesley Allen, John Hummel, Joseph Marsh, V.D. Hobaugh, J.S. Wall, Theodore Bonnell, Sanders Allen, David O. Terrell, S.N.

Woolman, Burr Woolman, Samuel McNary, Wm. F. Halstedd, Martin Lucas, Wm. Lytle, John Willelick, Samuel Brown, James Love, Harrison C. McRae, John Lobdell, Mark Hillsamer, A. Bish, John Bradford, Maurice Holoard, John Y. Paslett, Robert Lenfesty, Wm. Bollar, Francis Helm, Bates Helm, Henry Calentine, Stephen Conn, Jesse Bradford, George Camblin, Joseph Bradford, James Hamaker,

At an election begun and held at the district school No. 6, in Liberty township, in Grant county, Indiana, on Monday, the fourth day of November, 1866, for the purpose of electing twelve electors of president and vice president of the United States, the following persons appeared and voted, to with:

Spencer Readen, Daniel Thomas, Jas. Scott, Elias Baldwin, David Smitson, Charles Standfield, Thomas Baldwin, Hiram Jackson, Harvey Davis, Joseph W. Baldwin, William Wellington, Levi D. Pierce, David Jay, John Wilson, John Baldwin, Soloman Parsons, William Howel, Henry Willson, Abiga F. Jones, Thomas Orsborn, Parker Smith, Moses Rich, John Peack, James Swisher, Nathan Rich, John Rich, Peter Rich, Asa Peacock, Tredell Rush, Phineas Henly, James Pharington, Andrew Bubar, Samuel V. Standfield, Lewis Jones, Benjamin Havens, David Wright, Mahlon Neal, James Wright, Charles Baldwin, Henry H. Brown, Joseph Morgan, Jonathan Jones, Lindsey Butler, Hopkins Richeson, Nixon Rush

# GRANT COUNTY NEWS

On September 27, 1911, the *Marion Daily Chronicle* printed the following article on p. 11.

## COURT DOCKET OF 30 YEARS AGO

## GIVES NAMES OF MANY ATTORNEYS AND OFFICIALS SINCE DECEASED.

Among the debris found in the court house garret by Emory Brightman, is a bar docket of the Grant county circuit court for 1883. At that time Hon. Henry B. Sayler, of Huntington, was judge, Charles W. Watkins of Huntington, prosecutor, and Willis Vandevanter, now a justice of the United States Supreme bench, was deputy prosecuting attorney, Cyrus W. Neal, now of Indianapolis, was clerk, Charles Lenfesty, deceased, was sheriff. R.H. Jones and Wilson Addington, both deceased, were deputies. Of the Marion attorneys of that day only a few survive. The enrolled members of the bar at that time who are still living were R.T. St.John, Geo. W. Harvey, now in Mexico, John W. Lacey, now of Cheyenne, Wyo., E.L. Goldthwaite (it will be a surprise to many to know that he was a member of the Grant county bar), John T. Strange, Hiram Brownlee, Asbury E. Steele, L.D. Baldwin, John Kersey, H.J. Paulus, W.L. Lenfesty, Willis Vandevanter, and George Gibson. The members of the bar of that day who are now dead were John Brownlee, Asbury Steele, I. Vandevanter, James Brownlee, James F. McDowell, M.L. Marsh, Joseph L. Custer, Byron H.

Jones, A.M. Baldwin, Elijah Kitch, A.T. Wright, Geo. T.B. Carr, Rufus W. Bailey, J.H. Compton, James M. Wilson, H. Oliver, Richard Steele and Dan A. Banta. The members of the grand jury for the April term, 1883, were Ephriam Creviston, Nathan Overman, William F. Collins, John Gossoom, Perry Zirkle, David Wagner, of the petit jury, Samuel Haines, Micajah Weesner, Milton Cravens, Harrison Burke, George Egbert, Thomas Pugh, Andrew Ferguson, Levi Moorman, Lemuel Pearson, Andrew Mart, Jacob Friermood, David Wherry.

## GRANT COUNTY, WET OR DRY?

In 1911, during a debate about whether Grant County, Indiana should allow liquor to be sold under a local option, the following article appeared on p. 9 of the *Marion Daily Chronicle* for November 16, 1911:

## PETITIONED FOR A DRY COUNTY IN '35

The wet and dry fight in Marion and Grant county did not begin with the local option election held in Marion two years ago. Neither did it begin five or ten years ago. It is known that in 1835 a fight was being waged against the sale of liquor in Marion.

Grant county was first settled in 1823 and the county was organized in 1832. There were but a handful of settlers in the county at that time and Marion was but a small village in a little clearing in the dense timber. But the early settlers as well as those who live here today did not want saloons. They remonstrated against them. It is known that they succeeded in keeping many men from embarking in the liquor traffic who wanted.

Copies of the remonstrance filed with the board of commissioners in 1835 have been preserved. The following is a copy of one of the remonstrances and the voters who signed it:

To the Honorable Board of Commissioners of the County of Grant:

"The remonstrance of the undersigned freeholders and citizens of the township of Center in said county, respectfully showeth that they view with regret the great and from some appearances increasing evils of dissipation in this community, produced by the immoderate use of spirituous liquors; that they feel deeply sensible of the inability of establishing grogshops among us, and thereby, not only sanctioning the intemperate drinking of such of our fellow citizens as are already too much inclined to do it, but also opening the doors of disgrace and ruin and inviting the unwary youths of our country to come in; and that they believe that the general prosperity of the country would be much advanced were such shops to be excluded, now remonstrants therefore would respectfully remonstrate against the granting by your honorable body of any license, hereafter, to a person or persons as grocery keeper or grocery keepers, so establishing him, her, or themselves to retail spirituous or strong liquors within the limits of said township. Filed this day, January 11, 1835."

Signed by: "Henry Carter, John Pearson, William Murray, Cabel Morris, Bailey Pearson, William Murray, Alfred Tharp, William Jones, Daniel Jones, Eli Overman, John Pleasant, William Webb, Willis Jeffery, John Thomas, David Hiatt, Jeremiah Arnold, Joshua Small, Daniel Hiatt, Thomas Mason, Jesse Thomas, John Lamb, Edward Mason, G.C. Smith, Isaac Elliott, Nathan Cogshall, Silas Averman, George Shugart, John Benbow, John Shugart, Ephraim Overman, Thomas Lymens, Benjamin Kulcht, B. Bogue, Jesse Bogue, Joseph Ratliff, William Allen, Nathan Simons, Richard Jones, Warren Connley, Ruben Small, Jesse Small, George Carton, Jonathan Lamb, H. Simons, Robert McCracken, Lot Lundy and Henry Shugart."

## HAMILTON COUNTY RESIDENTS HEAD WEST

No Hamilton County newspapers exist for November 1839; the *Peru Gazette* for November 16, 1839, copied the following news item from the *Noblesville Intelligencer*.

## WESTERN EXPLORING COMPANY

On Saturday the 16th of October, a number of the citizens of Hamilton county, met in Noblesville, and organised a society of the above title. Its objects are, to send out persons to explore the far west, to seek out an eligible situation for the location of a colony, with the ultimate design of there building a city. The tract of country, which the society have more immediately in view, is that lying near the rocky mountains, and east, down the Platte river to the falls. Of the general character of this country we have very little intelligence; but, so far as information has reached us, we have no doubt, that a single view of its fertile prairies, large groves and majestic rivers, will fully compensate those enterprising gentlemen for their labors. There is little to fear in planting a colony in that country; its mineral resources, salt and Indian trade, will amply repay the hardy adventurer for the loss of all the comforts of a civilized country, when he may relinquish. The climate, too, is mild and healthy, strong inducements, inviting thither the lean faced, ague shaken settlers of the western States.

This society will hold a meeting in the court house at Noblesville on the 23d inst., where an address will be delivered explanatory of the object of the society, and the agents of the society, who are to explore the country, will then be appointed.

# LIST OF HARRISON COUNTY VOTERS 1818

(continued from March 1988)

Compiled by Catherine Summers

Harrison county was formed from Knox and Clark counties in 1808. Several other counties were later formed from Harrison, including Floyd 1 February 1819. Four elections were held in Harrison county in 1818. In March an associate judge was elected; the August election was for a representative to the U.S. Congress, a senator and three representatives to the Indiana legislature, a clerk of the circuit court, a coroner, a sheriff, and two county commissioners. In September a justice of the peace was elected in Corydon; and a clerk of the circuit court and a recorder in October.

Lists from Franklin, Posey, Morgan, Boone, Blue River, Corydon, and Harrison townships were published in the March 1988 *THG*.

## BOONE TOWNSHIP, March 1818

| | | |
|---|---|---|
| 1 Henry Grass | 18 Frederick Cotner | 35 David Cotner |
| 2 George Bentley | 19 George Snider | 36 John W. Gaither |
| 3 David Young | 20 Andrew Ellis | 37 Patrick Hunter |
| 4 Jesse Marsh | 21 John Cotner | 38 Paul French |
| 5 George Hooten | 22 William Tompson | 39 George Boone |
| 6 Adam Killion | 23 William Lunsford | 40 Adam D. Dodd |
| 7 David A. Killion | 24 Samuel Boone | 41 James Ludlow |
| 8 William Deal | 25 Squire Boone | 42 Henry P. Kean |
| 9 James Pell | 26 Jesse Chapple | 43 Richard Swacoick |
| 10 Jeramiah Wood | 27 Benjamin Vanator | 44 Isaac Williams |
| 11 John Rollins | 28 Jehew Sutton | 45 George Conrod |
| 12 Thomas Clark | 29 Philip Pearce | 46 George Young |
| 13 Enoch Rollins | 30 Mason Lunsford | 47 Jonathen Keller |
| 14 Eli Killion | 31 John McIntire | 48 Danniel Grass |
| 15 Lonard Killion | 32 Ignatius Able | 49 William D. Dolley |
| 16 James Barnet | 33 George Mcintosh | |
| 17 James Torr | 34 John Boone | |

## CORYDON, March 1818

| | | |
|---|---|---|
| 1 Henry P. Coburn | 5 David S. Collens | 9 David Morgan |
| 2 Robert A. New | 6 Samuel Redugh | 10 William H. Lilley |
| 3 Armstrong Brandon | 7 Patrick Flanigan | 11 Richard M. Heath |
| 4 Lyman Beeman | 8 Isaac Miles | 12 Jacob Conrad |

| | | |
|---|---|---|
| 13 Daniel C. Lane | 57 Samuel Camron | 101 John Sibard |
| 14 Joseph McMahan | 58 Philip Wiseman | 102 John McAdams |
| 15 Elijah Hurst | 59 Ezekiel Camron | 103 Jessee Craig |
| 16 Daniel French | 60 Isaac Boley | 104 Joseph Miles |
| 17 William Daggs | 61 Gilliam Harris | 105 Thomas Gwin |
| 18 Evan Morgan | 62 John Cole | 106 John Cumlar |
| 19 Benjamin Hurst | 63 Michael Kirkham | 107 Peter Coprass |
| 20 Levi Long | 64 James Smith | 108 Allen D. Thom |
| 21 James Eliott | 65 James Sands | 109 Eli Harrison |
| 22 Gordard Vigus | 66 Steven Smith | 110 Hugh Dyer |
| 23 James B. Slaughter | 67 Duncan McRay | 111 Isaac Cox |
| 24 Thomas Long | 68 John Louis | 112 George Spensor |
| 25 Christopher Boman | 69 Benjamin Role | 113 Walker K. Baylor |
| 26 Jacob Conrad, Jnr. | 70 Henry Conrad | 114 Richard Ellison |
| 27 Charles Dyer | 71 John Zenor | 115 Henry Bugher |
| 28 John Marford | 72 Ezekiel Harrison | 116 John Wade |
| 29 John Smith | 73 James Hubbard | 117 Tobias Broyles |
| 30 Robert Biggs | 74 John Morgan | 118 John Buckhanan |
| 31 Alexander Buckhanon | 75 Kinzey Veach | 119 Peter Cooprider |
| 32 George Gwin | 76 James Wiseman | 120 Volluntene Millar |
| 33 Edward Davis | 77 John Crawford | 121 Steven English |
| 34 Steven Langford | 78 James Smith | 122 Gilles McBean |
| 35 Abraham Hurst | 79 William Grant | 123 Jessee Brandon |
| 36 John Conrad | 80 John Denbo | 124 Richard French |
| 37 William Spensor | 81 Samuel Davison | 125 Israel Butt |
| 38 Philip Conrad | 82 Joseph Deckart | 126 Joshua Shields |
| 39 James Denbo | 83 Guy Davison | 127 Adam Sibord |
| 40 Charles Dyer, Jnr. | 84 William McRay | 128 James Newberry |
| 41 William Daggs | 85 Jessee Linzey | 129 James Dooley |
| 42 William Miller | 86 Robert Shields | 130 James Burd |
| 43 Edward Hughes | 87 David Shields | 131 Biram Combs |
| 44 George Shrake | 88 Jacob Zenor | 132 William Hurst |
| 45 Nathanul Applegate | 89 Samuel Cook | 133 William Gregory |
| 46 William Crawford | 90 Jehu Burket | 134 Thomas Gortny |
| 47 Abraham Watson | 91 Jacob Mauck | 135 Joseph Pearson |
| 48 Saml. Lettill | 92 Frances Crabb | 136 Philip Bell |
| 49 Beverly Hurst | 93 Peter Davison | 137 George Jonns |
| 50 James Watson | 94 James Kirkpatrick | 138 William Jonson |
| 51 John Harrison | 95 Elias Jefferes | 139 Edward Maddox |
| 52 Samuel Framer | 96 Jonathan Wright | 140 Andrew Kelly |
| 53 William Morgan | 97 John Hawerton | 141 Charles Toler |
| 54 Alexander McRay Jr. | 98 Louis Kenoyer | 142 Henry Rice |
| 55 William Crawford Sr. | 99 Samuel McGee | 143 Thomas Rite |
| 56 Jacob Lopp Jnr. | 100 John Harrod | 144 James Booth |

145 Isaac Ash
146 John T. Jameson
147 Carter Likens
148 Edward Davis
149 Joseph Kinkade

150 Dennis Pennington
151 Joseph Wheat
152 Eli Wright
153 Alexander Bohanon
154 Josiah Howell

155 Mason French
156 John McMahan
157 Alexander McRay

## BOONE TOWNSHIP, August 1818

1 Frederick Cotner
2 John Brown
3 John Stephens
4 William Lunsford
5 Thomas Young
6 George Snider
7 Daniel Grass
8 John F. Low
9 Robert Thompson
10 Henry Grass
11 Philip Pierce
12 George Hooton
13 Charles Butler
14 George Johns
15 John Smith
16 Thomas Burrass
17 Thomas Larue
18 Edward Larue
19 George Young
20 James Stephens
21 Henry Johns
22 Jacob Miller
23 Thomas Murdock
24 William Marsh
25 John B. Potts
26 Isaiah Boone
27 Anthony Dodds
28 James Bell

29 Peter Mcintosh
30 John B. Truman
31 Gary Hovis
32 Benjamin Stephens
33 George Evans
34 Thompson Kendall
35 James Holaday
36 James Read
37 Robert Mcintire
38 Meristeth Besheres
39 John Roblins
40 Garlin Overton
41 John Steepleton
42 Henry Thompson
43 John Parry
44 Patrick Hunter
45 David Young
46 Ignatius Abell
47 Paul French
48 Joseph Albin
49 George Mcintosh
50 Abel Bentley
51 Mason Lunsford
52 Henry P. Keen
53 Philip Albin
54 Thomas Jones
55 Philip Barger
56 Adam D. Dodds

57 Richard Mouldrin
58 John Mcintire
59 John Sands
60 William Smith
61 Samuel Boone
62 William Thompson
63 Jehu Sutten
64 Jacob Brown
65 Ezekiel Canada
66 Daniel Williams
67 Jesse Chapple
68 Thomas Beard
69 Benjamin Vernatta
70 George Boone
71 Amos Hall
72 George Conrad
73 Thomas Beshares
74 James Ayeres
75 Thomas Lane
76 John Pell
77 Isaac Williams
78 James Heady
79 Jacob Rowen
80 James Fox
81 Richard Swasick
82 Randol Smith
83 William Williams

## CORYDON, August 1818

1 James T. Robertson
2 Lunan Beeman
3 Jno McMechile
4 Danel Mussleman
5 Thos Long
6 Saml Smith

7 Robert Crosier
8 Charles Manwarren
9 George Jones
10 Joseph Bell
11 William Grant
12 Henry P. Coburn

13 David Craig
14 Daniel Davidson
15 John Woods
16 Abraham Harmon
17 Joseph Harmon
18 Isaac Houser

| | | |
|---|---|---|
| 19 Solomon Denbo | 63 John Wise | 107 Arta M Whipple |
| 20 John Denbo | 64 Elijah Mcdowel | 108 William Sharp |
| 21 John T. Jammeson | 65 Henry Warfield | 109 Philip Ekerd |
| 22 Daniel Trout | 66 Walter Pennington | 110 William Spencer |
| 23 Samuel Camron | 67 George Fipin | 111 Volentine Miller |
| 24 William Crawford | 68 James Elliot | 112 Thomas Gwartney |
| 25 William Miller | 69 William Conway Sr | 113 William Miller |
| 26 William Stephens | 70 William Conway | 114 Peter Copprass |
| 27 James Pittman | 71 John Gregory | 115 John Swank |
| 28 Joseph Merrill | 72 Elijah Johnson | 116 George J Shrake |
| 29 John Marlow | 73 Paul Matthews | 117 Philip Crieselius |
| 30 Tobias Broils | 74 Benjamin Adams | 118 William McGrew |
| 31 Frances Crable | 75 Frederick Canoyer | 119 Stafford Smith |
| 32 William Padget | 76 Peter Miller | 120 Abraham Rice |
| 33 Peter Vandvender | 77 Jacob Canoyer | 121 Stephen Westfall |
| 34 James Wiseman | 78 Joshua Harrison | 122 John Simler |
| 35 Ephraim Gwartney | 79 Simon Vanorsdol | 123 Isaac Meek |
| 36 Anthony Gwartney | 80 Peter Wise | 124 Peter Worlow |
| 37 Jesse Pallard | 81 Henry Miller | 125 Jesse West |
| 38 Daniel B. Fawver | 82 John Lopp | 126 Jesse Brandon |
| 39 Henry Histand | 83 Alexander Gilmore | 127 Sylvester Meek |
| 40 William Truett | 84 William Dane | 128 John Mcmertry |
| 41 William Goodman | 85 Elias Goowin | 129 Ezekiel Camron |
| 42 John Long | 86 Abijah Bayless | 130 David Shields |
| 43 Joseph Miles | 87 Samuel Davidson | 131 Edward Mattox |
| 44 John Miles | 88 Andrew Smith | 132 Edward Mattocks Jr |
| 45 Henry Houn | 89 Xpher Shuck | 133 Josiah Littell |
| 46 Isaac Cox | 90 Benjamin Aydelott | 134 Samauel Walks |
| 47 Stephen Smith | 91 Samuel Phremmer | 135 Stephen English |
| 48 Dudly Gresham | 92 John Vanorsdol | 136 Charles Blithe |
| 49 Joseph Ekerd | 93 Jonathan Wright | 137 Jacob Wise |
| 50 Henry Enlow | 94 John Shepherd | 138 Samuel Littell |
| 51 Nathanel Holdesaph | 95 Robert Shields | 139 John Dawson |
| 52 Jno Watkins | 96 Joseph Pearson | 140 William Kindal Jr |
| 53 James McCowen | 97 James Watkins | 141 Levi Wood |
| 54 William Potter | 98 George Albin | 142 Daniel Crandle |
| 55 Alexander McRea | 99 John B McRea | 143 Kinsey Veach |
| 56 Jno Margan | 100 Christopher Putty | 144 Joseph Mcmahon |
| 57 Mordica McRea | 101 William Gwartney | 145 Samuel Welman |
| 58 John Padax | 102 Joshua Shelds | 146 Peter Cooprighter |
| 59 Thomas Roden | 103 James Cubbage | 147 Isaac Miles Sr |
| 60 Samuel Cuningham | 104 Elijah Melton | 148 William Kendal |
| 61 Samuel McGee | 105 Reuben Duggin | 149 Henry Cresselis |
| 62 Daniel French | 106 Micajah Gwartney | 150 Abraham Heistand |

| | | | |
|---|---|---|---|
| 151 | Elias Jeffers | 195 | George Wise |
| 152 | John Cotner | 196 | Abraham Watson |
| 153 | Thomas Cuningham | 197 | Samul Watson |
| 154 | James Barton | 198 | Joseph Clark |
| 155 | Philip Wiseman | 199 | Thomas Grisham |
| 156 | Jesse Linsey | 200 | Philip Stine |
| 157 | Adam Kellian | 201 | John Maynard |
| 158 | Eli Kellian | 202 | Gellam Harris |
| 159 | John McKlehoe | 203 | Henry Richards |
| 160 | Lawrence Thompson | 204 | William Pennington |
| 161 | Henry Kirkam | 205 | Daniel Butler |
| 162 | Thomas Lewis | 206 | Lewis Combes |
| 163 | Josha Swank | 207 | Nathanel Applegate |
| 164 | John Cunningham | 208 | Thos Wheeler |
| 165 | Elisha Hubbard | 209 | Xhper Casner |
| 166 | Yelly Kindal | 210 | Dixon Pennington |
| 167 | John B Keller | 211 | George Yates |
| 168 | Daniel Deal | 212 | Joel Maberry |
| 169 | Charles Dyer | 213 | Stephen F Bennan |
| 170 | Robert Biggs | 214 | Jacob Casner |
| 171 | William Daggs Jr | 215 | Ephraim Broils |
| 172 | John Phiepes | 216 | Joseph Ellage |
| 173 | John Cline | 217 | William Lehue |
| 174 | Samuel Gilmore | 218 | James Smith |
| 175 | Levi Lastly | 219 | James Stephens |
| 176 | Gabriel North | 220 | Wright Bently |
| 177 | John Kennady | 221 | Daniel Cline |
| 178 | Adam Green | 222 | Robert A New |
| 179 | John Albin | 223 | Samul Briley |
| 180 | Frederick Peckle | 224 | John Plume |
| 181 | Charles Toler | 225 | Derick Applegate |
| 182 | John Hurst Sr | 226 | Allen D Thom |
| 183 | Jacob Fleshman | 227 | William Morgan |
| 184 | Robert Kirkam | 228 | Jacob Harmon |
| 185 | Thomas Gilmore | 229 | Daniel Foster |
| 186 | Jacob Mock | 230 | Jno Crawford |
| 187 | Pierce Jones | 231 | Jno Casner |
| 188 | Moses Dale | 232 | Jno Smith |
| 189 | Isaac Emely | 233 | James Barnet |
| 190 | David Brown | 234 | Stephen Smith |
| 191 | George Gwin | 235 | John Ewins |
| 192 | David Morgan | 236 | Danel C Lane |
| 193 | John Denham | 237 | John Dean |
| 194 | Frederick Bloom | 238 | David A Killian |

| | | | |
|---|---|---|---|
| 239 | David Askrien | 283 | Nathaniel Taylor |
| 240 | Abraham Stephens | 284 | Conrad Huddle |
| 241 | Joseph Mock | 285 | Davis Floyd |
| 242 | Hezekiah Burchfield | 286 | John Peterson Sr |
| 243 | Robert Davis | 287 | Samuel Hoskins |
| 244 | Martin Kurds | 288 | John Jackson |
| 245 | John Toler | 289 | William Russel |
| 246 | John Pittman | 290 | William Goldsmith |
| 247 | James Davis | 291 | John Miles |
| 248 | Samuel Redugh | 292 | Richard White |
| 249 | William Riley | 293 | John Harrison |
| 250 | Reuben Melton | 294 | Simon Grove |
| 251 | Frances Williams | 295 | Squire Boone |
| 252 | Luke Vaughn | 296 | Samuel J Black |
| 253 | John L Davis | 297 | Terry Scruchfield |
| 254 | David Cotner | 298 | Jno Critchfield |
| 255 | Jonathan Houser | 299 | Thos Rumley |
| 256 | James Ludlow | 300 | Reed Crandle |
| 257 | Benjamin Stephens | 301 | John Smith |
| 258 | Carrington Gresham | 302 | Joseph Denbo |
| 259 | Peter Charley | 303 | Faris Jones |
| 260 | John Scott | 304 | Samuel Smith |
| 261 | Alexander Matthews | 305 | Edward Davis |
| 262 | William Bennet | 306 | Isaiah Boone |
| 263 | Solomon Byrns | 307 | Henry Highfield |
| 264 | William Wright | 308 | John Cole |
| 265 | James Canady | 309 | Christian Swearings |
| 266 | James C   ? | 310 | Thos Conner |
| 267 | John Harberson | 311 | Daniel Arterbury |
| 268 | James Melton | 312 | William Roden |
| 269 | Eli Melton | 313 | Samul Black |
| 270 | John Wilson | 314 | Frederick Brown |
| 271 | Thomas Stephens | 315 | Jesse Crutchfield |
| 272 | William Rodes | 316 | Philip Gresham |
| 273 | James Mcmurtry | 317 | Joseph Kincade |
| 274 | Allen Roden | 318 | Edward Davis |
| 275 | Isaac Keller | 319 | Henry Brown |
| 276 | David Enlow | 320 | Jno Seton |
| 277 | Jonathan Keller | 321 | Elijah Hurst |
| 278 | Charles Peter | 322 | George Hup |
| 279 | Charles Mcdowel | 323 | William Harris |
| 280 | James Gregary | 324 | Lawson Brent |
| 281 | Lewis Caply | 325 | Andrew McCune |
| 282 | Anthony Keller | 326 | James Smith |

327 John Hockman
328 John H Riley
329 James Riley
330 Nathaniel Crandle
331 Philip Shrake
332 Jacob Conrad
333 James Bogard
334 Lewis Rodes
335 Thos Infield
336 Henry Pursel
337 William Terry
338 Christopher Linsey
339 James Crutchfield
340 Joseph Wheat
341 Patrick Flanagan
342 John Davis
343 Mason French
344 John Stevens
345 William Carpenter
346 Elijah Dyer
347 Abraham Mock
348 William Saffer
349 John McAdams
350 William Wiseman
351 James Pursell
352 James Hargrave
353 Peter Beard
354 John Winter
355 Benjamin Stephens
356 Edmond Davis
357 William Polston
358 Jacob Potts
359 James Dyer
360 William Hurst
361 Sack Pennington
362 Isaac Boley
363 Thos. McCune
364 Alexander McRea Jr
365 Alexander McRea Sr
366 Adam Burket
367 Thos Highfill
368 James Denbo
369 Benjamin Lastly
370 James Brune

371 Phelix Whimsey
372 David Melton
373 Hezekeah Coats
374 John Humphries
375 Henry Rice
376 Joel Wright
377 George Stonesipher
378 Gillis McBane
379 David Austin
380 John Snider
381 George Armstrong
382 Isaac Miles
383 Jonathan Paddax
384 James Brune
385 James Watson
386 William McRea
387 James Smith
388 Alexr F McRea
389 Caleb Crayton
390 Abraham Smith
391 Casheus Edwards
392 Ezekiel Davis
393 John Ellis
394 John Siberd
395 William Winters
396 Adam Sibert
397 Wilson Highfill
398 John Whitman
399 Arthur Ferguson
400 Henry Conrad
401 James Kindal
402 Moses Boone
403 James Sattenfield
404 William Ingleman
405 Jacob Ingleman
406 Laurence Pursel
407 Duncan McRea
408 Robert Ewing
409 William Crawford
410 Thos S Winter
411 Edward Long
412 Briant Bredin
413 John Flanagan
414 William H Smith

| | | | |
|---|---|---|---|
| 415 | Caleb Harrison | 459 | John Windle |
| 416 | John Polston | 460 | Eli Harrison |
| 417 | William Strawther | 461 | Andrew Johnson |
| 418 | Willis Atkins | 462 | William King |
| 419 | John Gileson | 463 | John Martin |
| 420 | Daniel A McRea | 464 | Richard Martin |
| 421 | James Sands | 465 | William Funk |
| 422 | Eli Wright | 466 | Henry Trobaugh |
| 423 | Jno Cooprighter | 467 | William Wilman |
| 424 | Levi Long | 468 | Alexander Blair |
| 425 | John Stonesiper | 469 | Robert Bell |
| 426 | Jesse Shields | 470 | William Daggs Sr |
| 427 | Daniel Row | 471 | John Bredon |
| 428 | George Brown | 472 | Joseph Cline |
| 429 | Danel Brown | 473 | Isaac Funk |
| 430 | Abraham Hurst | 474 | Abner Light |
| 431 | William Shepherd | 475 | Andrew Beeman |
| 432 | Daniel French Jr | 476 | Israel Butt |
| 433 | John Hughes | 477 | George Crutchfield |
| 434 | David Conrad | 478 | Medean Chamberlain |
| 435 | John Dunken | 479 | George Broils |
| 436 | James Boothe | 480 | Peter Chamberlain |
| 437 | Jacob Bline | 481 | Carter Likens |
| 438 | Samuel Houser | 482 | John Lehue |
| 439 | Nathaniel Buckhanon | 483 | Cornelius Lehue |
| 440 | John Wade | 484 | Michael Kirkam |
| 441 | Euriah Pursell | 485 | John Berust |
| 442 | Michael Pilgrim | 486 | Charles Sneed |
| 443 | Daniel Lamb | 487 | Peter Scott |
| 444 | John Parsons | 488 | Milo R Davis |
| 445 | James McBee | 489 | Andrew S Gibson |
| 446 | Thomas Marsh | 490 | John Harbaugh |
| 447 | Leonard Killian | 491 | Sylvanus Vigus |
| 448 | Jonathan Mock | 492 | Mason Bird |
| 449 | Laurence Pitman | 493 | James Bird |
| 450 | Andrew Potts | 494 | Patrick Bird |
| 451 | John Melton | 495 | Nathaniel Rigeway |
| 452 | Randal Melton | 496 | William Watkins |
| 453 | Hezekiah Pursell | 497 | William Gregory |
| 454 | John Smith | 498 | Thomas Byrne |
| 455 | Joseph Marsh | 499 | Peter Cooprighter |
| 456 | Edward B Wilson | 500 | Hugh Gilliland |
| 457 | Edward Tiler | 501 | Charles Smith |
| 458 | John Potts | 502 | John Danford |

| 503 Robert Long | 533 William McIntosh | 563 Samuel Lettell |
| 504 James Jemmison | 534 Christopher Bowman | 564 George Armstrong |
| 505 Samuel Bell | 535 Ezekiel Harrison | 565 Alexander Buckhanan |
| 506 James Bell | 536 Josiah Harrison | 566 Harbin H Moore |
| 507 Thos Smith | 537 Samuel Ruth | 567 Danil Bell |
| 508 John Baily | 538 Michael Bline | 568 Samul Beard |
| 509 John Sarver | 539 William Matheny | 569 Josiah Danford |
| 510 Edward Hughes | 540 Edward Pennington | 570 George Muck |
| 511 John Manson | 541 Hezekiah Davidson | 571 Jeremiah G Dean |
| 512 Jacob Collins | 542 Jesse Craige | 572 Samuel Flanagan |
| 513 James Kirkpatrick | 543 Francis Armstrong | 573 William Boone |
| 514 Henry Atkins | 544 Isaac Ash | 574 George Charley |
| 515 John Melton | 545 Michael Rodes | 575 Jorden Vigus |
| 516 Joel Evans | 546 Ebenezer McDonald | 576 William Kindal |
| 517 Thomas Rogers | 547 Christian Heistand | 577 Nathan Hughes |
| 518 James Gibbs | 548 Ninrod Maxwell | 578 Charles Martin |
| 519 William Carn | 549 George Mings | 579 Elijah Spencer |
| 520 Andrew Wiseman | 550 James Newberry | 580 Richd French |
| 521 Adam Broils | 551 James Hubbard | 581 Jacob Enfield |
| 522 Hiram G Boone | 552 Jesse Yandle | 582 Benjamin Crable |
| 523 William Stalions | 553 Samuel Mcmahan | 583 Jesse Melton |
| 524 William Johnson | 554 Henry Moeres | 584 George Shuck |
| 525 William Bell | 555 Timothy Wheeler | 585 Robert Mitchel |
| 526 Thos Posey | 556 Henry Hurst | 586 Samuel Neal |
| 527 Philip Bell | 557 Jacob Conrad | 587 Arthur McGauchey |
| 528 Jno Conrad | 558 Jacob Cresselus | 588 John Mcmahan |
| 529 Reuben Wright | 559 John Finly | 589 Beram Combs |
| 530 Jacob Wesner | 560 Reuben W Nilson | 590 Xpher Shuck |
| 531 Thos Elliot | 561 John Tipton | 591 William Stringfield |
| 532 Elisha Melton | 562 John Hurst | 592 Peter Sarver |

## BLUE RIVER TOWNSHIP, September 1818

| 1 Benjamin Stephens | 12 Richard Arnold | 23 Peter G Sensner |
| 2 John McMickal Jr | 13 Thomas Right | 24 William Connaway |
| 3 Thomas Carpenter | 14 Samuel McCurray | 25 Reed Crandle |
| 4 Samuel Flaningan | 15 Christein Swearings | 26 Nathaniel Crandle |
| 5 James Pilebs? | 16 John Whitman | 27 William Hanes |
| 6 John Smith | 17 Thomas S Winters | 28 James Barton |
| 7 Jacob Potts | 18 Caleb Harrison | 29 Daniel Bell |
| 8 John Miles | 19 William Carpenter | 30 William Smith |
| 9 Jacob Keith | 20 William Kethecirt | 31 David Austin |
| 10 Harmon Hegan | 21 Josiah Lincoln | 32 John Miles Sr |
| 11 Mason French | 22 John Herbaugh | 33 John R. Wynne |

## CORYDON, September 1818

1 Nathanel Holdcraft
2 Alexander McCray
3 Lyman Beaman
4 James Denbow
5 Henry P Coubern
6 Seml Davison
7 Nathanel Taylor
8 John Baysley
9 Andrew Potts
10 George Armstrong
11 Jacob Moch
12 Duncan McCray
13 ~~Edward Pennington~~
14 Joseph Miles
15 John Caps
16 Evin Hughes
17 Daniel B Fowns
18 John Tipton
19 Reuben Melton
20 ~~John Bollins~~
21 Edward Hughs
22 Anthony Gartna
23 Wm Potter
24 Jonathan Mock
25 George Brown
26 Francis Crab
27 John Parsons
28 Allexander Blair
29 Phillip Wiseman
30 Jacob Coonrod
31 Joseph McMahan
32 Wm Crawford
33 Willis Adkins
34 Benjn Hurst

35 Thos C. Davis
36 Robert Bell
37 Elijah Morgan
38 Saml Ruth
39 Jesse West
40 John McAdams
41 William Roden
42 Benjn Aydelott
43 Patriach Bird
44 Peter Baird
45 Robert Biggs
46 Wm Kindle
47 James Pittman
48 Hesekiah Davison
49 Edward B Wilson
50 Jordon Vigus
51 Wm Bennett
52 Thos Posey
53 William Kindle Snr
54 John McAdams Sr
55 Richard French
56 Wm Greyham
57 Haben H. More
58 Armstrong Brandon
59 James Melton
60 John Aydelott
61 A.F. McCray
62 David Craig
63 John Dorson
64 Stephen Smith
65 Eleven Cooper
66 Danel French
67 Saml. Cameron
68 Wm Ward

69 Allexander McCray
70 Laurence Percell
71 Daniel McCray
72 Jesse Meton
73 Robert Shields
74 Thos Lewis
75 P Flanigin
76 Dudley Gresim
77 John Finley
78 Joseph Kinkade
79 James Bird
80 Joseph Wheat
81 Allexander Gillmore
82 Wm H. Lilley
83 John Shepherd
84 Thos Gartney
85 John Flanagin
86 Adam Dodd
87 C H Manwaren
88 Alexander Buchanon
89 Jams Cubbage
90 David Shields
91 Elias Jeffers
92 William McGrew
93 Nathaniel Applgate
94 Julius Woodford
95 Selvenis Vigus
96 Wm Spencer
97 J T Jameson
98 Wm Wiseman
99 John Smith
100 George Armstrong
101 Wm Grant
102 James Newbery

## BOONE TOWNSHIP, October 1818

1 John B Potts
2 Ignatious Able
3 Andrew Elles
4 William Burrass
5 John Haney

6 George McEntosh
7 Eli Killion
8 Anthony Dodd
9 Mathew Robston
10 William Smith

11 Richard Swosick
12 William Marsh
13 Edward Stoker
14 Robert Croser
15 Jersey Marsh

16 Philip Beswick
17 Jacob Miller
18 William Deal
19 Garland Overton
20 Paul French
21 R.T. Whipple
22 Joseph Eckord
23 William Lunsford
24 Thomas Burrass
25 Mason Lunsford
26 Jacob Suthord
27 Isack Meak
28 Enock Rollins
29 Benjamin Vanata
30 Recard Selwell
31 John Stevens
32 Frederick Cotner
33 Ruben Duggens
34 Daniel Deal
35 John Brown
36 Seley Holdcroft
37 Benj Stevans
38 Edward Lane
39 Jahue Sutton

40 George Hooton
41 James Stevens
42 John B Keller
43 Henry Jons
44 George Johns
45 John Lane
46 Eligah Truel
47 Garey Norres
48 Thomas Young
49 Robert McIntire
50 George Bentley
51 John Keller
52 Thomson Kendall
53 Patrick Hunter
54 Jacob Brown
55 George Young
56 Jacob Rowan
57 George Boone
58 Henrey Grass
59 John Trueman
60 Christein Echord
61 David Young
62 Ephriam Norres
63 Richard Moreland

64 Samuel Hoskins
65 Thomas Lane
66 Henrey Coosenberey
67 Meraday Bershear
68 Moses Boone
69 Squire Boone
70 John Floyd
71 Jessey Chappel
72 George Conod
73 Robert Thompson
74 Henrey Thompson
75 Henrey P Kean
76 Peter McEntosh
77 William Thompson
78 John McIntere
79 James Pell
80 Jerrimeah Woods
81 Able Bentley
82 George Williams
83 John Saffers
84 Philip Barger
85 Thomas Jones

## CORYDON, October, 1818

1 William P. Thompson
2 George Jones
3 Limon Beaman
4 Jacob Conrad
5 Stephen T Beaman
6 Joshua Shields
7 Henry Rice
8 John McMyrtry
9 Daniel B Faun
10 Nathaniel Holcraft
11 John Long
12 Sylvanus Vigus
13 John Fauquar
14 James B Slaughter
15 Samuel Goldsmith
16 Solomon Denbo
17 Anthony Gortney

18 Dorsan Brent
19 Charles Butler
20 John Gregory
21 Thomas Fauquar
22 James Harper
23 Arthur Fergurson
24 William Truit
25 Reuben W Nelson
26 John Snyder
27 Henry P Coburn
28 George Armstrong
29 Fredric Kenoyorer
30 Dudley Gressom
31 Jacob Kenoyer
32 James Boothe
33 Jonathan Houser
34 Charles Smith

35 Henry Bugher
36 Adam Green
37 John Vanarsdel
38 Abraham Ivans
39 William Sharp
40 John Smith
41 Ebenezar Listen
42 Abraham Harrison
43 George Frank
44 Daniel Row
45 William Shepherd
46 George Kenoyer
47 Thomas C Spencer
48 John Denbo
49 William Daggs
50 Nathan Hughs
51 George Guin

52 Abijah Bayless
53 Isaac Williams
54 Jacob Conrad Junior
55 Alexander McRea
56 Dan Butler
57 Abner Lyght
58 Jehu Burket
59 Right Bentley
60 Robert Parks
61 Simon Vanarsdal
62 William Russel
63 James Barnet
64 William Kendall
65 James Denbo
66 John Morgan
67 Joel Wright
68 Elijah Morgan
69 John Hurst
70 Evan Morgan
71 Christopher Bowman
72 John Crawford
73 William Ward
74 Henery Canandey
75 Thos Rodin
76 Walter Pennington
77 Allen Rodin
78 Joseph McMahan
79 Samuel Smith
80 David A Killion
81 Lewis Kenoyer
82 Micheal Kenoyer
83 Edward MCown
84 Andrew Potts
85 James Wiseman
86 Jacob Harmon
87 Conrad Wise
88 William Long
89 Edward Pennington
90 Jessee Shields
91 David Sapenfield
92 Ezkial Kenada
93 Levi Wood
94 John Fox
95 Thomas Clark

96 Abraham Rice
97 Peirce Jones
98 Robert Shields
99 William Spencer
100 William H Lilly
101 Joel Mayberry
102 William H Potter
103 David Craig
104 Thos Long
105 James T Roberson
106 John Cooprider
107 William Pennington
108 Daniel Crandell
109 William Crawford
110 John McGinnis
111 George Hupp
112 Abraham Heistand
113 Peter Cooprider
114 Thomas Coner
115 John Martin
116 David Morgan
117 John Kotner
118 John Cline
119 Andrew Smith
120 Lawrence Pursel
121 Joseph Cline
122 Philip Stine
123 William Crawford
124 Chirstopher Shuck
125 Daniel Beadecum
126 Stephen Watkins
127 Eli Wright
128 Conrad Hudale
129 Stephen Smith
130 Biram Combs
131 Philip Bell
132 George Crutchfield
133 Elijah Hurst
134 Joseph Merrill
135 John Kesner
136 Joseph Wright
137 Philip Peirce
138 Benjamin Chitty
139 Armstrong Brandon

| | | | |
|---|---|---|---|
| 140 | Jessee Brandon | 184 | John Potts |
| 141 | Thomas Stevens | 185 | William Pagett |
| 142 | John Conrad | 186 | Frederic Brown |
| 143 | John Stonecipher | 187 | Edward Hughs |
| 144 | John Aydolett | 188 | Henry Brown |
| 145 | David Cotner | 189 | Jacob Mock |
| 146 | Alexander Blair | 190 | Joseph Mock |
| 147 | James Watkins | 191 | Micheal Pilgrim |
| 148 | Dennis Pennington | 192 | Andrew MCune |
| 149 | William W Hiefield | 193 | Gabriel North |
| 150 | Alexander Buchanan | 194 | William Miller |
| 151 | Joseph Miles | 195 | Thos MCune |
| 152 | Daniel French | 196 | Jacob Snyder |
| 153 | Daniel Kelser | 197 | William Burnett |
| 154 | David Shields | 198 | William Jones |
| 155 | Samuel Houser | 199 | Uriah Purcel |
| 156 | Jacob Tabler | 200 | Isom Harden |
| 157 | Samuel G Watson | 201 | David Melton |
| 158 | John Perkhiser | 202 | Conrad Frakes |
| 159 | Deric Applegate | 203 | Lawrence Pittman |
| 160 | James Jamisson | 204 | George Muck |
| 161 | Isaac Boyles | 205 | Hezekiah Purcel |
| 162 | Joshua Wilson | 206 | Jacob Mowry |
| 163 | Peter Wise | 207 | John Snyder Junior |
| 164 | John Melton | 208 | Martin Curts |
| 165 | Eli Melton | 209 | James Purcell |
| 166 | John Sybert | 210 | Mason Bird |
| 167 | John Melton Junior | 211 | Zachariah Cooplin |
| 168 | James Kendall | 212 | Frederick Bloom |
| 169 | Peter Warlow | 213 | Philp Shrake |
| 170 | James Melton | 214 | Daniel Brown |
| 171 | Stephen Westfall | 215 | James Pittman |
| 172 | Samuel Smith | 216 | Henry Trobough |
| 173 | John Crawford Junior | 217 | James MCune |
| 174 | Charles Sneed | 218 | Jacob Wise |
| 175 | Jacob Conrad | 219 | Henry Kirkam |
| 176 | Joseph Harmon | 220 | William McRea |
| 177 | David Mock | 221 | John Breeding |
| 178 | John McAdams | 222 | Thomas Grant |
| 179 | William Kendall | 223 | David Crable |
| 180 | John Copp | 224 | Jessee West |
| 181 | Archebald Allen | 225 | Daniel Foster |
| 182 | William Kendall | 226 | Abraham Mock |
| 183 | John Pittman | 227 | John Danford |

| | | | |
|---|---|---|---|
| 228 | Joseph Denbo | 272 | William Bell |
| 229 | Gideon Chamberlain | 273 | Fredereck Pickle |
| 230 | Nathan Richards | 274 | Joseph Wilson |
| 231 | Lewis Combs | 275 | John Smith |
| 232 | Ephraim Gortney | 276 | Levin Cooper |
| 233 | Joseph Potts | 277 | John Wade |
| 234 | Yelly Kendall | 278 | John Hurst Senior |
| 235 | Jessee C Summers | 279 | Stephen Smith |
| 236 | John Buchanan | 280 | Henry S Hiefield |
| 237 | Alexander F McRea | 281 | Jonathan Kelley |
| 238 | Jacob Hemp | 282 | John Symbler |
| 239 | Duncan McRea | 283 | Elias Jefferes |
| 240 | Robert Biggs | 284 | Samuel I. Black |
| 241 | Alexander Williams | 285 | Henry Wotson |
| 242 | John Smith | 286 | Thomas Gressom |
| 243 | George Brown | 287 | John Shepherd |
| 244 | William King | 288 | Daniel Cline |
| 245 | Peter Wolf | 289 | Samuel Davison |
| 246 | William Funk | 290 | Peter Cooprider Senior |
| 247 | Philip Acre | 291 | John Hessey |
| 248 | Elias Goodwin | 292 | Samuel Cambron |
| 249 | John Paddox | 293 | Abraham Watson |
| 250 | Thomas Gortney | 294 | Daniel C Lane |
| 251 | Charles Shaver | 295 | John Dorson |
| 252 | James Kirkpatrick | 296 | Charles Dyer |
| 253 | Henry Miller | 297 | William Watkins |
| 254 | Henry Warfield | 298 | John Denham |
| 255 | John Martin | 299 | Samuel Bell |
| 256 | Joseph Ellis | 300 | John McMahan |
| 257 | Jonathan Harberson | 301 | Hugh Dyer |
| 258 | Tobias Broils | 302 | Jonathan Paddox |
| 259 | Robert Lafollet | 303 | Ephraim Wendell |
| 260 | Christopher Linsey | 304 | William Engleman |
| 261 | Josiah Danford | 305 | William Gregory |
| 262 | John Combs | 306 | Willis Atkins |
| 263 | Philip Kimmel | 307 | Peter Vandevender |
| 264 | Levi Lessley | 308 | Isaac Keller |
| 265 | John Pittman Sen | 309 | James Bogard |
| 266 | Thos Innfield | 310 | James Watson |
| 267 | George Stonecipher | 311 | Thos C Davis |
| 268 | John Winter | 312 | Lawrence Thompson |
| 269 | Isaac Miles | 313 | Valentine Kenoyer |
| 270 | Ezekial Davies | 314 | Samuel Neil |
| 271 | Jacob Wisner | 315 | Anthony Windell |

316 Daniel French Junior
317 William Gortney
318 George Charley
319 Timothy Wheeler
320 Samuel Phfremer
321 John Phelmy
322 Henry Werts
323 Isaih Boone
324 Daniel Mussleman
325 Jacob Fleshman
326 Peter Charley
327 William Harper
328 Jermiah Winkle
329 Philip Wiseman
330 Paul Mathies
331 Adam Dodd
332 Patric Bird
333 James Bird
334 James Cubbage
335 Patric Flanagan
336 William Johnston
337 Ezekial Harrison
338 Elijah Dyer
339 John Ketterman
340 Jacob Kesner
341 David Byrns
342 Elijah Johnston
343 Feilding M Bradford
344 James Ayrs
345 John Hurst
346 Elijah Hubbard
347 Philip Gressom
348 Richard White
349 Alexander Gilmore
350 John Dyer
351 Joseph Eldige
352 Benjamin Adams
353 James McMyrtry
354 Edward Mattocks
355 John Bayley
356 Jessee Scrutchfield
357 James Smith
358 Levi Long
359 James Scrutchfield

360 George Armstrong
361 Carter Likens
362 John Windle
363 John Paisley
364 John Barnett
365 John Humphreis
366 Jacob Heck
367 William Goldsmith
368 William Daggs Sen
369 James Hubbard
370 Alexander McRea Junior
371 Jonathan Mock
372 William McGrew
373 Ephraim Fleshman
374 Cassius Edwards
375 Peter Beard
376 Benjamin Aydolett
377 John Mefford
378 Milo R Davis
379 John Lahue
380 William Boone
381 Hiram C Boone
382 Jocab Sapenfield
383 Isaac Houser
384 James Bruce
385 Jordan Vigus
386 Jessee Craig
387 Reubin Lettell
388 Jehu Ellis
389 George Booker
390 Arthur McGahy
391 Jonathan Wought
392 Ransdale Smith
393 Benjamin Crable
394 John McAdams Sen
395 Jessee Melton
396 Ephraim Broils
397 Micheal Rhodes
398 Cornelius Lahue
399 William Watson
400 James B Watson
401 George Yotes
402 John T Jamisson
403 William R. Stringfield

404  John Zenor
405  William Grant
406  James Flinn
407  James Evans
408  David Rhodes
409  Thomas Rogers
410  Westley Gaither
411  Edward B Wilson
412  William Lahue
413  Tary Scrutchfield
414  Ruebin Wright
415  William Rodin
416  Thomas Hiefield
417  Henry Conrad
418  Charles Dyer
419  Joseph Wheat
420  John Watkins

421  H.W. Heth
422  Joseph Paddox
423  Frederick Chamberlain
424  Miles Berry
425  Andrew Wiseman
426  William Fleshman
427  Thomas Galesby
428  Isaac Snyder
429  Anthony Keller
430  Joseph Kingkade
431  Joshua Swank
432  Jacob Blind
433  Robert A. New
434  Jacob Dull
435  John Dull
436  Lawraence Grissom
437  Peter Miller

## A HARRISON COUNTY DEATH

Another notice of a death, printed a distance from its occurrence:

Louis Sappenfield, living two miles south of Palmyra, in Harrison county, committed suicide by shooting himself in the forehead with a rifle the other day, because his wife refused to give him money to buy a farm with.  *The Greencastle Banner,* July 14, 1881.

# THE HENDRICKS COUNTY HOME CEMETERY

Submitted by Betty Bartley

In 1982, a four-lane highway was planned in Hendricks County, Indiana, which made it necessary to move the cemetery from what had been the Hendricks County Home. There were no markers on the graves. The State Highway Department and the Danville Public Library compiled a list of persons buried there. Information was obtained from records of the County Home and the County Health Department. Additional information was found in newspaper articles indexed at the Plainfield Public Library. Some of those buried in this cemetery were transients and unidentified bodies found in the county. The bodies were disinterred and moved to the Danville South Cemetery by a special Highway Department crew May 1982. A monument was erected and inscribed with the following names:

| | |
|---|---|
| Albertson, Phoebe | 23 Jun 1907 |
| Barker, Jemima | 13 Sep 1915 |
| Berry, Lucinda | 15 Dec 1915 |
| Berry, William B. | 5 Feb 1910 |
| Brock, William | 6 Feb 1904 |
| Buis, William C. | 20 Sep 1945 |
| Cox, Fred | 5 May 1919 |
| Crank, Homer | 15 Nov 1910 |
| Cummings, Infant | 9 Jul 1908 |
| Eakers, William | 7 Oct 1901 |
| Erskine, John | 22 Jun 1907 |
| Givens, Harry J. | 20 Aug 1906 |
| Hall, Mary | 6 Jan 1935 |
| Hatton, Melvina | 13 Apr 1916 |
| Hedges, Jane | 23 Jul 1901 |
| Henson, William | 13 Jun 1911 |
| Hockett, Isaac | 16 Jun 1913 |
| Hopson, Mary M. | 9 Jul 1919 |
| Hunt, Cantley W. | 17 Jan 1921 |
| Johnson, Homer | 19 Feb 1912 |
| Jones, William | 18 Dec 1915 |
| Lawrence, John | 1 Jan 1918 |
| McDaniel, Lizzie | 4 Feb 1925 |
| McOwen, William | 12 Nov 1910 |
| Mendenhall, Temple | 30 Jan 1937 |
| Millinger, Jacob | 3 Nov 1929 |
| Morphew, Robert | 29 Feb 1920 |
| Morphew, Sarah | 26 Jun 1900 |
| Patrick, Julia May | 12 May 1946 |
| Patrick, Lavender | 17 Sep 1902 |
| Pelk, William C. | 27 Aug 1937 |
| Pfaff, Elijah | 25 Nov 1909 |

| | |
|---|---|
| Poore, David | 20 Jan 1910 |
| Quackenbush, Mary | 14 May 1909 |
| Robers, Dorothy E. | 24 Sep 1901 |
| Rogers, Rupert | 5 Oct 1901 |
| Rutledge, Elijah H. | 8 Jun 1936 |
| Secrest, Buck | 28 Jun 1923 |
| Smith, Mary | 21 Dec 1914 |
| Spurling, James | 25 Dec 1901 |
| Sweat, Frank | 5 Jun 1935 |
| Tortonent, Alonzo | 17 Feb 1937 |
| Troubles, Cora | 7 Nov 1906 |
| Trowbridge, Louis | 3 Mar 1912 |
| Tubbs, James | 23 Apr 1901 |
| Underwood, William | 11 Dec 1929 |
| White, Thomas | 2 May 1911 |
| Williams, Lou | 14 Feb 1922 |
| Wood, Caroline | 25 Apr 1907 |
| Wood, James | 1 Dec 1906 |
| ----, Fred | 21 Dec 1910 |
| Unknown male infant | 15 May 1914 |
| Unidentified negro male | 25 May 1911 |
| Unknown male killed on RR | 6 Jan 1911 |
| 16 unknown persons | |

# HENDRICKS COUNTY MARRIAGES 1824-30

Hendricks County was formed by statute 20 December 1823; effective, April 1824 from parts of Delaware and Wabash Counties. In 1831, a small portion of Hendricks County was attached to Marion County; in 1868, the boundary between Hendricks and Morgan counties was changed. Marriage records were begun on 17 November 1824 in Marriage Book 1, a photocopy of which is in the Genealogy Division, Indiana State Library. The WPA indexed the Hendricks County Marriage books beginning with book 1, then going to book 2. Book 1 ends with 6 January 1831; book 2 begins with 29 October 1837. At a later date, a book which is now called book 1 1/2 was found. A photocopy of it in in the Genealogy Division. An index to books 1, 1½, and 2 was published in 1980 by Colleen A. Ridlen. The page numbers used in this transcription are those on the pages of Book 1. Page numbers in the WPA index begin with p. 29 and end with page 158 for the same information. Mrs. Ridlen uses the numbers used here.

| PAGE | DATE | GROOM—BRIDE |
|---|---|---|
| 1 | 17 Nov 1824 | James Reynolds-Rachel Demoss |
| | 9 Dec 1824 | Charles Merritt [of Marion Co.]-Jemima Leamon |
| 2 | 7 Feb 1825 | David Stutsman-Jane Nichols |
| | 5 May 1825 | Charles Wilcox [of Morgan Co.]-Alice Harrold |
| 3 | 9 Jun 1825 | James Fowler-Margrett Walker |
| | 21 Jul 1825 | David Jones-Elizabeth Ramsey |
| 4 | 7 Aug 1825 | John R. Hinton [of Monroe Co.]-Mary McCurry |
| 5 | 18 Aug 1825 | Amos Embree [of Morgan Co.]-Nancy Bray |
| 6 | 18 Aug 1825 | John Fowler-Elizabeth Benson |
| | 8 Sep 1825 | Erasmus Nicholus-Elizabeth Stanley |
| 7 | 8 Sep 1825 | William T. Matlock-Betsy Ballard |
| 8 | 7 Nov 1825 lic | Thomas L. Walker-Eppy Guynn |
| 9 | 18 Oct 1825 | Jonathan Jessup-Sarah Leaman |
| 10 | 25 Dec 1825 | George W. Neas-Cynthia Thompson |
| 11 | 9 Mar 1826 | William Jarrel-Peggy Horn |
| | 9 Mar 1826 | William Crumm-Polly Horin |
| 12 | 9 Mar 1826 | James Pope-Betsy Osborn |
| | 12 Mar 1826 | Mincher L. Cox [of Morgan Co.]-Sarah Nichols |

| PAGE | DATE | GROOM—BRIDE |
|------|------|-------------|
| 13 | 11 May 1826 | Alvin Dunn-Sarah Dunn |
|    | 20 Sep 1826 | John Hiatt-Jane Griffith |
| 14 | 19 Oct 1826 | Samuel M. Dunn-Nancy Walker |
|    | 5 Nov 1826 | Reuben Pearson [of Morgan Co.]-Elizabeth Wood |
| 15 | 16 Nov 1826 | William Moore-Betsey Moore |
|    | 22 Nov 1826 | William Harron-Catharine Cooper |
| 16 | 13 Apr 1827 | William Jones [of Morgan Co.]-Nelly Claypool |
|    | 13 Mar 1827 | Reuben Claypool-Isabel Adair |
| 17 | 22 Mar 1827 | Abraham Cook [of Morgan Co.]-Mary Carson |
|    | 1 Apr 1827 | Daniel Troxwell-Elizabeth Dicken |
| 18 | 4 Apr 1827 | David Evans-Sarah Walter |
|    | 20 Dec 1829 | Henry Young-Betsey Neas |
|    | 21 Jun 1827 | George Peck-Lucinda Samuel |
| 19 | 17 Jun 1827 | George Hartman-Polly Sawder |
|    | 30 Jun 1827 | Charles Williams-Elizabeth Staley |
| 20 | 29 Jul 1827 | George Walker-Sarah Lane |
|    | 7 Sep 1827 | Joshua Allen-Jane Turner |
| 21 | 15 Aug 1827 | Hiram Harrison-Jane Dunn |
|    | 23 Aug 1827 | James Demoss-Hannah Fox |
| 22 | 7 Sep 1827 | William Rushton-Polly Norman |
|    | 14 Sep 1827 | George W. Pope-Jane Cooper |
| 23 | 25 Sep 1827 | Joshua Marshill-Mary Cook |
|    | 4 Nov 1827 | Buriah Dunn-Hannah Dunn |
| 24 | 20 Dec 1827 lic | Isaac Talor-Mary McCracken |
|    | 19 Jan 1828 lic | Moorman Johnson-Sarah Bray |
| 25 | 30 Jan 1828 | William Chamnes-Polly Ann Bray |
|    | 31 Jan 1828 | Aaron Marshal-Susanna Matlock |
| 26 | 2 Dec 1827 | Samuel Louder-Lucretia Reynolds |
|    | 7 Sep 1827 | William Rushton-Polly Norman |
|    | 25 Dec 1827 | Wesley McKinley-Nancy McCoy |
| 27 | 9 Mar 1828 | Jesse Gibson-Molly Johnson |
|    | 10 Apr 1828 | Robert Cooper-Sarah Jessup |
|    | 12 Nov 1829 | John Sweateon-Sealy Hether |
| 28 | 22 Apr 1828 | William Moor-Betsy Myers |
|    | 20 May 1828 | James Merritt-Elizabeth Moore |
| 29 | 22 May 1828 | David Adams-Betsey Hale |
|    | 25 May 1828 | Benjamin Stuart-Judith Willis |
|    | 16 Oct 1828 | Samuel Jones-Nancy Ramsey |

| PAGE | DATE | GROOM—BRIDE |
|------|------|-------------|
| 30 | 31 Jul 1828 | Jesse Tindon-Fanny Sacre |
|  | 20 Jun 1828 lic | John Terner-Elizabeth Pennington |
|  | 7 Aug 1828 | Jesse Tindon-Fanny Sacre |
| 31 | 9 Sep 1828 | Hugh Barnhill-Phebe Huron |
|  | 12 Sep 1828 | Basil Jessup-Louisa Jackson |
|  | 23 Oct 1828 | Jacob Kenzer-Charity Owen |
| 32 | 26 Oct 1828 | Samuel Ballard-Isabel Eslenger [of Morgan Co.] |
|  | 16 Nov 1828 | William Dewitt-Mary Talbee |
|  | 18 Nov 1828 | Rollin Lindsey-Rosannah Matlock |
|  | 23 Nov 1828 | James Stamper-Elizabeth Lucky |
| 33 | 27 Nov 1828 | David R. Cox-Elizabeth Fox |
|  | 4 Dec 1828 | Thomas Nichols-Martha Hadley |
|  | 22 Feb 1829 | Joseph Herron-Louisa Ballard |
|  | 11 Dec 1828 | Gilberry Lawhorn-Elizabeth Williams |
| 34 | 28 Dec 1828 | Gideon Hufford-Elizabeth F. Barlow |
|  | 18 Dec 1828 | Elijah Thompson-Margaret Gwynn |
|  | 25 Dec 1828 | Menda Sloan-Pertina Saunders |
|  | 4 Jan 1829 | Abel Smith-Sally Bales |
| 35 | 8 Jan 1829 | George Leaman-Mariah G. Cook |
|  | 8 Jan 1829 lic | J.W. Lacy-Lucretia Davis |
|  | 12 Feb 1829 | George Daves-Susanna Staley |
| 36 |  |  |
| 37 | 4 Mar 1829 | Samuel Yates-Susannah Gibbons |
|  | 31 Mar 1829 | Isaiah Collins [of Morgan Co.]-Polly Blaekly |
|  | 2 Apr 1829 | Hiram Toney-Elizabeth Heather |
| 38 | 21 Apr 1829 | Hugh Decker-Latty Hether |
|  | 25 Apr 1829 | William Paul-Sally Matlock |
|  | 6 May 1829 | Andrew Roberts-Melinda Gibbons |
|  | 30 Apr 1829 | Paul Yount-Jane Stevenson |
| 39 | 4 May 1829 | Preston Pennington-Susanna Steward |
|  | 3 May 1829 | Eden Bayles-Betsey Davidson |
|  | 10 May 1829 | Armsted Jackson-Phebe Pope |
| 40 | May 1829 | Harmon Collins-America Blakely |
|  | 21 May 1829 | Harris Alman-Ruth Lakey |
|  | 7 Jun 1829 | Bartholomew Ballard-Polly Osborn |
| 41 | 5 Jul 1829 | Alexander Shawver-Harriett Gregory |
|  | 23 Jul 1829 | George Tyler-Lucinda Brown |
|  | 22 Jul 1829 | Willson Chettor-Polly Beattie |
|  | Jul 1829 | Philip Josep-Mary Mallet |

| PAGE | DATE | GROOM—BRIDE |
|------|------|-------------|
| 42 | 12 Aug 1829 | Asten Menefee-Polly Shockly |
|    | 14 Aug 1829 lic | Simeon Oatman-Margaret Matlock |
|    | 1 Sep 1829 lic | John Kenworthy-Keziah Lakey |
|    | 1 Sep 1830 | Isaac Prathor-Susannah Shelton |
| 43 | 20 Sep 1829 | James Anderson-Sarah S. Hampton |
|    | 8 Oct 1829 | John Shannon-Harriett West |
|    | 17 Oct 1829 | G.W. Carson-Nancy Matlock |
|    | 17 Oct 1829 | Silas Dooley-Betsey Kerkham |
|    | 22 Oct 1829 | Ira Scott-Rosey Neal |
| 44 | 22 Oct 1829 | Sanford Carter-Sally Vedila |
|    | 28 Oct 1829 | Abel Pennington-Sally Saunders |
|    | 4 Nov 1829 | **Willis McCalment-Mary Ann McClure** |
|    | 5 Nov 1829 | **William Hawkins [of Marion Co.]-Hannah Baxley** |
| 45 | 3 Dec 1829 | **Lewis Rin-Sophia Harriss** |
|    | 26 Nov 1829 | **James Brown-Lucinda Smith** |
|    | 13 Dec 1829 | **Daniel Turner-Martha Elender Walter** |
|    | 7 Dec 1829 | **Robert Davis-Sally Bryant** |
| 46 | 7 Dec 1829 | **William Williams-Rhoda Saunders** |
|    | 20 Dec 1829 | **Henry Young-Betsey Nees** |
|    | 3 Jan 1830 | **James Davis-Amanda Stoker** |
|    | 29 Nov 1829 | **William McCalment-Mary Ann McClure** |
| 47 | 24 Jan 1830 | **Jacob Harper-Nancy Staley** |
|    | 26 Jan 1830 lic | **Absolon Dunn-Rachel Gibson** |
|    | 11 Feb 1830 | **Jesse Hawkins-Martha Jones** |
|    | 13 Feb 1830 | **John Dunn-Sally Mires** |
| 48 | 20 Feb 1830 | **William Singleton-Nancy King** |
|    | 25 Feb 1830 | **William Logan-Sarah Faught** |
|    | 4 Mar 1830 lic | **Stephen Treat-Isabel Wood** |
|    | 17 Mar 1830 lic | **---- Reece-Elizabeth Wood** |
|    | 20 Mar 1830 lic | **Robert Tincher-Edith Ray** |
| 49 | 18 Apr 1830 | **James Trotter-Sally Whit** |
|    | 12 Apr 1830 | **Charles Johnson-Polly Jenkins** |
|    | 23 Feb 1830 | **Abram. Brown-Betsey McIntosh** |
|    | 8 May 1830 | **Elijah Dickerson-Polly Dodson** |
| 50 | 17 May 1830 | **James Merritt-Sarah Jessup** |
|    | 24 May 1830 lic | **Elijah Turner-Marry Mallet** |
|    | 1 Jun 1830 | **Ishmael Rains-Ann Jackson** |
|    | 13 Jun 1830 | **William Faught-Nancy Stevenson** |

| PAGE | DATE | GROOM—BRIDE |
|------|------|-------------|
| 51 | 27 Jul 1830 lic | John Poynter-Rebecca Sparks |
|    | 13 Aug 1830 | Samuel C. Strickland-Sally Bensenal |
|    | 13 Aug 1830 lic | Floyd Todd-Sally Prechett |
|    | 6 Sep 1830 | Alfred Waggoner-Julian Hufford |
|    | 19 Sep 1830 | Nathaniel Britton-Emeline Faught |
| 52 | 28 Aug 1830 lic | Isaac Williams-Sarah Lewis |
|    | 1 Sep 1830 lic | Benjamin Sacry-Mary Specklemier |
|    | 2 Sep 1830 | David Warren-Margaret Hether |
|    | 29 Sep 1830 | Ranson Carter-Elizabeth Asenia Fox |
| 53 | 10 Oct 1830 | Abraham Lewis-Hannah Wentworth |
|    | 4 Nov 1830 | James Todd-Jency Jones |
|    | 1 Nov 1830 | Samuel McClelland-Margaret Cooper |
|    | 30 Nov 1830 | Greenberry King-Margaret Singleton |
| 54 | 30 Nov 1830 | Thomas Singleton-Rhoda King |
|    | 6 Jan 1831 | Joseph Pearson-Sally Wilcox |
|    | 23 Dec 1830 | Jesse Thompson-Katharine Potts |

# FROM KNIGHTSTOWN, INDIANA TO CALIFORNIA

A visit to Knightstown, Indiana by a former resident then living in California prompted T.B. Deem to write an article "Knightstown Contributes to California," which appeared in the *Knightstown Banner* 15 July 1938. Mr. Deem lists former residents of Knightstown who had moved to the Sunshine State. Relatives still in the Knightstown area are often noted, as well as the dates of emigration and residences of some of the travellers.

Tressie Anderson (Los Angeles; daughter of N.W.C. Reeves)

Russell Armstrong (son of Sylvester Armstrong)

Maud Spencer Bell

Laura Berg (Riverside; daughter of Charles Stuart)

L.L. Boblett

Hattie Bowman (daughter of William Bowman)

Rev. & Mrs. R.F. Brewington (Fresno)

Nora Brown (daughter of W.J. Welborn)

____ Allee Bundy (wife of Jesse Bundy)

Carl Bundy (son of Jesse Bundy)

Jesse Bundy

Frank Butler (son of Edwin Butler)

Mrs. ____ Cassidy (Los Angeles; daughter of Frank Kennard)

Raymond Charles (son of Oliver Charles)

Mr. & Mrs. ____ Clifford

Mrs. Frank Collins (Patterson)

Stella Collins (Patterson; daughter of Mrs. Frank Collins)

Bessie Cameron Cook

Milo Cook (daughter of John V. Cook)

Carl Corwin (Pasadena; son of Joe Corwin)

Will Corwin (Pasadena; son of Joe Corwin)

Faye Crouse (son of H.M. Crouse)

____ Davis (Los Angeles; daughter of Mrs. Elmer Dill)

Ernest Davis (Los Angeles)

Jesse Davis (Fresno)

Charles Deem (Long Beach; son of George A. Deem; brother of Mrs. Cress)

Hazel Deem (Long Beach; daughter of George A. Deem)

Harry Elliott (nephew of Jesse Bundy)

Nannie Gregory Elliott (wife of Paul Elliott)

Paul Elliott

Frank Fithian

____ Glenn Fosburg (daughter of Nell Shanklin Glenn)

Blanche Freeman (Stanford; granddaughter of Morris F. Edwards)

Grace Mostler Furnace (Bakersfield; wife of Roy Furnace)

Roy Furnace (Bakersfield)

Philander Gard

Ross Gard (ca 1855; cousin of Moses and William Mitchell)

Sarah Gard

Serena Gard

Daisy Glendennin (daughter of Mrs. Sam McKee)

Nell Shanklin Glenn (daughter of Mrs. Long Shanklin)

Rufus Green (Stanford; brother of Alpheus Green)

Elmer Hall (Los Gatos; brother of Fred Hall)

Maggie Welborn Hancock (daughter of W.J. Welborn)

Charles Haney (Glendale)

Stella Charles Haney (Glendale; sister of Adah Fithian)

Dorothea Harper (daughter of Ada Fithian)

Frank Heaton (son of David Heaton)

John Heaton (son of David Heaton)

Leone Heaton (Long Beach; daughter of Mrs. Robert Heaton)

Louisa Heaton (daughter of David Heaton)

Mrs. Robert Heaton (Long Beach)

Ben Hensley

Hattie Hollingsworth (Santa Barbara; daughter of J.H. Hinshaw)

Lynn Hudelson (son of Emory Hudelson)

Hester Hughes (Ontario; daughter of Elmer Dill)

Charles Kennard (Los Angeles)

Frank Kennard (Los Angeles)

Levia Hittle Kennard (Los Angeles; wife of Charles Kennard)

W.R. Kerwood (Glendale)

Wayne Kerwood (Glendale; son of W.R. Kerwood)

Gertrude Grubbs Keyt

Gertrude Leisure (daughter of Fred Leisure)

John Leisure (son of Fred Leisure)

Ruby Leisure (Los Angeles; daughter of Elmer Dill)

Watson Leisure (widow of Fred Leisure)

Ella Mogul Lewis (wife of Walter Lewis)

Walter Lewis (brother of Harry Lewis)

Nora Wagoner Linton (Los Angeles)

Amos Maple (Whittier; son of John D. Maple)

Florence Maple (Whittier; daughter of John D. Maple)

John D. Maple (Whittier)

Moses Mitchell (ca 1855; son of John Mitchell)

Pinkney Mitchell

William Mitchell (ca 1855; son of John Mitchell)

Emma Moffitt (daughter of Frank Kennard)

—— Morrison (daughter of Ithamer Stuart; wife of John B. Morrison)

John B. Morrison

Frank Mostler (Bakersfield)

Robert S. Nancy

N.T. Nixon

Sophia Parker Nixon

Sarah Overman (Hollywood)

—— Parks (Los Angeles; daughter of Nathan Overman; wife of Perry Parks)

—— Parks (Los Angeles; daughter of Nathan Overman; wife of Taylor Parks)

Perry Parks (Los Angeles)
Taylor Parks (Los Angeles)
Miller Peder (1849)
Edna Pitts Peters (Los Angeles)
Earl Reddick (son of Earl Reddick)
Edna Carroll Roberts (Los Angeles; wife of Leonard Roberts)
Leonard Roberts (Los Angeles)
Mrs. Lon Shanklin (Bakersfield)
Maggie Shipley (Patterson; daughter of Mrs. Frank Collins)
Lawrence Spencer (Bernadino)
Margaret Starr (daughter of L.L. Boblett)
Mary Stifel (daughter of L.L. Boblett)

Hol. I. Stuart (Pasadena)
_____ Swain (Stanford; husband of Fanny Morgan Swain)
Fanny Morgan Swain (Stanford)
Fred Thornburg (Los Angeles)
Ruth Trimble (Los Angeles; daughter of Wilson Horn)
Don Vestal (son of Frank J. Vestal)
Carl Walling (son of Charles Walling)
Charles Walling
Elsie Johnson Walling (wife of Charles Walling)
Ada Newby Wilson
Lewis Wink, Sr. (1850; brother of Solomon Wink)
Sarah Jane Wright

# HONOR ROLL OF EARLY HUNTINGTON COUNTY PIONEERS

*The Warren Tribune* published the following list on page 29 of its January 31, 1931 edition. The list was taken from the county records office; land speculators were eliminated from the listing.

### 1833
Eli Mitchell
Samuel Jones
John D. Pulse
Fleming Mitchell
James Morrison
Lewis Purviance

### 1834
Ezekiel Fleming

### 1835
Denton Riggs
Joseph Stroup
Philip Loudermilk
Ezra C. Thompson
Simeon Huffman
William Coolman

### 1836
David Smith
Abel Johnson
Simeon Souers
Moses Sparks
Solomon Johnson
George H. Thompson
Ebenezer Thompson
John Dillon
Enoch Jones
John Alexander
Ezekiel Jones
John W. Priddy
Simeon Swaim
John Brawley
Daniel Stroup
Abner Leonard
John Leonard, Jr.
Geo. Blair
Aaron Back

George Beard
William Richards

### 1837
William Crum
Henry Mossburg
Abel Irwin
John C. Shafer

### 1838
Samuel Irwin
John McGrew
Leander Morrison
Andrew Irick
Jonathan Foust

### 1839
Isaac B. Dillon
James Coffield
Sergeant Clark
Robert Irwin
James Irwin
Jonathan Irwin
Bought from other purchasers
Peter Wire
Thomas McIlwain
William Gill
James Lynn
James Priddy
George Gephart
William Roberts
Ruel Wright
Jappa Rose
Joseph Eubank
Amos Sutton
Abram Sutton
Jacob McPherson

# EXCERPTS FROM JAY COUNTY NEWSPAPERS

*The Portland Weekly Sun*, June 16, 1881.

p. 3 Frederick Strausberg, living north of Portland, had the good luck to have a twelve pound boy make its appearance at his house on Thursday last. Another democratic victory.

Rev. A.C. Wilmore . . . visiting in Portland . . . moved with his parents to this county in infancy, remaining here until 1860. When at age of eleven years he moved to Huntington . . . He is the eldest great grand child of James C. Adair (twenty years deceased) and his second name, Cleeland, was given in his honor. Rev. Wilmore is an itinerate minister of the U.B. church and is the pastor at South Wabash, Indiana.

*The Portland Weekly Sun*, December 8, 1881.

p. 2 **Fair Haven Fancies** Married:  By Esquire C.E. Codder, at the bride's residence, Sabbath, November 27.  Miss Ellen Hartzell to Aaron Metts, both residents of this vicinity.

p. 3 **Local News** Married--On the 3rd inst., by J. Conkel, Justice of the Peace, Elijah Jordan and Sarah E. Thomas, all of this county.

Married--At the residence of the bride's parents, in Portland, Ind., by Jacob Conkle, Justice of the Peace, on the 3rd inst., George Lipps of Fort Recovery, Ohio, to Elizabeth Isenhart of Portland, Ind.

Mr. Calvin Q. Houck was married by Rev. Mr. Baker, on Tuesday, Nov. 29th, to Miss Emma J. Roush, at the residence of the bride's father.  *Marion Democrat*.

*The Portland Commercial*, August 16, 1888.

p. [4] Mr. and Mrs. T.S. Johnson, and Mr. and Mrs. W.A. Moorman, attended the golden wedding of Mr. and Mrs. Thomas Moorman, at Winchester last Thursday.

John Saunders did a good job of stonework on the foundations of N.H. Gable's new residence.

**NOTICE OF PARTNERSHIP** To whom it may concern:  Notice is hereby given that on the 1st day of May, 1888, I shall take my step son, Charles P. Snell, as a partner in the general merchandise business, at Kit, Indiana . . . the firm name of West & company.

Henry F. West

*The Portland Sun*, September 6, 1889.

p. 1 **At Rest The Editor of the "Sun" Passes Away**.  George M. Holloway has passed away . . . at 3:30 o'clock yesterday morning . . . The deceased was born in Shelby county, Ohio, April 3d, 1858 . . . interment at Green Park cemetery.

A very pleasant family re-union was held last Sunday at the residence of Mrs. Catherine Imel.  Mrs. Imel's children, eight in number, are all alive and were present:  Sarah Elvey, John Imel, Samuel Imel, Nancy Jetter, Ezra Imel, Elizabeth Coby, Nathaniel Imel and Thomas Imel.

Married.--Sept. 1., 1889, by W.L. Godfrey, J.P., Chas. N. Stratton and Sarah E. Lake.

Mrs. Joseph Detamore died at the home of her son John, on east Walnut street, Thursday morning at 6 oclock . . . Interment at Claycomb cemetery two miles west of Green post office. [*There is a death record for Barbara Detamore, age 69, September 5, 1889 in Jay Co. ed.*]

John Martin went to Huntsville, Ind., Tuesday, where he was married on the following day to Miss Lydia Patterson. [*No marriage license issued in either Jay or Madison counties. ed.*]

*The Portland Commercial*, February 6, 1890.

p. 1 Seth A. Winters of Portland, Ind., arrived in Minster [Oh.], Tuesday evening . . . visiting his sister, Mrs. C.M. Smith and family.

John L. Banks and wife, at the home of M.C. Culver, Riverside, were made happy Sunday morning, by the advent of a little girl. Grandpa Culver is quite elated at the appearance of his first grandchild. [*No birth record found in Jay Co., ed.*]

Freddie R., son of J.E., and Flora Bliss, died at the family residence on east Walnut street, Thursday, Jan. 30th, aged 6 years, 11 months and 28 days. Funeral services Friday, at 2 o'clock, conducted by Rev. J. Alex Adair. Interment in Green Park cemetery.

Harry O., infant son of J.H. and Nettie J. Davis, died in Ft. Recovery, O., Tuesday, Jan. 28th, of la grippe, or brain trouble. The funeral services were attended by Dr. D.S. Kinsey, A.W. Evilsizer and family, Mrs. J.F. Hill, Ruth Osborn, Myrtie and Fannie Long, and Mary Huey, of this city.

[*Obit.*] Melvin Warner of District no. 7, Jefferson township was born October 23, 1869 near Deerfield, Randolph County, Indiana. Came to Jefferson twp., this county in 1875. Survivors: father, mother, four brothers, one sister. [*Death certificate dated January 23, 1890 for Melvin M. Warner, ed.*]

*The Portland Commercial*, Women's edition, December 19, 1895.

p. 1 **Womens Relief Corps**. . . . Stephen J. Bailey Relief Corps., No. 77, was organized in September, 1877, and had for its first president, Mattie Mellinger. The following ladies have served as president since its organization: Mattie Melllinger, Nancy Gilpin, Carrie P. Bruner, Annie P. Davis, Mary E. Headington, May B. Malin, Lydia Bergman, Della F. Jones, Laura E. Headington and Esther Odle . . .

p. 3 **Sketch of Caroline Clark**. Caroline Clark was born at Eaton, Preble county, O., October 10, 1820. She came with her parents to Jay county, Indiana, March 8, 1829. They were the first family to stay in the county.

On April 14, 1861, when the first call for soldiers was made, her eldest son responded . . . went to Winchester, enlisted in Company E., Eighth Indiana volunteers . . . reenlisted in the Nineteenth Indiana. He died at Washington city, December 12, 1862. She joined the Relief Corps.

# THE PORTLAND MISSION
## JAY COUNTY, INDIANA

The following article was copied from *The Portland Commercial*, Womens edition, December 19, 1895, p. 2.

In the year 1837, the Rev. Mr. Lank was sent into this county to gather into societies the members who had settled in this frontier wilderness . . .

. . . in 1838 . . . was formed into a mission . . . known as Portland mission. Rev. Geo. W. Bowers was appointed pastor in charge. . . . Rev. James Havens . . . presiding elder.

The first organized . . . at house of John Kidder, in Pike township, Jay county. The members were John and Sarah Kidder, George and Polly Blazer.

The first quarterly meeting of Portland mission was held near Bear Creek, eight miles north of Portland, January 5, 1839 at . . . James Marquis. The members present were: Geo. W. Bowers, mission, P.C.; James Marquis and G.C. Whiteman, local preachers; Will Vail and David Baldwin, exhorters; Wm. Baldwin and Samuel Howe, class leaders.

The following classes were reported: Butternut, Wheat's, Gibson's, Marquis', Gray's, Debenbaugh's, Higgin's, Sutten's, Redkey's, Twibble's and Timberlack's.

First quarterly meeting . . . Feb. 6, 1841 was held in Portland. Present: B.H. Bradbury, P.E.; Elisha Bennett, L.D.; James Marquis and William Vail, local preachers; Henry L. Jinkins, Samuel Moore and Bennett King, stewards; Geo. Ritterhouse, Robert Kain, John Connor, Poindexter Manis and Abraham Lotz, exhorters; Louis Byram, Wm. Richardson, Wm. Baldwin, Arthur Bradley and Anthony Ritterhouse, class leaders.

At first quarterly conference held at Timberlake's school house, Dec. 4, 1852, a committee was appointed, viz.: J. Kidder, N. Bockoven and John Neeley, to estimate the necessary amount to build a church house at Kidders class.

In April, 1874 . . . pastors report . . ."I found 49 members. . . .J.W. Coffman, class leader. M. Adkinson, Eli Malin, W.C. Johnson and Wm. Shepard, stewards. Eli Mahin, Geo. Sebring, M. Adkinson, W.C. Johnson, Robert Huey, J.W. Headington, R.T. Hammons, R. Denney and Joe Malin were trustees."

# AN INDEX TO THE EARLIEST COURT RECORD
# IN JOHNSON COUNTY, INDIANA

*By Portia Christian\**

Johnson County, Indiana, was formed by statute December 31, 1822, to be effective May 5, 1823. The original book of the first court records is preserved in the Johnson County History Museum in the public records section. A microfilm copy of the record can be used in the Microfilm Department of the Johnson County Courthouse. Copies of pages of this book can be obtained at $1.00 per page from Brenda Smith, Microfilm Department, Johnson County Courthouse, Franklin, Indiana.

*ADAMS, Eli Nathan Hall, 19, 20, 21.*
*ADAMS, Elisha, jr., 19, 20, 21.*
*ADAMS, Elisha, sr., 19, 20, 21, 22.*
*ADAMS, George, juror, 196.*
*ADAMS, George Cook, 19, 20, 21.*
*ADAMS, James Cleland, 19, 20, 21.*
*ADAMS, Jane B., 19, 20, 21, 22, 23.*
*ADAMS, John, 19, 20, 21, 22.*
*ADAMS, Margaret, 20.*
*ADAMS, Marian Keturah, 19, 20.*
*ADAMS, Milton Phillips, 19, 20, 21.*
*ADAMS, Patrick, juror, 196.*
*ADAMS, William Campbell, 19, 20, 21, 22, 23.*
*ADULTERY, 33.*
*ADULTERY AND FORNICATION, 234-36.*
*AFFRAY, 4-5, 27-28, 29-30, 39-40, 40-41, 42-43, 58-59, 61-62, 67-68, 70-72, 75-77, 78-79, 79-80, 85-86, 93-94, 94-96, 110b-11, 113-15, 159-61, 165-67, 210-11, 222-24, 237-38, 241-43, 245-47, 262-63, 265-67, 276-77, 280-82, 282-83; aiding, 278-79.*

*\*Portia Christian grew up in Johnson County; her third great-grandfather was Amos Durbin who settled in Ninevah township in 1820. Miss Christian is a retired librarian with extensive experience in business and special subject university libraries. Since she returned to Johnson County in 1980 she has been associated with the county museum and the microfilm department in the court house as an indexer. She is now a part-time staff librarian/archivist at the Johnson County History Museum.*

ALEXANDER, John, 249; juror, 115, 116, 128, 172, 181, 183, 186, 188, 191.

ALEXANDER, William, 210; defendant, 212, 213.

APPEALS, 133-34, 173-74, 174-75, 176-77, 230-32, 232-33, 236-37, 269-71, 285-87, 287-88, 298-99.

ARNOLD, Henry, defendant, 250, 251, 264, 265.

ASSAULT AND BATTERY, 23-25, 30-31, 35-36, 37-38, 57-58, 69-70, 77-78, 84-85, 88-89, 90-91, 96-97, 98-99, 99-100, 109-110, 111-113, 115-117, 117-118, 119-20, 120-21, 121-22, 123-24, 158-59, 190-92, 195-96, 197-98, 198-99, 216-18, 218-20, 220-22, 238-39, 244-45, 257-59, 259-60, 277-78, 281-85.

ASSUMPSIT, 6-8, 55-56, 101-04.

ATWOOD, James, administrator, 252, 253, 254; juror, 86, 88, 91, 92, 94, 95, 100, 258.

ATWOOD, Thomas, deceased, 252, 253, 254; plaintiff, 124.

BAILEY, George, juror, 73, 75, 77, 213.

BAIRD, David, 98; defendant, 113, 160, 161.

BALEY, Perry, juror, 86, 88, 91, 92, 94, 95, 100.

BALLARD, Joab, 239.

BALY, George, juror, 209.

BANTA, David, juror, 257, 263, 265, 269, 273.

BARLEY, Edward, juror, 72.

BARLOW, William, 39, 40, 61; defendant, 45.

BARNETT, George, juror, 49.

BARNETT, John, defendant, 30, 70, 71, 93, 94, 95; juror, 26.

BARNETT, Spencer, bail, 94; foreman, 108, 109, 110b, 112, 115, 117, 119, 161, 166, 221; juror, 5, 220; witness, 236.

BARNETT, Thomas, juror, 24, 28, 131, 250, 255; security, 31, 94.

BARNETT, William, 112; administrator, 133; foreman, 250, 256, 259, 262, 264, 266, 267; juror, 163, 251, 258.

BARTHOLOMEW COUNTY, 13, 26, 254.

BARTHOLOMEW COUNTY SHERIFF, 12.

BASTARDY, 63-65, 110-110b.

BECK, Jacob, juror, 265.

BEELER, Hannah, Administrix, 287.

BELL, Benjamin, defendant, 249; security, 230.

BELL, Jacob, 49; defendant, 86, 87, 96, 97, 169, 171, 172, 177, 178, 179, 256, 257; security, 89, 166.

BELL, James, bail, 197; defendant, 110b, 165, 166, 167; security, 249.

BELL, Nathaniel, sr. 36; bail, 97; defendant, 46, 47, 60, 87, 177, 178, 179, 198; juror, 8, 9, 26, 48, 49; plaintiff, 132; security, 278.

BELL, Robert, 119, 292; defendant, 88, 89, 91, 92, 173, 197, 198; plaintiff, 230.

BELL FAMILY, 272, 273.

BELLER, Thomas, deceased, 287; plaintiff, 285, 286, 295

BERRY, Richard, 4, 5, 23, 24, 25, 29; defendant, 42.

BIGAMY, 214-16.

BISHOP, Lewis, 124, 225; defendant, 181, 182, 183, 184, 185; juror, 131.

BLANKENSHIP, George W., bail, 78, 79; juror, 26, 73, 75, 76.

BLYTHE, Benjamin J., plaintiff, 104, 105, 106.

BOND, 202.

BOOTH & NEWBY, 11, 202, 203; tavern, 206.

BOYD, George, juror, 235.

BOYD, James, juror, 208, 213.

BOYD, John, juror, 235.

BRACKENRIDGE, Robert, plaintiff, 50, 52, 54.

BRIGGS, George, security, 213.

BROCK, Elias, juror, 263.

BROCK, Martha, witness, 236.

BROOKVILLE, 1.

BROOKVILLE LAND OFFICE, 20.

BROWN, ----, attorney, 169, 170, 171, 271, 273.

BROWN, Andrew, defendant, 271, 273; juror, 86, 257; plaintiff, 127, 128.

BROWN, Anna, 63, 64, 65, 127.

BROWN, David, defendant, 273.

BROWN, Henry, juror, 95, 161, 251, 255.

BROWN, John, 49.

BROWN, Michael, juror, 5, 115, 116.

BROWN, R., 105.

BRUNEMER, Anthony, juror, 278, 280, 289.

BRUNK, John, juror, 164, 235, 269.

BRUNNEMER, Anthony, juror, 216

BURK, John, juror 213.

BURKHART, David, 4, 5, 110a; bail, 110, 110b; juror, 26, 163.

BURKHART, George, juror, 86, 88, 91, 92, 94, 95, 100.

BURKHART, Henry, 110a, 269; bail, 217; juror, 258, 262, 265.

BURKHART, William, 109; bail, 100; defendant, 4, 216, 217; juror, 24, 49, 115, 116, 128, 172, 215, 278, 280, 289; security, 215.

BURTON, Prettyman, juror, 128, 172.

BYERS, Henry, 250.

CALVIN, Hiram, bail, 222.

CALVIN, James, defendant, 176, 220, 221; juror, 164.

CALVIN, Thomas, defendant, 247, 248.

CALYER, Isaac, defendant, 267, 268.

CAMPBELL, John, foreman, 29, 30, 39, 40, 43, 48, 61, 67; juror, 131, 181,

DAVISSON, Jesse, defendant, 58; foreman 23, 25, 27, 35, 37, 45, 46, 57, 69, 71, 72, 74, 76, 87; juror, 72, 131.

DAWSON, John, security, 219.

DEARBORN, Thomas, 123.

DEMEREE, Peter, juror, 250, 251, 255.

DIVORCE, petition for, 14-15, 65-67, 136-38, 228-29, 240-41.

DOE, John, 106, 170.

DONALDS, James W., defendant, 55, 56; justice of the peace, 11.

DOTY, George, juror, 283.

DOTY, John, security, 163.

DOTY, Peter, juror, 73, 75.

DOWER, assignment, 199-201, 226.

DOWLING, Thomas, juror, 161.

DRAKE, Gideon, security, 75.

DUNHAM, Aaron, juror, 95; witness, 176.

DUNHAM, Jeremiah, juror, 72; plaintiff, 81; security, 248.

DUNN, Jane, 214.

DUNN, William, defendant, 169, 171; juror 161.

DURBIN, Amos, 45.

EADS, Thomas C., 1, 2.

EADS, William H., 1, 2.

EARLYWINE, Daniel, juror, 73, 75, 77; plaintiff, 138, 139, 140.

EARLYWINE, George, appellant, 132, security, 112.

EARLYWINE, Mary, estate of, 133, 134.

EDINBURGH, 25, 27, 202, 203.

ELLIOTT, John, juror, 181, 183, 186, 188, 191.

ELLIOTT, Thomas, juror, 196.

ESTRAY, 46, 74, 161-64, 274-75.

ETTER, Daniel, juror, 24, 28.

ETTER, William, defendant, 269, 270; juror, 5, 181, 183, 186, 188, 191; witness, 286.

FAYETTE COUNTY, 66.

FERRIN, Isaac, 37.

FLETCHER, Calvin, attorney, 16, 17, 18, 24, 26, 28, 29, 30, 36, 39, 41, 42, 43, 44, 45, 47, 48, 49, 55, 56, 57, 59, 61, 62, 64, 68, 69, 71, 73, 74, 76, 87, 139, 140, 141, 152, 154, 155, 169, 170, 171, 255, 271, 273, 292, 293.

FORNICATION, 207-09.

FOSTER, John, 114; deputy sheriff, 283; foreman, 276, 277, 279, 280; juror, 161, 196, 282, 284; justice of the peace, 134, 144.

FOSTER, Richard, juror, 115, 117, 128, 172.

FOSTER, William, bail, 7, 77, 91, 98, 141; security, 114.

FRARY, James, 259.

FREEMAN, Moses, juror, 259.
FREEMAN, William, juror, 131, 181, 183, 186, 188, 191, 258.
FULLER, John, 66.
GALLASPY, Robert, juror, 209.
GARRISON, William, juror, 161.
GARSHWILER, John, juror, 257, 262, 265, 269, 273.
GAUNCE, John, juror, 72, 73, 75, 77.
GIFFORD, Jesse, juror, 73, 75, 77, 259, 263.
GIFFORD, Peleg, juror, 283.
GILLASPY, George, juror, 208, 213, 235.
GILLASPY, James, juror, 181, 183, 186, 188, 191.
GILLASPY, Robert, juror, 213, 235.
GILLASPY, William, security, 238.
GILLCREES, Robert, customer, 168; juror, 26, 91, 163, 213.
GILLCREESE, Robert, juror, 209, 235, 263.
GILLMORE, Alexander, juror, 278, 289.
GILMORE, Alexander, juror, 215, 280.
GLENN, Archibald, foreman, 167, 181, 182, 183, 184, 186, 187, 188, 189, 190,
    191, 196, 197; justice of the peace, 63, 64, 132, 173, 198, 199, 200, 230, 231,
    287, 288.
GLENN, Henry, 89.
GLOVER, Joseph, Lawrence County sheriff, 107.
GOODMAN, Timothy S., plaintiff, 6, 8, 55.
GRAVES, Elizabeth, 208, 209; defendant, 234, 235.
GRAVES, George, 87.
GREGG, Harvey, attorney, 9, 10, 12, 13, 24, 26, 28, 31, 32, 33, 35, 37.
GRIFFITH, Samuel, juror, 209, 213, 235.
GRIFFITH, Thomas, juror, 181, 183, 186, 188, 191.
GROCECLOSE, Andrew, juror, 173, 208, 213, 235.
GROCECLOSE, John, bail, 129; juror, 24, 28, 115, 117, 172, 173, 251, 255,
    262; witness, 288.
GROUT, David, juror, 49.
HALLAM, William, juror, 24, 28.
HAMILTON, Jeremiah, defendant, 242, 243.
HAMNER, James, juror, 49.
HAMNER, Jemima, 65, 66, 67.
HAMNER, Joseph, 65, 66, 67.
HAMNER, William, juror, 86, 88, 91, 92, 94, 95, 100.
HARMONSON, Peter, defendant, 104, 106, 107.
HART, G.B., Bartholomew County sheriff, 12, 24, 26.
HARVEY, Isaac, juror, 24, 28.
HENDERSON, Thomas, juror, 161.

HENDRAN, Oliver, juror, 257, 263, 265, 269, 273.

HENDRICKS, David, 24, 25.

HENDRICKS, James, defendant, 93, 95.

HENDRICKS, Lewis, juror, 181, 183, 186, 188, 191.

HENDRICKS, Separate, 164, 165.

HENDRICKS, Squire, juror, 26, 28; plaintiff, 232, 233.

HENDRICKSON, James, defendant, 94, 95.

HENSLEY, Jeptha, defendant, 72, 73.

HENSLEY, Polly, defendant, 201, 202, 204, 205, 206.

HENSLEY, William R., defendant, 201, 202, 204, 205, 206.

HEROD, W., attorney, 102, 103.

HERRIOTT, Samuel, 19; bail, 125, 126; clerk, 151, 207, 228; security, 245.

HERROD, Saml., clerk, 151.

HESTER, Craven P., attorney, 142, 151, 152, 154, 157.

HETHER, Thomas, 164, 165.

HETHER, William, jr., 164, 165.

HICKERSON, Joseph, defendant, 98, 113, 114, 159, 160.

HILBOURN, Elias G., juror, 73, 75, 76; security, 68.

HILL, George, administrator, 224, 226, 227, 228; juror, 131, 181, 183, 186, 188, 191.

HILL, James, juror, 283.

HINES, Henry, 1, 2.

HOGS, estray, 74; malicious mischief, 91, 272; unmarked, 48-50, 74.

HOLEMAN, William, bail, 247; juror, 250, 251, 255.

HOLLAND, George B., 227, 228.

HOLLAND, John, defendant, 55, 56, 124, 125, 126.

HOLLANDBACK, George, juror, 72, 77.

HORTON, ----, 66.

HOUGHAM, Jonathan, juror, 49, 131.

HOUSLEY, Jane B., 19, 20, 22.

HUNT, Margaret, defendant, 50, 52, 54.

HUNT, Timothy, 6.

HUNT, William, defendant, 1, 2, 3, 4, 5, 6, 8, 50, 51, 52, 53, 54, 55, 56.

HUTTO, William, 212; defendant, 210, 211.

HUTTO, William, sr., bail, 211.

INDEBTEDNESS, 60, 104-08, 126-27, 164, 177-79, 252-55.

INTENTION TO BECOME A CITIZEN, 135-36.

ISRAEL, Isom, juror 262, 273, 283.

JENNINGS COUNTY SHERIFF, 15.

JERRELL, Henry, juror, 283.

JOHNSON, ----, attorney, 32.

JOHNSON, Charles, 284.

JOHNSON, Samuel, 30; Intent to become a citizen, 135, 136; juror, 49, 163.

JOHNSON COUNTY SEMINARY, 5, 62, 68, 80, 97, 110, 168, 188, 191, 194, 220, 239, 243b, 259, 260, 265, 266, 281, 283, 285.

JONES, Jefferson D., defendant, 245; juror, 257, 263, 265.

KAIGLY, John, commissioner, 200, 201.

KEATON, William, bail, 248; juror, 250, 251, 255.

KEELAND, William, 40, 41, 67, 68.

KEENY, Jonathan, plaintiff, 173.

KENARY, Michael, defendant, 243b, 244.

KEPHART, George, juror, 215, 278, 280, 289.

KEVIS, John, juror, 181, 183, 186, 188, 191.

KING, George, 7, 9.

KNAPP, Alfred, juror, 128, 250, 251, 255.

KNIGHT, William, defendant, 277, 278.

KOONS, Henry, juror, 263, 269.

KOONS, William, juror, 181, 183, 186, 188, 191.

KOONTS, Henry, juror, 257, 265.

LANE, Abraham, defendant, 273; plaintiff, 271.

LANE, Valentine, juror, 250, 251, 255.

LASH, Adam, juror, 24, 28, 209, 235.

LASH, James, security, 251.

LASH, Nancy, 110, 110a.

LAUGHLIN, Nathan, 292, 295, 296, 298; plaintiff, 287, 288, 290, 291.

LAWRENCE COUNTY SHERIFF, 107.

LEFFLER, Leonard, juror, 161.

LEGGIT, William, defendant, 117, 118.

LEONARD, William, witness, 236.

LETUS, George, security, 221.

LEWIS, Andrew, juror, 181, 183, 186, 188, 191, 283.

LEWIS, Isiah, 161.

LEWIS, Severe, defendant, 43, 44.

LONG, ----, reed maker, 290.

LOWE, Abraham, juror, 86, 283; justice of the peace, 285, 286; witness, 295.

LOWE, Jefferson, defendant, 120, 121; security, 97.

LOWE, Thomas, defendant, 63, 64, 65, 127, 128, 129, 172; juror, 72, 115, 116, 163; justice of the peace, 9, 47.

LYONS, Robert, juror, 263, 265, 269, 273.

MAGILL, William, juror, 215.

MALICIOUS MISCHIEF, 86-88, 91.

MARSHALL, Isaac, juror, 24, 28.

MARSHALL, Samuel, 140.

MARTIN, Charles, juror, 49.

MARTIN, William, juror, 131.

MARTINSVILLE, 151, 152.

MATTHEWS, James, defendant, 252, 253, 254, 255; witness, 236.

MATTHEWS, John S., defendant, 236.

McCASLAND, David, juror, 5.

McCASLIN, David, 99, 100; constable, 233.

McCOOL, William, juror, 257, 262, 265, 269, 273.

McCORD, John, juror, 115, 116, 164, 172, 196, 293, 294; witness, 292.

McGEE, Elijah, bail, 107.

McKINNEY, Hezekiah, bail, 80; security, 239.

McKINNEY, Joseph, clerk, 254.

McKINNEY, Samuel, juror, 262.

McKNIGHT, George, bail, 107.

MILLER, Alexander, 223.

MILLS, on White River, 142.

MILLS, Agnes, defendant, 224, 225, 227.

MILLS, Edward, defendant, 224, 225, 227.

MILLS, Elizabeth, defendant, 224, 225, 227.
MILLS, Elizabeth, widow, 224, 225, 226.

MILLS, James, defendant, 224, 225, 227.

MILLS, Martha, defendant, 224, 225, 227.

MILLS, Mary, defendant, 224, 225, 227.

MILLS, Richard, defendant, 224, 225, 227.

MILLS, Willis, defendant, 224, 225, 227.

MILLS, Willis S., deceased, 224, 225, 226, 227; juror, 5.

MITCHEL, Aaron, 243b.

MOORE, Levi, 85; defendant, 35, 36.

MOORE, Philip, juror, 5.

MOORE, Robert, 86; defendant, 123; witness, 176.

MORE, Robert, 221.

MORGAN COUNTY CIRCUIT COURT, 142-157.

MORRIS, ----, attorney, 6.

MORRIS, Bethuel F., 105, 106.

MOZINGO, John, juror, 86, 88, 91, 92, 94, 95, 100.

MULLENNEAX, Permenter, 48; juror, 5, 196.

MULLINEX, Permenter, security, 235.

MURPHEY, John, 84.

MURPHEY, Pierson, deputy recorder, 295; witness, 294.

MUSSELMAN, Daniel, defendant, 81, 82; juror, 73, 75, 77, 88, 91, 92, 94, 163.

MUSSELMAN, Henry, juror, 128, 172.

NEEDHAM, Thomas, juror, 86, 88, 91, 92, 94, 95, 100.

ROBINSON, Arthur, foreman, 77, 78, 79, 84, 85, 88, 90, 93, 95, 96, 97, 98, 99, 113, 160.

ROBINSON, Thomas, defendant, 39, 61, 62.

ROBINSON, William, juror, 289.

ROBINSON, William W., 3; deputy sheriff, 268; juror, 250; justice of the peace, 233, 251.

ROBISON, Jesse, foreman, 91.

ROBISON, Richard, bail, 62.

ROBISON, William C., defendant, 77, 78.

ROE, Amos, 266; defendant, 262, 263.

ROE, John, 9, 10, 121, 277.

ROE, Richard, 106, 170.

ROOK, Frederick, bail, 179.

ROSS, William, defendant, 161, 162, 163, 164.

RUDY, David, 272.

RUSSELL, Richard, witness, 236.

RUSSELL, Thomas, 116, 273; constable, 110a, 110b, 124, 236; defendant, 90, 91; juror, 236.

RUTHERFORD, William, juror, 5.

SACHET, Letus, defendant, 257, 258, 259.

ST. JOHN, Nathaniel, juror, 213, 250, 251, 255.

SANDERS, John S., constable, 133; juror, 131.

SANDERS, William, juror, 196.

SELBY, James, plaintiff, 101.

SELLS, Abraham, 16; juror, 5, 24.

SELLS, David, 272; plaintiff, 298, 299.

SELLS, John, administrator, 16.

SELLS, William, administrator, 16; juror, 215, 278, 280.

SEYBOLD, Mahlon, 174; constable, 132, 198; juror, 263; justice of the peace, 270, 299; witness, 286.

SHAFER, Elizabeth, 208, 209; defendant, 234, 235.

SHAFER, William Henry, 234.

SHAFFER, Simon, juror, 100.

SHAFFER, William, 209; juror, 26, 49.

SHIELDS, Elizabeth (Oldham), 14, 15.

SHIELDS, Robert, 14, 15.

SHIP, John, juror, 181, 216, 250, 251, 255.

SHIPP, John, juror, 183, 186, 188, 191, 278, 280, 289.

SLANDER, 139-42, 271-73.

SLAUGHTER, Moses, plaintiff, 269, 270.

SLOOS, Peter, constable, 286.

SMILEY, John, bail, 102; commissioner, 53; foreman, 239, 241, 242, 243, 243a, 243b, 244, 245, 246, 247, 249; sheriff, 1, 3, 28, 36, 38, 43, 47, 56, 62, 68, 70, 71, 73, 75, 76, 89, 91, 92, 94, 95, 97, 98, 100, 102, 106, 114, 125, 126, 128, 131, 139; security, 281, 285.
SMILEY, Samuel, juror, 283.
SMILEY, William, juror, 181, 183, 186, 188, 191, 257, 269, 273.
SMITH, Alice, 33.
SMITH, Hiram, foreman, 131.
SMITH, William, 57.
SMOCK, Isaac, foreman, 210, 212, 213, 214, 216, 217, 218, 219, 234, 235, 237.
SMOCK, James, juror, 86, 88, 91, 92, 94, 100.
SMOCK, Samuel, witness, 207.
SOME, Absolem, 4.
SPARKS, Zachariah, juror, 5.
SPEARS, William, defendant, 29, 42, 43; juror, 163, 257, 262, 265, 269.
SPRINGER, Edward, 279, 281; defendant, 260; juror, 24, 28, 259.
SPRINGER, William, bail, 243a, 275; defendant, 78, 79, 80, 276, 278, 279, 280; juror, 73, 75, 76.
SPRINGER, William G., bail, 110b, 218.
STAFFORD, Robert, security, 76.
STALLCUP, Elias, 31, 32, 33, 34.
STALLCUP, Ruth Hall, 31, 32, 33, 34.
STEAMBARGER, Frederick, 10, 11, 12, 13.
STEAMBARGER, Reuben, 10, 11, 12, 13.
STEVENS, David, juror, 161, 278, 279.
STEWART, Eleazer, defendant, 110, 110a.
STEWART, Eli, defendant, 240, 241.
STEWART, John, defendant, 99, 100, 109, 110.
STEWART, Lementa, plaintiff, 240, 241.
STOTT, Richard, sheriff, 15.
STOWERS, Traverse, juror, 283.
STOWERS, William, juror, 263.
SURETY OF THE PEACE, 8-9, 164-65.
SURFACE, ----, 292.
SUTTON, Catherine, defendant, 169, 171; plaintiff, 177, 178; widow, 199, 200, 201.
SUTTON, Cyrene, infant heir, 199, 200.
SUTTON, Elizabeth, defendant, 173; plaintiff, 169, 172.
SUTTON Isaac, juror, 258, 263, 265, 269, 283; security, 249; witness, 286.
SUTTON, Jonathan, deceased, 199, 200, 201.

WARREN, John, defendant, 298, 299.

WARREN, Separate, 165.

WATTS, Catharine, 295.

WATTS, Elisha, witness, 286.

WATTS, Isaac, defendant, 194.

WATTS, Israel, defendant, 193; witness, 134.

WATTS, James, 256.

WATTS, John, security, 249.

WATTS, Richard, 295.

WATTS, Samuel, defendant, 169, 171, 285, 286, 287, 288, 290, 291, 292, 293, 295, 296, 297; guardian, 200; juror, 95.

WEAKLEY, John, 282.

WEAVER, Thomas, juror, 115, 116, 128, 172.

WEBB, David, 70.

WELLS, Jesse, juror, 72; justice of the peace, 164, 165.

WHARTON, ----, witness, 290, 292.

WHARTON, Joseph, 295.

WHEELER, Isabel "Hebe", defendant, 201, 202, 204, 205, 206.

WHEELER, Nathan, defendant, 201, 202, 203, 205, 206; witness, 204.

WHISKEY, SALE OF, 181-83, 183-85, 188-90.

WHITCOMB, James, attorney, 62, 64, 68, 71, 72, 73, 75, 77, 78, 80, 84, 85, 86, 87, 88, 89, 91, 92, 94, 95, 96, 98, 100, 104, 106, 108, 109, 110, 110b, 111, 112, 113, 114, 116, 118, 119, 120, 121, 122, 123, 140, 141, 152, 154, 155, 158, 159, 160, 163, 165, 166, 167, 168, 182, 184, 185, 187, 189, 191, 192, 194, 195, 209, 210, 212, 216, 217, 219, 221, 223, 235, 254, 255.

WHITE, Isaac, juror, 73, 75, 77.

WHITE, Jacob, juror, 257, 262, 273.

WHITE, James, 125, 126.

WHITE LICK, 145.

WHITE RIVER, 142-43, 145, 148, 150, 294.

WHITE RIVER TOWNSHIP, 65,

WICK, Daniel B., attorney, 4, 5, 64, 83, 137, 217.

WICK, Samuel, justice of the peace, 151.

WICK, William W., attorney, 208, 220, 235, 238, 239, 242, 243a, 245, 246, 248, 249, 250, 251, 256, 257, 258, 260, 261, 263, 264, 265, 266, 268, 273, 275, 276, 277, 279, 281, 282, 283, 284, 285; plaintiff, 60.

WILEY, James, juror, 257, 262, 265, 269, 273.

WILKINS, Perryman, juror, 49.

WILLIAMS, Allen, defendant, 218, 219, 220.

WILLIAMS, Hugh, juror, 75, 76.

WILLIAMS, Isaac, juror, 115, 117, 128, 172.

WILLIAMS, Samuel, juror, 258.

# MARION COUNTY, INDIANA VOTERS, 1831;
## COMPARED WITH THE 1830 FEDERAL CENSUS
## OF MARION COUNTY*

Marion County was formed by statute, 1 April 1822. By 1830 when the federal census was taken, there were 1,075 heads of household and males 20 years of age and older in the county. Forty of the heads of household were female, leaving 1,035 possible voters. An election was held 1 August 1831 in the county courthouse to elect various officials. At this election, 975 males voted. The following comparison was made between the 1830 census and the 1831 voting list. Matching or near-matching names were found for 611 of the voters.

There was a constant movement of persons into and out of Marion County; therefore it seems valuable to print the voting list as an aid to locating persons who might not be identified with Marion County in other records. Although the election was physically held in Centre Township, voters resided throughout the county.

Poll Book of the Voters at the General Election held at the Court House in Centre Township Marion County, Indiana on Monday the first day of August in the year one thousand eight hundred and thirty one being the first Monday in August for the Election of a Governor of the State, Lieutenant Governor, Representative in Congress, State Senator, Representative, three County Commissioners and Coroner. Henry P. Coburn Inspector John Johnson and Jacob Calip being Judges J.P. Drake and Ansel Richmond being Clerks all duly sworn according to law.

| VOTERS NAMES | NO. | 1830 FEDERAL CENSUS | PAGE |
|---|---|---|---|
| Hervey Bates | 1 | Harvey | 349 |
| Edmund Harrison | 2 | | |
| Robert Dunken | 3 | | |
| Daniel Bower | 4 | | 423 |
| Z. Lake | 5 | Zenas | 363 |
| Samuel Smith | 6 | | 375 |
| Hugh Cambell | 7 | Campbell | 371 |
| Symon Smock | 8 | Simon | 377 |
| Caleb Scudder | 9 | | 351 |
| James Edgar | 10 | | 359 |
| William Renck | 11 | Rennick | 357 |

| VOTERS NAMES | NO | 1830 FEDERAL CENSUS | PAGE |
|---|---|---|---|
| F.T. Luce | 12 | Fleming Luse | 353 |
| Andrew C. Mann | 13 | Man | 379 |
| Andrew C. Cory | 14 | | |
| William Evans | 15 | | |
| Wm. Appleton | 16 | Applegate | 411 |
| Jacob Ringer, Sr. | 17 | | 365, 423 |
| Thomas Keeler | 18 | | 429 |
| Samuel Brison | 19 | | |
| David Bates | 20 | | |
| Benjamine Roberts | 21 | | 351 |
| John Sutherland | 22 | | 365 |
| Jeremiah Johnson | 23 | | |
| Eward Hutson | 24 | Edward Hudson | 399 |
| Geo. Hannah | 25 | Hanna | 407 |
| Zenas Cimberly | 26 | Kimberly | 371 |
| Cornelius Hardenbrook | 27 | | 377 |
| Francis Cassell | 28 | | |
| Caleb Kauble | 29 | | |
| Thomas Brunson | 30 | | |
| C.W. Vanhauten | 31 | Cornelius Vanhouten | 371 |
| Wm. Bagwell | 32 | | 361 |
| James Sulgrove, Sr. | 33 | | 391 |
| Moses Frazee, Jr. | 34 | | 361 |
| T.M. Smith | 35 | Thomas M. | 349 |
| Burr P. Dennis | 36 | | 373 |
| Joshua Stevens | 37 | Stephens | 357 |
| Solomon Decinger | 38 | | |
| Lyle McClong | 39 | Sigle McClung | 419 |
| G.B. Holland | 40 | George | 359 |
| Geo. Norwood | 41 | | 351 |
| Wm. Hannaman | 42 | | |
| Thos. Long | 43 | | |
| Wm. M. Lung | 44 | | |
| Wm. Bay | 45 | | 439 |
| Henry Bradley | 46 | | 363 |
| Wm. McLaughlin | 47 | | 369, 371 |
| John Blackburn | 48 | | |
| Eph. Elkins | 49 | | 425 |
| Jacob Ringer, Jr. | 50 | | 365, 423 |
| Peter Winchel | 51 | | 357 |
| John J. McLaughlen | 52 | | |
| J.W. Davis | 53 | Josiah W. | 357 |
| John Smith | 54 | | 375, 415, 427 |
| Isaac Coonfield | 55 | | |

| VOTERS NAMES | NO | 1830 FEDERAL CENSUS | PAGE |
|---|---|---|---|
| Josep Lake | 56 | | |
| John Merrygoold | 57 | Magoured | 401 |
| Sam L. Johnson | 58 | Samuel T. | 375 |
| Wm. McIvain | 59 | McIlvain | 419 |
| James Vansckles | 60 | | |
| Morgan Briant | 61 | | |
| David Lovett | 62 | | |
| Steph. Yager | 63 | | 439 |
| Jeremiah McCheseney | 64 | | |
| Jonathan Brunson | 65 | Bunson | 423 |
| Adam Broiles | 66 | Broils | 363 |
| Thos. Lewis | 67 | | |
| Thos. Lucas | 68 | | 409 |
| Coonrod Cullip | 69 | Conrad Collip | 429 |
| Harris Alman | 70 | Almond | 413 |
| Alfred Harison | 71 | Harrison | 349 |
| Josep P. Devall | 72 | Duvall | 371 |
| James Smither | 73 | | 441 |
| Henry Brenton, Jr. | 74 | | 383 |
| David Fisher | 75 | | 379 |
| Samuel McIlvain | 76 | | |
| J.B. McLain | 77 | Jacob, James, John McClain | 379, 381 |
| Jam. M. Christ | 78 | | |
| Alex. Wiley | 79 | Wylia | 349 |
| Moses McLain | 80 | McClain | 379 |
| A.H. Brian | 81 | Hampton Bryan | 377 |
| James McLain | 82 | | 441 |
| Hiram Bacon | 83 | | 419 |
| Nathl. Davis | 84 | | 351 |
| L.W. Heddy | 85 | | |
| Robt. Brenton | 86 | Brinton | 369 |
| Jacob Henshaw | 87 | | |
| Conrod Ringer | 88 | | 435 |
| Wm. McDowal | 89 | McDowell | 365 |
| Henry Hardin | 90 | Harden | 419, 435 |
| John Wilkins | 91 | | 355 |
| Wm. McLaughlin, Jr. | 92 | | 379, 435 |
| James M. Kiney | 93 | | |
| Milton Johnson | 94 | | 419 |
| John H. Burrows | 95 | Burroughs | 421 |
| Jas. Rodgers | 96 | | |
| Wm. Morris | 97 | | |
| Elijah Avery | 98 | | |

| VOTERS NAMES | NO | 1830 FEDERAL CENSUS | PAGE |
|---|---|---|---|
| Michael Sherer | 99 | Sharrar | 401 |
| Sampson Huffman | 100 | Simoson | 411 |
| Moses McDaniel | 101 | | |
| Thos. Fox | 102 | | |
| Adam Coprass | 103 | Coppers | 417 |
| Jas. McFarland | 104 | | 369 |
| Abraham Williams | 105 | | 359 |
| Wm. T. Sanders | 106 | | 371 |
| Arth. St. Clair | 107 | | 353 |
| Manual Michael | 108 | | |
| John Ungles | 109 | | 399 |
| John E. McLure | 110 | McClure | 353 |
| Wm. Mires | 111 | Myers | 371, 377 |
| Gor. Marcus | 112 | | 383 |
| Ricd. Berry | 113 | | 371 |
| Wm. Jones | 114 | | 375, 393 |
| John Ragin | 115 | Ragan, Reagan | 361, 425 |
| Noah Parr, Jr. | 116 | | 367 |
| John Brown | 117 | | 365, 373, 393, 407 |
| Alexander L. Wilson | 118 | | |
| David Burkheart | 119 | Burkhart | 361 |
| Anthony Mowser | 120 | | |
| Moses Tilley | 121 | Tilly | 371 |
| George Hanes | 122 | Hains | 443 |
| John Smither | 123 | | 441 |
| James Eaton | 124 | | 351 |
| Hezakiah Smith | 125 | | 375, 421 |
| John Culbertson | 126 | | |
| Andrew Smith | 127 | | |
| Wiley Smithers | 128 | | |
| John Groves | 129 | | 369 |
| Noah Parr, Sr. | 130 | | 367 |
| Prest. Lancaster | 131 | | 369 |
| Phil. Shirley | 132 | Philamon | 403 |
| Christian Biarly | 133 | Byerly | 417 |
| Bilip Harper | 134 | Philip | 401 |
| Wm. Smith | 135 | | 441 |
| James Smith | 136 | | 353, 415 |
| Barzilla French | 137 | | |
| Jonas Morie | 138 | | |
| James Carter | 139 | | 419, 445 |
| John McLaine | 140 | McClain | 381 |
| Jacob Coile | 141 | | |

| VOTERS NAMES | NO | 1830 FEDERAL CENSUS | PAGE |
|---|---|---|---|
| Joseph Roll | 142 | | |
| James M. Lellen | 143 | | |
| Terrel Winters | 144 | | |
| Wm. Gregory | 145 | | |
| L.B. Wilson | 146 | | |
| Jacob Morris | 147 | | |
| Chas. O'Neel | 148 | O'Neal | 365 |
| Elias D. Simpkins | 149 | | 429 |
| Ed. Wills | 150 | Wells | 421 |
| John Sailers | 151 | | |
| Joel Wadkins | 152 | | |
| Sam'l Leeper | 153 | | 421 |
| John St. Clair | 154 | | 419 |
| John McConnell | 155 | McConnel | 433 |
| James McCoy | 156 | | 423 |
| Wm. Brunson | 157 | | 423 |
| J.G. McIlvain | 158 | John G. | 423 |
| J.M. Johnson | 159 | John M. | 375 |
| Corson Vickers | 160 | | |
| Wm. Appleton | 161 | | |
| Oliver Morse | 162 | | |
| Benj. McFarland | 163 | | 377 |
| Saml. S. Seburn | 164 | | |
| George Landam | 165 | Landram | 365 |
| John Brady | 166 | | 421, 435 |
| Lewis O'Niel | 167 | O'Neal | 441 |
| Amuel Glympse | 168 | Emanael Glimpse | 393 |
| John North | 169 | | 435 |
| John McCullon | 170 | | |
| J.W. Brzilton | 171 | James Brazelten | 447 |
| Wm. Grrett | 172 | Garrett | 361 |
| Wolfcong Coffman | 173 | | |
| R.R. Brunson | 174 | Robert | 425 |
| Wm. Brison | 175 | | 413 |
| Thos. Martin | 176 | | 409 |
| John Pogue | 177 | Pouge | 371 |
| A.A. Hall | 178 | Abraham A. | 371 |
| Sam'l Eaton | 179 | | 355 |
| Wm Eddy | 180 | | |
| Daniel Hartman | 181 | Heartman | 445 |
| Peter Casteter | 182 | Castoter | 435 |
| Mordca Croper | 183 | | |
| H. Brenton | 184 | Henry Brinton | 375 |
| John Thompson | 185 | | 373, 379, 391 |

| VOTERS NAMES | NO | 1830 FEDERAL CENSUS | PAGE |
|---|---|---|---|
| Saml. Hooper | 186 | | |
| Pernal Coverdell | 187 | Coverdill | 377 |
| Lemon Chittonden | 188 | | |
| John Wright | 189 | | 377, 403 |
| Samuel Huston | 190 | | |
| Jacob Selgrove | 191 | | |
| Wm. Coverdell | 192 | | |
| Lewis Smithers | 193 | Smither | 441 |
| J.S. Cool, Dr. | 194 | | |
| Thos. Triggs | 195 | | |
| Benj. Newhouse | 196 | | 433 |
| Jacob Triggs | 197 | | 429 |
| George Hinton | 198 | | |
| Samuel Morrow | 199 | | 357, 419, 435 |
| Wm. Ramay | 200 | Ramsey | 425 |
| John Jackson | 201 | | 427 |
| J.S. Bell | 202 | | |
| Minor Roberts | 203 | | 409 |
| John Bowell | 204 | | |
| Joseph Pogue | 205 | | 367 |
| Robt. Martin | 206 | | |
| Rezin Ragin | 207 | Ragan | 389 |
| J.L. Cimberly | 208 | | |
| Thos. Hugins | 209 | | |
| Jacob Sherer | 210 | | |
| Jemison Hawkins | 211 | | 349 |
| Wm. Brenton | 212 | Brinton | 381 |
| Henry Bowlin | 213 | Bowling | 405 |
| Valentine Sherer | 214 | | |
| Math:w Allman | 215 | Almond | 413 |
| John Edins | 216 | | |
| Isaa Brown | 217 | | |
| C.J Hand | 218 | | |
| John West | 219 | | 423 |
| John Metsiker | 220 | Metsker | 425 |
| William Callon | 221 | | |
| James Kimberly | 222 | | |
| Seth Keeler | 223 | | |
| Parris H. Harris | 224 | | |
| Willis Adkins | 225 | Atkins | 425 |
| Abraham Cook | 226 | | |
| Isaac Jackson | 227 | | |
| Nicholas Cline | 228 | | 375 |
| Thos. Jackson | 229 | | |

| VOTERS NAMES | NO | 1830 FEDERAL CENSUS | PAGE |
|---|---|---|---|
| Noah Flood | 230 | | 365 |
| David Groves | 231 | | 403 |
| Robt. Callen | 232 | | |
| Joseph Johnson | 233 | Johnston | 433 |
| James Miller | 234 | | 415 |
| Alex. Hamelton | 235 | Hamilton | 365 |
| Wm. Hobson | 236 | | 427 |
| E.W. Fray | 237 | | |
| James Leonard | 238 | Lenard | 411 |
| Jonas Huffman | 239 | | |
| Jas. McIlvain | 240 | | 363 |
| J.B. Harmon | 241 | James | 445 |
| Mat Darringer | 242 | | |
| George Wright | 243 | | |
| Thos. Langford | 244 | Lankford | 367 |
| Caleb Hedges | 245 | | |
| Chas. McConnell | 246 | | |
| James Turner | 247 | | |
| David S. Vanblaricum | 248 | Vanblaraan | 415 |
| Enoch Arnold | 249 | | |
| William Read | 250 | | |
| Peter Brown, Jr. | 251 | | 365 |
| Luke Brion | 252 | Bryan | 411 |
| John Barringer | 253 | | |
| John Sherer | 254 | Sharrar | 403 |
| John W. Henesly | 255 | Hinesely | 421 |
| James Johnson | 256 | | 353, 377, 407 |
| Obediah Clark | 257 | | 379 |
| S.H. Patterson | 258 | | |
| Wm. Viney | 259 | | 379, 407 |
| James Martin | 260 | | 393 |
| Luke Brion | 261 | Bryan | 411 |
| James W. Johnson | 262 | | 353, 377, 407 |
| Henry Newhouse | 263 | | 433 |
| George Sherer | 264 | Sharrar | 403 |
| Robt. M. Ptterson | 265 | Patterson | 357 |
| John Watts | 266 | | 375 |
| Thos. Davis | 267 | | |
| Thos. Smock | 268 | | |
| Rob. Brown | 269 | | 361 |
| Nelson Hartsock | 270 | | 401 |
| Robt. Robertson | 271 | | 415 |
| Bedford Foster | 272 | | |

| VOTERS NAMES | NO | 1830 FEDERAL CENSUS | PAGE |
|---|---|---|---|
| Edmund Lovet | 273 | Edward Lovett | 379 |
| Lee Isaac | 274 | | |
| Jas. Brown | 275 | | 423 |
| Wilson Perkins | 276 | | |
| John Brady | 277 | | 421, 435 |
| Jas. Pool | 278 | | 441 |
| Wm. Williamson | 279 | | 407 |
| Wm. Henry Groves | 280 | | 443 |
| Daniel McDonald | 281 | | 421 |
| Wm. Myers | 282 | | 371, 377 |
| Wm. Ragin | 283 | Reagan | 355, 365 |
| John Jamison | 284 | | |
| Elsey Jackson | 285 | | |
| Jas. Hamilton | 286 | | 365, 369 |
| Joseph Sample | 287 | | |
| Abraham Ellis | 288 | | 375 |
| Benj. Pruette | 289 | | |
| David Croan | 290 | | |
| Simeon McBride | 291 | | |
| Wm. Davis | 292 | | 361 |
| Mathew Hickson | 293 | | |
| A.C. Read | 294 | Archibald C. Reed | 367 |
| Wm. McVay | 295 | | |
| Wm. Carbaugh | 296 | | |
| Prestin Lancaster | 297 | | 369 |
| John Lea | 298 | | |
| A.F. Morrison | 299 | Alexander F. | 394 |
| Thos. G. Keeler | 300 | | 429 |
| John Burrows | 301 | | |
| Francis Kitley | 302 | | |
| J.C. Busick | 303 | | |
| Letus Sackett | 304 | | |
| John Sherly | 305 | | |
| Henry Olinger | 306 | | |
| Philip McConnell | 307 | McCannel | 377 |
| Hugh L. Frazier | 308 | | |
| Joshua Hinesly | 309 | | 367 |
| John Reagin | 310 | Ragan, Reagan | 361, 425 |
| Evan Ballinger | 311 | Ballenger | 421 |
| John Sheet | 312 | | |
| Cader Carter | 313 | | |
| Chas. Orme | 314 | | |

| VOTERS NAMES | NO | 1830 FEDERAL CENSUS | PAGE |
|---|---|---|---|
| Hez. Smart | 315 | | |
| James Griswold | 316 | | 351 |
| Michael D. Faler | 317 | | |
| John Daily | 318 | | |
| Wm. McAdoe | 319 | McAdoo | 377 |
| James Porter, Sr. | 320 | | 429 |
| Ira Plummer | 321 | | |
| James Raines | 322 | | 411 |
| John Furgison | 323 | Forgason | 439 |
| Peter F. Newland | 324 | P.F. | 407 |
| J.M. Jones | 325 | Jesse, John | 359, 391, 405 |
| James Slone | 326 | Sloan | 407 |
| Alex. Noe | 327 | | |
| Jerry Day | 328 | | 369 |
| Conrad McLaine | 329 | | |
| Sam'l. Snodgrass | 330 | | 371 |
| Francis Baily | 331 | | 361 |
| John Caine | 332 | Cain | 351 |
| Samuel Ballinger | 333 | | |
| Harod Newland | 334 | | 357 |
| Daniel Groves | 335 | | 443 |
| Robt. Brewer | 336 | | 429 |
| Lewis Tilliard | 337 | | |
| Solomon Cook | 338 | | 365 |
| Andrew Wilson | 339 | | 371 |
| Elias Baldwin | 340 | | 363 |
| Eli Wills | 341 | Wells | 405 |
| Gliden True | 342 | | 349 |
| Jeremiah Johnson | 343 | | 349, 365 |
| Jesse Roberts | 344 | | |
| Avry Ward | 345 | | |
| Jacob Landis | 346 | | 361 |
| Benjamin Fowler | 347 | | |
| Alexus Riley | 348 | | |
| David McFall | 349 | | 383 |
| Otis Hobart | 350 | Hobert | 369 |
| Thos. Edmundson | 351 | Edmson | 419 |
| John Harrison | 352 | | 425 |
| Jacob Whitinger | 353 | Whiteinger | 423 |
| Archibald Clark | 354 | Archelus | 381 |
| James Furgison | 355 | Forgason | 403 |
| Jesse Admiah | 356 | Admire | 381 |
| Mecajah Wilson | 357 | Machagav Willson | 401 |
| John Jones | 358 | | 359, 405 |

| VOTERS NAMES | NO | 1830 FEDERAL CENSUS | PAGE |
|---|---|---|---|
| Joseph Pence | 359 | Pense | 413 |
| I.N. Sanders | 360 | Isaac N. | 367 |
| Abraham Sellers | 361 | | |
| Benjamine Pattison | 362 | Patterson | 409 |
| Greenup Eaton | 363 | | |
| Sim. Smith | 364 | Simon | 419 |
| John Johnson | 365 | | 353, 435 |
| Thos. Stoops | 366 | | 407 |
| Sidney Williams | 367 | | 409 |
| L.D. Wilson | 368 | | |
| Humphry Griffith | 369 | | 349 |
| David Stoops | 370 | | 407 |
| Wm. Roberts | 371 | | 409 |
| John Brinton | 372 | | |
| Joseph B. Hume | 373 | | |
| Daniel Crosser | 374 | Closer | 413 |
| Abraham Coble | 375 | | 415 |
| Wm. Helm | 376 | | |
| Joseph Coats | 377 | | 425 |
| Sam'l B. Roads | 378 | | |
| David Nigh | 379 | Knight | 393 |
| J.M. Bailey | 380 | | |
| George Bruice | 381 | | |
| John Smith | 382 | | 375, 415, 427 |
| John McCall | 383 | | |
| Westley Wilson | 384 | | |
| Robt. Leeper | 385 | | 423 |
| Fred Hartsell | 386 | | 387 |
| Lewis Huffman | 387 | | 425 |
| David Small | 388 | | 371 |
| Edward Lane | 389 | | |
| Robt. Huston | 390 | | |
| Samuel Davis | 391 | | |
| John Negley | 392 | | |
| Banabus Ball | 393 | Barney | 355 |
| James Darnell | 394 | | |
| Amos Harris | 395 | | |
| Isaac Roberts | 396 | | 409 |
| Oliver Shurtliff | 397 | Shirtleff | 447 |
| John Kitly | 398 | | |
| Edmund C. Johnson | 399 | | |
| James Hoglan | 400 | Hagland | 381 |
| Wm. Evans | 401 | | 383, 419 |
| John P. Cook | 402 | Cooke | 361, 389, 423 |

| VOTERS NAMES | NO | 1830 FEDERAL CENSUS | PAGE |
|---|---|---|---|
| Douglass Maguire | 403 | | 351 |
| Noah Jackson | 404 | | 427 |
| Franklin Hardin | 405 | | |
| Anthony Swain | 406 | | 447 |
| James Cochrane | 407 | | |
| Jesse Burket | 408 | Beurkett | 411 |
| Christly Aught | 409 | Alt | 387 |
| Richd. Gott | 410 | | 371, 405 |
| Smith McAll | 411 | McFall | 379 |
| Wm. McCoy | 412 | | 421, 431 |
| John Bolander | 413 | Bowlinder | 433 |
| James Darnell | 414 | | |
| Andrew Clark | 415 | Clarke | 435 |
| Robt. Hannah | 416 | | 367 |
| Wm. Banks | 417 | | 399 |
| James Pasley | 418 | | |
| Wm. Cummins | 419 | | |
| Joseph Snow | 420 | | 377 |
| Wm. H.P. Bristo | 421 | Bristow | 375 |
| Philip Harding | 422 | | 431 |
| James P. Coonfield | 423 | | 381 |
| Andrew Sherer | 424 | Sharrar | 403 |
| Simeon B. Adams | 425 | | 439 |
| Peter Smith | 426 | | 419 |
| Zeb Miller | 427 | | |
| Sam'l. True | 428 | | 383 |
| David Day | 429 | | |
| Joel Boland | 430 | Bowling | 379 |
| Matthew Day | 431 | | 433 |
| Eph. Arnold | 432 | | 379 |
| James DeLong | 433 | DeLany | 447 |
| Benj. Framan | 434 | Freeman | 399 |
| Chas. Campbell | 435 | | |
| Edmund Blackledge | 436 | | |
| Wm. DeFord | 437 | | 427 |
| Andrew Strane | 438 | | |
| Sam. Fulland | 439 | Fullen | 401 |
| Peter Smock | 440 | | 381 |
| Rufus Jennisson | 441 | Jenison | 403 |
| Amos Compton | 442 | | |
| Joseph Griffith | 443 | | 409 |
| Step. Pitts | 444 | | 365 |
| Absalem Cruise | 445 | | |
| Robert Kimberly | 446 | | |

| VOTERS NAMES | NO | 1830 FEDERAL CENSUS | PAGE |
|---|---|---|---|
| John Pasley | 447 | | |
| John Setter | 448 | Setters | 437 |
| James Ellis | 449 | Elles | 421 |
| David Allison | 450 | | |
| Otis Sprague | 451 | | 369 |
| Jed. Reed | 452 | | |
| Wm. Adams | 453 | | 399 |
| John Clark | 454 | | 435 |
| Thos. McCollum | 455 | | |
| Stephen Hankins | 456 | | 383 |
| Jesse Grace | 457 | | 359 |
| Nathan Johnson | 458 | | 427 |
| George Avery | 459 | Avey | 417 |
| John J. Bellis | 460 | | 439 |
| John Emory | 461 | Emry | 433 |
| Anothy Nichols | 462 | | |
| Wm. J. McIntosh | 463 | | 421 |
| Wm. T. McLaughlin | 464 | | 369, 371 |
| John Hawkins | 465 | | 351 |
| William Opord | 466 | Oppear | 437 |
| Daniel McRay | 467 | McCreery | 387 |
| Thopilus Watts | 468 | | |
| John Ellison | 469 | | |
| Lawrence Johnson | 470 | | |
| Andrew Slone | 471 | Sloan | 351 |
| Dan Smith | 472 | | 425, 439 |
| Peter Michael | 473 | Mechal | 423 |
| John Brown | 474 | | 365, 393, 407 |
| Saml. Duke | 475 | | 353 |
| Jacob Coverdale | 476 | Coverdell | 405 |
| James McIlvain | 477 | | 421 |
| Wm. Myers | 478 | | 371, 377 |
| Joseph Comer | 479 | | 387 |
| Jeremiah Fetherstone | 480 | Featherstan | 381 |
| Garret Garrison | 481 | | 429 |
| Hugh Blake | 482 | | |
| Thos. McClintock | 483 | | 365 |
| Mich. Vanblaricum | 484 | | 357 |
| Elijah Henderson | 485 | | |
| James McLaughlin | 486 | | 371, 377 |
| Noah Wright | 487 | | |
| Richd. Vanlandingham | 488 | | 367, 401 |
| Andrew Eller | 489 | | |
| David Trester | 490 | | |

| VOTERS NAMES | NO | 1830 FEDERAL CENSUS | PAGE |
|---|---|---|---|
| Cornelius Peterson | 491 | | |
| Saml. Frazir | 492 | | |
| James Leverton | 493 | | |
| Elijah McBride | 494 | | 393 |
| Harvy Wright | 495 | | |
| Adam Eller | 496 | | 435 |
| Bennett Pogue | 497 | | |
| S.C. Williams | 498 | Saml; Sidney | 409, 433 |
| Fred Bailer | 499 | Bailor | 363 |
| Geor. Smith | 500 | | 351 |
| Arch. Bruice | 501 | Bruce | 375 |
| James Hines | 502 | | 433 |
| Abel Seward | 503 | | |
| Moses Barker | 504 | | 441 |
| Gor. Metsiker | 505 | Metsker | 425 |
| Mathew Ethra | 506 | | |
| John Thompson | 507 | | 373, 379, 391 |
| Cyrus Cotton | 508 | | |
| Noble Banks | 509 | | |
| Arch. Todd | 510 | | |
| Wm. McClarin | 511 | | |
| Thos. Wilson | 512 | | 375 |
| Zadock Coverdale | 513 | | |
| Richd. Coverdale | 514 | Coverdill | 369 |
| David Forsett | 515 | | |
| Eph. Morrison | 516 | | 435 |
| John Parker | 517 | | 401 |
| Ralph Fults | 518 | | 419 |
| Nich. Swadley | 519 | | 355 |
| Zach. Lemasters | 520 | Lamaster | 375 |
| Jacob Southerland | 521 | Sutherland | 393 |
| Lambard Salter | 522 | Lambert | 381 |
| James McLaine | 523 | McClain, McLain | 381, 441 |
| James Epperson | 524 | | 387 |
| John Mansfield | 525 | | 431 |
| John McCormack | 526 | | |
| Nath'l Kidd | 527 | | |
| Robt. M. Cather | 528 | | |
| Fredrick Sheets | 529 | | 373 |
| Wm. Johnson | 530 | | 377 |
| Wilson McAlmot | 531 | | |
| James Braman | 532 | | 377 |
| Wm. Anold | 533 | Arnold | 359, 379 |
| Nicholas Porter | 534 | | 429 |

| VOTERS NAMES | NO | 1830 FEDERAL CENSUS | PAGE |
|---|---|---|---|
| Geor. McLaughlin | 535 | | |
| Hugh McDonald | 536 | | 437 |
| Wm. Harden | 537 | Harding | 419 |
| The. V. Denny | 538 | Theodore | 371 |
| Barnabas Blue | 539 | | |
| Joseph Nunn | 540 | | |
| Robt. Bruice | 541 | | |
| John Compton | 542 | | |
| James McLaughlin | 543 | | 371, 377 |
| John Patterson | 544 | | 409 |
| Uriah Dawson | 555 | | |
| Abraham Hayes | 556 | | |
| Benjamin Wilson | 557 | | |
| William Beaver | 558 | | |
| Wm. Tucker | 559 | | |
| John McFall, Jr. | 560 | | 371 |
| Chas. Neighbors | 561 | | |
| John Ferris | 562 | | |
| Isaac Reed | 563 | | 387 |
| Thos. Sheton | 564 | Shelton | 375 |
| James Merrit | 565 | | 387 |
| John Trester | 566 | | |
| George Leaman | 567 | | |
| Archillis Lancaster | 568 | | |
| Joseph Culberson | 569 | Culbertson | 437 |
| Henry L. Coffman | 570 | | |
| Aaron Coppock | 571 | | |
| Moses Frazee | 572 | | 361 |
| Joseph Chilress | 573 | Childers | 363 |
| Wm. Coats | 574 | | |
| Wm. Bacon | 575 | | 423 |
| Lawrence DeMott | 576 | | 377 |
| Wm. Garner | 577 | | 435 |
| James Parr | 578 | | 359 |
| Isaac Harding | 579 | Hardin | 409 |
| Rob't Large | 580 | | 437 |
| Benson Cornelius | 581 | Carnelius | 441 |
| John McConnal | 582 | McConnel | 433 |
| Edward Wright | 583 | | 387 |
| Wm. Wright | 584 | | 369 |
| Math. T. Noland | 585 | | |
| George Taffe | 586 | | |
| Alexander Botkin | 587 | Bodkin | 369 |

| VOTERS NAMES | NO | 1830 FEDERAL CENSUS | PAGE |
|---|---|---|---|
| Horatio McDowell | 588 | | 365 |
| Geor. Vanlandingham | 589 | Vanlaningham | 401 |
| Aaron Wright | 590 | | 387 |
| Nehimiah Smith | 591 | | |
| E.R. Smith | 592 | | |
| Samuel Merrill | 593 | | |
| Livingston Dunlap | 594 | | 353 |
| Dan. Wright | 595 | | 425 |
| Fieldin Clark | 596 | | 423 |
| Reuben Farnsworth | 597 | | |
| Wm. Quarles | 598 | | 349 |
| John Burns | 599 | | 363, 427 |
| Dann Bubtler | 600 | Butler | 425 |
| T.B.S. Hutson | 601 | Thos. Hudson | 403 |
| Wallace Levett | 602 | | |
| Henry S. Hinman | 603 | | |
| Jerm. Vanlandingham | 604 | | 433 |
| Abijah Hoover | 605 | | |
| Jonathan Soward | 606 | Seward | 419 |
| Isaac Simpkins | 607 | | |
| Adam Penz | 608 | Pence | 383 |
| R.G.H. Hannah | 609 | R.J.H. Hanna | 407 |
| Josep Smith | 610 | | 377 |
| Elishah Reddick | 611 | | 437 |
| Wm. Holmes | 612 | Homes | 409 |
| Saml. McCormach | 613 | McCormack | 363 |
| Wm. McCoy, Jr. | 614 | | 421, 431 |
| James Voris | 615 | Voorhis | 389 |
| Jordon Wright | 616 | | 415 |
| Andrew M. Smith | 617 | | |
| Wm. Winson | 618 | | |
| Jethro Duwese | 619 | Dewis | 409 |
| Isaac Kelly | 620 | | 385 |
| John Johnstone | 621 | Johnson | 353, 435 |
| Daniel Bollinger | 622 | | |
| Jonas Hoover | 623 | | |
| John Esra | 624 | | |
| Henry Brewer | 625 | | 383 |
| Harvy Steers | 626 | | |
| Robt. King | 627 | | |
| Henry Mondy | 628 | Monday | 393 |
| John Johnson | 629 | | 353, 435 |
| David Slone | 630 | | |
| Wm. Hawkins | 631 | | 391 |

| VOTERS NAMES | NO | 1830 FEDERAL CENSUS | PAGE |
|---|---|---|---|
| Wm. Montague | 632 | | |
| Jacob Case | 633 | | 401 |
| John Walden | 634 | | 439 |
| John Fox | 635 | | 411 |
| John Mussgrave | 636 | | |
| George Blackledge | 637 | | |
| Isaac Roll | 638 | | |
| Wm. Hooker | 639 | | 361 |
| Daniel Shorts | 640 | Shoots | 435 |
| Rob't Hamilton | 641 | | 403 |
| Francis Williams | 642 | | |
| Edward Winkels | 643 | | |
| John Walter | 644 | | 355 |
| John Ogle | 645 | | 371 |
| Elijah Dawson | 646 | | 419 |
| John Shingles | 647 | | 433 |
| Isaac Doty | 648 | | |
| David Mars | 649 | | 375 |
| Chas. McDougle | 650 | McDougal | 353 |
| John Boman | 651 | Bowman | 369 |
| Jacob Peggs | 652 | | 381 |
| George McLaine | 653 | McClain | 381 |
| Wm. Hughey | 654 | | 379 |
| John Burns | 655 | | 363, 427 |
| James P. Hannah | 656 | Hanna | 403 |
| Shadrck Lguat | 657 | Laguett | 363 |
| Wm. Smith | 658 | | 441 |
| John Bennett | 659 | | |
| Wm. Clark | 660 | | |
| Joseph Clark | 661 | | 401 |
| Nicholas McCarty | 662 | | 353 |
| Samuel Jennison | 663 | | 448 |
| David Sharp | 664 | | 423 |
| Joseph Glisten | 665 | | |
| James N. Huntington | 666 | | |
| L.L. Brown | 667 | Lewis | 433 |
| John Owins | 668 | | |
| Samuel Dabney | 669 | Dabeney | 375 |
| Wm. McLaine | 670 | McClain | 379, 435 |
| Jacob Smock | 671 | | 381 |
| John McCung | 672 | | |
| Wm. Aulphen | 673 | Alphen | 379 |
| Samuel Rooker | 674 | | |
| Myron Brown | 675 | | |

| VOTERS NAMES | NO | 1830 FEDERAL CENSUS | PAGE |
|---|---|---|---|
| James McDonnald | 676 | | |
| John Cloe | 677 | | 369 |
| Eph. Howard | 678 | | |
| John Jennison | 679 | | |
| Jonathan Cuningham | 680 | | |
| Geor. W. Johnson | 681 | G.U. | 415 |
| A. Shryock | 682 | | |
| Edmund Woodruff | 683 | | |
| John Hannah | 684 | J.W. Hanna | 407 |
| Wm. Jones | 685 | | 375, 393 |
| John Smith | 686 | | 375, 415, 427 |
| Wm. Cool | 687 | | 411 |
| Wm. G. Deckerson | 688 | Deckson | 435 |
| John G. Brown | 689 | | 373 |
| J.N. Mothershead | 690 | | |
| James Taffe | 691 | Taff | 363 |
| Elisha W. Lake | 692 | | 363 |
| Daniel A. Webb | 693 | | |
| Thos. Astren | 694 | Askins | 403 |
| Wm. Brown | 695 | | |
| Adam Thompson | 696 | | |
| Thomas Richardson | 697 | | 377 |
| William Bowls | 698 | Bowles | 387 |
| Richd. Vanlandingham | 699 | | 367, 401 |
| Joseph Selgrove | 700 | | |
| Thos B. Nelson | 701 | | |
| Julius Blackburn | 702 | | 367 |
| Thos. O'Neal | 703 | | 365 |
| Daniel Stuck | 704 | | 377 |
| Martin Brandon | 705 | | 401 |
| Wm. McCool | 706 | | |
| Lam. G. Mitchell | 707 | | |
| Joshua Glover | 708 | | 411 |
| Jacob Turner | 709 | | 377 |
| James Dabney | 710 | | 375 |
| Thos. Briant | 711 | Bryant | 383 |
| Norman Plummer | 712 | N.C. Plumer | 433 |
| Samuel Alexander | 713 | | |
| Francis McLaughlin | 714 | | 367 |
| Fredrick Tysinger | 715 | | 381 |
| Thomas Johnson | 716 | | 365 |
| James Pierce | 717 | | |
| Samuel Beeler | 718 | | 399 |
| S.B. Woodfield | 719 | Samuel Woodfil | 375 |

| VOTERS NAMES | NO | 1830 FEDERAL CENSUS | PAGE |
|---|---|---|---|
| Peter Conine | 720 | | |
| John Monday | 721 | | 393 |
| Henry Porter | 722 | | 351 |
| G.T. Russell | 723 | | |
| Caleb Bellows | 724 | | |
| James McDermott | 725 | | |
| Niel McInally | 726 | | |
| James McDermott, Jr. | 727 | | |
| Abner McNabb | 728 | | 359 |
| John Russell | 729 | | 381 |
| David Ringer | 730 | | |
| Wm. Rice | 731 | | 381 |
| Samuel Patten | 732 | | 367 |
| Isaac Stipp | 733 | | 365 |
| Joseph North | 734 | | 435 |
| Isaac Rennals | 735 | | |
| Lewis Darnell | 736 | | |
| Wm. Harman | 737 | Harmon | 445 |
| Samuel Goldsbery | 738 | Goldsberry | 357 |
| Zeb. Chill | 739 | | 355 |
| Willis Ball | 740 | | |
| Archibald Small | 741 | | |
| Wm. Smith | 742 | | 441 |
| Abraham Bowen | 743 | Booan | 425 |
| Thomas Donelin | 744 | Donnelan | 353 |
| James Givan | 745 | | |
| John Denny | 746 | | |
| John Neal | 747 | | |
| Peter Lemaster | 748 | | |
| Jacob Roberts | 749 | | 427 |
| John Tracee | 750 | Tracy | 381 |
| Joseph McClure | 751 | | |
| Archibald Lingenfelter | 752 | | 359 |
| Eliott M. Patterson | 753 | | |
| Thom. Woods | 754 | | 435 |
| Eli Boy | 755 | Bouie | 361 |
| Wm. Luckey | 756 | | |
| Huland Briant | 757 | | |
| David Johnson | 758 | | 367 |
| John Cook | 759 | Cooke | 389, 423 |
| A.W. Morris | 760 | | |
| David Williams | 761 | | |
| Chas. Ellison | 762 | | |

| VOTERS NAMES | NO | 1830 FEDERAL CENSUS | PAGE |
|---|---|---|---|
| Henry Wycoff | 763 | | 383 |
| Edward Brazilton | 764 | | |
| Matheas Dawson | 765 | Mathew | 431 |
| John Douglass | 766 | | 351 |
| Cary Smith | 767 | | 353 |
| Benadict Higden | 768 | | 353 |
| J.W. Fodery | 769 | John Foudray | 357 |
| James Kittleton | 770 | Kettleman | 355 |
| David Hoover | 771 | | |
| John H. Newland | 772 | | 357 |
| Squire Dawson | 773 | | 423 |
| James Luster | 774 | Lester | 355 |
| Jacob Lowks | 775 | Loucks | 355 |
| Andrew Hoover | 776 | | 393, 411 |
| Benj. J. Blythe | 777 | | 349 |
| Thomas S. Pierce | 778 | | |
| John Akles | 779 | | |
| Wm. Hull | 780 | | 375 |
| Benjamin Akles | 781 | | |
| John Smith | 782 | | 375, 415, 427 |
| Wm. H. Norrice | 783 | | |
| Andrew Hoover | 784 | | 393, 411 |
| Henry Hardin | 785 | Harden | 419, 435 |
| Cornelius Lowks | 786 | Loucks | 355 |
| Peter Negley | 787 | | 433 |
| Wm. McPherson | 788 | | |
| Thos. Johnson | 789 | | 365 |
| Hervey Gregg | 790 | Harvey | 353 |
| Eber Pierce | 791 | | |
| Reson Howard | 792 | Renyin | 411 |
| Daniel Clark | 793 | | 427 |
| Rob't Langford | 794 | Lankford | 369 |
| Wm. McCarty | 795 | | |
| Eli Watson | 796 | | |
| Wm. Christ | 797 | | 437 |
| Daniel Pattingill | 798 | Pattangill | 369 |
| Isaac Kinder | 799 | | 349 |
| John Holland | 800 | | 349 |
| Warren Baldwin | 801 | | |
| Jesse Combs | 802 | Coombs | 357 |
| James Selgrove | 803 | Sulgrove | 353 |
| Sylvester Vanlandingham | 804 | | |
| Sam. J. Patterson | 805 | | |
| Robt. F. Samuels | 806 | Samuel | 409 |

| VOTERS NAMES | NO | 1830 FEDERAL CENSUS | PAGE |
|---|---|---|---|
| John Stephens | 807 | | 427 |
| Leonard Eller | 808 | | |
| Butler Smith | 809 | | |
| H.L. Brown | 810 | Henry | 421 |
| Joseph Staten | .811 | | |
| Larkin Monday | 812 | | |
| Wilks Ragins | 813 | Reagan | 361 |
| Edward Hugins | 814 | Huggins | 351 |
| Henry Myers | 815 | | 393 |
| J.J. Corberly | 816 | Corbaley | 415 |
| Willis Prewett | 817 | | |
| James Hill | 818 | | 367 |
| Arch. Lemasters | 819 | Lamaster | 363 |
| Isaac Bailer | 820 | Baylor | 439 |
| Richard Watts | 821 | | 419 |
| John Richey | 822 | Ritchie | 375 |
| Joseph Howard | 823 | | |
| Thomas Pogue | 824 | | 373 |
| Isaac Stevens | 825 | Stephens | 429 |
| Wm. Cook | 826 | | |
| Ed. Nuby | 827 | Edmund Newby | 421, 427 |
| Daniel Ragin | 828 | Reagan | 421 |
| Rob't Hardin | 829 | Harding | 373 |
| Seth Bardwell | 830 | | |
| Wm. Johnson | 831 | | 377 |
| Joseph Rhodes | 832 | J.R. Roads | 411 |
| George L. Kinnard | 833 | Kenard | 415 |
| Samuel McClure | 834 | | |
| John Parr | 835 | | 367 |
| Wm. D. Rooker | 836 | | 421 |
| Harris Tyner | 837 | | |
| Joseph Wingate | 838 | | 361 |
| Jacob Darringer | 839 | Daringer | 399 |
| Mahlon Batty | 840 | Baty | 363 |
| Uriah Gates | 841 | | 359 |
| Abraham Hendrick | 842 | Hendricks | 441 |
| Wm. Boyce | 843 | | 371 |
| Eli Sulgrove | 844 | | 387 |
| Rob't Patterson | 845 | | 357 |
| Noah Sinks | 846 | | 371 |
| Payton Bristo | 847 | Bristow | 377 |
| W.D.J. Ungles | 848 | Wilford J. | 353 |
| John Jones | 849 | | 359, 405, 447 |
| Rob't Goudy | 850 | Goudie | 359 |

159

| VOTERS NAMES | NO | 1830 FEDERAL CENSUS | PAGE |
|---|---|---|---|
| Charles McBride | 851 | | 377 |
| Barrett Parrish | 852 | | 369 |
| Rob't A. Taylor | 853 | | 361 |
| Scipio Sedgewick | 854 | Sedwick | 377 |
| Sam'l Hardin | 855 | Harding | 407 |
| John Long | 856 | | |
| Edward Roberts | 857 | | 419 |
| Samuel P. Setters | 858 | | 419 |
| Aaron Aldridge | 859 | | 369 |
| Zach. Collings | 860 | Collins | 419 |
| David Eller | 861 | | 435 |
| John Givan | 862 | | 349 |
| James Sigerson | 863 | | |
| James Morrison | 864 | | 349 |
| Alex. Cambell | 865 | | |
| Jacob Mosley | 866 | | |
| Elisha Abner | 867 | | |
| John Frazee | 868 | | |
| John Phipps | 869 | | |
| Wm. Hardin | 870 | Harden | 419 |
| Francis Jamison | 871 | | |
| Mathias Tyson | 872 | | 367 |
| John VanBlaicum | 873 | Vanblaricum | 355 |
| Dan. Cool | 874 | | 369 |
| Thomas Johnson | 875 | | 365 |
| Milton White | 876 | | |
| John Ray | 877 | | 427 |
| Peter Ellis | 878 | | |
| John Barner | 879 | Barnett | 363 |
| Chas. Smith | 880 | | 349 |
| Samuel Perry | 881 | | |
| Benj. McFall | 882 | | |
| Wm. Costle | 883 | | |
| Thos. J. Todd | 884 | | 425 |
| D.P. Campbell | 885 | | |
| Elias Leming | 886 | Lemmon | 429 |
| Mathew Smock | 887 | | |
| Henry Allcorn | 888 | | 375 |
| Ed Watts | 889 | | |
| Wm. Morrison | 890 | | |
| Samuel Ray | 891 | | 353, 427, 429 |
| William Smith | 892 | | 441 |
| James M. Ray | 893 | | 357 |
| Benjamin Atherton | 894 | | 373 |
| Wm. Tichoner | 895 | Tichenor | 349 |
| Wm. Leningpetler | 896 | Lingenfelter | 359 |

| VOTERS NAMES | NO | 1830 FEDERAL CENSUS | PAGE |
|---|---|---|---|
| Richd. Williams | 897 | | 365 |
| Thos. McFarland | 898 | | |
| Abr. Harrison | 899 | | |
| Clvin Flecher | 900 | Calvin Fletcher | 351 |
| Morris Morris | 901 | | 361 |
| Jas. Tharp | 902 | | |
| Joel Leverton | 903 | | |
| Chas. Banks | 904 | | |
| Amos Hanaway | 905 | Hannaway | 359 |
| Dinnis White | 906 | | 351 |
| Isaac Coppock | 907 | Copper | 425 |
| Edward Davis | 908 | | |
| Aquilla W. Noe | 909 | | 355 |
| Israel Harding | 910 | | 407 |
| John Hooker | 911 | | |
| Laban Harding | 912 | | 371 |
| John Davis | 913 | | 359 |
| Nathaniel Cox | 914 | | 351 |
| James VanBlaricum | 915 | | 357 |
| Isaac Lake | 916 | | |
| Jonathan Ingold | 917 | Ingole | 429 |
| Samuel McFarland | 918 | | |
| Samuel Morrow | 919 | | 357, 419, 435 |
| James North | 920 | | 435 |
| Jeremiah Cranmer | 921 | | |
| Henry P. Coburn | 922 | | 357 |
| Jesse Wright | 923 | | 391 |
| Lemen Winchel | 924 | | |
| Ansel Richmond | 925 | | |
| Samuel Darnell | 926 | | |
| Ed Harding | 927 | Ead | 407 |
| James P. Drake | 928 | | 355 |
| Basil Brown | 929 | | |
| Jacob Collip | 930 | Colip | 351 |
| Rob't Tomlinson | 931 | Tumblestone | 383 |
| Wm. P. Carpenter | 932 | | 365 |
| Obed Foote | 933 | Foot | 349 |
| Samuel Woolly | 934 | | |
| Wm. Sanders | 935 | | 371 |
| Thomas H. Sharp | 936 | | |
| Homer Brooks | 937 | | |
| Samuel Henderson | 938 | | 351 |
| B.F. Morris | 939 | | 367 |
| John S. Hall | 940 | | 399 |
| John Johnson | 941 | | 353, 375, 435 |
| Alexander Frzier | 942 | Frazier | 349 |

| VOTERS NAMES | NO | 1830 FEDERAL CENSUS | PAGE |
|---|---|---|---|
| Isaac N. Phipps | 943 | | 353 |
| Hiram Brown | 944 | | 355 |
| John A. Tuttle | 945 | | |
| James Forsee | 946 | | 353 |
| Zechariah Wolly | 947 | | |
| Westley Batey | 948 | | |
| William Poland | 949 | Poling | 413 |
| Samuel Morrow | 950 | | 357, 419, 435 |
| Hubbard T. Loe | 951 | | |
| John Myers | 952 | | 393 |
| William McCaw | 953 | | 417 |
| William Adair | 954 | | |
| Henry Daugherty | 955 | | |
| James McDowall | 956 | McDowel | 365 |
| Jeremiah Collins | 957 | Collins | 351 |
| Benjamine Woods | 958 | | |
| Isaac Cox | 959 | | |
| Joseph Lefavour | 960 | Lafevour | 359 |
| Henry Brady | 961 | | 399 |
| Israel Philips | 962 | | 349 |
| George Tomlinson | 963 | Tumbleston | 383 |
| Michael Woods | 964 | | 413 |
| James K. Sleeth | 965 | | |
| David Buckhanan | 966 | Buchanen | 355 |
| Thomas S. Hitt | 967 | | |
| Edward Maguire | 968 | McGuire | 349 |
| James Aliman | 969 | | |
| James Blake | 970 | | |
| John Hobert | 971 | | 369 |
| Enoch Evans | 972 | | 367 |
| James Porter, Jr. | 973 | | 429 |
| John Blake | 974 | | 353 |
| Thos. Little | 975 | | |

The manuscript of the voters list is located in the William Henry Smith Library, Indiana Historical Society, document C390. Microfilm of the 1830 federal census of Marion County can be viewed in the Genealogy Division, Indiana State Library. The Indiana Historical Society has published an index to the 1830 census, now available on microfiche.

# OFFICIAL AND UNOFFICIAL MIAMI COUNTY MARRIAGE RECORDS THROUGH 1849

Compiled by Ruth Dorrel

Miami County's formation took place April 2, 1832, and its organization, March 1, 1834. The Peru courthouse burned March 16, 1843, with an apparent total loss of its contents. Attempts to recreate court records excluded marriage records. Local officials created a new marriage book and issued the first marriage license on March 30, 1843

For those persons who were married in Miami County prior to March 30, 1843, no official records are available. However, there are some marriage notes in early Peru newspapers. The *Gazette*, July 20, 1839-April 3, 1841 and October 9, 1841-October 8, 1842, is available both in the original and on mircofilm in the Newspaper Division of the Indiana State Library. Marriages prior to March 1843 have been extracted and are listed below. Following the newspaper marriage notes are the official marriage records for Miami County from March 30, 1843, to December 31, 1849.

*THE PERU GAZETTE*

August 24, 1839, p. 2 MARRIED--in Leesburg, in this county, on Sunday morning last by Augustus Brown, Esq., Mr. SAMUEL PIKE, ex-Editor of the "Peru, (IA) Forester," to Miss SARAH R. WAILEY, late of Lancaster, Pennsylvania.

December 14, 1839, p. 2 MARRIED--On the 8th inst. by Abraham H. Leedy, Esq. Mr. Robert Clendining to Miss Cynthia Clymer, both of this county.

January 18, 1840, p. 3 MARRIED--In this village on Tuesday morning last, by the Rev. Asa Johnson, Mr. J.M. Degrees, Druggist, to Miss Harriet Sophia, daughter of Col. Daniel Potter, formerly of Sheldon, N.Y.

January 25, 1840, p. 2 MARRIED--On Tuesday last, by John Clymer, Esq, Mr. George W. Osborn to Miss Cornelia Howes.

March 31, 1840, p. 2 MARRIED, On the evening of the 10th Instant by Rev. Asa Johnson, Mr. Michael Roughf of Wabash county, to Mrs. Mary Rhodes of this place.

On Sunday the 15th inst., by Jas B. Fulwiler, Esq., Mr. Henry Smith to Mrs. Anna Badger, all of Miami county.

March 28, 1840, p. 3 MARRIED On Sunday evening last of the Hon. Justice Fulwiler, Lemuel Price, Esq. of Richardville Prairie, to Miss Nancy Carpenter, second daughter of Isaac Carpenter, Esq., of Mill Avenue.

May 2, 1840, p. 3 MARRIED On Thursday the 23d ult., by John Bush, Esq., Mr. George W. Harvey, of this place to Miss Mirand Rhodes of Perry township, Miami county.

May 9, 1840, p. 3 MARRIED, On Thursday evening last, by Judge Bush, Mr. William H. Prince, merchant of Mexico, to Miss Nancy, daughter of Col. Humbert of this place.

May 23, 1840, p. 3  MARRIED, On Thursday the 14th inst., by J.L. Reyburn, Esq., Mr. Thomas Clayton to Miss Elizabeth Barne, all of this county.

June 6, 1840, p. 3  MARRIED, On Thursday, the 28th ult., by John Clymer, Esq., Mr. Andrew Woolpert to Miss Naomi Murden, all of this county.

On Saturday, the 30th ult., by Judge Fenimore, Mr. James Williams to Miss Lydia Rush, all of this county.

July 18, 1840, p. 3  MARRIED, At Woodmont, Wabash county, on the 14th inst., by Rev. Asa Johnson, Mr. Amos D. Seward to Miss Pleiades B. Barber.

August 22, 1840, p. 3  MARRIED, By Abraham H. Leedy, Esq., on the 22d ins., Mr. Daniel Leedy to Mrs. Elizabeth J. Nelson.

November 14, 1840, p. 2  MARRIED, Near Providence, Ohio, on Thursday the 5th November inst., by J. Van Allen, Esq., Mr. James B. Scott, one of the editors of this paper, to Sophia C. Griffith, of Henry county, Ohio.

November 28, 1840, p. 2  MARRIED On Thursday the 19th inst., by J.B. Fulwiler, Esq. Mr. Henry Howes to Miss Sarah Shadinger, all of this county.

MARRIED--In Dayton, Ohio, on the 26th ult., by the Rever Andrew Lomoreaci, Mr. Willis C. Fallis of this place, to Miss Mehatabel D. Phelps, of the former place.

December 5, 1840, p. 4  MARRIED--On the 26th ult. by the Rev. Mr. Ruslow, Mr. Henley James, of Grant county, IA, to Sarah, daughter of Jos. Holman of this county.

December 19, 1840, p. 3 MARRIED On Wednesday the 10th instant, by the Rev. Asa Johnson, Mr. Lewis D. Adkison to Mrs. Lucy A. Davis, both of this place.

--At the same time by the same, Mr. James T. Miller to Miss Mary L. Cole, both of this place.

January 16, 1841, p. 4  MARRIED, On Sunday evening last, by the Rev. Mr. Truslow, Mr. John Wiseman of this place to Miss Catharine Van Doran of Cass county.

Married in Wabashtown recently by the Rev. Asa Johnson, Mr. William Steel Jr. to Miss Eliza Dart.

Also, by the same, Mr. Joseph Myers to Miss Mary Dart, all of Wabash county.

Married recently at Chief Richardville's, in Huntington county, by the Rev. Mr. Benoit, Mr. Augustus A. Delmus of this place to Miss Felicia Gouin of the former place.

Married on the 12th inst., by the Rev. Mr. Truslow, Mr. Silas Enyart to Miss Martha J. Mowbray, all of this place.

February 13, 1841, p. 3  MARRIED--On Tuesday 19th ult. by Jno. A. Gilbert, Esq. Mr. Charles M. Oldham of this place, to Miss Lavina C. Long, of New Burlington, Ia.

MARRIED--On Tuesday 19th ult. by Rev. Mr. Templin, Mr. C.R. Tracy of this place, and Miss Adelia B. Crane of Charlottsville, Indiana.

March 20, 1841, p. 3  MARRIED--On the 4th inst. by the Rev. Mr. Martin, Mr. Francis Murphy of Cass county, to Miss Mary Ann Zern of Miami county.

October 16, 1841, p. 2  MARRIED--On Thursday 21st inst., by Rev. W. M. Reyburn, Mr. Ira Mendenhall to Mrs. Isabel E. Miller, all of this county.

December 3, 1841, p. 3  MARRIED.--On the 29th inst. by J. L. Rayburn, Esq. Mr. Martin Kenedy to Miss Eunice Hoover of this county.

--On the 2d inst. by the same, Mr. James Mowbray to Miss Sarah Jane Steenberger of this county.

March 19, 1842, p. 2  MARRIED--On Sunday last, by Anson Jewett, Esq. Mr. John Sutherland to the amiable and accomplished Miss Sarah Smith, both of this "nick of woods."

March 26, 1842, p. 2  MARRIED-- At Parkes-Port on the 19th instant, by the Hon. Chief Justice Fulwiler, Col. Joseph Bobain, of the Miami Consulate to Miss Mary, eldest daughter of the late Pierre Bonneventaurrer, Commissary on the Staff of Chief Godfroy.

January 15, 1842, p. 2  MARRIED--On the 28th inst. by Rev. A. Johnson, Mr. Robert Parks to Miss Elizabeth Burdsall, of this county.

| PAGE | DATE | GROOM — BRIDE |
|---|---|---|
| 1 | 30 Mar 1843 | John Barens-Elvira Love |
| | 30 Mar 1843 | Harmon Hiner-Margaret Young |
| | 3 Apr 1843 | Samuel Reins-Anna Carrey |
| | 5 Apr 1843 | Joseph Scott-Malinda Dabney |
| | 4 Apr 1843 | Stephen Bradley-Louisa Fenimore |
| | 19 Apr 1843 | George Pitsenberger-Sarah Kindle |
| 2 | 13 Apr 1843 | Elias Bills-Olinda B. Clymer |
| | 16 Apr 1843 | Noah S. Allebaugh-Sarah Ann Bryant |
| | 30 Apr 1843 | John Terhune-Barbara Ann Paul |
| | 19 May 1832 | Jonas Hoover-Elizabeth Alexander |
| | 4 Jun 1843 | George Shelner-Rebecca Carpenter |
| 3 | 7 Jun 1843 | Philip Gunckle-Sarah Snodgrass |
| | 7 Jun 1843 | Silas Wileman-Hannah Rhodes |
| | 29 Jun 1843 | Wyllys Hill-Abigail Goudy |
| | 7 Jul 1843 | Martin Craney-Mary Hayes |
| | 3 Aug 1843 | William Ryan-Nancy Walker |
| 4 | 4 Aug 1843 | William Landes-Elmyra Lawrence |
| | 27 Aug 1843 | Samuel K. Newman-Lydia Ann Harmon |
| | 1 Sep 1843 | Larkin Chambers-Elvina Malcom |
| | 29 Aug 1843 | Smalwood Axel-Sophia C. Hood |
| | 10 Sep 1843 | David Casebeer-Maria Cronk |
| 5 | 12 Sep 1843 | Robert Aker-Ann VanAmon |
| | 17 Sep 1843 | Ephraim Clayton-Rebecca Barnes |
| | 20 Sep 1843 | William Bear-Louisa VanAmon |
| | 22 Sep 1843 | Thomas Blackburn-Ruthe Lewis |
| | 28 Sep 1843 | Wm. C. Buchanan-Sarah F. Jeffery |
| 6 | 31 Sep 1843 | Joseph Alverd-Elizabeth Michael |
| | 28 Sep 1843 | William Masterson-Barbary Ann Champ |

| PAGE | DATE | GROOM — BRIDE |
|------|------|---------------|
|  | 5 Oct 1843 | Charles Gilbert-Susan Wallace |
|  | 10 Oct 1843 | John Tilden-Eliza Clendenin |
|  | 20 Oct 1843 | Amos Rank-Sarah Meek |
| 7 | 5 Nov 1843 | Jacob Zook-Roena Carlisle |
|  | 9 Nov 1843 | John B. McFarland-Lucinda Dennison |
|  | 23 Nov 1843 | Benjamin Watson-Sarah Overman |
|  | 26 Nov 1843 | Joseph Mull-Eliza Fouts |
|  | 3 Dec 1843 | Alfred Fisher-Martha Hays |
| 8 | 4 Dec 1843 | Samuel Adamson-Ann Clendennin |
|  | 7 Dec 1843 | Samuel David Rank-Elizabeth Shoemaker |
|  | 10 Dec 1843 | Alexander Willhelm-Isabel Barnes |
|  | 19 Dec 1843 | Wesley Wallich-Mary Ann Fisher |
|  | 26 Dec 1843 | Peter Long-Mary Ann Gallahan |
| 9 | 4 Jan 1844 | John D. Young-Clarissa Wait |
|  | 18 Jan 1844 | Thomas P. McCrea-Adeline Berry |
|  | 21 Jan 1844 | James Stephens-Emma O'Niel Good |
|  | 21 Jan 1844 | George Gaver-Mary Pendleton |
|  | 30 Jan 1844 | Daniel Hoffman-Sarah Hessong |
| 10 | 8 Feb 1844 | Jacob C. Miller-Frances Fiers |
|  | 2 Mar 1844 | Daniel Shewey-Jerusha Ply |
|  | 7 Mar 1844 | Tolcott L. Hurlbert-Sarah Ann Rhodes |
|  | 24 Mar 1844 | William Clingenpeel-Mary Allbaugh |
|  | 28 Mar 1844 | William Bowman-Nancy Austin |
| 11 | 11 Apr 1844 | Joseph Donner-Mary J. Homan |
|  | 11 Apr 1844 | William Parsons-Mary Price |
|  | 18 Apr 1844 | Samuel Fisher-Marcella Williams |
|  | 2 May 1844 | John Bargerhuff-Rachel McManis |
|  | 9 May 1844 | Israel Marquess-Araminta Doud |
| 12 | 3 May 1844 | N. C. Hall-Letitia Griswold |
|  | 20 May 1844 | James Calvin Fry-Christiana Browne |
|  | 21 May 1844 | David Jenkins-Sophia Jane Marshall |
|  | 13 Jun 1844 | George Ford-Elizabeth Swinehart |
|  | 17 Jun 1844 | David Peakok-Mary Black |
| 13 | 20 Jun 1844 | Harrison Hurd-Susana Wolf |
|  | 16 Jul 1844 | W.C. Kitchen-Elizabeth E. Slagle |
|  | 12 Aug 1844 lic | John Bay-Mary Pier |
|  | 15 Aug 1844 | Thomas Murden-Scynthia Ann Smith |
|  | 10 Aug 1844 | John M. Smith-Elizabeth Murden |
| 14 | 15 Aug 1844 | Ryleye Martin-Ruth Wilkinson |
|  | 19 Aug 1844 | John Wynn-Nancy Baming |
|  | 20 Aug 1844 | Charles Spencer-Louisa C. Crane |
|  | 24 Aug 1844 | Aaron S. Benedict-Cordelia Hill |
|  | 26 Aug 1844 | George Mouse-Katey Migh |

| PAGE | DATE | GROOM — BRIDE |
|------|------|---------------|
| 15 | Aug 1844 | Charles Brown-Sarah Bretten |
| | 26 Sep 1844 | Robert McFarland-Elener Spacht |
| | 26 Sep 1844 | Thomas Elliott-Elizabeth Fish |
| | 26 Sep 1844 | Isaac Miller-Ann Lybrooke |
| | 3 Oct 1844 | Elijah G. Chambers-Harriet Bard |
| | 3 Oct 1844 | John Mackay-Mary Ann Drake |
| 16 | 12 Oct 1844 | Saml. Beaty-Julia M Winnfield |
| | 22 Oct 1844 | John Shortridge-Anna York |
| | 23 Oct 1844 | Perry Newman-Sarah Moore |
| | 30 Oct 1844 | James Tracy-Margaret Fiers |
| | 17 Nov 1844 | William A. Soyer-Mary Baltimore |
| 17 | 27 Nov 1844 | Frederick Harter-Peggy Lennington |
| | 10 Dec 1844 | David O. Adkison-Harriet Henton |
| | 23 Dec 1844 | John Habbell-Catharine O'Mara |
| | 26 Dec 1844 | Henry Turnipseed-Phoeba Veal |
| | 5 Jan 1845 | Hiram Musselman-Delila Bowman |
| 18 | 9 Jan 1845 | James Bailey-Euphemia Drake |
| | 18 Jan 1845 | John Mous-Martha Minnich |
| | 18 Jan 1845 | Dennis Felty-Jane Miller |
| | 26 Jan 1845 | Wm. H.L. King-Angeline Clifford |
| | 22 Jan 1845 | Richard W. Jackson-Margaret Oliver |
| 19 | 29 Jan 1845 | James Peacock-Elizabeth Adamsen |
| | 8 Feb 1845 | Albert Cuffle-Rebecca Ann Newton |
| | 7 Feb 1845 | James M. Reyburn-Margaret Wallick |
| | 8 Feb 1845 | Charles Clarke-Betsey Noyer |
| | 15 Feb 1845 | John Price-Barbary Carpenter |
| 20 | 20 Feb 1845 | Riley Conner-Hester A.[Esther Ann] Williams |
| | 25 Feb 1845 | Chandler C. Moore-Fanny Gallahan |
| | 25 Mar 1845 | Moses Warren-Mary Ann Tann |
| | 16 Mar 1845 | David Haun-Elizabeth Davis |
| | 23 Mar 1845 | Samuel McConnehey-Elizabeth Hooks |
| 21 | 23 Mar 1845 | William Farmington-Scheiva Lear |
| | 26 Mar 1845 | Benajah Clark-Mary Smith |
| | 25 May 1845 | Simeon Crosby, Jr.-Sarah Davis |
| | 11 May 1845 | Harrison Grimes-Elizabeth Brower |
| | 6 May 1845 | Michael Henson-Catharine Ranck |
| 22 | 24 May 1845 lic | Caleb B. Bucknam-Evalina T. Lumsdon |
| | 29 May 1845 | John Miles-Martha Bartlett |
| | 1 Jun 1845 | Edward Emerson-Elizabeth P. Colvin |
| | 15 Jun 1845 | Daniel Collett-Sarah Shaddinger |
| | 15 Jun 1845 | William H. King-Barbara Bear |
| 23 | 26 Jun 1845 | Samuel Hinkle-Mary Ann Frazy |
| | 26 Jul 1845 | Samuel S. Hasten-Margaret Thompson |

| PAGE | DATE | GROOM — BRIDE |
|------|------|---------------|
|  | 7 Sep 1845 | Demas Garber-Catherine Onstott |
|  | 10 Aug 1845 | Levi Jones-Minerva Cook[Cools] |
|  | 28 Aug 1845 | Eli L. Butler-Mary Ann Smith |
| 24 | 9 Sep 1845 | Martin Landes-Abigail Raver |
|  | 14 Sep 1845 | James H. Stradley-Ann Eliza Grimes |
|  | 18 Sep 1845 | David Clemans-Hannah Beggs |
|  | 16 Sep 1845 | Alexander Jameson-Catherine Hoffman |
|  | 25 Sep 1845 | John P. Day-Malinda Swisher |
| 25 | 1 Oct 1845 | Ralph Giles-Susanna Zane [Zaio] |
|  | 4 Nov 1845 | Levi Tombaugh-Margaret Smith |
|  | 2 Oct 1845 | William Cox-Nancy Harter |
|  | 11 Oct 1845 | Andrew H. McFarland-Eliza Ann Kreider |
|  | 16 Oct 1845 | Henry Winter-Ann Jackson |
|  | 11 Oct 1845 | William M. Canfield-Hannah Reed |
| 26 | 9 Nov 1845 | Jno. S. Bishop-Nancy E. Wright |
|  | 13 Nov 1845 | Joseph Clare-Lucy Newten |
|  | 24 Nov 1845 | George Beck-Barbara Betzel |
|  | 4 Dec 1845 | George Taylor-Mary Hawknes |
|  | 26 Nov 1845 | William Bain-Elizabeth Lockwood |
| 27 | 29 Nov 1845 | William Weckler-Hannah Wattes |
|  | 4 Dec 1845 | Samuel A. Wiley-Calista Lease |
|  | 4 Dec 1845 | Henry Robinson-Tamar Snyder |
|  | 6 Dec 1845 | Hector Howes-Lydia Gilleland |
|  | 10 Dec 1845 | Mark Bower-Marian Patterson |
| 28 | 17 Dec 1845 | David Dannels-Delila Long |
|  | 21 Dec 1845 | Michael Dies-Elizabeth Barnet |
|  | 21 Dec 1845 | George W. Williams-Harriet Wikel |
|  | 22 Dec 1845 | Frederick Coleman-Barbara Hays |
|  | 22 Dec 1845 | Joseph F. Guyer-Margaret Martindale |
| 29 | 25 Dec 1845 | Austin Horrell-Elizabeth Hicks |
|  | 25 Dec 1845 | Wilson Gilleland-Lucinda Jane Bain |
|  | 1 Jan 1846 | Willis C. Brooks-Barbary Johnson |
|  | 31 Dec 1845 | William H. Harbert-Sarah McHenry |
|  | 1 Jan 1846 | John Finley-Minerva Jane Frazier |
| 30 | Jan 1846 | George W. Meek-Mary E. Sheehy |
|  | 8 Jan 1846 | John Close-Susanna Fickel |
|  | 9 Jan 1846 | Jacob Fry-Maria Landis |
|  | 14 Jan 1846 | Isaac Henderson-Mary Ann Gridley |
|  | 18 Jan 1846 | Benjamin Clark-Elizabeth Ozenbaugh |
| 31 | 17 Jan 1846 | William Shanklin-Amelia Griswold |
|  | 22 Jan 1846 | William Nicholson-Dorothy Hoover |
|  | 18 Feb 1846 | James Braffet-Lydia Slagel |
|  | 12 Feb 1846 | James McCrary-Sarah Larimer |
|  | 19 Feb 1846 | Peter Moury-Catharine Fears |

| PAGE | DATE | GROOM — BRIDE |
|------|------|---------------|
| 32 | 12 Feb 1846 | Samuel Edwards-Phoebe Edwards |
| | 17 Feb 1846 | Thomas J. Clemons-Drusilla Tracy |
| | 20 Feb 1846 lic | George Hackley-Ellen C. Breen |
| | 26 Feb 1846 | Elijah Barnes-Sarah Ann Burnett |
| | 1 Mar 1846 | John Bargerhoff-Sarah Biggs |
| 33 | 1 Mar 1846 | George Turnipseed-Sarah Veal |
| | 16 Mar 1846 | James McKee-Elmira McKee |
| | 15 Mar 1846 | Jackson Fernas-Susan Whitsinger |
| | 19 Mar 1846 | William H. Clawson-Asenath Adamson |
| | 29 Mar 1846 | Samuel Rosendale-Elizabeth Deeton |
| 34 | 1 Apr 1846 | Nelson Stanley-Charity Jonnes |
| | 2 Apr 1846 | William Love-Jemima Smith |
| | 3 Apr 1846 | Daniel Shuler-Mary Ann Sower |
| | 9 Apr 1846 | Lorenzo D. Bennett-Johanna Wallick |
| | 12 Apr 1846 | Thomas Powell-Ann Emry |
| 35 | 12 Apr 1846 | William Curte-Sarah D. Snodgrass |
| | 12 Apr 1846 | Stephen Rush-Lydia Fisher |
| | 14 Apr 1846 | Michael Welleck-Phebe Platz |
| | 21 Apr 1846 | Jacob Goudy-Elizabeth Fogerty |
| | 26 Apr 1844 | Samuel Stik-Harriet V. Tharp |
| 36 | 3 May 1846 | Henry King-Jane Berchel |
| | 9 May 1846 | Benjamin Fisher-Mary Elizabeth Rush |
| | 3 May 1846 | David Draper-Elizabeth Ballinger |
| | 10 May 1846 | Milnor Hawes-Sarah Ann Buck |
| | 14 May 1846 | George Clickard -Mary Branden |
| 37 | 28 May 1846 | Elias Cobble-Phoebe Ballinger |
| | 24 May 1846 | Elizabeth Shoop-Edna T. Cursey |
| | 21 May 1846 | James Guy-Dorothy Hurst |
| | 31 May 1846 | Joshua Jackson-Sarah Armentrout |
| | 19 Jun 1846 | Rudolph Stoner-Mary Ann Patterson |
| 38 | 23 Jun 1846 | John Whittenberger-Rebecca Ann Wadell |
| | 18 Jun 1846 | James Beard-Margaret Ellis |
| | 2 Aug 1846 | Patrick O'Morrow-Cessan Eakwright |
| | 16 Aug 1846 | Charles Bailey-Mariah Tayler |
| | 16 Aug 1846 | William Close-Elizabeth Fiers |
| 39 | 20 Aug 1846 | Azel Griffeth-Elvira Hobaugh |
| | 20 Aug 1846 | Daniel Landes-Mary Jane Hobaugh |
| | 23 Aug 1846 | Isaac R. Lentz-Elizabeth Hall |
| | 24 Aug 1846 | John W. Shults-Mariar Ann Munger |
| | 6 Sep 1846 | Joseph Hall-Catharine Finley |
| 40 | 27 Aug 1846 | James Kiser-Catharine Barlow |
| | 27 Aug 1846 | Joseph H. Reed-Frances E. Paul |
| | 10 Sep 1846 | Edward Means-Mary Powell |
| | 17 Sep 1846 | Edward More-Elizabeth Laymon |

| PAGE | DATE | GROOM — BRIDE |
|------|------|---------------|
|      | 24 Sep 1846 | Gabriel Hudson-Lavina Wright |
| 41   | 15 Oct 1846 | Joseph Stutz-Elizabeth Dice |
|      | 21 Oct 1846 | Joseph S. Shook-Julia Ann Bevis |
|      | 10 Nov 1846 | Thomas S. Smith-Louisa Jane Williams |
|      | 25 Oct 1846 | George Holcom-Eliza Grier |
|      | 25 Oct 1846 | John H. Neese-Joanna Caileff |
| 42   | 22 Oct 1846 | John H. Bryan-Amanda Clarke |
|      | Nov 1846 | James Sharpe-Jannett Thompson Lothen |
|      | 18 Nov 1846 | Robert Parks-Bridget Bruce |
|      | 29 Nov 1846 | Joseph Tyler-Nancy Tharp |
|      | 3 Dec 1846 | Philip Klingelsmith-Maria Wilson |
| 43   | 3 Dec 1846 | David Carlisle-Rachael Loudy |
|      | 3 Dec 1846 | Jefferson Hatfield-Frances Watson Mackey |
|      | 3 Dec 1846 | Reuben Dunman-Catharine Cinrose |
|      | 6 Dec 1846 | Thomas Henton-Julia Ann Dabney |
|      | 7 Dec 1846 | Thomas Martindale-Sarah Brown |
| 44   | 20 Dec 1846 | John Tully-Rachel Barnes |
|      | 23 Dec 1846 | Alex   Blake-Mary H. Todd |
|      | 24 Dec 1846 | Isaac Brown-Elizabeth Conall |
|      | 27 Dec 1846 | Frederick Hackley-Louisa Rector |
|      | 27 Dec 1846 | Andrew Williams-Margaret Armentrout |
| 45   | 31 Dec 1846 | Nathan Kimble-Mary Jane Price |
|      | 31 Dec 1846 | Lewis Rees-Ellen Love |
|      | 1 Jan 1847 | William Ward-Grace Ann Hill |
|      | 7 Jan 1847 | John Guy, Jr.-Elizabeth Peacock |
|      | 17 Jan 1847 | James A. Lockridge-Delany G. Tacket |
| 46   | 24 Jan 1847 | Simeon Wilkinson-Catharine Edwards |
|      | 28 Jan 1847 | James Stilwell-Elizabeth Bond |
|      | 31 Jan 1847 | Calvin S. Lore-Abigail Blake |
|      | 4 Feb 1847 | John Storm-Margaret Deeds |
|      | 1 Feb 1847 | Cyranus Marquess-Cinderella Wilkinson |
| 47   | 4 Feb 1847 | Peter Mount-Ellen Kidd |
|      | 11 Feb 1847 | Isaac Lehman-Eve Ann Hay |
|      | 25 Feb 1847 | Israel Frey-Sarah Ann Baber |
|      | 23 Feb 1847 | Joseph Gerard-Betsey Pickens |
|      | 25 Feb 1847 | Benjamin Jarnegan-Sarah Miller |
| 48   | 25 Feb 1847 lic | William Anderson-Mary Ann Shoemaker |
|      | 14 Mar 1847 | Minor Alley-Nancy Butler |
|      | 4 Mar 1847 | James Koohns-Polly Fisher |
|      | 18 Mar 1847 | Caleb Petty-Matilda Swisher |
|      | 18 Mar 1847 | David Baggs-Caroline Landgrave |
| 49   | 27 Mar 1847 | Matthew Lockridge-Elizabeth Newman |
|      | 2 Apr 1847 | Henry Daggy-Elizabeth Burnett |
|      | 8 Apr 1847 | Daniel Lockwood-Mary Bain |

| PAGE | DATE | GROOM — BRIDE |
|------|------|---------------|
| | 4 Apr 1847 | John Richardson-Margaret Hook |
| | 11 Apr 1847 | John Pasmore-Adeline Bailey |
| 50 | 11 Apr 1847 | Rogers O'Morrow-Mary Shaffer |
| | 22 Apr 1847 | Jeheil McCreary-Ann Winters |
| | Apr 1847 | Sherlock Johnson-Esther Bearss |
| | 23 Apr 1847 | John Clendenine-Casandra Tracy |
| | 29 Apr 1847 | Rufus T. Jones-Mary A. Bure |
| 51 | 6 May 1847 | Isaac Mooney-Elizabeth Webster |
| | 9 May 1847 lic | Aaron C. Scull-Miranda W. Beach |
| | 10 May 1847 | Michael Taylor-Araminta Woolpert |
| | 11 Jun 1847 | Gilford Barns-Martha J. Baker |
| | 11 May 1847 | Benjamin F. Hunter-Julia Ann Sharpe |
| 52 | 23 May 1847 | Josiah P. Kimball-Wealthy Masterson |
| | 28 May 1847 | Freiborn Davis-Mary J. Stevenson |
| | 28 May 1847 | Allen McGuire-Rebecca Jenkins |
| | 3 Jun 1847 | Hesekiah Tracy-Mary Jane Morgan |
| | 8 Jun 1847 | Samuel L. Clark-Mary Shirley |
| 53 | 29 Jun 1847 | Constantine Schuber-Malinda Hall |
| | 31 Jun 1847 | Jacob Bryant-Margaret Fickle |
| | 27 Jun 1847 | Lewis Hopper-Margaret Kinsey |
| | 1 Jul 1847 | Isaac Byers-Margarite Potterf |
| | 11 Jul 1847 | George Saunders-Amanda H. Davis |
| 54 | 23 Jul 1847 | Isaac Vandoren-Mary Shadinger |
| | 1 Aug 1847 | John Clarke-Winnifred Holloway |
| | 3 Aug 1847 | John Adams-Mary Ann Scott |
| | 5 Aug 1847 | Peter Clester-Sidney A.M. Wright |
| 55 | 8 Aug 1847 | Erastus Thomas Foster-Jane Going |
| | 15 Aug 1847 | James Hannons-Matilda Farlow |
| | 15 Aug 1847 | Jackson Ayres-Lucinda Farlow |
| | 19 Aug 1847 | John Peters-Elizabeth Bears |
| | 21 Aug 1847 | William Moss-Sarah Fouts |
| 56 | 26 Aug 1847 | James F. Beckner-Keziah Harp |
| | 26 Aug 1847 | Daniel Isley-Mary Grist |
| | 25 Aug 1847 | William Hawkins-Lavina White |
| | 29 Aug 1847 | Cyrus P. Fenemore-Mary M. Bryant |
| | 29 Aug 1847 | John Bowman-Nancy Fletcher |
| 57 | 27 Aug 1847 | William Smith-Mary Runnion |
| | 29 Aug 1847 | John B. Ross-Sarah Donaldson |
| | 2 Sep 1847 | Amos R. Appleton-Hannah Ann Savilla |
| | 2 Sep 1847 | George W. Nicklesen-Emily Cole |
| | 9 Sep 1847 | Joseph W. Frazee-Minerva C. Fish |
| 58 | 10 Sep 1847 | Robert Watson-Catharine J. Sellers |
| | 16 Sep 1847 | Jesse Pearson-Rebecca Thomas |
| | 5 Oct 1847 | Lewis Watts-Margaret Newhard |

171

| PAGE | DATE | GROOM — BRIDE |
|------|------|---------------|
|      | 7 Oct 1847 | William Bacon-Lovica Culiff |
|      | 14 Oct 1847 | George W. Malcom-Susan Irwin |
| 59   | 14 Oct 1847 | Christian Clymer-Ann Woolley |
|      | 17 Oct 1847 | Eber Fenimore-Mary Shepard |
|      | 21 Oct 1847 | Alfred Murphy-Julia Ann Dixon |
|      | 21 Oct 1847 | Elias Vanamon-Sarah Koler |
|      | 21 Oct 1847 | Rufus Reeves-Ann Maria Middelkauff |
| 60   | 24 Oct 1847 | Thomas B. Harper-Activus Bond |
|      | 27 Oct 1847 | William Jenkins-Sarah E. McLaughlin |
|      | 9 Nov 1847 | William Matthews-Phebe Drake |
|      | 11 Nov 1847 | Martin Martindale-Polly Cady |
|      | 11 Nov 1847 | Orange Fisher-Sarah Ann Garver |
| 61   | 12 Nov 1847 | Larkin Antrim-Elizabeth McCombs |
|      | 18 Nov 1847 | Charles R. Harper-Lucy Waterman |
|      | 20 Nov 1847 | Robert Cleland-Mary Ann Guier |
|      | 20 Nov 1847 | Isaiah Tuttle-Mary Highland |
|      | 12 Dec 1847 | Olly Paul-Cassandra Benner |
| 62   | 28 Nov 1847 | Henry Mower-Rachael Bowman |
|      | 25 Nov 1847 | Henry Sharpe-Sarah Ann Kinzie |
|      | 26 Nov 1847 | Turner Sullivan-Angeline Bryant |
|      | 26 Nov 1847 | Hugh Masterson-Mary Snodgrass |
|      | 28 Nov 1847 | William Coulter-Sophia Howes |
| 63   | 2 Dec 1847 | Abijah Cox-Mary E. Bright |
|      | 24 Dec 1847 | John P. Buck-Ann Blankingshipp |
|      | 5 Dec 1847 | Emmer D. Robbins-Alice Clendennin |
|      | 22 Dec 1848[47] | John Belew- Mamine Woolpert |
|      | 19 Dec 1847 | John Baber-Elizabeth Homan |
| 64   | 21 Dec 1847 | John Shugart-Rebecca Guyer |
|      | 30 Dec 1847 | George Alvord-Mary Ann Mason |
|      | 30 Dec 1847 | Thomas Skillman-Maria Gunkle |
|      | 31 Dec 1847 | Samuel Benner-Jane Jenkins |
|      | 1 Jan 1848 | Wm. K. Sherwin-Cornelice Lawrence |
| 65   | 12 Jan 1848 | Joseph Fisher-Elizabeth Brewer |
|      | 20 Jan 1848 | Andrew Onstott-Elizabeth Thompson |
|      | 26 Jan 1848 | John L. Willard-Louis Culef |
|      | 30 Jan 1848 | William Ewes-Nancy Jane Whaley |
|      | 31 Jan 1848 lic | James Welsh-Mary Ann Richason |
| 66   | 1 Feb 1848 lic | Job Morris-Julia Ann Clayton |
|      | 8 Feb 1848 | Abel M. Hawk-Harriet Smith |
|      | 9 Feb 1848 lic | Alfred Hall-Rachael Ann Largent |
|      | 17 Feb 1848 | John I. Hill-Eliza Wadell |
|      | 27 Feb 1848 | Charles S. Stryker-Lydia Jane Davis |
| 67   | 27 Feb 1848 | William Thomas-Frances Givens |
|      | 27 Feb 1848 | John Hartelroad-Mahala White |

| PAGE | DATE | GROOM — BRIDE |
|------|------|---------------|
|      | 26 Feb 1848 lic | Nelson Young-Elizabeth Sharpe |
|      | 29 Feb 1848 | Edward Potmen-Teressa B. Clickert |
|      | 1 Mar 1848 | James Tittsworth-Lucinda Laurence |
| 68   | 5 Mar 1848 | Isaiah Tombaugh-Jane Antrim |
|      | 6 Mar 1848 | Gilbert N. Smith-Susan Benner |
|      | 9 Mar 1848 | Charles M. Broune-Sarah Jane Graham |
|      | 7 Mar 1848 | Frederick Maison-Susanna Graebner |
|      | 13 Mar 1848 | William Browne-Polly Ward |
| 69   | 2 Apr 1848 | Wm. H.L. King-Nancy Beggs |
|      | 23 Jun 1848 | William Baldwin-Harriet D. Beaver |
|      | 30 Mar 1848 | Peter Holland-Nancy Crispin |
|      | 30 Mar 1848 | Elzyran Lawham-Milly Adams |
|      | 3 Apr 1848 | William Cline-Lucy Leach |
| 70   | 3 Apr 1848 | Alexander Abrams-Sarah Cain |
|      | 9 Apr 1848 | Amos Wooley-Ann Long |
|      | 19 Apr 1848 lic | Christopher Lesly-Eliza Jane Vierge |
|      | 1 May 1848 | Joseph Faust-Clara Beck |
|      | 28 Jun 1848 | Joseph Runnells-Catharine Busick |
| 71   | 7 May 1848 | George W. Onstott-Louisa Smith |
|      | 25 May 1848 | John A. McHenry-Margaret Reyburn |
|      | 22 May 1848 | Abraham R. Kripp-Caroline Berry |
|      | 3 Jun 1848 | Henry Deter-Catharine Wade |
|      | 4 Jun 1848 | Andrew Rush-Elizabeth Britton |
| 72   | 23 Jun 1848 | Daniel Petty-Sarah Swoverland |
|      | 19 Jun 1848 lic | Nathan B. Cook-Sarah Jane Ptomey |
|      | 23 Jun 1848 lic | Jacob Hochstetler-Elizabeth Shetler |
|      | 24 Jun 1848 | John P. Robinson-Anna Gilbert |
|      | 28 Jun 1848 | John Conklin-Polly Flagg |
| 74   | 29 Jun 1848 | Elijah Husher-Maria Cory |
|      | 9 Jul 1848 | Noah Sinks-Mary Ann Jackson |
|      | 20 Jul 1848 | Augustus Hunter-Sarah Ann Day |
|      | 30 Jul 1848 | Daniel F. Whitesel-Nancy Petty |
|      | 4 Aug 1848 lic | George W. Spicer-Sidney Brown |
| 75   | 7 Aug 1848 lic | Philip Cool-Nancy A. Krider |
|      | Aug 1848 lic | Phineas Cook-Sarah Pearson |
|      | 19 Aug 1848 | Joel Adams-Nancy Hays |
| 76   | 5 Aug 1848 | Nicholas Smith-Susannah Barnhart |
|      | 8 Aug 1848 | Phineas Cook-Sarah Pearson |
|      | 30 Aug 1848 | Jacob Snyder-Ester Bolan |
|      | 31 Aug 1848 | John P. Brown-Mary Mayers |
|      | 1 Sep 1848 | James H. Kizer-Harriet Jebeau |
| 77   | 7 Sep 1848 | Isaac P. Brannaman-Martha Jane Barret |
|      | 10 Sep 1848 | Addison Tinson-Mansy Jackson |
|      | 9 Sep 1848 lic | Lewis Elkins-Rachael Thomas |

| PAGE | DATE | GROOM — BRIDE |
|------|------|---------------|
|  | 10 Sep 1848 | Eli Hoove-Elizabeth Turnipseed |
|  | 14 Sep 1848 | David W. Young-Barbara Maria Moyer |
| 78 | 12 Sep 1848 lic | Eli S. Middlkauff-Elizabeth Lee |
|  | 24 Sep 1848 | Avery Carvey-Angelina King |
|  | 27 Sep 1848 | Robert Stitt-Mary Frazier |
|  | 28 Sep 1848 | John Barnhart-Harriet Higgins |
|  | 4 Oct 1848 | Lewis Stewart-Nancy Jane Brandon |
| 79 | 5 Oct 1848 | Thomas Timmons-Freelove Miller |
|  | 7 Oct 1848 | Nathan B. York-Sally Stomes |
|  | 12 Oct 1848 | William Jones-Matilda Jane Shoemaker |
|  | 8 Oct 1848 | Sylvester Omeara-Nancy Hopper |
|  | 15 Oct 1848 | James Witham-Mahala Davis |
| 80 | 19 Oct 1848 lic | William Hooks-Josephine Miller |
|  | 27 Oct 1848 | David Edwards-Charity Wildman |
|  | 25 Oct 1848 | George Cockley-Jane Holman |
|  | 2 Nov 1848 | Sampson Sher-Elizabeth Raymer |
|  | 2 Nov 1848 | John E. Johnson-Mary Cox |
| 81 | 3 Nov 1848 lic | Jacob Benner-Catharine Armentrout |
|  | 8 Nov 1848 lic | John Albaugh-Ruth Wilkeson |
|  | 16 Nov 1848 | Adam Rader-Leah Ann Nichelson |
|  | 19 Nov 1848 | Christopher Kessler-Sarah B. Fenimore |
|  | 16 Nov 1848 | Calvin Tracy-Harriet Dexter |
| 82 | 19 Oct 1848 | John Nelson Hurst-Lydia A. Sullivan |
|  | 2 Nov 1848 | Henry Hall-Magdaleny Rickel |
|  | 16 Nov 1848 lic | Stephen Segraves-Sarah Essick |
|  | 26 Nov 1848 | Daniel Deeds-Sarah Tilden |
|  | 31 Nov 1848 | Hosea Woolpert-Siger Caroline Orum |
| 83 | 30 Nov 1848 lic | Benton Lane-Ellen Birdsall |
|  | 8 Dec 1848 | Klingensmith-Lydia Hostetler |
|  | 10 Dec 1848 | John Bohn-Elizabeth Demouth |
|  | 11 Dec 1848 | Marcus Harter-Lucinda Kessler |
|  | 31 Dec 1848 | Abraham Hicks-Susannah Farlow |
| 84 | 24 Dec 1848 | William A. Beckner-Helen Man Brown |
|  | 28 Dec 1848 | Lewis F. Bowyer-Naomi E. Pugh |
|  | 23 Dec 1848 lic | William Bullock-Cecilia Benner |
|  | 28 Dec 1848 | Robert S. Donaldson-Sarah E. Curry |
|  | 7 Jan 1849 | Joseph Miller-Leah Keim |
| 85 | 10 Jan 1849 lic | Washington Benner-Sarah Bolen |
|  | 11 Jan 1849 | John Hoffman-Susannah Sidener |
|  | 11 Jan 1849 lic | Absalom W. Chalmers-Mary Snodgrass |
|  | 21 Jan 1849 | John J. Wertz-Ann Louisa Ellis |
|  | 1 Feb 1849 | Ebenezar E. Tilden-Sarah Ann McGinley |
| 86 | 31 Dec 1848 | Jacob Barhart-Mary Fisher |
|  | 7 Jan 1849 | James Fiers-Nancy Close |

| PAGE | DATE | GROOM — BRIDE |
|------|------|---------------|
|      | 5 Jan 1849 | Reece Bickell-Jane Jones |
|      | 11 Jan 1849 | Charles Talbott-Martha Ann Woodkirk |
|      | 7 Jan 1849 | Eli P. Mendenhall-Elizabeth Hup |
| 87   | 18 Feb 1849 | James Wright-Elizabeth Moore |
|      | 25 Feb 1849 | James Harvey Sayers-Eliza Jane Marquess |
|      | 22 Apr 1849 | James Fornash-Betsy Thomas |
|      | 4 Apr 1849 | Otto P. Webb-Elizabeth Shobert |
| 88   | 23 Mar 1849 | Levin S. Lesh-Malita McManes |
|      | 27 Mar 1849 | Cornelius S. Foley-Margaret Ritchey |
|      | 1 Apr 1849 | Aaron Tombaugh-Sarah Antrim |
|      | 29 Mar 1849 | George W. Layton-Nancy Loveall |
|      | 1 Apr 1849 | Daniel Seltenright-Sarah Wentrote |
| 89   | 5 Apr 1849 | John B. Redd-Brittania Hurst |
|      | 7 Apr 1849 | Benjamin G. Martindale-Margaret Guyer |
|      | 7 Apr 1849 | Lewis Evans Beane-Julia Ann Jenkins |
|      | 7 Apr 1849 lic | Washington Poor-Anna Poor |
|      | 10 Apr 1849 | Thomas G. Horton-Harriet M. Fenimore |
| 90   | 12 Apr 1849 | Nathaniel Clingenpeel-Eliza Ann Buck |
|      | 19 Apr 1849 | John Quincy Adams Howes-Orpah Ann Murden |
|      | 22 Apr 1849 | Abraham Nell-Katharine Hochstettler |
|      | 22 Apr 1849 | Peter Bonnevonchin -Sarah Carpenter |
|      | 30 Apr 1849 lic | Benjamin F. Dice-Elizabeth Gunkle |
| 91   | 6 May 1849 | Joseph H. Finley-Mary Jane Close |
|      | 26 May 1849 | Bloomville O. Bond-Anna Barnes |
|      | 3 Jun 1849 | Christopher Keesy-Hannah Dryer |
|      | 3 Jun 1849 | Thomas B. Swisher-Ester Conner |
|      | 5 Jun 1849 | William Pitsenberger-Susannah Tharp |
| 92   | 10 Jun 1849 | Adam Lambert-Eve Mason |
|      | 14 Jun 1849 | Joseph Watson-Elizabeth Moore |
|      | 14 Jun 1849 | Henry D. Moore-Jane Richison |
|      | 17 Jun 1849 | Henry Nell-Catharine English |
|      | 24 Jun 1849 | William Kessler-Jane Bunn |
| 93   | 1 Jul 1849 | Orris Blake-Sarah Ann Todd |
|      | 3 Jul 1849 lic | Jonathan Clingenpeel-Hester Buck |
|      | 10 Jul 1849 | Charles Hartman-Anna Youngblodt |
|      | 9 Jul 1849 | Martin Weaver-Eleanor Guyer |
|      | 17 Jul 1849 | Isaac Harter-Rachael Rankin |
| 94   | 15 Jul 1849 | Abraham Hoover-Louiza Young |
|      | 22 Jul 1849 | Cornelius Snyder-Malinda Smith |
|      | 2 Aug 1849 | Walter C. Shaw-Rebecca Keller |
|      | 23 Jul 1849 | Jacob Freestone-Patsy Wildman |
|      | 30 Jul 1849 | Hubert Albachten-Elizabeth Hartman |
| 95   | 29 Jul 1849 | David H. Hume-Minerva Jane Frazier |
|      | 4 Aug 1849 | Levi P. Hill-Christenia Tilden |

| PAGE | DATE | GROOM — BRIDE |
|------|------|---------------|
|      | 16 Aug 1849 | Ebenezar Humrickhouse-Minerva Lewis |
|      | 19 Aug 1849 | Benjamin Rector-Rachael J. Smith |
|      | 23 Aug 1849 | Daniel Vanaman-Elenor Small |
| 96   | 30 Aug 1849 | Samuel Bain-Experience Busick |
|      | 30 Aug 1849 | James M. Colvin-Sarah Spray |
|      | 30 Aug 1849 | George Dillman-Hannah Clingenpeel |
|      | 2 Sep 1849 | James Shahan-Sarah R. Adams |
|      | 6 Sep 1849 | John Truax- Eliza Walter |
| 97   | 5 Sep 1849 | John Shoemaker-Catherine Close |
|      | 5 Sep 1849 | Jonathan Stutesman-Emily Elizabeth Moore |
|      | 9 Sep 1849 | William L. Logan-Harriet F. King |
|      | 14 Sep 1849 | Aquilla Watson-Lucinda Moore |
|      | 16 Sep 1849 | David Countryman-Mary Crull |
| 98   | 23 Sep 1849 | John Barker-Elizabeth Long |
|      | 21 Sep 1849 | Andrew Howman-Fanny Bragg |
|      | 24 Sep 1849 | Robert Bean-Catharine Benner |
|      | 25 Sep 1849 | Noah Ausman-Hannah Veal |
|      | 26 Sep 1849 | Franklin Michael-Tilara Shiffert |
| 99   | 4 Oct 1849 | George P. Kuns-Sarah Ann Brower |
|      | 30 Sep 1849 | Joseph Shirley-Nancy M. Striker |
|      | 7 Oct 1849 | Philip Parcels-Eleanora E. Jackson |
|      | 31 Oct 1849 | Leopold Platts-Susan Vandurmer |
|      | 9 Oct 1849 | George Taylor Elliott-Viena Miner |
| 100  | 13 Oct 1849 | John Walter-Kesia Ash |
|      | 14 Oct 1849 | Cornelius Barnhuzel-Nancy Thompson |
|      | 16 Oct 1849 | Parker Hollingsworth-Polly Pearson |
|      | 17 Oct 1849 | John W. Brown-Irinda Kenworthy |
|      | 21 Oct 1849 | James A. Crispen-Harriet Harsh |
| 101  | 25 Nov 1849 | Robert Watson-Elizabeth Tumelson |
|      | 21 Oct 1849 | William Wilson-Mary Amanda Shoup |
|      | 27 Oct 1849 | John W. Thomas-Elizabeth Ann Wilson |
|      | 28 Oct 1849 | Daniel Trahune-Mary Ann Jessup |
|      | 2 Nov 1849 | Jacob C. Rader-Eliza A. Wilson |
| 102  | 4 Nov 1849 | Michael W. Confer-Julia Ann Armstrong |
|      | 5 Nov 1849 lic | Alfred Perry Sellers-Mary Jane Cole |
|      | 11 Nov 1849 | David J. Bumgarner-Mary Catharine Fansler |
|      | 14 Nov 1849 | Henry P. Howes-Mary Ann Conner |
|      | 15 Nov 1849 | Zeri M. Baldwin-Rachael S. Ptomey |
| 103  | 11 Nov 1849 | Wesley Benner-Maria Louisa Beane |
|      | 11 Nov 1849 | Joseph Bullock-Lavina Hudson |
|      | 13 Nov 1849 lic | Jacob F. Reeves-Mary Jane VanHousen |
|      | 15 Nov 1849 | Henry Rosenthal-Rebecca Slaughter |
|      | 29 Nov 1849 | David H. Conrad-Catharine Garber |

# FEDERAL CENSUS MORTALITY SCHEDULES

Family historians use the population schedules of the Federal Census extensively in their search for information concerning ancestors. Some are not aware that added information is available on other census schedules which were compiled simultaneously with the population schedules.

One additional schedule which provides valuable information is the Mortality Schedule, which was compiled during the censuses of 1850, 1860, 1870, and 1880. This schedule lists deaths during the proceeding twelve months (i.e., the 1860 population census was to reflect the conditions as of 1 June 1860; therefore, the mortality schedule was to include all deaths from 1 June 1859 through 31 May 1860). Technically, if a person died 1 June 1860, that person's information was to be included on the population schedule. Fortunately, or unfortunately, the Assistant Marshals who gathered the information did not understand their orders, or ignored them. We thus find deaths on the mortality schedule which did not occur during the stipulated period; births on the population schedule which occured after the appointed date, etc. In some cases, a person appeared on both the population and mortality schedule!

The information gathered for the mortality schedules for 1850, 1860, and 1870 was: name of person, age, sex, color, free or slave, married or widowed, place of birth, month of death, occupation, cause of death, number of days ill. In 1880, the following information was also collected: person's length of residence in the United States, the place the cause of death was contracted, and the name of the attending physician.

The National Archives offered the original volumes of the mortality schedules to the various states. The Indiana volumes are available in the Genealogy Division of the Indiana State Library. An everyname index on cards is also there. A compilation of the 1850 mortality schedule for Indiana was done by Lowell M. Volkel in 1971. Copies of this transcription can be found in the Genealogy Division of the Indiana State Library. The 1860 mortality schedule for Pike County, Indiana is printed below to illustrate the information available. The categories color, and Free and slave are omitted in the transcription for Pike County, as no entries were made in those columns.

Abbreviations used in this transcription are: A = Age, M in age column = months; W in age column = weeks; S = sex, in the sex column, F = female, M = male; in the third column, the M indicates martal status, M = married, W = Widow or widower; BP = Birthplace; standard PO abbreviation are used for states in birthplace column.; MO = month; OCC = Occupation; CD = Cause of death; DU = Duration.

## PIKE COUNTY, INDIANA
## 1860 MORTALITY SCHEDULE

Transcribed by Clarice June Hale

### CLAY TOWNSHIP

| NAME | A | S | M | BP | MO | OCC | CD | DU |
|------|---|---|---|----|----|-----|----|----|
| Kelly, John F | 1 | M | | IN | AP | | laryngitis | 6 |
| Fredrick, Mary | 63 | F | | IN | AG | | typhoid fever | 60 |
| Fredrick, Michel | 70 | M | W | IN | SE | farmer | typhoid fever | 6 |
| White, Alonzo P. | 1M | M | | IN | JE | | unknown | 14 |
| Ewing, John | 55 | M | M | Ireland | NO | farmer | typhoid fever | 21 |
| Decker, Lucinda | 24 | F | M | IN | JA | | consumption | 1 yr |
| Nixon, Isabel | 1M | F | | IN | MR | | epilepsey | 3 |
| Traylor, Hannah | 37 | F | M | IN | AP | | unknown | 8 hr |
| Fredrick, Martha I | 5 | F | | IN | MY | | inflamation of brain | 4 |
| McCrary, Thos | 2 | M | | IN | SE | | cholera infantum | 21 |

### TOWN OF PETERSBURGH

| NAME | A | S | M | BP | MO | OCC | CD | DU |
|------|---|---|---|----|----|-----|----|----|
| Warren, John | 6M | M | | IN | SE | | chills and fever | 14 |
| McClure, Catherine | 28 | F | M | IN | JE | | consumption | 4 mo |
| McClure, Telitha | 1M | F | | IN | JL | | epilepsey | 12 |
| Stratton, _____ | 1M | F | | IN | MY | | epilepsey | 11 |
| Hammond, Lola | 1M | F | | IN | JA | | lung fever | 7 |
| Rice, Fredrick W | 1 | M | | IN | MR | | measles | 14 |
| Smith, Carissa | 9 | F | | IN | JE | | unknown | 1 |
| Hawthorn, Margaret | 73 | F | | PA | FE | | pneumonia | 8 |
| Wright, Catherine | 82 | F | W | VA | OC | | typhoid fever | 56 |
| Ackaline, John B | 1M | M | | IN | FE | | unknown | 3 |
| Griffin, Ann | 36 | F | | IN | FE | | typhoid fever | 14 |
| Benedict, Allice | 2 | F | | IN | FE | | typhoid fever | 21 |
| Jackson, Ethelbert | 2M | M | | IN | JA | | erysipelas | 6 |
| Thomas, George | 2M | M | | IN | MR | | whooping cough | 1 |
| Denison, Ida J | 7M | F | | IN | JL | | flux | 21 |
| Hutchens, Laura E | 4 | F | | IN | AP | | croup | 3 |
| Battles, John | 31 | M | M | VA | DE· | farmer | pneumonia | 4 |
| McElwain, Elizabeth | 75 | F | W | NY | AG | | unknown | 6 |
| Cahill, Thos. | 2 | M | | IN | JL | | cholera infantum | 6 |
| Hawthorn, John | 8M | M | | IN | OC | | scarlet fever | 28 |

179

## MADISON TOWNSHIP

| NAME | A | S | M | BP | MO | OCC | CD | DU |
|------|---|---|---|----|----|----|----|----|
| Sapingfield, George | 3M | M | | IN | AP | | unknown | 60 |
| Slater, Mary D | 9 | F | | IN | FE | | consumption | 1 yr |
| Haskins, Lusebra | 4 | F | | IN | MY | | burned to death | 10 |
| Selby, Malinda A. | 20 | F | M | IN | JL | | remittant fever | 14 |
| Burkhart, Sarah | 1 | F | | IN | JL | | flux | 21 |
| Selby, William | 1 | M | | IN | OC | | inflamation of brain | 1 |
| Hollon, Betsy J. | 3M | F | | IN | FE | | unknown | 2 hrs |
| Snyder, Solomon B | 1M | M | | IN | MR | | croup | 2 |
| McGowan, John N. | 20 | M | | IN | MR | farmer | inflamation brain | 21 |
| Fowler, Lyman | 1M | M | | IN | JL | | unknown | 1 |
| McConnell, Martha | 3 | F | | IN | JA | | scalded | 2 |
| Williams, William | 5 | M | | IN | JA | | inflamation bowels | 21 |
| Noland, Joel J. | 36 | M | M | NC | SE | farmer | carbunkle | 21 |
| Borders, Susanna | 47 | F | M | NC | MR | | hemorage of womb | 90 |

## JEFFERSON TOWNSHIP

| NAME | A | S | M | BP | MO | OCC | CD | DU |
|------|---|---|---|----|----|----|----|----|
| Cowan, Mary A | 1 | F | | IN | SE | | fever, unknown kind | 11 |
| Peach, William | 1M | M | | IN | DE | | cause not known | few hr |
| Hancock, Milton | 8M | M | | IN | SE | | hives | 7 |
| Lockhart, Sarah | 1M | F | | IN | JL | | unknown | 1 |
| Downey, Alexander C | 2 | M | | IN | JA | | winter fever | 14 |
| Walker, _____ | 9M | M | | IN | OC | | inflamation bowels | 4 wks |
| Foster, Margaret E | 2 | F | | IN | DE | | croup | 2 |
| Stobough, Rebecca J | 1M | F | | IN | JA | | pneumonia | 2 |
| Brown, Mary E | 1M | F | | IN | JL | | epilepsy | 3 |
| Brown, Geo W | 33 | M | M | OH | SE | farmer | pneumonia | 8 |
| Rodarmel, Amanda | 7 | F | | IN | JL | | congestive chills | 14 hr |
| Sullivan, Mary Ann | 11M | F | | IN | JE | | fits | 5 |
| Brown, Jas B | 1 | M | | IN | JL | | congestion of brown | 21 |
| Brown, Caroline O | 1 | F | | IN | AP | | congestion of brown | 14 |
| Brown, Perry | 39 | M | M | TN | MY | physician | consumption | 6 mo |
| Baldwin, John S | 50 | M | M | SC | MR | shoe-maker | penumonia | 12 |
| Denton, Julia E | 13 | F | | IN | MR | | typhoid fever | 8 |
| Finch, Clarry | 3 | F | | IN | FE | | lung fever | 3 wk |
| Parker, Hariet E | 1 | F | | IN | AG | | croup | |
| Beck, Catherine A* | 1 | F | | IN | AG | | choked | 15 min |
| Lindsey, Elijah | 54 | M | M | KY | JA | farmer | billious cholic | |
| Weldon, Benj D | 25 | M | M | IN | SE | farmer | pul consumption | 8 mo |
| Hurst, Elzira | 1M | F | | IN | AP | | brain fever | 1 |
| Whaley, Goodlet | 1 | M | | IN | AG | | chills and fever | 8 mo |

*Remarks: Catherine A Beck while eating green corn, inhaled a quantity & died instantly.

| NAME | A | S | M | BP | MO | OCC | CD | DU |
|------|---|---|---|-----|-----|-----|-----|-----|
| Mattison, _____ | 1M | M | | IN | SE | | unknown | 3 |
| Mattison, _____ | 1M | M | | IN | SE | | unknown | 3 |
| Coleman, Jane | 36 | F | M | VA | FE | | typhoid fever | 3 mo |
| May, Lydia Ann | 1 | F | | IN | MY | | lung fever | 14 |
| Traylor, Amanda | 13 | F | | IN | AG | | erysipelas | 4 |
| Abbott, Frank | 6 | M | | IN | MR | | scarlet fever | 6 |
| Alcorn, Solomon | 32 | M | M | IN | FE | farm lab | pneumonia | 3 wk |
| McCain, Mary | 49 | F | M | SC | FE | | cold plague | 12 |

## WASHINGTON TOWNSHIP, END OF PETERSBURG

| NAME | A | S | M | BP | MO | OCC | CD | DU |
|------|---|---|---|-----|-----|-----|-----|-----|
| Cox, Henry E | 1M | M | | IN | AP | | inflamation of brain | 3 |
| McGan, Barney | 50 | M | M | Ireland | DE | farmer | pneumonia | 20 |
| McGan, Rosey | 42 | F | M | Ireland | DE | | pneumonia | 20 |
| Caton, Mary | 15 | F | | IN | MR | | pul consumption | 1 yr |
| Kinman, Iberilla | 26 | F | M | IN | MY | | pul consumption | 6 mo |
| Chamness, Catherine | 9M | F | | IN | SE | | diarhea | 3 |
| Chamness, Charlotta | 23 | F | M | IN | AP | | pneumonia | 5 |
| Willson, Evy M | 2M | F | | IN | AG | | cholera infantum | 10 |
| Benjamin, Thos | 1M | M | | IN | FE | | unknown | 1 hr |
| Benjamin, Blanch | 6 | F | | IN | SE | | unknown | 90 |
| Jackson, Nancy A | 25 | F | M | IN | JA | | quinzy | 14 hr |
| McCain, Henrietta | 18 | F | | IN | NO | | unknown | 3 wk |
| Arnold, Richard | 22 | M | | IN | JE | farmer | typhoid fever | 6 wk |
| Nash, James | 2 | M | | IN | SE | | brain fever | 14 |
| Miley, Wilsey | 36 | M | M | IN | SE | farmer | consumption | 1 yr |
| Shay, Timothy | 72 | M | W | Ireland | OC | farmer | chronic sore leg | 2 yr |
| Miley, Jeremiah | 25 | M | M | IN | SE | farmer | consumption | 3 mo |
| Palmer, Robt C | 2 | M | | IN | AG | | cholera infantum | 23 |
| Evans, Mary J | 3 | F | | IN | DE | | pneumonia | 9 |
| Brenton, William | 3M | M | | IN | JL | | cholera infantum | 6 |
| Clark, Delphi A | 31 | F | M | KY | MR | | consumption | 3 mo |
| Miley, David | 61 | M | M | KY | JL | farmer | chronic diarhea | 13 mo |
| Willis, Albert | 1M | M | | IN | OC | | thrush | 8 |
| Willis, Wm H | 1M | M | | IN | OC | | thrush | 8 |
| Beck, Elizabeth | 1 | F | | IN | SE | | billious fever | 60 |
| Rusher, William F | 1M | M | | IN | SE | | unknown | 15 hr |

## MONROE TOWNSHIP

| NAME | A | S | M | BP | MO | OCC | CD | DU |
|------|---|---|---|-----|-----|-----|-----|-----|
| Ferguson, John T | 1 | M | | IN | DE | | burn | 15 |
| Harden, Malinda E | 2 | F | | IN | MY | | salisation | 6 |
| Harger, Andrew | 20 | M | | IN | SE | farmer | typhoid fever | 9 |
| Roberts, Wm J | 4M | M | | IN | JE | | smothered | |
| Slater, John | 1 | M | | IN | JE | | inflamation of brain | 3 |

| NAME | A | S | M | BP | MO | OCC | CD | DU |
|------|---|---|---|----|----|----|----|----|
| Sharp, Loranzo D | 6 | M | | IN | MR | | pneumonia | 9 |
| Grissom, Levi | 11M | M | | IL | OC | | inflamation of brain | 3 |
| Skinner, Wm H | 2W | M | | IN | JA | | fits | 7 |
| Coleman, Eliza | 38 | F | | IN | MR | farmer | measles | 15 |
| Williams, Levi C | 11D | M | | IN | AP | | croup | 2 |
| Slater, Malinda | 60 | F | W | KY | MR | | consumption | 80 |
| Henning, Thom | 2 | M | | IN | JA | | croup | 2 |
| Ross, Albert E | 3M | M | | IN | SE | | yellow thresh | 8 |
| Richeson, Peter I | 11M | M | | IN | AG | | diarea | 3 |
| Pancake, Mary | 45 | F | | KY | JA | farmer | t fever | 11 |
| Ferguson, Peter | 57 | M | M | KY | NO | farmer | palsy | 5 |
| Retherford, David | 18 | M | | IN | DE | farm lab | sinking chill | 2 |
| Tisdal, Warner | 1 | M | | IN | SE | | unknown | 12 |

## LOCKHART TOWNSHIP

| NAME | A | S | M | BP | MO | OCC | CD | DU |
|------|---|---|---|----|----|----|----|----|
| Byrd, Serena A | 4 | F | | IN | NO | | fever | 6 |
| Scales, John | 50 | M | M | IN | AP | farmer | pneumonia | 2 |
| Strong, S M | 1 | M | | IN | AG | | rickett | 180 |
| Marshall, Elias J | 5 | M | | OH | MY | | scarlot fever | 7 |
| Tooly, _____ | | F | IN | JA | | | borne dead | |
| McMertery, James N | 8M | M | | IN | JA | | colra in phanton | 6 |
| Miller, _____ | | F | IN | OC | | | born dead | |
| Posey, Mary | 60 | F | M | KY | JE | blind | intermittent fever | 14 |
| Lynch, Edward | 22 | M | M | IN | AG | farmer | consumption | 160 |
| Kinder, Wm L | 2 | M | | IN | MY | | unknown | 15 |
| Stewart, Sarah C | 6 | F | | IN | OC | | unknown | 3 |
| Stewart, _____ | 1D | M | | IN | JA | | unknown | 1 |
| Clam, Wm E | 3 | | | OH | MR | | croup | 1 |
| Houchin, Chester-field | 31 | M | M | IN | OC | farmer | consumption | 20 |
| Houchin, _____ | 40 | F | | KY | NO | | milk sickness | 8 |
| Numan, Darethee | 63 | M | | Germany | MY | farm lab | billious fever | 13 |

## PATOKA TOWNSHIP

| NAME | A | S | M | BP | MO | OCC | CD | DU |
|------|---|---|---|----|----|----|----|----|
| Risley, Mary | 15 | F | | IN | MR | | consumption | 42 |
| Campbell, James M | 3M | M | | IN | FE | | inflamation of brain | 9 |
| Davidson, Edth | 69 | F | | VA | NO | lady | consumption | 160 |
| Crow, John H | 7 | M | | IN | AG | | typhoid fever | 81 |
| Roadearmel, _____ | 1 | F | | IN | NO | | unknown | 1 |
| Anderson, Ellen | 6M | F | | IN | SE | | inflamation of brain | 1 |
| Richardson, Elijah | 1 | M | | IN | DE | | croup | 4 |
| Spredgins, F H | 11D | M | | IN | FE | | croup | 11 |
| Beedles, Rebeca | 31 | F | M | KY | MR | farmer | pneumonia | 21 |

| NAME | A | S | M | BP | MO | OCC | CD | DU |
|------|---|---|---|----|----|----|----|----|
| Hecock, _____ | 1 | M | | IN | MR | | unknown | 1 |
| Ashby, _____ | 1D | M | | IN | NO | | unknown | 1/2 |
| McCanlass, _____ | 3M | F | | IN | JL | | unknown | 1/2 |
| Ridge, Manida | 16M | F | | IN | AP | | inflamation of brain | 4 |
| Massy, James J | 1M | M | | IN | MR | | croup | 1 |
| Hedges, Henry | 14 | M | | IN | MR | | unknown | 1 |
| Beck, _____ | 4H | M | | IN | MR | | unknown | 4 hr |
| Bee, A W | 24 | M | M | OH | AG | merchant | unknown | 7 |
| Collins, Laura A | 11 | F | | IN | JL | | milk sickness | 15 |
| Mellon, Eliza J | 19 | F | | IN | FE | | consumption | 90 |
| Milton, John | 6D | M | | IN | DE | | unknown | 6 |

LOGAN TOWNSHIP

| NAME | A | S | M | BP | MO | OCC | CD | DU |
|------|---|---|---|----|----|----|----|----|
| Gillum, Eliza | 24 | F | M | NC | JE | | hemorage | 10 |
| Brittingham, Teena | 24 | F | M | IN | SE | | consumption | 10 |
| Shoaft, _____ | | | M | IN | SE | | unknown | |
| Adkinson, _____ | 5D | M | | IN | JA | | croup | 1 |
| Rickard, Peter | 67 | M | M | NC | AP | farmer | dropsy | 90 |
| Loveless, _____ | 11D | | | IN | MY | | carbuncle | 11 |
| Blase, _____ | | | F | IN | MY | | borne dead | |
| Loveless, Mary | 32 | F | M | IN | DE | farmer | pneumonia | 7 |

# SPENCER COUNTY GUARDIANS' REPORTS, 1871
Abstracted by Ruth Dorrel

In Indiana guardians were appointed, usually by the probate court to manage assets of minors or persons who were determined unable to handle their own affairs. Reports were made periodically to the court giving a financial accounting, and sometimes stating other information of interest to the court and to present day family historians.

In Spencer County, Indiana, these reports were recorded in the probate court records until June, 1871 when a separate book, Guardians Report Probate was begun. Volume 1 of the Guardians Report covered the period 1 June 1871 through April 1975. Abstracts of the reports for 1871 are given below. These records were microfilmed as part of the CRIMP program. A copy of the film is located in the Genealogy Division, Indiana State Library. All 1871 guardianship records were recorded by J.W. Laird, clerk. Persons wishing a copy of the complete report may contact the Genealogy Division, or the Recorder, Spencer County Courthouse, Rockport, Indiana 47635.

DECEASED: Aaron Thrallkill
GUARDIAN: Mary Thrallkill
HEIRS: Unnamed
SWORN: 8 May 1871
RECORDED: 21 June 1871
p. 1

DECEASED: Jane Staats
GUARDIAN: Augustus Ergeman
MINOR HEIRS: Unnamed female
MISC: Ward lives with guardian and attends school.
SWORN: 2 May 1871
RECORDED: 21 June 1871
pp. 2-3

DECEASED: Alfred R. Wright
GUARDIAN: John E. Wright
HEIRS: Christopher C. Wright, Ellis W. Wright, Elizabeth Tuley, Margaret Wright.

MISC: Guardianship of last two named discharged.
SWORN: 8 May 1871
RECORDED: 21 June 1871
pp. 4-5

DECEASED: Daniel Miller
GUARDIAN: May Hamilton
HEIRS: Unnamed
SWORN: 6 May 1871
RECORDED: 21 June 1871
p. 6

DECEASED: Barbara Long
GUARDIAN: Adam Long
INFANT HEIR: John A. Long
SWORN: 18 May 1871
RECORDED: 21 June 1871
p. 7

DECEASED: Anthony Miller
GUARDIAN: Adam Long

**184**

INFANT HEIRS: Samuel H. Miller, Jacob L. Miller and Jonathan Miller

MISC: Samuel H. Miller has died since last report [May 1869] without issue, never having been married, leaving Rosanah Kruger, Adam Miller, Margaret Dufendock, Jacob S. Miller, Jonathan Miller his brothers and sisters and John A. Long the child and heir of Barbara Long, who was a sister of said deceased.

SWORN: 8 May 1871

RECORDED: 22 June 1871

pp. 8-9


DECEASED: John W. Small

GUARDIAN: Mathias McKey

HEIRS: William Small, Henrietta Small, John F. Small

MISC: Henrietta and John F. reside with guardian.

SWORN: 6 May 1871

RECORDED: 23 June 1871

pp. 10-11


DECEASED: Rodolf Trachsel

GUARDIAN: Frederick Hartloff

HEIRS: Unnamed

MISC: Heirs received pension and live with guardian in Spencer County.

SWORN: 8 May 1871

RECORDED: 23 June 1871

p. 12


DECEASED: Levi McCoy

GUARDIAN: Elenor McCoy

INFANT HEIRS: Ida E. McCoy, Masiah A. McCoy

MISC: Wards live with guardian who is their mother and are being sent to school.

SWORN: 6 May 1871

RECORDED: 23 June 1871

p. 13


DECEASED: Caleb Lindsay

GUARDIAN: George Beck

MINOR HEIR: Rhoda A.E. Lindsay

MISC: Heir received a pension.

SWORN: 29 April 1871

RECORDED: 23 June 1871

pp. 14-15


GUARDIAN: Isaac Varner

HEIRS: May F. Varner, Jacob F. Varner, Ann Varner

MISC: Wards are all yet young.

SWORN: 8 May 1871.

RECORDED: 23 June 1871

pp. 15-16


DECEASED: Henry Wolf

GUARDIAN: Anton Holinda

HEIRS: Frank Wolf, Elizabeth Wolf

MISC: Mother of these wards is now married to the guardian.

SWORN: 2 May 1871

RECORDED: 23 June 1871

p. 16


DECEASED: Jacob Brenner

GUARDIAN: James I. Jones

HEIRS: Anna Brenner, Charles Brenner

MISC: Wards reside with mother.

SWORN: 8 May 1871

RECORDED: 24 June 1871

pp. 17-18


GUARDIAN: John E. Wright

WARD: James W. Wright, insane

SWORN: 8 May 1871

RECORDED: 24 June 1871

pp. 19-20

185

DECEASED: Lewis D. Adams
GUARDIAN: Christian Kramer
HEIRS: Lewis D. Adams, Dora B. Adams and others
MISC: Two heirs live in Spencer County.
SWORN: 9 May 1871
RECORDED: 24 June 1871
p. 21

GUARDIAN: Absolem R. Gentry
WARD: Francis A. Gentry
MISC: Ward has arrived at full age and has married Willis Wilkinson. Discharged from guardianship.
SWORN: 9 May 1871
RECORDED: 24 June 1871
p. 22

DECEASED: Sylvester J. Masterson
GUARDIAN: Aaron Masterson
HEIR: Clarissa Masterson
MISC: Heir received a pension.
SWORN: 9 May 1871
RECORDED: 29 June 1871
p. 23-24

DECEASED: Jacobina Raaf
GUARDIAN: Christian Kruger
MINOR HEIRS: Elizabeth Blesah, John Blesah, William Blesah
MISC: Wards are niece and nephews of guardian and are living among their relatives.
SWORN: 9 May 1871
RECORDED: 29 June 1871
pp. 24-25

DECEASED: John Foster
GUARDIAN: Wolfe Vogel
HEIRS: John G. Foster, Lawrence Foster, George Foster, John Foster, Jr.
MISC: George and John, Jr. are now of full age.

SWORN: 10 May 1871
RECORDED: 29 June 1871
pp. 26-27

DECEASED: Winfield S. Brenton
GUARDIAN: William H. Johnston
MINOR HEIRS: Heirs of A. Brenton: Phoebe E. Brenton, Henrietta Brenton, Izora Brenton, Henry T. Brenton
MISC: Winfield S. Benton was of age
on the 27 day of 1869 and received his share of the estate on 10 January 1870. Henrietta Brenton married Genodia S. Crooks 18 November 1869 and received her share.
SWORN: 10 May 1871
RECORDED: 29 June 1871
pp. 27-28

DECEASED: Daniel Miller
GUARDIAN: Barney Frank
MINOR HEIRS: John Miller, Margret Miller
MISC: John Miller was twenty one years of age on the 4 June 1870. Margarett Miller was married to Thomas Wilmot on 10 November 1870. Final settlement made 29 December 1870.
SWORN: 10 May 1871
RECORDED: 30 June 1871
pp. 28-29

GUARDIAN: George Herath
WARD: Elizabeth Graner
SWORN: 10 May 1871
RECORDED: 30 June 1871
pp. 30-31

DECEASED: Nicholas Fisher
GUARDIAN: Mary M. Fisher

HEIRS: Bernard Fisher, Mathias Fisher, Elizabeth Fisher, John Fisher, Margaretta Fisher, Susanah Fisher
MISC: Wm. A. Fisher co-guardian and an heir. 7 heirs. Wm. A. Fisher's guardianship discharged.
SWORN: 18 April 1871
RECORDED: 30 June 1871
pp. 31-32

DECEASED: William and Margaret Kelley
GUARDIAN: William Woodward
MINOR HEIRS: Martha Kelley, Samuel Kelly, Thomas Kelly
MISC: William and Margaret Kelley were heirs of John Woods, deceased.
SWORN: 9 May 1871
RECORDED: 30 June 1871
pp. 32-33

DECEASED: William Bradshaw
GUARDIAN: William W. Hamilton
HEIRS: Daniel Bradshaw, Nancy Bradshaw, Stephen Bradshaw, Thomas Bradshaw, Mary Bradshaw, Elizabeth Bradshaw, Elizia Bradshaw
MISC: Daniel Bradshaw is now of age.
SWORN: 9 May 1871
RECORDED: 30 June 1871
GUARDIAN: James Parker
WARD: Calvin Durfees
SWORN: 10 May 1871
RECORDED: 30 June 1871
pp. 34-36

DECEASED: William S. Cooper
GUARDIAN: John Meeks

MINOR HEIRS: Lydia Anne Cooper, Martha Jane Cooper, Laura Cooper, Albert Cooper
MISC: Wards received a pension, and reside with their mother America Brenner in Spencer County and attend school.
SWORN: 10 May 1871
RECORDED: 1 July 1871
pp. 37-39

DECEASED: Mechack Newton
GUARDIAN: James Varner
MINOR HEIRS: Sarah F. Newton, Eliza E. Newton
MISC: Wards received a pension, reside with guardian and attend school.
SWORN: 8 May 1871
RECORDED: 1 July 1871
pp. 40-41

DECEASED: Charles Dickerson
GUARDIAN: Louisa Dickerson
HEIRS: Hellen M. Dickerson, Mary M. Dickerson
SWORN: 11 May 1871
RECORDED: 1 July 1871
p. 42

DECEASED: George A. Divine
GUARDIAN: Matilda Divine
HEIRS: John H. Divine, Charles W. Divine, Samuel V. Divine, Frederick M. Divine, Martha Elizabeth Divine, Electa J. Divine Margrett I. Divine
MISC: Heirs received a pension. John H. Divine died, leaving his mother this guardianship, his brothers and sisters are his heirs. Mother inherited 1/2 of John's part. Samuel N. Divine is

now of age. Martha E. is now wife of Stewart Gerard, is now over 18 yrs.
SWORN: 10 May 1871
RECORDED: 3 July 1871
pp. 43-44

DECEASED: Daniel Osborn
GUARDIAN: Jordan P. Jones
FORMER GUARDIAN: William Allen
HEIRS: Emery J. Osborn, Alice Osborn, William S. Osborn, Lane B. Osborn
SWORN: 11 May 1871
RECORDED: 3 July 1871
pp. 45-47

GUARDIAN: Herman H. Castens
WARD: Mary Briggerman
SWORN: 11 May 1871
RECORDED: 3 July 1871
p. 48

DECEASED: William R. Tuley
GUARDIAN: John B. Chrisney
HEIRS: Unnamed
MISC: Heirs received a pension.
SWORN: 11 May 1871
RECORDED: 3 July 1871
p. 49

DECEASED: Joel Newman
GUARDIAN: Charles F. Nelson
MINOR HEIRS: Jonathan Newman Marcus L. Newman, Isabell Newman
MISC: Jonathan Newman has arrived at full age, his guardianship discharged.
SWORN: 10 May 1871
RECORDED: 3 July, 1871
pp. 50-51

DECEASED: Reuben Dewit
GUARDIAN: Barney Frank
MINOR HEIR: Oscar Dewit
MISC: Ward lives with guardian.
SWORN: 10 May 1871
RECORDED: 5 July 1871
p. 51

GUARDIAN: William J. Miller
WARD: Catherine Burkdoll, insane
SWORN: 12 May 1871
RECORDED: 6 July 1871
pp. 52-53

DECEASED: Isaiah Piatt
GUARDIAN: Isaac N. Burnes
HEIRS: William H. Piatt
MISC: Heir received a pension.
SWORN: 11 May 1871
RECORDED: 6 July 1871
pp. 53-54

DECEASED: Ferdinand Sheib
GUARDIAN: John Lisch
HEIR: Peter Sheib
SWORN: 5 May 1871
RECORDED: 6 July 1871
pp. 55

DECEASED: Thomas Ulerick
GUARDIAN: Lehew Conner
HEIRS: Unnamed
SWORN: 12 May 1871
RECORDED: 6 July 1871
p. 56

GUARDIAN: A. Hacklman
WARD: John F. Nox
SWORN: 11 May 1871
RECORDED: 6 July 1871
p. 57

DECEASED: James K. Crowder
GUARDIAN: J.J. Gwaltney
MINOR HEIRS: Rhoda M.

Crowder, James M. Crowder
MISC: Heirs received pension.
SWORN: 10 May 1871
RECORDED: 6 July 1871
pp. 58-59

DECEASED: P.E. Livengood
GUARDIAN: J.B. Livengood
MINOR HEIRS: Anna R.
Livengood, Wm. H. Livengood
SWORN: 10 May 1871
RECORDED: 6 July 1871
p. 60

DECEASED: Louis B. Shivels
GUARDIANS: John T. Karrk
HEIRS: Unnamed
SWORN: 11 May 1871
RECORDED: 6 July 1871
p. 61

DECEASED: Geo. W. Masters
GUARDIAN: Ira Broshears
HEIRS: William P. Masters (the
eldest), and others unnamed
MISC: Heirs received a pension.
William P. was taken to his
grandfather in Boone Co Ky for
the purpose of getting an education
in Dec 1869.
SWORN: 13 May 1871
RECORDED: 7 July 1871
p. 62

GUARDIAN: John G. Shackleford
WARD: Kenneth Smith
MISC: No assets ever known.
Ward is now of age, guardianship
discharged.
SWORN: 13 October 1871
RECORDED: 13 November 1871
p. 63

GUARDIAN: Sanford Palmer

FORMER GUARDIAN: Horace
Palmer
WARD: Sarah Palmer
MISC: Balance due paid to R.S.
Hicks, attorney for Sarah Palmer
who has married John W. Holder.
Discharged from her guardianship.
SWORN: 6 September 1871
RECORDED: 14 November 1871
p. 64-68

DECEASED: Wayne Montgomery
GUARDIAN: Jordan P. Jones
MINOR HEIRS: William H.
Montgomery, America B.
Montgomery,
Nelson W. Montgomery, Anna E.
Montgomery
MISC: Money had been received
from estate of Matilda Montgomery.
America B. Montgomery married
John T. Taylor, Her guardianship
discharged.
SWORN: 12 October 1871
RECORDED: 20 November 1871
pp. 69-70

DECEASED: Riley Main
GUARDIAN: Allen Brooner
HEIRS: Unnamed
SWORN: 12 October 1871
RECORDED: 20 November 1871
p. 71

DECEASED: Maranda Murphy
GUARDIAN: John Arnold
MINOR HEIRS: Andrew J. Arnold,
Sarah H. Arnold
MISC: Wards reside with guardian
and attend school.
SWORN: 10 October 1871
RECORDED: 20 November 1871
p. 72

DECEASED: George Anderson
GUARDIAN: William N. Combs
MINOR HEIRS: Unnamed
MISC: Heirs received pension.
SWORN: 11 October 1871
RECORDED: 20 November 1871
p. 73

DECEASED: Robert Miller
GUARDIAN: Enfield Miller
HEIRS: Unnamed
SWORN: 20 September 1871, C.E.
DeBruler
RECORDED: 20 November 1871
p. 74

DECEASED: Abel Crawford
GUARDIAN: William Thompson
HEIRS: Delia Crawford, Caroline
Crawford, Ruth Crawford, Samuel
A. Crawford, Ada Ann Crawford.
MISC: Guardianship discharged for
Delia & Caroline. Heirs received
pension. Ruth Crawford became 16
on 20 October 1867.
SWORN: 10 October 1871
RECORDED: 20 November 1871
pp. 75-77

DECEASED: Joseph Braddle
GUARDIAN: Geor. W. Scherginger
HEIR: Unnamed female
MISC: Heir has married Aloys
Ebner. Her guardianship dis-
charged.
SWORN: 9 October 1871
RECORDED: 20 November 1871
p. 78

DECEASED: E.C. Prince
GUARDIAN: Riley Prince
MINOR HEIRS: Elva A. Prince,
William A. Prince, Mary Ann
Prince, Martha L. Prince
MISC: Guardianship of Elva A.

Prince, now of age, discharged.
William A., Mary Ann and
Martha L. reside with guardian.
SWORN: 20 November 1871, Calvin
E. DeBruler
RECORDED: 20 November 1871
p. 79

GUARDIAN: Joel S. Tillman
WARD: Davis M. Hammond
MISC: Guardianship resigned.
SWORN: 10 October 1871
RECORDED: 20 November 1871
p. 80

DECEASED: James S. Lamar
GUARDIAN: Charles F. Nelson
MINOR HEIRS: David R. Lamar,
Edwinia C. Lamar
MISC: David R. Lamar has arrived
at full age. His guardianship
discharged.
SWORN: 11 October 1871
RECORDED: 20 November 1871
pp. 81-82

DECEASED: George W. Clark
GUARDIAN: John G. Stuteville
MINOR HEIRS: Mary E. Clark,
John S. Clark
MISC: Heirs received a pension.
SWORN: October 12, 1871
RECORDED: 20 November 1871
pp. 83-85

DECEASED: Isaac Varner
GUARDIAN: Lydia Hancock
MINOR HEIR: Alice Varner
MISC: Heir received a pension.
SWORN: 12 October 1871
RECORDED: 20 November 1871
pp. 86-87

DECEASED: George Stauber
GUARDIAN: Marin Hess
HEIRS: Unnamed

SWORN:  10 October 1871
RECORDED:  20 November 1871
p. 88

DECEASED:  John Masterson, Sr.
GUARDIAN:  Hugh E. Masterson
HEIRS:  Mary A. Masterson,
Sylvester Masterson, John
Masterson
SWORN:  15 September 1871
RECORDED:  20 November 1871
p. 89

GUARDIAN:  James Razor
WARD:  Barbara Blish, an insane
adult.
SWORN:  12 October 1871
RECORDED:  20 November 1871
p. 90

DECEASED:  Harvey Evans
GUARDIAN:  Malvira Evans
HEIRS:  Unnamed
SWORN:  9 October 1981
RECORDED:  20 November 1871
p. 91

GUARDIAN:  John S. Hammon
FORMER GUARDIAN: Joel S.
Tilman
WARD:  Davis M. Hammon

MISC:  Davis W. Hammon is
about 19 years of age and in college
in Elberfield in the state of Illinois.
SWORN:  11 October 1871
RECORDED:  27 November 1871
p. 92

GUARDIAN:  Wm. B. Richardson
WARD:  Josephing Harkey
SWORN:  11 October 1871
RECORDED:  27 November 1871
p. 93-94

DECEASED:  Orlando Bennett
GUARDIAN:  Fernando D. Waugh
MINOR HEIR:  Orlando L. Bennett,
SWORN:  13 October 1871
RECORDED:  27 November 1871
p. 95

DECEASED:  Amansus Philips
GUARDIAN:  John H. Huffman
INFANT HEIRS:  George Philips,
Daniel Philips
MISC:  Heirs received a pension.
Wards live with their mother
Elender J. Hays in Perry County,
Indiana.
SWORN:  October 10 1871
RECORDED:  27 November 1871
p. 96

DECEASED:  Rudolph Kaiser
GUARDIAN:  Michael Eisler
HEIRS:  Unnamed wards
MISC:  Wards live with mother in
Spencer County.
SWORN:  October 1871
RECORDED:  27 November 1871
p. 97

DECEASED:  James T. Morgan
GUARDIAN:  John Puller
HEIRS:  John Morgan, Wm. S.
Morgan, Mary E. Price, Amanda
Morgan, Elizabeth Morgan, Lulu
Morgan, David H. Morgan, James
T. Morgan, Robert L. Morgan
SWORN:  12 September 1871, R.S.
Hicks.
pp. 98-100

DECEASED:  Peter Rynacker
GUARDIAN:  Helena Rynacker
HEIRS:  Unnamed
SWORN:  9 October 1871

RECORDED: 27 November 1871
p. 101

DECEASED: John Heubschenan
GUARDIAN: Jno Polston
HEIR: John Heubschenan and others
MISC: Ward John now 21 years of age; his guardianship discharged. Other wards unnamed.
SWORN: 9 October 1871
RECORDED: 27 November 1871
p. 102

DECEASED: James McLellan
GUARDIAN: Joshua B. Selby
HEIRS: James O. McLellan, Serilda McLellan
MISC: Heirs received a pension.
SWORN: 9 October 1871
RECORDED: 27 November 1871
p. 103

DECEASED: Zacharia Skelton
GUARDIAN: Robert J. Skelton
HEIRS: Unnamed
SWORN: 10 October 1871
RECORDED: 27 November 1871
p. 104

DECEASED: Nicholas Kohler
GUARDIAN: Jobst Scherzer
HEIRS: Unnamed
MISC: Heirs received a pension.
SWORN: 9 October 1871
RECORDED: 27 November 1871
p. 105

DECEASED: Jacob Brenner
GUARDIAN James I. Jones
HEIRS: Anna Brenner, Emma Brenner, Charles Brenner
MISC: Wards reside with mother in Spencer County and Charles attends school.

SWORN: 11 October 1871
RECORDED: 27 November 1871
p. 106

DECEASED: Geo. W. Masters
GUARDIAN: Ora Broshears
HEIRS: Unnamed
MISC: Guardian asks to be relieved from reporting.
SWORD: 13 October 1871
RECORDED: 27 November 1871
p. 107.

DECEASED: Geo. W. Masters
GUARDIAN: Wm. Woodward
FORMER GUARDIAN: Ira Broshears
MINOR HEIRS: William P. Masters, Charles Masters, Daniel D. Masters
MISC: Heirs received a pension.
SWORN: 18 October 1871
RECORDED: 27 November 1871.
p. 108

DECEASED: Mary H. Eisler
GUARDIAN: Conrad Hetzel
HEIRS: Unnamed
MISC: Father of wards: William Eisler. Guardianship terminated.
SWORN: 10 October 1871
RECORDED: 29 November 1871
p. 109

DECEASED: Joseph Cox
GUARDIAN: C.E. Coombs
HEIRS: Sarah E. Cox, Cordelia F. Cox
MISC: Both heirs received monies from C.E. Cox's share of estate.
SWORN: 11 October 1871
RECORDED: 29 November 1871
pp. 110-11

DECEASED: Grant Dunigan

192

GUARDIAN: Nancy A. Dunigan
MINOR HEIRS: Lora, Fanny,
William, Belle Dunigan
SWORN: 10 October 1871
RECORDED: 29 November 1871
pp. 112-13

DECEASED: Thomas Jackson
GUARDIAN: George V. Sutton
MINOR HEIR: William Jackson
SWORN: 11 October 1871
RECORDED: 29 November 1871
p. 114

DECEASED: Bernard Walters
GUARDIAN: Thomas H. Brown
HEIRS: Henry D. Walters,
FranciscoWalters
MISC: Henry has arrived at full
age. His guardianship discharged.
SWORN: 12 October 1871
RECORDED: 30 November 1871
pp. 115-18

DECEASED: Jesse Hurst
GUARDIAN: Joseph Varner
HEIRS: Sarah S. Hurst, Letitia
Hurst.
MISC: Received money from Albert
Bayless in bastardy suit. Clement
Pierciall, administrator of Jesse
Hurst estate. Heirs received a pen-
sion. Guardian posted bond, Gust-
avus Woodward and John Meeks,
sureties. Sarah Hurst resides in

Spencer county with Mrs. Elias
Emswick. Letitia resides with the
guardian.
SWORN: 10 October 1871
RECORDED: 30 November 1871
pp. 119-21

DECEASED: John Jackson
GUARDIAN: Mary Jackson
MINOR HEIRS: Missouri Jackson,
Catherine Jackson, Arvilla Jackson,
John Jackson
MISC: Missouri Jackson is now
married to a Mr. Simpson. Arvilla
Jackson has received her share.
SWORN: 10 October 1871
RECORDED: 30 November 1871
pp. 122-23

GUARDIAN: J.A. Haaff
WARD: William Haaff
MISC: George H. Haaff signed
report.
SWORN: 9 October 1871
RECORDED: 30 November 1871
p. 123

DECEASED: John Foster
GUARDIAN: Wolf Vogle
HEIRS: George Foster, John Foster,
John G. Foster
MISC: Heirs are now all of age,
guardianships discontinued.
RECORDED: 30 November 1871
p. 124

# STARKE CO. INDIANA MARRIAGES 1850-79

Transcribed by Ruth Dorrel

Starke Co., Indiana was formed by statute from parts of St. Joseph and attached territory, and was organized January 15, 1850. The first marriage license issued in Starke Co. was in September 1850. The first land entry in what is now this county was in 1832. Hence, civil records for the area prior to 1850 should be in St. Joseph Co. Books A and B of marriages are found on microfilm in the Genealogy Division of the Indiana State Library. Licenses are in chronological order in the order in which they were issued. Three dates are on most of the records: date license applied for and issued; date returned and recorded; and the date the marriage occured. Dates the marriages occured are used in this transcription except in those few cases when the license was never returned. This transcription is of Book A and the first 259 pages of Book B in order. In 1974, Ruth Slevin transcribed both books, placing the names in alphabetical order by grooms and by brides. This compilation is in the Genealogy Division of the State Library. Also in the Genealogy Division are three marriage indexes for Starke Co. The first, although titled *Index to Marriage Applications Starke County 1840-1920* Inc., actually begins with April 19, 1905. The second, titled *Index to Marriage Records, Starke County, 1896-1938*, begins with July 27, 1896. The third, although titled *Index to Marriage Transcripts Starke County 1899-1938*, also begins with April 19, 1905. As far as can be determined no records exist of marriages between April 1890 and July 27, 1896. The remainder of Book B will be published in a later issue of THG.

## BOOK A

| PAGE | DATE | GROOM — BRIDE |
|------|------|---------------|
| 1 | 24 Sep 1850 | James Cannon-Nancy Lane |
| | 26 Apr 1851 | Abraham Welch-Elizabeth Collins |
| 2 | 11 May 1851 | Samuel Tinkey-Catherine Kibler |
| | 29 May 1851 | James Evans-Mary J. Graham |
| 3 | 12 Jun 1851 | David F. Woods-Francis Cunningham |
| | 19 Feb 1852 | Solomon K. Ulery-Margaret McGowen |
| 4 | 28 Mar 1852 | Andrew W. Porter-Rebeca Mahan |
| | 19 May 1852 | Solon O. Whitson-Sarah Turner |
| 5 | 9 Jun 1852 | Charles Humphreys-Martha Abbott |
| | 28 Jun 1852 | George W. Hardy-Mary McColm |
| 6 | 26 Jul 1852 | Jacob Bogarth-Charlotty Short |
| | 4 Aug 1852 | Samuel L. Vanblaricum-Mary Ann Wyant |
| 7 | 4 Nov 1852 | Moses Hershberger-Mary Burke |
| | 3 Nov 1852 | Abraham Kinsey-Anna Griggs |
| 8 | 27 Nov 1852 | Adam Lambert-Rachel Ann Tilman |
| | 30 Dec 1852 | Daniel Dunklebarger-Sarah Jane Bell |

| PAGE | DATE | GROOM — BRIDE |
|---|---|---|
| 9 | 29 Dec 1852 lic | J.D. Meece-Alvira M. Patterson |
|  | 16 Jan 1853 | Stephen W. Jackson-Margaret Cherry |
| 9a | 20 Jan 1853 | Erastus Flanagan-Catharine Ann Addington |
|  | 3 Feb 1853 | John F. Tracy-Mary Jane McCullough |
| 10 | 17 Feb 1853 | Nathaniel M. Garard-Nancy Bright |
|  | 12 Apr 1853 | Benjamin F. Wyant-Mary Martha Vanblaricum |
| 11 | 14 Apr 1853 | James M. Williams-Sarah Vinson |
|  | 17 Apr 1853 | Tilley Page-Mary Crysmore |
| 12 | 19 Apr 1853 | John M. Morris-Elizabeth Shaw |
|  | 22 May 1853 | Samuel B. Coffin-Catharine Hatter |
| 13 | 24 May 1853 | Bryant L. Vinson-Louisa Vanblaricom |
|  | 26 Jul 1853 | Hiram Jones-Elizabeth Vannote |
| 14 | 29 Sep 1853 | William A. Turnbull-Eliza Osborn |
|  | 12 Nov 1853 | John W. Osborn-Sarah Mishler |
| 15 | 20 Dec 1854[3] | Robert C. Wood-Elizabeth Koontz |
|  | 23 Feb 1854 | Alfred Humphreys-Frances Adalade Jackson |
| 16 | 9 Mar 1854 | William H. Jackson-Hannah Manwell |
|  | 19 Mar 1854 | Jonathan Phillips-Susannah Brown |
| 17 | 20 Mar 1854 | William Miller-Anna Kibler |
|  | 30 Mar 1854 | George Graham-Elizabeth McFarland |
| 18 | 9 Apr 1854 | Isaac Bascome-Melissa Farrow |
|  | 12 Jun 1854 | Thomas Slight-Susanah Mariah Fry |
| 19 | 3 Aug 1854 | Paul W. Sult-Elizabeth Kibler |
|  | 27 Jul 1854 | William Lany-Catharine Stephenson |
| 20 | 25 Jul 1854 | John S. Inman-Catharine Watkins |
|  | 6 Aug 1854 | John N. Morris-Elizabeth Mishler |
| 21 | 28 Sep 1855[4] | John Cunningham-Ellen Taylor |
|  | 25 Oct 1854 | Henry H. Hill-Elizabeth Ann Bozarth |
| 22 | 2 Jan 1855 | William Shuster-Jane Wolfinbarger |
|  | 25 Jan 1855 | Allen Humphreys-Permelia Witehead |
| 23 | 1 Mar 1855 | Amos Fry-Catharine O'Neal |
|  | 13 Mar 1855 | N.H.K. Foss-Martha Ann Brown |
| 24 | 19 Mar 1855 | John W. Turnbull-Juliann Blew |
|  | 27 Mar 1855 | Jacob G. Black-Adaline Short |
| 25 | 25 Mar 1855 | Willard Fletcher-Susanna Peoples |
|  | 1 Apr 1855 | David Conner-Rachel Truax |
| 26 | 16 Apr 1855 | David McCumber-Caroline Coffin |
|  | 1 Jul 1855 | Edward A. Tibbets-Harriet Humphreys |
| 27 | 7 Oct 1855 | John Shirley-Lydia Parker |
|  | 21 Oct 1855 | Samuel Parker-Elizabeth Chapman |
| 28 | 28 Oct 1855 | Albert B. Willey-Joannabeck Prettyman |
|  | 4 Oct 1855 | James H. Parker-Sarey Romig |
| 29 | 27 Nov 1855 | John Phelps-Harriett E. White |
|  | 23 Dec 1856[5] | Isaac Romig-Mary Good |
| 30 | 23 Dec 1855 | James S. Mounts-Mary Ann Akers |
|  | [25 Dec 1855] | George S. Dumont-Keziah Pettis |

| PAGE | DATE | GROOM — BRIDE |
|------|------|---------------|
| 31 | 14 Feb 1856 | George A. Anderson-Mariah Koontz |
|    | 21 Feb 1856 | George T. Turnbull-Mary Ann Akkridge |
| 32 | 1 Apr 1856 | Cornelius Short-Barbary Ellen McFarlin |
|    | 10 Apr 1856 | Benjamin A. Dunklebarger-Mary E. Bascome |
| 33 | 11 Apr 1856 | Joshua Timmons-Emaly Lewis |
|    | 28 Apr 1856 | David Beebe-Mary Lane |
| 34 | 25 May 1856 | Henry Tuman-Mary Ann Fletcher |
|    | 5 Jun 1856 | Peter Shaw-Martha Jane Fletcher |
| 35 | 5 Jun 1856 | Conrad Groshause-Liza Jane Demasters |
|    | 11 Sep 1856 | Joseph Romig-Mactiline Shirk |
| 36 | 25 Sep 1856 | Jacob A. Bellhimer-Elizabeth Smith |
|    | 19 Oct 1856 | Jacob Snyder-Sarah Adaline German |
| 37 | 27 Oct 1856 lic | Orlow Green-Elizabeth Alhert |
|    | 7 Nov 1856 | James Milford Dickson-Mary Elizabeth Bright |
| 38 | 9 Nov 1856 | William A. Wolverton-Margaret M. Brundage |
|    | 12 Dec 1856 | George Evans-Mary Elizabeth Bell |
| 39 | 13 Dec 1856 | Silas E. Timmons-Julia Ann Short |
|    | 31 Jan 1857 | Silas Howard-Sarah Blew |
| 40 | 15 Feb 1857 | Aaron McCumber-Phebe Jane Fletcher |
|    | 18 Feb 1857 | Isaac B. Turner-Matilda Ann Maxy |
| 41 | 19 Feb 1857 | David Conner-Elizabeth Eskridge |
|    | 1 Mar 1857 | William Lock-Eliza Jane Way |
| 42 | 1 Mar 1857 | William H. Fletcher-Tabitha Wyant |
|    | 15 Mar 1857 | Peter Miller-Esther Ann Bascom |
| 43 | 19 Mar 1857 | Joshua O.B. Prettyman-Mary Bootes |
|    | 12 Apr 1857 | Joseph Heminger-Amanda Williams |
| 44 | 31 May 1857 | James M. Tucker-Margaret A. Collins |
|    | 3 Jun 1857 | Joshua J. Collins-Sarah Ann Fry |
| 45 | 1 Jun 1857 | John Lock-Melinda J. Myers |
|    | 21 Jun 1857 | George W. Crismore-Mary Ann Foster |
| 46 | 16 Jul 1857 | John T. Jones-Martha Humphreys |
|    | 17 Jul 1857 | Luther Coffin-Mary McCumber |
| 47 | 2 Sep 1857 | William T. Cox-Phebe Cox |
| 48 | 27 Aug 1857 | Rendel L. Short-Martha Ann Elkins |
|    | 6 Sep 1857 | Henry C. Petro-Sarah J. Adair |
| 49 | 20 Sep 1857 | Nathan McCumber-Nancy Jane Welch |
|    | 20 Sep 1857 | Charles Wm. Moses-Sarah Francis Welsh |
| 50 | 18 Oct 1857 | Ralph Williams-Jane Watkins |
|    | 19 Oct 1857 lic | Barney Leffert-Margaret Rothermel |
| 51 | 5 Nov 1857 | Hiram Abbot-Cathrine Rowland |
| 52 | 5 Nov 1857 | Andrew W. Porter-Mary Slocum |
|    | 15 Nov 1857 | Joseph Argo-Susan Heminger |
| 53 | 26 Nov 1857 | John Collins-Ellen Reede |
|    | 30 Nov 1857 | Hiram Turnbull-Almira Cole |
| 54 | 8 Dec 1857 | William T. Landon-Elisabeth Case |
|    | 23 Dec 1857 | William Anderson-Elizabeth J. Jackson |

| PAGE | DATE | GROOM — BRIDE |
|------|------|---------------|
| 55 | 24 Dec 1857 | Alexander M. Hedglen-Martha Jane Maxey |
|    | 11 Jan 1858 lic | Constance Vurpillat-Elizabeth Rothermel |
| 56 | 31 Jan 1858 | Elias Romig-Elizabeth Foster |
|    | 28 Jan 1858 | Lorenzo L. Williams-Sarah L. Pike |
| 57 | 11 Feb 1858 | John C. Lain-Margaret Hann |
|    | 21 Feb 1858 | Daniel Mishler-Margaret Jane Walters |
| 58 | 7 Mar 1858 | Alvan E. Clark-Catharine Bradly |
|    | 19 Mar 1858 | Augustus Fritz-Henrietta Drager |
| 59 | 23 Mar 1858 | Jacob Walters-Margaret Mishler |
|    | 21 Apr 1858 | Cornelius Stevenson-Chloe Crites |
| 60 | 22 Apr 1858 | George W. Hemminger-Mary Vincent |
|    | 26 Apr 1858 | John Vanarsdalen-Mary West |
| 61 | 27 May 1858 | John W. Garrett-Martha Hann |
|    | 22 Jul 1858 | Samuel Koontz-Sarah Sult |
| 62 | 24 Jul 1858 | George Anderson, Jr.-Cynthia Jane Monroe |
|    | 8 Aug 1858 | James Evans-Phebee Brundrige |
| 63 | 29 Aug 1858 | John Daum-Elvira Smith |
|    | 5 Aug 1858 | David Dewit-Susannah Carr |
| 64 | 4 Jul 1858 | James Martin-Nancy Ann Lucas |
|    | 7 Oct 1858 | Joseph Austin-Delila Dial |
| 65 | 4 Nov 1858 | William Cellers-Christena Foster |
|    | 31 Jul 1858 | Isaac Thomas-Julia Turnbull |
| 66 | 29 Nov 1858 | Lafayette Abbott-Elizabeth Williams |
|    | 5 Dec 1858 | James J. Thompson-Mary Lain |
| 67 | 21 May 1859 | William Haines-Mary J. Daugherty |
|    | 30 Dec 1858 | Philip Crites-Dorothy Reed |
| 68 | 6 Jan 1859 | John Miller-Sarah Lain |
|    | 6 Jan 1859 | Benjamin S. Bell-Nancy R. Williams |
| 69 | 16 Jan 1859 | Wingate Prettyman-Catharine Jones |
|    | 27 Jan 1859 | George W. Cook-Elizabeth C. Kephart |
| 70 | 11 Feb 1859 | John McGill-Mary Miller |
|    | 30 Mar 1859 | Henry H. Wyant-Angeline Hagle |
| 71 | 22 Apr 1859 | Milford C. Dixson-Sarah E. Peoples |
|    | 28 Apr 1859 | George Vannote-Mary Ann Deen |
| 72 | 3 Jun 1859 | John J. Justice-Mary J. Payne |
|    | 12 Jun 1859 | John E. Smith-Lydie E. Barton |
| 73 | 14 Aug 1859 | Abel G. Monroe-Mary E. Monroe |
|    | 22 Aug 1859 | David Hemminger-Hester A. Peoples |
| 74 | 18 Sep 1859 | John E. Short-Armenia P. Jackson |
|    | 12 Oct 1859 | Mathias J. German-Harriet Smith |
| 75 | 18 Jan 1860 | Thomas E. Quicksell-Angeline Sult |
|    | 22 Jan 1860 | James Evans-Axa Ann Kepperlin |
| 76 | 5 Feb 1860 | John B. Poter-Catharine Leese |
|    | 9 Feb 1860 | James P. Fry-Mahala Jane Collins |
| 77 | 14 Feb 1860 | Aaron Monroe-Elizabeth Koontz |
|    | 1 Mar 1860 | Samuel Shivley-Susana Koontz |

| PAGE | DATE | GROOM — BRIDE |
|------|------|---------------|
| 78 | 25 Mar 1860 | Wm. Hamilton Parker-Mary Canaan |
|  | 5 Apr 1860 | Okeley Askridge-Elizabeth Vanasdlan |
| 79 | 15 Apr 1860 | Sylvester Bascome-Eliza Elston |
|  | 8 Jun 1860 | James Clark-Ranchael Steinsback |
| 80 | 10 Jun 1860 | James Canaan-Matilda Fry |
|  | 20 Jun 1860 | Loima Gates-Sarah J. Cory |
| 81 | 28 Jul 1860 | Joseph Hemminger-Susana Ranstead |
|  | 2 Sep 1860 | Harvey C. Green-Ruth Cannan |
| 82 | 11 Sep 1860 | Phillip Weller-Mary Ditrick |
|  | 7 Oct 1860 | Hiram A. Hall-Alvira Monroz |
| 83 | 27 Nov 1860 | John Dawson-Margaret E. Petro |
|  | 27 Nov 1860 | Jacob Emich-Elizabeth Hay |
| 84 | 5 Dec 1860 | Eli M. Lambert-Louesa C. Armer |
|  | 26 Dec 1860 | George W. Myers-Mary Jane Kinsey |
| 85 | 27 Dec 1860 | Henson Lock-Druzilla Persis Way |
|  | 2 Jan 1861 | Matthias T. HKepner-Louisa B. Spoor |
| 86 | 21 Jan 1861 | Jessee Fletcher-Elizabeth J. Coffin |
|  | 29 Feb 1861 | Morris Stack-Mary Hays |
| 87 | 21 Mar 1861 | Jesse Slight-Mary Elizabeth Corbin |
|  | 30 May 1861 | Jonathan Sanford-Caroline Hepner |
| 88 | 12 May 1861 | Martin D. Prickett-Mary Ann Bell |
|  | 15 May 1861 | William C. Spoor-Henrietta C. German |
| 89 | 26 May 1861 | Adrian V.H. Foote Julia A. Thornton |
|  | 7 Jul 1861 | Willoughby M. McCormack-Sarah Smalley |
| 90 | 10 Aug 1861 | Joab G. Brown-Eve Christena Goon |
|  | 12 Aug 1861 | Francis Yager-Matilda Koontz |
| 91 | 17 Aug 1861 | John W. Bockover-Violet Case |
|  | 30 Aug 1861 | Robert Johnston-Louisa McIlvain |
| 92 | 6 Sep 1861 | Francis M. Fletcher-Susan Cole |
|  | 13 Oct 1861 | George Briggs-Julia Ann Hay |
| 93 | 30 Oct 1861 | Jacob Walder-Margaret Working |
|  | 7 Nov 1861 | Martin Eisenhour-Sarah Ann Sherck |
| 94 | 24 Nov 1861 | Granville P. Edwards-Catharine Collins |
|  | 25 Dec 1861 | James Topper-Rebecca Case |
| 95 | 30 Dec 1861lic | Frederick Hoffman-Sarah Hackelroth |
|  | 1 Jan 1862 | William H.H. Coffin-Eliza E. Blythe |
| 96 | 6 Jan 1862 | August Fretzsha-Jane Sult |
|  | 23 Jan 1862 | Michael Miller-Martha Ann Short |
| 97 | 4 Feb 1862 | Leonard Leonard-Ellen Collins |
|  | 23 Feb 1862 | Francis Barton-Elizabeth Sult |
| 98 | 20 Mar 1862 | Pernel Dennis-Melissa A. Hann |
|  | 20 Mar 1862 | Spencer Brinkley-Sarah Hackelrode |
| 99 | 1 May 1862 | John Miller-Lucretia J. German |
|  | 8 May 1862 | Daniel Harris-Edith Brinkley |
| 100 | 15 May 1862lic | Albert H. Taylor-Mary Baughman |
|  | Jun 1862 | Michael P. Eisenhour-Matilda Sherck |

| PAGE | DATE | GROOM — BRIDE |
|------|------|---------------|
| 101 | 3 Jul 1862 | Wayland Fletcher-Sarah Jane Scott |
| | 28 Jul 1862 | Joseph R. McCumber-Sarah Cole |
| 102 | 26 Jul 1862 | Charles Barton-Amazetta Dillon |
| | 1 Sep 1862lic | Samuel Osborn-Amanda McCumber |
| 103 | 26 Oct 1862 | William Netherton-Elender Hann |
| | 23 Nov 1862 | James White-Catharine Keefe |
| 104 | 8 Jan 1863 | George F. McCormick-Martha Jane Larew |
| | 22 Jan 1863 | John Brandall-Catharine Sherck |
| 105 | 14 Feb 1863 | Wm. Elmendorff-Hattie L. Sandford |
| | 26 Mar 1863 | Peter Dipert-Florilla Cupp |
| 106 | 27 Mar 1863 | Josephus H. Prettyman-Sarah S. Larew |
| | 26 Feb 1863 | Stiles Rose-Isabel Long |
| 107 | 25 Apr 1863 | Jefferson Seagraves-Caroline Yahne |
| | 14 Jun 1863 | James Holderman-Margaret E. Taylor |
| 108 | 6 Jul 1863 | James F. Miller-Samantha C. Ellis |
| | 10 Jul 1863 | Walter G. Rogers-Emma Shoup |
| 109 | 25 Jul 1863lic | William M. Rooker-Catharine Davison |
| | 22 Aug 1863 | Lewis Timm-Wilhelmena Freiday |
| 110 | 24 Sep 1863 | Joshua N. German-Elizabeth Daisey |
| | 16 Oct 1863 | Daniel Poor-Mary J. Goldsberry |
| 111 | 20 Oct 1863 | John H. Geller-Ruth Green |
| | 1 Nov 1863 | Robert Johnson-Saloma Goon |
| 112 | 29 Oct 1863 | George Jones-Telitha Fletcher |
| | 5 Nov 1863 | Andrew J. Miller-Georgiana Brinkman |
| 113 | 13 Nov 1863 | William H. Myers-Mary Ellen Osborn |
| | 14 Nov 1863 | Abraham J. Gingrich-Mary Ann Secrest |
| 114 | 1 Dec 1863 | Robert H. Bender-Elvira J. Morris |
| | 12 Dec 1863 | Austin Dial-Edna Beatty |
| 115 | 20 Dec 1863 | Elias C. Hagle-Susannah Dean |
| | 31 Dec 1863 | Asa Brown-Harriet Prettyman |
| 116 | 17 Jan 1864 | Truman M. Smith-Elmira Justice |
| 117 | 7 Feb 1864 | John Reselka-Mary Ken |
| | 14 Feb 1864 | Jacob Quigley-Louisa J. Couch |
| 118 | 14 Feb 1864 | Franklin Miller-Catharine Kelver |
| 119 | 10 Mar 1864 | Joshua King-Margaret A. Cannon |
| | 12 Mar 1864 | Wilson Simcox-Martha J. Larew |
| 120 | 17 Mar 1864 | Jesse Roose-Julia A. Anderson |
| | 17 Mar 1864 | William Truax-Mary E. Cline |
| 121 | 17 Mar 1864 | Cyrus Huey-Laura M. Wood |
| | 24 Mar 1864 | Philip Awald-Lydia Koontz |
| 122 | 27 Mar 1864 | Jacob Reed-Harriet Anderson |
| 123 | 12 May 1864 | David Brandal-Martha Hornig |
| | 12 Jun 1864 | Henry Sult-Susan Shively |
| 124 | 5 Jun 1864 | Aurelius W. Hoffman-Eliza Jane Personett |
| | 11 Jul 1864 | William H. West-Nancy Jane Smith |
| 125 | 17 Jul 1864 | William Ayers-Nancy P. Wood |
| | 14 Aug 1864 | Stephen C. Lark-Margaret Fallis |

| PAGE | DATE | GROOM — BRIDE |
|------|------|---------------|
| 126 | 22 Oct 1864 | Daniel Peoples-Armaretta Reed |
|  | 31 Oct 1864lic | John Roup-Sophia Gaston |
| 127 | 6 Nov 1864 | Nicholas Lock-Esamel Staner |
|  | 5 Nov 1864 | Jefferson Segraves-Achsah Ann Kris |
| 128 | 4 Dec 1864 | Ezekiel Cole-Jemima Bright |
|  | 5 Feb 1865 | Amos Horner-Eliza Emigh |
| 129 | 25 Mar 1865 | William Hagle-Cordelia Mercer |
|  | 9 Mar 1865 | Nathaniel Rebstock-Nancy Ann Stewart |
| 130 | 8 Apr 1865 | Joseph J. McCormick-Adaline Kelly |
|  | 11 May 1865 | Isaac Roose-Olita Taylor |
| 131 | 23 Jun 1865 | James M. Davis-Sarah E. Kelly |
|  | 5 Jul 1865 | Jesse Lattemer-Elizabeth Shafer |
| 132 | 15 Jul 1865 | Albert Stevenson-Sarah Jane Petro |
|  | 3 Nov 1858 | Joel Dunkelbarger-Harriet M. Sleight |
| 133 | 10 Aug 1865 | Milton Haines Chapman-Rachel Collins |
|  | 10 Sep 1865 | William N. Patmore-Edith E. Stoops |
| 134 | 26 Sep 1865 | Michael Tenme-Anna Spletstover |
|  | 17 Sep 1865 | Charles C. Hine-Mary E. Jarrett |
| 135 | 28 Sep 1865 | John Fetters-Emely M. Hawkins |
|  | 11 Oct 1865 | James Hamilton-Hannah Elizabeth Ludlow |
| 136 | 15 Oct 1865 | Solomon Speelman-Mary A. Larimar |
|  | 13 Oct 1865 | Charles Booth-Sarah Secrest |
| 137 | 22 Oct 1865 | Levi Stevenson-Rosanna Gould |
| 138 | 12 Nov 1865 | James A. Bell-Sarah Catharine McFarland |
|  | 12 Nov 1865 | James Short-Cristena Westhaver |
| 139 | 22 Nov 1865 | George W. Scofield-Vashti L. Personett |
|  | 25 Nov 1865 | John C. Larrew-Catharine Jackson |
| 140 | 3 Dec 1865 | Caleb S. Bootes-Sarah A. Prettyman |
| 141 | 14 Dec 1865 | Asbury Evans-Alvira Evarts |
|  | 12 Dec 1865 | George W. Vankirk-Mary Kinsey |
| 142 | 17 Dec 1865 | Henry B. Wyatt-Sarah Ann Adair |
|  | 17 Dec 1865 | Allen Cole-Cetharine Wyant |
| 143 | 25 Dec 1865 | Jacob Garnart-Mary S. White |
|  | 25 Dec 1865 | Hiram A. Deen-Leona Gould |
| 144 | 25 Dec 1865 | John H. Bernard-Eliza A. Taylor |
|  | 25 Dec 1865 | David S. Couchman-Cynthia E. Brewer |
| 145 | 10 Jan 1866 | Alva H. Scofield-Martha A. Speelman |
|  | 14 Jan 1866 | Albert Moser-Laura Jane Miller |
| 146 | 11 Jan 1866 | Phillip B. Waterhouse-Julian Thomas |
|  | 17 Jan 1866 | L.A. Garner-Arena Morris |
| 147 | 20 Jan 1866 | Ebenezer Baughman-Harriet German |
|  | 29 Jan 1866 | Clinton Chapman-Phebe Castleman |
| 148 | 22 Feb 1866 | William Kelly-Mary C. Spellman |
|  | 20 Feb 1866 | Daniel Hay-Rebecca Simmons |
| 149 | 1 Mar 1866 | Samuel Nepstosk-Catharine Stewart |
|  | 4 Mar 1866 | Elvin Ellis-Charity Boots |

| PAGE | DATE | GROOM — BRIDE |
|------|------|---------------|
| 150 | 11 Mar 1866 | Henry Wineger-Rebecca Lemon |
|     | 20 Mar 1866 | Harvy J. Good-Sarah F. Thompson |
| 151 | 8 Apr 1866 | John Reed-Eliza J. Parker |
|     | 9 Apr 1866 | Stephen N. Matlock-Winnie J. Andrew |
| 152 | 10 Apr 1866 | William Simmons-Sarah Grove |
|     | 22 Apr 1866 | John Henry McFarland-Mary Westhaver |
| 153 | 26 Apr 1866 | John Wolfram-Elizabeth Groshouts |
|     | 8 May 1866 | Artemius Hanes-Menervia J. Stringback |
| 154 | 30 Apr 1866 | Alfred Taylor-Nancy J. Bennett |
|     | 30 Apr 1866 | Cornelius Tanner-Adelia Cory |
| 155 | 22 Apr 1866 | Morrison Lawrence-Maransa Ellis |
|     | 15 Jul 1866 | C.M. Hervey-Leah Elizabeth Goon |
| 156 | 27 Jul 1866 | Alfred Quin-Mahala Jane Taylor |
|     | 16 Aug 1866 | Robert J. Faris-Sarah M. Williams |
| 157 | 19 Sep 1866 | Manuel Lawrence-Martha Ellis |
|     | 22 Sep 1866 | Lewis W. Parsloe-Sarah A. Wyatt |
| 158 | 23 Sep 1866 | Jonathan Bascom-Martha Cole |
|     | 28 Sep 1866 | George Canaan-Rosanna Stevenson |
| 159 | 9 Oct 1866 | James K. Smith-Marietia Jones |
|     | 1 Oct 1866 | Dennis Willard-Erne E. Linder |
| 160 | 14 Oct 1866 | Martin Whitmore-Keziah C. Bell |
|     | 18 Oct 1866 | Isaac Reed-Susannah Gurnsy |
| 161 | 21 Oct 1866 | Jesse L. Critchfield-Martha A. Miller |
|     | 21 Oct 1866 | Eli E. Ham-Nancy A. Swartz |
| 162 | 4 Dec 1866 | Levi Stevenson-Malinda J. Myers |
|     | 23 Dec 1866 | George Hann-Rebecca M. Wynegar |
| 163 | 1 Jan 1867 | John Veal-Rebecca Canaan |
|     | 27 Jan 1867 | John Hardy-Mary E.J. Whett |
| 164 | 24 Jan 1867 | John Downey-Jane Canon |
|     | 27 Jan 1867 | Joseph Akers-Nancy C.J.A. Heath |
| 165 | 21 Feb 1867 | Barnhart Hasty-Margaret Kelly |
|     | 28 Feb 1867 | Phillip Groshaus-Eliza Humphreys |
| 166 | 3 Mar 1867 | Andrew J. Nutter-Amelia M. Scott |
|     | 20 Mar 1867 | Robert V. Brinkly-Elvira Houghton |
| 167 | 7 Mar 1867 | Royal H. Tremain-Mahalia S. Wise |
|     | 22 Mar 1867 | William Haolloway-Elizabeth Learman |
| 168 | 12 Mar 1867 | James Vanloon-Kasiah Strayer |
|     | 13 Mar 1867 | John S. Given-Louvisa Cartright |
| 169 | 27 Mar 1867 | Henry J. Headley-Lydia L. Kitchel |
|     | 17 Mar 1867 | Joseph F. Chapman-Emeline Turner |
| 170 | 24 Mar 1867 | Oliver H.P. Beatty-Terrissa A. Crabs |
|     | 7 Apr 1867 | James M. Scott-Sarah Swartz |
| 171 | 23 Apr 1867 | Henry L. White-Enestine Long |
|     | 14 Apr 1867 | John Cougle-Sarah Coats |
| 172 | 13 Apr 1867 | Andrew J. Graham-Elizabeth Long |
|     | 20 Apr 1867 | Levi Sherow-Henrieta Hoag |

| PAGE | DATE | GROOM — BRIDE |
|------|------|---------------|
| 173 | 22 Apr 1867 | Conrad Susdorf-Christena Brown |
| | 27 Apr 1867lic | Wallace L. Daggy-Caroline Bladen |
| 174 | 29 Apr 1867lic | Mikel Micheaaelson-Christena Pearson |
| | 2 May 1867 | John Heminger-Elizabeth Rocks |
| 175 | 16 May 1867 | John A. Rovenstine-Rosetta A. Gould |
| | 5 Jun 1867 | Andrew J. Uncapher-M.E.L. McCormick |
| 176 | 20 Jun 1867 | David A. Wynegar-Mary E. McCune |
| | 27 Jun 1867 | James Eskridge-Eve Deen |
| 177 | 29 Jun 1867 | William Ausem-Lovesa Swartz |
| | 4 Jul 1867 | William G. Pierson-Sarah E. Chaney |
| 178 | 4 Jul 1867 | George W. Justice-Ellen N. Pierson |
| | 3 Jul 1867 | Wallace L. Gould-Sarah Jane Swartzell |
| 179 | 21 Jul 1867 | Andrew Groshaus-Maria Koontz |
| | 12 Aug 1867 | John H. Vosburgh-Eveline Ford |
| 180 | 18 Aug 1867 | Samuel Freet-Abegal Catherine Coates |
| | 18 Aug 1867 | William McCormick-Sabena S. Davis |
| 181 | 25 Aug 1867 | William Speelman-Hannah Hatter |
| | 8 Sep 1867 | John H. Huff-Hannah M. Myers |
| 182 | 15 Sep 1867 | Peter Werner-Malinda McPheron |
| | 10 Oct 1867 | John Reed-Thursy Wedington |

## BOOK B

| | | |
|------|------|---------------|
| 1 | 6 Oct 1867 | Orin Humphreys-Mary Emigh |
| | 17 Oct 1867 | Joseph H. Wynegar-Esther M. Payn |
| 2 | 16 Oct 1867 | Aaron N. Prettyman-Lavanna C. Larew |
| | 20 Oct 1867 | John Head-Syntha Ann Nitcher |
| 3 | 28 Oct 1867 | William Keller-Edith E. Palmore |
| | 24 Oct 1867 | John Brown-Matilda C. Lain |
| 4 | 3 Nov 1867 | Frederick Cramer-Jane Howard |
| | 14 Nov 1867 | James M. Tucker-Hannah W. Lain |
| 5 | 19 Dec 1867 | Josiah Scott-Mary Angeline Seymour |
| | 5 Jan 1868 | Jacob Emig-Lovena Orris |
| 6 | 29 Jan 1868 | Sidney H. Smith-Sarah Talbert |
| | 28 Jan 1868 | Robert Milton Bailey-Harriet Baughman |
| 7 | 30 Jan 1868 | John E. Collins-Margarett C. Prettyman |
| | 16 Feb 1868 | Joseph Long-Rebecca Ann Bell |
| 8 | 16 Feb 1868 | Joseph H. Williams-Maggie H. Masterson |
| | 27 Feb 1868 | Ephraim Wilson-Julima H. Brown |
| 9 | 22 Feb 1868 | John P. Smart-Elizabeth Ann Horner |
| | 27 Feb 1868 | Reily H. Craig-Mary Bliss |
| 10 | 1 Mar 1868 | William J. Good-Mary M. Wolfram |
| | 5 Mar 1868 | William Anderson-Calesta C. Hartsock |
| 11 | 1 Mar 1868 | Seth Eskridge-Mary Ellen Clinger |
| | 6 Apr 1868 | Urias J. Wise-Emma J. Haggerty |
| 12 | 22 Mar 1868 | William N. Conner-Alice A. Shoup |
| | 24 Mar 1868 | Samuel Davis-Mary Genrick |

| PAGE | DATE | GROOM — BRIDE |
|------|------|---------------|
| 13 | 30 Mar 1868 | Daniel Garbison-Harriet S. Wilson |
|  | 3 Apr 1868 | F.M. Abbott-Sarah Jane Loring |
| 14 | 8 Apr 1868 | Cornelius Stevenson-Betsy Niles |
|  | 7 May 1868 | James H. Baker-Sarah Elston |
| 15 | 18 May 1868 | John N. Wyant-Sarah Sinclier |
|  | 3 Jun 1868 | John M. Lockwood-Lucretia Miller |
| 16 | 15 Jun 1868 | Samuel Lepard-Jane E. Davis |
|  | 29 Jun 1868 | Andrew Holloway-Jemima A. Davis |
| 17 | 2 Jul 1868 | Jesse Lindsey-Isabel Stilwell |
|  | 5 Jul 1868 | Samuel Taylor-Mary L. Hardsock |
| 18 | 15 Aug 1868 | Thomas B. Wade-Ellen Cole |
|  | 23 Aug 1868 | Silas W. Howard-Sarah A. Seymour |
| 19 | 11 Aug 1868 | John Williams-Martha McMahan |
|  | 23 Aug 1868 | Solamon Florian-Caroline Working |
| 20 | 26 Aug 1868 | John E. Mills-Catherine Cole |
|  | 28 Aug 1868 | Frederick Burns-Augustine M. Cosnet |
| 21 | 13 Sep 1868 | Richard M. Jackson-Emily Alice Auguster Potter |
|  | 16 Sep 1868lic | Philip Trapp-Mary Jane Chapman |
| 22 | 20 Sep 1868 | John Shrader-Louvisa Bremer |
|  | 23 Sep 1868 | Lewis C. Foust-Elizabeth Jane Craig |
| 23 | 10 Oct 1868 | Arther J. Metcalf-Hester A. Grove |
|  | 29 Oct 1868 | Walter Lightcap-Eliza Jane Stewart |
| 24 | 1 Nov 1868 | George Deerduff-Eliza Anderson |
|  | 4 Nov 1868 | George W. Baker-Alice C. Mulvain |
| 25 | 5 Nov 1868 | Amos Heath-Sarah Adamson |
|  | 9 Nov 1868 | Daniel Hay-Clarinda Pangle |
| 26 | 3 Dec 1868 | Amos Z.T. Heath-Nancy Jane McFarlin |
|  | 8 Dec 1868 | John Akers-Sarah W. Jarrett |
| 27 | 13 Dec 1868 | Alfred T. Ricks-Mary Jane Terry |
|  | 20 Dec 1868 | Francis M. Shoup-Martha Ricks |
| 28 | 25 Dec 1868 | Samuel Koontz, Jr.-Martha Morrow |
|  | 3 Jan 1869 | Paul Sult-Mary E. Smith |
| 29 | 6 Jan 1869 | William H. Stevenson-Sarah Ellen Canaan |
|  | 7 Jan 1869 | Lewis W. Youngs-Maria E. Gieger |
| 30 | 24 Jan 1869 | Josephus N. Peelle-Marthey M. McCrackin |
|  | 10 Feb 1869 | John W. Henshaw-Mary Heminger |
| 31 | 10 Mar 1869 | James Hepshire-Ellen Taylor |
|  | 21 Mar 1869 | George Lightcap-Ellen Herrod |
| 32 | 29 Apr 1869 | William F. Childers-Barbara E. Shon |
|  | 6 May 1869 | Levi T. Bell-Amanda E. Stewart |
| 33 | 11 May 1869 | William L. Peck-Elvira Jane Shaw |
|  | 22 May 1869 | George Butler-Annie Williams |
| 34 | 27 May 1869 | William J. Bell-Martha E. Sherley |
|  | 27 May 1869 | Jacob Avault-Sarah Jane Jolly |
| 35 | 28 Jul 1869 | Lewis Keller-Nettie Craig |
|  | 28 Jul 1869 | James B. Bagwell-Rebecca Elizabeth Clearwater |

| PAGE | DATE | GROOM — BRIDE |
|------|------|---------------|
| 36 | 16 Jul 1869 | Nathan Winfield Scott-Margaretta Stevenson |
|    | 8 Aug 1869 | A.B. Morrow-Emma Elmendorf |
| 37 | 22 Aug 1869 | George H. Byers-Lucey McBratney |
|    | 12 Sep 1869 | Jacob Myers-Nancy Done |
| 38 | 22 Sep 1869 | John Baker-Ellen Wynegar |
|    | 16 Sep 1869 | Charles Prettyman-Catherine Canaan |
| 39 | 10 Oct 1869 | John Reed-Thersia Weddington |
|    | 10 Oct 1869 | William G. McCormick-Mary Uncapher |
| 40 | 12 Oct 1869 | Samuel Taylor-Elizabeth Bonner |
|    | 17 Oct 1869 | Jacob Slocum-Deliah Sanford |
| 41 | 31 Oct 1869 | Henry S.C. Heath-Isabel H. Adair |
|    | 30 Oct 1869 | Edward Jones-Phebe Ann Monroe |
| 42 | 4 Nov 1869 | John W. Bevilhymer-Almeda White |
|    | 21 Nov 1869 | Daniel Koontz-Celia M. Brinkly |
| 43 | 21 Nov 1869 | Christopher Owens-Anna B. Roller |
|    | 28 Nov 1869 | Joseph N. McCormick-Martha A. Gurnsey |
| 44 | 9 Dec 1869 | William H.A. Smyth-Martha Baldwin |
|    | 5 Dec 1869 | John P. Haskins-Mary Ann Rathburn |
| 45 | 9 Dec 1869 | Andrew M. Smith-Sarah E. Justice |
|    | 11 Dec 1869 | Lewis Lahmon-Rhoda Ann Barns |
| 46 | 16 Dec 1869 | William H. Shafer-Sarah Ann Brandle |
|    | 24 Dec 1869 | Udorus Trowbridge-Mary E. Wyland |
| 47 | 29 Jan 1870 | Joseph B. Barnum-Lucinda Myers |
|    | 10 Jan 1870 | William Murphy-Ellen Pew |
| 48 | 23 Jan 1870 | Daniel Kreis-Caroline Baker |
|    | 27 Jan 1870 | Jacob B. Roller-Sarah Ann Lawrence |
| 49 | 22 Feb 1870 | James Wells-Sarah S. McCormick |
|    | 20 Feb 1870 | Stephen McLaughlin-Marantha Lawrence |
| 50 | 11 Mar 1870 | James M. Johnson-Rachel Morrow |
|    | 20 Mar 1870 | J. Leroy Cozens-Martha E. Hand |
| 51 | 22 Mar 1870 | Vine Welsh-Mary Ann Haines |
| 52 | 5 Apr 1870 | Martin M. Munroe-Lydia A. Fleming |
|    | 7 Apr 1870 | John A. Patmore-Jemimah S. McFarlin |
| 53 | 14 Apr 1870 | Samuel W. Lane-Angeline Replogle |
|    | 8 May 1870 | Elias Dipert-Elizabeth Jolly |
| 54 | 19 May 1870 | Lemuel E. Lower-Minerva V. Mulvin |
|    | 31 May 1870 | Jeremiah Gingrick-Ellen Brockert |
| 55 | 27 Jul 1870 | James A. Clements-Josephine Banta |
|    | 3 Aug 1870 | Charles H. Baker-Sarah C. Headly |
| 56 | 1 Sep 1870 | Martin Garn-Sarah Hawkins |
|    | 10 Sep 1870 | Erastus M. Birch-Betsy Ann Baker |
| 57 | 17 Sep 1870 | William Miller-Mary Ann Long |
|    | 29 Sep 1870 | John W. Grindle-Susan Phillips |
| 58 | 6 Oct 1870 | Samuel F. Rock-Susan Jane Hutcheson |
|    | 29 Oct 1870 | John Goff-Christian Menser |
| 59 | 20 Nov 1870 | Julius C. Hatter-Lovisa Hill |
|    | 4 Dec 1870 | Simeon Brown-Rody Jane George |

| PAGE | DATE | GROOM — BRIDE |
|------|------|---------------|
| 60 | 27 Dec 1870 | Jonas Miller-Elizabeth Stutzman |
|    | 27 Dec 1870 | John N. King-Maria L. Pedrick |
| 61 | 1 Jan 1871 | Fredrick Stahl-Austina Wolfram |
|    | 9 Jan 1871 | Edward Trexlar-Mary Zedick |
| 62 | 1 Jan 1871 | William W. Garner-Anna F. Moore |
|    | 8 Jan 1871 | William Rosenberger-Bellmina Baker |
| 63 | 24 Jan 1871 | James J. Lawrene-Sena P.F. Heath |
|    | 22 Jan 1871 | George S. Rockwell-Katie Pope |
| 64 | 2 Feb 1871 | Peter G. Wynegar-Margaret A. Baker |
|    | 5 Feb 1871 | Peter Awald-Jane Koontz |
| 65 | 16 Feb 1871 | Immanuel Griffin-Susanah Garrison |
|    | 26 Feb 1871 | William Lawrence-Elizabeth A. Byers |
| 66 | 26 Mar 1871 | Jonass Dipert-Julia Barns |
|    | 1 Apr 1871 | Daniel Dunkelbarger-Lydia M. Gillson |
| 67 | 2 Apr 1871 | William S. Cartright-Sarah Jane Deen |
|    | 3 Apr 1871 | Robert Taylor-Julia Gardner |
| 68 | 11 Apr 1871 | Conrad Susdorf-Mary Goon |
|    | 15 Apr 1871 | John Dawson-Margaretta Gardner |
| 69 | 23 Apr 1871 | William Wyner-Paulina Ott |
|    | 8 June 1871 | Henry S. Miulle-Laura J. Moshier |
| 70 | 6 Jul 1871 | William Perry-Anna Jarrett |
|    | 17 Jun 1871 | John Grinelle-Martha Watkins |
| 71 | 29 Jul 1871 | John Traver-Malinda Butler |
|    | 17 Aug 1871 | Willis W. Worley-Eliza A. Taylor |
| 72 | 20 Aug 1871 | Stephen Stevenson-Hannah E. West |
|    | 3 Sep 1871 | James Baldwin-Elizabeth Myers |
| 73 | 10 Sep 1871 | Theodore Herr-Mary Swartzell |
|    | 24 Sep 1871 | William Grary-Sarah J. Stevenson |
| 74 | 12 Oct 1871 | Mahlon S. Brown-Mary A. Sharp |
|    | 11 Nov 1871 | John Karns-Sarah E. Bonner |
| 75 | 14 Dec 1871 | Alexander Horner-Nancy J. Brown |
|    | 21 Dec 1871 | Levi Stephenson-Nancy Eskridge |
| 76 | 7 Jan 1872 | Cornelius Phillips-Louisa Newton |
|    | 7 Jan 1872 | John O. Coonfare-Percilla Myers |
| 77 | 19 Jan 1872 | David F. Wisner-Sarah F. Crose |
|    | 11 Feb 1872 | Andrew J. Laramore-Rosana Hill |
| 78 | 27 Jan 1872 | Conrad Cup-Maranda Cole |
|    | 13 Feb 1872 | Charles Laramore-Mary E. Emigh |
| 79 | 15 Feb 1872 | Mathias Collins-Frances M. Lybrook |
|    | 5 Mar 1872 | John Eckert-Henrietta Leska |
| 80 | 20 Mar 1872 | William H. Dean-Minerva Weeks |
|    | 24 Mar 1872 | James A.D. Robinson-Anna L. Fletcher |
| 81 | 4 Apr 1872 | William Seagraves-Martha J. Cole |
|    | 9 Apr 1872 | Patrick Flynn-Mary Ellen Kays |
| 82 | 4 May 1872 | Jacob Cole-Sarah E. Dunkelbarger |
|    | 5 May 1872 | George W. Favorite-Emma Rodgers |

| PAGE | DATE | GROOM — BRIDE |
|------|------|---------------|
| 83 | 14 May 1872 | Julius Roskie-Augusta Koontz |
| | 20 May 1872 | William W. Canaan-Mary R. Wright |
| 84 | 16 Jun 1872 | John K. Harrison-Frances A. Smith |
| | 7 Jul 1872 | Milford C. Dixon-Jane Eskridge |
| 85 | 5 July 1872 | John W. Williams-Mary Ellen Phillips |
| | 15 Jul 1872 | David Fetters-Martha Pettis |
| 86 | 14 Jul 1872 | William W. Bonner-Margaret Wyland |
| | 31 Jul 1872 | Franklin Peterstauf-Henrietta Cres |
| 87 | 13 Aug 1872 lic | James Loftus-Maria Nolan |
| | 10 Sep 1872 | William H. Cozens-Feriby Nave |
| 88 | 5 Sep 1872 | Joseph Laudermilk-Laura J. Hagle |
| | 13 Sep 1872 | James Brazill-Ann Connly |
| 89 | 2 Sep 1872 | Phillip Awalt-Susana M. Fleming |
| | 15 Sep 1872 | Jacob A. Hill-Hariet E. Laramore |
| 90 | 26 Sep 1872 | George Knachall-Rebecca Lower |
| | 24 Sep 1872 | T.J. Thompson-Elizabeth R. German |
| 91 | 28 Sep 1872 | Henry Bender-Mary Meek |
| | 29 Sep 1872 | Leonard Long-Mary S. Garberson |
| 92 | 28 Sep 1872 | John Canaan-Marietta Scott |
| | 29 Sep 1872 | John S. Collins-Emma Hay |
| 93 | 22 Oct 1872 | John Drake-Celia Boles |
| | 25 Oct 1872 | John Newport-Elizabeth Shricker |
| 94 | 29 Oct 1872 lic | Thomas Griffith-Mary Crolly |
| | 2 Nov 1872 | Samuel G. Kline-Amanda Swartzell |
| 95 | 7 Nov 1872 | William Reed-Catharine E. Roller |
| | 10 Nov 1872 | James Thompson-Christina Working |
| 96 | 9 Nov 1872 | Brittain Larue-Elizabeth Hand |
| | 20 Nov 1872 | E.W. Davis-Sue Patesel |
| 97 | 5 Dec 1872 | John Miller-Elmira S. Bennett |
| | 6 Dec 1872 | John H. Wright-Sarah E. Lawrence |
| 98 | 10 Dec 1872 | Jacob Hartz-Barbara Goppert |
| | 28 Dec 1872 | George W. Swartzell-Eliza Morris |
| 99 | 30 Dec 1872 | Edwin P. Curtis-Emeline P. Cozens |
| | 9 Jan 1873 | John W. Lain-Artenecy Nimrod |
| 100 | 6 Jan 1873 | Elijah W. Cannon-Zorie Patesel |
| | 9 Feb 1873 | Michael J. Freet-Sarah Ann Anderson |
| 101 | 9 Mar 1873 | Albert Mosher-Nancy Ann Lain |
| | 23 Mar 1873 | Thomas Reed-Elnora Vanasdall |
| 102 | 26 Mar 1873 | Abraham Sult-Caroline Marsh |
| | 29 Mar 1873 | Martin D. Puckett-Mary Jane Vanasdall |
| 103 | 30 Mar 1873 | John Krimm-Mary Toleson |
| | 6 Apr 1873 | Francis E. Cartwright-Mary E. Sanderlin |
| 104 | 29 Apr 1873 | James A. Surpless-Mary Ann Spicer |
| | 1 May 1873 | Levi Lower-Sarah Porter |
| 105 | 25 May 1873 | Benjamin West-Elizabeth Thompson |
| | 25 May 1873 | John Haines-Mary Thompson |

| PAGE | DATE | GROOM — BRIDE |
|------|------|---------------|
| 106 | 29 May 1873 | Peter F. Munn-Harriett Geddes |
|  | 8 Jun 1873 | Wilfrid Stranger-Almira Speelman |
| 107 | 20 Jun 1873 | George W. Vories-Charlotte Personate |
|  | 20 Jul 1873 | William McCartney-Sarah A.F. Simpson |
| 108 | 20 Jul 1873 | Theadore A. Smith-Elizabeth J. Bagwell |
|  | 7 Sep 1873 | Amos Laramore-Martha Gibbs |
| 109 | 14 Sep 1873 | Thomas Seamore-Ellen D. Taylor |
|  | 16 Sep 1873 | Frank Whitlock-Sarah Coats |
| 110 | 28 Sep 1873 | George W. Coffin-Annie M. Patrick |
|  | 23 Oct 1873 | Wingate Prettyman-Arrena Hillabold |
| 111 | 9 Nov 1873 | Daniel Mayer-Charlotte Smith |
|  | 6 Nov 1873 | Isaac Werner-Casie Ann McPheron |
| 112 | 1 Dec 1873 | Isaac D. Lauderback-Mary E. Wharton |
|  | 4 Dec 1873 | Lemuel Seagraves-Elizabeth Porter |
| 113 | 17 Dec 1873 | John W. Swartzell-Mary Kline |
|  | 17 Dec 1873 | Jared W. Wilson-Mary E. Taylor |
| 114 | 23 Dec 1873 | Wiley Johnson-Julia Ann A. Batson |
|  | 25 Dec 1873 | Emanuel Geller-Julia Hall |
| 115 | 24 Dec 1873 | Filmore T. Spoor-Mary Scott |
|  | 25 Dec 1873 | John W. Hutchinson-Nancy Ann Simmons |
| 116 | 31 Dec 1873 | Alonzo Sharpe-Lovisa E. Short |
|  | 11 Jan 1874 | Samuel Heflick-Elizabeth Swartz |
| 117 | 4 Jan 1874 | Nathaniel B. Batson-Mary M. Anderson |
|  | 14 Jan 1874 lic | Joseph W. Hubbell-Ollie M. Hathaway |
| 118 | 26 Jan 1874 | Samuel B. Romine-Elizabeth Garverson |
|  | 1 Feb 1874 | John Dawson-Malinda Penwright |
| 119 | 5 Feb 1874 | David S. Shefer-Lydia P. Bridgeman |
|  | 15 Feb 1874 | Frederick J. Nave-Nancy A. Tucker |
| 120 | 14 Feb 1874 | William R. Beatty-Sarah E. Gurnsey |
|  | 5 Mar 1874 | Frederick Wright-Anna Ross |
| 121 | 4 Mar 1874 | John Donnell-Dorothy Isabel Murphey |
|  | 22 Mar 1874 | John Whitesel-Rosetta Shanks |
| 122 | 13 Apr 1874 | John S. Deboise-Rebecca J. Lampson |
|  | 26 Apr 1874 | William Rowe-Cora Annis |
| 123 | 13 Jun 1874 | Noyes S. Chamberlin-Nancy B. Byers |
|  | 16 Jun 1874 | William P. Uncapher-Josephine Davis |
| 124 | 5 Jun 1874 | Henry C. Rogers-Carrie Beatty |
|  | 19 Jun 1874 | Nicholas Archer- Mary R. Strope |
| 125 | 19 Jun 1874 | Alfred Myers-Emma Simpson |
|  | 28 Jun 1874 | Tobias Good-Cyntha Jane Hartsock |
| 126 | 4 Jul 1874 | Edward A. Tucker-Eliza E. Nelson |
|  | 5 Jul 1874 | Henry Secrist-Jennie Perry |
| 127 | 30 Jul 1874 | George Winsell-Eliza Armstrong |
|  | 8 Aug 1874 | Charles Baker-Anna B. Koeppel |
| 128 | 29 Jul 1874 lic | Patrick McMannis-Mariah Nollen |
|  | 5 Aug 1874 | Warren S. Terry-Barbara A. Emigh |

| PAGE | DATE | GROOM — BRIDE |
|------|------|---------------|
| 129 | 16 Aug 1874 | Jonathan W. Heath-Mary E. Snyder |
|     | 27 Aug 1874 | Philander Lowery-Sarah Jane Berry |
| 130 | 3 Sep 1874 | John C. Longwell-Mary A. Drake |
|     | 24 Sep 1874 | William H. Tucker-Susanah Hagle |
| 131 | 15 Nov 1874 | William B. Pierce-Sarah L. Lish |
|     | 1 Oct 1874 | Adam Almandinger-Mary E. Prettyman |
| 132 | 4 Oct 1874 | Alonzo G. Hagle-Eliza J. Bickel |
|     | 4 Oct 1874 | Jacob Bozarth-Phebe Westhaver |
| 133 | 4 Nov 1874 | Benton Watkins-Sarah E. Loring |
|     | 12 Nov 1874 | Daniel A. Wiltfong-Elizabeth Huffman |
| 134 | 5 Dec 1874 | Charles Dautenhahn-Johannie Klittick |
|     | 2 Dec 1874 | John Lohse-Auguste Kane |
| 135 | 5 Dec 1874 | Matthias D. Harness-Clarisa A. Albertson |
|     | 6 Dec 1874 | Daniel Hoffacker-Susan Secrist |
| 136 | 20 Dec 1874 | Henry Ely-Henrietta Morris |
|     | 17 Jan 1875 | James P. Lain-Alice Mosher |
| 137 | 4 Jan 1875 lic | George F. Jones-Elizabeth Seagrist |
|     | 2 Feb 1875 | Henry Richmond-Elizabeth Finch |
| 138 | 21 Feb 1875 | James A. Giles-Sarah Lower |
|     | 4 Mar 1875 | John W. Thompson-Rosella J. Brown |
| 139 | 7 Mar 1875 | Samuel W. Holderman-Sarah A. Shelly |
|     | 8 Mar 1875 | John McVicker-Mary C. Myers |
| 140 | 26 Mar 1875 | Samuel K. Uncapher-Eva A. Shultze |
|     | 27 Mar 1875 | Abington Baker-Maria Thompson |
| 141 | 30 Mar 1875 | Daniel S. Biggs-Lizzie A. Ekins |
|     | 8 Apr 1875 | William T. Jolly-Caroline Minser |
| 142 | 9 Apr 1875 | William J. Rice-Anne T. Page |
|     | 14 Apr 1875 | George Harbaugh-Elizabeth Benson |
| 143 | 14 Apr 1875 | Daniel Rowell-Mary Ann Wheeler |
|     | 25 Apr 1875 | Gotleib Hankey-Augusta Spinner |
| 144 | 25 Apr 1875 | George W. Lower-Lilus Hershey |
|     | 2 May 1875 | John Yount-Elizabeth French |
| 145 | 2 May 1875 | Walter F. Williams-Alwilda A. Crabbs |
|     | 6 May 1875 | Orvill W. Edwards-Louisa Justice |
| 146 | 6 Jun 1875 | Lambert M. Ford-Mary E. McDaniel |
|     | 21 Jun 1875 | Edward Short-Armilda Sharp |
| 147 | 13 Jun 1875 | William Snyder-Sarah Brown |
|     | 1 Jul 1875 | Paul Wegner-Augusta Louise Adem |
| 148 | 3 Jul 1875 | Tobias Troyer-Fanny Troyer |
|     | 2 Aug 1875 | Willard Mann-Thurza Reed |
| 149 | 5 Aug 1875 | Robert Rodgers-Vasti L. Personette |
|     | 19 Aug 1875 | Matthew E. Martin-Lovina E. Kreis |
| 150 | 15 Aug 1875 | Thomas J. Fletcher-Sarah E. Cochran |
|     | 14 Aug 1875 | John Tully-Lucy J. Stutsman |
| 151 | 21 Aug 1875 | Orin B.C. Heath-Martha Jones |
|     | 22 Aug 1875 | Daniel C. Allen-Elizabeth J. Lopp |

| PAGE | DATE | GROOM — BRIDE |
|------|------|---------------|
| 152 | 24 Aug 1875 | Silas W. Howard-Eliza J. Seymour |
|  | 26 Aug 1875 | Willard R. Wilson-Rebecca J. Thornburg |
| 153 | 2 Sep 1875 | Albanus K.M. Heath-Julia Bickel |
|  | 12 Sep 1875 | William McCormick-Caroline Rendsbaugher |
| 154 | 9 Sep 1875 | Arthur M. Bennett-Emma C. Lee |
|  | 25 Sep 1875 | William C. Inks-Nancy Stevenson |
| 155 | 2 Oct 1875 | William Tilden-Isabelle Castle |
|  | 11 Oct 1875 | William W. Butts-Lille M. Chamberlain |
| 156 | 16 Oct 1875 | George Eskridge-Sarah E. Troyer |
|  | 29 Oct 1875 | Andrew Collins-Martha Simpson |
| 157 | 25 Oct 1875 | Isaac F. Dawson-Mary Hizer |
|  | 4 Nov 1875 | Wilson P. Jones-Mellissa Sharp |
| 158 | 11 Nov 1875 | John R. Phillips-Margaret L. Dunkelberger |
|  | 17 Nov 1875 | Frank M. Batchelder-Rebecca J. Peelle |
| 159 | 21 Nov 1875 | Daniel Lefevre-Elizabeth Groshans |
|  | 30 Nov 1875 | Charles H. Chapman-Anna DeCamp |
| 160 | 5 Dec 1875 | Oliver P. Justice-Rosilla Hazen |
|  | 13 Dec 1875 | Sherman McBratney-Sarah C. McCune |
| 161 | 12 Dec 1875 | Henry H. Cannon-Rhoda C. Kepperling |
|  | 14 Dec 1875 | Joseph Floran-Magdalena Working |
| 162 | 15 Dec 1875 | Vernon Vankirk-Catharine Jones |
|  | 22 Dec 1875 | John W. Willhelm-Elizabeth Ringleben |
| 163 | 23 Dec 1875 | James J. Willhelm-Margaret E. Grounds |
|  | 24 Dec 1875 | Nathaniel G. Edwards-Mary E. Collins |
| 164 | 11 Jan 1876 | William Pierson-Malinda Yoder |
|  | 9 Jan 1876 | William Dawson-Ruth Ann Sloan |
| 165 | 11 Jan 1876 | Walter C. Baker-Mary M. Wyeth |
|  | 13 Jan 1876 | Conrad Groshans-Sarah Jane Gould |
| 166 | 30 Jan 1876 | Simon A. Vanasdal-Jerusha M. Freet |
|  | 30 Jan 1876 | Luther W. Carpenter-Rachael Johnson |
| 167 | 12 Feb 1876 | Henry Cartwright-Louisa Smith |
|  | 13 Feb 1876 | Theadore R. Bennett-Mary J. Brooke |
| 168 | 17 Feb 1876 | Francis M. Fletcher-Orlivia Coffin |
|  | 6 Mar 1876 | John Butcher-Olive O. Personett |
| 169 | 9 Mar 1876 | Horace Pownall-Amanda Lemler |
|  | 30 Mar 1876 | George A. Williams-Ella M. Crabbs |
| 170 | 26 Mar 1876 | Charles Harberman-Mena White |
|  | 8 Apr 1876 | Gamaliel W. Robinson-Mary Ann Troyer |
| 171 | 30 Mar 1876 | David Reniker-Susannah Hoff |
|  | 2 Apr 1876 | George H. Summers-Mary Jane Dunkelbarger |
| 172 | 9 Apr 1876 | Oskar Cartwright-Selena Lemler |
|  | 15 Apr 1876 | John Bigler-Mary Reed |
| 173 | 12 Apr 1876 | Isaac Fletcher-Mary Ann Turner |
|  | 16 Apr 1876 | Augustus J. White-Frances Lightcap |
| 174 | 16 Apr 1876 | Frank Dusek-Anna Fialova |
|  | 19 Apr 1876 | James C. Nelson-Abagail E. Riley |

| PAGE | DATE | GROOM — BRIDE |
|------|------|---------------|
| 175 | 20 Apr 1876 | Matthias J. Haskins-Jennetta Brooks |
|     | 20 Apr 1876 | John W. Seagraves-Della May Spoor |
| 176 | 22 Apr 1876 | Wilson T. Loring-Emma L. Savery |
|     | 29 Apr 1876 | George W. Conner-Emma Humphreys |
| 177 | 11 May 1876 | Samuel Davis-Nancy Gingrich |
|     | 1 Jun 1876 | Michael Kelley-Josephine M. Malaney |
| 178 | 12 Jun 1876 | Hiram M. Waterman-Flora Triplett |
|     | 25 Jun 1876 | Byron D. Rowell-Lucinda J. Deringer |
| 179 | 18 Jun 1876 | William H. Tucker-Lucretia E. Shoemaker |
|     | 27 Aug 1876 | Henry Lightcap-Augusta Ross |
| 180 | 30 Aug 1876 | Joseph Laudermilk-N. Caroline Clements |
|     | 10 Sep 1876 | Havilah C. Netherton-Susan Burris |
| 181 | 21 Sep 1876 | Samuel Greiner-Isabell Coil |
|     | 5 Oct 1876 | Jacob Baughman-Alice Hughs |
| 182 | 16 Oct 1876 | Silas Seagraves-Sarah Isabell Adams |
|     | 22 Oct 1876 | George W. Bell-Lavina E. Willey |
| 183 | 28 Oct 1876 | George J. Bowers-Matilda D. Bell |
|     | 2 Nov 1876 | James F Huey-Sarah M. Dunkelbarger |
| 184 | 3 Nov 1876 | John L. Armstrong-Harriet M. Swartz |
|     | 12 Nov 1876 | Thomas Bell-Jemima Nave |
| 185 | 2 Dec 1876 | John W. Marion-Nancy E. Collins |
|     | 28 Dec 1876 | Amos Osborne-Alice A. Sickman |
| 186 | 31 Dec 1876 | Joseph B. Hoag-Lydia Cox |
|     | 7 Jan 1877 | William McDaniel-Martha Jane Smith |
| 187 | 2 Jan 1877 | John Phillips-Catharine Phillips |
|     | 8 Jan 1887 | Thomas J. Fletcher-Mary Hanes |
| 188 | 20 Jan 1877 | J. Frank Malana-Elle R. McColester |
|     | 27 Jan 1877 | William J. Scott-Arabe Huston |
| 189 | 25 Jan 1877 | John A. Jones-Dora A. Petro |
|     | 28 Jan 1877 | William Parker-Maggie E. Wolfe |
| 190 | 1 Feb 1877 | William Smith-Anna Gentry |
|     | Feb 1887 | Milton P. Graves-Maggie J. McCune |
| 191 | 7 Feb 1877 | Thomas B. Frane-Amelia D. Hani |
|     | 19 Feb 1877 | Theodore Dufford-Mary A. Hitchcock |
| 192 | 20 Feb 1877 | John Giles-Christena Spicer |
|     | 25 Feb 1877 | Alvin C. Willhelm-Helen H. Spoor |
| 193 | 4 Jan 1877 | Oliver M. Fields-Sarah S. Wells |
|     | 4 Mar 1877 | George Vannote-Nancy A. Fuston |
| 194 | 9 Apr 1877 | Thomas Jolley-Elizabeth Crim |
|     | 12 Mar 1877 | George W. Spicer-Sarah Anna Smalley |
| 195 | 25 Mar 1877 | Samuel Lower-Arrena Akers |
|     | 1 Apr 1877 | Jesse Jackson-Izore Emigh |
| 196 | 3 Apr 1877 | James Nye-Cordelia E. Foss |
|     | 13 Apr 1877 | Charles Baker-Minna Ballnow |
| 197 | 27 Apr 1877 | Thomas Coil-Elizabeth Jane Depert |
|     | 29 Apr 1877 | Alison T. Burris-Sarah E. Ashley |

| PAGE | DATE | GROOM — BRIDE |
|------|------|---------------|
| 198 | 21 Jun 1877 | William McCune-Sarah J. Payne |
|  | 1 Jul 1877 | William Mires-Elizabeth Smith |
| 199 | 3 Sep 1877 | William Knapp-Nancy Janette Albertson |
|  | 8 Sep 1877 | Conrad Awald-Rhoda Brinkly |
| 200 | 9 Sep 1877 | Stephen D. Howard-Mary E. Freet |
|  | 15 Sep 1877 | William H. Haskins-Clarry J. Avery |
| 201 | 12 Sep 1877 | William Myres-Elizabeth Fuston |
|  | 25 Sep 1877 | Benjamin F. Shafer-Mary E. Kintzel |
| 202 | 28 Sep 1877 | Carl Dommer-Otile Stauk |
|  | 14 Oct 1877 | Frank Shindelar-Anna Yanouskovec |
| 203 | 30 Sep 1877 | Leonard C. McCrackin-Hariet Davidson |
|  | 10 Oct 1877 | Aaron Speelman-Maggie B. Collins |
| 204 | 14 Oct 1877 | Christopher Schessler-Elizabeth Soellner |
|  | 25 Oct 1877 | William Sable-Mary Ott |
| 205 | 25 Oct 1877 lic | Corneilious Philips-Rosell Surpluss |
|  | 25 Oct 1877 lic | August Hupp-Carolina Litky |
| 206 | 27 Oct 1877 | William Sawyer-Syntha J. Anderson |
|  | 3 Oct 1877 | James Townley-Margret Bussing |
| 207 | 30 Oct 1877 | William J. Berry-Elizabeth Baldwin |
|  | 4 Nov 1877 | Joseph Miller-Mary McFarland |
| 208 | 11 Nov 1877 | Robert Hall-Mary Gingerich |
|  | 15 Nov 1877 | Clayton Grove-Media Fletcher |
| 209 | 2 Dec 1877 | John B. Hill-Allis Potter |
|  | 28 Nov 1877 | Peter W. Hannan-Matilda J. Walker |
| 210 | 2 Dec 1877 | Schyler C. Norrice-Sarah J. Uncapher |
|  | 1 Dec 1877 | Adam Ringleben-Caroline W. Geoice |
| 211 | 13 Dec 1877 | Samuel Parks-Samantha Reffer |
|  | 26 Dec 1877 | August Gusmer-Caroline Ross |
| 212 | 25 Dec 1877 | William P. Chadwick-Louvina Peelle |
|  | 4 Jan 1878 | William Will-Beatha Weiche |
| 213 | 1 Jan 1878 | William Kris-Elizabeth Seagraves |
|  | 6 Jan 1878 | Silas W. Howard-Mary A. Welsh |
| 214 | 2 Jan 1878 | William H. Coldrain-Ida M. Loring |
|  | 9 Jan 1878 lic | Joel Vail-Martha E. Fletcher |
| 215 | 10 Jan 1878 | David J. Yoder-Mary J. Drake |
|  | 26 Jan 1878 | John Cooper-Lidia E. Bennett |
| 216 | 29 Jan 1878 | George Vannote-Analiza Dickson |
|  | 28 Jan 1878 | John Casper-Ambrosia Gentry |
| 217 | 3 Feb 1878 | George W. Armstrong-Idora A. Ford |
|  | 7 Feb 1878 | Allanson Mills-Sarah Mosher |
| 218 | 16 Feb 1878 | Daniel Lenlen-Mary Ellen Ruth Dean |
|  | 11 Feb 1878 | Leblens Scott-Eliza Reed |
| 219 | 24 Feb 1878 | David M. Thomas-Allice Baker |
|  | 26 Feb 1878 | Henry P. Tracey-Susan Clark |
| 220 | 28 Feb 1878 | Solomon Brandal-Elizabeth Brooke |
|  | 5 Mar 1878 | Daniel Scott-Amanda Seamore |

| PAGE | DATE | GROOM — BRIDE |
|---|---|---|
| 221 | 23 Mar 1878 | Orrin Humphreys-Eliza Homer |
|  | 23 Apr 1878 | Milo D. Eatinger-Olive Allen |
| 222 | 27 Apr 1878 | Joseph Garbinson-Mary E. Truax |
|  | 28 Apr 1878 | Joel Vail-Alice D. Jolly |
| 223 | 28 Apr 1878 | George M. Berdine-Laurea Branerd |
|  | 30 Apr 1878 | Jacob Kleckner-Anna E. Geiselman |
| 224 | 2 May 1878 | B.F. Chance-Ellie May Werner |
|  | 2 May 1878 | Isaac Short-Louisa A. Hurshey |
| 225 | 26 May 1878 | John H. Gould-Catherine S. Brown |
|  | 3 Jun 1878 | William Will-Hester J. Penright |
| 226 | 8 Jun 1878 | Cyrus A. Huey-Elizabeth A. Dunklebarger |
|  | 20 Jun 1878 | Alva Welsh-Mary C. Thornburg |
| 227 | 19 Jun 1878 | Maon H. Mills-Sarah J. Lowery |
|  | 4 Jul 1878 | Samuel O. Bean-Ruth Ann Dawson |
| 228 | 23 Jul 1878 | Elizah Queer-Christena Wright |
|  | 20 Aug 1878 | Leverndon Sebridge-Jane Bergel |
| 229 | 24 Aug 1878 | George W. Sult-Sarah A. Thompson |
|  | 25 Aug 1878 | Nelson G. Bryant-Hannah J. Laramore |
| 230 | 1 Sep 1878 | Samuel Bevialhimer-Nancy J. Esties |
|  | 8 Sep 1878 | James Cavin-Racheal Troyer |
| 231 | 8 Sep 1878 | Daniel Troyer-Sarah McCartney |
|  | 7 Sep 1878 | Cornealious Garison-Susan S. Gentry |
| 232 | 15 Sep 1878 | Ed D. Vandolsen-Mary A. Jones |
|  | 16 Sep 1878 | Nicholas Amnoldi-Anna Schram |
| 233 | 20 Sep | |
|  | 3 Oct 1 | |
| 234 | 29 Sep | |
|  | 10 Oct | |
| 235 | 17 Oct | |
|  | 17 Oct | |
| 236 | 26 Oct | |
|  | 26 Oct | |
| 237 | 16 Nov | |
|  | 28 Nov | |
| 238 | 12 Dec | stleman |
|  | 22 Dec | |
| 239 | 27 Dec | |
|  | 19 Dec | |
| 240 | 22 Dec | |
|  | 1 Jan | |
| 241 | 8 Jan | |
|  | 14 Jan | |
| 242 | 8 Feb | |
|  | 8 Feb 1879 | Robert J. Boyd-Rebecca Segrist |
| 243 | 2 Mar 1879 | Michael N. Mills-Mary C. Welsh |
|  | 16 Mar 1879 | George W. Tanner-Barbra Troyer |

| PAGE | DATE | GROOM — BRIDE |
|------|------|---------------|
| 244 | 5 Apr 1879 | Allen Sanders-Cynthia A. Brown |
|  | 17 Apr 1879 | Samuel V. Black-Lavina C. Eatinger |
| 245 | 27 Apr 1879 | Henry G. Burbank-Margret Scott |
|  | 1 May 1879 | George A. Scott-Aggie L. Musselman |
| 246 | 8 May 1879 | John A. Palmore-Ann D. Cutshall |
|  | 8 May 1879 | Francis W. Williams-Mary Fry |
| 247 | 6 Jun 1879 | Matthias D. Harness-Nancy J. Knapp |
|  | 31 May 1879 | Benjamin F. Dunkelbarger- Jane Brown |
| 248 | 5 Jun 1879 | Henry A. Croco-Mary E. Castlman |
|  | 8 Jun 1879 | John Sayer-Flora Leake |
| 249 | 11 Jun 1879 | Merideth Wentz-Eliza Coil |
|  | 30 Jun 1879 | Adam Ireland-Adaline Bark |
| 250 | 1 Jul 1879 | William Swartzell-Jane E. Tilden |
|  | 19 Jul 1879 | Harry B. Chappelear-Mattie Felton |
| 251 | 21 Aug 1879 | Arkey Purkey-Josephine Archibald |
|  | 22 Aug 1869 | Isaac Kramer-Emma Finch |
| 252 | 30 Aug 1879 | William Christoph-May M. Leiby |
|  | 27 Aug 1879 | Benjamin D. Foust-Mary Winegar |
| 253 | 31 Aug 1879 | Jesse Schroder-Fidilla Ditto |
|  | 11 Sep 1879 | Francis Earl-Isabelle Morrow |
| 254 | 19 Sep 1879 | Abraham Jones-Jennie Stewart |
|  | 25 Sep 1879 | John H. Hiatt-Mary E. Petomey |
| 255 | 1 Oct 1879 | Jacob Merket-Emma Simmons |
|  | 4 Oct 1879 | Stephen Cole-Henrietta Crabbs |
| 256 | 19 Oct 1879 | Henry H. Pelle-R. Jesse Chadwick |
|  | 13 Nov 1879 | William Fedrick-Delila Austin |
| 257 | 2 Nov 1879 | Bradford A. Louderback-Josephine Brazier |
|  | 18 Nov 1879 | William Mosier-Nannia Tufts |
| 258 | 15 Nov 1879 | Joshua Bedee-Sarah J. Jones |
|  |  | Loring |
| 2 |  | ahala Welsh |

# STARKE COUNTY INDIANA MARRIAGES

## 1880-April 6, 1890

Starke County, Indiana was formed by statute from parts of St. Joseph and attached territory, and was organized January 15, 1850. The first marriage license issued in Starke County was in September 1850. The first land entry in what is now this county was in 1832. Hence, civil records for the area prior to 1850 should be in St. Joseph Co. Books A and B of marriages are found on microfilm in the Genealogy Division of the Indiana State Library. Licenses are in chronological order in the order in which they were issued. Three dates are on most of the records: date license applied for and issued; date returned and recorded; and the date the marriage occured. Dates the marriages occured are used in this transcription with the exception of those few cases when the license was never returned to the clerk's office. The March 1989 issue of *THG* published Book A and the first 46 pages of Book B. This transcription is of the remainder of Book B. In 1974, Ruth Slevin transcribed both books, placing the names in alphabetical order by grooms and by brides. This compilation is in the Genealogy Division of the State Library. Also in the Genealogy Division are three marriage indexes for Starke Co. The first, although titled *Index to Marriage Applications Starke County 1840-1920 Inc.*, actually begins with April 19, 1905. The second, titled *Index to Marriage Records, Starke County, 1896-1938*, begins with July 27, 1896. The third, though titled *Index to Marriage Transcripts Starke County 1899-1938*, also begins with April 19, 1905. As far as can be determined, no records exist of marriages between April 1890 and July 27, 1896.

## BOOK B

| PAGE | DATE | GROOM — BRIDE |
|---|---|---|
| 259 | 13 Jan 1880 | Julius Hine-Johanna C. Lukin |
| 260 | 7 Mar 1880 | George S. Singleton-Sarah Calhoon |
| | 5 Jan 1880 lic | Elijah Rice-Dora Summers |
| 261 | 8 Jan 1880 | Lon E. Bernethy-Callie J. Murphey |
| | 11 Jan 1880 | Frederick Awald-Malinda Dipert |
| 262 | 10 Jan 1880 | John B. Collins-Susan Watkins |
| | 21 Jan 1880 | Ezekiel Keller-Carrie Rost |
| 263 | 25 Jan 1880 | John W. Walters-Mary Franklin |
| | 25 Jan 1880 | William M. Short-Isabel E. Lane |
| 264 | 1 Feb 1880 | B. H. Armstrong-Margaret Byres |
| | 3 Feb 1880 | Samuel S. Wright-Francis R. Sharpe |
| 265 | 12 Feb 1880 | Joseph E. DeMont-Margret J. Shaw |
| | 15 Feb 1880 | David Walters-Sarah E. Garvison |
| 266 | 22 Feb 1880 | Scott R. Geddes-Almira F. Batson |
| | 6 Apr 1880 | John Tucker-Kate McCoy |
| 267 | 18 Apr 1880 | Joseph Kadrowski-Augusta Jankowski |
| | 31 May 1880 | Andrew Kirtch-Evia Menzer |

**214**

| PAGE | DATE | GROOM — BRIDE |
|------|------|---------------|
| 268 | 20 May 1880 | Charls Demonte-Maria E. Horner |
|     | 31 May 1880 | Benjamin Headley-Sarah A. Palmer |
| 269 | 10 Jun 1880 | John B. Shafer-Hannah Bennett |
|     | 30 Jul 1880 | George H. Warner-Flora D. Payne |
| 270 | 12 Jun 1880 | Frank Welsh-Maria Umbenheuer |
|     | 17 Jun 1880 | Wesley P. Griffen-Eva Humphryes |
| 271 | 4 Jul 1880 | William H. Hornby-Laovina Isabel Rinebolt |
|     | 17 Jul 1880 | Charles T. German-Ida V. Adkins |
| 272 | 31 Jul 1880 | John F. Jolly-Phebe Ann Dipert |
|     | 12 Aug 1880 | Alfred A. Sphung-Ellmirah J. Adams |
| 273 | 18 Aug 1880 | Michael Restow-Caroline Tiemm |
|     | 20 Aug 1880 | John L. Camel-Sarah E. Baldwin |
| 274 | 21 Aug 1880 | Isaac Morrow-Hariet Allen |
|     | 31 Aug 1880 | Henry B. Allen-Jennie Lish |
| 275 | 19 Sep 1880 | Leander Clinger-Mary M. Hurshey |
|     | 23 Sep 1880 | Jeremiah L. Clearwater-Tobitha Harison |
| 276 | 26 Sep 1880 | Samuel L. Collins-Matilda Dunkelbarger |
|     | 26 Sep 1880 | Chancy M. Wright-Mary E. Tinner |
| 277 | 27 Sep 1880 | Daniel Hilderbrand-Clara Spoor |
|     | 3 Oct 1880 | Soloman Romig-Josephene Hill |
| 278 | 5 Oct 1880 | James M. Tucker, Jr.-Anna Tufts |
|     | 7 Oct 1880 | William Dunkelbarger-Lucy J. Stanridge |
| 279 | 12 Oct 1880 | Athanasious B. Ellas-Sarah M. Spoor |
|     | 17 Oct 1880 | J. Edward Fairchilds-Rebecca A. Wertsbaugher |
| 280 | 29 Oct 1880 | James W. Adair-Alma H. Shatto |
|     | 1 Nov 1880 | Albert C. Stevenson-Estor Green |
| 281 | 7 Nov 1880 | Samuel A. Bechtol-Mary A. Osborn |
|     | 7 Nov 1880 | James D. Harness-Mary C. Roose |
| 282 | 4 Nov 1880 | Henry A. Woodworth-Mary Koontz |
|     | 11 Nov 1880 | Philip Awald-Rhoda Awald |
| 283 | 11 Nov 1880 | John H. Banty-Clary Tilden |
|     | 22 Nov 1880 | Frank M. Geddes-Emma J. Tucker |
| 284 | 14 Nov 1880 | William Peelle-Rosa Windish |
|     | 21 Nov 1880 | Thomas H. Short-Martha J. Clements |
| 285 | 30 Nov 1880 | Joseph Dreis-Emley Munsonburgh |
|     | 23 Nov 1880 | Michael D. Falvey-Anna McLaughlin |
| 286 | 5 Dec 1880 | Henry Carter-Sarah Turner |
|     | 7 Dec 1880 | James C. Potter-Amanda J. Ellis |
| 287 | 14 Dec 1880 | Hiram G. Shilling-Alice S. Prettyman |
|     | 15 Dec 1880 | Zachriah P. Hunt-Mary Cooper |
| 288 | 2 Dec 1880 | George Bender-Emma Schussler |
|     | 15 Dec 1880 | Duglass Patsell-Mary Allie Adair |
| 289 | 23 Dec 1880 | Clayton W. Nichols-Zella F. Ammons |
|     | 31 Dec 1880 | John Heminger-Sarah H.F. Archibald |
| 290 | 1 Jan 1881 | Elijah W. Cannon-Mary Martilla Boyles |
|     | 6 Jan 1881 | Lewis Brenner-Mary A. Seagraves |

| PAGE | DATE | GROOM — BRIDE |
|------|------|---------------|
| 291 | 13 Jan 1881 | George M. Rarick-Nancy Shock |
| | 13 Jan 1881 | Abel Patrick-Elizabeth Finch |
| 292 | 30 Jan 1881 | James W. Brown-Anna J. Hall |
| | 3 Feb 1881 | Cyrus W. Hecox-Hester Loring |
| 293 | 3 Feb 1881 | Joseph A. Headley-Sarah E. Clark |
| | 3 Feb 1881 | Joseph E. Jones-Annie Nealis |
| 294 | 16 Feb 1881 | Monroe Baldwin-Frances T. Hopkins |
| | 20 Feb 1881 | Charles W. Favorit-Jane Davis |
| 295 | 22 Feb 1881 | Fredrick Minebury-Laura Taylor |
| | 3 Mar 1881 | Essex B. Ketchum-Mary B. Bickle |
| 296 | 12 Mar 1881 | William Dial-Vashti L. Schofield |
| | 17 Mar 1881 | Henry Redman-Rosa Mann |
| 297 | 20 Mar 1881 | Morgan Welsh-Emma H. Stanton |
| | 27 Mar 1881 | Wallace U. Earl-Mary E. Ipe |
| 298 | 4 Apr 1881 | Virgil M. Demoss-Olive Jane Calaway |
| | 6 Apr 1881 | Levi Stevenson-Jane Smith |
| 299 | 7 Apr 1881 | Andrew J. Jackson-Sadie Phillips |
| | 12 Apr 1881 lic | James C. Stephenson-Lilly W. Lee |
| 300 | 17 Apr 1881 | Samuel W. Cooper-Susan Osborn |
| | 20 Apr 1881 | William H. Knapp-Lousa Allen |
| 301 | 28 Apr 1881 | Addison Morrow-Anna J. Clark |
| | 2 Jun 1881 | Nathan M. Jarrett-Mary R. Werner |
| 302 | 7 Jun 1881 | John P. Tucker-Mary Ester Tracy |
| | 12 Jun 1881 | William Hopp-Polina Hentz |
| 303 | 12 Jun 1881 | Christ Schricker-Anna M. Meier |
| | 18 Jun 1881 | Joseph M. Kris-Joannah Foltz |
| 304 | 3 Jul 1881 | George Troaster-Amelia Henz |
| | 25 Jun 1881 | Alexander Scott-Mary E. Inks |
| 305 | 25 Jun 1881 | Ralph Hill-Adda Hornsby |
| | 8 Jul 1881 | William J. Hyne-Amanda A. Eatinger |
| 306 | 2 Jul 1881 | Joshua Bede-Hannah Strimback |
| | 24 Jul 1881 | Calvin Cherry-Ida May Niles |
| 307 | 5 Aug 1881 | Thomas Hart-Mary Ann Hornby |
| | 21 Aug 1881 | Edward Schrock-Mary Jones |
| 308 | 13 Sep 1881 | Frank Robison-Rachel Beatty |
| | 14 Sep 1881 | William Deen-Lora Burge |
| 309 | 15 Sep 1881 | Henry A. Jackson-Jane Hillabold |
| | 17 Sep 1881 | Owen Ritter-Ella Warner |
| 310 | 24 Sep 1881 | Steven Nave-Clara Meek |
| | 24 Sep 1881 | John M. McDonald-Martha Ann Hagle |
| 311 | 29 Sep 1881 | Benjimin F. Williams-Frances E. Singleton |
| | 6 Oct 1881 | Orlando Austin-Mary E. Kepperling |
| 312 | 9 Oct 1881 | John A. Hubbartt-Marcia F. Taylor |
| | 16 Oct 1881 | Franklin Ross-Josephine Summers |
| 313 | 16 Oct 1881 | John Sult-Lizzie Long |
| | 15 Nov 1881 | Frank Iten-Mary Daily |

| PAGE | DATE | GROOM — BRIDE |
|------|------|---------------|
| 314 | 20 Oct 1881 | Sylvanus N. Tilberry-Mary E. Bell |
|  | 23 Oct 1881 | Andrew J. Switzer-Lidia McCumber |
| 315 | 24 Oct 1881 | Joseph Clements-Milley Kelley |
|  | 26 Oct 1881 | Addam Bickel-Mary Stewart |
| 316 | 30 Oct 1881 | Jesse Brown-Flora Flowers |
|  | 2 Nov 1881 | Egbert E. Page-Ettie M. Hepner |
| 317 | 17 Nov 1881 | Charles Harman-Lucinda Mann |
|  | 24 Nov 1881 | Albert E. Barnes-Adoria J. Morton |
| 318 | 23 Nov 1881 | Andrew B. Barnes-Delia Ford |
|  | 23 Jan 1882 | Michael J. Kenefick-Mary Carroll |
| 319 | 7 Dec 1881 | Joseph Wyland-Sarah Lucinda Pierce |
|  | 11 Dec 1881 | George E. Dunkelberger-Jenna M. Morton |
| 320 | 18 Dec 1881 | George E. Patrick-Martha E. Fletcher |
|  | 15 Dec 1881 | Frank Diehl-Emma Cannon |
| 321 | 17 Dec 1881 | John E. Osborn-Eliza J. Nealis |
|  | 21 Dec 1881 | Henry W. Garner-Mattie M. Hepner |
| 322 | 2 Dec 1881 | Millard F. Jones-Adaline McLaughlin |
|  | 21 Dec 1881 | Augustus H. Knosman-Ida Ammons |
| 323 | 8 Jan 1882 | Martin Lefever-Maggie Hanby |
|  | 5 Jan 1882 | Henry Baumgardt-Clara Long |
| 324 | 6 Jan 1882 | Franklin Hains-Mary R. Troyer |
|  | 15 Jan 1882 | Frank Calaway-Emma H. Fite |
| 325 | 20 Jan 1882 | John Michael Haines-Henrietta Hornby |
|  | 26 Jan 1882 | Oliver Swanson-Mary M. Stoker |
| 326 | 28 Jan 1882 | Levi N. Nave-Dora Summers |
|  | 29 Jan 1882 | Fredrick Fite-Emily Simmons |
| 327 | 2 Feb 1882 | Josiah York-Sarah J. Shoemaker |
|  | 19 Feb 1882 | William H. Dunkelbarger-Viola A. Martindale |
| 328 | 22 Feb 1882 | Samuel R. Byres-Caroline E. Cormick |
|  | 25 Feb 1882 | Jacob H. Paul-Sarah Koontz |
| 329 | 3 Mar 1882 | George Favorite-Mira Hersing |
|  | 16 Mar 1882 | William Bickel-Mary E. Harkins |
| 330 | 18 Mar 1882 | Joseph H. Crabbs-Nancy Cole |
|  | 20 Mar 1882 | George W. Peniston-Jemima Stigleman |
| 331 | 4 Apr 1882 | William A. Campbell-Aley Stephenson |
|  | 13 Apr 1882 | Jacob J. Cromley-Mary P. Loring |
| 332 | 17 Apr 1882 | Samuel F. Meldin-Cora Bell Thompson |
|  | 25 May 1882 | Leonard Kinsey-Nellie Vandalen |
| 333 | 9 May 1882 | Charles Will-Sarah Gingrich |
|  | 25 May 1882 | Abner R. Wentz-Ettie Knachel |
| 334 | 27 May 1882 | William Kimerer-Mary Anderson |
|  | 1 Jun 1882 | Charles Milner-Hannah Maude Holland |
| 335 | 2 Jun 1882 | William Marsh-Malinda Bickle |
|  | 17 Jun 1882 | George Dearduff-Ruth A. Beem |
| 336 | 6 Jul 1882 | William H. Witham-Emma Breeding |
|  | 22 Jul 1882 | James M. Lerch-Violna Finch |

| PAGE | DATE | GROOM — BRIDE |
|------|------|---------------|
| 337 | 1 Aug 1882 | William L. Fletcher-Huldah Loring |
| | 20 Aug 1882 | George F. Morgan-Sarah A. Dipert |
| 338 | 20 Aug 1882 | Robert J. Fallis-Sarah J. Fletcher |
| | 20 Aug 1882 | Jeremiah H. Brickles-Maggie J. Gibbs |
| 339 | 14 Sep 1882 | John D. Inks-Mary Williams |
| | 17 Sep 1882 | Samuel C. Rector-Nellie Summers |
| 340 | 23 Sep 1882 | Henry Kash-Rilla Davis |
| | 8 Oct 1882 | August Barke-Augusta Seifert |
| 341 | 7 Oct 1882 | Jesse C. Stanton-Sindarilla Berry |
| | 13 Oct 1882 | Fredrick Geissel-Elisabeth Goldstein |
| 342 | 31 Oct 1882 | August A. Dommer-Emma Schinosliski |
| | 7 Dec 1882 | John Cannon-Mary A. DeCamp |
| 343 | 24 Oct 1882 | Leroy S. Gillespy-Minnie Glazebrook |
| | 29 Oct 1882 | John R. Hawkins-Lucinda Hill |
| 344 | 26 Oct 1882 | Oscar Golding-Mary Geisleman |
| | 28 Oct 1882 | John D. Mosher-Lilly M. Dunkelbarger |
| 345 | 5 Nov 1882 | Charls M. Dunkelbarger-Mary Lawrance |
| | 1 Nov 1882 | James Cavin-Frances H. Dickson |
| 346 | 12 Nov 1882 | Joseph Fite-Sarah M. Morton |
| | 19 Nov 1882 | Samuel M. Smith-Rosa L. Hardy |
| 347 | 23 Nov 1882 | William O. Mulvane-Emma Hichcock |
| | 24 Nov 1882 | Stephen A. Finch-Susan Philo |
| 348 | 25 Nov 1882 | William Edward Berry-Allie Patesel |
| 349 | 24 Dec 1882 | William H. Mitchel-Agnes Riffle |
| | 28 Dec 1882 | Charles Foryth-Lucy Sult |
| 350 | 31 Dec 1882 | William Cunningham-Sarah Frich |
| | 30 Dec 1882 | John W. Cochran-Olive J. Reed |
| 351 | 1 Jan 1883 | Joseph Cannon-Hannah Speelman |
| | 12 Jan 1883 | Isaac Hayes-Carrie McCray |
| 352 | 28 Jan 1883 | Edward Groshands-Loretta Bennett |
| | 1 Feb 1883 | Charles Wesley Colwell-Rebecca Ellen Hiatt |
| 353 | 7 Feb 1883 | Lewis German-Clara A. Clements |
| | 29 Dec 1882 | Carlton W. Voris-Jennie D. Robinson |
| 354 | 24 Feb 1883 | Henry Guernsey-Allie M. McCormack |
| | 15 Feb 1883 | Oliver P. Marks-Lovina C. Black |
| 355 | 12 Mar 1883 | John R. Eskridge-Elizabeth Fletcher |
| | 20 May 1883 | Seben Sebens-Christina Schultz |
| 356 | 31 Mar 1883 | William J. McDonald-Victoria E. Williams |
| | 11 Apr 1883 | William A. Hiatt-Frances M. Records |
| 357 | 13 Apr 1883 | Jacob Simmons-Louisa Peters |
| | 31 Apr 1883 | J.F. Rich-Emly Turner |
| 358 | 22 Apr 1883 | Daniel Coffin-Susanah Reynolds |
| | 1 May 1883 | Charley Johns-Chathrine Schebart |
| 359 | 15 May 1883 | George Heltzler-Lanie Caroline McCormick |
| | 12 May 1883 | Joseph Frank-Louisa J. Hawkins |

| PAGE | DATE | GROOM — BRIDE |
|------|------|---------------|
| 360 | 10 May 1883 | James William Clark-Mary Barnes |
|     | 20 May 1883 | Albert B. Davis-Mary E. Heath |
| 361 | 5 Jun 1883 | Henry Miller-Matilda Brown |
|     | 31 May 1883 | Charles E. Baird-Emma R. Dull |
| 362 | 21 Jun 1883 | S.H. Jones-Ladora Staufer |
|     | 23 Jun 1883 | Stephen Tucker-Victoria E. Stanton |
| 363 | 29 Jun 1883 | Robert Raynelds-Josephine Shaw |
|     | 30 Jun 1883 | All Stepenson-Nancy Jane Bevelhymer |
| 364 | 14 Jul 1883 | John Baseney-Margaret J. Favorite |
|     | 17 Jul 1883 | D.G. Harrington-Leuis Hadach |
| 365 | 29 Jul 1883 | Nahum O. Peacock-Mary E. Bowers |
|     | 31 Jul 1883 | James Singleton-Matilda Noonan |
| 366 | 7 Aug 1883 | Reuben Coffin-Sarah Shilling |
|     | 30 Jul 1883 | Jason W. Heath-Lydia A. Fike |
| 367 | 18 Aug 1883 | Myron E. Tuttle-Emma Brazier |
|     | 29 Aug 1883 | Meredith Moor-Martha J. Thompson |
| 368 | 30 Aug 1883 | Frank Windisch-Mary Willhelm |
|     | 3 Aug 1883 | Albert Warn-Margaret R. Taylor |
| 369 | 21 Oct 1883 | Philander Lowery-Mary E. Davidson |
|     | 1 Nov 1883 | Benjamin Moorman-Mary E. Hay |
| 370 | 13 Oct 1883 | Wilhelm Tismer-Julia White |
|     | 6 Oct 1883 | August J. Olson-Nancy E. McCumber |
| 371 | 3 Nov 1883 | John Boyle-Norah Casey |
|     | 20 Oct 1883 | Adelbert C. Brown-Josephene Flowers |
| 372 | 27 Oct 1883 | Isaac D. Osborn-Adaline Dunkelberger |
|     | 28 Oct 1883 | Obed H. Depert-Clara A.V. Crouch |
| 373 | 16 Nov 1883 | Frederick Well-Tilla Weil |
|     | 11 Nov 1883 | Harmen Rank-Alma Chapman |
| 374 | 13 Nov 1883 | George Hann-Rosena Bower |
|     | 25 Nov 1883 | William Nintz-Caroline Fedke |
| 375 | 28 Nov 1883 | William L. Fairchild-Sarah E. Hiler |
|     | 1 Dec 1883 | Levi Williams-Clara Trump |
| 376 | 2 Dec 1883 | Amos Cunningham-Olive Ausim |
|     | 2 Dec 1883 | Cornelius C. Cutter-Frances O. Anderson |
| 377 | 26 Dec 1883 | William Teets-Adelia Wilde |
|     | 20 Dec 1883 | Arthur J. Chaplin-Lyde A. Reed |
| 378 | 13 Dec 1883 | William B. Atkins-Elmira Cooper |
|     | 13 Dec 1883 | John Hamilton-Laura Smith |
| 379 | 24 Dec 1883 | William J. Volkamer-Mariah Rock |
|     | 24 Dec 1883 | Willis Savery-Julia Bazney |
| 380 | 24 Dec 1883 | Fredrick A. Chaple-Eliza J. Krisy |
|     | 25 Dec 1883 | Charles J. Lundin-Emma Jane Prettyman |
| 381 | 5 Jan 1884 | Isaac Hardsock-Rosetta E. Dean |
|     | 17 Jan 1884 | William S. Easterday-Susannah A. Romig |
| 382 | 21 Jan 1884 | John Heartz-Maggie Brookman |
|     | 2 Feb 1884 | Paul Sult-Etta E. Talyor |

| PAGE | DATE | GROOM — BRIDE |
|------|------|---------------|
| 383 | 19 Feb 1884 | John H. Bernard-Mahala Taylor |
|     | 23 Feb 1884 | Joseph Sellers-Emma Casper |
| 384 | 25 Feb 1884 | Pleasant M. Thompson-Mary A. Roberts |
|     | 16 Mar 1884 | Peter Wolf-Mabel Coil |
| 385 | 15 Mar 1884 | George Willhelm-Manerva Kline |
|     | 22 Mar 1884 | Johnathan Collins-Emma C. Berry |
| 386 | 28 Mar 1884 | Abel Patrick-Eliza Kniss |
|     | 1 Apr 1884 | Henry W. Huret-Ruth Watkins |
| 387 | 6 Apr 1884 | George W. Osborn-Lanora Leighty |
|     | 10 Apr 1884 | Andrew J. Stevens-Laura A. Young |
| 388 | 14 Apr 1884 | William H. Thornburg-Genetta Ashley |
|     | 19 Apr 1884 | Frank M. Johnson-Mary E. Thomas |
| 389 | 20 Apr 1884 | Alexander Horner-Katharine Edwards |
|     | 27 Apr 1884 | William P. Castleman-Mary A. Fedders |
| 390 | 29 Apr 1884 | Benjamin Welsh-Catharine Walsh |
|     | 4 May 1884 | Lewis M. Steutsman-Samina M. Gappert |
| 391 | 3 May 1884 | Charles Trumbul-Anna Cochran |
|     | 8 May 1884 | John A. Bunner-Letitia Bickel |
| 392 | 31 May 1884 | Lorenzo P. Hiatte-Lucy May Reed |
|     | 1 Jun 1884 | John Brown-Elizabeth A. Taylor |
| 393 | 24 Jun 1884 | James E. Jolly-Jennie M. McDonald |
|     | 4 Jul 1884 | Amos Bertram Depert-Lydia C. Menser |
| 394 | 23 Jul 1884 | Lincan Clark-Elida M. Inman |
|     | 9 Aug 1884 | John H. Rehard-Amanda Chambers |
| 395 | 14 Aug 1884 | William A. Lane-Mary L. Owens |
|     | 21 Aug 1884 | Andrew J. Thompson-Anna M. Swanson |
| 396 | 21 Aug 1884 | William Etter-Ella Johnson |
|     | 8 Sep 1884 | Levi B. Hummel-Alvina E. Warner |
| 397 | 8 Sep 1884 | Cornelius J. Rock-Bertha A. Rank |
|     | 15 Sep 1884 | John Welsh-Ella Daly |
| 398 | 24 Nov 1884 | August F. Luken-Louisa C. Hutt |
|     | 3 Oct 1884 | Rudolph Pett-Emeline M. Ferch |
| 399 | 4 Oct 1884 | John C. Myers-Sarah E. Lark |
|     | 28 Nov 1884 | Leonard Dietz-Antona Schmidt |
| 400 | 19 Oct 1884 | August Born-Bertha Tonart |
|     | 14 Oct 1884 | Charles Born-Louisa Hantz |
| 401 | 15 Oct 1884 | Albert F Belger-Matilda Warner |
|     | 28 Oct 1884 | Leander Morris-Carline Clearwater |
| 402 | 28 Oct 1884 | George W. Coats-Mary Jane Spicer |
|     | 6 Nov 1884 | Alfred A. Garner-Ella E. Ford |
| 403 | 23 Nov 1884 | James A. McCrackin-Lottie Avery |
|     | 23 Nov 1884 | Jacob Simmons-Mary Myers |
| 404 | 3 Dec 1884 | James H. Beach-Frances L. Dunkelberger |
|     | 25 Dec 1884 | Isaac Holmes-Mary B. Selock |
| 405 | 23 Dec 1884 | Frank L. Hay-Sarah C. Laramore |
|     | 25 Dec 1884 | Samuel Blockson-Jennie Duboice |

| PAGE | DATE | GROOM — BRIDE |
|------|------|---------------|
| 406 | 24 Dec 1884 | James A. Bell-Catharine Brazier |
| | 24 Dec 1884 | Samuel G. Evans-Mary J. Kriss |
| 407 | 28 Dec 1884 | Huston Crum-Maggie Loy |
| | 30 Dec 1884 | Frank C. Moyer-Varilla Chambers |
| 408 | 5 Jan 1885 | Frederick J. Zelch-Henrietta A.W. Barbknecht |
| | 20 Jan 1885 | Elmer E. Masterson-S. Jennie Chidester |
| 409 | 12 Feb 1885 | George A. Talbert-Ida M. Patch |
| | 14 Feb 1885 | A. Alincoln Gurnsey-Martha J. Page |
| 410 | 2 Mar 1885 | Jacob A. Deem-Laura B. Heath |
| | 11 Apr 1885 | Albert Novark-Mary James |
| 411 | 14 Apr 1885 | Danial Faltz-Ella Smith |
| | 19 Apr 1885 | Grangcott Carl Rux-Pulina Ernst |
| 412 | 21 Apr 1885 | Jacob Vogelgesang-Flra Logan |
| | 26 Apr 1885 | Michael Daley-Augusta Shultz |
| 413 | 5 May 1885 | Martin Schricker-Annie M. Roller |
| | 28 Apr 1885 | Sturgis S. Yeley-Ennie E. Sherman |
| 414 | 7 May 1885 | Joseph Lancaster-Alice T. Rebstock |
| | 10 May 1885 | Abney Hay-Maggie Dincan |
| 415 | 12 May 1885 lic | Max Caskoske-Kate Jankoske |
| | 13 May 1885 | Robert R. Roberts-Harietta Glazebrook |
| 416 | 21 May 1885 | Edgar Hapeman-Florence M. McCray |
| | 1 Jun 1885 | George Vannote-Lydia F. Rhodes |
| 417 | 17 May 1885 | John W. Good-Annie M. Clements |
| | 10 Jun 1885 | Rob. W. Jones-Ella E. Vail |
| 418 | 8 Jul 1885 | Charles Bartholomew-Lillie Randall |
| | 20 Apr 1885 | Edward Monroe-Caitty B. Fults |
| 419 | 18 Jul 1885 lic | William H. Liehtz-Mattie Coffin |
| | 23 Jul 1885 | Peter Hartz-Ida Shanks |
| 420 | 28 Jul 1885 | Daton Shanks-Flora B. Smith |
| | 9 Aug 1885 | James A. Cunningham-Susan C. Inks |
| 421 | 16 Aug 1885 | John E. Hartford-Ida A. Gibbs |
| | 18 Aug 1885 | Charles Barkey-Agnes M. Beard |
| 422 | 23 Aug 1885 | Alfred A. Savery-Adie R. Groshaus |
| | 28 Aug 1885 | John Dizon Inks-Mary E. Fry |
| 423 | 30 Aug 1885 | Carl Wilhelm Mylues-Dorthea Knoke |
| | 3 Sep 1885 | Nathan M. Coffin-Ella Bonar |
| 424 | 11 Sep 1885 | John W. Stewart-Clara E. Wolfgang |
| | 14 Sep 1885 | Jesse C. Stanton-Sussen Hiller |
| 425 | 15 Sep 1885 | John W. Lee-Ciddie V. Stephenson |
| | 15 Sep 1885 | John Armstrong-Idora Armstrong |
| 426 | 16 Sep 1885 | Thomas M. Callaway-Marcie L. Hart |
| | 19 Sep 1885 | George M. Hathaway-Jennie Davis |
| 427 | 21 Sep 1885 | Andrew Dagget-Sarah J. Hopper |
| | 23 Sep 1885 | Andrew Jankoenski-Mary Podach |
| 428 | 24 Sep 1885 | George Holman Trevor-Nacy Ella Beatty |
| | 26 Sep 1885 lic | Joseph C. Hathaway-Eliose Hoyt |

| PAGE | DATE | GROOM — BRIDE |
|------|------|---------------|
| 429 | 4 Oct 1885 | George W. Scott-Sarah E. Stephenson |
| | 2 Oct 1885 | John W. Ridenour-Retta Davis |
| 430 | 7 Oct 1885 | Sigle Shoemaker-Emily C. Wamsley |
| | 17 Oct 1885 | William Hanes-Julia Ann Shelden |
| 431 | 16 Nov 1885 | Joseph Parrish-Sophrona Cannon |
| | 25 Oct 1885 | Michael J. Welch-Luety Matilda Groshaus |
| 432 | 3 Nov 1885 | William E. Oppy-Annie E. Swartz |
| | 15 Nov 1886 [85] | Abel Patrick-Elizabeth Patrick |
| 433 | 17 Nov 1885 | Israel Frees-Emma J. Sheely |
| | 18 Nov 1885 | Levi Ashley-Luella Wood |
| 434 | 16 Nov 1885 lic | Joseph Parrish-Saprona Cannon |
| | 19 Nov 1885 lic | Charles W. Hanes-Sarah A Howard |
| 435 | 23 Nov 1885 | Samuel J.S. Thomas-Tillie E. Woofgang |
| | 26 Nov 1885 | Watson K. Woodroff-Mary A. Vandalson |
| 436 | 15 Jan 1886 | Mathew Binger-Molly Turnbull |
| | 24 Dec 1885 | William P. Fletcher-Susie H. Tucker |
| 437 | 10 Jan 1886 | George Parish-Sarrah E. Campbell |
| | 8 Jan 1886 lic | David Miller-Rebecca Boyd |
| 438 | 12 Jan 1886 | G. August Rank-Catharine Walter |
| | 11 Feb 1886 | Peter Wetherholt-Nancy A. Steward |
| 439 | 18 Feb 1886 | William O'Conner-Laury Badgley |
| | 4 Feb 1886 | George Langenbahn-Jane Horner |
| 440 | 4 Feb 1886 | Alfred Myers-Katie A. Hanselman |
| | 8 Feb 1886 | John W. Cox-Augusta Waddington |
| 441 | 20 Feb 1886 | George W. Miller-Angelia E. Loring |
| | 20 Feb 1886 | Liman F. Emigh-Ella Cidister |
| 442 | 26 Feb 1886 | William H. Emigh-Mary S. Reich |
| | 15 Mar 1886 | William A. Phillips-Martha Ann Coleman |
| 443 | 21 Mar 1886 | Samuel A. Good-Kattie Casper |
| | 23 Mar 1886 | Orpheus Shaw-Ruthan Poter |
| 444 | 22 Mar 1886 | William H. Peckham-Bettie Cole |
| | 27 Mar 1886 | Christian Emigh-Rebecca A. Williams |
| 445 | 31 Mar 1886 | Joseph A. Townall-Clary B. Green |
| | 25 Apr 1886 | Jacob A. Cannon-Widdie Boyles |
| 446 | 27 Apr 1886 | Schuyler C. Shilling-Amanda E. Collier |
| | 1 May 1886 | Arthur A. Albertson-Louis R.L. Spicer |
| 447 | 9 May 1886 | Marcellus Lucas-Bertha V. Clemans |
| | 29 May 1886 | Swain Post-Retta Speelman |
| 448 | 2 Jun 1886 | Wilson T. Loing-Mary C. Jolly |
| | 14 Jun 1886 | James Jana-Anna Kegebine |
| 449 | 26 Jun 1886 | Frederick A.A.O. Rouse-Lydia A. Munroe |
| | 21 Jun 1886 | Edward E. Anderson-Sarah J. Yaukey |
| 450 | 1 Jul 1886 | Jasper N. Cochran-Louis D. Adair |
| | 6 Jun 1886 | Samuel Baker-Rosetta Whitzell |
| 451 | 25 Jul 1886 | Jason G. Diamond-Lovina Eatinger |
| | 29 Jul 1886 | Jacob B. Reeg-Cornelia E. Short |

| PAGE | DATE | GROOM — BRIDE |
|------|------|---------------|
| 452 | 3 Aug 1886 | Joseph Kolars-Mary Smith |
| | 29 Jul 1886 | Benjamin P. Fallis-Geneva Stevenson |
| 453 | 8 Aug 1886 | Franklin Watkins-Josephene Simpson |
| | 12 Aug 1886 | Charles R. Fletcher-Flora Foster |
| 454 | 2 Sep 1886 | John H. Shafer-Eliza J. Geiselman |
| | 6 Nov 1886 | John Guke-Mary E. Conner |
| 455 | 2 Sep 1886 | A.D. Thomas-Mary A. Adams |
| | 23 Sep 1886 | William H. Shontz-Daisy D. Koonsman |
| 456 | 19 Sep 1886 | Charles E. Dener-Anna E. Williams |
| | 1 Oct 1886 | Perry Chance-Elizabeth N. Chitester |
| 457 | 1 Oct 1886 | Caleb Hill-Rena Rank |
| | 14 Oct 1886 | John Swarts-Tabitha L. Shafer |
| 458 | 17 Oct 1886 | Thomas Cooper-Mary Alice Quigly |
| | 21 Oct 1886 | Joseph Swarts-Mariah Stephenson |
| 459 | 1 Nov 1886 | James Anderson-Catharine M. Fry |
| | 2 Nov 1886 | Joshua Beaty-Anna Roupe |
| 460 | 3 Nov 1886 | Valentine L. Shultz-Sarah F. Shively |
| | 31 Nov 1886 | Elijah Rice-Sarah A. Swarts |
| 461 | 24 Nov 1886 | John Redd-Ladora A. Staufer |
| | 25 Nov 1886 | Moses Menser-Emma Geiselman |
| 462 | 28 Nov 1886 | Frederick Marsh-Clara Alice Shafer |
| | 1 Dec 1886 | John M. Lane-Jennie Keller |
| 463 | 18 Apr 1886 | John W. Watterhouse-Rosa L. Baldwin |
| | 5 Dec 1886 | William Dunkelbarger-Maggie Speelman |
| 464 | 19 Dec 1886 | Isaac J. Butterfield-Alice Tucker |
| | 31 Oct 1886 | William Callaway-Mary M. Brown |
| 465 | 18 Dec 1886 | Aaron T. Vail-Mabel M. Kilgore |
| | 20 Dec 1886 | James S. Thompson-Manela S. Campbell |
| 466 | 28 Dec 1886 | Edward G. Loser-Luella G. Willson |
| | 12 Jan 1887 | Charles Kinderman-Mena Parduien |
| 467 | 1 Jan 1887 | Obed R. Deen-Ettie T. Hisey |
| | 2 Jan 1887 | Oscar D. Hitchcock-Rosa E. Leiby |
| 468 | 17 Jan 1887 | Frank Kolar-Mary Burjanck |
| | 9 Dec 1886 | Theadore Jordan-Bartha Happes |
| 469 | 23 Jan 1887 | Calvin G. Harless-Lovina Prettyman |
| | 16 Jan 1887 | James C. Dipert-Allie Crim |
| 470 | 13 Jan 1887 | John C. Smith-Lydie E. Barton |
| | 22 Jan 1887 | Louis T. Long-W. Newman |
| 471 | 21 Jan 1887 | Plinna Nave-Allie M. Hay |
| | 26 Jan 1887 | Owen Daily-Maggie Walsh |
| 472 | 25 Jan 1887 | Joseph Francis-Anna Messler |
| | 1 Feb 1887 | Mathew Kays-Mary Finn |
| 473 | 27 Feb 1887 | Otis F. Smith-Emma A. Davis |
| | 28 Feb 1887 | Mark E. Wright-Jasophene Favorite |
| 474 | 5 Mar 1887 | Joseph N. McCormick-Ella A. Carpenter |
| | 8 Mar 1887 | William E. Roose-Ida E. Veach |

| PAGE | DATE | GROOM — BRIDE |
|------|------|---------------|
| 475 | 10 Mar 1887 | John W. Rock-Louisa L. Rank |
|  | 12 Mar 1887 lic | Tobias H. Cole-Louisa S. Foster |
| 476 | 16 Mar 1887 | Jacob Wolfgang-Matilda Gates |
|  | 20 Mar 1887 | Artillis R. Taylor-Susana Adams |
| 477 | 23 Mar 1887 | Daniel Trayer-Sarah Beede |
|  | 30 Mar 1887 | William E. Payne-Eva M. Chritchfield |
| 478 | 9 Apr 1887 | Thomas Hill-Ruth Davidson |
|  | 14 Apr 1887 | Stacy Hill-Luella Willson |
| 479 | 18 Apr 1887 | James A. Tomlison-Luisa J. Mulvain |
|  | 24 Apr 1887 | Julius Michalski-Louiza Schultz |
| 480 | 7 Apr 1887 | Albert B. Fletcher-Jennie E. Scudder |
|  | 1 May 1887 | Franklin D. Weed-Emma J. Cox |
| 481 | 21 May 1887 | August Batten-Augusta Fleming |
|  | 17 May 1887 | Edgar W. Shilling-Flora M. Spiker |
| 482 | 19 May 1887 | Jacob A. Dean-Ida J. Hiler |
|  | 19 May 1887 | Kirk Rodgers-Sarah Conner |
| 483 | 26 May 1887 | Charles H. Lane-Bertha A. Roberts |
|  | 1 Jun 1887 | Nathaniel W. Littrel-Lanora Sharp |
| 484 | 2 Jun 1887 | Elias W. Green-Ella Warren |
|  | 7 Jun 1887 | Alvyron C. Naylor-Lillie Staufer |
| 485 | 8 Jun 1887 | Fredrick Shultz-Augusta Stark |
|  | 21 Jun 1887 | Robat R. Roberts-Ninnie R. McCray |
| 486 | 26 Jun 1887 | George H. Baker-Clara Denor |
|  | 29 Jun 1887 | Clement L. Rogers-Martha B. Laramore |
| 487 | 30 Jun 1887 | Noah Bennett-Lisetta Schroder |
|  | 2 Jul 1887 lic | August Schmidt-Ottilie Guse |
| 488 | 18 Jul 1887 | Lisha Robins-Elizabeth Welch |
|  | 31 Jul 1887 | Dennie O'Brien-Clara E. Yager |
| 489 | 14 Aug 1887 | Rebbert Myers-Orah A. Peeler |
|  | 22 Aug 1887 | Abijah Gilmore-Amanda M. Willson |
| 490 | 23 Aug 1887 | William W. Gust-Ida M. Gilmore |
|  | 25 Aug 1887 | J. M. Cormack-Ida Hull |
| 491 | 2 Sep 1887 | Amos A. Shaffer-Nancy E. Long |
|  | 10 Sep 1887 | Robin B. Stiles-Augusta May Swahn |
| 492 | 3 Sep 1887 | William Carpenter-Emma Ballenger |
|  | 7 Sep 1887 | Albert White-Mary Emigh |
| 493 | 8 Sep 1887 | John Menier-Minnie A. Miller |
|  | 17 Sep 1887 | Henry Brunder-Bartha Stuck |
| 494 | 26 Sep 1887 | William H. Stailey-Jennie R. McVey |
|  | 2 Oct 1887 | George M. Sprague-Harriett Grenert |
| 495 | 2 Oct 1887 | Daniel E. Sharp-Phebe R. Short |
|  | 1 Oct 1887 | Elias Jones-Francis Turner |
| 496 | 6 Oct 1887 lic | John Ernst-Emma H. Neumann |
|  | 10 Oct 1887 | Charles W. Wright-Ida M. Smith |
| 497 | 10 Oct 1887 | John W. Stephenson-Almina A. Spicer |
|  | 31 Aug 1887 | William Truby-Libbie Cole |

| PAGE | DATE | GROOM — BRIDE |
|------|------|---------------|
| 498 | 12 Oct 1887 | William E. Mattern-Mary A. Miner |
| | 13 Oct 1887 | A.J. Webster-Emily Roby |
| 499 | 30 Oct 1887 | William Caloway-Ceila Brattain |
| | 1 Nov 1887 | George W. Fairchilds-Sarah Conner |
| 500 | 2 Nov 1887 | William Lewis-Harretta Basney |
| | 6 Nov 1887 | Georg F. Philippi-Alice D. Tibbs |
| 501 | 8 Nov 1887 | Andrew J. Shell-Arvila James |
| | 16 Nov 1887 lic | John B. Shafer-Laura O. Stephenson |
| 502 | 27 Nov 1887 | George A. Rough-Elizabeth Stickler |
| | 8 Dec 1887 | Charles Blue-Florence Taylor |
| 503 | 24 Dec 1887 | Henry C. Hawblitzel-Lizzie Anderson |
| | 15 Dec 1887 | Howard M. Chapel-Clarra A. Windish |
| 504 | 25 Dec 1887 | David W. Trayer-Mahley J. Scott |
| | 25 Dec 1887 | George B. Tucker-Mary E. Romig |
| 505 | 24 Dec 1887 | John L. Christopher-Ida B. Coffin |
| | 29 Dec 1887 | Albert C. Wolfram-Ella M. Wright |
| 506 | 1 Jan 1888 | Grant R. Rockwell-Della M. Ridgeway |
| | 1 Jan 1888 | Phillip Woodworth-Matilda Koontz |
| 507 | 8 Jan 1888 | Robert A. McCrackin-Madora A. Bascum |
| | 19 Jan 1888 | August F. Erdman-Addie M. Adams |
| 508 | 19 Jan 1888 | George F. Hasker-Annah E. Hissong |
| | 4 Feb 1888 | James E. Quadlin-Mary E. Stevens |
| 509 | 7 Feb 1888 | Charles A. Williams-Mary L. Dilts |
| | 15 Feb 1888 | Elijah Ballenger-Emeline Walters |
| 510 | 29 Feb 1888 | Henry Arnd-Emma Finn |
| | 4 Mar 1888 | George W. Harden-Tressie J. Coffin |
| 511 | 2 Mar 1888 | Edward J. Curtis-Permelia E. Curtis |
| | 12 Mar 1888 | Albert F. Singleton-Florence Henselman |
| 512 | 15 Mar 1888 | James B. Fry-Martha J. Gurnsey |
| | 17 Mar 1888 | James B. Welsh-Dora M. Justice |
| 513 | 29 Mar 1888 | William Willson-Mary Hull |
| | 1 Apr 1888 | Charles Strew-Augusta Linling |
| 514 | 2 Apr 1888 | William H. Morris-Ettie C. Wamsley |
| | 8 Apr 1888 | Herman Hine-Sarah Lukin |
| 515 | 8 Apr 1888 | Hamlin Hardesty-Catharine M. Wolfram |
| | 8 Apr 1888 | Schuyler Fletcher-Sarah E. Speelman |
| 516 | 8 Apr 1888 | Jeremiah Clearwater-Tabitha Harrison |
| | 15 Mar 1888 | William C. Larren-Jessie W. Smith |
| 517 | 28 Apr 1888 | John Guiselman-Mary M. Smith |
| | 1 May 1888 | Eli B. Weed-Mary E. Davis |
| 518 | 3 May 1888 | N.L. Gurnsey-Mattie L. Larch |
| | 5 May 1888 | A.C. McCumber-Mary E. Dunkelbarger |
| 519 | 21 May 1888 | Charles Carey-Anna Foote |
| | 22 May 1888 | John L. Miller-Clara C. Brundrige |
| 520 | 30 May 1888 | John D. Inks-Elizabeth Trich |
| | 7 Jun 1888 lic | Elcany S. Matteson-Mary L. Faltz |

| PAGE | DATE | GROOM — BRIDE |
|---|---|---|
| 521 | 11 Jun 1888 | William Stevenson-Amelia C. Windel |
| | 26 May 1888 | George W. Anderson-Sarah M. Weed |
| 522 | 3 Jul 1888 | George Goppert-Elizabeth Pfugsfaupt |
| | 28 Jun 1888 | John W. Grindle-Mary J. Simmons |
| 523 | 6 Jul 1888 | George Richey-Minnie A. Willhelm |
| | 2 Jul 1888 | William Turner-Samanth Davis |
| 524 | 19 Jul 1888 | Merrit W. Shaw-Celestien Apllis Hull |
| | 1 Aug 1888 | Certiz O. Townsend-Icepene Dillon |
| 525 | 9 Aug 1888 | Sidney J. Childs-Mary R. Hall |
| | 7 Aug 1888 | Lewis Shultz-Lena Shultz |
| 526 | 19 Aug 1888 | Joseph Bahr-Emeline Taylor |
| | 23 Aug 1888 | Charles M. French-Ida A. Hazon |
| 527 | 31 Aug 1888 lic | William T. Buchanan-Kitty O'Neil |
| | 8 Sep 1888 | Eldo Johnson-Dolla V. Adams |
| 528 | 9 Sep 1888 | Sydney F. Leazenby-Alice R. Thomas |
| | 16 Sep 1888 | Daniel E. Dunkelbarger-Arwilda Troyer |
| 529 | 16 Sep 1888 | John E. Joseph-Mauda O. Yoder |
| | 26 Sep 1888 | George Schoonover-Laura M. Davis |
| 530 | 9 Oct 1888 | Alonzo Sharp-Eliza Wennegar |
| | 16 Oct 1888 | Jerry Falvy-Margaret Fitzgerald |
| 531 | 2 Oct 1888 | Charles C. Reprogle-Margarett Payne |
| | 5 Nov 1888 lic | Francis Arthur-Mary K. Zindorf |
| 532 | 12 Nov 1888 | Edward G. Nix-Nettie D. Reprogal |
| | 17 Nov 1888 | Jacob Fowley-Emma E. Vinson |
| 533 | 24 Nov 1888 | Jonathan D. Heath-Prissilla M. James |
| | 24 Nov 1888 | Thomas Wooderson-Matilda C. Harkins |
| 534 | 2 Dec 1888 | Samuel J. Brown-Sarah B. Archer |
| | 10 Dec 1888 | Myron A. Garrison-Ida Hazon |
| 535 | 15 Dec 1888 | Albert Vandalen-Mary E. Hacker |
| | 15 Dec 1888 | Charles M. Hart-Ida L. Larren |
| 536 | 20 Dec 1888 | William Turnburg-Della V. Smith |
| | 23 Dec 1888 | William T. Joseph-Rachel E. Hawkins |
| 537 | 24 Dec 1888 | William Hagle-Matilda Cavender |
| | 27 Dec 1888 | A.M. Deck-Jane E. Swartzel |
| 538 | 28 Dec 1888 | Nathan Scott-Ida Cherry |
| | 29 Dec 1888 | Isaac R. Short-Mary L. Lain |
| 539 | 31 Dec 1888 | William D. Dunfee-Cora Wolf |
| | 4 Jan 1889 | John D. Clark-Elizabeth Bradley |
| 540 | 26 Mar 1889 | John Hill-Sarah E. Robbin |
| | 27 Jan 1889 | James E. Bogart-Olive J. Davis |
| 541 | 6 Feb 1889 | Georg W. Smith-Alice Hisey |
| | 14 Feb 1889 | Sherman W. Tracy-Alice M. Carr |
| 542 | 16 Feb 1889 | George W. Martin-Anna L. Quigley |
| | 3 Mar 1889 | Adam F. Sider-Lilla M. Yeager |
| 543 | 17 Mar 1889 | Edward Krupski-Augusta Hupp |
| | 7 Mar 1889 | Peder Rhoda-Albertine Andem |

| PAGE | DATE | GROOM — BRIDE |
|------|------|---------------|
| 544 | 5 Mar 1889 | Lenard Long-Mary Badkins |
| | 7 Mar 1889 | Seward Rinehard-Dora Uncapher |
| 545 | 9 Mar 1889 | Jones G. Closson-Elizabeth E. Caloway |
| | 14 Mar 1889 | Harvey Landers-Ella A. McCormick |
| 546 | 30 Mar 1889 | S.A. McCrackin-Rachel Davidson |
| | 1 Apr 1889 | James R. German-Rosa B. Cavender |
| 547 | 2 Apr 1889 | Daniel W. Dunkelberger-Mary Richey |
| | 6 Apr 1889 | James Valoon-Anna Johnson |
| 548 | 10 Mar 1889 | Jessey F. Coffin-Mary E. Rebstock |
| | 10 Apr 1889 | Freeman T. Stanton-Rosa Hanselman |
| 549 | 9 Apr 1889 | Albian D. Swank-Berth E. Koontz |
| | 14 Apr 1889 | George T. Lindley-Emma C. Yager |
| 550 | 20 Apr 1889 | George W. Grave-Corie A. Pettis |
| | 23 Apr 1889 | Martin Buterbaugh-Elizabeth Stocker |
| 551 | 24 Apr 1889 | George Collins-Laura C. Stephenson |
| | 22 Apr 1889 | Frederick C. Coleman-Eliz S.C. Ptomy |
| 552 | 22 Apr 1889 | William C. Ripley-Caroline M. Keller |
| | 27 Apr 1889 | Thomas J. Mitchel-Lavina Vankirk |
| 553 | 2 May 1889 | John Fisher-Emma Long |
| | 5 May 1889 | Elmer E. Foote-Ida M. Cupp |
| 554 | 8 May 1889 | Schuyler Rorick-Abby J. Horner |
| | 7 May 1889 | Patrick Brazzel-Katie Kays |
| 555 | 16 May 1889 | Henry Kruger-Eliza Spinner |
| | 9 May 1889 | Ellis B. Cross-Ora Ebert |
| 556 | 21 May 1889 | Peter P. Bushbaum-Anna Schram |
| | 29 May 1889 | Heber Lankford-Lula M. Ammons |
| 557 | 1 Jun 1889 | Samuel Cavinder-Ida Alise Smith |
| | 9 Jun 1889 | Franklin Scott-Rosetty Sprague |
| 558 | 12 Jun 1889 | Rits L. Callahan-Clara D. Sherman |
| | 13 Jun 1889 lic | David Hitchcock-Augusta Bearnt |
| 559 | 19 Jun 1889 | Edward Lucas-Mary McKinsey |
| | 25 Jun 1889 | Kirk Rodgers-Cora Standon |
| 560 | 26 Jun 1889 | John M. Shouts-Rennie L. Ayers |
| | 2 Jul 1889 | Granville Emrick-Minnie Minnear |
| 561 | 8 Jul 1889 | John E. Smith-Margaret Uncapher |
| | 10 Jul 1889 | Charles M. Longwell-Eliza Summers |
| 562 | 13 Aug 1889 | Nathan McCumber-Zella Fallis |
| | 14 Aug 1889 | Walter Carpenter-Issabella Mock |
| 563 | 24 Aug 1889 | Henry T. Anderson-Emma H. Gorden |
| | 16 Aug 1889 | Charles Shultz-Anna Kaston |
| 564 | 24 Aug 1889 | Franklin Stanton-Bertha Kiser |
| | 25 Aug 1889 | John D. Hacked-Faima Huls |
| 565 | 27 Aug 1889 | Charles B. Atkins-Barbara Ann B. Emigh |
| | 29 Aug 1889 | Charles B. Fletcher-Dolly P. Brader |
| 566 | 5 Sep 1889 | Daniel S. Nave-Izora C. Horner |
| | 22 Sep 1889 | Franklin Grenart-Eliza J. Caywood |

| PAGE | DATE | GROOM — BRIDE |
|------|------|---------------|
| 567 | 24 Sep 1889 | Frank M. Leslie-Juliette C. Henderson |
|  | 29 Oct 1889 | Grant Emigh-Hattie J. Broadstreet |
| 568 | 3 Oct 1889 | William S. Smith-Hattie Davis |
|  | 6 Oct 1889 | Henry Foursythe-Mary A. Hiland |
| 569 | 5 Oct 1889 | James W. Hall-Dortha Diltz |
|  | 5 Oct 1889 | George W. Garbinson-Cora Ballinger |
| 570 | 12 Oct 1889 | Barton W. Murphy-Lillian M. Whitmore |
|  | 15 Oct 1889 | Samuel G. Kline-Amanda Kline |
| 571 | 15 Oct 1889 | Frank M. Parker-Ida M. Rector |
|  | 20 Oct 1889 | Gottleib Pflughaupt-Theressa Knacht |
| 572 | 24 Oct 1889 | Alexander H. Henderson-Loutetia Bickel |
|  | 31 Oct 1889 | Charles Farver-Ida Groshaus |
| 573 | 1 Nov 1889 lic | Amos Murry-Nannie E. Pope |
|  | 2 Nov 1889 Lic | Dalbert Liby-Lovina Joice |
| 574 | 9 Nov 1889 | George W. Megill-Alice J. Harrison |
|  | 10 Nov 1889 | James C. Hemminger-Fary B. Miller |
| 575 | 10 Nov 1889 | Edward Harrison-Sarah Peeler |
|  | 23 Jan 1890 | John Lefever-Lottis Crab |
| 576 | 16 Nov 1889 | Abram D. Harker-Clary Harker |
|  | 17 Nov 1889 | Charles Burket-Lucy Susdorf |
| 577 | 17 Nov 1889 | Charles E. Patrick-Anna Fletcher |
|  | 21 Nov 1889 | Frederick Lumbert-Emma McCroy |
| 578 | 2 Nov 1889 | Frank Konaposek-Anna Carving |
|  | 4 Dec 1889 | Perra Smith-Amelia Sellears |
| 579 | 30 Nov 1889 | John E. Masterson-Anna E. Harttley |
|  | 22 Dec 1889 | Ishmael T. Bunch-Emm L. Upp |
| 580 | 22 Dec 1889 | Bert McVey-Amelia Baker |
|  | 24 Dec 1889 | William V. Speelman-Sophronia Parish |
| 581 | 26 Dec 1889 | James R. Colden-Louella Geiselman |
|  | 24 Jan 1890 | William D. Wolf-Katie A. Mock |
| 582 | 26 Jan 1890 | Oliver Jorden-Ida M. Hartz |
|  | 2 Feb 1890 | Herman W. Childs-Eliza Smith |
| 583 | 2 Feb 1890 | Elmer E. Horner-Ida M. Cooper |
|  | 8 Feb 1890 | Fred Smith-Amelia Bitters |
| 584 | 9 Feb 1890 | John Patch-Tracy Doll |
|  | 10 Feb 1890 | Charles Nickols-Charlatie Fry |
| 585 | 13 Feb 1890 | Frank H. Clements-Frances D. Geisleman |
|  | 24 Feb 1890 | Andrew J. Clark-Sarah P. Snyder |
| 586 | 22 Feb 1890 | Elmer E. Johnson-Pearl Lung |
|  | 5 Mar 1890 | Mark McCormick-Leonora Howe |
| 587 | 25 Mar 1890 | Thomas McGinnis-Mausuria Shively |
|  | 6 Apr 1890 | Eli Smith-Mary E. Dipert |

## MILITARY DEATHS IN *THE LAFAYETTE DAILY JOURNAL—*
## *RAILROAD EDITION*
### November-December 1861

*The Daily Journal-Railroad edition*, in 1861 was a one-page newspaper printed on both sides. The first page, naturally, was filled with national news of the Civil War which had just begun. However, page 2 often contained local news, and news of Indiana regiments in the war. Military deaths reported are listed below. The "official" list of Civil War veterans was issued in 8 volumes; compiled by the Indiana Adjutant General, William H.H. Terrell, it is titled *Report of the Adjutant General of the State of Indiana . . .*, published between 1866-69. The Archives Division of the Indiana Commission on Public Records has a card index to Indiana Civil War soldiers. Both Terrell and the Archives index purport to have been compiled from the official rosters of the units involved. The newspaper reports have been compared with the above two sources. If discrepancies were found, the differing information has been entered in brackets [] if the differing source is Terrell; in braces ( ) when differing information was found in the Archives index.

### MILITARY ITEMS

The following Indiana soldiers died in the hospitals and camps around St. Louis during the last week.

Oct. 26—Ruben Going. Captain Pool's Company, 25th Indiana regiment. [Goen] (Company G)

Oct. 17—Davie Peace, Company A, 24th Indiana. [Pace, October 27] (no death date)

Oct. 17—Snyder, Company not known, 8th Indiana. [Matthias, Company F, October 2] (Lewis Snyder, no death date)

Oct. 30—Lewis Walker, Company A, 24th Indiana. [October 31]

Oct. 30—Milton Jackson, Company D, 24th Indiana. [musician, no death date listed] (no death date)

Oct. 31—Andrew Stephenson, Company K, 8th Indiana. [Anderson Stevenson, October 21] (Anderson Stevenson)

Oct. 31—Amos French, Company F, 24th Indiana. [not listed]

Nov. 1—Henry Whiper, Company G, 23d Indiana. [Whipker, 22d regiment, December 1] (Whipker, 22d regiment, December 1)

Nov. 2—Samuel Kelmes, Company D, 25th Indiana. [Kellmus] (not listed)

Nov. 2—Alfred H. Baldwin, Company I, 25th Indiana.

Nov. 2—Isaac Shannon, Company G, 25th Indiana.

Nov. 2—John Stanton, Company I, 25th Indiana. [Corporal, no death listed] (no death listed)

November 7, 1861.

## Military Items

A correspondent of the St. Louis Democrat, writing from Georgetown, reports the following dead in the hospital at that place from Indiana regiments:

George B. Gilley, Company E, 18th Indiana regiment, died Oct. 30th of typhoid fever.

John Harmiken, Co. K, 22d Indiana, Oct. 20. [Honaker, no death listed] (Honaker, no death date listed)

John Spaulding, Co. C, 22d Indiana, Oct. 20. [George W., October 21] (George W., October 21)

Thomas Phipps, Co. H, 23d Indiana, Oct. 21. [22d regiment, company I] (22d regiment, company I, October 25)

Thomas F. Emmons, Co. C, 25th Indiana, Oct. 20. [not listed] (not listed)

Isaac S. Taylor, Co. E, 25th Indiana, Oct. 26. [October 20] (October 20)
November 11, 1861.

## Military Items

The following named Indiana soldiers died in the hospital at Otterville, Missouri between the 1st and 12th of November.

Nov. 3d—Edward Harris, 18th regiment, Co. I. [not listed]

Nov. 4—Abraham Epsy, 25th regiment, Co. I. [no death listed] (not listed)

Nov. 9—Andrew Rhoads, 8th regiment, Co. F. (not listed)

Nov. 11—John Shields, teamster. [not listed] (not listed)

Nov. 11—George Cron, 25th regiment, Co. F. [not listed] (not listed)
November 21, 1861.

The funeral of Elisha Kise, a private in Capt. Ferkins' company, of the 10th regiment, who was killed on the 20th inst. in Kentucky, will take place at Lebanon to day. He was the son of Lieut. Col. Kise of the 10th. [no death listed] (no death listed)
November 23, 1861.


## MILITARY ITEMS

The following is the weekly report of the mortality among the Indiana soldiers in the hospitals and camps in the vicinity of St. Louis. It is furnished by Mr. John A. Smithers, Undertaker, 113 Chestnut street. Friends or relatives can obtain any information relative to their burial place, or for their removal, by calling on or addressing Mr. Smithers as above.—All communications from abroad promptly answered by him:

December 1, John H. Chesler, Co. C., 25th Indiana. [Chissler] (Chissler)

December 1, Rice Johnston, Co. K., 25th Indiana.

December 5, Alexander Robertson, Co. E., 18th Indiana.

December 5, Francis M. Locke, Co. E., 22d Indiana. (December 6)

December 5, Samuel Clements, Co. A., 26th Indiana. [Clemens, December 6]

December 7, Oliver Garrison, Co. D., 8th Indiana.
December 12, 1861.

A private in the 40th regiment named McGuire, was buried yesterday. We believe this is the only death that has occurred in the regiment. [Edward, enlisted December 6, died at Lafayette December 12] (Edward Maguire, died December 12)

December 14, 1861.

The State Sentinel says the following is the weekly report of the mortality among the Indiana soldiers in the hospitals and camps around St. Louis. It is furnished by Mr. John A. Smithers, Undertaker, 113 Chestnut street. Friends or relatives can obtain information in reference to their burial, or for their removal, by calling on or addressing Mr. Smithers, as above. All communications from abroad answered promptly by him:

Dec. 9—Louis Hartman, Co. I, 23d Indiana. [22d regiment, December 18] (not listed)

Dec. 13—Wm. N. Stewart, Co. D., 22d Indiana. [November 13] (November 13)

Dec. 13—William Berry, Co. I., 8th Indiana.

Dec. 13—Willian Stinnett, Co. A., 25th Indiana.

Dec. 14—F.M. Hoyt (drummer), Co. —, 22d Indiana. [Hoit, Francis M., Company A, December 10] (Francis M. Hoit, no death listed)

December 19, 1861.

A special dispatch to the Louisville Journal says Lieut Saxe, of the 1st Indiana German regiment was killed at the battle of Mumfordsville on Tuesday, together with seven privates. [Max Sachs, December 17]

December 20, 1861.

Among the reported deaths in the army of the Potomac, we see the names of B. Bridge, of the 16th, and A. Fielding, of the 19th Indiana regiments. [not listed] (not listed)

December 21, 1861.

The remains of Joseph R.T. Gordon, son of Major Jonathan W. Gordon, of the Eleventh U.S. Infantry, were interred at Indianapolis, on Friday, with impressive military ceremonies. The remains were brought on by Cap. Patten of the 6th Indiana. [Ninth Indiana regiment, December 13] (Ninth regiment, December 13)

December 23, 1861.

The following is the list of the Indiana soldiers who died in Otterville [Missouri] between the 15th of November and the 18th of December:

Nov. 15—Henry Fecklin, company —, 24th. [Fickling, Nov —] (Company H, died Nov —)

Nov. 23—Ezekiel Melvin, company A, 24th. [no death listed]

Nov. 24—R.E. McPherson, company B, 26th. [not listed]

Nov. 25—John Balthus, company D, 24th. [1861] (died Nov)

Nov. 26—D.H. Newland, company C, 26th. [Daniel H. Newlin]

Nov. 27—Jacob C. Johnson, company C, 26th. [Corporal, November 22]

Nov. 30—Wm. Legrand, company F, 26th.

Dec. 2—James Hull, company C, 24th. [1861]

Dec. 2—Calvin Reeves, company E, 24th. [died 1862] (not listed)

Dec. 4—Wm. Chenoworth, company G, 26th.

Dec. 4—John B. Johnson, company D, 24th. [died Nov 1862]

Dec. 5—John A. Shyrock, company B, 26th. [Shrihauk] (Shrihawk)

Dec. 6—Samuel R. Auld, company I, 24th. [no death listed]

Dec. 7—William Scarlet, company F, 24th. [December 9]

### Deaths in Indiana Regiments

The following are the names of Indiana soldiers who died in the hospital in St. Louis during the week ended December 21st.

Dec. 16—Elias Wheatley, Co. D, 25th Indiana. [December 18] (not listed)

Dec. 17—E.P. Richmond, Co. D, 18th Indiana. [Edwin R.] (Edwin R., died Nov —)

Dec. 18—Wm. H. Houts, Co. F, 18th Indiana. [Houtz, musician]

Dec. 18—Absalom Lee, Co. E, 18th Indiana. [December 19] (Anslum, December 19)

Dec. 19—James Baxter, Co. K, 25th Indiana.

Dec. 19—Thomas J. Hill, Co. G, 18th Indiana. [September 19] (September 22)

Dec. 19—Isom M. Edwards, Co. B, 25th Indiana. [John M.]

Dec. 20—Fred H. Ellsberry, Co. B, 8th Indiana. (Frederich H.)

December 25, 1861.

### Col. Willich's Regiment [32d regiment]

The Louisville Journal publishes the following list of killed . . . on the part of Col. Willich's regiment in the skirmish on Tuesday, the 17th inst., near Mumfordsville, on the Louisville and Nashville railroad, having been carefully compiled from the best sources of information.

Lieutenant Max Sachs, company C, killed.

Private John Fellerman, company B, killed.

Private Fr. Schuhmacher, company C, killed. [Schumacher, Frederick] (not listed)

Private Henry Lohse, company C, killed.

Private Richard Wehs, company C, killed. [Wehe]

Private Tim Schmidt, company F, killed. [Theodore]

Private George Kiefer, company F, killed. [Garri]

Private Charles Reuber, company F, killed. [Reuter] (Christopher Reuter)

Private Ernest Schiemann, company F, killed. [Schimann]

Private Daniel Schmidt, company G, killed.

Private George Burkhardt, company G, killed.

Private Carl Knapp. company C, died since of wounds. [Knab, December 19] (Charles Knab, December 19)

Private Wm. Stabs, company C, died since of wounds. [not listed]

## LOSS OF THE INDIANA 9TH AND 13TH

These two regiments engaged in the battle at Camp Alleghany [December 13] under General Milroy, met with the following losses:

### THIRTEENTH IND. REGIMENT
### KILLED

Private William Day, Co. B.
Second Lieutenant Joseph P. Jones, Co. K.

### NINTH IND. REGIMENT
### KILLED

Private Daniel S. Souders, Company A.    [David S. Souder]
Private Jackson Kilmer, Company A.
Sergeant Thomas R. McKay, Company E.    [Mackey]
Private Walter H. Pangborn, Company F.
Private Joseph Gordon, Company F.    [Company G]
Private Perry Knowles, Company G.    [Nouls]    (not listed)
Private Charles Wilson, Company G.
Corporal Benj. F. Huntington, Company H.
December 28, 1861.

# THE UNION COUNTY POORHOUSE IN THE 1860 CENSUS

By Ruth Dorrel and Nancy Newby

The U.S. marshals who did the enumeration of the population in 1860 were paid so much per person listed and a fee for mileage based on a formula. Therefore, it behooved the said marshals to enumerate as many individuals as possible, especially if a number of them could be listed at one spot. The double listing of the Union County, Indiana poorhouse illustrates the reasoning of two marshals, each contending (and possibly rightly so), that he was the person to enumerate the inhabitants of the Union County poor farm. How did this problem originate?

The Indiana State Constitution of 1816 in Article IX, Section 4 states " . . . and also to provide one or more farms to be an asylum for those persons, who by reason of age, infirmity, or other misfortunes, may have a claim upon the aid and benefecince of society; on such principles, that such persons may therein, find employment, and every reasonable comfort and lose, by their usefulness, the degrading sense of dependence."[1]

Until 1836, the paupers in Union, Fayette and Franklin counties were under the charge of township officers who let the contracts for maintenance of the unfortunate poor to the lowest responsible bidder. In 1834, the counties of Franklin, Fayette and Union petitioned the Indiana State Legislature to create a joint asylum or poor farm for the three counties. "On the 26th of December, 1834, the Commissioners of the three counties met at Fairfield, in Franklin County, for the purpose of jointly erecting an asylum for the poor of the three counties. Subsequently, a farm situated in Fayette County was purchased of Thomas Clark, and the Commissioners met at thereon August 10, 1835 and agreed to "build an asylum, to be in readiness by the first Monday in May next [1836]."[2]

This joint asylum was maintained until 1856 when the three counties decided to maintain separate facilities. Since the poor farm then in use in Fayette County was jointly owned, it was necessary to sell it. Strangely enough, the Fayette County Commissioners did not want to purchase it, but chose to provide a different facility. When bids for the then poor farm were let, the joint property was purchased in June 1856 by the Union County Commissioners. Thus, the Union County poor farm was physically located in Fayette County, and remained so until 1870.

In 1860, the U.S. census was taken by counties, and by townships within counties. When the Asst. U.S. Marshal in Fayette County was doing his enumeration, he reasoned that the inhabitants of the Union County Poor Farm were physically present in Jackson Township, Fayette County; therefore he should enumerate them. He did so on June 5, 1860. By law, the information obtained was to be the situation as of June 1 of that year. On pages 579-80, he

listed twenty-one inhabitants of the "Asylum for the Poor for Union County."
When the enumerator for Union County was doing his job, he reasoned that the
residents of the Union County Asylum rightfully were residents of that county,
even though physically in Fayette. For whatever reason, on August 10, 1860,
those persons were again listed, but this time in Union County. Interestingly
enough, the situation as of June 1, was apparently ignored; for some residents
listed on June 5 are missing from the second listing, and others have been added.

This mistake by the two U.S. Marshals gives us a chance to check the
information, and may give an insight into the reliability of census records. It
also resulted in an overcount of population for one of the two counties.

The information from Fayette County is listed with the corresponding information from Union County listed below it in brackets.

| NAME | AGE | SEX | RACE | BIRTHPLACE | HANDICAP |
|------|-----|-----|------|------------|----------|
| Sipio Newton | 102 | M | B | Kentucky | Pauper |
| [Scipio Newton | 103 | M | B | Virginia] | |
| | | | | | |
| Jacob Douthard | 82 | M | W | N. Carolina | Pauper |
| [Jacob Douthard | 84 | M | B | N. Carolina] | |
| | | | | | |
| Mary Wilson | 75 | M | W | N. Carolina | Pauper |
| [Dorcia Wilson | 70 | F | W | N. Carolina] | |
| | | | | | |
| Mary Morgan | 75 | F | W | N. Carolina | Blind |
| [no matching person] | | | | | |
| | | | | | |
| Sarah McGreer | 65 | F | M | Indiana | Insane |
| [Sarah McGreer | 52 | F | W | N. Carolina | Insane] |
| | | | | | |
| James Crow | 50 | M | W | Ireland | Insane |
| [James Crow | 55 | M | W | Ireland | Insane] |
| | | | | | |
| John Owens | 50 | M | W | Ireland | Insane |
| [John Owens | 50 | M | W | Ireland | Insane] |
| | | | | | |
| Elnor Ferensworth | 44 | F | W | Virginia | Idiotic |
| [Ellen Farnsworth | 44 | F | W | Virginia | Insane] |
| | | | | | |
| Mary A. Wilson | 40 | F | W | Virginia | Idiotic |
| [Mary A. Wilson | 40 | F | W | Indiana | Insane] |
| | | | | | |
| Jas. Bull | 42 | M | W | Ohio | Pauper |
| [James Bolls | 42 | M | W | Ohio] | |
| | | | | | |
| Wm. Wilson | 32 | M | W | Indiana | Idiotic |
| [William Wilson | 37 | M | W | Indiana | Insane] |
| | | | | | |
| Jesse Williams | 30 | M | W | Indiana | Idiotic |
| [Jesse Wilson | 34 | M | W | Indiana | Insane] |
| | | | | | |
| Esther Revels | 37 | F | B | N. Carolina | Pauper |
| [Esther Revels | 35 | F | B | N. Carolina] | |

| NAME | AGE | SEX | RACE | BIRTHPLACE | HANDICAP |
|------|-----|-----|------|------------|----------|
| Edmon Revels | 29 | M | B | N. Carolina | Pauper |
| [Edmon Revels | 29 | M | B | N. Carolina] | |
| Eliza Perdue | 30 | F | W | Indiana | Idiotic |
| [Eliza Perdue | 30 | F | W | Indiana] | |
| Letitia Finch | 28 | F | W | Indiana | Pauper |
| [Louticia Finch | 28 | F | W | Indiana] | |
| Woodson Perdue | 26 | M | W | Indiana | Pauper |
| [Woodson Perdue | 28 | M | W | Ohio | Insane] |
| Eliza Scudder | 25 | F | W | Indiana | Pauper |
| [Eliza Scudder | 40 | F | W | Ohio] | |
| Catherine Michel | 13 | F | M | N. Carolina | Blind |
| [Catharine Mitchel | 14 | F | M | Indiana] | |
| Alex Bondon | 7 | M | B | N. Carolina | Pauper |
| [Alexander Bowden | 7 | M | B | Indiana] | |
| John Finch | 2 | M | W | Indiana | Pauper |
| [John F. Finch | 3 | M | W | Indiana] | |

As can be seen by the above information, all persons listed on June 5 by the Fayette County enumerator were also listed by the Union County enumerator except one. Possibly, she had died. However, on August 10, the Union County enumerator listed these additional persons:

| NAME | AGE | SEX | RACE | BIRTHPLACE | HANDICAP |
|------|-----|-----|------|------------|----------|
| Mary Reveles | 70 | F | B | N. Carolina | |
| George Perdue | 22 | M | W | Indiana | Insane |
| Wm. T. McGreer | 35 | M | W | Indiana | Insane |

By comparing the entries, it is apparent that the two Asst. U.S. Marshals listed different information about some persons. Some questions arise. Is it possible that Mary Morgan (75, W, b. NC) in Fayette Co. is the same person as Mary Reveles (70, B, NC) in Union Co? Could it be that the information was given to the marshals by the keeper of the Asylum, or did the marshal see each person individually? Could it be that the marshal from Union County did not physically go to Fayette County to do his enumeration, but only copied from records in the Union County courthouse? The latter seems possible, for his spelling of names seems to be more reliable.

In comparing the two listings of the same individuals, the agreement of sex and race seem to be the most accurate. Only in one case of each is there a disagreement. Differences in ages are the most numerous, with birthplace differences in second place.

What does this tell us about the accuracy of the 1860 federal census? It seems to the compilers that the census should be used as a starting point, but not as the gospel in determining exact spellings of names, ages, bithplaces, and even of sex and race; and in some cases, such as this, place of residence. Other sources should be used to confirm or deny the accuracy of the census data.

1. Kettlebrough, Charles, *Constitution Making in Indiana*, Indianapolis, Indiana Historical Bureau (1951) 1:114.
2. *Atlas of Union County Indiana* . . . Chicago, J.H. Beers & Co., 1884, p. 9.

# WHITE'S INDIANA MANUAL LABOR INSTITUTE

Submitted by Ronald L. Woodward*

*The Wabash Weekly Courier*, March 30, 1883, p. 2 contained the following paragraph:

### Thirty Little Indians.

Last Tuesday morning thirty Indian children from the Indian Territory, for whom provision had been made at White's Institute, south of the city, arrived here and were immediately taken to their new home, where they will complete their education. They were an intelligent looking set of redskins and wore the garb of civilization; in appearance they did not differ from the Indians on the reservation in this county. They are all pretty well advanced in their studies, being able to read quite well. Some have completed the Third reader and are struggling valorously through the meshes of the Fourth. All in all they are a respectable lot of kids who will some day possibly make useful citizens. Preparations for their reception at the Institute were consummated last week and they are now comfortably settled.

The White's Indiana Manual Training Institute was established in 1850 with funds willed to the Indiana Yearly Meeting of Friends by Josiah White, a Philadelphia Quaker. The state of Indiana granted a charter to the institution on October 25, 1852. In 1860 the first building was erected; three students were admitted in the spring of 1861. Students were to be admitted at no charge regardless of color. In 1882, the Indian Aid Society with the cooperation of the Indian Bureau arranged to send Indian children from the Sac and Fox Agencies in Indian Territory to White's Institute for terms of three years. The federal government paid expenses for these students. At one time eighty-seven Indians from thirteen different tribes were students there. In 1892 when the Indian Aid Society withdrew its support, no further Indians were admitted under this program. The institution became an orphans' home until 1903, when the first ward of a juvenile court was admitted. The institution is still in operation, funded by the Indiana Yearly Meeting of Friends with the aid of grants by three foundations. Children, ages 9 to 18, now reach White's through the juvenile courts. Schooling is available from the third grade through high school.

The original book containing the following information is at White's Institute, a photocopy is in the Wabash County Museum.

Admitted March 26, 1883

| NAME | AGE | SEX | TRIBE | DATE DISMISSED |
|------|-----|-----|-------|----------------|
| David Badfish | 10 | M | Sac and Fox | March 29, 1886 |
| Frank Bazhaw | 11 | M | Pottawatomie | March 29, 1886 |
| Willie Bazhaw | 9 | M | Pottawatomie | March 29, 1886 |

*Ronald L. Woodward is the Wabash County historian.

| NAME | AGE | SEX | TRIBE | DATE DISMISSED |
|------|-----|-----|-------|----------------|
| Daniel Clinton | 14 | M | Modoc | March 29, 1886 |
| Samuel Edmonds | | M | Shawnee | July 4, 1883 |
| Ruth Garrett | 13 | F | Seneca | March 29, 1886 |
| Louise Harden | 15 | F | Pottawatomie | March 29, 1886 |
| Harry Hunter | 16 | M | Ab Shawnee | March 29, 1886 |
| Clark Jim | 10 | M | Modoc | March 29, 1886 |
| Andrew Johnson | 10 | M | Pottawatomie | March 29, 1886 |
| Sadie Johnson | 13 | F | Pottawatomie | March 29, 1886 |
| Willie Jones | 12 | M | Sac and Fox | March 29, 1886 |
| John Karaho | 12 | M | Seneca | March 29, 1886 |
| Frank Keokuk | 11 | M | Sac and Fox | March 29, 1886 |
| Lillie Lawver | 13 | F | Modoc | March 29, 1886 |
| Janie Monroe | 12 | F | Sac and Fox | March 29, 1886 |
| Lydie Monroe | 14 | F | Sac and Fox | March 29, 1886 |
| Cora Pickering | 14 | F | Modoc | March 29, 1886 |
| David Pooler | 12 | M | Ottaway | March 29, 1886 |
| Anna Senache | 9 | F | Sac and Fox | March 29, 1886 |
| Lucy Thorp | 9 | F | Sac and Fox | November 12, 1883 |
| Amos Valier | 13 | M | Quapaw | March 29, 1886 |
| Mary Jane White-crow | 11 | F | Seneca | March 29, 1886 |
| Cooper Wilson | 13 | M | Ab Shawnee | March 29, 1886 |
| Reid Winney | 11 | M | Seneca | March 29, 1886 |
| Henry Young | 15 | M | Wyandotte | March 29, 1886 |
| Lizzie Young | 10 | F | Wayndotte | March 29, 1886 |

Admitted July 12, 1883

| | | | | |
|------|-----|-----|-------|----------------|
| Willie Chauncy | 12 | M | Seneca | March 29, 1886 |

Admitted February 24, 1884

| | | | | |
|------|-----|-----|-------|----------------|
| Daniel Goodthunder | 14 | M | Sioux | February 28, 1887 |
| Clara Graham | 9 | F | Sioux | February 28, 1887 |
| James Hayes | 15 | M | Sioux | February 28, 1887 |
| Amelia Jones | 15 | F | Sioux | April 28, 1886 |
| Alex LaPlant | 16 | M | Sioux | February 28, 1887 |
| Charles LaPlant | 9 | M | Sioux | February 28, 1887 |
| Julia LaPlant | 17 | F | Sioux | February 2 8, 1887 |
| James Robb | 15 | M | Sioux | July 25, 1889 |
| Joseph Samuels | 17 | M | Sioux | February 28, 1887 |
| John Selwyn | 10 | M | Sioux | February 28, 1887 |
| Gertie Simmons | 8 | F | Sioux | February 28, 1887 |
| Jenet Strickler | 17 | F | Sioux | June 16, 1886 |
| Mary Trimmer | 10 | F | Sioux | died December 7, 1886 |
| William Walker | 16 | M | Sioux | February 28, 1887 |

| NAME | AGE | SEX | TRIBE | DATE DISMISSED |
|------|-----|-----|-------|----------------|
| **Admitted March 4, 1884** | | | | |
| Mark Black | 13 | M | Sioux | April 8, 1886 |
| Mary Brothers | 15 | F | Sioux | February 28, 1887 |
| George Howe | 13 | M | Sioux | June 16, 1886 |
| James Moccasin | 15 | M | Sioux | February 28, 1887 |
| Maggie Moccasin | 10 | F | Sioux | October 26, 1886 |
| John Pattie | 17 | M | Sioux | April 6, 1888 |
| Reba White | 4½ | F | Sioux | died April 5, 1885 |
| **Admitted June 4, 1884** | | | | |
| Ida Stevenson | 13 | F | Sioux | July 5, 1887 |
| **Admitted July 3, 1884** | | | | |
| Nellie Allen | 9 | F | Sioux | July 5, 1887 |
| Mattie Bissonette | 14 | F | Sioux | July 5, 1887 |
| Louise Curry | 11 | F | Sioux | July 5, 1887 |
| Millie Curry | 14 | F | Sioux | July 5, 1887 |
| Jane Edgewalk | 17 | F | Sioux | July 5, 1887 |
| Rosa Fast Hourse | 13 | F | Sioux | died April 3, 1885 |
| Maggie Pulliam | 12 | F | Sioux | July 5, 1887 |
| Susie Rooks | 14 | F | Sioux | August 5, 1890 |
| Louise Rultan | 12 | F | Sioux | August 5, 1890 |
| **Admitted July 4, 1884** | | | | |
| Lizzie Hope | 12 | F | Sioux | August 5, 1887 |
| **Admitted December 3, 1884** | | | | |
| Ruth Taber | 22 | F | Modoc | March 19, 1886 |
| Mary Jane Winney | 12 | F | Seneca | July 2, 1888 |
| **Admitted May 12, 1885** | | | | |
| Marian Kist | 15 | F | Modoc | May 1, 1886 |
| Elwood N. Modoc | 9 | M | Modoc | December 9, 1889 |
| **Admitted March 6, 1886** | | | | |
| Maggie Baldwin | 13 | F | Pottawatomie | July 2, 1889 |
| Jefferson Bennett | 19 | M | Wyandotte | February 1, 1887 |
| Rosetta Bourhannais | 14 | F | Pottawatomie | July 2, 1888 |
| Ellen Crawford | 15 | F | Seneca | August 4, 1886 |
| George Crawford | 12 | M | Seneca | April 9, 1889 |
| Frank Lofland | 20 | M | Wyandotte | May 26, 1887 |
| Josie Lofland | 12 | F | Wyandotte | May 26, 1887 |
| Siddie Long | 19 | F | Wyandotte | died November 11, 1887 |
| Martha Punch | 14 | F | Wyandotte | |
| Minnie Schiffbauer | 13 | F | Wyandotte | July 1, 1889 |

| NAME | AGE | SEX | TRIBE | DATE DISMISSED |
|------|-----|-----|-------|----------------|
| Fannie Spicer | 14 | F | Seneca | February 4, 1896 |
| Clar Talsier | 10 | F | Pottawatomie | July 2, 1889 |
| Sabie Tyner | 17 | F | Shawnee | July 2, 1889 |
| Peter Whipple | 12 | M | Pottawatomie | July 2, 1889 |

Admitted Arpil 6, 1886

| | | | | |
|------|-----|-----|-------|----------------|
| Willie Canalas | 16 | M | Ab Shawnee | September 18, 1889 |

Admitted April 26, 1886

| | | | | |
|------|-----|-----|-------|----------------|
| Louise Abilene | 8 | F | Comache | July 2, 1889 |
| Moveretta Abilene | 13 | F | Comanche | July 2, 1889 |
| Rachel Edge | 18 | F | Caddo | July 2, 1889 |
| Stephen Harrold | 18 | M | Cheyenne | August 30, 1887 |
| Samuel Johnson | 25 | M | Uchee | August 2, 1889 |
| Earnest Lefthand | 17 | M | Araphoe | April 6, 1888 |
| Lena Rabitaille | 15 | F | Wyandotte | April 25, 1889 |
| Waldo Reed | 18 | M | Cheyenne | August 5, 1890 |
| John Tyler | 18 | M | Cheyenne | May 14, 1889 |
| Hugh Wind | 10 | M | Ottaw | April 25, 1889 |

Admitted May 4, 1886

| | | | | |
|------|-----|-----|-------|----------------|
| Rosa Bassett | 12 | F | Seneca | April 25, 1889 |
| Cora Brown | 14 | F | Wyandotte | July 1, 1889 |
| Allen Johnson | 16 | M | Wyandotte | April 9, 1889 |
| Service Karaho | 12 | M | Seneca | July 2, 1889 |
| Peter McLain | 17 | M | Peoria | July 1, 1889 |
| Alexander Spicer | 17 | M | Sencea | December 23, 1887 |
| Alfred Whitecrow | 18 | M | Seneca | February 1, 1887 |
| Janie Zane | 15 | F | Wyandotte | June 18, 1889 |
| Katie Zane | 13 | F | Wyandotte | February 5, 1889 |

Admitted July 13, 1886

| | | | | |
|------|-----|-----|-------|----------------|
| Addie Beaver | 15 | F | Shawnee | July 14, 1891 |
| Sadie Johnson | [16] | F | Pottawatomie [readmitted] | July 2, 1888 |

Admitted August 11, 1886

| | | | | |
|------|-----|-----|-------|----------------|
| Joseph Crawford | 10 | M | Seneca | July 1, 1889 |
| Emeline McLain | 14 | F | Peoria | July 13, 1889 |
| Elizabeth Mahiner | 12 | F | Miami | July 13, 1889 |
| Lulu White | 14 | F | Peoria | July 13, 1889 |

Admitted January 26, 1887

| | | | | |
|------|-----|-----|-------|----------------|
| Clayton Wind | 12 | M | Ottawa | April 20, 1889 |

| NAME | AGE | SEX | TRIBE | DATE DISMISSED |
|------|-----|-----|-------|----------------|

**Admitted April 22, 1887**

| Louis Dagenette | 8 | M | Ottawa | August 5, 1890 |

**Admitted August 11, 1887**

| George Cottier | 7 | M | Sioux | August 5, 1890 |

**Admitted August 19, 1887**

| Frank Bissonette | 13 | M | Sioux | August 5, 1890 |
| Jackson Bissonette | 18 | M | Sioux | August 5, 1890 |
| Lillie Bissonette | 17 | F | Sioux | August 5, 1890 |
| Theresa Bissonette | 14 | F | Sioux | died May 13, 1890 |
| Nancy Black Eyes | 17 | F | Sioux | June 19, 1888 |
| Samuel Broken Rope | 18 | M | Sioux | April 20, 1888 |
| Elizabeth Carlow | 8 | F | Sioux | |
| Henry Cottier | 10 | M | Sioux | August 5, 1890 |
| Rosa Flies | 16 | F | Sioux | August 5, 1890 |
| Julia Goodwin | 8 | F | Sioux | August 5, 1890 |
| Louise Goulette | 14 | F | Sioux | August 5, 1890 |
| Elmore Little Chief | 16 | M | Cheyenne | August 5, 1890 |
| Buffalo Lone Wolf | 8 | M | Sioux | August 5, 1890 |
| Emily Lone Wolf | 13 | F | Sioux | July 31, 1889 |
| Nathan Lone Wolf | 10 | M | Sioux | July 31, 1889 |
| Mable Noflesh | 18 | F | Sioux | August 5, 1890 |
| Oscar Pretty Back | 13 | M | Sioux | August 5, 1890 |
| Vina Red Horse | 16 | F | Sioux | July 31, 1989 |
| Rosanna Rooks | 7 | F | Sioux | |
| Mary Shoulder | 16 | F | Sioux | |
| Martin Thunder Hawk | 17 | M | Sioux | August 5, 1890 |
| Moses Two Bulls | 13 | M | Sioux | died June 2, 1890 |
| Willie White Wolf | 13 | M | Sioux | August 5, 1890 |
| Josephine Wolf Soldier | 16 | F | Sioux | August 5, 1890 |
| Lizzie Wolf Soldier | 15 | F | Sioux | June 19. 1888 |

**Admitted November 8, 1887**

| James Brown | 12 | M | Wyandotte | July 5, 1889 |

**Admitted August 27, 1888**

| Emma Howling Wolf | 17 | F | Cheyenne | |
| Josie Rodd | 14 | F | Pottawatomie | |
| Leah Sands | 15 | F | Cheyenne | |
| Anna Senache | 9 | F | Sax & Fox | |
| | | | [readmitted] | July 14, 1891 |
| Katie May Talsier | 11 | F | Pottawatomie | July 2, 1889 |

| NAME | AGE | SEX | TRIBE | DATE DISMISSED |
|---|---|---|---|---|
| Rosa Talsier | 10 | F | Pottawatomie | July 2, 1889 |
| Senia Talsier | 10 | F | Pottawatomie | July 2, 1889 |
| Rhoda Thurber | 14 | F | Pottawatomie | July 8, 1890 |

Admitted September 3, 1888

| | | | | |
|---|---|---|---|---|
| Mary Brown | 10 | F | Wyandotte | July 5, 1889 |
| Ida Crawford | 12 | F | Seneca | July 8, 1891 |
| Lucy Spicer | 13 | F | Seneca | July 8, 1891 |
| Ida Splitlog | 12 | F | Seneca | |
| Susie Whitecrow | 13 | F | Seneca | July 8, 1891 |
| Mary Jane Winney | [15] | F | Seneca | |
| | | | [readmitted] | |

Admitted November 11, 1888

| | | | | |
|---|---|---|---|---|
| Emma V. Young | 9 | F | Wyandotte | February 5, 1889 |

Admitted May 30, 1889

| | | | | |
|---|---|---|---|---|
| Allen Johnson | [19] | M | Wyandotte | |
| | | | [readmitted] | February 20, 1890 |

Admitted August 10, 1889

| | | | | |
|---|---|---|---|---|
| Louise Abilene | [11] | F | Comanche | |
| | | | [readmitted] | |
| Pio Abilene | 10 | M | Comanche | |
| Clyde Bear Robe | 17 | M | Cheyenne | February 2, 1891 |
| Roscoe Conkling | 9 | M | Wichita | |
| Horace Greely | 8 | M | Wichita | |
| Carl Grey | 10 | M | Wichita | |
| John Haddon | 8 | M | Keechi | |
| Pauline Lane | 13 | F | Keechi | |
| Oleanda Roache | 8 | F | Comache | |
| Ebon Rose | 10 | M | Wichita | |
| Charley Swift | 14 | M | Wichita | |
| Oliver Tyler | 18 | M | Cheyenne | |
| Edward Williams | 17 | M | Cheyenne | |
| Joseph Williams | 17 | M | Cheyenne | |

Admitted August 14, 1889

| | | | | |
|---|---|---|---|---|
| Alma Allen | 12 | F | Sioux | |
| Nellie Allen | [12] | F | Sioux | |
| | | | [readmitted] | |
| Jennie Bissonette | 13 | F | Sioux | |
| Adolph Curry | 15 | M | Sioux | |
| Susie Curry | 17 | F | Sioux | |
| Victoria High Wolf | 17 | F | Sioux | |
| Julia Hornbeck | 14 | F | Sioux | |

| NAME | AGE | SEX | TRIBE | DATE DISMISSED |
|------|-----|-----|-------|----------------|
| Susie Hornbeck | 11 | F | Sioux | |
| Lottie Peck | 12 | F | Sioux | |
| Lewis Wolf Ears | 16 | M | Sioux | |

Admitted August 18, 1889

| | | | | |
|------|-----|-----|-------|----------------|
| Carrie Noflesh | 12 | F | Sioux | died March 19, 1890 |

Admitted August 23, 1889

| | | | | |
|------|-----|-----|-------|----------------|
| Susie Johnson | 11 | F | Wyandotte | July 1, 1890 |
| Naomi Kanho | 12 | F | Seneca | |
| Daniel Spicer | 13 | M | Seneca | |
| Jacob Spicer | 12 | M | Seneca | |
| Minnie Spicer | 16 | F | Seneca | |
| Alex Splitlog | 16 | M | Seneca | |
| Inez Splitlog | 11 | F | Seneca | |
| Jacob Splitlog | 12 | M | Seneca | |
| Clara Whitecrow | 8 | F | Seneca | |
| Jacob Whitecrow | 10 | M | Seneca | |
| Thomas Winney | 14 | M | Seneca | |

Admitted August 24, 1889

| | | | | |
|------|-----|-----|-------|----------------|
| John Bull Bear | 17 | M | Sioux | |

Admitted December 28, 1889

| | | | | |
|------|-----|-----|-------|----------------|
| Mary Spicer | 17 | F | Seneca | |

Admitted August 24, 1890

| | | | | |
|------|-----|-----|-------|----------------|
| Louise Goulette | [17] | F | Sioux [readmitted] | |
| Mary Iron Teeth | 16 | F | Cheyenne | |
| Elmore Little Chief | [19] | M | Cheyenne [readmitted] | |
| Buffalo Lone Wolf | [11] | M | Sioux [readmitted] | |
| Ida Shot-In-The-Face | 14 | F | Cheyenne | |
| Willie White Wolf | [16] | M | Sioux [readmitted] | |
| Creighton Yankton | 17 | M | Sioux | |

Admitted September 2, 1890

| | | | | |
|------|-----|-----|-------|----------------|
| Johnson Punch | 15 | M | Wyandotte | |

Admitted September 9, 1890

| | | | | |
|------|-----|-----|-------|----------------|
| Frank Bullard | 13 | M | Sioux | |
| Nellie Carlow | 8 | F | Sioux | |

**244**

| NAME | AGE | SEX | TRIBE | DATE DISMISSED |
|------|-----|-----|-------|----------------|
| Amy Hill | 8 | F | Sioux | |

Admitted September 19, 1890

| | | | | |
|------|-----|-----|-------|----------------|
| George Bent | 13 | M | Cheyenne | |
| Budd Howling Wolf | 10 | M | Cheyenne | |

Admitted October 2, 1890

| | | | | |
|------|-----|-----|-------|----------------|
| Bonniface Abilene | 9 | M | Comanche | |
| David Haddon | 8 | M | Comanche | |
| Steven Roache | 10 | M | Comanche | |

Admitted October 9, 1890

| | | | | |
|------|-----|-----|-------|----------------|
| Hattie Hicks | 14 | F | Wyandotte | |

Admitted December 18, 1890

| | | | | |
|------|-----|-----|-------|----------------|
| Gertie Simmons | [11] | F | Sioux [readmitted] | |

Admitted December 20, 1890

| | | | | |
|------|-----|-----|-------|----------------|
| John Dillon | 11 | M | Sioux | |
| Frank Fast Horse | 14 | M | Sioux | June 24, 1891 |
| Willie Fast Horse | 15 | M | Sioux | |
| Thomas Marshall | 15 | M | Sioux | |

Admitted February 21, 1891

| | | | | |
|------|-----|-----|-------|----------------|
| Kittie Peltiere | 15 | F | Pottawatomie | |

Admitted June 20, 1891

| | | | | |
|------|-----|-----|-------|----------------|
| John Block | 19 | M | Caddo | |

Admitted September 3, 1891

| | | | | |
|------|-----|-----|-------|----------------|
| Ida Crawford | [15] | F | Seneca [readmitted] | |
| Lucy Spicer | [16] | F | Seneca [readmitted] | |
| Susie Whitecrow | [16] | F | Seneca [readmitted] | |

*Wabash Weekly Courier,* April 10, 1885, p. 3

**Deaths at White's Institue.** Since the sixty Indian children who were brought from the Wild West to this county for education, have been pursuing their studies at White's Institute, south of the city, they have enjoed remarkably good health, and none have been seriously ill during their two years' sojourn there. Some four or five weeks ago, however, one of the older girls was stricken down with an affection of the throat and lungs, which developed into hasty consumption and after lingering along for over a month, suffering most intensely, she on Saturday morning expired. Fifteen hundred miles from her prairie home, surrounded by fair-skinned strangers the daughter of the Sioux quietly passed to the Great Beyond, and savage though she was her death cast a gloom over the inmates of the Institute to whose minds the memory of the sad event will long linger. The funeral occurred Sunday and was of an impressive character. P.S. Since the above was written another one of the Indian children at the Institute has died.

*The Wabash Weekly Times,* December 10, 1886, p. 8

Mary Trimmer, a young Indian girl from Pine Ridge, Dakota agency, died at White's Institute Tuesday evening. The girl was quite a favorite among the teachers, being very bright and affectionate. She was thirteen years old. The funeral took place yesterday afternoon. She was buried in the Institute cemetery.

## LAGRO, INDIANA TOWN CENSUS, 1853
### Submitted by Ron Woodward

Lagro, Wabash County, Indiana town was named for LeGros, a Miami Indian chief who lived in the area. The town was settled around 1829, and thrived when the construction of the Wabash and Erie Canal brought increased activity to the community. The census of 1853, listed below showed a population of 373 persons. Mr. Woodward has checked this 1853 census against both the 1850 and 1860 federal censuses of the town. The original manuscript is in the Wabash County Historical Museum, Wabash, Indiana.

## CENSUS OF THE POPULATION OF THE TOWN OF LAGRO, WABASH COUNTY & STATE OF INDIANA AS TAKEN ON THE SEVENTH (7TH) DAY OF MAY 1853

| | | | | | |
|---|---|---|---|---|---|
| * | Warner Bartholomew | 3 | * | Issachu Stirk | 7 |
| * # | Elijah W. Benjamin | 8 | # | W. Warner | 3 |
| # | W.B. Barlow | 9 | * # | Jas. Ditton | 3 |
| * | A.T. Stephenson | 15 | # | Dr. Saml. St.John | 5 |
| * # | Dennis Ryan | 5 | # | Dr. J.D. St.John | 1 |
| * | Wash. C. Stevens | 4 | | R.T. St.John | 1 |
| # | Thos. B. McCarty | 2 | * | Wm. Bennett | 7 |
| * # | Jirah Barlow | 5 | * | Marcus Tracy | 3 |
| # | Wm. Orcutt | 2 | * # | G. Bradley Wheeler | 4 |
| * | Wm. T. Shively | 7 | | D.D. Beardsley | 2 |
| | Isaac Bedsaul | 5 | | J.T. Scarlet | 12 |
| | John Kiser | 7 | | John W. Gossette | 3 |

Ron Woodward is the county historian for Wabash County, Indiana.

| | | | |
|---|---|---|---|
| * # | George Stutsman | 3 |
| * # | Alex Taylor | 6 |
| | Mrs. Widow Finan | 2 |
| * # | Thos. J. Ridge | 4 |
| | W. Montgomery | 6 |
| | Rev. J.J. Elrod | 2 |
| | W. Price | 6 |
| * # | George Billings | 6 |
| | W. Tingman | 7 |
| * | Robert Ramsey | 2 |
| # | Alex. Duncan | 7 |
| | ---- Albright | 4 |
| * | Jos. Hopkins | 9 |
| * # | Benedict W. Lowry | 9 |
| * | Francis D. Johnson | 5 |
| | Jas. Nolan | 3 |
| * # | W.B. Cadwell | 1 |
| * | Alex McGuire | 5 |
| | | 210 |
| | | |
| * | Dr. Thos Hamilton | 3 |
| | Mrs. Widow Ring | 5 |
| * | John E. Townsend | 2 |
| * # | Henry Townsend | 2 |
| * # | Charles Ditton | 7 |
| * # | Dr. J.H. Depuy | 4 |
| * | David Dedrick | 4 |
| * | Mrs. R. English | 5 |
| | Robert Jane | 2 |
| * | Gabriel Young | 6 |
| | Wm. B. Keefer | 4 |
| * # | A. Myres | 4 |
| | J. Little | 8 |
| * | Phillip Shaffer | 5 |
| * # | Mrs. Alice Wright | 5 |
| * # | Wm. Murgotten | 4 |
| * | J.W. Stephenson | 8 |
| * # | J.L.P. Anthony | 4 |
| * | Jos. Roach | 7 |
| | Wm. Rowan | 6 |
| * | Robert S. Goudy | 6 |

| | | | |
|---|---|---|---|
| | Mrs. Malone | 2 |
| | F.J. Collier | 3 |
| # | Martin Sweetman | 5 |
| * # | Simeon S. Wiltse | 1 |
| | M. Levi | 1 |
| # | John Watkins | 4 |
| | W. Forbs | 1 |
| | Jos. Kregg | 3 |
| | H.S. Cooper | 1 |
| | S. Wallace | 3 |
| | Dr. Wolverton | 1 |
| | B.W. Bishop | 4 |
| | J. McDevitt | 5 |
| | L. Tingman | 7 |
| * | John G. Quinn | 3 |
| | W. Milligan | 4 |
| | A.C. Schull | 4 |
| | Mrs. Widow Murphy | 2 |
| | Mrs. Rassella Depat | 3 |
| * | Albridge Henderson | 2 |
| | J. Christe | 4 |
| | | 166 |
| | | |
| | H. D. Lowry | 3 |
| * | Jno. K. Murphy | 6 |
| | Sprig Murphy | 6 |
| | Robert Gilbert | 6 |
| * # | Hugh McNown | 8 |
| | Edmond Hennessy | 8 |
| | M. Rowan | 9 |
| * # | Rev. Ryan | 3 |
| * | J.E. Filson | 2 |
| # | B.H. Lasselle | 1 |
| | Jacob Yount | 1 |
| | Christ. Haltz | 5 |
| | Thos. Gordon | 2 |
| * # | Timothy Reagin | 4 |
| | ---- Keefer | 6 |
| | | 67 |

247

STATE OF INDIANA          SCT
WABASH COUNTY

Personally came before me the undersigned notary public in and for said county James Kerr who being duly sworn on his oath says that he is the person who took the above census of the town of LaGro, and that the same is the full census of said town as taken by him as he verily believes.

James Kerr

Subscribed and sworn to before me this
9th day of May, A D 1853
R.G. St. John
Notary Public
*   Appeared in 1850 census.
#   Appeared in 1860 census.

# BIBLE RECORDS

Bible records are valued by family historians for many reasons. Often, they are the only source of exact birth, marriage, and death dates; they record births and deaths of infants who may not be mentioned in any other source; they give clues to the family historian as to the migration of the families.

When submitting Bible records for publication, send the information from the title page: publisher, place of publication, and date of publication. If possible, send photocopies of the family history information along with a typewritten transcription. Include any interesting facts about the history of the Bible, and other material found in it, such as newspaper clippings, death notes, wedding announcements, etc.

Several Bible records have been submitted for publication in the past few months. They are printed below.

## NOAH LANE-REBECCA WALTER BIBLE

Submitted by Jane Murrow Atherstone

This Bible record was found in a Bible published in 1842. At least two different hands recorded the information. Papers found in the Bible are also transcribed.

Inside front cover: Rebecca Walter
Front flyleaf: Rebecca Walter's Bible Bought in the Year of our Lord 1844
Next page: Rebecca Walters Bible Bought in the year of our Lord-1846

Marriages:

Noah Lane and 1851
Rebeca Walter was
Maraid the 13 of March

Noah Sherman Lane
    and
Hattie Frances Roman
was married Oct. 3rd 1892

Births:

William Martin Lane
Was bornd the 6 day of
1871

Noah Sherman Lane
was born November 21th
January 1852

Luis Edward Lane Was bornd
the 7 day of November 1853

Dora Eveline Lane
Born April 11th 1893

Charles Francis Lane
Born & Died March 22. 1895

Willis F Lane was bornd
June the 26 1858

Margaret Ann Lane 1860
was bornd November the 5
1860

Joseph M. Lane was born
May the 18 1866

James Marlin Lane was born
September 29th 1868

Deaths:
William Martin Lane
Died the 21 day of Febuary
his age was six wheaks and
four days

Luis Edward Lane died
the 3 day of October 1855

Elbert Lane
Born March 21 1897

Franz Delaven Lane
Born Nov 5 1898

Letitia Lane
Born July 18th 1902

Willis F. Lane Died
July the 24 1860

Joseph M. Lane died
May the 18 1866

Lucinda Jane Martin
Died Dec 14 1920

Old paper found in Bible:
Noah Lane Born Marion co Indianna in the Year 1830 August 28
Rebecca Walters Bornd Center co Penslvania in 1831 September the first
Noah Lane and Rebecca Walters was Married March 1851

## DANIEL AND LOLA HAVENS BIBLE RECORDS

Submitted by Dorothy Vekasi

### FAMILY REGISTER

Husband, Daniel Frame Havens
  Born May 8th 1865
Wife, Lola Temprance Havens
  Born Sep 3rd 1865
Married, April 18, 1889

### CHILDREN'S NAMES

Mable Havens Born Feb 16 1890
Georgia Havens Dec 1st 1891
Charles Howard Havens Sep 4 1896
Madalene Havens Nov 28 1902

### MARRIAGES

Charles Howard Havens and
  Virginia Eva Rea (Nov 9,
  1897) April 22, 1919.
Madalene Havens and Joe
  Henry Wildermuth (July 6
  1896) January 10, 1923

### DEATHS

Mabel Havens Dec 3 1891
Georgia Havens Oct 20th 1894
Lola T. Havens March 15 1922
Daniel Frame Havens April 4 1937
Charles Howard Havens Dec. 16 1956
Joe Henry Wildermuth Dec. 30 1972
Madeleine Havens Wildermuth Feb. 22
  1979

Richard Lee Wildermuth-Helen Cole (Oct. 19, 1925) Aug. 30, 1947
Dorothy Ann Wildermuth-Michael Eugene Vekasi (June 9, 1925) Aug 17, 1947

## Marriages-Grandchildren

Richard Joe Wildermuth-Kathay Lee Chichester (Nov. 13, 1947) June 18 1971
David Lee Vekasi-Wanda Lou Waldo (2-14-51) Dec. 23, 1972
James Michael Vekasi-Mary Holcomb (6-15-50) April 19, 1974
William Howard Vekasi-Debra Schneider (3-18-53) 6-18-1974
Polly Wildermuth-John Richter July 16, 1983

## Children

Katherine Madeleine Havens-daughter of Howard and Virginia Havens.  May 14, 1923.
Children of Joe and Madeliene Wildermuth.  Richard Lee Wildermuth, June 22,  1924; Dorothy Ann Wildermuth, January 4, 1926.
Children of Richard & Helen Wildermuth.  Richard Joe Wildermuth, July 8, 1948; Polly Wildermuth, July 28, 1951.
Children of Dorothy and Michael Vekasi. James Michael, 6-25-1950; David Lee, 7-22-1951; William Howard, 2-21-1953.
Dau. of Dick & Kathy Anne Wildermuth, b. July 8, 1985.

## Great Grand Children

Joseph Michael Vekasi, b. 6-17-1975, son of David & Wanda Vekasi. Kathleen Erin Vekasi, 3-16-78.
Dau. of Jim and Mary Vekasi, Sarah Marie Vekasi, 9-9-78.
Dau of Bill and Debra Vekasi.  Andrea Madeleine Vekasi 9-29-81.
Kristin Elizabeth Vekasi, b. 4-14-81.
Alison Catharine Vekasi, b. 7-31-84

## JOHN HILL BIBLE

Submitted by George C. Parker

Family Record.

Births.

John Hill, son of Benjamin Hill and Mary his wife, was born in the State of North Carolina, Randolph County, on the 20th day of the 2nd mo 1797.

Births.

Mary and Martha Hill, daughters of ditto born ditto 8th day of 1st mo 1819

Benjamin C. Hill son of ditto, born ditto 19th day of the 4th mo 1820.

Dinah Hill, daughter of
Joseph Cox and Dinah his
wife, was born in the same
State and County, on the 4th
day of the 9th mo 1792.

Joseph Hill, son of John
Hill and Dinah his wife, was
born in the State of Indiana
Wayne County, on the 19th
day of the 2nd mo 1818.

Nathan Clarke Hill son of ditto,
born ditto. 3rd day of the 12th mo
1821.

Ervin Hill, son of ditto, born
ditto 29th day of the 4th mo 1823.

Sarah Ann Hill daughter of ditto,
born ditto. 7th day of the 8th mo
1824.

William R. Hill son of ditto. born
in Rush County Ind. 19th of 7th mo
1827

### Births.

Miriam Jane Hill daughter of
ditto, born ditto on the
24th day of the 3rd mo 1831.

Mary Ann Hill daughter of
John and Dinah was born the
6th day of 2nd mo 1836.

### Deaths.

Martha (Hill) Binford deceased 8 mo

Nathan C Hill deceased 6 mo 7th
1904 age 82 yr & 4 days

Mary Ann Binford deceased 1st 30th
1902 age 68 years 11 mos and 24
days

### Family Record.

### Deaths

Mary Hill deceased the 16th
day of the 2nd month 1819.
aged 1 mo and 7 days.

Benjamin C Hill deceased the
17th of 1st mo 1837. Aged
16 years 8 months and 28
days.

Ervin Hill deceased 19th day
of the 3rd month 1844. aged
20 years 10 Months and 21
days

William R Hill deceased 27th
day of 9th month 1846 Aged
19 years 2 months and 8 days

### Deaths

John Hill deceased the 20th day of
the 10th month 1846 aged 49 years
and 8 months.

Sarah Ann Hodson deceased 11th day
of the 2nd month 1851 aged 26 years
six months and 4 days

Dinah Hill deceased the 30th of the
11th month 1867. Aged 75 years 2
months and 26 days

Joseph Hill deceased 18th day of
7th month 1871 aged 53 years 4
months and 29 days

Family record

Marriages.

John Hill and Dinah Cox were married among the Society of Friends, in Wayne County Indiana at West Grove Meeting house, on the 27th day of the 2nd Mo 1817.

## LYDIA BELL MACY BIBLE

Submitted by George C. Parker

Family Record.

Deaths.                    Deaths.

John M. Macy son of Stephen and Rebecca Macy deceased 5th mo. 19th 1887.
Lydia B. Macy daughter of John & Lydia Bell deceased 4th mo. 15th 1891.
Josephine M. Parker daughter of John M. & Lydia B. Macy deceased 5th mo. 1st 1894.

Family Record.

Births.                    Births.

Rebecca Bell daughter of John and Sarah Bell was born 4th mo. 21st 1804.

Abigail Bell daughter of John and Lydia Bell was born 4th Mo. 14th 1814.

Lydia Symons daughter of Jesse and Sarah Symons was born 4th mo. 21st 1780.
Margaret Bell daughter of John and Lydia Bell was born 5th mo 6th 1810

Lydia Bell daughter of John and Lydia Bell was born 3rd mo. 11th 1816.
Martha Bell daughter of John and Lydia Bell was born 1st mo. 29th 1818.

Jesse Bell son of John and Lydia Bell was born 4th mo. 26th 1812.

Family Record.

Marriages                    Marriages

John Bell son of Lancelot and Miriam Bell and Sarah Bundy daughter Josiah and Mary Bundy were married 12th mo. 30th 1789.

John M. Macy son of Stephen and Rebecca Macy and Lydia Bell daughter of John and Lydia Bell were married 12th mo. 20th 1855.

253

John Bell son of Lancelot and Miriam Bell and Lydia Symons daughter of Jesse and Sarah Symons were married 2nd mo 19th 1809.

Clarkson H. Parker son of John and Miriam J. Parker and Josephine Macy daughter of John M. & Lydia B. Macy were married 10th mo. 25th 1883.

Family Record.

### Births

John B. the son of Lancelot Bell and Miriam his wife was born 1nd Mo. 6th 1768.

Mary M. the daughter of John and Sarah Bell was born 3rd Mo. 3rd 1792.

Miriam Bell daughter of John and Sarah Bell was born 8th Mo. 5th 1795.

### Births

Josiah Bell, son of John and Sarah Bell was born 1st Mo. 11th 1798.

Lancelot Bell son of John and Sarah Bell was born 11th mo. 3rd 1790.

Sarah Bell daughter of John and Sarah Bell was born 1st Mo. 15th 1800.

Thomas Bell son of John and Sarah Bell was born 4th Mo. 17th 1802.

## PARKER FAMILY BIBLE

Submitted by George C. Parker

Family Record

### Births.

Samuel Parker was bornd the 20th of 2nd mo 1793

Rebecca Parker my wife was bornd the 4th of 6th mo 1792

Joseph C Parker wass bornd the 13th of 11th mo 1815

Silas Parker wass bornd the 29th of the 9th mo 1817

James B. Parker was bornd the 8th of the 9th mo 1819

Blandina Parker was bornd the 9th day of the 11th month 1821.

### Deaths.

Our son Joseph C. Parker Departed this life 27th of 10th mo 1816

Our daughter Blandina Parker Departed this life the 21th of the 1st mo about half past 3 in the morning in date 1822

Josiah Parker Departed this life the 7th of 9th mo 1846. about twenty minutes After six oclock in the morning aged 18 years and 11 moths 10 days

Samuel Parker Departed this life the 12th 6th mo 1847 about nine oclock in the evening aged 54 years 3 mos 3 we 3 day

254

James Binford was Bornd the 3rd of 4th mo 1756

Hannah Binford his wife was born the 15th of 6th mo 1757

James Binford Departed this life the 3rd day of 10th mo 1824 his age 68 and 6 months

Hannah Binford Departed this life the 18th of 7 month 1845 Aged 88 years and 3 weeks and 2 Days

Joshua Binford Departed this life the 5th of 1st mo 1844 Aged 64 years and Two days

## Family Record

### Births.

John P Parker wass Bornd the 16 of 4th mo 1823

Josiah Parker was bornd the 17 of 9th mo 1827

Hannah J. Parker was bornd the 17th day of 2nd mo 1830

Martha Ann Parker wass bornd the 5th of 3rd mo 1832

Angeline B [Pa]rker was bornd [the] 26th of the 10th [mo] 1834

### Deaths

James B. Parker died 8 mo 6th 1881 aged 61 years 10 mo & 12 d

## Marriages

Samuel and Rebecca Parker wass Maried the 15 of the 1st month 1815

## JOHN PEELE PARKER BIBLE

Submitted by George C. Parker

### Family Record

#### Births

John P. Parker Was born the 16th of 4 mo 1823
Miriam Jane Parker was born the 24th of 3rd 1831
Clarkson Parker was born the 9th of 7th mo 1853
Almira Parker was born the 12th of 8th mo 1854
Benjamin Franklin Parker was born the 13th of 7th mo 1856

Alice Parker was born the 1th of 1 mo 1858
Samuel Murray Parker Was born 8 mo 23th 1860
Hannah Ann Parker was born 9 mo 5th 1862
John Oscar Parker was born 8 mo 25th 1874

## Family Record.

Deaths

Hannah Ann Parker Deceased 3 mo 9th 1863 Ages 6 months and 4 days
John P. Parker deceased 8th and 7th 1896. ag 72 yrs 10 ms. 21 days Seventh in
  evening about 9 oclock
Miriam J. Parker. deceased 7 mo. 23, 1906. age 75 yrs. 3 mo 29 da.

## Family Record.

Marriages.

John P. and Miriam Jane Parker Was Married the 23 of 4 mo. 1851

## THE POWELL FAMILY BIBLE

### Submitted by Geraldine Hale Schlecht

This Bible was found several years ago in very poor condition. Five pages survive in the possession of Margaret Bomkamp of Muscoda, Wisconsin. The first page is an engraving depicting the visit of the Magi. The remaining four pages contain the following information.

p. 2

### Marriages

Richard Powel fammily Register of him and his wife Anne Powel.
Richard Powel he was born February the 14th Day 1790 in England Corsham
  Wilsher County.
Anna Powel she was born in year 1797.
George Powel he was born March the 14th Day 1819.
Charles Powel he was born the 26th day of May 1821.
Joseph Powel he was born the 18th Day of May 1823.
Samuel Powel he was born the 15th Day of November 1825.
Richard and Anne Powel Daughter of George Sheets was Married July 3rd
  1817.
Peter Wolf and Susannah Powell was married August 27 1848.
Joseph Powell and Rebecca Jane Carson was married December 30th 1849.

p. 3

### Births

Richard Powel was born February 14th 1790.
Anne Sheets was born in the year 1797.
John Burlington Powel son of Richard and Anne Powel was born April 4th
  1818.

George Powel was born March 24th 1819.
Charles Powel was born May 26th 1821.
Joseph Powel was born May 18th 1823.
Samuel Powel was born November 15th 1825.
Susanah Powel was born April 29th 1828.
Elizabeth Ann Powel was born February 15th 1830.
Isaac James Powel was born in Lafayette December 14th 1831.

Richard Powell was born June 12th 1834.
Rebeca Powell was Born October 17th 1838.
George Lott Powell son of Joseph and Rebeca Jane Powell was born November the 11th in the year 1854.
Margaret Anna Powell was born April the 4th 1857.
John Carson Powell was born December the 28th 1859.
Richard Powell was born January the 6th 1862.
Amy Susannah Powell was born February the 7th in year 1863.

p. 4

Births and Deaths

Joseph Wolf son of Peter and Susannah Wolf was born December 8th in the year 1849
Phillip Wolf son of Petter and Susannah Wolf was born January the 27th in the year 1852
Joseph Milton Powell was born February the 13th 1865.
Mary Catharine Powell was May the 31st 1867.
Asher Townsend Powell was born January 11th 1874

John Burlington Powel son of Richard and Anne Powel Departed this life June 12th 1818.   Aged 2 months and 8 days.
Charles Powel Departed this life July 18th 1830.   Aged 9 years, 4 months and 22 days.
Elizabeth Ann Powel Departed this life March 20th 1830.   Aged 1 Month and 1 week.
Samuel Powel Departed this life October 28th 1830.   Aged four years eleven months and thirteen days.
Richard Powell son of Richard and Anne Powel Departed this life August 9th 1835.   Aged one year one month and twenty eight days.

p. 5

Deaths

Rebeca Powell Daughter of Richard and Any Powel Departed Life November 9th 1838.
Richard Powell Departed this Life May 17th 1844.   Aged 54 years two months three days.
Richard Powell the son of Joseph and Rebecca Jane Powell Departed this Life January the 24 1862.
Joseph Milton Powell Died March th 17th 1870.

# JOHNSON COUNTY BIBLE RECORDS

Submitted by Mary Ann Plummer

Wayne B. Walters donated three Bibles to the Johnson County Historical Museum, 149 West Madison Street, Franklin, Indiana 46131. They may be examined at the museum which is open Tuesday through Friday from 10 A.M. to 12 P.M. from 1 to 4 P.M. Saturday hours are from 10 A.M. to 3 P.M.

## THE DOTY-VANDIVIER BIBLE

This Bible was printed in Philadelphia in 1877 by William W. Harding. An inscription on the front page states: "Jan. the 1st 1878 A Holy Bible pressented to Clarance . R. Doty by his Grandfather John Doty

### MARRIAGE CERTIFICATE

This Certifies that Clarence R. Doty and Minnie B. Vandivier Were solemnly united by J.C. Rhodes in the Holy Bonds of Matrimony at Franklin on the twenty fifth day of September in the year of our Lord one Thousand eight hundred and eighty nine   Conformably to the Ordinance of God and the Laws of the State.   In Presence of            Signed

### BIRTHS

William Abraham was
born Jan. 28, 1815

Maria Abraham
born Sept. 18, 1817

William A. Doty
Born April 8, 1844

Sarah A. Doty
born Oct. 2, 1847

Clarence R. Doty
born Feb. 16, 1866

Minnie B. Vandivier
born Jan 5, 1871

Pearl M. Doty
born Feb 9, 1891

Florence Marie Doty
was born June 24, 1895
passed away Dec. 24, 1949,
5 A. M.

Lillian Vandivier
was born June 8, 1901

Wayne B. Walters born
Dec. 25, 1894

Rosemary Walters born
Feb. 19, 1922

Florence Jean Paris, born
Aug. 22, 1924.

Richard and Ruth Paris
born May 31, 1932

Patricia Ann Reynolds
Born Oct 27 19 2
weighed 10 lbs. 4 oz.

Michael Taylor Reynolds
son of Ruth Parris and Martin
Reynolds born Sun nite Mch 7, 1954
8 lbs.

Larry Wayne born 5:30 a.m.
Friday Jan 2, 1959.

Wayne B. Walton &
Pearl Maria Doty were
married by A.T.
Belknap Dec. 30, 1916

William A. Doty and
Sarah A. Abraham
married Dec. 1, 1864

Clarence R. Doty
and Minnie B. Vandivier
married Sept. 25, 1889.

Wayne B. Walters and
Pearl B. Doty married
Dec. 30, 1916.

Russel A. Paris and
Florence Marie Doty were
married Sept. 3, 1919.

Mark N. Adams and
Lillian V. Doty married
Jan. 22. 1938.

The following notes were written on page opposite the Deaths in the Record Section of this Bible.
"Richard's baby born   Kay"
"Wilda Walters passed away Mon. Jan. 30, 1956 at 4 o'clock, we in Sebring Fla. Jess Patterson brought us telegram.   Wayne talked with Fay Walters at 9:45 about funeral, etc.   burried Thurs. Feb 2 at 2:o'clock.   Mountain roads too slick for us to return.   Road conditions bad in Franklin same time."

"Gracie Merrick Dill Simpson passed away Oct. 1, 5 A.M. at Johnson Co. Memorial hospital, been a patient there 17 days.   funeral Friday 3, at 2 P.M. at Rhiel Vandivier funeral home.   We took Mom to call of Thurs. eve Oct. 2 at Vandivier funeral home."

## DOTY-ABRAHAM BIBLE

This Bible was published in Cincinnati in 1868.   The inscription on the flyleaf reads:   "S.A. Doty's Book Presented to Her by Her Husband Sept. 29th, 1868."

### FAMILY RECORD

### MARRIAGES

William A. Doty
and
Sarah A. Abraham
married
Dec. 1st, 1864

William Abraham
& Maria Arnold
married Oct. 7, 1840

Clarence R. Doty
and
Minnie B. Vandivier
married
September 25,
1889

Pearl M. Doty
and
Wayne B. Walters
married
Dec. 30, 1916.

F. Marie Doty and
Rusell Paris
married Sept. 3
1919

BIRTHS

William A. Doty was
born Apr. 8th 1844

Sarah A. Abraham
was born
Oct. 2nd, 1841,

Clarence R.
Son of W.A. Doty
and Sarah A. Doty
was born
Feb. 16th 1866

Pearl M. Doty
born Feb. 9, 1891
daughter of Clarence
& Minnie Doty

DEATHS

William A. Doty
died Dec. 24, 1874
age 30 yrs.

Sarah A. Doty
Dec. 8, 1924 77 yrs.

Clarence R. Doty
died Sept. 25, 1933
67 yrs. 5 mo.

Minnie B. Doty passed
away Aug. 7-62
age 91 yrs. 7 mo.

Mrs. Russell (Marie)
Paris passed away
Dec. 24, Johnson Co.
hospital 1949

Russell Paris (Marie's
husband married
Emma) passed away
Jan 17, 72 at hospital

BIRTHS

William Abraham
born Jan. 28, 1815

Maria Arnold
born Sep. 18, 1817

Richard A. Abraham
born July 4, 1842

Julia Abraham
Sep. 28, 1844

James A. Abraham
born March 4, 1850

DEATHS

John A. Abraham
died April 10, 1856

William Abraham
Died Jan. 22, 1894.

Maria Abraham
Died June 1, 1904

Richard A. Abraham
Died June 16, 1923

Julia Province
Died

260

John A. Abraham
born Sep. 7, 1852

Maria L. Abraham
born Mar. 20, 1855

William R. Abraham
born Sep. 23rd 1858

### BIRTHS

John Doty was
born Oct. 14, 1826

Nancy T. Doty
was born Apr 4, 1823

Florence Marie Doty
Born June 24, 1895
Daughter of Clarence
& Minnie Doty

Lillian Vandivier Doty
was born June 8, 1901
daughter of Clarence &
Minnie Doty.

Rosemary Walters
was born Feb. 19, 1921
daughter of Wayne B.
and Pearl M. Walters

Sarah A. Doty died
Dec. 8, 1924

Louisa Harris died

James A. Abraham
died

### DEATHS

James M. Doty died
Nov. 25 A.D. 1874 age 22 y 6 mo 23
d

Sena A. Doty died
Nov. 14, A.D. 1874 age 17 y, 10 mo.
19 D.

William A. Doty died
Decem. 24, A.D. 1874
age 30 y 8 mo. 16 days

Lewis Doty died
Janr. 4, 1875 age
10 y, 7 mo. 3 days

John A. Doty died
Sept. 27, 1819 age 21 y

Angelina Clary
died Aug. 30, 1881
aged 25 yr. 7 mo. 24 d.

Nancy Doty died
June 2nd 1888

Rachael Badgley
died May 25, 1892

Copy written on yellow ruled memo paper found in family record pages of this Bible.

Mary Ann Vandivier
died Sept. 23, 1892

James H. Vandivier
was born in Mercer County,
Ky. Feb. 13, 1823.
and is the son of Peter and
Sarah (Garshwiler) Vandivier

Mary Ann (Buckner) Vandivier
was born in Kentucky
May 29, 1832
and is the daughter of
Avery and Margaret (Sturgeon)
Buckner.

James H. Vandivier and
Mary Ann Buckner
was married November
16, 1848.

James H. Vandivier
Died Sept. 11, 1907
Age 84 yrs. 6 mos. 29 days

## WALTERS-MULLENDORE BIBLE

This Bible was published in Indianapolis by the Indianapolis Book & Stationary Co., copyright 1872-90.

"What God Hath Joined Together Let Not Man Put Asunder" This Certifies that the rite of Holy Matrimony was Celebrated Between John I. Walters of Franklin and Wilma Mullendore of Franklin on Jan. 28th, 1894 at the bride's home By Rev. Ephriam Pond. Witness: Strather Herod Margaret Herod

### MARRIAGES

| | |
|---|---|
| Wayne B. Walters<br>- Pearl M. Doty | Dec. 30, 1916 |
| Guy F. Walters<br>- May Sluyter | Dec. 24, 1918 |
| Roscoe Walters<br>- Fay Deputy | Oct. 8, 1919 |
| Edelle Walters<br>- Ralph Dragoo | Oct. 6, 1926 |
| Max Walters<br>- Josephine Newkirk | Aug. 26, 1933 |
| Merle Walters<br>- Dru Fisk | March 28, 1943 |
| John I. Walters<br>- Wilda Mullendore | Jan. 28, 1894 |

(Copy of note pinned to Marriages Page)
219 E. 17th St. #3 Indianapolis, Ind. 3-3-43 Dear Folks:-Well well and well-- Merle and I have decided to "Middle Aisle it" on Sunday March 28, 1943 at the

3rd Christian Church at 17th and Broadway, here in the city. We will be very happy if all 3 of you can come to the wedding, which will be a very informal affair. Just a plain war time wedding but just as sincere as the biggest wedding that was ever performed. We were very sorry to hear that Pearl had been sick and sincerely hope she has completely recovered by now, and the whole family is in good health. Yours very truly, Drue

## BIRTHS

Wayne B. Walters was born Dec. 25th 1894

Margaret Edelle Walters was born May 13, 1906

Guy Thomas Walters was born December 4, 1896

Roscoe Forest Walters was born March 23rd, 1899

Hugh Maxwell Walters was born September 13th, 1901

Frances Merle Walters was born October 15, 1903

## DEATHS

| | |
|---|---|
| John I. Walters | Feb. 10th, 1940 |
| Edelle Walters Dragoo | Feb. 20, 1932 |
| Margaret Herod | Feb. 4th, 1926 |
| Strather Herod | Aug. 19th, 1903 |
| Maude Kersey | Oct. 28th, 1925 |
| John Kersey | March 21st, 1913 |
| Jessie Hartling | April 1939 |
| Henry Hartling | July 1915 |
| Virgil Hartling | Nov. 1941 |
| Blanche Holt, Ax | Feb. 16th, 1922 |

(Copy of notebook sheet inserted in this Bible after recorded Deaths)

## BIRTHS

William Mullendore, March 19, 1840
Margaret E. Nay, April 23, 1847
Mazy & Catherine Mullendore, Aug. 18, 1867
Jessie U. Mullendore, Jan. 19, 1869

Infant daughter, Nov. 10, 1870
Maude M. Mullendore, May 27, 1872
Infant Son, Mar. 3, 1875
Wilda W. Mullendore, Jan. 19, 1876
Strather E. Herod, Nov. 14, 1846
Mapel Clare Herod, Nov. 25, 1883
Ralph T. Herod, Nov. 22, 1885

DEATHS

Catherine Mullendore, Feb. 15, 1868
Mazy Mullendore, Sept. 8, 1868
Infant Son, Mar. 6, 1875
William E. Mullendore, Nov. 5, 1875
Infant daughter, Nov. 22, 1870
Mapel Clare Herod, July 18, 1884
Strather E. Herod, Aug. 19, 1903

(Newspaper clipping dated Feb. 10, 1940)
J.I. Walters, 66, of Franklin Dies (photograph)  John I. Walters, 66 years old, a
farmer living near Franklin, died Wednesday following an illness of nine
months.  Mr. Walters was born near Franklin, Aug. 10, 1873, and had lived in
the community all his life.  He was a member of the Young Creek Christian
Church and of the Improved Order of Red Men.  Survivors are the widow, Mrs.
Wilda Walters; five sons, Wayne B. Walters and Roscoe F. Walters of Franklin,
and the Rev. Guy T. Walters of Mellott, H. Max Walters of Connersville, and F.
Merle Walters of Indianapolis, a member of the advertising department of The
Star; three sisters, Mrs. John Coy of Franklin, Mrs. Lewis Royce of El Reno,
Okla., and Mrs. Frank Mullikin of Franklin, and four brothers, Young P.
Walters of Indianapolis, Lewis Walters of Franklin, Clarence Walters of
Trafalgar, and Benton Walters of Franklin.  Funeral services will be held at 11
o'clock tomorrow morning in the Vandivier funeral home in Franklin.  Burial
will be in Franklin.

(Copy of newspaper clipping pasted on back of notebook sheet inserted)

Feb. 20, 1932  Mrs. Ralph F. Dragoo Dies Early Saturday  Had Suffered Heart
Attack--Rites at Christian Church Monday Afternoon.  Mrs. Margaret Edelle
Dragoo, wife of Ralph F. Dragoo and formerly one of the best known young
women of the Franklin community, died suddenly Saturday morning at her
home in Indianapolis, following a heart attack.  She had not been in good
health for some time, but her condition had not been serious and the death at 2
o'clock came as a great shock to members of the family and to her many friends
throughout the county.  Funeral services will be held from the Franklin Christian church Monday afternoon at 2 o'clock and will be conducted by the Rev.
Crafton, of the Garfield Baptist church at Indianapolis.  Burial will be in
Greenlawn cemetery.  Friends are invited to call at the residence, 1318 Finley
street, Indianapolis, at any hour before noon Monday, when the body will be
brought here for the services.  Mrs. Dragoo was the daughter of Mr. and Mrs.

Greenlawn cemetery. Friends are invited to call at the residence, 1318 Finley street, Indianapolis, at any hour before noon Monday, when the body will be brought here for the services. Mrs. Dragoo was the daughter of Mr. and Mrs. John I. Walters, well known residents of the Jollity community, and was one of the most popular young women of that community. She attended the Franklin schools, graduating from the Alva Neal high school and was a student at Franklin college for one year before her marriage six years ago to Ralph F. Dragoo. Before her marriage, she was Youngs Creek correspondent for The Star and filled her duties with great satisfaction. She had resided in Indianapolis since her marriage. Surviving with the husband is a daughter, Margaret Louise; the parents, Mr. and Mrs. John I. Walters, and five brothers, Wayne Walters and Roscoe F. Walters, both Franklin; Rev. Guy T. Walters, Bluffton; H. Max Walters, of Connersville, and Merle Walters, of Indianapolis.

## GRIMES FAMILY BIBLE
Submitted by Oscar J. Curtis*

### Births.

Ervin Grimes, son of Thomes Grimes and Nancy Woodard Grimes, born September 19th 1828,
Sarah Rogers Daughter of Benjamin Rogers and Elisabeth Arnold Rogers Born March 14th 1834.
Our Baby boy was born July 6th 1870
Lura L. Grimes Born August 14th 1871 (half past 3 o'clock P M)
Elenor Pearl Grimes Born April 26th 1874 8 oclock P.M.
Sarah Margaret Wright born August 4, 1908 (5 o'clock A.M.)

### Marriages.

Ervin Grimes and Sarah Rogers were married November 18th 1868

### Deaths.

Our Baby boy died July 6th 1870
Sarah Rogers Grimes died December 15, 1904
Ervin Grimes died July 16, 1910
Eleanor Grimes Wright died Nov. 18, 1917
Sarah Margaret Wright died Nov. 18 1917
Lura Grims Anderson Died July 21 1936 Four clock In evening

*Oscar J. Curtis is a member of the Family History Committee of the Indiana Historical Society. He has submitted several Bible records which he has gathered. The Grimes Bible was published in 1868.

# BIBLE RECORDS OF DAVID C. WIGGINS

Submitted by Peggy Ann Hobson*

[first page]
Marriages

Lorenzo Delton Bouse & Burtrude Jane Wiggins   Feb. 20--1912
Forest Glenn Bouse & Vena Martin   Feb. 20--1930
Sarah Jewel Bouse & Franklin Rockey   Mar. 13--1937

[second page]
Marriages
George Stephen Wiggins & Anna Paulene Sandman   Oct 6th 1887
William Milton Wiggins & Alice Ann Rouls   Mar. 1880
Sarah Ellen Wiggins & Albert N. Springer   Sept. 4-1890
Ida May Wiggins & John Edward Stewart   Oct 1892
Anna Victory Wiggins & Hubert W. Bunch   Feb. 20-1902
Bertha Jane Wiggins & Lorenzo Bouse   Feb 20--1902
David Chester Wiggins & Clara Alice Kindes   May 9--1906

[third page]
Births
Lorenzo Delton Bouse was Born Feb. 20th 1875
Bertha Jane Bouse was Born Aug 28th 1876
Forest Glenn Bouse was born Sept 5--1904
Sarah Jewel Bouse was born Mar. 10th 1915

[fourth page]
Births
of
David L. Wiggins Family

| | | |
|---|---|---|
| David L. Wiggins | | June 1--1836 |
| Mary Nagle | " | June 1--1838 |
| Jane Elsworth | " | Aug 21--1862 |
| Elizabeth Martha | " | Nov. 6--1863 |
| George Stephen | " | Jan 18--1865 |
| William Milton | " | Oct 18--1866 |
| Sarah Ellen | " | Sept 4--1868 |
| Mary Rosa | " | Sept 12-1870 |

*This Bible was purchased in a garage sale in Indianapolis in 1988.   The title page gives no indication of the date purchased.   Much of the book is gone, Peggy Ann Hobson has preserved the pages containing family history.   She also researched newspapers to find the obituaries and marriage notice reproduced after the Bible records.

| Emma Leona | : | | |
| | : --" | | Aug. 20-1872 |
| Ida May | : | | |
| Anna Victory | " | | Dec   13-1874 |
| Burthude Jane | " | | Aug 28--1876 |
| David Chester | " | | July 8--1882 |

| [fifth page] | | Deaths |
| Elizabeth Martha Wiggins | | Jan. 1-1864 |
| Mary Rosa | " | |
| Emma Leona | ", | Jan 14-1874 |
| John Elsworth | " | Oct.---1873 |
| Mary (Nagle) | " | Aug 7 1911 |
| John Edward Stewart | | July    1915 |
| Alice Ann (Rouls) Wiggins | | Jan    1921 |
| David L. Wiggins | | Nov 3--1921 |
| Anna Paulene (Sandman) W. | | Dec    1934 |
| Lorenzo Delton Bouse | | June 15 1935 |
| Albert Newton Springer | | Oct 1   1937 |
| Clara Alice (Kinder) W. | | April 30 1936 |
| William Milton Wiggins | | Dec 24 1927 |
| David Chester Wiggins | | Aug 21 1949 |
| George Stephen Wiggins | | Oct 15 1950 |
| Ida May Stewart | " | April 19 1958 |
| Sarah Ellen Springer | " | April 21 1958 |
| Anna Victory " Bunch | | Sept 21 1958 |
| Hubert H [Harden] | | Feb 10   1961 |
| Bertha J. Bouse | | April 3 1970 |

[sixth page]                              Deaths
Lorenzo Delton Bouse passed away June 15, 1935
Forest Glenn Bouse passed away Nov. 17th 1942

**ROCKEY-BOUSE**   Franklin J. Bouse and Sarah Jewel Bouse of Tipton were married Saturday afternoon at the parsonage of the Albright church in Atlanta. The single ring ceremony was read by Rev. Wilson S. Parks. They were attended by Miss Vivian Sells and Roderick Hobbs. Following the ceremony the young couple left for a short honeymoon trip.

Mr. Rockey is the son of Joe Rockey, deceased, who was one of the large land owners of the north part of this township and Miss Bouse, the daughter of L.D. Bouse, also deceased. She is a graduate of the class of 1933 of the Tipton High School. (*Tipton Daily Tribune*, 15 March 1937, p. 3)

The funeral services of the late Mrs. David Wiggins were conducted Thursday morning at 10 o'clock at the Albright church, and there were many of the friends of the deceased there to pay their last respect. The burial was at Arcadia. (*Tipton Daily Tribune*, 10 August 1911, p. 4)

**PIONEER PASSED AWAY**.  David C. Wiggins Sr. Died at Home of Daughter, Mrs. L.D. Bouse.

David C. Wiggins Sr., aged pioneer, died at the home of his daughter, Mrs. Delt Bouse, four miles southwest of Tipton, Thursday afternoon at three-thirty, following an illness lasting nearly five months, from complications incident to his advanced years, he being past eighty-five years old.   During the last few weeks his condition was such that his death was expected at any time.

The funeral services will be held Saturday morning at ten-thirty o'clock at the Albright church with Rev. Brewer of Cicero, in charge of the ceremonies and the burial will take place at the Arcadia cemetery.

Besides his children he is survived by 25 grandchildren, and thirteen great grandchildren.   His wife preceded him into the beyond Dec. 7th 1910.   Since her death he made his home the greater part of the time with his children.

Mr. Wiggins was born in Lancaster county, Pennsylvania, June 1, 1836, and while he came from German stock and was reared in a German community, he never talked the language until he was eighteen years of age.   His father was Stephen Wiggins, of Irish extraction, and his mother was Elizabeth Bowman, of German extraction, she talking the language quite fluently.   Young Wiggins was thrown entirely among German association at the age of eighteen and then it was that he took up the language.   He soon mastered the tongue and could talk that language better than he could the English tongue.   At the age of twenty-two he began to learn the trade of a blacksmith in the town of Buck, Pa.   On the 23rd of January, 1862, at Lancaster, Pa., he was joined in marriage to Mary Nagle, she being twenty-two years of age, and she was also born on June 1.   She was a native of Lancaster county.   Her father was John Nagle and her mother was Martha Shoaff, the father being English and the mother German.

In 1865, when they had been married three years, they moved to Arcadia, Mrs. Wiggins having a brother, William Nagle, living there.   Mr. Wiggins followed the trade of a blacksmith for a time, but later took a lease on the farm of Sylvester Gwinn, who at this time is one of the heaviest land owners in Hamilton county.   On this lease he accumulated a sufficient amount of money to buy a farm of his own and he purchased thirty acres in Hamilton county, which he afterward exchanged for eighty acres in Tipton county, getting the farm of William Russell, father of James Russel, now of Tipton.   The land was mostly swamp and heavily timbered.   Seven years later he bought an additional forty acres that adjoined the original farm.   Six years later he added another forty.   In 1908 he bought forty more, this giving him 200 acres that today would bring the top price in this county, as it is one of the best farms in the county.

It took a good deal of courage to attempt the making of a home in that section, as it was in the heart of the Devil's Den, one of the most uninviting sections of the country at that time.   Today it is a garden spot.

Mr. Wiggins was not a soldier in the war of the rebellion, but it was not his fault that he did not get to the front, as he made two applications and each time was refused because of a crippled arm.

He served Tipton county as county commissioner for three years, he going into office in 1898, and was also a member of the county council.

Mr. and Mrs. Wiggins were the parents of ten children, seven of whom are living, they being George Wiggins, of Hamilton county; William Wiggins, of

Tipton; Mrs. Albert Springer, of Tipton; Mrs. Ida Phelps, of Indianapolis; Mrs. Hubert Bunch, of near Windfall; Mrs. Delt Bouse, of Tipton county, and David C. Wiggins, of Tipton county. The deceased children are Lizzie, Rosa and Emma.

Both Mr. and Mrs. Wiggins were members of the Evangelical church, having their membership at the Albright church on the county line. They held membership in that church for more than a quarter of a century. (*Tipton Daily Tribune* 4 November 1921, p. 8)

**DEATH CLAIMS WM. WIGGINS** Former Business Man and Long Time Resident of City is Dead. Illness was Baffling.

Monday morning at 7 o'clock William Wiggins, 58, died at the home of his son, Walter Wiggins southwest of Tipton, death ending an illness of several months during which time his condition had been rapidly growing worse and the nature of his illness baffled physicians. One week ago Thursday he went to the home of his sister, Mrs. Hubert Bunch in the Hazel Dell community near Windfall and while there became bedfast. He was taken to the home of his son, Walter in the Ogle & Little ambulance Friday of last week.

William Wiggins had been a resident of Tipton county for the past fifty years coming here from Hamilton county with his father and mother David L., and Mary Nagle Wiggins in 1877 and settling on what is known as the Wiggins farm southwest of Tipton. The father came to Hamilton county from Pennsylvania in 1865 following his trade as blacksmith and farming until his removal to this county when all of his attention was devoted to his farm.

The son grew to manhood in this county and was known as one of the reliable and trustworthy men of this section, being honored by being elected to the office of trustee of this township, an office which he filled with credit. The father was a former county commissioner and served in other capacities. Both parents are deceased.

William Wiggins was married to Miss Alice Rouls, sister of D.S. Rouls of Tipton, her death occuring a number of years ago. He is survived by several children, Walter at whose home he died; Ray who resides in Atlanta; Clifford, unmarried, of Tipton and Mabel, unmarried, who is employed as an instructor in the Methodist home for orphans in Honolulu. He is also survived by two brothers, George Wiggins of Cicero and David C. Wiggins , southwest of Tipton, four sisters, Mrs. Ella Springer of Detroit, Mich.; Mrs. Ida Stewart of Indianapolis; Mrs. Hubert Bunch of Hazel Dell and Mrs. Bertha Bouse residing west of Atlanta.

William Wiggins was formerly engaged in the implement business in the rooms now occupied by the postoffice and the Ogle & Little Undertaking establishment, this business being closed out and he entered the office of trustee. After serving his term as trustee he for a time was engaged in the real estate business being a partner in the Clark-Miner firm. Later he opened the International Harvester store on Court street a business he was conducting at the time of his death.

William Wiggins was a member of the West Street Christian Church and a man who enjoyed and commanded the respect and confidence of all, being strictly upright in his dealings and in his mode of living and his passing is a matter of sincere regret to the many friends he had in this community. *Tipton Daily Tribune* 26 December 1927, p. 1)

**BOUSE FUNERAL.** The Albright Evangelical church, west of Atlanta, was filled Monday afternoon when friends and relatives gathered there to pay their last respects to Delt Bouse, a resident of that community, whose death occurred suddenly early Saturday morning. The body was surrounded by numerous beautiful floral pieces, silent tributes to the memory of this splendid friend and neighbor.

Rev. Francis Willard of Dayton, O., former pastor of the Albright church conducted the services, assisted by Rev. Park, the present pastor. Burial was in the Normanda cemetery. (*Tipton Daily Tribune*, 17 June 1935, p. 5)

### DAVID WIGGINS RITES PLANNED

Funeral services for David C. Wiggins, 67, who died Sunday at the Scott Nursing home in Lafayette, are planned at 2:30 p.m. Tuesday at Young's Funeral home. Rev. Ben Kendall, former pastor of the Kemp Methodist church, will be in charge of rites and burial will be in Fairview cemetery. Masonic rites will be conducted at the grave.

Mr. Wiggins, who resided at 222 West Adams street, died at 2 a.m. Sunday after being in failing health for several months. His condition has been critical for the past two weeks. The body is lying in state at Young's Funeral home.

Born in Tipton county July 8, 1882, David Chester Wiggins was the son of David L. and Mary (Nagle) Wiggins. He attended public schools in Tipton county and spent most of his entire life here. On May 19, 1906, he was married to Clara Kinder who preceded him in death April 10, 1936. Three children born to the couple died in infancy.

Mr. Wiggins was engaged in farming southwest of Tipton in the earlier years of his married life. Later he was employed with the Tipton Ice Cream company, the Inland Alkaloid company and, until his sickness, the Oakes Manufacturing company. He was a member of the Kemp Methodist church, Austin lodge No. 128, F. and A.M. Commandery, Order of the Eastern Star and Modern Woodmen of America.

Survivors are a brother, George, of Noblesville; four sister, Mrs. Bertha Bouse, with whom he had been making his home for the past 13 years, Mrs. Hubert Bunch, near Windfall, Mrs. Ida Steward of Indianapolis and Mrs. Ella Springer of Detroit, Mich., and several nieces and nephews. (*Tipton Daily Tribune 22 August 1949*, p. 1)

### FORMER TIPTON MERCHANT DIES

George S. Wiggins, 85, died Sunday afternoon at the home of his son, Harry Wiggins, in Noblesville after an illness of two years.

Funeral services will be Wednesday from the Coaltram Funeral home in Noblesville, Wednesday at 2 p.m. with Rev. Donald Barnes of Lapel officiating. Interment will be in the Arcadia cemetery. The body is at the son's home, 1194 Wayne street, Noblesville, where friends may call.

Born in Lancaster, Pa., Jan. 18, 1865, he was the son of David L. [and] Mary Wiggins. From Pennsylvania they moved to Hamilton county, near Arcadia, and in 1877 came to Tipton county where he was a farmer, road contractor and merchant. On October 30, 1934 he moved to Noblesville where he retired, and his wife Anna P. Wiggins, died a year later.

His father, David L. Wiggins, was a commissioner on the first Tipton County board of commissioners, also served as president of the board.

He was a member of the Methodist church, and Modern Woodmen of America lodge.

Survivors include three children: Harry of Noblesville; Mrs. Cora E. Holliday, Noblesville, and Mrs. Maude E. Russell, Evansville; a daughter in law Mrs. Ruth Wiggins, Noblesville; four sister, Mrs. Ella Springer, Detroit, Mich.; Mrs. Ida Stewart, Indianapolis, Mrs. Hubert Bunch Windfall and Mrs. Bertha Bouse of Tipton. Other relatives include neices and nephews, 13 grandchildren, 29 great grandchildren, and two great, great grandchildren. (*Tipton Daily Tribune*, 16 October 1950, p. 1)

Mrs. Bertha J. Bouse Dies After Illness

Mrs. Berth J. Bouse, 93, route 2 Sheridan, died at 2 p.m. Thursday in Riverview hospital, Noblesville following an extensive illness.

Services will be at 2 p.m. Monday in Nichols Funeral Home. Friends may call any time Sunday. Burial will be in the Normandie Cemetery.

Bertha Bouse was born Aug. 28, 1876 in Hamilton Co. the daughter of David and Mary (Sara) Wiggins. She married Dolton Bouse on Feb. 20, 1902 in Tipton. Dolton Bouse died on June 15, 1935.

Bertha Bouse was a member of Kemp United Methodist Church. Survivors include a daughter Mrs. Frank (Sara) Rockey, Sheridan; four grandchildren and 10 great grandchildren. (*Tipton Daily Tribune*, 4 April 1970, p. 1)

## BIBLE OF BENJAMIN RENARD
### Submitted by Oscar F.Curtis*

Benjamin Ranard   Bible Price $1.12 1/2   Cts   Bought of John Camb[es?] Jan 6th 1840.

This 18th of July 1851 From the Time of Purchase to the Preasant date is ten years eight months and twelve days   Simeon Ranard

### Births of the Benjaman Ranard

Son of William Ranard and Sopha his wife Was born Oct 29th 1771

Elizabeth Ranard wife of Benjamin Ranard was born February th 27 1783

Catharine Ranard daughter of Benjam Ranard and Elizabeth his wife was born May 24th 1804

Sophia Ranard Ranard daughter of Benjamin Ranard and Elizabeth his wife was born May 21th 1806

Jacob M Ranard Son of Benjamin Renard and Elizabeth his wife Was born September th 29 1808

Joel Ranard son of Benjamin Ranard and Elizabeth his wife Was born Novem   ber 12th 1810

William Ranard Son of Benjamin Ranard and Elizabeth his wife was born December 30th 1812

Elias Ranard son of Benjamin Ranard and Elizabeth his wife was born January 4th 1815

Eli Ranard son of Benjamin Ranard and Elizabeth his wife was born January 28th 1818

Daniel Ranard Son of Benjamin Ranard and Elizabet his wife was born June 30th 1820

*Oscar F. Curtis is a member of the Family History Committee of the Indiana Historical Society.  The Renard Bible was published in New York in 1834. Page 72 of Blanchard, Charles, *Counties of Clay and Owen, Indiana, Historical and Biographical* . . .  Chicago, F.A. Battey & Co., 1884, states that Benjamin and Elizabeth (Massey), born in Kentucky and North Carolina, respectively came to Owen County in 1830. The same paragraph gives the birthplace of Elias Ranard as Pulaski County, Kentucky. Apparently the Renards did not arrive in Indiana until after the 1830 census was taken. In 1840, Benjamin, Daniel, and Joel Ranard are all enumerated on p. 171 of the Owen County census.  By 1860, the only one of this family listed in Owen County was Joel, age 49, born in Kentucky.

**Births**

Simeon Ranard Son of Benjanam Ranard and Elizbeth his wife was born Oct the 13 1823

Elizabeth Ranard Daughter of Benjamin Ranard and Elizabeth his wife was born April 9th 1828

Catharine Stogsdill was born November the 14 1836

Emilia Stogsdill was born November 15 1830

Josiah G. Ranard Son of Simeon Ranard and Emilia his wife was born February 15th 1850

**Deaths**

Josiah G. Ranard Son of Simeon Ranard and Emilia his wife Departed this Life February 22th 1850

Elzabeth Ranard Wife of Benjamin Ranard died or Departed this life January 16th 1845 Aged 61 years 10 months and 19 days

Benjamin Ranard departed this life September 16 1855

Catharine Bray Daughter of B and E Ranard departed this life September

Sophia Stogsdill Daughter of B and E Ranard departed this life Aprile 11 1837

Jacob M Ranard departed this life September 1852

William Ranard departed this life November 3 1859

Daniel Ranard departed this life December 20 1858

Simeon Ranard departed this life February 17 1863

## DUNBAR FAMILY BIRTHS
Submitted by Bernadine Betlach

### BIRTHS

Johnathan Arnold Dunbar was born in Lee, Oneida Co., N.Y. July 4 1822

Harriet Dunbar was born in Rome Onida Co N.Y. Dec 5 1824

Julius E. Dunbar was born in Florence, Onida Co N.Y. Aug 20th 1856

Anna Gertrude Dunbar was born in LaPorte, LaPorte Co Ind. Dec 10 1864

Wallace Dunbar was born in Benton Harbor, Barien Co Mich Jan. 8 1888

Baby "Grace" B.H. Mich Oct 31 1886

Harriet A Dunbar was born in Benton Harbor Sept 3 1889

Erma G. Dunbar St. Joseph Mich May 4 1891

Lois Dunbar Benton Harbor Mich Jan 22 1893

Josephine Dunbar B.H Mich Feb 27 1894

Raymond J. Dunbar B. H. Mich Apr 10 1897

# WILLIAM POLK HARMON BIBLE
Submitted by Elizabeth J. Glenn

William Polk Harmon was born in Chatham County, NC, Feb. 27, 1807 to George and Amelia (Polk) Harmon. He moved to Henry Co., Indiana in 1829 and there married Mary B. Leeson, daughter of Richard Largent and Jane (Dooley) Leeson on April 24, 1834. The title page and the first few pages of Genesis are missing from this Bible.

## MARRIAGES
William P. Harmon and Mary B. Leeson Was Married April 24th 1834.
William Barton and Sinai Jane Harman Was Married May the 4th 1857.
James B. Tull and Sarah C. Harman Was Married August the 18th 1862.
John D. Armfield and Ruth Senoria Harmon Was Married Septembr 26th 1866
George W. Broyls and Eliza M. Harmon was Maried Augest the 21 1872
Moses Dooley Harmon married April 12 1870 to Inez Clendenen
Martha Elizabeth Harmon was married To Joseph A. Stephenson
Clarinda E. Harmon was married To Frank Legg
Martissa Selina Harmon was married to Walter Beech
Edmund F. Harmon was married to Rosa Savage
Thomas L. Harmon was married to Alice Myrely
Henry Harmon was married to Mary Montgomery

## BIRTHS
James Silvester Harmon Was Born March 15th 1835
Sinah Jane Harmon Was Born May 8th 1837
Nancy Melvina Harmon Was Born November 29th 1838
George Luther Harmon was Born June 23d 1840
Sarah Caroline Harmon was Born December 29th 1841
John Allen Harmon Was Born July 9th 1843
Ruth Seonora Harmon Was Born February 24, 1845
Mary Eliza Harmon Was Born January 11th 1847
Moses Dooley Harmon Was Born September 5 1848
Martha Elizabeth Harmon was Born July 23d 1850
Richard Largent And Wiliam Henry Harmon Was Born May 8th 1852
Clarinda Elen Harman Was bornd August the 16th 1854
Martissa Selina was Born November the 2d 1856
Edmund fremont Harman was born June the 2 1858
thomas Linkon harman was born March the 4 1860

## DEATHS
George Luther Harmon Departed this life July 12th 1848
Richard Largent Harmon Depared this life May 13th 1852 aged five days
Nancy Melvina harman Departed this life october the first 1853
James sylvetter harman Departed this life september the 22 1856

John Allen Harman Departed this life August the 30th 1864 Aged 21 years 1
 month and 22 days
Sina Jane Barton Departed this life March the 10 1869
Sarah C Tull Died September the 5 1870
Ruth S Armfield Died April the 5 1872
Mary E. Broyles Departed tis life August the 21 1872
Clarissa Legg Died February 5 1875
Martha E. Stephenson Died April 11, 1875
Mary B. Harmon Died August 1887
William P. Harmon Died April 10, 1899
Martissa S. Beach Died
William H. Harmon Died

## CAMPBELL FAMILY BIBLE
Submitted by Oscar F. Curtis

### FAMILY RECORD
### MARRIAGES.

George W. Campbell and Annie J. Campbell were Married November 20th
1866;

### BIRTHS

George W. Campbell was Born August 12th 1843;
Annie J. Campbell was Born January 31st 1848:
Charles T. Campbell was Born June 3d 1868.
Minnie Campbell was Born August 24th 1869.
Fannie R. Campbell was Born December 23d 1871
Noble C. Campbell was Born August 6th 1875.
Earl H. Campbell was Born October 15th 1884,

### DEATHS

George W. Campbell Died November 25 1906, aged 63 yrs. 3 mo. 12 days.
Charles T. Campbell Died June 7, 1868
Minnie Campbell Died January 10 1871.
Earl H. Campbell Died October 17, 1884,

### MARRIAGES

Fannie R. Campbell and Sherman Botts were married April 16, 1891
Noble C. Campbell and Roxie E. Smyth were married October 23d 1897.

Oscar J. Curtis has submitted thirty-three Bible records from the collection at
the Monroe County Historical Society. Mr. Curtis was elected to the Family
History Committee of the Indiana Historical Society in November 1989. The
Campbell Bible was published in 1876, all entries appear to be in the same
handwriting.

# BASSETT FAMILY BIBLE

Submitted by Dorothy Kekasi

This Certifies Charles H. Bassett of Fairfield and Mary A. Kyger of Brookville were united by me in the Bonds of Holy Matrimony At Brookville on the 25th day of August in the year of our Lord 1863. In Presence of T.T. Smith, W.H. Jones; Signed Rev. Crawford.

Charity Line Kyger born Aug 31 1810
Charity Line Kyger Mother born Nov 17 1781
mother Margaret Lines
father Henry Lines father
Daniel Kyger born Mar 6 1807
Alphus Kyger born Oct 2 1828
T. Verd Kyger born Mar 26 1831
Melvinia Kyger born Mar 1st 1833
Viena Kyger Armfield born June 14 1835
Martha Jane Kyger Stonner born Nov 31st 1837
Mary Ann Kyger Bassett born Oct 6th 1840
Candice Kyger Bell born Feb 6 1843
Amanda Jane Kyger Fish born April 6, 1845
Adda Jane Kyger (Enslinger) born June 1 1847

## BIRTHS

Charles Hill Bassett Born Aug 25th 184-
Mary Ann Kyger Born Oct 6th 1840
Leora Temprance Bassett Born Sep 3rd 65
[Lew]is Watson Bassett Born Feb 4 1869
Gertrude Bassett Born Apr 11th 1872
Grace Caroline Bassett Born June 23 1876
Orris Welman Bassett Born Aug 23 1878
Harry Hershall Bassett Born Sep 5th 1880
Walter Scott Bassett Born Apr 8th 1884

## MARRIAGES

D.F. Havens to Leora T. Bassett April 1889 by Rev. G.W. Winchester
Gertrude B to F.O. Hodson May 8 1895 by Rev. J.W. Guild
Caroline to Chas R Allison Dec 6 1898 by Rev
Orris Welman to Mary E Haines Feb 15th 1902 by Rev Beaty
Walter Scott to Golda Tegarden Jan 7 1908 by Rev
Mary A Kyger to Chas H. Bassett Aug 25th 1863 by Rev John Crawford

mother of Mary A Bassett   Charity Kyger born Aug 31 1810
father of Mary Kyger Bassett   Daniel Kyger born Mar 6 1807   Chairty & Daniel married 1827
mother of Chas Hall Bassett   Elizabeth Dubois Bassett born
father of Chas Hall Bassett   Nathanal Bassett born

# JOURNAL OF WILLIAM H. MOORE

Transcribed and Submitted by Irene Moore Lindsey*

The Reverend William H. Moore was born near Rising Sun, Indiana, 6 January 1821, and died at Brookville, Indiana, 9 August 1908. He was graduated from Miami University, Oxford, Ohio, in 1841. The next year he assisted the Reverend McKinney at Rising Sun. In 1843 he entered the New Albany Theological Seminary and was licensed to preach by the Presbytery of Salem, Indiana, on 27 June 1845. Moore kept journals of his ministerial labors. The following are portions of the journal dealing with his duties in and near Rising Sun. Moore's first nine years of the ministry were spent in the southern part of Indiana in Presbyterian churches of Jeffersonville, Port Fulton, Dillsboro, Versailles, and Rising Sun. In 1855, he left Indiana to answer a call to Harrison, Ohio. His third journal includes this first ministry in Rising Sun. Another journal covering a later period in Rising Sun is in the process of being transcribed. Moore used abbreviations freely in his journal. A list of these is found at the end of this transcript.

Rising Sun Ind. Ap. 4" 1853
Journal of Ministerial labours
performed by W.H. Moore
Vol" 3d.

Sab. April 3d. 1853 Preached at R.S. in A.M. from Psalm CXI: 10.f.c. Lecture at night. Acts IX:10-19. Monday P.M. set out for Presbytery to meet at Metamora, Franklin Co. Ind. Rode as far as Mr. Rowlands & put up for the night; next day in company with Msrs. Rowland & McCabe reached Metamora. Was chosen Moderator. After a pleasant session Pres. adjourned thursday night. Rode next day to Versailles & put up for the night. Visited next day Mr. Carter's & Mr. Lingle's & staid all night at Mr. Ecklis.

Sab. April 10". Preached at Stringtown Ps. CXI: 10.f.c. Rode to Dillsborough & preached same at 4.P.M. Bro P. from L. came and preached at night. Next day spent in visiting from house to house. Bro. P. preached again at night. Quite an interesting state of feeling among the members. Returned home next day.

*Mrs. Lindsey, great-granddaughter of William H. Moore, recently retired as acting Director of the Smith Library of Regional History, a Division of the Lane Public Library, Oxford, Ohio.

Sab. Ap. 17" 1853  Preached in the church in A.M.  1 Pet. IV:18.  Called in P.M. to preach a funeral discourse on the occasion of the death of James Moor of East Bend, Ky. one of the friends & companions of my early days.  A voice seemed to come to all in this providence, saying "Be ye also ready."  Spoke on the occasion from Eccl. III:2 "A time to die."  Remained with the afflicted friends all night.  Sat. rode to I. McCabes on way to Versailles.

Sab. Ap. 24"  Preached in V. at 11.  I Cor. XV:55-57, a fun. ser. on the death of Mrs. Carter a member of the church.  Larger audience than usual.  Session rec'd Mr. H. Papet on ex.  In P.M. Preached from I Pet. IV:18.

Next day April 25" 1853 rode two miles north of Napoleon & united in marriage Mr. I. MCabe & Miss Sarah McFatridge.  Returned home next day.

Sab. May 1st. 1853.  at R.S.  Preached in A.M.  Mark IV:24 f.c.  Lecture in P.M. Acts IX:19-31.  Wednesday evening commenced the monthly concert of prayer for Foreign Missions.  Saturday rode to Mr. Harris(?) in Ripley Co. & put up for the night.

Sab. May 8" 1853.  preached at 11 at Stringtown.  Heb. XII:2 f.c.  Rode to Dillsborough & preached at 4 P.M.  Mark 1:14,15.  Session received Mrs. Rebecca Windsor on ex. & 8 childrn were baptized, after which preached a sermon on baptism.  Acts XVI. 15 f.c.  Returned home in P.M.

Sab. 15" at R.S. in A.M.  Jas. I:17.  Rode in P.M. to Pleas. Ridge & preached for Bro. Sheldon Is. IX:6.  Returned & preached here at night.  John XII: 21 l.c.

Sat. 21st rode to Mr. Lingle's on way to Versailles.

Sabbath May 22d. 1853.  Preached in V. at 11 & at 3. same as last Sab.  Rode to I. Mc's in the evening and home next morning.

Sab. 29" at Dillsborough in A.M.  Col II:6.  Previous to the sermon Session rece'd John P. Rowland & wife on examination.  Preached in P.M. at Pleasant Grove from the parable of the ten virgins.  Mar XXV:1-13.  Returned home next day.

Sab. June 5"  Preached in R.S. in A.M. Ps. XCIX:9.  Rode in P.M. to Mr. Wilson's & preached I John III:2.  returned & preached in town at night-- parable of ten virgins.  Friday rode to Stringtown & at night heard Rev. Holliday P.E. of the M.E. Ch. preach.  Next day preached at 11 Luke XIVC:46,47, also at night I Kings XVIII:21st.  Session received on certificate from the regular Baptist church Mrs. Sarah McCabe

Sabbath June 12" 1853.  Preached in Stringtown at 11  Ps. XCIX:9.  Previous to sermon received on prof. of his faith Mr. James Scudder.  After sermon administered the L's Supper.  Collection for For. Missions $4.00.  Preached in P.M.  I Jno:III:2.  Returned home next day.

Rising Sun June 17"  Candlelighting preached I John III:2.  On Sab. at 11 Luke XVIII: 18 preparatory to the communion.

Sab. June 19"  Is LIII:4,5 & admistered the Lord's Sup.  Session rec'd on ex. Mr. Gus Hillis.  Preached at night  Rev. XXII:17.

Friday 24" rode in Buggy with Rev. D. Lattimore to Aurora & from there to Dillsborough in Omnibus, then walked to Mr. Perlu's where remained all night. Next morn rode on horse to Mr. Bod--'s in neighborhood of Versailles. Preached at night in V. Rev. XXII:17.

Next morn (Sab. June 26") at 11 Ps. XCIX 9. In P.M. Luke XVIII:18 Rode to Mr. Rowland's next day & home on day following.

June 29" 1853 at 1/2 past 7 & 8 P.M. united in marriage Mr. S.A. Adams & Miss Agnes L. Coles & Mr. Reuben James & Miss Rebecca B. Moore.

Sab. July 3d. at R.S. in A.M. and P.M. John X:11 & Acts IX:32-43

Friday 8" Started for Dillsborough, rode to Esq. Wilder's & staid all night. Rode to D. next morn. Bro. Sheldon of the N.S. church came & preached at 11 & at night.

Sab. July 10" Communion sermon Preached in A.M. Is LIII:4,5. Collection for For. Missions 5.00. In P.M. sermon to sabbath school children on occasion of the death of Eliz. Wilson, one of their number. Ser. from Eccl. XII:1. Next morn set out for Brookville to attend a called meeting of Pres. reached there 1/2 past 4 P.M. Preached at candlelighting John IV:13,14. Pres. adjd next day. Rode to Manchester on the way home, where arrived next day.

Sab. July 17"--1853 Preached in R.S. 1/2 past 10 A.M. John XVIII:40. In the Meth. Ch. at 5 1/2 P.M. 1 Cor. III:21,22 & in my own ch. at night Acts X:1-8. Called on in the morning to marry a couple but declined on accoun. of engagements & the impropriety of performing such service on the sabbath.

Frid. July 22d. Rode to Versailles. Bro. Stryker of Kingston, Ind. came and preached at candlelighting; next day at 11 & at night.

Sab. 24" Bro. S. preached again at 11 & at 4. Administered the sacraments of baptist & Lords Sup. the former to a greyheaded man by the name of Coomes. Collected $3.00 for For. Missions. Returned home on Monday.

Sab. 31st. Preached in A.M. & P.M. Acts XXVI:24,25 & Rvs V:1-5. Attended the fun. of Saml. Jelly Jr. at 2 P.M. Rev. Morris made remarks to a large audience of all ages & classes.

Sat. Aug. 6" 1853. Rode to neighborhood of Stringtown Ripley Co. & put up for the night. Preached next morn Sab. 7" from Acts XXVI:24,25 same as last sab. Preached in P.M. at I. McCabe's house. John XVIII:40. "Not this man, but Barrabbas." Returned home next day.

Sab. Aug. 14" Preached here in A.M. Dan. V:27. Lecture in P.M. Acts X:9-24. Thursday rode to Dillsborough and preached at night John XX:24-31. returned home next day.

Sab. 21st. At home preached in A.M. Ps. CL:1. In P.M. Acts X:24-35. Sat rode to Versailles & preached next day.

Sab. 28" Dan. V:27, in P.M. John X:11.

Sab. 4" Sept. Preached in R.S. in A.M John XV:5. Rode in P.M. to Mr. Wilson's and preacher ----

Sat. 10" Rode to Dillsborough with Mr. Fisher on way to Presbytery. Preached in D.

Sab. Sept. 11, 1853. A.M. & at night I Cor. XIII:5. "Charity not her own." and John IV:46-53. Next morn set out for Pres. at Liberty; reached there tuesday P.M. Preached the opening sermon I Cor IX:16.1.c.

Sept 13" After a protracted but pleasant session reached home friday night.

Sab. 18" Preached in R.S. A.M. & P.M. I Cor XIII:5 & Acts X:34,38. Prayer meeting on Wednesday evening. Commenced lecturing on 2d. Cor. Sat. rode to Mr. Haire's on the way to Ver. in company with Miss C. Haire. Preached next morning & P.M.

Sab. 25" in Versailles John XV:5 & Acts X:34-38. Received Mrs. I.(?) Sutton by Letter & Mrs. Papet on examina.

Sab. Oct. 2d. In R.S. John VIII:44. Lec. in P.M. Acts X:39,43.

Sat. P.M. Oct. 8" rode to I. McCabe's. Owing to a storm did not preach Sab. A.M. but in P.M. Jer. VIII:20. Session received Miss Rachel Fleming on examination. Returned home next day.

Wednesday, Oct. 12" 1853. rode to Dillsborough & preached at night same as last sab. After preaching rode to I. Rowland's & put up for the night. Rode next morn to Mr. Henry Mullen's where I united in marriage Mr. John Mullen & Miss Nancy Mullen--returned home same day.

Sat. 15" Preached in R.S. at 11 A.M. preparatory to the Lord's Supper. from Rev. 11:5, at night from John IV:46-53.

Sab. 16" Jer. VIII:20 & administered the Lord's Supper. Lecture at night Acts X:44-48. Wednesday evening started in company with Bro. Fisher to Synod to meet at Franklin, where we arrived next day about 10 A.M. Synod met at candlelighting and after a pleasant & harmonious Session adjourned monday night between 11 & 12 o'clock. Reached home tuesday night. Rode to Shelbyville on saturday during the Session of Synod and preached Sab. Oct. 23d. 1853 in A.M. & at night Jer. VIII:20 & Mat. XIX:16.

Sab. Oct 30" At Dillsborough. Addressed sabbath school in A.M. & preached at 11--Rev. II:5--rode to the country & addressed the Pleasant Grove Sab. school--returned to D & preached at night John IV:46-53. returned home next day.

Sab. Nov. 6" At home. Preached at 11 John VI:68. Lecture at night Acts XI:1-18. Friday P.M. rode to D. on way to Stringtown, met Bro. S.S. Potter who delivered a temperance address to a large & attentive audience made some remarks(?) myself after him. Next morn rode to S. where Bro. P. preached at 11 & at night--weather unfavorable & but few in attendance.

Sab. Nov. 13" Session received Miss Jane Eckles on examination. After sermon by Bro. P. administered the Lords Supper to an unusually attentive and solemn audience. Bro. P. preached again at night--rode myself to Dillsborough & preached at night to a large & very attentive audience from Jno VI:68. Session rec'd John Hair on examination. Returned to S. next morning & found that there was some interest in the church. Collected $5.00 for Dom. Miss. Bro. P. preached at 11 & I at night same as night before--a number of inquirers.

Tuesday A.M. Bro. P. preached--also at night, after which Session received John Thompson, Wm. Hair, Saml. Hair, Ruth Eckles, Mary McCabe, Marian Knapp, Laura Knapp, & Caroline Stockwell, on examination--all young persons. Wednesday night  Bro. P. preach'd again, after which Session receive Miss Rebecca McFatridge on examination--making 11 in all.  The Misses Knapp, I. Thompson & Miss Stockwell & Miss McFatridge were baptized. Returned home next day with a heart refresh'd and grateful for what the Lord had done in us & by us.  To his name be the praise.

Sab. Nov. 20" 1853. At home.  Preached in A.M. from Heb. VII:24,25. Lecture at night Acts XI:19-24.  Wednesday sent for to go to Dillsborough to marry a couple.

Thursday Nov. 24" 2 O'clock P.M. united in marriage Demas Perlu & Miss Rebecca Ann Wheaton.  Remained in the neighborhood until Sat. then rode to Versailles, where I preached next day Sab. 27" same as last sab. & lecture in P.M.  Returned to D. next day & home the day following.  Friday P.M. rode to Lawrenceburgh to assist Bro. P. sacramental meeting.  Preached at night John IV:46-53.  Also next day in A.M. & at night.  Luke XVII:20 l.c. Heb. VII:24,25.

On Sab. Dec. 4" John XV:5.  Assisted at the L's Sup. in P.M. & pr'ch'd at night Acts XXVI:24,25.  Some seven or eight in all but two, received on exam. Returned home next day in the P.M.

Sat. P.M. Dec. 10" 1853. rode to Dillsborough.  Preached next day Sab. at 11 & at night II Cor. V:17 & John VII: 45,46.  Returned home next day.   James Wilson formerly an elder & at his death a member of R.S. ch. died Sab. Dec. 11" 1853 about 9 1/2 P.M.  His end was peace.  Attended the funeral and made some remarks from Num. XXIII:10 l.c.  Wednesday morning between two and three o'clock, died Mrs. Elizabeth Young, also a member of this church.  She died trusting in Christ.  Thus in the short space of a few days the Lord has called away two from the number of this little flock.  How are we who remain called upon to exercize new diligence in the discharge of every christian duty.

Sab. Dec. 17" Preached at R.S. in A.M. & at night.  John VII:45-46 & Acts XI:25-30.  Friday A.M. prepared a temperance sermon to preach in the evening at Dillsborough, but when I reached there found the audience so much smaller than usual, concluded to postpone it, & preached from Acts XI:22:26.  Rode to Stringtown & preached next morn at 11 John VII:45,46.  Rode in P.M. to Versailles & preached at night Acts XI:19-16.

Sabbath Dec. 25" 1853. Preached in V. in A.M. & at night.  Ezk. XVIII:4 and Luke XIV: 13 f.c.  Called next day on my way home to see Miss Margaret White who had long been confined to a sick bed.  Found her resigned to the Lord's will.  Conversed, read the scriptures, sung and prayed with her & the rest of the family, & rode on to Dillsborough, where I visited with the sons of temperance.  Returned home next day.

Sab. Jan. 1st. 1854. Preached in R.S. in A.M. & at night Jer. XXVIII:16. "This year thou shalt die" & Acts XII:1-10.

Saturday Jan. 7" 1854. Rode to I. McCabe's in Ripley Co. & preached at night, same as last sab. in A.M.

Sab. 8" At Stringtown in A.M. and at night. Prov. IV:23. "Keep thy hearth with all dilligence," &c. Luke XIX:41-44. Returned home next day.

R.S. Sab. Jan 15, in A.M. from I Tim. III:16. At night from Acts XII:11-19. Friday A.M. started for Dillsborough on way to Versailles. Reached Aurora a little after noon, was detained by rain until 3 P.M. rode then to Mr. Perlu's & after taking some refreshment, walked over to Pleasant Grove schoolhouse & preached to some 12 or 15 persons from II Cor VIII: 9. went to Peter Rowland's & remained all night. Sat morn. very cold. rode to V. on way called to see Joseph Vandolah Jr. a young man sick of consumption, seemed alarmed at my presence, gave little evidence of a preparation for death. Bro. S.S. Potter reached V. in the evening.

Sab. Jan 22d. 1854. New church dedicated. Bro. P. preached the sermon. Collected $114.00 to aid in paying for the house. After sermon Session received five persons to the fellowship of the church, but all but one on examination. Tuesday seven more were received on profession of their faith. Meeting closed Wednesday night. Preached I Tim III:16. Congregation elected two additional elders. J. Hendricks and F. Mullan.

Sab. 29" At R.S. Preached in A.M. Is. LII:7 Dom. Miss. sermon In P.M. Acts XII:20-25.

31st. Died this morning W.G. Cadwell's little daughter. called & conversed & prayed with the afflicated parents. Attended the funeral next day. Made remarks from Christ's words. "Suffer little children to come unto me" & Mat. XIX:14. Friday P.M. Rev. I.C. Harrison from Boone Co. Ky. came & preached at night. next day at 11. & at night.

Sab. Feb. 5" 1854 Levi H. Howard died this morning, had visited him two or three times during his sickness, found him during his last hours somewhat concerned about his future prospects, but gave no wellgrounded evidence of a preparation for death. Bro. Harrison preached at 10 1/2 A.M. raised $25.00 for Dom. Missions. Communion in P.M. Bro. H. Preached again at night. Mond. 2 O'clock P.M. Attended the funeral of Mr. Howard in the church. Preached from Amos IV:12. "Prepare to meet thy god." Buried with Masonic honors. Bro. Harrison preached again at night & the night following, when our meetings closed. Sat. P.M. rode to Dillsborough and preached next day--Sab. 12" in A.M. & at night. Mat. X:32,33, & Acts XII:5,6. Bro. S.S. Potter came next day and preached at night. Preached myself next day at 11 from Is. I:10-18. Bro. P. at night in D. & I at Pleasant Grove from Rev. III:20. Session received on examination Mr. Peter Rowland and Wife. Returned home on wednesday & same evening united in marriage Mr. Wm. N. Grur & Miss Margaret H. Espey.

Sab. Feb. 19" 1854.   At R.S.   Preached in A.M. I:Tim. III:15--, in P.M. lecture from Acts XIII:1 & 2.   Friday P.M. rode to Dillsborough & preached at night from II Kings VI:16. temperance sermon.   Rode next morn to Stringtown & preached at 11 from Acts XVII:16, rode on to Mr. Lingle's & preached at night II Cor VIII:9.   Rode next morn Sab. 26" to Versailles, found that Satan had gained an advantage over some in the church & caused heartburnings & dissensions among them.   Preached at 11 from I Tim. III:15.   In P.M. from John XIII:34-35   After which ordained Francis Mullan an elder and installed him with Jamison Hendricks.   Returned home on tuesday.

Sab. March 5" 1854.   Preached at R.S. in A.M. Mat. X:32-33.   Rev. W. Terrill Agt. of Am. Bible Soc. preached in P.M. & raised a collection of $15.75.   Attended the M.E. church at night & heard Bro. T. again.

Sab. March 12" At R.S. in A.M. & at night--P's LXIII:5-6 and Luke XXII:42,43.   Sat. rode to Mrs. Fleming's, Mt Hope church & preached next day.

Sab. 19" at Stringtown in A.M. & P.M. same as last sabbath.   Rode to Mr. Lewis' in evening & remained all night, returned home next day.   Wednesday Rev. H.H. Cambern called, Ag't for Hanover College, obtained a scholarship of $100.   Friday A.M. rode to Sparta to assist Bro. Potter, preached at night in the Baptist church II Cor. VIII:9. rode through the neighborhood next day hunting up those desirous of having a presbyterian church organized.   Rode to Mr. A.M. Sutton's in P.M. on way to Versailles.

Sab. March 26" 1854 Rode to V. where met Bro. Cambern who pr'ch'd in A.M. & P.M.   Preached myself at night II Cor V:17.   Monday spend the forepart of the day in endeavoring to reconcile the Elders who were at variance on account of a part of them being connected with a secret Soc. but could not succeed.   Rode to John Mullan's in P.M. & remained all night.   Home next day.

Sab. Ap. 2" Preached in R.S. A.M. & P.M. II Cor. IV:17, Acts XIII:13-41. Friday P.M. rode to Dillsborough & preached at night Luke XXIII:42-45.   Also saturday A.M. I Tim III:15 l.c. and baptized 3 children of Peter Rowland. Preached at night Col. III:11 l.c.

Sab. Ap 9" Preached in A.M. II Cor. IV:17 & administered the Lords Sup. Preached at night Mat. XII:31,32, oweing to a storm but few in attendance. Returned home next day.

Tuesday evening, April 11" 1854. united in marriage Wm Wallace Wiswell of Cin. O. & Almira Augusta Hathaway of this place.

Sab. 16" At R. S. A.M. & P.M. Rev. 1:7 & Acts XIII:44-52.   Next morn set out for Presbytery to meet at Greensburgh; reached V. at night and preached Luke XXIII:42-45.   Rode to G. next day in company with Elder Hendricks. Pleasant services of Pres.   Rev. I. Stuart received from the N.S.   Pres. closed thursday P.M. Rode as far as Napoleon next morn & preached in the neighborhood at 11 from II Cor. IV:17.   Preached in the Baptist church near town at night John IV:14. Rode next day in company with Elder McCabe to the neighbood of Versailles & put up for the night with Elder Mullan. Preached in V. next morn

Sab. April 23d. 1854. A funeral sermon from Mat. XXIV:44, on the occasion of the death of Mrs. Sarah Mullan wife of I. Mullan Sr. and a member of this church. She died in the triumph of faith one week before. Preached in the P.M. Rev. I:7. Returned home next day. Sat. A.M. rode to Sparta as one of com. appointed to organize a church there. Preached at night in the Methodist church John IV:14. Bro. Potter of L. preached next day Sab. 30" at 11. At 3 P.M. organized the church with 16 members & administered the ordinances of baptism and the L's Sup. Preached at night Ps. CXXXVII:5,6 & next morn three miles from S. from Job XXV:4. Returned home in P.M.

Sab. May 7" At R.S. in A.M. and P.M. Ps LXXXIV:11 & Acts XIV:1-7.

Sat. May 13" 1854 Rode to I. McCabes where preached next morn Sab. 14" in A.M. Ps. LXXXIV:11. Rode to Dillsborough in P.M. & preached II Cor. IV:17. After preaching a messenger came for me to preach a funeral discourse on the occasion of the drowning of Charles Borders & his daughter Sarah, on their way to hear me preach in the morning. The family were in a waggon & attempted to cross Hogan's creek (which was high on account of previous rains) the waggon was upset & the Father & eldest Daughter were drowned. Attended the funeral next day at 2 P.M. and preached to a large and attentive audience in the Freewill Baptist church from Mat. XXIV:44. Truly death meets us wherever we go. Returned home same night. Thursday night took the Mail Boat for Lawrenceburgh on way to Kingston, to assist Bro. Stryker. Took cars next morning for Greensburgh, reached K. in P.M. Preached sat. May 20" 1854 in A.M. Ps. LI:4. P.M. II Cor. IV:17.

Sab. May 21" in A.M. & P.M. Psalm XCIX:9 & Rev. 1:7. Returned to Lawrenceburgh next day, and home day following.

Sat. May 27" Rode to Versailles.

Sab. 28" preached in A.M. Luke XX:34-36. Rode to the Ripley church in P.M. & preached Rev. I:7. Next morn rode to Kingston & purchased a horse & buggy; returned as far as I. Mullans in P.M. Next day reached Versailles, where was detained until day following by rain and high water.

Sat. June 3" Preached at R.S. in A.M. preparatory to the communion. Mat. XXII:37,38.

Sab. 4" Preached in A.M. Heb. IX:24 & dispensed the L. Supper. Rec'd Mr. Jas. Campbell from the church of Burlington Ky. Lecture in P.M. Acts XIV:8-18.

Sat. June 10" 1854. Rode to Dillsborough. Preached next day at 11 Mat. XXII:37,38. Rode to Stringtown & preached in P.M. same as last sat. A.M.

Sab. June 18" Preached in R.S. in A.M. Luke VII:22 l.c. Lecture in P.M. Acts XIV:18-28. Friday 23d. rode to V. in company with Rev. I.C. Harrison, who preached at night & next day at 11. Preached myself at night Mat. XXII:37,38.

284

Sab. June 25" Mr. H. preached in A.M. preached at night myself Luke VII:22 l.c. Received two members Miss E. White & Miss Helen Craigmiles. Returned home next day.

Sab. July 2d. Preached in A.M. I Sam. XX:3 l.c. Lecture in P. M. Acts XV:1-9.

July 4" Sabbath School celebration in R-S. made some remarks to the teachers. Sat. rode to Mr. Hair's.

Sab. July 9" Preached at Stringtown A.M. & P. M. I Sam XX:3 l.c. & Ps CL:1 m.cc. Ordained one elder & received two members Mrs. Boarders & Mr. Mills & baptized three children. Returned home next day. Started same night with Wife & two children for Indianapolis, arrived there next day at noon. Quite unwell with sore throat & lungs; remained over sabbath not being able to Preach Sab. July 16" 1854. Returned home on tuesday. Sat. rode to A.M. Sutton's on way to Ver.

Sab. July 23d. Preached in V in A.M. only II Cor. VII:1 on account of throat. Received two members Mrs. White & Daughter. Returned home next day.

Sab. July 30" In R.S. in A.M. only same as last sabbath.

Sab. Aug 6" At Dillsborough in A.M. Ex. XII:23. At Milton in P.M. Luke XV:10. Monday evening called to attend the funeral of Mr. Wintzell's child at the River in a boat made a few remarks, sung & prayed.

Sab. 13" In R.S. in A.M. Col 1:19. Lecture in P.M. Acts XV:6-12. Tuesday P.M. went to Indianapolis, returned home next day, having travelled 96 miles in 5 1/2 hours. Friday P.M. rode in company with Rev. I.C. Harrison to Mr. Rowland's on way to Stringtown. Sab. 11 A.M. Mr. H. preached; in P.M. preached myself Acts XV:5-11.

Sab. Aug 20" 1854. Mr. H. preached at 11 & I at night Luke XV:10. Mr. H. also at 11 next day & I at night at the Pleasant Grove School house Col. I:19. on the way from meeting conversed with a young man who was quite serious-- directed him to Ct as an all-sufficient Savior. Returned home next day. . . .

Sab. 26" [*sic*] Rode to Mr. Kitts' neighborhood of V. & preach'd at night Ex. XII:23. Preached next day in V. in A.M. & P.M. Col. I:19 & Est IV:16. Home next day.

Sab. Sept 3d. At R.S. Preached A.M. & P.M. I Cor XV:20 & Acts XV:13-18. Mond. started for Presbytery to meet at Sardinia. On way called to see Mrs. Nelson, sick, very sick. Reached Mr. Hair's & staid all night. Next day rode to S. with Elders Hair, Rowland & F. Mullan. After a very harmonious & pleasant session, Pres. adjourned thursday noon. Reached V. same night. Rode to neighborhood of Dillsborough next day & at night preached in the Pleasant Grove school house from Mark XVI:15-18 by request.

Next day Sab. Sept 10" 1854. Preached in D. in A.M. & P. M. I Cor XV:20 & I Thes. V:22. Also next day at 1 P.M. a funeral discourse on the death of Mr. Savage's child--Job I:21 l.c. After which returned home.

Sab. 17" At R.S. in A.M. from Jno. III:20,21. Lecture in P.M. Acts XV:22-31 Friday rode to Dillsborough having been sent for to attend the funeral of Joseph Vandolah, a member of the church. Preached at 10 A.M. Amos IV:12 "Prepare to meet they God." Rode in P.M. to I. McCabe's on way to Versailles. Sat. A.M. rode to V. with Elder Hair in company. Found an unpleasant difficulty existing in the church.

Sab. Sept. 14" 1854. Preached in A.M. & P.M. Jonah III:4-9 & Ps. XVII:15 l.c. Monday commenced process again. H. Papet charged by I. Hendricks with slander. Session after placeing a copy of the charge in the hand of the accused, adjourned to Oct 5" 10 A.M. Returned home on tuesday. On way visited Bro. Perlu Roland sick, prayed with him; also C. Eggleston a young man low with consumption, conversed & prayed with him. Fearful he is not prepared for what is before him.

Sat. Sept 30" Sent for to go to D. to attend the funeral of Mrs. Gelvin, formerly Miss McClain. Funeral at 2:o'clock. John XIII:7. Returned same evening.

Preached in R.S. Sab. Oct 1" in A.M. only. John XVI:33. Wednesday P.M. rode to D. & preached at night. Mat. VII:24-27. Rode next morn in company with Elders Perlu and Rowland, to Versailles. Session of Dillsborough Church, by the invitation issued the case of I. Hendricks versus H. Papet. Charge sustained & he suspended from the privileges of the church. Saturday rode to Mr. Hair's

Sab. Oct 8" 1854. Preached at Stringtown in A.M. & at night. John XVI:33 & III:19-21. Returned home next day, and found Mother much worse, and at 1/4 before 8 P.M. her spirit calmly winged its way to God who gave it. She gave evidence that her long & severe affliction had not been in vain. Funeral services on wednesday at 2 P.M. Rev. T.G. Beheral (M.E.) preached from Job XIV:14.

Sab. 15" At Dillsborough in A.M. only. Luke X:2. Pulpit in R.S. occupied by member of N.S. Synod. Returned home in P.M. Monday evening started to New Albany with Wife & youngest child to visit friends & attend meeting of Synod. Synod met thursday evening & was opened by I.G. Monforth the last Mod. present from Rev. VIII:4.

Sab. 22d. Rev. C. Leavenworth preached before Synod & in P.M. sacrament of the L's supper was administered, quite an interesting service. Synod closed Monday p.m. Returned home on friday.

Sab. Oct 29" 1854. A. R.S. in A.M. only. Rvs. VIII:1.

Sab. Nov 5" At Stringtown in A.M. & at night. Rev. VIII:1 & Ps CXXII:6. Mond. morn went with Elder Hair to se Mr. Bruce & Wife both sick, conversed & prayed with them. Returned hom in P.M. Sat. rode to D. Preached at 3 P.M. Rvs. XII:1. Congregation elected 3 elders. John Rowland, V. Wilson and I. McClain.

Preached next day Sab. 12" in P.M. & at night I Peter I:8 & Ps. CXXII:6. heard Rev. Mellendar, Meth. in the morn. "Is it well with the child." II Kings

IV:26. funeral sermon. Very disagreeable day congregation smaller than usual, but attentive. Monday spent in visiting. Returned home next day.

Sab. 19: At home. Preached in A.M. II Cor. V:20-21. Lecture in P.M. Acts XVI:9-15. Thursday 23d called to attend the funeral of Mrs. Isabella Monroe, a member of the R.S. church. preached from Psalm CXIX:164-168--a text selected by the deceased before her death.

Sat. Nov. 25" 1854. Started for Versailles. Storms & cold, did not ride further than P. Rowland's that night. Rode to V. next morn

Sab. 26" preached in A.M. & P.M. last time I Pet 1:8 & II Cor V:20-21. People very discouraged at my leaving them. Visited some of them next day & found them quite disheartened.

Thursday--public thanksgiving. Union meeting in Main St. church. Rev. Mr. Collard (Meth) preached & myself & other ministers took part in the exercises.

Sat. Dec. 2d Rode to I. McCabe's & put up for the night, preached next day

Sab. 3d. in Stringtown in A.M. & at night. Ps L:14. Thanksgiving. Acts XVI:14,15. Session received on examina. Mr. Robt. Mills & Wife. Mr. Jos. Allen & Jacob Boarders. Returned home next day.

Sab. 10" At home in A.M Eccl. IX:18 l.c. lecture in P.M. Acts XVI:16-24. Friday evening at Dillsborough Acts XVI:14,15.

Sat. A.M. Jno. XIII:34,35. at night Gen. VI:3

Sab. 17" in A.M. I Jno. IV:13. Lord's sup. administered. At night Eccl. IX:18 l.c.

Sat. Dec 23d. 1854. Preached in the church at R.S. from Rvs. VIII:32 Expected to have an election of Trustees & Elders, but owing to the small num. present. defered three weeks. Wednesday evening at 8 1/4 o'clock died Mrs. Janet Jamieson in the triumph of faith. Friday A.M. endeavored to improve the solemn occasion from Ps. CXVI:15. "Precious in the sight of the L. is the death of his saints." In P.M. started for Stringtown, but owing to bad roads did not get further than Elder Rowland's rode next morn to S. and preached at 11 from Rvs. VIII:32. at night from Eccl. IX:18 l.c. Session received Mr. Jas. Mills & Wife & Miss Lavina Boarders. Rec'd $6.00 for Dom. Missions.

Sab. 31st. Preached at 11 Is. LIII:3 f.c. Administered the L's Supper. Preached at night Gen. VI:3. Rode next day as far as Perlu Rowland's & remained until next day, when returned home.

Sat. Jan. 6" 1855. rode to Pleasant Grove & preached in schoolhouse at night Gen. III:22-24. Rode to D.(?) next morn & heard Rev. Mellender (M.E.) preach, "Bodily exercise profiteth little" etc. Preached in P.M. & at night Luke XIII:24 and Gen. VII:1. Returned home next day after making two visits in families belonging to the congregation. Friday P.M. Rev. I.S. Potter came & preached at night, also next morn at 11 & baptized three children. Congregation elected three Trustees & one Elder. Session Rec's Mrs. Margaret McAlister. Sat. night preached from Rvs. XIII:11 also on Sab. 14" Jan. 1855, at 11 & at night. Is. LIII:3 f.c. & Ps. CXI:10 also on monday night Luke XIV: 18

f.c. on Tuesday night I Pet IV:18.  meeting closed Sat. rode to Mr. Hair's on way to Stringtown.  Sab. 21st. heavy rain few present at meeting.  preached from Rvs. XIII:11 at night at I. McCabe's I Pet. IV:18.  Monday detained by high waters.  Visited two or three families  Returned home next day.  Sat Rode to Lawrenceburgh to exchange with Bro. Potter, he going to Dillsborough

Sab. 28" Preaching in L. A.M. & P.M.  Heb. IX:24 & Rvs. XIII:11.  Went at night to the Methodist church & heard Rev. Gilmore Prov. XIII:18.

Sab. Feb 4: 1855  Preached in A.M. at R.S. Rvs. XII:2 f.c.  Lecture at night Acts XVI:35-40.  Sat. rode to Mr. Hair's on way to Stringtown

Sab. 11" Preached in S. in waggonmaker's shop at 11 A.M. same as last sab. Invited to hold our meeting in Baptist church at night, where I lectured same as last Sab. night.  Returned home on Monday.

Sat. 17:  Rode to schoolhouse in neighborhood of Dillsborough & preached at night II Cor. XII:7-10.  In D. next morn Sab. 18" & night.  Is XII:1 & Prov. XV:3.  Returned home next day.

Tuesday 20" united in marriage Chas. E. Young and Mrs. Euphresine Sparks. Thursday rode with wife to Mr. Phil. Rowlands on my way to Sparta to assist Bro. Potter at a communion.  Rode to S. next morn. set out immediately in visiting families talking and praying with them.  Preached at night Acts XVI:35-40.  Sat. spent the forepart of the day in going from house to house, meeting at 2 P.M.  Bro. P. preached  congregation elected two additional elders.  After meeting visited two families.  Preached at night Prov. XV:3.

Sab. Feb. 25" 1855  Bro. Potter preached in A.M. administered the ordinances of baptism & the L's Sup. myself.  Preached at night Rev. I:7 after which Bro. P. addressed the elders elect & ordained them.  Preached next morn at 10 Phil. III:7,8.  Session received in all nine persons on profession of their faith. Returned in P.M. to Mr. Rowlands.  Next morn rode with wife to Mr. W. Hair's in Ripley Co. & in P.M. united in marriage Armstrong Eckle & Miss Cynthia Hair.  Returned home next day, Wednesday 28"  Sat. rode to A.M. Suttons in vicinity of Stringtown & remain'd all night.  Preached next day Sab. March 4" 1855 in S. in A.M. only Is XLIII:12 l.c.  Rode to Versailles & preached at night Is. XII:1.  Congregational meeting, agreed to bury their difficulties & try and go on as formerly.  Returned home next day.

Thursday March 8" united in marriage John Neaman & Miss Julia Debber. Sat. rode to neighborhood of Dillsborough and preached in Pleasant Grove Schoolhouse from Rev. 1:7.

In D. next morn Sab. March 11" 1855.  Before sermon united in marriage I.C. Younker & Miss Isabella McClain.  Preached in A.M. Phil III:8.  P.M. Is XLIII:12 l.c.  At night attended a prayer meeting in the P. Grove schoolhouse & made some remarks at the close.  Agent of Amer. B.S. in R.S. collected from my people $11 for the cause.

Sab. March 18" at R.S. in A.M. Is. XII:1.

In P.M. Sat. 24" rode to Sparta to fill an appoint. of Pres.

Sab. 25" Preached in A.M. and at night Heb. III:8 & II Tim. III:16. Received two members & baptized 5 children. Returned home in P.M. next day.

Sat. March 31st. rode to Pleasant Grove schoolhouse & preached at night Jno. III:18.

Sab. Ap. 1st. In Dillsborough A.M. & at night Ps LXXIII:28 f.c. & Tim III:16. Next morn started for Pres. to meet at Rushville. Rode to V. & from there with Elder Hendricks. After a very pleasant session Pres. adjourn'd thursday evening. Preached at candlelighting same as last sat. night. Reached home saturday evening.

Sab. Ap. 8" 1855 preached in R.S. in A.M. & P.M. Is XLIII:12 l.c. & II Tim III:16.

Sat. 14" Rode to Mr. Hair's Ripley Co. and endeavored to reconcile Mer's Eckles & Fox who were at variance. accomplished nothing.

Sab. 15" Preached at Stringtown at 11 A.M. Rode to Versailles & preached at 3 P.M. Heb. XII:15 & Ps. LXXIII:28 f.c. Bro. Potter from Lawrenceburgh also at V. who preached at night. Succeeded in reconciling parties at variance in the church. Rode over to Stringtown in P.M. and brought those at variance there together & succeeded in a settlement. My throat very sore and painful. Rode home next day, very uncomfortable. Commenced doctoring my throat immediately in the hope that I would be able to fill my appointments next sab. but I was disappointed.

Sab. 22d. April 1855 laid up with a cold & inflamed throat, unable to go & hear the gospel preached, let alone preach it myself. Tried to say "Thy will be done."

Sab. 29" At R.S. in A.M. only Ps. LXXIII:28 f.c. in P.M. attended the funeral of Mrs. Jefferson A. French in the M.E. Church. Think sometimes the L. is about to lay me by as unfit for his service. "Let him do what seemeth good in his sight.

Sab. May 6" At Stringtown in A.M. CXVIII:8,9 [*sic*]. At I. McCabe's in P.M. Rvs. VI:23.

Sab. 13" At Dillsborough in A.M. & P.M. II Sam. VI:11 & Gal. VI:7,8.

Sab. 20" at R.S. A.M. & P.M. same as on the 6".

Sat. May 26" 1855 rode to Versailes where I preached next day 27". by appointment of Pres. In A.M. & P.M. Ps CXXXIII:1 & Mark II:27. Also addressed sab. school in P.M. Next morning visited Miss Mary Lingle a member of the church, sick for some time, conversed & prayed with her & the family. found her calm & trusting in Cr.

Sat. June 2d. rode to Dillsborough. Sab. preached in A.M. & P.M. Luke VII:19-22. Mat. XI:23,24. Monday A.M. visited--Elder Perlu in company--Mr. Chi family--new settlers, from Newport, Ky. Returned home in P.M.

Sab. June 10" at R.S. in A.M. & P.M. Psalm CXXXIII:1 & Luke VII:19-22.

Sat. June 16" rode to Mr. H's on way to S. where preached in A.M. Sab. June 17" Rvs XIII:21 l.c. in P.M. at I. McCabe's Heb. IV:15-16. Rode to vicinity of D. next day & home the following.

Sat. June 23d. rode to D. & preached at 11 A.M. Is. IX:6 "His name shall be called wonderful." Prayer meeting at 4 P.M.

Sab. 24" Preached in D. in A.M. & P.M. Acts X:33 & Rvs. VIII:21st "The glorious liberty of the children of God." Visited Mrs. Eggleston a member of the church, very low with consumption. Found her resigned to the L's will & willing to depart. Returned home next day.

Tuesday morning June 19" [sic] Mrs. E. died, was sent for to attend her funeral. Rode out next morn & preached in the church from P CXVI:15. Returned home same day. Sat. 11 A.M. Preached in R.S. Ps LXVI:13,14.

Sab. July 1st 1855 Preached in R.S. A.M. & P.M. & administered the L's sup. Rvs. VIII:21 l.c. & Heb. IV:14-16. Rec'd on certif. Mrs. Sarah Hardin. Sat. rode to neighborhood of Stringtown, preached next morn. Sab. 8". Ps. LXVI:13,14. in P.M. at I. McCabe's Gen. VII:1 f.c. returned home next day. Sab. morn (15") rode to Dillsborough & preached in A.M. in P.M. at Pleasant Grove. Ps. IX:10, Acts XXVI:24,25. home next day.

Sab. 22d. In R.S. in A.M. & P.M. Titus III:8 two discourses. In P.M. was sent for to go & see Thos. Whiteford a young man, very sick. Conversed & prayed with him & the family remained all night. He died tuesday morning was sent for to attend his funeral, which I did next day & discoursed from Mat. XXIV:44. He gave comfortable evidence that his soul was found in Jesus hands. Returned home in P.M. & suffered the remainder of the day with rheumatism.

Sat. 28" Rode to Versailles in company with T.R.B.

Sab. July 29" 1855. Preached in V. A.M. & P.M. Luke VII:19-2 & Ps. IX:10. Returned home next day. Sat. A.M. rode to Dillsborough & preached at 11 & 5 P.M. Phil. II:5 & Job XXI:14,15. Also on Sab. Aug 5" in A.M. & administered the ordinances of Baptism & the L's Sup. In A.M. Mark XVI:15 in P.M. Titus III:8. Collection for Board Dom. Miss. $2.50. Returned home next day.

Sab. Aug 12" At R.S. in A.M. & P.M. Phil. II:5 & Ps. IX:10.

Sat. 18" Rode to Mr. Hair's in Ripley Co.

Sab. Aug. 19" 1855. Preached at Stringtown in A.M. Ex. XX:7. In P.M. rode to Versailles & preached I Thes. IV:13,14, a funeral discourse on the death of Miss Mary Lingle, her infant niece & infant sister. Returned home next day. Friday rode to the vicinity of Ripley Church Ripley Co. On Sat. preached in A.M. & P.M. Phil. II;5; Acts X:33.

Sab. Aug. 16" in A.M. addressed the S. school; preached at 11: Is. IX:6 & administered the ordinances of baptism & the L.S. In P.M. Luke XV:10. Weather unfavorable & few in attendance. Returned home next day.

Sab. Sept. 2d. At R.S. in A.M. & P.M. John VII:37 & Mark XVI:15.

Fri. 7" Rode to Mr. Perlu's on way to Stringtown.

Sat. 8" rode to S. and preached at 11 A.M. & 4 P.M. Gal. V:22,23 & II Pet. 1:4 f.c.

Sab. 9" in A.M. & P.M. Luke XXIV:46,7 & James II:10 administered the ordinances of baptism & the Lords Supper.

Sab. 16" Appointment at D. did not go on acct. of rain and sickness of Wife. Preached in R.S. in A.M. Luke XVIII:9-14.

Tuesday 18" 1855 Presbytery met at Connersville, did not go on acct of sickness of Wife.

Sat 22d. Rode to Harrison O. & preached next day in A.M. & at night. II Tim. III:14 and Rvs. VIII:21 l.c. Returned home next day.

Sat. Sept. 29" Rode to Mr. Stopher's and attended his funeral. Preached from Deut. XXXII:29. Rode in P.M. to D. when hearing that Mr. McClain was very sick went to see him & remained all night, rode next morn Sab. 30" to Mr. Perlu's to breakfast & then to Stringtown where preached at 11 A.M. from Phil. IV:4 in P.M. at Mr. Robt. Mills Job XXV:4 f.c. Return'd home next day. Friday P.M. rode to Lawrenceburg on way to Providence church to assist Bro. Golladay. Sat morn rode to the church & preached Job XXV:4 f.c. also at night Luke XIV:17 on Sab. Oct. 7" in A.M. Luke XV:10. Bro. G. at night. Returned home next morning. Sat. rode to the neighborhood of Harrison, O.

Sab. 14 Oct. 1855 Preached in Harrison at 1/2 past 10 A.M. & at night. Mat. XVI:26 & Mat. XI:28. Some prospect of an invitation to labour with this people. Returned home next day. Wednesday morn set out with I.E.C. to attend synod at Indianapolis. Reached there in safety, by a kind Providence. Thursday spent in visiting the State Fair. At candlelighting Synod met & was opened with a sermon by the Mod'r C. Leavenworth. After a harmonious session Synod adjourned on monday at 12 A.M. Returned home on tuesday, found all well.

Sab. 28" Preached in R.S. in A.M. only Phil.IV:4, probably my farewell to this people.

Sab. Nov. 4" Preached at Dillsborough Heb. IX:24. last sermon. Visited Pleasant G. in P.M. & preached from Heb. XI:24

Sat. 10" rode to Harrison & next day Sab. Nov 11" 1855 preached my first sermon as the supply of this church Heb. IX:24. At night Is. XII:1.

Nov. 14" Left Rising Sun with family and household goods for Harrison. Reached Lawrenceburgh about 3 o'clock next morn. Friends from H. met us with waggon & carriages & took us there same evening. remainder of goods left to be brought up on Canal boat.

Sab. Nov 18" 1855. Preached in H. in A.M. & at night. Phil. IV:4.

Thursday thankgiving day. Union meeting in our church Endeavored to preach from Ps. XCV:1.

## SUMMARY OF ASSIGNEMENTS FOLLOWING 1853-55 MINISTRY IN RISING SUN

November 11, 1855-Began ministry at Harrison, Ohio

May 3, 1857-Last sermon at Harrison. "Obliged to suspend my labors on account of my health."

May 5, 1857-Removed to Rising Sun, Ind. "hoping that rest from ministerial labour would [restore] my health."

October 1857-Commenced preaching regularly at Rising Sun, Dillsborough, & Sparta

July 1, 1860-Last sermon at Rising Sun church, "having engaged to take charge of churches of Reading & Pisgah In Cincinnati Presbytery.

July 18, 1860-Started with family and household goods for Reading. "Next morning waggons & carriages met us at the River & conveyed us & goods to Reading where we arrived about noon July 19, 1860, and goods in the P.M.

January 4, 1861 (Friday)-Fast day proclaimed by President of the U.S. in view of the threatened dissolution & civil war. Preached at 11 from Jonah III:5-10.

January 27, 1861-Last entry in Journal. "Preached at Pisgah."


## ABBREVIATIONS USED IN JOURNAL

| | |
|---|---|
| ex. | examination |
| Bro. P. | Brother S.S. Potter |
| Cr. | Christ |
| D. | Dillsborough |
| Dom. Mission | Domestic Mission |
| For. Mission | Foreign Missions |
| L. | Lawrenceburg |
| L.'s Sup | Lord's Supper |
| M.E. | Methodist Episcopal |
| Pres. | Presbytery |
| prof. | profession |
| R.S. | Rising Sun |
| S. | Stringtown or Sparta |
| Sab. | Sabbath |
| V. | Versailles |

# FINNEY COUNTY KANSAS OBITUARY ABSTRACTS
## 1884-1889
Compiled by Katherine Kelley Powell
and
Patricia Douglas Smith*

Obituaries from 1879 through 1911 have been abstracted from newspapers in Finney County. An every name and place index is included. Notices of those persons showing a connection with Indiana from 1884 through 1889 are included here.

**AMBURS**, W.C., who had been ill for a long time, on Tuesday night. *The Kalvesta Herald*, 24 February 1888.

**AMBURS**, William C., aged 40 years, at his residence three miles south of Kalvesta on the evening of the 21st. He was a native of North Carolina where he lived until after the war of the rebellion. He then moved to Indiana and eleven years ago came to Kansas, settling in Butler county. While there he united with the Regular, and subsequently with the Missionary Baptist church, with which he remained until two years ago when he came to Hodgeman county, becoming a member of the society formed in Kalvesta about a year ago. He leaves a wife and eight children. The funeral was attended by a large concourse of friends who followed the remains to the cemetery near Wittrup. *The Kalvesta Herald*, 2 March 1888.

**BERKEY**, Jonas, father of Mrs. John Cochran at his home in Salem, Ind. Mrs. Cochran leaves for Salem tonight accompanied by her husband, son Charley, and Dr. Neal, a son-in-law of the deceased. *The Garden City Irrigator*, 23 October 1886.

**BREWER**, Mrs. Hannah, age about 36, on Monday at her homestead from consumption. She came here a year ago locating three miles northeast of town. She had hoped to return to relatives in Indiana during the last weeks of her life, but was prevented by a man named Kerchival who had contested her claim. She was taken to Partridge Tuesday for burial. A nephew, Mr. Hamilton of Hutchinson, arrived shortly before her death. *The Terry Eye*, 12 May 1887.

*Taken from *Finney County, Kansas Obituary Abstracts and Death Notices, 1879-1911*, compiled by Katherine Kelley Powell and Patricia Douglass Smith. Published by Stanley C. Smith and Patricia D. Smith, P.O. Box 1, Garden City Kansas 67846-0001. The newspapers are held by the Kansas State Historical Society. Microfilm copies are available for use at the Finney County Historical Society and the Garden City Community College.

**CHARLES**, Miss Rose, a step-daughter of Mrs. I.R. Dodds, at Fairmount, Ind., on June 23. *Terry Eye*, 4 July 1889.

**CONOVER**, Moses L.. age 16, Sunday of typhoid fever at the residence of J.C. Wolfe on E. 6th street. He was a brother of Mrs. Wolfe, coming from Greencastle, Ind. Funeral yesterday under auspices of the Fire Department of which he was a member. Burial in city cemetery. *The Garden City Sentinel*, 17 August 1887.

**CONOVER**, Moses L., age 17, of typhoid fever on Sunday, August 14. A brother of Mrs. J.C. Wolf, he came here recently from Greencastle, Ind. Funeral from the Wolf home today, and attended by the fire department of which he was a member. Burial in city cemetery. *The Garden City Herald*, 18 August 1887.

**CRAFTON**, Thomas, from injuries suffered when he jumped off train at Pierceville last week. Interment at Hillsboro, Ind. *The Garden City Irrigator*, 22 January 1887.

**CRAWFORD**, Martin Bowman [editor of the *Hatfield News*] on March 16, after a long illness. He was born February 20, 1851 in Columbiana county, Ohio. In 1874 he edited the *Booneville* [Ind.] *Standard*, and on March 22 that year he married Miss Fannie K. Thompson in Sullivan, Ind. After editing the *Terre Haute Daily Courier* he came to Garden City in February 1886 where he edited the *Daily Sentinel*. In 1887 he became editor of the *Hatfield News* and also was appointed postmaster. He leaves his wife and only son Harry. The funeral was held March 18 at the homestead three miles south of Terry, and burial on the homestead north of the residence at his request. Services were conducted by Rev. L.D. Willingham and Rev. Albert Godley. *The Terry Eye*, 21 March 1889.

**CRAWFORD**, M.B., age 38, March 16 at his home in Hatfield, from lung hemorrhage. The funeral was conducted by Rev. Godley of the Christian church, with the Tyrian Lodge of this place in charge of the burial. He was a member of the Masonic lodge of Brownsville, Ind. *The Finney County Democrat*, 23 March 1889.

**CRAWFORD**, Martin B., age 38, on Saturday, March 16 near Hatfield of hemorrhage of the lungs. Born February 20, 1851 in Columbiana county, Ohio, he married Miss Fanny K. Thompson in 1887 at Sullivan, Ind. Was publisher in Indiana before coming here in 1886, where he was with the *Sentinel*, then published the *Hatfield News* until six weeks ago. Funeral Monday with Tyrian Lodge and Rev. Albert Godley in charge. Burial near home on the claim. *The Garden City Sentinel*, 23 March 1889.

**CRAWFORD**, Martin B., editor of the *Hatfield News*, on March 16, after an illness of seven weeks which began with a severe hemorrhage of the lungs. The funeral was from the family residence March 18, largely attended by the people from the surrounding country, Terry, and Garden City. The services were conducted by Rev. A. Godley, assisted by Rev. Willingham of Garden City, and hymns were sung by the Hatfield Choir. The Masonic fraternity of Garden City conducted their ritual at the interment, as the remains were laid to rest on the homestead, in accordance with the wishes of the deceased. Mr. Crawford had been a member of the Presbyterian church in Terre Haute, Ind., and was a member of the Union church here. *The Hatfield News*, 30 March 1889. [The body was removed and reinterred in Garden City cemetery on December 20, 1892. The newspaper ceased with Mr. Crawford's death.]

**DALE**, Mr. Father of the Dale Brothers of the cornice works, in Bedford, Ind., Tuesday. Interment was on Thursday. *The Finney County Democrat*, 13 April 1889.

**DRYBREAD**, W.E., at the Aurora Hotel in Richfield on Monday. Formerly of Edinburg, Ind. He took a claim 10 miles west of the city last December. Burial was in Grand View cemetery Monday at Richfield. *The Garden City Sentinel*, 31 August 1887.

**HOPKINS**, Mrs. Frances, age 74y, 18d, on September 7 at home of daughter, Mrs. Kate Minard in Garden City. Born in Muskingum county, Ohio, daughter of William and Elizabeth Barkus, she married in Wabash county, Ind., Joseph Hopkins in 1838. He died in central Missouri in 1877. In 1881 Mrs. Hopkins came with her children to Garden City, one of whom is W.R. Hopkins. She was a member of the Methodist Church. *The Garden City Sentinel*, 14 September 1887.

**McHATTON**, Jesse L., age 55y, 11m, on Sunday, July 3. Born in Indiana, was a Civil War veteran, and came to Garden City in 1885. He married first, Miss Mary Dawson who died and second, Miss Lou Hardwick who survives. A son who died last winter in New Mexico was brought here for burial. The deceased was a member of the Methodist church. *The Garden City Sentinel*, 6 July 1887.

**McHATTON**, Jesse L., age 55y 11m, at his home here. Born in Indiana he servied in the Civil war from Illinois, and came to Garden City in 1885. He married first, Mary Dawson who died. He is survived by his widow, the former Lou Hardwick. *The Garden City Herald*, 7 July 1887.

**MORGAN**, Charles F., age 23, son of Charles Morgan of Derby, Ind., died last Saturday at the Bartholomew hotel where he had been ill with fever for several weeks. The remains were returned to his former home for burial. *The Garfield County Call*, 25 November 1887.

**NEWBY**, William, of this place, accidentally killed himself Tuesday near Cimarron when reaching for his gun in his wagon to shoot a jackrabbit. He recently came here with his people from the east. *The Garden City Irrigator*, 20 November 1884.

**NEWBY**, William F., age 32y 11m, 18d, on Tuesday, November 25 from an accidental gunshot when lifting his fun from wagon to shoot a rabbit. Was born December 7, 1851 at Waynesville, Ind. Funeral by Elder A.C. McKeever of the Christian church. Burial in city cemetery. *The Garden City Sentinel*, 3 December 1884.

**PIERCE**, W.W., father of Mode M. Pierce, and a former resident, on Monday in Warsaw, Ind., at the age of 63 years. *The Garden City Herald*, 12 September 1889.

**PIERCE**, W.W., father of Judge M.M. Pierce, on the 2nd inst. at his home in Warsaw, Ind. *The Garden City Sentinel*, 14 September 1889.

**RHEUBOTTOM**, Mrs. Eva, nee Dragoo, age 19, on August 19 at Lakin. Formerly of LaGrange, Ind. she married F.P. Rheubottom last March 25. Funeral was conducted by the Rev. Lowrance of Garden City and burial in Lakin cemetery. *The Garden City Sentinel*, 27 August 1884.

**RHUEBOTTOM**, Mrs. F.P., age 19, on Tuesday, at Lakin, formerly of Kendallville, Ind. Funeral conducted by Rev. Lowrance of Garden City, and burial in the cemetery west of Lakin. *The Garden City Irrigator*, 28 August 1884.

**SMITH**. A child, age 3, of Mr. and Mrs. F.S. Smith of this place on Sunday, while on visit in Indiana with its mother. *The Garden City Irrigator*, 22 January 1887.

**SMITH**, Mrs. G.W., on Wednesday at Albany, Ind. She was a former resident of Ravanna. *The Ravanna Record*, 3 November 1888.

**SMITH**. Theo R. Smith returned Wednesday evening from Indiana where he had gone to pay his last respects to his departed mother. The remains of his father were taken up and sent east for burial last week. *The Ravanna Chieftain*, 15 November 1888.

**Smith**, George W., suddenly on Wednesday, apparently from an old wound suffered while in the service of his country as a lieutenant in the 49th Indiana Inf. He came to Kansas in 1885, first settling on a claim south of Ravanna, later moving to this city. He was a member of the Masonic Order, Odd Fellows, and Knights of Pythias. The remains were interred with Masonic honors at the Ravanna cemetery in the presence of a large number of friends and neighbors. His wife and two children survive. *The Ravanna Record*, 28 October 1887

**SMITH**, George W., aged nearly 48 years, at his residence in the Hoffman block Tuesday night. He came to this place in June, with his family who have been in the millinery business while he has been employed by N. Hoffman. Born in Floyd county, Ind., he came to Kansas in its infancy. He suffered from injuries suffered during the war. His funeral was held Thursday, the 27th under the auspices of the Masonic Lodge of which he was a member. Lodges from Dodge City and Cimarron in attendance. *The Ravanna Chieftain*, 27 October 1887. [3 November issue states A.K. Smith of Parsons, Kan. was in attendance at the funeral of his brother G.W. Smith.]

**SMITH**, Geo., on Tuesday October 25, at Ravanna after a short illness. The funeral was held at Ravanna. He was the father of Mrs. J.B. Murphy and Theo Smith of Ravanna. He was a member of lodges at Greenville and New Albany, Ind. *The Essex Sunbeam*, 28 October 1887.

**TEITELBAUM**, Sarah, age 32y 8m, 15d, wife of Samuel Teitelbaum, on April 2 of heart disease. The family came here last October from Vincennes, Ind. [Burial in Jewish cemetery.] *Garden City Irrigator*, 17 April 1884.

**THOMPSON**, Blanche, age 4, oldest child of Mr. and Mrs. T.A. Thompson about a week ago at Terre Haute, Ind., of diptheria. Mr. Thompson was working in Hutchinson when summoned by telegram but could not reach Terre Haute in time. *The Hatfield News*, 19 January 1889.

**THOMPSON**, Mrs. Mary A., wife of Dr. J.J. Thompson, and mother of Mrs. M.B. Crawford, at the family home in Sullivan, Ind., Monday, of cancer. *The Hatfield News*, 21 March 1888.

**WEIR**, Mrs. Sophia A., near Pierceville December 13 of heart disease. Formerly a resident of Indiana, was a sister of Rev. T.C. Smith, known to readers as president of U.C. College, Merom, Ind. Funeral conducted by Rev. Albert Godley. *The Garden City Sentinel*, 22 December 1888.

**WHITMER**, Mrs. J., on Monday, at family home on East 7th street after a long illness. Remains taken to former home in Indiana by husband. *The Garden City Irrigator*, 23 January 1886.

**WHITMER**, Mrs. J., at family home north of Garden City yesterday after long illness. Leaves husband who will take her remains to Indiana for burial. *The Garden City Sentinel*, 27 January 1886.

**WHITSON**, Ethel, little daughter of Mr. and Mrs. John Whitson on Monday, December 10, in Indiana where she had been visiting relatives with her mother. The funeral was from the home of Mrs. Whitson's father, Mr. Paul who lives near Seymour, Ind. Burial was in the cemetery there. *The Hatfield News*, 22/29 December 1888.

**WOLF**, Mrs. L.J., age 61, at her home 2 1/2 miles northwest of here on Wednesday. She leaves a large family. *The Kansas Sod House*, 24 June 1887.

**WOLF**, Mrs. Mary A., formerly Mary A. Richards, was born in Lancaster county, Pennsylvania, March 27, 1826 and died at her home two and one half miles northwest of this place June 22, 1887, aged 61y 2m and 26d. She married L.J. Wolf at Richville, Elkhart County, Ind., November 26, 1854. She joined the M.E. Church at 16 years of age. She and her husband moved to Garfield County in December 1886. She leaves a husband and three children, two here and one in Warsaw, Ind. *The Ravanna Chieftain*, 30 June 1887.

**WOLF**, Mrs. Mary A., formerly Mary A. Richards, was born in Lancaster county, Pa., on March 27, 1826, and died at her home north of this place on June 22, 1887, age 61y 2m 5d. She married L.J. Wolf at Richhill, Elkhart county, Ind., November 16, 1854. They came to Garfield county in December 1886. Her husband and three children survive, one living in Warsaw, Ill. *The Kansas Sod House*, 1 July 1887.

# HOOSIER OFFICERS ON THE OHIO RIVER, 1931

Ethel C. Leahy, on pages 616 through 624 of her *Who's Who on the Ohio River and its tributaries*, lists the officers in the several supervising inspection districts from 1925 through 1930. Those with Indiana addresses are listed below.

Masters, Masters and Pilots and Pilots in the Seventh
Supervising Inspection District, Pittsburgh, Pa., 1925-30.
Cincinnati, Ohio

**Masters and Pilots**
Campbell, Milton, Jeffersonville
Chandler, William S., Aurora
First Class Pilots
Grimm, Walter C., Jeffersonville
Weddell, Dee, Vevay

**Mates**
Evans, William, Madison
McAdams, William G., Rising Sun
McKay, William R., Vevay

6th Supervising Inspection District
Louisville, Kentucky

**Masters**
Ballard, Joe G., Mauckport
O'Brien, James J., Jeffersonville
Pratt, Coburn, Madison
Spellman, George F., Jeffersonville
Suter, William H., Madison
Masters and Pilots
Ash, Leon, Vevay
Bottorff, Charles W., Jeffersonville
Brasher, Gilbert W., Jeffersonville
Donaldson, Peter C., Jeffersonville
Houser, Ed J., Jeffersonville
King, Harry H., Madison
Knight, Charles A., New Albany
Monroe, George A., Madison
Pfeiffer, Harry D., Jeffersonville
Smith, Albert, Jeffersonville
Smith, Mitchell P., Jeffersonville

Pilots
Crecelius, Charles S., Corydon

Dean, Daniel D., Bethlehem
Haycox, James A., Tell City
Heady, John P., Vevay
Lime, William A., Indianapolis
Mason, Leonard, Madison
Singer, Jesse, Bethlehem
Singleton, Jesse A., Mauckport
Smith, Sanford B., Bethlehem
Turner, Edward M., Madison
Turner, Selby, Madison

**Evansville District**

**Masters**
Carr, Howard M., Evansville

**Masters and Pilots**
Ashcraft, Clarence C., Evansville
Barnard, Austin A., Evansville
Briedenbach, Charles F., Evansville
Brown, John H., Evansville
Flesher, Grove K., Mt. Vernon

298

Fuchs, Charles F., Tell City
Gordon, Leander, Hanover
Groff, William A., Mt. Vernon
Hall, Emmett M., Terre Haute
Hamilton, Harry A., Evansville
Hornbrook, Sanders C., Evansville
January, Henry S., Evansville
Kirk, Charles, Evansville
Lunn, William, Evansville
McCoy, William E., Evansville
McNutt, Charles, Evansville
Mann, Robert P., Evansville
Morris, David G., Evansville
Nelson, James M., Mt. Vernon
Price, Steven E., Evansville
Sanderson, William C., Evansville
Sproule, James V., Evansville
Sullivan, Charles, Evansville
Thompson, James B., Evansville
Veatch, John O., Evansville
Williams, Jefferson H., Evansville
Williams, Thomas A., Evansville
Williams, William N., Evansville

Pilots, First and Second Class
Ashcraft, Clarence C., Evansville
Beiling, Louis G., Evansville
Blair, John P., Griffin
Cook, William, New Harmony
Eades, Jackson H., Evansville
Gerhart, Alvin R., Evansville
Gosnell, Charles J., Terre Haute
Groff, William A., Evansville
Hamilton, Harry A., Evansville
Hockman, Carson, Mt. Vernon
Johnson, O. Theodore, Evansville
Jones, Owen P., Evansville
McClure, James B., Evansville
Pfaffin, Leland G., Newburgh
Riggs, Henry D., Evansville
Schaad, Christ, Jr., Evansville
Schneider, George T., Evansville
Scholey, David, Mt. Vernon
Steele, Val M., Evansville
Stevens, Charles E., Evansville
Sullivan, Charles, Evansville
Wall, James, Evansville
Wingfield, Cecil

## WHO WAS WHO ON THE OHIO RIVER IN 1931
by Ruth Dorrel

In 1931, a volume titled *Who's who on the Ohio River and its tributaries*, was published in Cincinnati by Ethel C. Leahy. The book contains information about the history of the Ohio River as well as the biographies of persons working and living in and on the river. Mrs. Leahy states in her introduction that "this book is of the Ohio River . . . Hundreds of letters were mailed . . . Fifty thousand letters were sent out; twelve thousand were returned; . . . five hundred sixty-five were found acceptable."

The following biographies of persons with Hoosier connections were extracted.

**ARTMAN**, Elmer Carol, born Old Augusta, Indiana 31 March 1867 to Delia Klinqensmith (of near New Augusta) and James Alexander Artman (of near Pittsburgh, Pennsylvania); widower of Anna Mohr; son, E.C. Artman, Jr. Residence, Metropolis, Illinois.  pp. 384-85.

**ASH**, Leon, born Lamb, Indiana 6 January 1890 to Mary J. (of Cannan, Indiana) and Joseph B. Ash (of Lamb); married. Residence, Vevay, Indiana. p. 385.

**ASHCRAFT**, Clarence C., born Grayson, Kentucky, 22 December 1887 to Alice (of Henry County, Kentucky) and James J. Ashcraft (of Grayson). Married; two children. Residence, Evansville, Indiana.  p. 385.

**BAILEY**, Arnold J., born Hurricane, West Virginia 13 March 1890 to Annie M. Brouyette (of Gallipolis, Ohio) and Lucian Losure Bailey (of Hurricane); married Harriet Evelyn ----; one daughter. Residence, Newburgh, Indiana.  p. 387.

**BAIN**, Jarvis Johnson, born 2 May 1880 to Sallie Johnson (of Morgantown, Indiana) and James Gallagher Bain (of Martinsville, Indiana); married Ethel Ralston; two children. Residence, Fort Leavenworth, Kansas.  p. 387.

**BAKER**, Anne I., born Dickinson County, Kansas to Nancy T. Baker (of Paris, Illinois and Henry Baker (of Evansville, Indiana). Residence, Paducah, Kentucky. Obituary, Miss Baker died July 22, 1931.  p. 387-88.

**BALLARD**, Joe G., born Mauckport, Indiana 14 April 1874 to Emma Brandenburg (of Mauckport) and Richard H. Ballard (of Jasper, Indiana); married Cora B. Trotter; one child. Residence, Mauckport.  p. 386.

**BARRY**, Dennie Francis, born Warren, Massachusetts 11 January 1891 to Katherine Dennie (of Raleigh, Massachusetts) and James J. Barry (of Warren); married Ruth Ellis; two daughters. Residence, Jeffersonville, Indiana. p. 388.

**BARTLES**, Frank, born Meade County, Kentucky, 1852 to Abigail Crecelius (of Harrison County, Indiana) and E.M. Bartles (of Tennessee); married Tina Perry; no children. Residence, Bartles, Kentucky, p. 388.

**BEAR**, George Howard, born Cincinnati, Ohio 21 September 1881 to Gertrude Knighton and Oliver Franklin Bear (of Madison, Indiana); married Vivian Blanche Wilson (of Mobile, Alabama); no children. Residence, Paducah, Kentucky, p. 390.

**BEELER**, Jerome Durham, born Evansville, Indiana 23 April 1899 to Estella Durham (of Evansville) and Addison G. Beeler (of Boonville, Indiana); married Helen Tucker; two children. Residence, Evansville. p. 390-91.

**BELL**, Joseph, born Meade County, Kentucky 24 February 1865 to Mary Weathers (of Crawford County, Indiana) and John Bell (of Tennessee); married Nellie Williams; no children. Residence, Leavenworth, Indiana. p. 391.

**BETTS**, Isaac W., born Ironton, Ohio 6 September 1868 to Mary Ann Carver (of Grayson, Kentucky) and Isaac J. Betts (of Jackson, Ohio); married Eulallie Gamache; two children. Residence, Jeffersonville, Indiana. p. 394.

**BICKEL**, Charles A., born Louisville, Kentucky 6 October 1885 to Caroline Bauer (of Louisville) and Phillip Bickel (of Corydon, Indiana); married; one child. Residence, Wilkinsburg, Pennsylvania. p. 394.

**BONDURANT**, Graham, born Madison, Indiana 12 November 1875 to Lulu (of Kentucky) and Richard Bondurant (of Brooksburg, Indiana); married; three children. Residence, Florence, Indiana. pp. 395-96.

**BRASHER**, Gilbert Wymond, born Boone, Kentucky 14 March 1887 to Anna E. and Robert Brasher (of Boone County, Kentucky); married. Residence, Jeffersonville, Indiana. p. 397.

**BREIDENBACH**, Charles F., born Hawesville, Kentucky 20 June 1857 to Mildred (of Frankfort, Kentucky) and Edward H. Breidenbach (of Cologne, Germany); married Nannie Cheaney; three children. Residence, Evansville, Indiana. p. 398.

**BROWN**, Claude, born Vevay, Indiana to Isabel Todd (of Moorefield, Indiana) and John Francis Brown (of Craig, Indiana); married Jennette Lanham; no children. Residence, Charleston, West Virginia. p. 399.

**BROWN**, William H., born Brazil, Indiana 31 May 1874 to Mary E. and Benjamin Brown (of Crooksville, Ohio); Residence, Paducah, Kentucky. p. 399.

**CALLIS**, Ballard S., born Dubois County, Indiana 17 November 1887 to Nannie and Arthur Callis, Sr.; married; one child. Residence, Westport, Kentucky. p. 403.

**COLE**, George P., born Jeffersonville, Indiana 19 July 1878 to Eliza (of Utica, Indiana) and Jabez R. Cole (of Utica, Tennessee); married; no children. Residence, Louisville, Kentucky.  p. 408.

**CONNER**, Walter Scott, born New Albany, Indiana 13 December 1860 to Ellen Childs (of New Albany) and James Wesley Conner (of New Albany); married Lillian S. Halstead; three children.  Residence, Louisville, Kentucky. p. 409.

**CONWAY**, Ancil H., born Rown Hill, Kentucky 25 July 1897 to Martha (of Rown Hill) and Wm. T. Conway (of Readyville, Kentucky); married; one child.  Residence: U.S. Engineers Office, Lock 43, Evans Landing, Indiana. p. 409.

**CURRAN**, Charles William, born Louisville, Kentucky 18 October 1868 to Isabella McKennon (of County Antrim, Ireland) and Jerome Boone Curran (of Louisville); single.  Residence: Madison, Indiana.  p. 412.

**DEAN**, Daniel J., born Scott County, Indiana 27 May 1864 to Phoebe Richey (of Scott County) and Jerry Dean (of Kentucky); married Nioma Haycox; two children.  Residence, Bethlehem, Indiana.  p. 413.

**DeGARIS**, James Parvin, born Princeton, Indiana 11 June 1855 to Virginia Evans (of Washington, D.C.) and James DeGaris (of Louisville, Kentucky); married Laura Alice Vaught; four children.  Residence, Evansville, Indiana. p. 413.

**DIGGS**, William S., born Cincinnati, Ohio 10 February 1862 to Elizabeth Addington (of Wayne County, Indiana) and Marshall W. Diggs (of Randolph County, Indiana); married Emma Hensel; two children.  Residence, Mount Lebanon, Pennsylvania.  p. 414.

**DONALDSON**, Peter Campbell, born Pittsburgh, Pennsylvania 15 June 1881 to Eliza Campbell (of Pittsburgh) and Peter Donaldson (of Pittsburgh); married; no children.  Residence, Jeffersonville, Indiana.  p. 415.

**DURFEE**, Charles, born Illinois 21 November 1863 to Lucretia Moore (of Rising Sun, Indiana) and William Durfee (of Zanesville, Ohio); married Lucy Berry; two children.  Residence, Golconda, Illinois.  p. 417.

**ELLIS**, Roy C., born Georgetown, Indiana 23 May 1879 to Catherine Tyler (of Georgetown) and Miles Ellis (of Georgetown); married Mollie F. Neafus; three children.  Residence, New Albany, Indiana.  p. 419.

**FISKE**, William P., born New Albany, Indiana 22 March 1878 to Katie Stephens (of Cleveland, Ohio) and Peleg Fiske (of New Albany); married Carrie Elouse Sylva; no children.  Residence, Nashville, Tennessee, p. 421.

**FOWKE**, Gerard (born Charles Mitchell Smith), born Charleston Bottom, Mason County, Kentucky 25 June 1855 to Sibella Mitchell (of Charleston Bottom) and John D. Smith/Smythe (of County Wexford, Ireland); grandmother, Elizabeth Fowke.  pp. 422-23.

**FRETAGEOT**, Arthur E., born New Harmony, Indiana 12 December 1873 to Kate Bolton (of New Harmony) and Achilles H. Fretageot (of New Harmony); widower of Stella Spencer; one daughter. Residence, New Harmony, p. 424.

**FUCHS**, Charles F., born Cannelton, Indiana 29 March 1877 to Jenny Spencer (of Indiana) and Frederick L. Fuchs (of Germany); married Annie Steele; one child. Residence, Evansville, Indiana. p. 424.

**GARBER**, Michael Christian, born Madison, Indiana 7 April 1850 to Ellen Schell (of Schellsburg, Pennsylvania) and Michael Christian Garber (of Garber, Stanton, Virginia); widower of Blanche Goode; six children. Residence, Madison. Obituary, Mr. Garber died 14 July 1930. p. 426.

**GARDNER**, Stonewall Jackson, born near Paducah, Kentucky 20 April 1863 to Ellen D. Lawrence (of Tennessee) and William Gardner (of Tennessee); married Margaret Carney; three children. Residence, New Albany, Indiana, p. 426.

**GILLHAM**, Robert Patterson, born Cincinnati, Ohio 9 January 1854 to Margaret Ann Catherine Thompson (of Rockport, Indiana) and Alfred Gillham (of Twelve Mile, Kentucky); married Tillie Patzhold and Edith H. Oehlmann; five children. Residence, Cincinnati. pp. 427-28.

**GORSUCH**, James Arnold, Jr., born Greenville, Ohio to Ella May Curtis (of Dayton, Ohio) and John Arnold Gorsuch (of Zanesville, Ohio); single. Residence, Jeffersonville, Indiana. p. 429.

**GRAHAM**, Everett E., born Vevay, Indiana 5 March 1881 to Martha Lester (of Bennington, Indiana) and Robert T. Graham (of Ghent, Kentucky;) married Lena M. Brooks; one child. Residence, Vevay. pp. 430-31.

**GREGORY**, Whitney Irwin, born Clark County, Missouri 27 October 1886 to Anna Elizabeth Goodwin (of Indiana) and Perrin Burkett Gregory (of West Virginia); married Mary Rose Sheehy; six children. Residence, Paducah, Kentucky. p. 433.

**GROFF**, William Allen, born Belmont, Illinois 23 July 1882 to Sophia (of Baden, Germany) and James William Groff (of Belmont); married; no children. Residence, Mt. Vernon, Indiana. p. 433.

**HALL**, George G., born Kearney, Missouri 8 July 1889 to Mary B. (of Missouri) and Edgar Price Hall (of Missouri); married; two children. Business address, Madison, Indiana. p. 434.

**HARRY**, Elmer George, born Lawrenceburg, Indiana 27 August 1890 to Celeste Wehrling (of Aurora, Indiana) and Isadore L. Harry (of France); married Georgia Elizabeth Kunz; 2 daughters. Residence, Greendale, Indiana. p. 435.

**HEATHERINGTON**, Jacob Park, born Bellaire, Belmont County, Ohio 16 January 1870 to Eliza Penn (of Hopedale, Harrison County, Ohio) and Hamden Heatherington (of Bellaire); married Kathryn Chambers; one daughter. Residence, Madison, Indiana. p. 436.

**HENDRIX**, Walter Willits, born Letts, Louisa County, Iowa 8 August 1877 to Rachel Charlotte Willits (of Monmouth County, Illinois) and William Hendrix (of Wayne County, Indiana); married Eva Belle Power; two children. Residence, Pittsburgh, Pennsylvania. pp. 436-37.

**HOCKMAN**, Robert Carson, born Henderson, Kentucky 12 September 1884 to Lenora Carson (of Indiana) and Benjamin F. Hockman (of Indiana); married Nena Martin; one daughter. Residence, Mt. Vernon, Indiana. p. 438.

**HOLZER**, Charles Elmer, born Sherwood, Ohio 29 July 1887 to Susan Frances Kintner (of Defiance County, Ohio) and William Henry Frederick Holzer (of Fort Wayne, Indiana); married Alma Vornholt October 1914; five children. Residence, Gallipolis, Ohio. p. 440.

**HOUSER**, Edward J., born Jeffersonville, Indiana 31 August 1873 to Charlotte Durgee (of Harrison County, Indiana) and John W. Houser (of Harrison County); married Viola M. Consley; four children. Residence, Jeffersonville. p. 441.

**HOWARD**, Edmonds John, born Jeffersonville, Indiana 10 May 1910 to Loretta M. Wooden (of Kent, Indiana) and James Edmonds Howard (of Jeffersonville); single. Residence, Jeffersonville, p. 442.

**HOWARD**, James Edmonds, born Jeffersonville, Indiana 2 October 1876 to Laura A. Burke (of Louisville, Kentucky) and Edmonds J. Howard (of Madison, Indiana); married Loretta Maud Wooden; three children; grandfather, James Howard, born Manchester England 1 December 1814). Residence, Jeffersonville. pp. 441-42.

**HOWARD**, Loretta Maud, born Kent, Indiana 10 May 1885 to Martisha Catherine Hendricks (of Kent) and William Earl Wooden (of Madison, Indiana); married James Edmonds Howard; two daughters and one son. Residence, Jeffersonville. p. 442.

**HOWE**, James G., born Carrollton, Kentucky 18 December 1893 to Sallie Goslee (of New Castle, Indiana) and J.B. Howe (of Champlain, Illinois). single. Residence, Carrollton. pp. 442-43.

**IGERT**, Louis Henry, born Leavenworth, Indiana 1 August 1883 to Mary Vernie (of Milltown, Indiana) and Peter Igert (of Frenchtown, Indiana); married Emma Vawter; two children. Residence, Paducah, Kentucky. p. 444.

**IRWIN**, William J., born Newport, Kentucky 12 October 1886 to Elizabeth Linscott (of Rising Sun, Indiana) and Jesse P. Irwin (of Sistersville, West Virginia); married Rose Hackhaus; one child. Residence, Norwood, Ohio. pp. 444-45.

**JENCKES**, Virginia E. Somes, born Terre Haute, Indiana 6 November 1879 to Mary Oliver (of Hopkinsville, Kentucky) and James Ellis Somes (of Vincennes, Indiana); widow of Ray Greene Jenckes; one daughter; great-grandfather, Henry Vanderburgh. Residence, Terre Haute. p. 446.

**JEREMY**, William M., born Prescott, Wisconsin 20 October 1876 to Sarah Bush (of South Bend, Indiana) and Joseph J. Jeremy (of Cromwell, Ontario, Canada); widower; four children. Residence, Cairo, Illinois. p. 446.

**JOHNSON**, Edward Mead, born Dundaff, Pennsylvania 1855 to Louise Wood (of Goshen, New York) and Sylvester Johnson (of New London, Connecticut); married Helena Dalton; four children. Business address, Evansville, Indiana. pp. 446-47.

**JOHNSON**, Joseph Sylvester, born Pike County, Indiana 18 May 1879 to Lydia Ellen Nixon (of Oakland City, Indiana) and Stephen Samuel Johnson (of Vicksburg, Mississippi); married Nettie E. McCoy; six children. Residence, Rockport, Indiana, p. 447.

**JONES**, Owen Pennel, born Ceralvo, Kentucky 16 January 1893 to Blanche (of Ceralvo) and Pennel Jones (of Ceralvo); married; no children. Residence, Evansville, Indiana. p. 448.

**KING**, Harry H., born Madis
Lanham (of Indiana) and Robert Ki
child. Residence, Madison. p. 45

**KNOBLOCH**, Thomas C., bor
Mary E. (of McKeesport, Pennsyl
mond, Ohio); married; no childre
452.

**KOENIG**, Bert, born Evansvill
(of Buffalo, New York) and Albe
Lydia Norwood, 1912; one child.

**LANG**, Walter John, born Ev
Jaucht (of Evansville) and John Wa
Wuetherich; no children. Reside

**LEE**, William P., born Jeffersor
(of Jeffersonville) and George C
Tomlin; one daughter. Residence

**LEPPER**, William C., Sr., bor
Copes (of Cincinnati) and Benjar
Mary A. Evans; six sons and four daughters. Residence, Columbus, Indiana. pp. 456-57.

**LEPPER**, William C., Jr., born Napoleon, Indiana 1880 to Mary A. Evans (of Brownsville, Pennsylvania) and William Conrad Lepper (of Cincinnati, Ohio); married Edith Klooz; one child. Residence, Hollywood, California. p. 457.

**McKAY**, Arthur, born Switzerland County, Indiana 2 October 1872 to Mary Banta (of Switzerland County) and Frances M. McKay (of Coles County, Illinois); single. Residence, Pittsburgh, Pennsylvania. p. 465.

**McNUTT**, Charles, born Troy, Indiana 1871 to Mary Ellen Seay (of Troy) and Charles R. McNutt (of Troy); married Antoinette Stuteville; no children. Residence, Evansville, Indiana. p. 466.

**MANN**, Henry H., born Henderson County, Kentucky 22 September 1877 to Virginia Smith (of Henderson County) and Thomas J. Mann (of Hartsville, Tennessee); married Blanche White; no children. Residence, Evansville, Indiana. p. 460.

**MANN**, Robert Preston, born Henderson County, Kentucky 9 July 1896 to Earnest J. Johnson (of Hartsville, Tennessee) and Albert Preston Mann (of Henderson County); married second Addie A. Underwood McDowell (of Cave-in-Rock, Illinois); no children. Residence, Evansville, Indiana. pp. 459-60.

**MAURER**, Edward, born Grant County, Kentucky 24 July 1877 to Rebecca Cook (of Indiana) and Joseph Maurer (of Germany); married Martha Board; two children. Residence, Louisville, Kentucky. p. 461.

**MAURER**, John J., born Grant County, Kentucky 5 July 1880 to Rebecca Cook (of Indiana) and Joseph Maurer (of Germany); married Lucinda Clore. Residence, Ghent, Kentucky. pp. 461-62.

**MILLER**, Knox Emerson, born Norton, Kansas 26 November 1886 to Martha Washington Whiteman (of Xenia, Ohio) and Joseph Medford Miller (of Montezuma, Iowa); married Noxie Bliss; three children. Residence, Evansville, Indiana. pp. 467-68.

**MILLER**, Robert V., born Eureka, Indiana 23 December 1884 to Sadie E. Wade (of Rockport, Indiana) and Frank M. Miller (of Enterprize, Indiana); married Tina May Brown; two children. Residence, Rockport. p. 467.

**MILLER**, William H., born Warsaw, Illinois 15 August 1858 to Louise Henrietta Leyhe (of Germany) and Peter Miller (of Germany); married Jennie Knowles and Laura E. Church; four children; brothers, William H. and Frank. Residence, Madison, Indiana. p. 468.

**MONROE**, George A., born Madison, Indiana 17 May 1874 to Nancy Love Slater (of Jefferson County, Indiana) and George W. Monroe (of Jefferson County); married Hulda W. Alexander; two children. Residence, Madison. p. 469.

**MOODY**, Fred E., born Aurora, Indiana 21 September 1891 to Mary E. Tague (of Switzerland County, Indiana) and George W. Moody (of Switzerland County); married Ruby J. Stegall; one child. Residence, Fullerton, Kentucky. p. 469.

**NEWBERGER**, Lee Reeve, born Roann, Indiana 2 May 1896 to Octavia (of Indiana) and Orlie R. Newberger (of Indiana); married Ruth Freitag; no children. Residence, Bedford, Indiana. p. 472.

**OATMAN**, Thomas J., born New Albany, Indiana 12 December 1858 to Amanda McDonald (of Kentucky) and J. Harvey Oatman (of Kentucky);

married Theresa Peege; four children.   Obituary, Mr. Oatman died Louisville, Kentucky 24 August 1931.   Residence, Louisville.   p. 474.

**OHL**, John William, born Evansville, Indiana 18 September 1880 to Mary Ellen Boyd (of Cannelton, Indiana) and Conrad Lawrence Ohl (born on Atlantic Ocean); married Rose M. Wilhelm; four children.   Residence, Evansville.   p. 474.

**PEAK**, John M., born Madison, Indiana 8 June 1884 to Mary Jane (of Jefferson County, Indiana) and John B. Peak (of Jefferson County); married; three children.   Residence, Paducah, Kentucky.   p. 477.

**PFEIFFER**, Harry D., born Jeffersonville, Indiana 5 September 1871 to Emma (of Jeffersonville) and Jacob J. Pfeiffer (of Louisville, Kentucky); married Fannie Lewis; one son.   Residence, Jeffersonville, p. 477.

**PULLEM**, Harry H., born Jeffersonville, Indiana 12 September 1886 to Addie Taylor (of Jeffersonville) and William H. Pullem (of Oswego, New York); married Eva A. Harper; two sons.   Residence, Point Pleasant, West Virginia, p. 479.

**RADER**, Wilfred Bennett, born Charleston, Virginia 13 July 1860 to Louisa Cobb and Bennet Rader; married Minnie Levan; no children.   Residence, New Albany, Indiana, p. 480.

**RIGGS**, Henry David, born Calhoun, Kentucky 14 August 1868 to Mary Harriett Ward (of Kentucky) and David Riggs (of Kentucky); married Laura Timmons; two children.   Residence, Evansville, Indiana, p. 482.

**ROSS**, John Graham, born Madison, Indiana 15 June 1890 to Blanche Reynolds (of Wirt, Indiana)and John Isom Ross (of Madison); married Linda Clements; four children.   Residence, Madison.   p. 485.

**ROWBOTTOM**, Harry E., born Aurora, Indiana 3 November 1884 to Anna (of England) and James Rowbottom (of England); married Elizabeth Margaret Rohsenberger 16 June 1915; one son.   Residence, Evansville.   pp. 485-86.

**SCHIPPER**, Alfred Andrew, born Aurora, Indiana 10 February 1894 to Emma Doerr (of Carrollton, Kentucky) and Frank Anthony Schipper (of Aurora); married Mary Magdalene Monohan; no children.   Residence, Louisville, Kentucky.   p. 486.

**SEABROOK**, Edward Corrie, born New Albany, Indiana 13 October 1871 to Mary Emma Wolf (of Indiana) and John Wesley Seabrook (of Indiana); married Mary E. Daughter; five children, including sons, Earl and Paul; grandfathers, Daniel Seabrook and Lexington Wolf.   Residence, New Albany.   p. 487.

**SINGER**, Jesse George, born Trimble County, Kentucky 1 August 1880 to Lizzie Fernoy (of Trimble County) and James Harvey Singer (of Trimble County); married; four children.   Residence, Bethlehem, Indiana.   p. 491.

**SINGLETON**, Jesse A., born Mead County, Kentucky 19 January 1874 to Ellen Stiles (of Mead Company) and George Singleton (of Mead County);

Residence, Evansville, Indiana. p. 501.

**WAINMAN**, John Frederick, born Evansville, Indiana 1896 to Elnora Goings (of Louisville, Kentucky) and John Nelson Wainman (of Pittsburgh, Pennsylvania); married; two children. Residence, Evansville. p. 503.

**WATKINS**, Frank L., born 4 February 1873 to Sarah (of England) and G.W. Watkins (of Mitchell, Indiana); married, four children. Residence, Green Castle, Kentucky. p. 506.

**WELBORN**, James Y., born Stewartsville, Indiana 28 January 1873 to Martha Stinnette (of Elklon, Kentucky) and George W. Welborn (of Evansville, Indiana); widower; three children. Residence, Evansville, p. 507.

**WHITLOCK**, John W., born Rising Sun, Indiana 1871 to Adeline and William H. Whitlock; married; four children. Residence, Rising Sun. pp. 508-09.

**WILDER**, Daniel A., born Warrick County, Indiana 11 July 1887 to Julina E. (of West Virginia) and William S. Wilder (of Tennessee); married; one child. Residence, Golconda, Illinois. p. 509.

**WRIGHT**, Admiral W., born Grantsburg, Indiana 8 September 1868 to Mary Miller (of Leavenworth, Indiana) and George W. Wright (of Leavenworth); married; no children. Residence, Metropolis, Illinois. p. 513.

**STROUBE**, Owen L., born Rockport, Indiana 13 January 1900 to Zelma Smith (of Ohio County, Kentucky) and George Stroube (of Grandview, Indiana); married Virginia May Taylor; no children. Residence, Golconda, Illinois. p. 495.

**THACKER**, Frank L., born Madison, Indiana 1862 to Mary Elizabeth Scott (of Madison) and Isaac Thacker (of Shawneetown, Illinois); married Anna Hunter; three children. Residence, Wirt Junction, Kentucky. p. 498.

**THOMPSON**, Samuel Albert, born Richmond, Indiana 2 January 1855 to Margaret Elizabeth Fryar (of Wayne County, Indiana) and John Lewis Thompson (of Augusta County, Virginia); married Elizabeth Gatch Mears and Elizabeth E. Stewart; four children. Residence, Washington, D.C. p. 499.

**TURNER**, Selby, born Jefferson County, Indiana 31 July 1885 to Mary Elizabeth Kennedy (of Indiana) and John Thomas Turner (of Kentucky); married Katherine Anetta Keller; four children. Residence, Madison, Indiana. p. 500.

**VAIL**, Joel, born Slaine County, Illinois 1882 to Elizabeth (of Clermont County, Ohio) and John Vail (of Clermont County). Residence, Mount Vernon, Indiana. p. 501.

**VANZANT**, Leonard, born Knob Lick, Kentucky 23 February 1886 to Eugenia Pedigo (of Knob Lick) and U.G. Vanzant (of Knob Lick); married Greta May Hart; three sons. Residence, Leavenworth, Indiana. p. 501.

**VEATCH**, John Oatman, born Mount Vernon, Indiana 16 June 1867 to Margaret Oatman (of Mount Vernon) and Virgil S. Veatch (of Mount Vernon); married Carrie C. Rottmayer 1889; five children; descendant of Betsy Ross.

married Lou M. Rowe; one daughter. Residence, Mauckport, Indiana. p. 491.

**SLIDER**, Chester C., born New Albany, Indiana 13 February 1890 to Anna L. (of New Albany) and E.R. Slider (of New Albany); married; one son. Residence, Louisville, Kentucky. p. 491.

**SMITH**, David Ernest, born Morgantown, West Virginia, 12 October 1880 to Sarah Abbie (of Woodbury, Kentucky) and Eldridge Anderson Smith (of Vevay, Indiana); married; three children. Residence, Richardsville, Kentucky. pp. 491-92.

**SMITH**, Sanford B., born Bethlehem, Indiana 8 August 1872 to Martha E. (of Eminence, Kentucky) and Abraham G. Smith (of Keokuk, Iowa); married; five children. Residence, Bethlehem. p. 492.

**SMITH**, William R., born Evansville, Indiana 9 May 1881 to Rebecca A. Martin (of Smithland, Kentucky) and W.H. Smith (of Richmond, Virginia); married Eleanor Estell Jordan 1915; three children; grandfather Admiral R. Smith. Residence, Paducah, Kentucky. p. 492.

**SNIDER**, Frank, born Florence, Indiana 8 September 1872 to Charlotte Miller (of Markland, Indiana) and John N. Snider (of Bedford County, Pennsylvania); married Katie Luck; one child. Residence, Florence. p. 493.

**WYLLIE**, Harry R., born East Liverpool, Ohio 1 September 1876 to Fannie Arnold (of Richmond, Indiana) and John R. Wyllie (of England); married Harriette McAdoo; no children. Residence, Ritter Park, West Virginia, p. 514 .

# OBITUARY INDEX, INDIANA HISTORY BULLETIN
## Compiled by Ruth Dorrel

*The Indiana History Bulletin*, published by the Indiana Historical Bureau, began to print in 1930, as part of its report of the Annual meeting of the Indiana Historical Society, obituaries of members of the Historical Society who had died in the preceding year. This listing continued until 1965. The following is an index to those obituaries. Copies of the *IHB* are available in many libraries.

Achenbach, W. N. (1880-1948), 27:7
Adams, Winifred Brady (1871-1955), 33:6
Ade, George (1866-1944), 22:24
Alexander, Nell G. Boruff (1871-1954), 32:6
Allen, Josiah G. (1861-1944), 22:25
Alsop, George R. (1851-1933), 11:98
Amos, Willard Hildreth (1856-1949), 27:7
Anderson, Emil V. (1875-1958), 36:3
Andrew, Jesse C. (1889-1955), 33:6
Andrew, Thomas M. (ca 1882-1955), 33:6
Antrim, Elbert M. (1885-1961), 39:33
Arbuckle, Lloyd (1906-1960), 38:6
Ashby, W. Hurley (1894-1948), 26:8
Atherton, John W. (1877-1947), 25:26
Atwater, Carleton W. (1885-1964), 42:32
Austin, Ennis R. (1863-1951), 29:5
Axtell, Harry A. (1871-1948), 27:7
Ayres, Frederic Murray (1872-1940), 18:42

Backman, Lucie DuChemin (1865-1945), 23:10
Badolett, LeRoy J. (1889-1957), 35:6
Baer, Paul Frank (1894-1930), 8:468a
Baker, Albert (1851-1942), 20:65
Baker, Fannie Knowlton (1856-1932), 10:357
Baker, George Bramwell (1866-1937), 15:40
Baker, Thaddeus R. (1873-1956), 34:13
Ball, Bertha Crosley (1875-1957), 35:6
Ball, Elizabeth Brady (1867-1944), 22:25
Ball, George A. (1862-1955), 33:7
Ball, Walter J. (1853-1943), 21:30
Ballard, C. William (1893-1963), 41:25

*Pamela Bennett, Editor of the *Indiana History Bulletin*, has granted permission to publish this index.

Barker, William L. (1857-1937), 15:41

Barkley, Ida Douglass (1844-1929), 7:158

Barkley, Merrill B. (1875-1964), 42:32

Barnaby, Charles H. (1870-1945), 23:10

Barnett, Henry Clay (1848-1945), 23:11

Barnett, John (1851-1935), 13:28

Barr, J. Allen (1873-1950), 28:7

Barry, Charles L. (1878-1951), 30:5

Bartholomew, Henry S. K. (1862-1952), 30:5

Bartlett, Charles H. (1853-1937), 15:41

Barton, James M. (1858-1943), 21:31

Bates, Esther Felkner (1896-1959), 37:91

Bates, Frank G. (1868-1955), 33:7

Bates, Howard Haywood (1901-1962), 40:25

Batty, Bernard (1879-1958), 36:4

Baudendistel, William V. (ca 1886-1960), 38:6

Baum, William, (1878-1939), 17:31

Baxter, Arthur R. (1876-1957), 36:4

Baxter, Mary Alice Jordan (1849-1933), 11:99

Beamer, John V. (1896-1964), 42:32

Beard, Charles A. (1875-1948), 26:8

Beard, Mary Ritter (1876-1958), 36:4

Beardsley, Charles S. (1874-1962), 40:25

Beardsley, Helen M. Brown (1873-1958), 36:5

Beck, Charles H. (1876-1959), 37:91

Beck, Earl (1895-1954), 32:6

Beeler, A. Dale (1893-1963), 41:25

Beitner, George B. (Mrs.) (1860-1940), 19:50

Beldon, Roy H. (1891-1958), 36:5

Benham, Fred R. (1904-1954), 32:7

Bennett, Harry W. (1858-1936), 14:24

Berry, Mrs. C. M. (d. 1951), 29:5

Berry, Irene Wasson (1886-1955), 33:8

Bertsch, Harry Dorsett (1864-1937), 15:42

Biddle, Ward G. (1891-1946), 24:34

Binford, Florence Clark (d. 1939), 17:31

Binford, Frank L. (1886-1954), 32:7

Binford, John Clark (1892-1944), 22:26

Birge, Edward Bailey (1868-1952), 30:5

Bishop, Martha C. (1865-1950), 28:7

Black, Glenn A. (1900-1964), 41:126; 42:32

Blair, George W. (1887-1953), 31:5

Blessing, Geraldine White (d. 1933), 11:100

Blunk, Sanford M. (1878-1946), 25:27
Bock, William H. (1893-1954), 32:7
Bogardus, Frank Smith (1874-1931), 9:157
Bogner, Stella Milholland McCafferty (1875-1961), 39:33
Bohn, Arthur (1862-1948), 26:9
Bomberger, Ida Griffin (d. 1954), 32:8
Bomberger, Louden Lane (1875-1958), 37:91
Botkin, John W. (ca 1878-1958), 37:91
Bottorff, Amanda L. (1863-1957), 35:6
Bowen, Crate D. (ca 1872-1959), 37:92
Bowers, Claude G. (1878-1958), 36:5
Bowles, Cora Johnston (1878-1938), 16:26
Bowman, Lewis S. (1867-1960), 38:6
Bowsher, Delevan D. (1868-1949), 28:8
Bracken, Leonidas Locke (1877-1942), 20:66
Bradbury, Robert B. (1881-1937), 15:42
Braden, Fannie Dumont (1840-1934), 13:29
Brady, Arthur W. (1865-1933), 11:100
Bradshaw, Flora Gros (1872-1961), 39:33
Brady, Caroline H. McCulloch (d. 1935), 13:29
Branson, George (1852-1942), 20:67
Bray, Perry A. (1861-1938), 17:
Breen, William B. (1859-1930), 8:277
Brengle, Fred E. (1889-1963), 41:25
Brennan, William A. (1886-1961), 39:33
Breunig, LeRoy C. (1875-1958), 36:5
Brevoort, Eliza Haddon McClure (1866-1959), 37:92
Brewster, James B. (1872-1946), 24:35
Briggs, William A. (1873-1958), 36:5
Brimelow, William (1891-1954), 32:8
Brooks, Lorabel Wallace (1868-1936), 14:25
Brooks, Susan (1860-1935), 13:29
Brown, Austin H. (1890-1954), 32:8
Brown, Charles W. (1868-1929), 7:159
Brown, Cornelia Garvin (1863-1931), 9:158
Brown, Gertrude (1881-1953), 31:5
Brown, Hilton U. (1859-1958), 36:6
Brown, Hiram (1859-1938), 17:29
Brown, Raymond D. (1886-1959), 37:92
Browne, Chester G. (1876-1949), 27:8
Brumfield, India (1862-1950), 28:8
Bruner, Henry Lane (1861-1945), 23:12
Bryan, Enoch Albert (1855-1941), 19:52
Bryan, William Lowe (1860-1955), 33:8

Bryant, Willis S. (1888-1963), 41:25
Burgan, Edgar O. (1876-1947), 25:28
Burnet, Harry Bentley (1861-1931), 9:158
Burns, Lee (1872-1957), 35:6
Butler, Amos W. (1860-1937), 15:43
Byers, Russell T. (1875-1955), 33:8

Caldwell, Alma Brenton (1868-1942), 20:68
Caldwell, Edward (1861-1949), 27:8
Calvert, Cecil K. (1886-1948), 27:9
Campbell, Jessamine Morris (1861-1942), 20:68
Canis, Edward N. (1871-1933), 12:98
Canis, Ruth Adah Cushman (d. 1935), 14:25
Carey, John Newman (Mrs.) (1859-1937), 16:27
Carlisle, Anne Studebaker (1868-1931), 9:159
Carter, Larue De Pew (1880-1946), 24:36
Carter, Laura Beeler (1861-1943), 22:26
Carter, Vinson (ca 1840-1932), 10:358
Cates, Dudley (1887-1954), 32:9
Cauble, Elizabeth Tucker (1871-1945), 23:12
Cavanaugh, Robert B. (1881-1960), 38:6
Chamberlain, Harry (1872-1960), 38:7
Chambers, D. Laurance (1879-1963), 41:25
Chaney, John Crawford (1854-1940), 18:42
Chapman, Edwin G. (1861-1937), 15:44
Chartrand, Joseph (1870-1933), 11:101
Chase, Charles Warren (1877-1942), 20:69
Chase, James R. (1908-1952), 30:6
Clark, Cecil Pratt (1894-1962), 40:26
Clark, Edmund D. (1869-1938), 16:28
Clark, George L. (1892-1961), 39:34
Clarke, Grace Julian (1865-1938), 16:29
Clearwaters, John F. (ca 1867-1932), 10:358
Cleveland, Chester W. (1898-1961), 39:34
Clifford, Emily Orr (1886-1952), 30:6
Cline, Joanna C. Stevenson (1853-1935), 13:30
Clough, George J. (1883-1951), 29:5
Clowes, George H. A. (1877-1958), 36:6
Coate, Alvin T. (1870-1955), 34:13
Coffin, Annie Morrison (1840-1938), 17:29
Coffin, Charles E. (1849-1934), 12:99
Coffin, Florence Worth (1868-1961), 39:34
Coffing, McMannomy (1890-1958), 36:6
Cole, Ella S. Barnett (1861-1942), 20:70

Coleman, Christopher Bush (1875-1944), 21:355; 22:27
Coleman, Juliet Brown (1880-1953), 31:6
Combs, Charles N. (1879-1960), 38:7
Condit, H. Allen (1868-1935), 13:30
Conrad, Jeannette Wilson (d. 1950), 29:5
Cook, Clarence A. (1871-1962), 40:26
Cooper, Minnie D. Marshon (1869-1953), 31:6
Coquillard, Alexis (1882-1955), 33:9
Cornuelle, Herbert C. (ca 1893-1936), 14:25
Costelo, David (1856-1939), 17:32
Cottman, George Streibe (1857-1941), 19:53
Coulter, Stanley (1853-1943), 21:32
Courtright, William A. (1866-1939). 17:32
Coval, Willis Nixon (1881-1951), 29:5
Cox, Charles Herbert (1866-1940), 18:43
Cox, Dale (1902-1958), 36:6
Cox, Miles Standish (1887-1929), 7:159
Craig, Evelyn M. (ca 1875-1963), 41:26
Crain, Joseph (ca 1844-1932), 10:359
Crandall, Arthur W. (1894-1963), 41:26
Crane, Mary Campbell (1867-1943), 22:27
Craven, Arthur (1872-1952), 31:6
Crawford, Clifford E. (1877-1934), 13:31
Creigmile, Robert Alexander (1867-1941), 19:54
Crider, Edward C. (1869-1938), 16:30
Cuthbertson, Harry K., Jr. (1924-1954), 32:8
Cutter, Fred P. (1869-1956), 34:14

Dahmen, Corinne Schenck (d. 1936), 15:44
Dalton, John Eric (1901-1960), 38:7
Daniels, Wylie J. (1888-1951), 29:5
Danner, Effa Morrison (1874-1949), 27:10
Davidson, Helen Chick (1872-1940), 18:44
Davidson, Lyman C. (1879-1951), 29:5
Davies, Frederick R. (1874-1946), 24:37
Davis, Charles S. (1877-1954); 32:9, 65
Davis, Irene Addington (1887-1961), 39:34
Davis, Lawrence B. (1879-1946), 24:37
Davis, William J. (1856-1940), 18:44
Dawson, Ruth Moorhead (1886-1956), 35:7
Day, David I. (ca 1888-1955), 33:9
Deam, Charles C. (1865-1953), 31:7
DeBruler, Eva (1870-1942), 20:71
Deery, Paul A. (1895-1964), 42:33

Dennis, William C. (1878-1962), 40:26
Denny, Mary Adeline (1849-1930), 8:277
Dickinson, Charles (1888-1956), 34:14
Dickore, Marie (1883-1964), 42:33
Dickover, Mark L. (1869-1962), 40:26
Dillan, Florence Eva (1867-1944), 22:28
Dillingham, Thomas J. (1889-1957), 35:7
Doane, Waring L. (1896-1955), 33:9
Doney, Emma Louisa Knowlton (1862-1942), 20:71
Donnan, Laura (ca 1854-1930), 8:277
Dooley, Hazeltine Hinkle (d. 1930), 8:278
Dorsey, Leroy H. (1887-1954), 32:10
Douglass, Benjamin Wallace (1882-1939), 17:33
Draper, Luther O. (1867-1938), 16:30
Drum, John (1904-1960), 39:34
Dugan, Henry F. (1889-1957), 35:7
Duling, G. Harold (1909-1964), 42:33
Dunbar, James W. (1860-1943), 21:33
Duncan, Frank C. (1873-1949), 27:10
Dunkin, Martha K. Howard (1900-1960), 38:7
Dunlap, Theo M. (1888-1964), 42:33
Dunlavy, Edwin Wesley (1874-1953), 31:7
Dunn, Charlotte Jones (1869-1956), 34:14
Dunn, Jacob Piatt (1855-1924), 1:119

Earl, Elizabeth Claypool (1856-1931), 9:159
Ebbinghouse, August F. (Mrs.) (d. 1933), 11:101
Eberhart, Frederick G. (Mrs.) (ca 1867-1953), 31:8
Eddy, Eugenia Schenck (1862-1936), 14:26
Edmison, John P. (1869-1957), 35:7
Edwards, Alice Shirk (ca 1855-1931), 9:160
Edwards, Richard A. (1851-1947), 25:29
Ehrnschwender, Karl S. (1890-1962), 40:26
Elliott, George B. (1868-1953), 31:8
Elliott, Harry (1878-1931), 9:160
Elliott, Mary Sewall (ca 1879-1962), 40:30
Elliott, Phoebe Stoker (1855-1940), 18:45
Ellis, Theodore W. (ca 1910-1963), 41:26
Ellwood, Willard M. (1871-1954), 33:10
Elston, Isaac Compton, Jr. (1873-1964), 42:33
Emhardt, Adolph G. (1908-1961), 39:35
Emmert, Philip J. (1841-1934), 12:99
English, Henry King (1853-1939), 17:34
Ensminger, Leonard A. (1878-1963), 41:26

Fox, David E. (1877-1956), 34:14
Franck, Georgianna Garman (1893-1963), 41:27
French, Alice Moore (ca 1863-1934), 13:33
Fretageot, Nora Chadwick (1858-1937), 15:45
Friedley, Harmon H. (1849-1932), 10:360
Friedley, Roy M. (1877-1958), 36:7
Friesner, Ray C. (1894-1952), 30:7
Funk, Kate Douglass (1867-1951), 29:6
Funkhouser, Elmer (1885-1964), 42:34
Furbee, Ellen G. Knowlton (1860-1949), 27:11

Gaar, Julia Meek (1859-1944), 22:29
Gaesser, Theobald T. (1861-1934), 12:102
Gall, Albert (d. 1949), 28:8
Gallaher, Florence (d. 1951), 29:6
Garber, William S. (d. 1933), 11:102
Gardner, Alonzo M. (1860-1941), 20:63
Garman, Harry Otto (1880-1952), 30:7
Gary, Abraham L. (1868-1953), 31:10
Gatch, Willis D. (1877-1962), 40:27
Gaul, Cyril (1884-1946), 24:40
Gavin, Frank E. (1854-1936), 14:26
Gavisk, Francis H. (1856-1932), 10:360
Gennett, Hazel Reid (ca 1887-1959), 37:92
Geringer, Joseph J. (1880-1949), 27:12
Gerken, Carl A. (ca 1889-1954), 32:11
Gibbons, George Lee (1869-1951), 29:7
Gibson, Walter (ca 1879-1963), 41:27
Gildersleeve, W.H. (ca 1875-1959), 37:92
Gillie, George W. (1880-1963), 41:27
Gilpin, Levi Lambdin (1844-1931), 9:161
Gladden, Claude M. (d. 1959), 37:93
Gladden, Elijah A. (1860-1936), 14:26
Glossbrenner, Alfred M. (1869-1938), 16:30
Glossbrenner, Harry Wishard (1883-1964), 42:34
Godchaux, Leon (1894-1957), 35:8
Godfroy, Clarence (ca 1882-1962), 40:27
Goodrich, James Putnam (1864-1940), 18:45
Goodwin, Clarence L. (1859-1935), 13:33
Goossens, Emile J. (1903-1959), 37:93
Gorman, Robert (1906-1964), 42:34
Grau, Lydia (d. 1930), 8:278
Gray, Mark Roy (1883-1947), 25:30
Graydon, Katherine Merrill (1858-1934), 12:102

Green, Lot (1904-1964), 42:34
Greenly, Albert H. (ca 1881-1960), 39:35
Greist, Oliver Howard (1871-1947), 25:31
Griffin, Mary Jane (1874-1961), 39:35
Griffith, Albert H. (1871-1948), 27:12
Grills, Merton W. (1872-1958), 36:7
Grimes, Margie M. (1891-1963), 41:27
Grover, Emily Monroe (ca 1879-1961), 39:38
Grubbs, Samuel Bates (1871-1942), 20:74
Guthrie, William A. (1851-1936), 14:27

Habbe, John F. (1858-1930), 8:279
Hack, Elizabeth Miller (1878-1961), 39:35
Hadley, Chalmers (1872-1958), 36:7
Haerle, Elisabeth L. (1898-1957), 35:8
Haerle, George C. (1867-1932); 11:97
Haines, Matthias Loring (1850-1941), 20:64
Halberstadt, Loring C. (1891-1963), 41:28
Hall, Joseph Emmett (1884-1943), 21:34
Hamilton, Dora Miller (ca 1862-1933), 11:103
Hamilton, Frank A. (1872-1937), 15:45
Hamilton, Frances Frazee (1866-1930), 8:279
Hanan, John W. (ca 1861-1931), 9:161
Hannon, J. Walter (1890-1955), 34:14
Harding, Walter B. (ca 1872-1938), 16:31
Hargrave, Frank F. (ca 1878-1962), 40:27
Hargrave, Homer P. (1895-1964), 42:35
Harker, Mark H. (1912-1962), 40:27
Harris, Edward H. (1880-1937), 15:45
Harrison, Cleves (1881-1963), 41:28
Hart, William L. (1889-1963), 41:28
Hartsough, Mary M. (d. 1961), 39:36
Hasselman, Ida Blood (1853-1938), 16:32
Hassmer, Joseph A. (1865-1952), 30:7
Hatfield, Mary Wright (1883-1957), 35:8
Haugh, May Blake (1866-1935), 14:28
Haworth, Paul Leland (1876-1938), 16:33
Haymond, Claude J. (1877-1930), 8:280
Hays, Walter L. (1895-1962), 40:27
Hays, Will H. (1879-1954), 32:11
Hazen, David W. (1879-1944), 22:30
Heberhart, Charles E. (1877-1943), 21:34
Heberhart, William G. (d. 1932), 10:361
Heitger, Louis C. (1907-1958), 36:8

Hendren, Gilbert R. (1910-1961), 39:36
Hendricks, Allan (1864-1949), 27:13
Hendricks, Thomas A. (1875-1955), 33:10
Hendrickson, Edmonia DeSouchet (1860-1944), 22:31
Henley, Eunice D. (ca 1893-1979), 37:93
Henley, Howard E. (1882-1963), 42:35
Henley, Lillian E. (1880-1950), 28:8
Hepburn, William M. (1889-1963), 41:28
Herod, Henry L. (1875-1935), 13:34
Heron, Katherine (d. 1933), 11:103
Herr, Ben (1897-1961), 39:36
Herr, Shirl (1875-1936), 14:28
Herron, Josephine (1873-1952), 30:7
Hersch, Jennie Rae (1886-1941), 19:55
Heusler, Basil (1860-1942), 20:74
Heywood, Henry B. (1865-1930), 8:280
Hibben, Evadne Hayward (1882-1961), 39:36
Hibben, George (1868-1939), 19:50
Hibben, Mae B. (d. 1951), 29:7
Hickman, Warren Reynolds (1906-1951), 29:7
Hidy, Rex L. (1889-1961), 39:36
Hiestand, Joseph E. (d. 1959), 37:93
Hitch, Othniel (1885-1949), 27:13
Hitz, Benjamin D. (1890-1949), 27:14
Hoadley, C. Vergil (1876-1964), 42:35
Hobbs, Martha Sayles (d. 1932), 10:361
Hochgesang, Robert C. (1887-1960), 38:8
Hogate, Jessie (ca 1875-1930), 8:280
Holcomb , James Irving (1876-1962), 40:28
Holland, Emory Edward (d. 1949), 28:8
Holliday, Alexander R. (1877-1931), 9:162
Holliday, Evaline MacFarlane Rieman (1853-1929), 7:160
Holliday, Florence Baker (1870-1947), 25:31
Holliday, Frederick T. (1898-1951), 29:7
Holtman, Barbara Richwine (1945-1964), 42:35
Honeywell, Mark C. (1874-1964), 42:35
Hoover, Guy Israel (1872-1943), 21:35
Hopkins, Louis Bertram (1881-1940), 18:46
Hornbrook, Henry Hallam (1870-1935), 13:34
Hoss, Henry G. (1882-1960), 38:8
Howe, Sue (1877-1956), 34:15
Howe, Thomas Carr (1867-1934), 12:103
Hubbard, Ella Hurst (1864-1954), 32:12
Hubbard, Walter John (1863-1951), 29:7

Huddleston, Fred R. (1888-1944), 22:31
Huff, Fannie Wright (1873-1941), 20:65
Hugg, Martin M. (1858-1938), 16:34
Humbert, Russell J. (1905-1962), 40:28
Hummel, Zennia M. (1872-1940), 19:51
Hussey, Mary Bradshaw (1840-1929), 7:160
Hutcheson, William L. (1874-1953), 31:10
Hyde, James H. (1876-1959), 37:93

Iglehart, John Eugene (1848-1934), 11:263; 12:104
Insley, William H. (1870-1962), 40:28
Irwin, Nettie (1860-1939), 18:41
Irwin, William G. (1866-1943), 22:32

Jackson, Phyllis Wynn (1898-1959), 37:93
Jamieson, Walter A. (1890-1957), 35:8
Jessup, Alfred (ca 1848-1937), 16:35
John, Don D. (1894-1957), 35:8
Johnson, Emsley W. (1878-1950), 28:9
Johnson, Louis (1873-1951), 29:7
Johnson, Nell Shute (d. ca 1961), 39:36
Johnson, Sylvester (1882-1956), 34:15
Jones, Frank L. (1872-1953), 32:12
Jones, Robert S. (1878-1956), 34:15
Jones, S. Florence (1900-1961), 40:28
Joyce, Thomas C. (1898-1960), 39:36
Judah, John M. (1848-1936), 14:28

Kackley, Sarah Atkins (1870-1934), 12:104
Karrer, Marie (1898-1951), 29:7
Katterjohn, Monte M. (1891-1949), 27:15
Kautz, Frederick Rollin (1864-1939), 17:34
Kearby, Delbert Oscar (1879-1947), 25:32
Keister, Edna Mattox (1875-1955), 33:10
Kelley, Elizabeth Spease (1875-1944), 22:32
Kelley, Luther E. (1870-1933), 11:103
Kendrick, Charlotte Phelps (1908-1955), 33:10
Kent, Arthur S. (1868-1947), 26:11
Kern, Flora Work (1873-1937), 15:46
Kershner, Bruce Lesher (1871-1949), 27:15
Ketcham, Flora McDonald (1846-1938), 16:35
Kettleborough, Charles (1878-1938), 16:34
Kilgore, Charles T. (1913-1963), 41:28
Kimble, Horace V. (1868-1942), 20:75
Kimble, Ralph P. (1887-1961), 39:37

Kingsbury, Edward D. (1867-1954), 32:12
Knisely, Alexander (1851-1931), 9:162
Knoblock, Otto M. (1859-1935), 13:35
Knowlton, Lovina (1869-1947), 25:33
Koch, Edward William (1882-1946), 24:41
Kohlmeier, Albert L. (1883-1964), 42:36
Kolb, Mary Gallahan (1896-1963), 41:28
Korbly, Margaret Elizabeth Crim (1879-1942), 20:76
Kothe, William J. (1899-1956), 34:15
Kryter, Charles C. (1873-1944), 23:14
Kuehn, Alfred L. (ca 1878-1960), 38:8

LaFollette, Harvey Marion (1858-1929), 7:161
Land, William Jesse Goad (1865-1942), 20:76
Landon, Hugh McK. (1867-1947), 25:33
Lapenta, Vincent Anthony (1883-1946), 24:42
Lathrop, Louis E. (ca 1862-1934), 12:105
Laut, William F. (1873-1954), 32:13
Leak, Roscoe R. (1884-1964), 42:36
Leech, Leona (1880-1932), 10:361
Leeds, Rudolph Gaar (1886-1964), 42:36
Lemmon, Walter S. (1893-1958), 36:8
Lesh, Ora Wilkens (1866-1940), 18:47
Levey, Meta Carpenter (ca 1865-1959), 37:94
Lewis, Montgomery S. (1887-1954), 32:13
Lieber, Carl H. (1866-1929), 7:161
Lieber, Richard (1869-1944), 22:33
Lilly, Josiah Kirby (1861-1948), 26:11
Littell, Clarence G. (1882-1959), 37:94
Little, Lindley P. (1868-1939), 17:35
Lockridge, Lillian (1909-1961), 39:37
Lockridge, Ross F. (1877-1952), 30:8
Lockwood, Virgil H. (1860-1932), 10:362
Long, Benjamin Franklin (1872-1940), 19:51
Long, Fred W. (1881-1961), 39:37
Loy, Clarence O. (1887-1952), 30:8
Luhrs, Henry E. (1901-1962), 41:29
Lutz, Philip, Jr. (1888-1947), 25:34
Lynch, William O. (d. 1957), 34:35
Lynn, Charles J. (1874-1958), 36:8
Lyon, Marcus Ward, Jr. (1875-1942), 20:77
Lyons, Michael W. (1872-1952), 30:8

McCollough, Ethel F. (d. 1950), 28:9
McConnell, Maude W. (1869-1950), 29:8

McCulloch, Carleton B. (1871-1949), 27:16
McCulloch, Maud Boyer (1865-1945), 24:43
McDermott, Joseph T. (1886-1960), 38:9
McDonald, Mary Belton (1862-1945), 24:43
McKee, Edward Lodge (ca 1856-1929), 7:162
McKinney, E. Kirk (1892-1961), 39:37
McMahan, William N. (1876-1946), 24:44
McMurray, Arthur G. (1889-1957), 35:9
McNally, Edwin M. (1896-1962), 40:28
McNamee, Wilbur Armstrong (1860-1942), 20:78
McNitt, Esther Uhl (d. 1941), 19:56
McNitt, James D. (1845-1935), 13:36
McNutt, Harry F. (ca 1884-1936), 14:29
McNutt, James Roy (1893-1942), 20:78
MacBeth, Lucia Holliday (1879-1955), 33:15
Mace, William Harrison (1852-1938), 16:36
Madden, John J. (1869-1930), 8:281
Maish, David Fudge (1859-1941), 19:57
Makemson, Charles L. (1885-1953), 31:10
Malan, Clement T. (1883-1961), 39:38
Mann, Mary Abegail (1901-1945), 23:15
Mardis, Joseph K. (1909-1964), 42:36
Marlowe, Fred Marion (1897-1920), 8:468c
Marmon, Elizabeth Carpenter (1849-1940), 18:47
Marshall, Charles B. (1895-1955), 33:15
Marshall, Norma McKay (1884-1960), 39:38
Marshall, Thomas Worth (1872-1952), 30:8
Marsters, Mary E. Coleman (1871-1957), 35:9
Martin, Florence J. (1876-1963), 41:29
Martin, Gary (1847-1933), 11:104
Martindale, Charles T. (1857-1936), 14:29
Mason, Augustus Lynch (1859-1939), 17:35
Matter, Milton (1887-1947), 25:35
Matthew, William H. (ca 1872-1931), 9:163
Mattingly, Ezra (1864-1938), 16:36
Maxwell, Howard (1865-1930), 8:281
May, Blanche Allen (1875-1952), 30:9
Mayer, Josephine Kiefer (1863-1934), 12:105
Mayhill, Dora Thomas (1884-1963), 41:29
Meissner, Mary Nordyke (1865-1944), 22:34
Merrill, Celine Lodge McKee (1867-1944), 23:15
Merry, Earl W. (1897-1964), 42:36
Metzger, Albert E. (1865-1931), 9:163

Miesse, Harry (1865-1954), 32:13

Miesse, Lulu M. (1888-1945), 23:16

Miller, Edith (1878-1958), 36:8

Miller, Frederick A. (1868-1954), 32:14

Miller, Grace Moore (1865-1952), 30:9

Miller, Hugh Th. (1867-1947), 25:36

Miller, J. Don (1881-1960), 38:9

Miller, John Robert (1845-1932), 10:362

Miller, Marion Clinton (1906-1940), 19:51

Miller, Nettie Sweeney (1876-1960), 38:9

Miller, Owen Lambe (1865-1941), 19:57

Miller, Robert G. (1871-1953), 31:10

Miller, Thomas (ca 1877-1962), 40:29

Miller, Winfield (1853-1947), 26:12

Millikan, Mabel Warner (1885-1962), 40:29

Millis, Fred Clark (1892-1951), 29:8

Millspaugh, Flora Hardin (1858-1945), 23:16

Milner, Jean S. (1893-1964), 42:37

Minturn, Joseph Allen (1861-1943), 21:36

Misselhorn, Adele C. Knight (1870-1957), 35:9

Mitchell, William C. (1854-1935), 13:36

Mitten, Arthur G. (1866-1938), 16:33

Moeller, Velma Whiteleather (1897-1964), 42:37

Moffat, James E. (1883-1957), 35:9

Moffett, Dorothy Dell (1904-1949), 27:17

Moffett, Paul G. (1900-1948), 26:13

Moll, Theophilus J. (1872-1930), 8:281

Montgomery, Walter H. (1889-1963), 41:29

Moore, Deborah Duane (d. 1958), 36:9

Moore, Ethel MacDowell (1884-1950), 28:10

Moore, Jesse C. (1868-1957), 35:9

Moore, Julia Harrison (1865-1939), 17:36

Moore, Perry G. (1845-1931), 9:164

Moores, Charles W. (d. 1923), 1:20

Moores, Charles W. (1903-1956), 34:16

Moores, Charles W. (Mrs.), (1871-1950), 28:10

Moran, Thomas Francis (d. 1928), 6:43

Morgan, Raymond C. (1868-1953), 31:11

Morrill, Edward (1888-1962), 40:29

Morris, Charles R. (1874-1947), 25:36

Morris, Donald S. (1878-1964), 42:37

Morris, Ernest M. (1882-1951), 29:8

Morris, John H. (1892-1963), 41:30

Morris, Martha Tucker (1867-1948), 26:13

Morrison, Florence I. (d. 1954), 32:14
Morrison, H.C. (Mrs.) (ca 1860-1932), 10:363
Mote, Carl H. (1884-1946), 24:44
Mother Mary Helene (ca 1846-1932), 31:11
Mottier, David Myers (1864-1940), 18:48
Moulder, Martha M. Carter (ca 1846-1932), 10:363
Mumford, Eugene Bishop (1879-1961), 39:38
Murphy, Maurice (d. 1930), 8:282
Myers, Burton D. (1870-1951), 29:8
Myers, William A. (1869-1955), 33:15

Nanz, Robert H. (1885-1957), 35:10
Nedwick, Rhoda (ca 1901-1959), 37:94
Neimeyer, Harry D. (1906-1956), 34:16
Nelson, Carl W. (1887-1958), 36:9
Neuenschwander, Wilbur E. (1885-1954), 32:14
New, Harry S. (1858-1937), 15:46
Newby, Arthur C. (1865-1933), 11:104
Newcomb, Florence S. (ca 1858-1935), 14:30
Newsom, Annie McEwen (1868-1939), 17:36
Niblack, Sarah Lydia (ca 1868-1933), 11:104
Nicholson, Meredith (1866-1947), 26:14
Niezer, Charles M. (1877-1941), 19:58
Noble, Thomas B. (1897-1958), 37:94
Noblitt, Quentin (1882-1954), 32:15
Noel, James W. (1867-1944), 22:34
Nolan, Val (1892-1940), 18:49
Noland, Stephen C. (1887-1962), 40:29
Norris, Joe L. (1906-1962), 41:30
Norton, Daniel F. (1894-1956), 34:16
Nowlin, Ambrose E. (ca 1843-1931), 9:164
Nugent, Walter C. (1879-1960), 39:38

Oakes, Mansur B. (1873-1946), 24:45
O'Bannon, Lew M. (1864-1943), 21:37
O'Bannon, Lillian Keller (1867-1939), 17:37
Obenauer, Hattie Studabaker (1861-1938), 16:38
O'Brien, Cornelius (1883-1953), 31:11
O'Brien, William H. (1855-1933), 11:105
Oilar, Arthur L. (1891-1940), 18:49
Olin, Frank W. (1853-1941), 19:58
Olive, George S., Sr. (1881-1962), 40:29
Oliver, Joseph Doty (1850-1933), 11:106
Orth, Albert A. (1899-1963), 41:30
Osborn, Chase Salmon (1860-1949), 27:18

Osborne, Clarence W. (1852-1932), 10:363
Otis, Frederick Bishop (1863-1945), 23:17
Overbay, Arthur S. (1896-1955), 33:16
Owens, Alonzo C. (1885-1950), 29:8

Pagani, Humbert P. (1878-1954), 32:15
Pangborn, Anne Porter (d. 1951), 29:8
Parker, Albert G., Jr. (1892-1958), 36:9
Parry, St. Clair (1861-1931), 10:363
Patterson, Evelyn McFarland Holliday (1881-1952), 31:12
Patton, Anna Pearl Miller (1886-1962), 40:29
Patton, William H. (Mrs.) (d. 1951), 29:9
Payne, Felice Smith (1896-1964), 42:37
Payne, Gavin L. (1869-1939), 17:37
Paynter, Lawrence W. (1871-1951), 29:9
Paynter, Maud M. Stratton (1877-1964), 42:38
Pearson, Esther (1900-1931), 9:165
Pence, George (1852-1929), 7:162
Perkins, Edgar A., Sr. (1866-1956), 34:16
Perkins, Edgar A., Jr. (1896-1959), 37:94
Perkins, Frances Owens (1886-1962), 40:30
Perkins, Samuel Elliott III (1878-1941), 19:59
Perry, Oran (1838-1929), 7:163
Phelps, Hal C. (1876-1949), 27:18
Philhower, Charles A. (1878-1962), 40:30
Pike, Edna Jones (1883-1961), 39:38
Pinnick, Rufus E. (1867-1932), 10:364
Pittenger, Lemuel A. (1873-1953), 31:12
Platter, Amelia Waring (1854-1940), 18:50
Ploch, Carl A. (1884-1961), 39:39
Poland, Jennie Kirkpatrick (1889-1958), 36:9
Polley, Frederick (1875-1957), 35:10
Poorman, Alfred P. (1877-1952), 30:9
Poorman, Sarah Elizabeth Ellmaker (1876-1935), 13:37
Poston, Clement L. (1901-1964), 42:38
Power, Richard L. (1896-1960), 38:9
Pratt, Mary A. (1882-1943), 21:38
Pratt, Sarah Smith (1853-1942), 21:38
Preston, Abraham Lincoln (1860-1935), 13:37
Probasco, Margaret O'Neill (d. 1930), 8:282
Purcell, George W. (1888-1952), 30:9
Putnam, James William (1865-1940), 18:50
Pyle, Dan (1875-1964), 42:38

Rabb, Ada Hall (1869-1940), 18:51

Rabb, Albert Livingston (1893-1939), 17:39
Rabb, Kate Milner (1866-1937), 15:47
Ramsay, Frank P. (1865-1929), 7:164
Ramsey, Rolla R. (1872-1955), 33:16
Ransburg, Harper J. (1886-1963), 41:30
Rappaport, Leo M. (1879-1959), 37:94
Rauh, Samuel Elias (1853-1935), 13:38
Ray, Cary T. (ca 1859-1962), 40:30
Reade, Anna Ruth (1879-1957), 35:10
Reed, Della Shoup (1859-1941), 19:60
Reilly, Peter C. (1869-1952), 30:10
Remy, Charles F. (1860-1948), 26:15
Rennick, Percival Graham (1864-1938), 16:38
Reser, William M. (1863-1943), 21:39
Rettig, Nellie Stevens (1859-1932), 10:364
Rice, Jessie Pearl (1901-1949), 27:19
Richards, Clement J. (1881-1938), 16:39
Richardson, Willis (1896-1964), 42:38
Richter, Lucile Lane (1894-1961), 39:39
Rielag, Raymond (1886-1935), 13:39
Ristine, Theodore H. (d. 1931), 9:165
Robertson, Eleanor M. (1879-1951), 30:10
Robinson, Mary Yandes (1864-1953), 31:13
Rockwood, William M. (1874-1945), 23:17
Roebuck, Wesley S. (1861-1953), 32:15
Rogers, Aaron Grigsby (1849-1934), 12:106
Rogers, Ada C. Adamson (1856-1931), 9:166
Rose, Frederick Dodds (1882-1945), 23:18
Rose, Gladys Walcott (1884-1958), 36:9
Ross, Frances McIntire (1856-1940), 18:51
Row, Ella Yater (1863-1937), 15:48
Rowan, Margaret B. (d. 1964), 42:38
Ruby, Charles E. (1890-1958), 36:10
Runnels, Alice Barteau McCullough (1854-1948), 26:15
Rupel, Ernest (1892-1964), 42:38
Russell, John F. (1870-1943), 21:40
Russo, Anthony John (1898-1940), 18:52

Sallee, Alva Charles (1883-1951), 29:9
Sample, Sallie S. (1856-1937), 15:48
Sanders, Everett (1882-1950), 28:10
Sanders, Ura (1868-1959), 37:95
Sansberry, Charles T. (d. 1930), 8:283
Sansberry, Maud Mahorney (1875-1957), 35:10

Santarelli de Brasch, Laura Morton (1884-1954), 32:16
Scherrer, Anton (1878-1960), 38:9
Schiltges, William B. (1890-1964), 42:39
Schnitzius, Henry J. (1897-1957), 35:11
Schofield, Everett M. (1884-1963), 41:30
Schrichte, Elizabeth Pattison (1865-1952), 30:11
Schrum, John Luther (1860-1941), 19:60
Schumm, Lorenz G. (1891-1959), 37:95
Schwab, Lenora (1868-1957), 35:11
Scott, George A. (1862-1964), 42:39
Sears, Louis M. (1885-1960), 38:10
Sees, John Vincent (1875-1946), 24:45
Segur, Margaret Bartlingck (1876-1953), 31:13
Shaffer, John C. (1853-1943), 21:41
Shanks, William Carey (1874-1945), 23:19
Shaw, Archibald (1847-1940), 18:53
Sherry, M. Evan (1877-1954), 32:16
Shields, Jesse Leroy (1882-1962), 40:30
Shilts, John H. (1862-1943), 21:42
Shipp, Margaret Mandeville (1883-1961), 39:39
Shirk, Joseph Henry (1881-1953), 31:13
Shirley, William C. (1839-1932), 11:98
Shreve, Oscar (Mrs.) (d. 1964), 32:39
Simmons, Abram (1857-1941), 19:60
Simms, Daniel W. (1862-1931), 9:166
Sims, Frederick Augustus (1867-1947), 25:37
Sims, Lester P. (d. 1948), 26:16
Sinclair, Robert S. (1872-1937), 16:26
Sisson, Winfield E. (1893-1946), 24:46
Small, Albert G. (1867-1955), 33:16
Smeltzly, Eleanor (d. 1957), 36:10
Smith, Albert Preston (1873-1937), 15:49
Smith, Bettie Dufour (1868-1936), 14:30
Smith, Harry A., Sr. (1875-1958), 36:10
Smith, Henry Lester (1876-1963), 41:31
Smith, Ulysses Howe (1865-1953), 31:13
Sollenberger, Danna H. (ca 1873-1935), 13:39
Somes, Joseph H.V. (1898-1962), 40:30
Sonner, Wenonah E. (1877-1955), 33:17
Sparks, Frank Hugh (1891-1964), 42:39
Squibb, Alexander Hamilton (1869-1953), 31:14
Springhorn, Sophia Simon (1873-1931), 9:167
Stalker, Althea Winslow (1869-1947), 25:38

Stantz, Guy (1884-1955), 33:17
Staples, Marston Reviere (1884-1962), 40:30
Starkey, William Carleton (1881-1949), 27:20
Stempfel, Theodore (1863-1935), 14:30
Stevenson, James R. (1901-1964), 42:40
Stevenson, Kenyon (1895-1957), 35:11
Stinson, Arthur E. (1879-1957), 35:11
Stockbridge, Adda Ashley (1859-1947), 25:39
Stolz, Charles (d. 1931), 9:167
Stoops, Harry M. (1866-1936), 14:31
Stoops, Marmaduke McClellan (1862-1951), 29:9
Stoops, William T. (1890-1955), 33:17
Storen, Mark (1857-1934), 12:106
Stout, Elmer W. (1876-1962), 40:31
Stout, William Hovey (1870-1950), 28:11
Stratton, Hetty Champ (1876-1963), 41:31
Stratton, Melvin (1872-1960), 38:10
Straus, Simon William (1866-1930), 8:283
Stuart, Mary Howell (1867-1943), 21:43
Studebaker, Ada L. (1866-1954), 32:16
Studebaker, Clement W. (1861-1934), 12:107
Stukenberg, August (1862-1933), 12:98
Stull, Reginald Brentz (1888-1941), 19:61
Sturgis, Charles E. (1867-1957), 35:12
Sullivan, George William (1884-1959), 37:95
Summers, Roy (1882-1947), 25:39
Suverkeup, John W. (1870-1953), 31:14
Swift, Ella Lyon (1852-1933), 11:107
Switzer, George Washington (1854-1940), 18:53
Syron, Rose Alexander Sheldon (1885-1957), 35:12

Talkington, Edgar (1877-1959), 37:96
Taylor, Frank Bursley (1860-1938), 16:40
Taylor, Herbert C. (1878-1964), 42:40
Taylor, Isabelle Houghton (1859-1932), 9:114; 10:365
Taylor, Mary (1875-1964), 42:40
Taylor, William Mode (1865-1947), 25:40
Teel, William Ross (1866-1945), 23:19
Teetor, Charles N. (Mrs.) (d. 1951), 29:9
Temple, Clarabelle Hillis (1865-1948), 26:16
Terhune, Rufus W. (1866-1946), 24:46
Thistlethwaithe, Daisy Richey (1879-1957), 35:12
Thom, Jay Webb (1894-1962), 40:31
Thomas, Albert A. (1883-1942), 20:78

**328**

Thomas, Lucy Adams (1879-1951), 29:9
Thomas, Nora E. (1895-1944), 22:35
Thompson, Charles Nedeker (1861-1949), 27:20
Thompson, Rebecca J. (1844-1940), 18:54
Thompson, William H. (1878-1945), 23:20
Thornton, Irene Blackledge (1868-1942), 20:79
Thornton, William W. (1851-1932), 10:365
Tippy, Worth M. (1868-1961), 39:39
Tolle, Mary Mason (1881-1964), 42:40
Travis, Frank F. (1884-1963), 41:31
Traylor, Bomar (1876-1929), 7:164
Turner, Mabel Johnson (1876-1964), 42:40

Vance, Ohmer D. (ca 1892-1955), 33:17
Vandeveer, Welzie Wellington (1887-1964), 42:40
Vandeventer, Nellie Rainbolt (1896-1962), 40:31
VanDorn, Samuel (1870-1959), 37:96
VanNatter, Francis M. (1892-1960), 38:10
VanWinkle, Benjamin A. (1853-1933), 11:107
Venn, Florence (1882-1939), 17:39
Verhoeff, Mary (d. 1962), 40:31
Vernon, Anna Gurley (1876-1954), 32:17
Vernon, Noah H. (1872-1941), 19:62
Vestal, Allan P. (1879-1946), 24:47
Voigt, John G. (1887-1953), 31:14
Vonnegut, Anton (1881-1964), 42:41
Vonnegut, Emma Schnull (1857-1939), 17:40
Voris, Myrtillus J. (1860-1944), 23:21
Vrooman, Henry W. (1865-1930), 8:284

Waddington, Ralph B. (1889-1963), 41:31
Wade, Margaret A. (d. 1939), 17:40
Wagner, Joseph M. (1890-1955), 34:17
Wagner, Sarah Hill Fletcher (1855-1939), 17:41
Wainwright, Guy A. (1889-1956), 34:17
Wainwright, Lucius M. (1860-1931), 9:167
Wainwright, W. W. (1854-1929), 7:164
Walcott, Benjamin D. (1854-1933), 11:108
Waldenmaier, Benjamin C. (1876-1956), 34:17
Walk, Carl F. (1870-1963), 41:31
Walk, Julia E. F. (1869-1948), 27:21
Walker, Elizabeth Harrison (1897-1955), 34:17
Walker, John M. (1874-1960), 38:11
Wallace, Lew III (1918-1954), 32:17

Walton, Cora Parker (1864-1951), 29:10
Wampler, Frank (d. 1932), 10:366
Ward, Louis C. (1878-1931), 9:167
Warnock, Clarence O. (1886-1943), 22:35
Washburn, Will W. (1900-1956), 35:12
Watkins, Everett C. (ca 1883-1955), 33:18
Watkins, Oscar L. (1861-1945), 23:21
Watson, Phil M. (1875-1938), 16:41
Wayne, J. Lloyd III (d. 1948), 26:17
Weatherholt, Wallace (1887-1960), 38:11
Webb, Zelia K. (1883-1955), 33:18
Weer, Marjorie Stalnaker (1895-1959), 37:96
Weer, Paul Wiley (1886-1956), 34:18
Weisenburger, Lewis (1845-1932), 10:366
Welborn, Anne Acton (1871-1945), 23:22
Wells, Mary Wheeler (1897-1964), 42:41
Wentworth, Edward N. (1887-1959), 37:96
Wetherill, Richard Benbridge (1859-1940), 18:54
Wetzel, Julian S. (1867-1937), 15:49
Wheatley, Ella Cockrum (1859-1943), 21:44
Wheeler, Homer H. (1872-1945), 23:22
Wheeler, Lawrence M. (1898-1952), 30:11
Wheeler, Walton M. (1908-1960), 38:11
Wheeler, Walton Mark (1864-1951), 29:10
White, Roy Barton (1883-1961), 39:39
Wieser, Nannie Mooney (1860-1933), 11:108
Wilcox, Hattie M. (d. 1929), 7:65
Williams, Charles N. (1856-1939), 17:41
Williams, Howard (1871-1938), 16:41
Williams, Kenneth P. (1887-1958), 36:10
Williams, Oscar H. (1874-1951), 29:10
Williams, Sarah I. (1870-1961), 40:31
Williams, Walter Owen (1860-1949), 27:22
Willoughby, Benjamin M. (1855-1940), 19:52
Wilmore, Augustus C. (1849-1933), 11:108
Wilson, Elsie Newsom (1877-1946), 24:48
Wilson, George Robert (1863-1941), 19:62
Wilson, George Steele (1905-1963), 41:31
Wilson, Thomas J. (1863-1937), 15:49
Wilson, William T. (1854-1943), 21:44
Winger, Otho (1877-1946), 24:48
Winton, Gendron M. Whaley (1894-1962), 40:31
Wipperman, Franklin H. (1861-1943), 21:45

# HOOSIERS IN FULTON COUNTY, ILLINOIS

### Submitted by D.B. Allman

Apparently there was a migration of Hoosiers, mainly from southern Indiana to Fulton County, Illinois, in the 1830s. The following biographies of Hoosiers were excerpted from *History of Fulton County, Illinois* . . . (Peoria: Chas. C. Chapman Co., 1879; reprinted 1970). The original and the reprint copies are available in the Genealogy Division, Indiana State Library.

Christina (**Babbitt**) **Abbott**, b. Scott County, Indiana to Daniel **Babbitt**; married John W. **Abbott** in Fulton County 1837; children who all were born in Fulton County: Alexander (died age 25); Bethany, deceased; Cynthia, deceased; Daniel; Elizabeth, deceased; George B.; Jacob; Jeremiah; John W.; Nancy C.; Sarah L. (died age 21); Silas, deceased; Stephen A. (died age 17); William A., deceased; to Fulton County 1827. p. 726

John **Abbott**, b. Indiana 10 January 1835 to Alexander and Nancy (**Doty**) Abbott; married Margaret **Barkley** 1854; 3 sons, 4 daughters; to Fulton County 1845. p. 683

Isaac F. **Babbitt**, born Hamilton County, Ohio 18 March 1810 to Stephen **Babbitt** of Washington County, Pennsylvania; married Samantha **HURLEY** (born Hamilton County 6 July 1810) 13 January 1829; 5 children; married Ailsie **Phelps**; 6 children; lived Indiana 1824-32; to Fulton County 1842. p. 885

James **Babbitt**, born Fayette County, Ohio 9 April 1813; married Mary A. **Randall** 5 November 1837; children: Jonathan J.; Delilah; James; Eliza J.; Sarah C.; Edwin; Azuba; Wilford; 4 deceased; grandniece: Estelle **Babbitt**; lived Indiana 1818-29. p. 885

Jonathan **Babbitt**, born Fayette County, Ohio 13 March 1811 to Job **Babbitt**; to Indiana 1818; to Springfield, Illinois 1829; to Fulton County 1830. pp. 885-86

Jesse **Beaman**, b. Pennsylvania 1799; married Nancy **Pool** (born North Carolina 10 May 1805 to Joseph **Pool**), Indiana before 1840; died Fulton County 1858; Children: John W. (born Schuyler County, Illinois 15 July 1843); William, deceased, and six others; to Illinois ca 1840; to Indiana; to Menard County, Illinois; to Fulton County 1850. pp. 749-50

James H. **Blair**, born Lawrence County, Indiana 1833; 3 children; to Fulton County 1853. p. 750

G.W. **Brewer**, born Indiana 28 October 1838 to Bincent (born Indiana) and Elizabeth (born Indiana) **Brewer**; married Mary Ann **Peggs** (born England 1839), Otto, Illinois; 4 children; to Fulton County 1856. p. 714

Joseph **Brown**, born 1842 to Jonas and Margaret **Brown** of Pennsylvania; married Serilda **Zimmerman** (born Fulton County 1848) 1866; lived Indiana; to Fulton County 1865. p. 761

William C. **Buckner**, born Crawford County, Indiana 2 June 1818 to Henry **Buckner** (born Kentucky); married Christian **Church** 1837; to Fulton County 1833. p. 762

John **Butler**, born Greenbrier County, Virginia 26 July 1802; to William and Tacy (**Gray**) **Butler**; married Mary **Adney** (died Kansas 12 November 1875) 25 April 1822; daughter: Mary Helen; 6 other children living; 6 deceased; uncle: Isaac **Butler**; to Gallia County, Ohio 1804; to St. Joseph County, Indiana 1833; to Warren County Illinois, 1839. p. 887

E.T. **Campbell**, born Indiana 25 February 1835; married Matilda **Shawver** (born Ohio 1835) Fulton County 1859; children: Charles; Anna; Susana. p. 793

George W. **Clark**, born Gallia County, Ohio 27 August 1847; married Julia A. **Smith**, Fulton County 1846; to Indianapolis 1849; to Gallia County; to Indianapolis; to Iowa 1854; to Indianapolis 1857; to Gallia County; to Schuyler County, Missouri 1858; to Fulton County by 1869. p. 717

Henry **Coons**, born Indiana 25 May 1832 to David **Coons** (died Fulton County September 1876); married Lucy **Dodge** (daughter of George **Dodge**) 7 January 1872; daughter: Emma (born 16 December 1875); to Bernadette Township, Fulton County 1852. p. 699

Elizabeth **Craig**, married William **Craig**; son: John (born Fulton County 18 November 1858); lived Indiana; to Fulton County 1844. p. 717

John W. **Dimmitt**, born Jefferson County, Virginia 25 December 1802; married Rachel **Grinard** (born Mason County, Kentucky 15 August 1807) 22 September 1825; children: James P.; William V.; Betsey A.; Pratt; 5 others deceased; to Kentucky 1818; to Indiana 1839; to Peoria County, Illinois 1850; to Fulton County 1850. pp. 699-700

Pratt **Dimmitt**, born Montgomery County, Indiana 20 October 1846 to John W. and Rachel (**Grinard**) **Dimmitt**; married Margaret J. **Wheeler** (born Young Hickory Township, Fulton County) 30 March 1871; children: Warder D.; Burton J.; Eldana; 1 other; to Peoria County, Illinois 1850; to Fulton County 1850. p. 700

Franklin **Dunn**, born Indiana 1830 to Franklin and Melinda **Dunn**; married Mary **Barkley** (daughter of Joseph **Barkley**); 3 children; to Fulton County 1854. p. 795

O.D. **Evans**, married Irene **Kelly** (daugher of John H. and Nancy (**Carter**) **Kelly**); lived Wayne County, Indiana. p. 556

Frederick **Fisher**, died Fulton County 5 July 1876; married Sarah **Fouts** (born Clark County, Indiana 5 October 1807); children: Barbara, deceased; Jacob; John; Henry; Cynthia (born Fulton County; married David **Copple**, lived Indiana 1879); lived Clark County 1825-27; to Fulton County 1831. p. 483-84

Jacob **Fisher**, born Clark County, Indiana 1825, to Frederick and Sarah (**Fouts**) **Fisher**; married Charlotte **Bauman** Van Buren County, Iowa 1 January 1856; child: Olive (born 21 August 1858); to Fulton County 1831. p. 483-84

John **Fisher**, born Washington Township, Clark County, Indiana 2 October 1827 to Frederick and Sarah (**Fouts**) **Fisher**; married Melissa **Maxwell** 10

October 1850; Children: Josephine (born 17 August 1851); Alice (born 6 June 1854, married Frederick M. **Fouts** 21 December 1876); Willard (born 17 January 1859); Leonard (born 17 October 1861); Charles (born 7 April 1864); Attie (born 17 August 1869); Dolly B. (born 1 October 1871); to Fulton County 1831  pp. 483-84

Elizabeth (**Leadmon**) **Foutch**, born Indiana; married F.M. **Foutch** (born Sangamon County, Illinois 1833 to John and Rhoda (**Ray**) **Foutch**) 1854; 4 children living; 1 child deceased; to Fulton County 1835.  p. 717

John **Foutch**, born Virginia, died Sangamon County, Illinois 1845, married Nancy **Wherrott**; children: John (born Kentucky 1806); 4 others; to Indiana 1807; to Sangamon County, Illinois 1823.  p. 718

Andrew **Fouts**, born Clark County, Indiana 1807 to Daniel **Fouts** (son of Jacob **Fouts** (from Germany), died age 92), married Eliza Ann **Hufford** (born Buford County, Kentucky to George **Hufford**) January 1834; son: Martin; brother: Emsley; to Fulton County 1829.  p. 484

Dougan **Fouts**, born Indiana to Jacob **Fouts**; died 16 March 1862; married Sarah **Hutchinson** (born Virginia to Zachariah **Hutchinson**); children: Eleanor (married Cyrus **Babcock**); Elizabeth (married Archibald **Carver**); Rebecca (married John **Carleton**); Harriet (married George **Hammitt**); Sarah (married John **Provard**); Nancy (married T.J. **Kelly**); Francis M. (married Alice **Fisher**, daughter of John **Fisher**).  p. 484

Jacob **Fouts**, born North Carolina 1788 to Jacob **Fouts**; died October 1874; married Eleanor **Dougan** (born North Carolina 1790; died 17 November 1858); children: Dougan; Rebecca; Jacob; William; Sarah; Thomas; Elizabeth J.; Levi; Lewis; Francis C.; Malcom C.; to Fulton County from Indiana ca 1831.  p. 487

Allen H. **Harrod**, born Scott County, Indiana 4 January 1831 to William (born Louisville, Kentucky; died 28 January 1835) and Elizabeth (**New**) (born North Carolina 6 December 1876 to Jethro **New**) **Herrod**; married Ailcy **Cox** (born Canton, Illinois 7 December 1830 to James **Cox** of Fulton County) 1850; 5 children; married Eliza J. **Babbitt** (daughter of James **Babbitt**) 16 March 1876; daughter: Silva New (born 10 September 1877); cousin: John C. **New** (of Indianapolis); to Illinois 1848.  p. 889

Sarah (**Johnson**) **Hinds**, born Clark County, Indiana to Henry (born Virginia; died 6 July 1869) and Martha (**Steel**) (died 4 March 1859) **Johnson**); married Jacob **Hinds** (born 25 May 1817) Canton Township, Fulton County 1840; children: John; Frank; Alice; Em.  p. 489

A.L. **Hoover**, born Wayne County, Indiana 1843 to John **Hoover**; married Della J. **Knotts** (daughter of N.C. **Knotts** of Pennsylvania) Baltimore, Michigan; 1 child; to Ann Arbor, Michigan; to Eaton, Indiana; to Vermont, Fulton County.  p. 920

David **Johnson**, born Clark County, Indiana 26 March 1825 to Richard M. and Catherine (**Fouts**) **Johnson**; married Charlotte **Walling** (born Ohio to Louis and Cynthia (**Peirce**) **Walling**) 17 June 1849; children: Cynthia Ellen (born 8 March 1854; married Joseph **DeArmand**); Charles H. (born 5 November 1855;

died 15 January 1879); George Delmer (born 30 January 1859); Sarah Annas (born 3 February 1862); Luella (born 27 November 1868); to Fulton County 1827. pp. 490-91

Lemuel **Johnson**, born Indiana 1 March 1823 to Richard M. and Catherine (**Fouts**) **Johnson**; married Margaret **Weller** 16 March 1857; children: Richard M. (born 1 December 1857); Douglas (born 1 September 1865); to Fulton County 1827. p. 491

Richard M. **Johnson**, born Randolph County, North Carolina 8 Aug 1797 to Josiah and Sarah (**Wright**) **Johnson**; died 8 February 1879; married Catharine **Fouts** (daughter of David (died age 91) and Mary (died age 84) **Fouts**); children: Sarah (born Indiana 21 November 1820); Lemuel; David (born Indiana 16 March 1825); Emsley (born Fulton County 22 December 1829); Mary Ann (born Fulton County 7 September 1831; died 3 December 3, 1872); Martha (born Fulton County 22 February 1833); Elisha and Elijah (born Fulton County 28 May 1836); Julia Ann (born Fulton County 28 May 1840; married William **Bocock**); to Fulton County 1827. p. 491

Allen **Keefauver**, born Washington County Indiana, 23 March 1853 to John and Elizabeth (**Young**) **Keefauver**; married Mary **Suydam** 16 February 1875; daughter: Jessie (born 16 November 1875); to Joshua Township, Fulton County 1855. p. 634

Isaac **Lamb**, born Floyd County, Indiana 20 March 1818 to Benjamin and Nancy **Lamb** of North Carolina; married 20 February 1836; 7 sons; 4 daughters; to Fulton County 1841. p. 635

David **McNeill**, born New Hampshire; died 30 September 1867; married Mary **Cole** 19 December 1819; 1 child; married Sarah (**Smith**) **Huff** 31 March 1841; brother: Parker **McNeill**; to New York; to Indiana 1820; to Fulton County 1827. pp. 754-55

Joseph **Mayall**, born Indiana 12 October 1834 to James and Eliza (**Shields**) **Mayall**; married Alla **Doisey** (born Virginia ca 1843) 29 September 1864; children: Willard L.; Dessa S.; Affa V.; Arta M.; Emanuel R.; Emues C.; Sada E.; Lima, deceased; to Illinois 1862. p. 859

W.H. **Nance**, born Floyd County, Indiana 24 December 1814 to William (born Virginia; died Adams County, Illinois, age 68, married Rockingham County, North Carolina; to Kentucky; to Adams County Illinois, 1836) and Nancy (**Smith**) (died age 82) **Nance**; married Susan **Lane** (daughter of Joab and Hannah **Lane**) 14 April 1836; 1 daughter; to St. Louis, Missouri 1848; to Vermont, Fulton County 1849. p. 932

William **Norton**, born South Bend, St. Joseph County, Indiana 24 Aug 1844 to George C. (born New York) and Tamar (**Stockdale**) (born England) **Norton**; married 16 January 1873; children: Archilli C. (born 20 November 1873); George H. (born 16 November 1875; one other (born 30 June 1878); to Fulton County 1864. p. 690

Thomas **Nott**, born Roxbury, Washington County Ohio, 17 Feb 1809 to Samuel (of New Hampshire) and Amy **Van Clief** (born New Jersey to Peter **Van**

**Clief**) married Celesta **Kent** (daughter of Jabe and Catharine (**Johnson**) **Kent**) Ohio 13 March 1828; son: Stephen H. (born Vermillion County, Indiana 10 May 1840); grandfather: Thomas **Nott** (born England); to Indiana; to Fulton County 1841. p. 834

Joseph **Ogden**, born Marietta, Ohio 1796 to John and Mary (**Hinich**) **Ogden** (born Pennsylvania); married Mary **Watkins** (born Green County, Kentucky 9 January 1818); 8 children; to Fulton County 1833; to Indiana 1834; to Fulton County 1845. p. 737

Richard **Osborn**, to Fulton County from Indiana 1836. p. 765

Thomas **Pool**, born La Porte County, Indiana 31 March 1833 to John and Elizabeth (**Fulton**) **Pool**; married Chartlotte **Leeper**, Fairview Township, Fulton County 16 January 1857; 7 children, 1 deceased; brother: Joseph; brother-in-law: John **Leeper**; to Montgomery County, Indiana 1837; to Wayne County, Indiana 1840; to Fulton County 1843. p. 893

John **Prickett**, born Indiana 7 September 1838 to Isaiah (born Ohio) and Eliza P. (born Ohio) **Prickett**); married Margaret **Lenhart** Illinois 15 February 1866; children: Della E.; Mary J.; J.H.; William F.; Hattie M.; to Fulton County 1852. p. 808

William **Provine**, born Clark County, Indiana to William (born Tennessee) and Mary (**Buchanan**) **Provine**; married Pauline **Scott** (daughter of Martin **Scott** of Kentucky) 1838; 11 children, 4 deceased; to Macomb, Illinois 1836; to Vermont, Fulton County 1847; to Abington, Illinois; to Vermont, Fulton County; to Tennessee, Illinois 1858; to Bushnell, Illinois; to Vermont, Fulton County. p. 926

George C. **Putman**, born Indiana 3 October 1814 to Reading and Stacy (**Combs**) **Putman**; married Charlotte **Crosthwait** 1834; children: 5 boys; 2 girls; 3 boys deceased; to Fulton County 1821. p. 877

Jonas **Rawalt**, born Northumberland County, Pennsylvania to John **Rawalt** (born Pennsylvania); married ---- (died 27 October 1878) Clark County, Indiana 1825; children: John, deceased; Enoch; Henry, deceased; Seth, deceased; James; Mary (married William M. **Ganson**); Benjamin; Elizabeth (married Mr. **Winship**); Jonas R.; to Fulton County 1829. p. 845

George W. **Smith**, born Indiana 1843 to Jacob (died 1872) and Sarah (**Lells**) (died 1857-58) **Smith**; 5 brothers; to Fulton County 1848. p. 742

Peter S. **Tarter**, Sr., born Washington County, Indiana 18 December 1827 to Frederick M. (born Richmond, Virginia 22 January 1800) **Tarter**; brother: Enos; grandfather: Peter; to Clay County, Illinois 1829; to Fulton County 1834. p. 673

Henry **Walker**, born New York City; married Mary **Hines** La Porte, Indiana; children: Emily, deceased; Jefferson, deceased; Job; Alfred, deceased; Harriet, deceased; Leonidas, deceased; Meredith; Ann; Arthur; to Canton, Fulton County 1834. p. 578

Samuel **Warner**, born Ohio; married Sarah **Carter** Indiana; children: George (born Harrison County, Ohio 1850; married Lucinda **LeMasters** 1871);

children: Lillie V.; David; Ira; 4 others; to Indiana; to Harrison County Ohio; to Fulton County 1858.   p. 757

Jacob R. **Welch**, born Clay County, Indiana 27 June 1835 to James **Welch** (born Kentucky; died Kentucky 1835); married Almeda **Baughman** (daughter of Gabriel **Baughman**) 16 October 1862; children: Sarah Melinda, deceased; 5 sons; 2 other daughters; to Kentucky; to Illinois 1852.   p. 709

Thomas W. **Wilson**, born Harrison County, Indiana 1835 to Joseph (born East Tennessee) and Margaret (**Armstrong**) or Mary M (**Rogers**) **Wilson**; married Martha A. **Deweese** Indiana; children: Sarah P.; Joseph W.; John W.; Mary S.; Margaret E.; Charles S.; Amos L.; DeLefayette; Nandora; Laura B.; Emmet C.; Lewie E.; Martha A.; Hays; Thomas; Gertrude; to Fulton County 1855.   p. 758

Lewis P. **Wright**, born Harrison County, Indiana 1844 to William (born Indiana) and Melinda (**Wiseman**) (born Virginia) **Wright**; married Harriet **Murray** (daughter of St. Clair **Murray**) 30 August 1866; children: Charley; John W.; Sarah; Elmer; Edmund; to Fulton County 1856.   p. 758

# INDEX

**339**

| | | | | | | |
|---|---|---|---|---|---|---|
| Adams | Mark N. | 259 | Akers | Arrena | 210 |
| | Mary | 60 | | Benjamin | 42 |
| | Mary A. | 223 | | Carrie | 5 |
| | Milly | 173 | | John | 203 |
| | Milton Phillips | 125 | | Joseph | 201 |
| | Patrick | 125 | | Joshua | 38 |
| | Ray(Mrs.) | 7 | | Lavina | 35 |
| | S.A. | 279 | | Martin | 37 |
| | Sarah Isabell | 210 | | Mary Ann | 47,195 |
| | Sarah R. | 176 | | Rebecca | 39 |
| | Simeon B. | 150 | | Sarah | 44 |
| | Susan | 46 | Akin | Mary Ann | 47 |
| | Susana | 224 | | William | 22 |
| | Wm. | 151 | Akkridge | Mary Ann | 196 |
| | William Camp. | 125 | Akles | Benjamin | 158 |
| | Wm. Henry | 177 | | John | 158 |
| | Winifred Brady | 310 | Albach | James R. | 57 |
| Adamsen | Elizabeth | 167 | Albachten | Hubert | 175 |
| Adamson | Ada C. | 326 | Albaugh | John | 174 |
| | Asenath | 169 | Albertson | Arthur A. | 222 |
| | David | 85 | | Clarisa A. | 208 |
| | John | 83,85 | | Nancy Janette | 211 |
| | John | 85 | | Phoebe | 111 |
| | Joseph | 85 | Albin | George | 98 |
| | Moses | 86 | | John | 99 |
| | Samuel | 166 | | Joseph | 97 |
| | Sarah | 203 | | Philip | 97 |
| Addington | Catharine Ann | 195 | Albright | ---- | 247 |
| | Elizabeth | 302 | Alcorn | Solomon | 181 |
| | Irene | 314 | Alden | Deborah | 25 |
| | William | 89 | | Whiting(Mrs.) | 8 |
| | Wils | 91 | Alderson | Samuel B. | 45 |
| Ade | George | 310 | Aldridge | Aaron | 160 |
| Adem | Augusta Lou. | 208 | | Christopher | 24 |
| Adkins | Donald Ray | 77 | Alexander | Elizabeth | 165 |
| | Elender | 22 | | Hulda W. | 306 |
| | Henry C. | 85 | | James | 19,21,82 |
| | Ida V. | 215 | | John | 121,126 |
| | Lucy | 77 | | Joseph | 59 |
| | Raymond | 77 | | Margaret | 37 |
| | Willis | 104,145 | | Nell G. Boruff | 310 |
| Adkinson | ---- | 183 | | R. | 88 |
| Adkinson | M. | 124 | | Rose | 328 |
| Adkison | David O. | 167 | | Samuel | 156 |
| | Lewis D. | 164 | | William | 126 |
| Admiah | Jesse | 148 | Alhert | Elizabeth | 196 |
| Admire | Jesse | 148 | Aliman | James | 162 |
| Adney | Mary | 333 | Allbach | James R. | 57 |
| Affleck | Vita S. | 8 | Allbaugh | Mary | 166 |
| Afflick | Charlotte | 41 | Allburn | John | 68 |
| Aken | Myron(Mrs.) | 3 | | Lucy P. | 68 |
| Aker | Robert | 165 | Allcorn | Henry | 160 |

| | | | | | | |
|---|---|---|---|---|---|---|
| Allebaugh | Noah S. | 165 | Alsmon | John | 49 |
| Allen | Alma | 243 | Alsop | George R. | 310 |
| | Amer | 81 | Alt | Christly | 150 |
| | Archebald | 107 | Alverd | Joseph | 165 |
| | Daniel C. | 208 | Alvord | George | 172 |
| | Hariet | 215 | Ambrose | George | 85 |
| | Henry B. | 215 | Amburs | William C. | 293 |
| | James | 85 | Ammon | George W. | 90 |
| | James M. | 90 | Ammons | Ida | 217 |
| | John | 18,85 | | Lula M. | 227 |
| | John P. | 38 | | Zella F. | 215 |
| | Joseph | 24,87,287 | Anderson | Alexander | 212 |
| | Joshua | 114 | | Benjamin | 43 |
| | Josiah G. | 310 | | Edward E. | 222 |
| | Lousa | 216 | | Eliza | 203 |
| | Nellie | 240,243 | | Ellen | 182 |
| | Olive | 212 | | Emeline | 34 |
| | Rebecca | 54 | | Emil V. | 310 |
| | Samuel | 26,55 | | Frances O. | 219 |
| | Sanders | 90 | | George | 190 |
| | Sarah | 34 | | George, Jr. | 197 |
| | Saunders | 88 | | George A. | 196 |
| | Thomas | 34 | | George W. | 226 |
| | Wesley | 81,90 | | Graham | 22 |
| | William | 93,188 | | Harriet | 199 |
| Alley | Ann | 51 | | Henry T. | 227 |
| | Asby Christan | 52 | | Isaac | 85,88 |
| | David | 61 | | James | 18,21,116,223 |
| | Elihu | 53 | | James K. | 51 |
| | Fanna | 56 | | Joseph R. | 85 |
| | Hosea | 60 | | Julia A. | 199 |
| | James | 51 | | Lizzie | 225 |
| | Jane | 59 | | Lura Grims | 265 |
| | Joycey | 62 | | Marcey | 32 |
| | Minor | 170 | | Mary | 217 |
| | Rachel | 49 | | Mary M. | 207 |
| | Samuel | 61 | | Nancy P. | 33 |
| | Wesley | 88 | | Sarah Ann | 206 |
| Allfree | E.(Mrs.) | 7 | | Syntha J. | 211 |
| Allison | Caroline | 276 | | Tressie | 118 |
| | Chas. R. | 276 | | William | 42,170,196,202 |
| | David | 151 | Anderton | Delight T. | 10 |
| | Elizabeth | 45 | Andrew | Jesse C. | 310 |
| | Susannah | 55 | | Sarah | 54 |
| Allman | Mathew | 145 | | Thomas M. | 310 |
| Allsman | John | 49 | | Winnie J. | 201 |
| Allsmon | William | 57 | Andrews | Richard D. | 50 |
| Alman | Harris | 115,142 | Angel | John | 43 |
| Almandinger | Adam | 208 | | Samuel | 35 |
| Almond | Harris | 142 | Aninger | Henry | 47 |
| | Mathew | 145 | Annis | Bertha | 63 |
| Alphen | Wm. | 155 | | Charles | 63 |

| | | | | | |
|---|---|---|---|---|---|
| Annis | Cora | 207 | Argo | Joseph | 196 |
| | Effa B. Beasley | 67 | Armentrout | Catharine | 174 |
| | Everett A. | 63 | | Margaret | 170 |
| | G. | 64 | | Sarah | 169 |
| | Idie | 64 | Armer | Louesa C. | 198 |
| | | | Armfield | John D. | 274 |
| | | | | Ruth S. | 275 |
| | | | | Viena Kyger | 276 |
| | | | Armstrong | Absolem | 58 |
| | | | | Adell Jane | 47 |
| | | | | B.H. | 214 |
| | | | | Eliza | 207 |
| | | | | Emma | 3 |
| | | | | Francis | 103 |
| | | | | George | 42,101,103,104, 105,109 |
| | | | | George W. | 211 |
| | | | | Harriet M. | 1 |
| | | | | Idora | 221 |
| | | | | John | 24,221 |
| | | | | John L. | 210 |
| | | | | Jonathan E. | 58 |
| | | | | Julia Ann | 176 |
| | | | | Margaret | 337 |
| | | | | Mary Ann | 47 |
| | | | | Russell | 118 |
| | | | | Sylvester | 118 |
| Applegate | ---- | 30 | | Tabitha | 24 |
| | Deric | 107 | | William | 44 |
| | Derick | 99 | Arnd | Henry | 225 |
| | Edward | 40 | Arnes | Daniel | 212 |
| | Hesekiah | 27,28 | Arnett | Thomas | 49 |
| | Hesi. | 29 | Arnold | Abbigail | 57 |
| | Mary | 33 | | Andrew J. | 189 |
| | Nathanel | 99 | | Elisabeth | 265 |
| | Nathanul | 96 | | Enoch | 146 |
| | Nelly | 27,30 | | Eph. | 150 |
| | Wm. | 141 | | Fannie | 309 |
| Appleton | Amos R. | 171 | | Henry | 126 |
| | Wm. | 141,144 | | Jeremiah | 93 |
| Applgate | Nathaniel | 104 | | John | 189 |
| Arbuckle | Lloyd | 310 | | Maria | 259 |
| Arbuthnot | Sarah Milburn | 80 | | Marie | 260 |
| | John | 80 | | Mary | 47 |
| | Nancy | 79 | | Minnie | 6 |
| | Nicholas | 207 | | Richard | 103,181 |
| | Polly | 18 | | Sarah H. | 189 |
| | Sarah B. | 226 | | Wm. | 152 |
| | Thomas | 80 | Arterbury | Daniel | 100 |
| Archibald | Josephine | 213 | Arthur | Francis | 226 |
| | Sarah H.F. | 215 | Arthurholtz | David | 89 |
| Archor | Daniel | 83 | Artman | E.C., Jr. | 300 |

| | | | | | | |
|---|---|---|---|---|---|---|
| Artman | Elmer Carol | 300 | Audl | Samuel R. | 232 |
| | James Alex. | 300 | Aught | Christly | 150 |
| Ash | Isaac | 97,103 | Auld | Samuel R. | 232 |
| | Joseph B. | 298 | Aulphen | Wm. | 155 |
| | Kesia | 176 | Ausem | William | 202 |
| | Leon | 298,300 | Ausman | Noah | 176 |
| | Mary J. | 300 | Austen | Jane | 59 |
| Ashbrook | Absalom C. | 42 | Austin | David | 101,103 |
| Ashby | ---- | 183 | | Delila | 213 |
| | Chain Miles | 42 | | Ennis R. | 310 |
| | Earl | 77 | | Joseph | 197 |
| | Joseph A. | 44 | | Kisiah | 51 |
| | Ronald Dean | 77 | | Nancy | 166 |
| | Tate | 67 | | Olive | 219 |
| | Tommie | 77 | | Orlando | 216 |
| | W. Hurley | 310 | Avault | Jacob | 203 |
| Ashcraft | Alice | 300 | Averman | Silas | 93 |
| | Clarence C. | 298,299,300 | Avery | Clarry J. | 211 |
| | James J. | 300 | | Elijah | 142 |
| Ashley | Adda | 328 | | George | 151 |
| | Genetta | 220 | | Lottie | 220 |
| | Levi | 222 | Avey | George | 151 |
| | Sarah E. | 210 | Awald | Conrad | 211 |
| Ashton | Isaac S. | 36 | | Frederick | 214 |
| Askins | Thos. | 156 | | Peter | 205 |
| Askridge | Okeley | 198 | | Philip | 199,215 |
| Askrien | David | 100 | | Rhoda | 215 |
| Aston | Anina | 41 | Awalt | Phillip | 206 |
| | Elizabeth | 45 | Ax | Blanche Holt | 263 |
| | Jesse | 37 | Axel | Smalwood | 165 |
| | Richard | 23,25 | Axt | Bertha K. | 9 |
| Astren | Thos. | 156 | Axtell | Harry A. | 310 |
| Athen | Wm. W. | 87 | Aydelott | Benjamin | 98,104 |
| Atherton | Benjamin | 160 | | John | 104 |
| | Honour | 54 | Aydelotte | Cynthia A. | 65 |
| | John W. | 310 | | James R. | 65 |
| Athon | Electious | 47 | | N.A. | 65 |
| Atkins | Charles B. | 227 | | S.P. | 65 |
| | Charlotte | 37 | | Walter R. | 65 |
| | Gideon | 45 | Aydolett | Benjamin | 109 |
| | Henry | 33,103 | | John | 107 |
| | Joseph | 41 | Ayeres | James | 97 |
| | Mary | 35 | Ayers | Anna L. | 65 |
| | Sarah | 320 | | Clarence | 67 |
| | William B. | 219 | | David E. | 65 |
| | Willis | 102,108,145 | | Della A. | 65 |
| Atkinson | Cephas | 83 | | Loda | 67 |
| | Charles | 82,83 | | Rennie L. | 227 |
| | Eli | 55 | | William | 199 |
| Atwater | Carleton W. | 310 | Ayres | Frederic Murray | 310 |
| Atwood | James | 126 | | Jackson | 171 |
| | Thomas | 126 | | S.D. | 86 |

**344**

| Surname | Given name | Page |
|---|---|---|
| Baker | George H. | 224 |
| | George W. | 203 |
| | Henry | 300 |
| | James | 38 |
| | James H. | 203 |
| | John | 204 |
| | Joseph | 78 |
| | Margaret A. | 205 |
| | Marion | 7 |
| | Martha J. | 171 |
| | Nancy T. | 300 |
| | Samuel | 222 |
| | Sarah H. | 73 |
| | Susannah | 41 |
| | Thaddeus R. | 310 |
| | Walter C. | 209 |
| | William | 73 |
| Baldwin | A.M. | 92 |
| | Abira | 85 |
| | Alfred H. | 229 |
| | Charles | 91 |
| | Clarinda | 56 |
| | D.C. | 89 |
| | David | 83,124 |
| | David H. | 35 |
| | Dillon | 85 |
| | Ebenezer | 34 |
| | Elias | 86,91,148 |
| | Elizabeth | 211 |
| | H. | 85 |
| | I. | 82 |
| | Isaac | 82 |
| | James | 205 |
| | James A. | 84 |
| | John | 85,91 |
| | John S. | 180 |
| | Joseph W. | 84,91 |
| | L.D. | 91 |
| | Lindsey | 85 |
| | Maggie | 240 |
| | Martha | 204 |
| | Monroe | 216 |
| | Moses | 89 |
| | Richa | 84 |
| | Rosa L. | 223 |
| | Sarah E. | 215 |
| | Thomas | 84,85,91 |
| | Thornburgh | 177 |
| | Warren | 158 |
| | William | 124,173 |
| | Zeri M. | 176 |
| Bales | Sally | 115 |
| Baley | Perry | 126 |
| | William | 84 |
| Ball | Banabus | 149 |
| | Barney | 149 |
| | Bertha C. | 310 |
| | Elizabeth B. | 310 |
| | George A. | 310 |
| | Walter J. | 310 |
| | Willis | 157 |
| Ballard | Bartholomew | 115 |
| | Betsy | 113 |
| | C. William | 310 |
| | Joab | 126 |
| | Joe G. | 298,300 |
| | Louisa | 115 |
| | RichH. | 300 |
| | Samuel | 115 |
| | Wm. | 85 |
| Ballenger | Elijah | 225 |
| | Emma | 224 |
| | Evan | 147 |
| Ballinger | Cora | 228 |
| | Elizabeth | 169 |
| | Evan | 147 |
| | Isaac | 83 |
| | James | 83 |
| | John | 86 |
| | Joseph | 83 |
| | Phoebe | 169 |
| | Samuel | 148 |
| | Minna | 210 |
| Ballnow | John | 231 |
| Balthus | Mary | 167 |
| Baltimore | George | 126 |
| Baly | Nancy | 166 |
| Baming | William | 50 |
| Banes | John A. | 87 |
| Banion | Chas. | 161 |
| Banks | Hiram | 57 |
| | John L. | 123 |
| | Noble | 152 |
| | Wm. | 150 |
| Banning | Corinna | 8 |
| | Florida | 7 |
| Banta | Dan A. | 92 |
| | David | 126 |
| | Josephine | 204 |
| | Mary | 305 |
| | John H. | 215 |
| Banty | John | 46 |
| Baptiste | ---- | 65 |
| Barber | A.L. | 65 |

| | | | | | | |
|---|---|---|---|---|---|---|
| Barteau | Alice | 326 | Bassett | Nathanal | 276 |
| Bartelow | Cornelius | 56 | | Orris Welman | 276 |
| | Malinda | 59 | | Rosa | 241 |
| Bartels | Anna | 71 | | Walter Scott | 276 |
| Bartholomew | Charles | 221 | Bastion | Henry | 39 |
| | Henry S.K. | 311 | | Mariah | 58 |
| | Joseph | 17,24 | Baston | Maria | 58 |
| | Warner | 246 | Batchelder | Frank M. | 209 |
| Bartles | E.M. | 301 | Bateman | Elizabeth | 43 |
| | Frank | 301 | Bates | David | 141 |
| Bartlett | Charles H. | 311 | | Esther F. | 311 |
| | Martha | 167 | | Frank G. | 311 |
| Bartlingck | Margaret | 327 | | Harvey | 140 |
| Bartlow | Cornelius | 56 | | Hervey | 140 |
| | Isabella | 55 | | HowH. | 311 |
| | Mahalla | 52 | | James | 47 |
| | Malinda | 59 | | Mabel C. | 10 |
| Bartmass | M.W.(Mrs.) | 8 | | Martin | 84 |
| Bartness | M.W.(Mrs.) | 15 | Batey | Westley | 162 |
| Barton | Charles | 199 | Batkin | Hamilton | 88 |
| | Francis | 198 | Batson | Almira F. | 214 |
| | James | 99,103 | | Julia Ann A. | 207 |
| | James M. | 311 | | Nathaniel B. | 207 |
| | Lydie E. | 197,223 | Batten | August | 224 |
| | Sina Jane | 275 | Battles | John | 179 |
| | William | 274 | Battram | L.F. | 70 |
| Barwick | Elijah | 56 | | Louis F. | 70 |
| | Neoma | 57 | | Sarah Luhring | 70 |
| | Seth E. | 60 | Batty | Bernard | 311 |
| Bascom | Esther Ann | 196 | | Mahlon | 159 |
| | Jonathan | 201 | Baty | Mahlon | 159 |
| Bascome | Isaac | 195 | Baudendistel | William V. | 311 |
| | Mary E. | 196 | Bauer | Blanche | 10 |
| | Sylvester | 198 | | Caroline | 301 |
| Bascum | Madora A. | 225 | | Georgia | 10 |
| Baseney | John | 219 | Baughman | Almeda | 337 |
| Bash | Chas.(Mrs.) | 3 | | Ebenezer | 200 |
| | John | 82 | | Gabriel | 337 |
| | Simon | 82 | | Harriet | 202 |
| Basney | Harretta | 225 | | Jacob | 210 |
| Bassett | Charles H. | 276 | | Mary | 198 |
| | Chas. Hall | 276 | Baum | William | 311 |
| | Elizabeth D. | 276 | Bauman | Charlotte | 333 |
| | Gertrude | 276 | Baumgardt | Henry | 217 |
| | Grace C. | 276 | Baxley | Hannah | 116 |
| | Harry H. | 276 | Baxter | A.M.(Mrs.) | 5 |
| | Leora T. | 276 | | Allen | 57 |
| | Leora Temper. | 276 | | Arthur R. | 311 |
| | Lewis Watson | 276 | | James | 232 |
| | Mary A. | 276 | | Mary Alice J. | 311 |
| | Mary Ann K. | 276 | | Matilda | 52 |
| | Mary Kyger | 276 | | Perthany | 40 |

| | | |
|---|---|---|
| Baxter | Thomas | 90 |
| Bay | John | 166 |
| | Wm. | 141 |
| Bayles | Eden | 115 |
| Bayless | Abijah | 98,106 |
| | Albert | 193 |
| Bayley | John | 109 |
| Baylor | Isaac | 159 |
| | Walker K. | 96 |
| Baysley | John | 104 |
| Bazhaw | Frank | 238 |
| | Willie | 238 |
| | Willie | 238 |
| Bean | Robert | 176 |
| | Samuel O. | 212 |
| Beane | Lewis Evans | 175 |
| | Maria Louisa | 176 |
| Bear | Barbara | 167 |
| | George Howard | 301 |
| | Oliver F. | 301 |
| | William | 165 |
| Bear Robe | Clyde | 243 |
| Beard | Agnes M. | 221 |
| | Charles A. | 311 |
| | George | 121 |
| | James | 169 |
| | Mary Ritter | 311 |
| | Peter | 101,109 |
| | Samul | 103 |

| | | |
|---|---|---|
| Beard | Thomas | 97 |
| Beardlsey | D.D. | 246 |
| | Charles S. | 311 |
| | D.D. | 246 |
| | Helen M.B. | 311 |
| Bearnt | Augusta | 227 |
| Bears | Elizabeth | 171 |
| Bearss | Esther | 171 |
| Beatman | John | 88 |
| Beattie | Polly | 115 |
| Beatty | Carrie | 207 |
| | Edna | 199 |
| | James Edgar | 77 |
| | Lora Princess | 77 |
| | Nacy Ella | 221 |
| | Oliver H.P. | 201 |
| | Rachel | 216 |
| | William R. | 207 |
| Beaty | ----(Rev.) | 276 |
| | Joshua | 223 |
| | Robert | 87 |
| | Samuel | 86,167 |
| Beaver | Addie | 241 |
| | Catharine | 177 |
| | Harriet D. | 173 |
| | William | 153 |
| Bechtel | Jacob | 89 |
| Bechtol | Mabel Ethel | 8 |
| | Samuel A. | 215 |
| Beck | ---- | 183 |
| | Catherine A. | 180 |
| | Charles H. | 311 |
| | Clara | 173 |
| | Earl | 311 |
| | Elizabeth | 181 |
| | George | 168,185 |
| | Jacob | 126 |
| Becker | Adeline C. | 9 |
| | Gladys C. | 10 |
| Beckford | Lewis C. | 82 |
| | Thomas | 82,85 |
| Beckner | James F. | 171 |
| | William A. | 174 |
| Bede | Joshua | 216 |
| Bedee | Joshua | 213 |
| Bedleicome | Nathan | 39 |
| Bedlicome | Nathan | 39 |
| Bedsaul | Isaac | 246 |
| Bee | A.W. | 183 |
| Beebe | David | 196 |
| Beece | Ewan | 90 |
| Beech | Walter | 274 |

| | | | | | | |
|---|---|---|---|---|---|---|
| Benner | Samuel | 172 | Bernethy | Lon E. | 214 |
| | Susan | 173 | Berry | Adeline | 166 |
| | Washington | 174 | | Benjamin F. | 41 |
| | Wesley | 176 | | C. M.(Mrs.) | 311 |
| Bennet | Jane | 51 | | Caroline | 173 |
| | William | 100 | | Emma C. | 220 |
| Bennett | Arthur M. | 209 | | Irene Wasson | 311 |
| | Elisha | 124 | | John | 18 |
| | Elmira S. | 206 | | Lucinda | 111 |
| | Hannah | 215 | | Lucy | 302 |
| | Harry W. | 311 | | Miles | 110 |
| | Jefferson | 240 | | Richard | 127,143 |
| | Jesse | 51 | | Sarah Jane | 208 |
| | John | 155 | | Sindarilla | 218 |
| | Lidia E. | 211 | | William | 231 |
| | Lorenzo D. | 169 | | William B. | 111 |
| | Loretta | 218 | | William E. | 218 |
| | Nancy J. | 201 | | William J. | 211 |
| | Noah | 224 | Bershear | Meraday | 105 |
| | Orlando | 191 | Bertenshaw | John | 57 |
| | Orlando L. | 191 | Bertram | Ed. L. | 74 |
| | Rosa | 2 | | Edward | 74 |
| | Theadore R. | 209 | | Edward L. | 74 |
| | Wm. | 104,246 | | Ella | 74 |
| Benninghoff | Ellen M. | 10 | | Ella May | 74 |
| Benoit | ----(Rev.) | 164 | | Elmer E. | 74 |
| Benoy | F.T.(Mrs.) | 2 | | Emma | 74 |
| | Grace | 6 | | Minnie | 74 |
| Bensenal | Sally | 117 | | William | 74 |
| Benson | Elizabeth | 113,208 | Bertsch | Harry D. | 311 |
| | G.E.(Mrs.) | 2 | Berust | John | 102 |
| | Isaac | 89 | Beshares | Thomas | 97 |
| | Robert | 42 | Besheres | Meristeth | 97 |
| Bent | George | 245 | Beshore | Peter | 87 |
| Bentenshaw | John | 57 | Besse | James | 34 |
| Bentley | Abel | 97 | Beswick | Philip | 105 |
| | Able | 105 | Betts | Isaac J. | 301 |
| | George | 95,105 | | Isaac W. | 301 |
| | Right | 106 | | Mary | 43 |
| | William | 3 | Betzel | Barbara | 168 |
| Bently | Wright | 99 | Beurkett | Jesse | 150 |
| Benton | Alva | 59 | Bevard | David | 87 |
| | David | 54,62 | | Jonathan | 88 |
| Berchel | Jane | 169 | | Willard | 81 |
| Berdine | George M. | 212 | | Wm. | 87 |
| Berg | Laura | 118 | Bevelhymer | Nancy Jane | 219 |
| Bergel | Jane | 212 | Bevialhimer | Samuel | 212 |
| Bergman | Lydia | 123 | Bevilhymer | John W. | 204 |
| Berk | Harrison | 89 | Bevis | Julia Ann | 170 |
| Berkey | Jonas | 293 | Biarly | Christian | 143 |
| Berkshire | Rebecca | 42 | Bickel | Addam | 217 |
| Bernard | John H. | 200,220 | | Charles A. | 301 |

| | | | | | | |
|---|---|---|---|---|---|---|
| Bickel | Eliza J. | 208 | Bissel | Anthony | 51 |
| | Julia | 209 | Bissonette | Frank | 242 |
| | Letitia | 220 | | Jackson | 242 |
| | Loutetia | 228 | | Jennie | 243 |
| | Phillip | 301 | | Lillie | 242 |
| | William | 217 | | Mattie | 240 |
| Bickell | Reece | 175 | | Theresa | 242 |
| Bickle | Malinda | 217 | Bitters | Amelia | 228 |
| | Mary B. | 216 | Bix | John | 86 |
| Biddle | Anna | 7 | Bixby | Chas. W.(Mrs.) | 2 |
| | Ward G. | 311 | Black | Amon W. | 87 |
| Biewand | C.N.(Mrs.) | 3 | | Glenn A. | 311 |
| Bigger | James | 21 | | Jacob G. | 195 |
| Biggs | Daniel S. | 208 | | Jane | 35 |
| | Gincy | 27 | | Lovina C. | 218 |
| | Jincy | 31 | | Margaret | 36 |
| | Robert | 96,99,104,108 | | Mark | 240 |
| | Sarah | 169 | | Mary | 166 |
| | Susannah | 34 | | Samuel I. | 108 |
| Bigler | John | 209 | | Samuel J. | 100 |
| Bilby | Elizabeth | 59 | | Samuel V. | 213 |
| Bill | Naomi A. | 14 | | Samul | 100 |
| Billings | George | 247 | | Thomas H. | 60 |
| Bills | Elias | 165 | | William | 45,87 |
| | Polly | 56 | Black Eyes | Nancy | 242 |
| Binfor | Martha Hill | 252 | Blackburn | Absolem H. | 55 |
| Binford | Florence C. | 311 | | Blanche | 8 |
| | Frank L. | 311 | | Catharine | 55 |
| | Hannah | 255 | | Drusilla | 59 |
| | James | 255 | | Helen | 8 |
| | John Clark | 311 | | James | 52 |
| | Joshua | 255 | | John | 141 |
| | Martha Hill | 252 | | Julius | 156 |
| | Mary Ann | 252 | | Thomas | 165 |
| Binger | Mathew | 222 | Blackledge | Edmund | 150 |
| Birch | Erastus M. | 204 | | George | 155 |
| Bird | Benjamin | 82,83 | | Harvey | 54 |
| | Edward | 87 | | Irene | 329 |
| | James | 83,102,104,109 | Bladen | Caroline | 202 |
| | James, Sr. | 82 | Blades | Mary | 50 |
| | Mason | 102,107 | | Matilda | 58 |
| | Patriach | 104 | Blaekly | Polly | 115 |
| | Patric | 109 | Blair | Alexander | 102,107 |
| | Patrick | 102 | | Allexander | 104 |
| Birdsall | Ellen | 174 | | Cornelius L. | 39 |
| Birge | Edward Bailey | 311 | | Geo. | 121 |
| Bish | A. | 91 | | George W. | 311 |
| | Abraham | 89 | | James H. | 332 |
| Bishop | B.W. | 247 | | John P. | 299 |
| | Jno. S. | 168 | | Sally | 46 |
| | Lewis | 127 | | Samuel | 49 |
| | Martha C. | 311 | Blaisdel | Chas.(Mrs.) | 1 |

351

| | | | | | | |
|---|---|---|---|---|---|---|
| Blake | Abigail | 170 | Blythe | Eliza E. | 198 |
| | Alex | 170 | Boader | Isaac | 88 |
| | Hugh | 151 | Board | Martha | 306 |
| | James | 162 | Boarders | ----(Mrs.) | 285 |
| | John | 162 | | Jacob | 287 |
| | May | 318 | | Lavina | 287 |
| | Orris | 175 | Bobain | Joseph | 165 |
| Blakely | America | 115 | Boblett | L.L. | 118,120 |
| Blankenship | George W. | 127 | Bock | William H. | 312 |
| Blankingshipp | Ann | 172 | Bockoven | N. | 124 |
| Blase | ---- | 183 | Bockover | John W. | 198 |
| Blazer | David | 56 | Bocock | Alfred | 81 |
| | George | 124 | | Julia Ann | 335 |
| | Polly | 124 | | William | 335 |
| Blazier | David | 56 | Bodkin | Alexander | 153 |
| Bledsoe | Bessie E. | 6 | Bodle | Thomas | 86 |
| Blesah | Elizabeth | 186 | Bogard | James | 101,108 |
| | John | 186 | Bogardus | Frank Smith | 312 |
| | William | 186 | Bogart | James E. | 226 |
| Blessing | Geraldine W. | 311 | Bogarth | Jacob | 194 |
| Blew | Juliann | 195 | Bogner | Stella M. Mc. | 312 |
| | Mary Ann | 59 | Bogue | B. | 93 |
| | Sarah | 196 | | Jesse | 86,93 |
| Blind | Jacob | 110 | Bohanon | Alexander | 97 |
| Bline | Jacob | 102 | Bohn | Arthur | 312 |
| | Michael | 103 | | John | 174 |
| Blinn | Samuel | 86 | | W.A.(Mrs.) | 2 |
| Blish | Barbara | 191 | Bohne | Gertrude | 9 |
| Bliss | Flora | 123 | Boilean | Elijah C. | 38 |
| | Freddie R. | 123 | Bolan | Ester | 173 |
| | J.E. | 123 | Boland | Joel | 150 |
| | Mary | 202 | Bolander | John | 150 |
| | Nancy | 42 | Boldorson | Andrew | 19 |
| | Noxie | 306 | | Betsy | 19 |
| Block | John | 245 | | Daniel | 19 |
| Blockson | Samuel | 220 | | David | 19 |
| Blondoit | Clara | 10 | | Eve | 19 |
| Blonham | Ephraim | 90 | | Fany | 19 |
| Blood | Ida | 318 | | Henry | 19 |
| Bloom | David | 24 | | John | 19 |
| | Frederick | 99,107 | | Lany | 19 |
| | Peter | 20 | | Peter | 19 |
| Bloor | John | 35 | | Polly | 19 |
| Blue | Barnabas | 153 | | Sally | 19 |
| | Charles | 225 | | Thomas | 19 |
| | Isaiah | 82 | Boldwin | John H. | 22 |
| | Mary Ann | 59 | Bole | Wm. | 88 |
| | Membrance | 82 | Bolen | Sarah | 174 |
| Blunk | Mary | 33 | Boles | Celia | 206 |
| | Sanford M. | 312 | | Luella C. | 5 |
| Blystone | Morning | 6 | Boley | Isaac | 96,101 |
| Blythe | Benj. J. | 127,158 | Bolin | Samuel | 43 |

352

| Bowles | Cora Johnston | 312 | Boyer | Fredrick | 25 |
|---|---|---|---|---|---|
| Bowles | William | 156 | | John | 25 |
| Bowlin | Henry | 145 | | Maud | 322 |
| Bowlinder | John | 150 | Boyle | John | 219 |
| Bowling | Henry | 145 | Boyles | Charles | 43 |
| | Joel | 150 | | Isaac | 107 |
| Bowls | William | 156 | | Lydia | 41 |
| Bowman | Aaron | 20 | | Mary Matilla | 215 |
| | Catherine | 34 | | Widdie | 222 |
| | Christopher | 103,106 | Bozarth | Elizabeth Ann | 195 |
| | David C. | 71 | | Jacob | 208 |
| | Delila | 167 | Bracken | Leonidas L. | 312 |
| | Elisha | 33 | Brackenridge | Robert | 127 |
| | Eliza | 39 | Bradburn | Catharine | 58 |
| | Elizabeth | 43,268 | Bradbury | B.H. | 124 |
| | George | 86 | | John L. | 85 |
| | Hattie | 118 | | Robert B. | 312 |
| | Isaac | 42 | Braddle | Joseph | 190 |
| | Jane | 20 | Braden | Fannie Dumont | 312 |
| | Jane E. | 3 | Brader | Dolly P. | 227 |
| | John | 21,86,155,171 | Bradford | Casper | 90 |
| | Joseph | 23 | | Daniel | 81 |
| | Lane | 20 | | Feilding M. | 109 |
| | Leonard | 21 | | George | 25 |
| | Lewis S. | 312 | | George, Sr. | 88 |
| | Mabel C. | 71 | | Jesse | 91 |
| | Mary | 23 | | Joel Daniel | 88 |
| | Peter | 88 | | John | 84,91 |
| | Prudence L. | 5 | | Joseph | 88,91 |
| | Rachael | 172 | | Lewis C. | 84 |
| | Sarah | 20 | | Moses | 86 |
| | William | 23,24,118,166 | | Susannah | 17 |
| Bown | John | 60 | | William | 17 |
| Bowne | John | 60 | | Wm. R. | 88,90 |
| Bowsher | Delevan D. | 312 | Bradley | Arthur | 124 |
| Bowyer | Lewis F. | 174 | | Elizabeth | 226 |
| Boxell | John | 81,87 | | Henry | 141 |
| | John, Jr. | 88 | | Stephen | 165 |
| | Joseph | 81,88 | Bradly | Catharine | 197 |
| | R.B. | 88 | Bradshaw | Daniel | 187 |
| | Thomas | 88 | | Elizabeth | 39,187 |
| | William | 81,88 | | Elizia | 187 |
| Boy | Eli | 157 | | Flora Gros | 312 |
| Boyce | Wm. | 159 | | Mary | 187,320 |
| Boyd | George | 127 | | Nancy | 187 |
| | Georgiana | 4 | | Stephen | 187 |
| | James | 127 | | Thomas | 187 |
| | John | 127 | | William | 187 |
| | Mary Ellen | 307 | Brady | Arthur W. | 312 |
| | Rebecca | 222 | | Caroline H.M. | 312 |
| | Robert J. | 213 | | Elizabeth | 310 |
| Boyer | Christopher | 25 | | Henry | 162 |

| | | | | | | |
|---|---|---|---|---|---|---|
| Brady | John | 87,144,147 | Breeding | John | 107 |
| | Winifred | 310 | Breedlove | George | 42 |
| Braffet | James | 168 | | William B. | 42 |
| | John | 82 | Breen | Ellen C. | 169 |
| Braffett | Silas | 82 | | William B. | 312 |
| Bragg | Fanny | 176 | Brees | Samuel | 59 |
| Braman | James | 152 | Breese | Samuel | 59 |
| Brand | Sarah | 41 | Breeze | Robert, Jr. | 20 |
| Brandal | David | 199 | Breidenbach | Charles F. | 301 |
| | Solomon | 211 | | Edward H. | 301 |
| Brandall | John | 199 | | Mildred | 301 |
| Branden | Mary | 169 | Bremer | Louvisa | 203 |
| Brandenburg | Emma | 300 | Brengle | Fred E. | 312 |
| Brandle | Sarah Ann | 204 | Brennan | William A. | 312 |
| Brandon | Armstrong | 95,104,106 | Brenner | America | 187 |
| | Jesse | 98 | | Anna | 185,192 |
| | Jessee | 96,107 | | Charles | 185,192 |
| | Martin | 156 | | Emma | 192 |
| | Nancy Jane | 174 | | Jacob | 185,192 |
| | W.G. | 86 | | Lewis | 215 |
| Branerd | Laurea | 212 | Brent | Dorsan | 105 |
| Branham | Jane | 34 | | Lawson | 100 |
| Brannaman | Isaac P. | 173 | | William | 39 |
| Brannan | Grace | 8 | Brenton | A. | 186 |
| Brannen | Jeruse | 51 | | H. | 144 |
| Bransford | Edward | 51 | | Henrietta | 186 |
| Branson | Coomes | 84 | | Henry, Jr. | 142 |
| | George | 312 | | Henry T. | 186 |
| | Thomas | 84 | | Izora | 186 |
| Brasher | Anna E. | 301 | | Marion | 3 |
| | Gilbert W. | 298,301 | | Phoebe E. | 186 |
| | Robert | 301 | | Robt. | 142 |
| Brattain | Ceila | 225 | | William | 145,181 |
| Bratton | George | 20 | | Winfield S. | 186 |
| Brawley | John | 121 | Bresnahan | Marie P. | 14 |
| Bray | Catharine | 273 | Bretsford | Thomas | 86 |
| | Nancy | 113 | Bretten | Sarah | 167 |
| | Perry A. | 312 | Breunig | LeRoy C. | 312 |
| | Polly Ann | 114 | Brevet | Louis | 43 |
| | Sarah | 114 | Brevoort | Eliza H. Mc. | 312 |
| Brazelten | James | 144 | Brewer | ----(Rev.) | 268 |
| Brazier | Catharine | 221 | | Bincent | 332 |
| | Emma | 219 | | Cynthia E. | 200 |
| | Josephine | 213 | | Elizabeth | 172,332 |
| Brazill | James | 206 | | G.W. | 332 |
| Brazilton | Edward | 158 | | Hannah | 293 |
| Brazzel | Patrick | 227 | | Henry | 154 |
| Breckwinkle | Carrie | 77 | | John | 83 |
| | Frank | 77 | | Mary Ann | 332 |
| Bredin | Briant | 101 | | Robt. | 148 |
| Bredon | John | 102 | | Stephen, Sr. | 83 |
| Breeding | Emma | 217 | Brewington | R.F. | 118 |

355

| | | | | | | |
|---|---|---|---|---|---|---|
| Brewster | Edith M. | 4 | Broadhead | Sarah | 54 |
| | James B. | 312 | Broadrick | Geo. | 85 |
| Brian | A.H. | 142 | Broadstreet | Hattie J. | 228 |
| Briant | Huland | 157 | Broadwell | Jacob, Jr. | 49 |
| | Morgan | 142 | Brock | Christena | 45 |
| | Thos. | 156 | | Elias | 127 |
| Brickles | Jeremiah H. | 218 | | Elijah | 36 |
| Bridge | B. | 231 | | Martha | 127 |
| Bridgeman | Lydia P. | 207 | | William | 111 |
| Bridges | Jesse | 86 | Brockert | Ellen | 204 |
| | William | 38 | Brogan | Robert U. | 74 |
| Bridgewater | Elender | 33 | Broiles | Adam | 142 |
| Briedenbach | Charles | 298 | Broils | Adam | 103,142 |
| Briggerman | Mary | 188 | | Ephraim | 99,109 |
| Briggs | George | 127,198 | | George | 102 |
| | William A. | 312 | | Tobias | 98,108 |
| Bright | Frank (Mrs.) | 7 | Broken Rope | Samuel | 242 |
| | Jemima | 200 | Bromfield | Robert | 89 |
| | Mary E. | 172 | Brookbank | Emley | 51 |
| | Mary Eliza. | 196 | Brooke | Elizabeth | 211 |
| | Nancy | 195 | | Mary J. | 209 |
| Brightman | Emory | 91 | | Thomas J. | 212 |
| Briley | Samul | 99 | Brookman | Maggie | 219 |
| Brimelow | William | 312 | Brooks | George | 49 |
| Brimmer | Mary | 6 | | Homer | 161 |
| Brindley | Eliza | 45 | | Isaac | 36 |
| | Joseph | 33 | | Jenetta | 210 |
| Brinkley | Edith | 198 | | Jose | 84 |
| | Spence | 87,198 | | Larkin | 85 |
| Brinkly | Celia M. | 204 | | Lena M. | 303 |
| | Rhoda | 211 | | Lorabel W. | 312 |
| | Robert V. | 201 | | Susan | 312 |
| Brinkman | Georgiana | 199 | | Willis C. | 168 |
| Brinton | Henry | 144 | Brooner | Allen | 189 |
| | John | 149 | Broshears | Ira | 189,192 |
| | Robt. | 142 | | Ora | 192 |
| | Wm. | 145 | Brothers | Mary | 240 |
| Brion | Luke | 146 | Brouhard | Sarah | 54 |
| Briscoe | Dolly | 42 | Broune | Charles M. | 173 |
| Brison | Elizabeth | 57 | Brouyette | Annie M. | 300 |
| | Samuel | 141 | Brower | Elizabeth | 167 |
| | Wm. | 144 | | John | 90 |
| Bristo | Payton | 159 | | Sarah Ann | 176 |
| | Wm. H.P. | 150 | Brown | ---- | 68,127 |
| Bristow | Elizabeth | 38 | | Abram. | 116 |
| | Payton | 159 | | Adelbert C. | 219 |
| | Wm. H.P. | 150 | | Andrew | 127 |
| Britter | James M. | 86 | | Anna | 127 |
| Brittingham | Teena | 183 | | Asa | 199 |
| Britton | Elizabeth | 173 | | Augustus | 163 |
| | Nathaniel | 117 | | Austin H. | 312 |
| Broaderick | Robert | 85 | | Basil | 79,161 |

| Brown | Benjamin | 301 | Brown | Juliet | 314 |
|-------|----------|-----|-------|--------|-----|
|  | Bernice M. | 14 |  | Julima H. | 202 |
|  | Caroline O. | 180 |  | L.L. | 155 |
|  | Catherine S. | 212 |  | Lewis | 155 |
|  | Charles | 167 |  | Lida | 331 |
|  | Charles W. | 312 |  | Lucinda | 115 |
|  | Charlotte | 45,46 |  | M.B. | 68 |
|  | Christena | 202 |  | Mahlon S. | 205 |
|  | Claude | 301 |  | Margaret | 332 |
|  | Cora | 241 |  | Martha Ann | 195 |
|  | Cornelia G. | 312 |  | Mary | 243 |
|  | Cynthia A. | 213 |  | Mary E. | 180,301 |
|  | Danel | 102 |  | Mary M. | 223 |
|  | Daniel | 107 |  | Matilda | 219 |
|  | David | 99,127 |  | Michael | 127 |
|  | Edmund | 82 |  | Myron | 155 |
|  | Edward, Jr. | 42 |  | Nancy | 34 |
|  | Elizabeth | 34,38,41 |  | Nancy J. | 205 |
|  | Frederick | 100 |  | Nora | 118 |
|  | Fredric | 107 |  | O.H. | 68 |
|  | George | 102,104,108 |  | Osker J. | 212 |
|  | Geo. W. | 180 |  | Perry | 180 |
|  | Gertrude | 312 |  | Peter, Jr. | 146 |
|  | H.L. | 159 |  | Polly | 23 |
|  | Helen M. | 311 |  | R. | 127 |
|  | Helen Man | 174 |  | Rachael | 177 |
|  | Henry | 100,107,127, |  | Raymond D. | 312 |
|  |  | 159 |  | Rob. | 146 |
|  | Henry H. | 91 |  | Robert B. | 82 |
|  | Hilton U. | 312 |  | Rosella J. | 208 |
|  | Hiram | 162,312 |  | Samuel | 23,35,88,91 |
|  | Isaac | 145,170 |  | Samuel J. | 226 |
|  | J.W. | 86 |  | Sarah | 36,170,208 |
|  | Jacob | 97,105 |  | Serilda | 332 |
|  | James | 41,116,147,242 |  | Sidney | 173 |
|  | Jas. B. | 180 |  | Simeon | 204 |
|  | James W. | 216 |  | Susannah | 195 |
|  | Jane | 213 |  | Thomas H. | 193 |
|  | Jane E. | 5 |  | Tina May | 306 |
|  | Jeanette | 7 |  | William | 40,41,156 |
|  | Jesse | 217 |  | William(Mrs.) | 7 |
|  | Joab G. | 198 |  | William H. | 301 |
|  | John | 23,36,60,97,105, | Browne | Chester G. | 312 |
|  |  | 127,143,151,202,220 |  | Christiana | 166 |
|  | John | 37 |  | William | 173 |
|  | John Francis | 301 | Brownlee | Hiram | 91 |
|  | John G. | 156 |  | James | 86,91 |
|  | John H. | 298 |  | John | 86,91 |
|  | John P. | 173 | Broyles | Mary E. | 275 |
|  | John W. | 176 |  | Tobias | 96 |
|  | Jonas | 332 | Bruce | ---- | 286 |
|  | Joseph | 84,332 |  | Arch. | 152 |

| | | | | | | |
|---|---|---|---|---|---|---|
| Buraker | Joshua | 90 | Burns | Thomas | 47 |
| Burbank | Henry G. | 213 | Burnworth | David | 86,90 |
| Burchfield | Hezekiah | 100 | Burrass | Thomas | 97,105 |
| Burd | James | 96 | | William | 104 |
| Burdette | Ada Feifel | 7 | Burris | Alison T. | 210 |
| Burdsall | Elizabeth | 165 | | Susan | 210 |
| Bure | Mary A. | 171 | Burroughs | John H. | 142 |
| Burford | Nancy | 41 | Burrows | John | 147 |
| Burgan | Edgar O. | 313 | | John H. | 142 |
| Burge | Lora | 216 | | Louisa Ann | 32 |
| Burger | Nancy | 42 | Burson | Henry | 85,87 |
| Burjanck | Mary | 223 | | John | 87 |
| Burk | John | 60,127 | | Jonathan | 87 |
| | M. | 87 | | Samuel | 86 |
| | Michael | 82 | | Seth | 86 |
| Burkdoll | Catherine | 188 | Burton | Charles | 33 |
| Burke | Harrison | 92 | | Elizabeth | 37 |
| | James | 36 | | Mary | 38,47 |
| | Laura A. | 304 | | Prettyman | 127 |
| | Mary | 194 | | William | 90 |
| Burket | Adam | 101 | Bush | ----(Judge) | 163 |
| | Charles | 228 | | Ida D. | 3 |
| | Jehu | 96,106 | | Isaac | 50 |
| | Jesse | 150 | | John | 163 |
| Burkhardt | George | 232 | | Sarah | 305 |
| Burkhart | David | 127,143 | Bushbaum | Peter P. | 227 |
| | George | 127 | Busick | Catharine | 173 |
| | Henry | 127 | | Experience | 176 |
| | Sarah | 180 | | J.C. | 147 |
| | William | 127 | Busing | ---- | 74 |
| Burkheart | David | 143 | | Brett C. | 74 |
| Burkholder | Isaac | 52 | | Charles | 74 |
| | Zilla M. | 3 | | Frank C. | 73 |
| Burks | Sarah Ann | 42 | | Herbert F. | 74 |
| Burnes | Isaac N. | 188 | | Judy | 74 |
| Burnet | Harry Bentley | 313 | | Maria | 74 |
| Burnett | Alexander | 46 | | Sarah M. | 73 |
| | Elizabeth | 170 | Bussing | Margret | 211 |
| | Sarah Ann | 169 | Butcher | John | 209 |
| | William | 107 | Buterbaugh | Martin | 227 |
| Burnikel | Clara C. | 78 | Butler | Amos W. | 313 |
| | George | 78 | | Charles | 97,105 |
| | John G. | 78 | | Dan | 106 |
| Burns | Catula | 35 | | Daniel | 99 |
| | Elias B. | 90 | | Dann | 154 |
| | Frederick | 203 | | Edwin | 118 |
| | John | 154,155 | | Eli L. | 168 |
| | Joshua | 66 | | Frank | 118 |
| | Lee | 313 | | George | 203 |
| | Maude | 66 | | Isaac | 333 |
| | R. Hobart | 66 | | John | 333 |
| | Rosella | 66 | | Lindsey | 91 |

| | | | | | |
|---|---|---|---|---|---|
| Buraker | Joshua | 90 | Burns | Thomas | 47 |
| Burbank | Henry G. | 213 | Burnworth | David | 86,90 |
| Burchfield | Hezekiah | 100 | Burrass | Thomas | 97,105 |
| Burd | James | 96 | | William | 104 |
| Burdette | Ada Feifel | 7 | Burris | Alison T. | 210 |
| Burdsall | Elizabeth | 165 | | Susan | 210 |
| Bure | Mary A. | 171 | Burroughs | John H. | 142 |
| Burford | Nancy | 41 | Burrows | John | 147 |
| Burgan | Edgar O. | 313 | | John H. | 142 |
| Burge | Lora | 216 | | Louisa Ann | 32 |
| Burger | Nancy | 42 | Burson | Henry | 85,87 |
| Burjanck | Mary | 223 | | John | 87 |
| Burk | John | 60,127 | | Jonathan | 87 |
| | M. | 87 | | Samuel | 86 |
| | Michael | 82 | | Seth | 86 |
| Burkdoll | Catherine | 188 | Burton | Charles | 33 |
| Burke | Harrison | 92 | | Elizabeth | 37 |
| | James | 36 | | Mary | 38,47 |
| | Laura A. | 304 | | Prettyman | 127 |
| | Mary | 194 | | William | 90 |
| Burket | Adam | 101 | Bush | ----(Judge) | 163 |
| | Charles | 228 | | Ida D. | 3 |
| | Jehu | 96,106 | | Isaac | 50 |
| | Jesse | 150 | | John | 163 |
| Burkhardt | George | 232 | | Sarah | 305 |
| Burkhart | David | 127,143 | Bushbaum | Peter P. | 227 |
| | George | 127 | Busick | Catharine | 173 |
| | Henry | 127 | | Experience | 176 |
| | Sarah | 180 | | J.C. | 147 |
| | William | 127 | Busing | ---- | 74 |
| Burkheart | David | 143 | | Brett C. | 74 |
| Burkholder | Isaac | 52 | | Charles | 74 |
| | Zilla M. | 3 | | Frank C. | 73 |
| Burks | Sarah Ann | 42 | | Herbert F. | 74 |
| Burnes | Isaac N. | 188 | | Judy | 74 |
| Burnet | Harry Bentley | 313 | | Maria | 74 |
| Burnett | Alexander | 46 | | Sarah M. | 73 |
| | Elizabeth | 170 | Bussing | Margret | 211 |
| | Sarah Ann | 169 | Butcher | John | 209 |
| | William | 107 | Buterbaugh | Martin | 227 |
| Burnikel | Clara C. | 78 | Butler | Amos W. | 313 |
| | George | 78 | | Charles | 97,105 |
| | John G. | 78 | | Dan | 106 |
| Burns | Catula | 35 | | Daniel | 99 |
| | Elias B. | 90 | | Dann | 154 |
| | Frederick | 203 | | Edwin | 118 |
| | John | 154,155 | | Eli L. | 168 |
| | Joshua | 66 | | Frank | 118 |
| | Lee | 313 | | George | 203 |
| | Maude | 66 | | Isaac | 333 |
| | R. Hobart | 66 | | John | 333 |
| | Rosella | 66 | | Lindsey | 91 |

| Butler | Louisa J. | 1 | Calaway | Olive Jane | 216 |
| | Malinda | 205 | Caldwell | Alma Brenton | 313 |
| | Mary | 333 | | D.H.(Mrs.) | 4 |
| | Mary Helen | 333 | | Edward | 313 |
| | Nancy | 42,170 | Calentine | Henry | 91 |
| | Susan | 44 | | Henry J. | 88 |
| | Tacy | 333 | Calhoon | Sarah | 214 |
| | William | 38,333 | Calintine | Abraham | 88 |
| Butt | Israel | 96,102 | Calip | Jacob | 140 |
| Butterfield | Isaac J. | 223 | Callahan | Elizabeth | 35 |
| Butterfield | Roger(Mrs.) | 1 | | Rits L. | 227 |
| Butts | William W. | 209 | | Winifred | 7 |
| Byerly | Christian | 143 | Callan | Ann Eliza | 47 |
| | David | 37 | Callaway | Thomas M. | 221 |
| | David, Jr. | 40 | | William | 223 |
| | Elizabeth | 40 | Callen | Robt. | 146 |
| | Solomon | 47 | Callis | Arthur, Sr. | 301 |
| Byers | Elizabeth A. | 205 | | Ballard S. | 301 |
| | George H. | 204 | | Nannie | 301 |
| | Henry | 127 | Callon | William | 145 |
| | Isaac | 171 | Caloway | Elizabeth E. | 227 |
| | Nancy B. | 207 | | William | 225 |
| | Russell T. | 313 | Calvert | Cecil K. | 313 |
| Byles | Isaac | 32 | Calvin | Hiram | 127 |
| Byram | Louis | 124 | | James | 127 |
| Byrd | Serena A. | 182 | | Thomas | 127 |
| Byres | Margaret | 214 | Calyer | Isaac | 127 |
| Byres | Samuel R. | 217 | Camack | James | 84 |
| Byrn | Alice | 41 | Cambell | Alex. | 160 |
| | Matthew M. | 41 | | Hugh | 140 |
| | Patrick | 41 | Cambern | H.H. | 283 |
| Byrne | Alice | 41 | Cambes | John | 272 |
| | Patrick | 41 | Camblin | David L. | 88 |
| | Thomas | 102 | | Enoch | 90 |
| Byrns | David | 109 | | G.W. | 88 |
| | Solomon | 100 | | George | 91 |
| | | | | Jonathan | 88 |
| C---- | James | 100 | | Milton | 88,90 |
| Cade | Phebe | 54 | Cambridge | Elizabeth | 61 |
| Cadwell | W.B. | 247 | | John | 61 |
| | W.G. | 282 | Cambron | Samuel | 108 |
| Cady | Polly | 172 | Camdin | E.E. | 88 |
| Cahill | Thos. | 179 | Camebridge | Elizabeth | 61 |
| Caileff | Joanna | 170 | | John | 61 |
| Cain | Daniel | 89 | Camel | John L. | 215 |
| | John | 148 | Cameron | Saml. | 104 |
| | John M. | 87 | Cammel | ---- | 28 |
| | Sarah | 173 | Cammick | Sally Milburn | 80 |
| | Wm. M. | 87 | Camp | Cecil A. | 63 |
| Caine | John | 148 | | Rosa E. | 63 |
| Calahan | Louretta J. | 212 | Campbell | Alexander | 88 |
| Calaway | Frank | 217 | | Anna | 333 |

| Surname | Given | Page | Surname | Given | Page |
|---|---|---|---|---|---|
| Carpenter | Rebecca | 165 | Carter | Ranson | 117 |
| | Sarah | 175 | | Sanford | 116 |
| | Thomas | 103 | | Sarah | 337 |
| | Walter | 227 | | Thomas | 128 |
| | William | 101,103,224 | | Vinson | 313 |
| | Wm. P. | 161 | | William | 60,128,212 |
| Carr | ---- | 29,30 | Carton | George | 93 |
| | Alice M. | 226 | Cartright | Louvisa | 201 |
| | Catharine | 53 | | William S. | 205 |
| | Elisha | 19,27,28 | Cartwright | Francis E. | 206 |
| | Geo. T.B. | 92 | | Henry | 209 |
| | Howard M. | 298 | | Oskar | 209 |
| | James | 88 | Carver | Archibald | 334 |
| | John | 27,88 | | Elizabeth | 334 |
| | Joseph | 24,26 | | Mary Ann | 301 |
| | Nancy | 27,28 | Carvey | Avery | 174 |
| | Susannah | 197 | Carving | Anna | 228 |
| | Thomas | 19 | Case | Amanda | 57 |
| | William | 25 | | Benjamin | 42 |
| Carrel | Eliza | 49 | | Elisabeth | 196 |
| Carrey | Anna | 165 | | Jacob | 155 |
| Carrol | Adam | 128 | | Rebecca | 198 |
| | Bartholomew | 128 | | Sarah | 44 |
| | Samuel | 45 | | Violet | 198 |
| Carroll | Mary | 217 | Casebeer | David | 165 |
| Carson | G.W. | 116 | Casey | Norah | 219 |
| | Israel | 60 | Caskoske | Max | 221 |
| | Joseph | 88 | Casner | Jacob | 99 |
| | Lenora | 304 | | Jno. | 99 |
| | Maria | 60 | Cason | Mary | 53 |
| | Mary | 53,114 | Casper | Emma | 220 |
| | Rebecca Jane | 256 | | John | 211 |
| | Thomas | 90 | | Kattie | 222 |
| | William | 53 | | Xhper | 99 |
| | William W. | 61 | Cass | John | 25 |
| Carter | ---- | 277 | Cassell | Francis | 141 |
| | ----(Mrs.) | 278 | | Oliver | 46 |
| | Cader | 147 | Cassidy | ----(Mrs.) | 118 |
| | Charity | 36 | Cast | Elisha | 86 |
| | George | 85 | Castens | Herman H. | 188 |
| | Henry | 85,93,215 | Casteter | Peter | 144 |
| | Isaac | 128 | Castle | Isabelle | 209 |
| | James | 143 | Castleman | Mary | 45 |
| | James F. | 88 | | Melissa Isab. | 212 |
| | John | 49 | | Phebe | 200 |
| | Larue De Pew | 313 | | William P. | 220 |
| | Laura Beeler | 313 | Castlman | Mary E. | 213 |
| | Levi | 88 | Casto | William | 52 |
| | Liles | 37 | Castoter | Peter | 144 |
| | Martha M. | 323 | Cates | Dudley | 313 |
| | Nancy | 333 | Cather | Robt. M. | 152 |
| | Nicholas | 27 | Cathers | Mary | 50 |

| | | | | | | |
|---|---|---|---|---|---|---|
| Caton | Mary | 181 | Chaple | Fredrick A. | 219 |
| Catterlin | Noah F. | 128 | Chaplin | Alice B. | 4 |
| Catum | W. | 86 | | Arthur J. | 219 |
| Cauble | Elizabeth T. | 313 | Chapman | Alma | 219 |
| Cavanaugh | Robert B. | 313 | | Charles H. | 209 |
| Cavender | Matilda | 226 | | Chrystal J. | 76 |
| | Rosa B. | 227 | | Clinton | 200 |
| Cavin | James | 212,218 | | Edwin G. | 313 |
| Cavinder | Samuel | 227 | | Elaine Turnbloom | 76 |
| Caywood | Eliza J. | 227 | | Elizabeth | 195 |
| Cellers | William | 197 | | Jean | 76 |
| Chadwick | Nora | 317 | | Joseph F. | 201 |
| | R. Jesse | 213 | | Mary Jane | 203 |
| | William P. | 211 | | Michael Ray | 76 |
| Chalmers | Absalom W. | 174 | | Milton Haines | 200 |
| Chamberlain | Allurad | 61 | | Russell | 76 |
| | Catharine | 43 | Chappel | Jessey | 105 |
| | Frederick | 110 | Chappelear | Harry B. | 213 |
| | Gideon | 108 | Chapple | Jesse | 95,97 |
| | Harry | 313 | Charles | Oliver | 118 |
| | Lille M. | 209 | | Raymond | 118 |
| | Medean | 102 | | Rose | 294 |
| | Nancy | 38 | Charley | George | 103,109 |
| | Peter | 102 | | Peter | 100,109 |
| | Pierce | 41 | Chartrand | Joseph | 313 |
| Chamberlin | Noyes S. | 207 | Chase | Charles Warren | 313 |
| Chambers | Amanda | 220 | | James R. | 313 |
| | D. Laurance | 313 | Chate | Edward | 128 |
| | Elijah G. | 167 | | John | 128 |
| | H.K.(Mrs.) | 8 | Chauncy | Willie | 239 |
| | Kathryn | 303 | Cheaney | Nannie | 301 |
| | Larkin | 165 | Chenoweth | Mahala | 44 |
| | Leah | 60 | Chenoworth | Wm. | 232 |
| | Varilla | 221 | Cheoworth | Wm. | 232 |
| Chamnes | William | 114 | Cherry | Calvin | 216 |
| Chamness | Catherine | 181 | | Elizabeth | 53 |
| | Charlotta | 181 | | Ida | 226 |
| Champ | Barbary Ann | 165 | | Margaret | 195 |
| | Hetty | 328 | | Marion S. | 14 |
| Chance | B.F. | 212 | Chesler | John H. | 230 |
| | Jane | 57 | Chettor | Willson | 115 |
| | Lufamey | 53 | Chew | Margaret | 41 |
| | Perry | 223 | | Nancy | 33 |
| | Redden | 81 | | Sarah | 40 |
| | Reddin | 88 | | Susan | 37 |
| | Wm. | 88 | Chi | ---- | 289 |
| Chandler | C.J.(Mrs.) | 9 | Chichester | Kathay Lee | 251 |
| | William S. | 298 | Chick | Helen | 314 |
| Chaney | John Crawford | 313 | Chidester | S. Jennie | 221 |
| | Sarah E. | 202 | Chids | Sarah | 33 |
| Chapel | Howard M. | 225 | Childers | Joseph | 153 |
| Chapin | Elizabeth E. | 5 | | William F. | 203 |

| Clarke | John | 171 | Cleveland | Chester W. | 313 |
| Clary | Angelina | 261 | Clevenger | Job | 83 |
| Claudius | Augustus | 86 | Clickard | George | 169 |
| Clawson | William H. | 169 | Clickert | Teressa B. | 173 |
| Clay | Virginia Adelme | 5 | Clifford | ---- | 118 |
| Claypool | Elizabeth | 315 | | Angeline | 167 |
| | Nelly | 114 | | Emily Orr | 313 |
| | Reuben | 114 | | Samuel | 86 |
| Clayton | Catharine | 51 | Clifton | Elizabeth | 49 |
| | Ephraim | 165 | Cline | Benjamin | 82 |
| | Hannah | 57 | | Catherine | 43 |
| | Julia Ann | 172 | | Daniel | 99,108 |
| | Thomas | 164 | | Joanna C. S. | 313 |
| Clearwater | Carline | 220 | | John | 99,106 |
| | Jeremiah | 225 | | Joseph | 102,106 |
| | Jeremiah L. | 215 | | Mary E. | 199 |
| | Rebecca Eliz. | 203 | | Nicholas | 145 |
| Clearwaters | John F. | 313 | | William | 173 |
| Cleary | Bessie V. | 10 | | William C. | 128 |
| | Julia G. | 9 | Clingenpeel | Hannah | 176 |
| Cleland | Robert | 172 | | Jonathan | 175 |
| Clemans | Bertha V. | 222 | | Nathaniel | 175 |
| | David | 168 | | William | 166 |
| Clemants | Nancy | 60 | Clinger | Leander | 215 |
| Clemens | Penelope | 6 | | Mary Ellen | 202 |
| | Samuel | 230 | Clinton | Daniel | 239 |
| Clements | Ann | 39 | Clithe | Charles | 98 |
| Clements | Annie M. | 221 | Cloe | John | 156 |
| | Clara A. | 218 | Clore | Lucinda | 306 |
| | Frank H. | 228 | Close | Catherine | 176 |
| | James A. | 204 | | John | 168 |
| | Joseph | 217 | | Mary Jane | 175 |
| | Linda | 307 | | Nancy | 174 |
| | Martha J. | 215 | | William | 169 |
| | N. Caroline | 210 | Closer | Daniel | 149 |
| | Nancy | 60 | Closson | Jones G. | 227 |
| | Samuel | 230 | Cloud | James | 87,90 |
| Clemons | Thomas J. | 169 | | Joseph | 87,90 |
| Clendenen | Inez | 274 | | Noah | 81,87 |
| Clendenin | Eliza | 166 | | Ramey S. | 50 |
| Clendenine | John | 171 | | Thomas C. | 81,87 |
| Clendennin | Alice | 172 | | William | 88,90 |
| | Ann | 166 | Clough | George J. | 313 |
| Clendenning | Elenor | 19 | Clover | Nancy | 52 |
| | Thomas | 19 | Clowes | George H.A. | 313 |
| Clendenon | Elenor | 19 | Clymer | Christian | 172 |
| | Thomas | 19 | | Cynthia | 163 |
| Clendining | Robert | 163 | | John | 163,164 |
| Clester | David | 83 | | Olinda B. | 165 |
| | Jacob | 82 | Coal | Charles | 81 |
| | Peter | 171 | Coalscott | Ralph | 54,62 |
| | Thomas | 82 | Coate | Allen | 85 |

| Coleman | Jane | 181 | Collins | Mathias | 205 |
|---|---|---|---|---|---|
| | John | 128 | | Nancy E. | 210 |
| | Juliet Brown | 314 | | Rachel | 200 |
| | Lydia | 128 | | Ruth | 44 |
| | Martha Ann | 222 | | Samuel L. | 215 |
| | Mary E. | 322 | | Spencer | 27 31 |
| | Sarah Jane | 64 | | Stella | 118 |
| | Seth | 128 | | William F. | 92 |
| | Thomas | 85 | | Zach. | 160 |
| Coles | Agnes L. | 279 | Collip | Conrad | 142 |
| Colescott | Ralph | 54 | | Jacob | 161 |
| Colier | Isaac | 128 | Colly | Isaac | 56 |
| Colip | Jacob | 161 | Colter | John | 87 |
| Collard | ----(Rev.) | 287 | Colvin | Elizabeth P. | 167 |
| Collens | David S. | 95 | | James M. | 176 |
| Collet | James | 55 | Colwell | Charles Wesley | 218 |
| Collett | Daniel | 167 | | John, Jr. | 50 |
| | Eleanora Peace | 45 | Colyer | David | 59 |
| | James | 55 | Combes | Lewis | 99 |
| | Lydia | 58 | Combs | Beram | 103 |
| Collier | Amanda E. | 222 | | Biram | 96,106 |
| | F.J. | 247 | | Charles N. | 314 |
| | Isaac | 128 | | Jesse | 158 |
| Collings | Zach. | 160 | | John | 108 |
| Collins | Andrew | 209 | | Lewis | 108 |
| | Cater'n | 27 | | Stacy | 336 |
| | Catharine | 198 | | William N. | 190 |
| | Caty | 31 | Comer | Joseph | 151 |
| | Elizabeth | 4,194 | Comparet | Irene | 9 |
| | Ellen | 198 | | Irma | 10 |
| | Ephraim | 42,89 | Compton | Amos | 150 |
| | Frank(Mrs.) | 118,120 | | Harriet | 44 |
| | George | 227 | | J.H. | 92 |
| | Harmon | 115 | | John | 153 |
| | Henry(Mrs.) | 21 | | Martin | 84 |
| | Humphrey Q. | 86 | | Nathan | 86 |
| | Isaiah | 115 | Conall | Elizabeth | 170 |
| | J.H. | 89 | Condit | H. Allen | 314 |
| | Jacob | 103 | Coner | Thomas | 106 |
| | James | 85 | Cones | Elizabeth | 49 |
| | Jeremiah | 162 | Confer | Michael W. | 176 |
| | John | 196 | Conine | Peter | 157 |
| | John B. | 214 | Conkel | J. | 122 |
| | John E. | 202 | Conkle | Jacob | 122 |
| | John S. | 206 | Conklin | Andrew | 45 |
| | Johnathan | 220 | | Caroline E. | 3 |
| | Joshua J. | 196 | | Frances L. | 4 |
| | Laura A. | 183 | | John | 173 |
| | Maggie B. | 211 | | Mary Ann H. | 44 |
| | Mahala Jane | 197 | Conkling | Roscoe | 243 |
| | Margaret A. | 196 | Conley | Reese | 128 |
| | Mary E. | 209 | Conn | Ephraim | 88,90 |

| Conn | Ezra | 88 | Cook | Bessie Cameron | 118 |
|------|------|-----|------|------|-----|
| | George | 81,88,90 | | Clarence(Mrs.) | 5 |
| | Stephen | 88,91 | | Clarence A. | 314 |
| Connaway | William | 103 | | George W. | 197 |
| Connell | George G. | 128 | | John | 157 |
| Conner | Benjamin | 43 | | John M. | 90 |
| | David | 195,196 | | John P. | 149 |
| | Ester | 175 | | John V. | 118 |
| | George W. | 210 | | Mahlon | 84 |
| | James | 40,128 | | Mariah G. | 115 |
| | James | 40 | | Mary | 53,114 |
| | Jefferson | 46 | | Milo | 118 |
| | John | 19,87,128 | | Minerva | 168 |
| | John Wesley | 302 | | Moses | 21 |
| | Lehew | 188 | | Nancy | 21 |
| | Lewis, Sr. | 86 | | Nathan B. | 173 |
| | Lewis, Jr. | 86 | | Peter S. | 83 |
| | Mary Ann | 176 | | Philip | 45 |
| | Mary E. | 223 | | Phineas | 173 |
| | Nelson | 86 | | Polly | 54 |
| | Riley | 167 | | Rebecca | 306 |
| | Sarah | 224,225 | | Samuel | 96 |
| | T.H. | 85 | | Silas | 85 |
| | Thomas | 36,100,177 | | Solomon | 148 |
| | Walter Scott | 302 | | Wiliam | 58 |
| | Warren | 88 | | William | 159,299 |
| | William N. | 202 | Cooke | John | 157 |
| Connley | Warren | 93 | | John P. | 149 |
| Connly | Ann | 206 | Cooksee | Polly | 55 |
| Connor | John | 124 | Cooksey | Mary | 53 |
| Conod | George | 105 | | Polly | 55 |
| Conover | Moses L. | 294 | | William | 53 |
| Conrad | David | 102 | Cooksy | Polly | 55 |
| | David H. | 176 | Cool | Dan. | 160 |
| | George | 97 | | J.S.(Dr.) | 145 |
| | Henry | 96,101,110 | | Philip | 173 |
| | Jacob | 95,101,103,105, | | Wm. | 156 |
| | | 107 | Cooley | David F. | 54 |
| | Jacob, Junior | 96,106 | Coolman | William | 121 |
| | Jeannette Wilson | 314 | Cools | Minerva | 168 |
| | John | 96,103,107 | Cooly | John | 49 |
| | Philip | 96 | Coombs | ----, Sen. | 28 |
| Conrey | Abraham | 59 | | Ann | 27 |
| Conrod | George | 95 | | C.E. | 192 |
| Consley | Viola M. | 304 | | Hannah | 27,28,30 |
| Conway | Ancil H. | 302 | | Jesse | 19,20,158 |
| | Martha | 302 | | Joel | 23 |
| | William | 98 | | John | 19 |
| | William Sr. | 98 | | Margaret | 19 |
| | Wm. T. | 302 | | Nancy | 19 |
| Conwell | James | 88 | | Rachel | 27,28 |
| Cook | Abraham | 114,145 | | William | 19,27,28,29 |

| | | | | | | |
|---|---|---|---|---|---|---|
| Coombs | Wm., Sen. | 30 | Coppers | Adam | 143 |
| | William, Jun. | 27,28,29 | Copple | Cynthia | 333 |
| Coomes | ---- | 279 | | David | 333 |
| Cooms | Daniel | 58 | Coppoch | John | 85 |
| Coon | Jacob | 88 | Coppock | Aaron | 153 |
| | Michael | 88 | Coppock | Isaac | 161 |
| Coonfare | John O. | 205 | Copprass | Peter | 98 |
| Coonfield | Isaac | 141 | Coprass | Adam | 143 |
| | James P. | 150 | Coprass | Peter | 96 |
| Coonrod | Jacob | 104 | Coquillard | Alexis | 314 |
| Coons | David | 333 | Corbaley | J.J. | 159 |
| | Emma | 333 | Corberly | J.J. | 159 |
| | Henry | 333 | Corbin | Mary Eliza. | 198 |
| | Lucy | 333 | Corder | James | 90 |
| | William | 128 | | Robert | 84 |
| Cooper | Abigail S. | 34 | Corey | Joseph D. | 88 |
| | Albert | 187 | | Stephen | 88 |
| | Catharine | 114 | | William D. | 88 |
| | Eleven | 104 | Cormack | J.M. | 224 |
| | Elmira | 219 | Cormick | Caroline E. | 217 |
| | George | 34 | Corn | Joseph | 83 |
| | H.S. | 247 | Cornelius | Benson | 153 |
| | Hardin | 86 | Cornuelle | Herbert C. | 314 |
| | Ida M. | 228 | Corwin | Carl | 118 |
| | Jane | 114 | | Joe | 118 |
| | John | 211 | | Will | 118 |
| | Laura | 187 | Cory | Adelia | 201 |
| | Levin | 108 | | Andrew C. | 141 |
| | Lydia Anne | 187 | | Maria | 173 |
| | Margaret | 55,117 | | Sarah J. | 198 |
| | Martha Jane | 187 | Cosner | Henry | 21 |
| | Mary | 215 | | John | 21 |
| | Minnie D. M. | 314 | Cosnet | Augustine M. | 203 |
| | Nathaniel | 89 | Costelo | David | 314 |
| | Robert | 114 | Coster | Nicolas | 31 |
| | Samuel W. | 216 | Costle | Wm. | 160 |
| | Thomas | 57,223 | Cothrell | Edith M. | 4 |
| | William | 42 | Cotner | David | 95,100,107 |
| | William S. | 187 | | Frederick | 95,97,105 |
| Cooplin | Zachariah | 107 | | John | 95,99 |
| Cooprider | John | 106 | Cottier | George | 242 |
| | Peter | 96,106 | | Henry | 242 |
| | Peter, Senior | 108 | Cottingham | Andrew | 45 |
| Cooprighter | Jno. | 102 | | Catharine | 34 |
| | Peter | 98,102 | | Lydia | 40 |
| Coosenberey | Henrey | 105 | Cottman | George Streibe | 314 |
| Coovert | Jean | 27,28 | Cotton | Cyrus | 152 |
| Copes | Sarah | 305 | | Margaret | 57 |
| Copic | John | 82 | Coubern | Henry P. | 104 |
| Copler | Matthias | 82 | Couch | Louisa J. | 199 |
| Copp | John | 107 | Couchman | David S. | 200 |
| Copper | Isaac | 161 | Cougle | John | 201 |

| | | | | | | |
|---|---|---|---|---|---|---|
| Crouse | H.M. | 118 | Cunningham | John | 99,195 |
| Crow | James | 235 | | Margaret | 6 |
| | John H. | 182 | | William | 218 |
| Crowder | James K. | 188 | Cup | Conrad | 205 |
| | James M. | 189 | Cupp | Florilla | 199 |
| | Mary | 38 | | Ida M. | 227 |
| | Nancy | 38 | Curran | Charles William | 302 |
| | Rhoda M. | 188 | | Jerome Boone | 302 |
| | Wiley | 35 | Curry | ---- | 31 |
| | William | 41 | | Adolph | 243 |
| Crowders | Nancy | 38 | | James | 20,27,29 |
| Crowel | John | 85 | | Louise | 240 |
| Cruise | Absalem | 150 | | Millie | 240 |
| Crull | Mary | 176 | | Mitilda | 61 |
| Crum | Huston | 221 | | Sarah E. | 174 |
| | William | 121 | | Susie | 243 |
| Crumley | Amanda S. | 1 | Cursey | Edna T. | 169 |
| Crumm | William | 113 | Curte | William | 169 |
| Cruse | Benjamin | 128 | Curtis | Annadale E. | 14 |
| Crutchfield | George | 102,106 | | Arthur | 33 |
| | James | 101 | | Edward J. | 225 |
| | Jesse | 100 | | Edwin P. | 206 |
| Crysmore | Mary | 195 | | Ella May | 303 |
| Cubbage | James | 98,109 | | Job | 88 |
| | Jams | 104 | | Josiah | 47 |
| Cubberly | Wm. B. | 86 | | Permelia | 225 |
| Cuffle | Albert | 167 | | R.A.(Mrs.) | 4 |
| Culberson | Joseph | 153 | Curtiss | Alfred | 81 |
| Culbertson | Davidson | 88,90 | | Job | 81 |
| | John | 143 | Curts | Martin | 107 |
| | Joseph | 153 | Cushman | Ruth Adah | 313 |
| Culef | Louis | 172 | Custer | Joseph L.. | 91 |
| Culiff | Lovica | 172 | Cuthbertson | Harry K., Jr. | 314 |
| Cullip | Coonrod | 142 | Cutler | Jacob | 128 |
| Cully | Julia Ann | 50 | Cutshall | Ann D. | 213 |
| Culver | Benjamin | 128 | Cutsinger | Jacob | 128 |
| | M.C. | 123 | | Martin | 128 |
| | Nathaniel | 128 | Cutter | Cornelius C. | 219 |
| Cumings | Frank | 212 | | Fred P. | 314 |
| Cumlar | John | 96 | | Joshua | 32 |
| Cummings | ---- | 111 | | | |
| | Delilah | 36 | Dabeney | Samuel | 155 |
| Cummins | John | 46 | Dabney | James | 156 |
| | Lucinda | 55 | | Julia Ann | 170 |
| | Thomas | 55 | | Malinda | 165 |
| | Wm. | 150 | | Samuel | 155 |
| Cuningham | Jonathan | 156 | Dagenette | Louis | 242 |
| | Samuel | 98 | Dagget | Andrew | 221 |
| | Thomas | 99 | Daggs | William | 96,105 |
| Cunningham | Amos | 219 | Daggs | William, Sr. | 102,109 |
| | Francis | 194 | | William, Jr. | 99 |
| | James A. | 221 | Daggy | Henry | 170 |

| | | | | | | |
|---|---|---|---|---|---|---|
| DeCamp | Mary A. | 218 | Denbow | James | 104 |
| Decinger | Solomon | 141 | Dener | Charles E. | 223 |
| Deck | A.M. | 226 | Denham | John | 99,108 |
| Deckart | Joseph | 96 | Denison | Ida J. | 179 |
| Decker | Joseph | 38 | Dennelsbeck | Jacob | 48 |
| | Lucinda | 179 | Denney | R. | 124 |
| | Sarah | 38 | Dennie | Katherine | 301 |
| Deckerson | Wm. G. | 156 | Dennis | Anthony | 44 |
| Deckson | Wm. G. | 156 | | Burr P. | 141 |
| Dedrick | David | 247 | | Pernel | 198 |
| Deeds | Daniel | 174 | | William C. | 315 |
| | Margaret | 170 | Dennison | Georgia L. | 5 |
| Deem | Charles | 118 | | Lucinda | 166 |
| | George A. | 118 | Denny | John | 19,157 |
| | Hazel | 118 | | Mary Adeline | 315 |
| | Jacob A. | 221 | | The. V. | 153 |
| | T.B. | 118 | | Theodore | 153 |
| Deen | Eve | 202 | Denor | Clara | 224 |
| | Hiram A. | 200 | Denton | Julia E. | 180 |
| | Mary Ann | 197 | Deoing | Caroline | 36 |
| | Obed R. | 223 | Depat | Rasella | 247 |
| | Sarah Jane | 205 | | Rassella | 247 |
| | William | 216 | Depert | Amos Bertram | 220 |
| Deerduff | George | 203 | | Elizabeth J. | 210 |
| Deery | Paul A. | 314 | | Obed H. | 219 |
| Deeton | Elizabeth | 169 | Deputy | Fay | 262 |
| Deford | Catharine | 61 | Depuy | J.H. | 247 |
| DeFord | Wm. | 150 | Deringer | Lucinda E. | 210 |
| DeGaris | James | 302 | DeSouchet | Edmonia | 319 |
| | James Parvin | 302 | Detamore | Barbara | 123 |
| Degrees | J.M. | 163 | | John | 123 |
| DeLany | James | 150 | | Joseph(Mrs.) | 123 |
| Deliaferis | Ann | 56 | Deter | Henry | 173 |
| Dell | Dorothy | 323 | Detzer | A.J.(Mrs.) | 4 |
| Delmus | Augustus A. | 164 | Devall | Indiann | 52 |
| DeLong | James | 150 | | Josep P. | 142 |
| Demasters | Liza Jane | 196 | Devenish | James | 34 |
| Demeree | Peter | 129 | DeVilbiss | Laurinda M. | 7 |
| Demine | Mary | 47 | Devoe | David | 86 |
| DeMont | Joseph E. | 214 | Deweese | Martha A. | 337 |
| Demonte | Charls | 215 | | Nancy | 52 |
| Demoss | Benjamin F. | 212 | Dewis | Jethro | 154 |
| | James | 114 | Dewit | David | 197 |
| | Rachel | 113 | | Oscar | 188 |
| | Virgil M. | 216 | | Reuben | 188 |
| DeMott | Lawrence | 153 | DeWitt | Isaac | 35 |
| Demouth | Elizabeth | 174 | | William | 115 |
| Dempster | James | 33 | Dewyre | Thomas | 52 |
| Denbo | James | 96,101,106 | Dexter | Harriet | 174 |
| | John | 96,98,105 | | John L. | 53 |
| | Joseph | 100,108 | Dial | Austin | 199 |
| | Solomon | 98,105 | | Delila | 197 |

| | | | | | | |
|---|---|---|---|---|---|---|
| Dial | William | 216 | Dimmitt | Eldana | 333 |
| Diamond | Jason G. | 222 | | James P. | 333 |
| Dice | Benjamin F. | 175 | | John W. | 333 |
| | Elizabeth | 170 | | Margaret J. | 333 |
| Dick | Annie B. | 4 | | Pratt | 333 |
| | Mary Emma | 4 | | Rachel | 333 |
| Dicken | Elizabeth | 114 | | Warder D. | 333 |
| | Richard W. | 89 | | William V. | 333 |
| Dickens | Elizabeth | 37 | Dincan | Maggie | 221 |
| Dickerson | Charles | 187 | Dinklage | Katherine M. | 14 |
| | Elijah | 116 | Dipert | Elias | 204 |
| | Hellen M. | 187 | | James C. | 223 |
| | Louisa | 187 | | Jonass | 205 |
| | Mary M. | 187 | | Malinda | 214 |
| Dickey | James | 53 | | Mary E. | 228 |
| Dickinson | Charles | 315 | | Peter | 199 |
| Dickore | Marie | 315 | | Phebe Ann | 215 |
| Dickover | Mark L. | 315 | | Sarah A. | 218 |
| Dickson | Analiza | 211 | Ditrick | Mary | 198 |
| | Frances H. | 218 | Ditto | Fidilla | 213 |
| | James Milford | 196 | Ditton | Charles | 247 |
| Diehl | Frank | 217 | | Jas. | 246 |
| Dies | Michael | 168 | Divine | Charles W. | 187 |
| Dietz | Leonard | 220 | | Electa J. | 187 |
| Diggins | Cora A. | 4 | | Frederick M. | 187 |
| Diggs | Marshall W. | 302 | | George A. | 187 |
| | William S. | 302 | | John H. | 187 |
| Dilinger | Nicholas | 40 | | Margrett I. | 187 |
| Dill | Elmer | 119 | | Martha E. | 188 |
| | Elmer(Mrs.) | 118 | | Martha Eliz. | 187 |
| | Gracie Merrick | 259 | | Matilda | 187 |
| Dillan | Florence Eva | 315 | | Samuel N. | 187 |
| Dille | James | 83 | | Samuel V. | 187 |
| Dillinger | Lucinda | 44 | Dixon | Julia Ann | 172 |
| | Miles | 35 | | Milford C. | 206 |
| | Theny Perkins | 39 | Dixson | Elizabeth | 51 |
| Dillingham | Thomas J. | 315 | | Milford C. | 197 |
| Dillman | George | 176 | Doan | Bernice | 75 |
| Dillon | Albert | 84 | | Jerry L. | 75 |
| | Amazetta | 199 | | Jerry R. | 75 |
| | Icepene | 226 | | John | 41 |
| | Isaac B. | 121 | | Linda D. | 75 |
| | J.P. | 87 | Doane | Waring L. | 315 |
| | James | 89,90 | Dochterman | Erma | 7 |
| | Jesse | 84 | Dockham | Chase C. | 38 |
| | John | 121,245 | Dodd | Adam | 104,109 |
| Diltry | Andrew, Jr. | 87 | | Adam D. | 95 |
| Dilts | Mary L. | 225 | | Anthony | 104 |
| Diltz | Andrew, Sr. | 86 | Dodds | Adam D. | 97 |
| | Dortha | 228 | | Anthony | 97 |
| Dimmitt | Betsey A. | 333 | | I.R.(Mrs.) | 294 |
| | Burton J. | 333 | Dodge | George | 333 |

| | | | | | | |
|---|---|---|---|---|---|---|
| Dowden | Nancy | 21 | Dufendock | Margaret | 185 |
| | Sephaniah | 21 | Duff | William | 82 |
| | Thomas | 21 | Dufford | Theodore | 210 |
| | William | 21 | Dufour | Bettie | 327 |
| Dowling | Thomas | 129 | Dugan | Henry F. | 315 |
| Downey | Alexander C. | 180 | | J. | 90 |
| | John | 201 | | John | 81,88 |
| Downin | Francis C. | 50 | Duggens | Ruben | 105 |
| Downs | ---- | 28 | Duggin | Reuben | 98 |
| | Alen B. | 82 | Duggins | James | 45 |
| | Pricilla | 27,29 | Duglas | Susanna | 53 |
| | Thomas | 17,27 | Duke | Emma E. | 64 |
| Doyle | Ellen M. | 10 | | Green | 83 |
| | Michael | 88,90 | | J.W. | 64 |
| Drager | Henrietta | 197 | | John W. | 64 |
| Dragoo | Edelle Walters | 263 | | N.A. | 64 |
| | Eva | 296 | | Nancy A. | 64 |
| | Margaret Edelle | 264 | | Saml. | 151 |
| | Margaret Louise | 265 | | William P. | 64 |
| | Ralph | 262 | Duling | Edmund | 83 |
| | Ralph F. | 264,265 | | G. Harold | 315 |
| Drake | Euphemia | 167 | | Thomas D. | 83 |
| | Gideon | 129 | Dull | Emma R. | 219 |
| | J.P. | 140 | | Jacob | 110 |
| | James P. | 161 | | John | 110 |
| | John | 206 | Dumont | Fannie | 312 |
| | Mary A. | 208 | | George S. | 195 |
| | Mary Ann | 167 | Dunbar | Anna Gertrude | 273 |
| | Mary J. | 211 | | Erma G. | 273 |
| | Patsey | 62 | | Harriet | 273 |
| | Phebe | 172 | | Harriet A. | 273 |
| | Leonora I. | 1 | | James W. | 315 |
| Draper | David | 169 | | Johnathan A. | 273 |
| | John | 86 | | Josephine | 273 |
| | Joshua | 86 | | Julius E. | 273 |
| | Luther O. | 315 | | Lois | 273 |
| | Noah | 86 | | Raymond J. | 273 |
| Dreis | Joseph | 215 | | Wallace | 273 |
| Druck | Jacob | 82 | Dunbeck | Thelma Louise | 316 |
| | John | 82 | Duncan | Alex. | 247 |
| Drum | John | 315 | | Frank C. | 315 |
| Drummond | James | 21 | | James | 41,80 |
| Drybread | W.E. | 295 | | Joshua | 80 |
| Dryer | Hannah | 175 | Dunfee | William D. | 226 |
| Drysdale | Elizabeth | 38 | Dunham | Aaron | 129 |
| | William | 38 | | Jeremiah | 129 |
| Duboice | Jennie | 220 | Dunigan | Belle | 193 |
| Dubois | Elizabeth | 276 | | Fanny | 193 |
| | Mary | 50 | | Grant | 192 |
| DuChemin | Lucie | 310 | | Lora | 193 |
| Duckwall | John | 88,90 | | Nancy A. | 193 |
| Duerner | Audrey L. | 75 | | William | 193 |

| | | | | | | |
|---|---|---|---|---|---|---|
| Eckles | Ruth | 281 | Eggleston | ----(Mrs.) | 290 |
| Ecklis | ---- | 277 | | C. | 286 |
| Eckord | Joseph | 105 | Ehle | Helen A. | 10 |
| Eddins | James | 41 | Ehrman | Mary | 8 |
| Eddins | Jane | 38 | Ehrnschwender | Karl S. | 315 |
| | Maria | 41 | Eikenbury | Sameul | 52 |
| Eddy | Eugenia S. | 315 | Eisberg | ---- | 72 |
| | Wm. | 144 | Eisberg | Freddie W. | 72 |
| Edgar | James | 140 | | John F. | 72 |
| | Mary E. | 1 | | Lydia M. | 72 |
| | Sarah H. | 11 | | M. | 72 |
| Edge | Rachel | 241 | | Marie L. | 72 |
| Edgerton | Urban | 50 | | Mary | 72 |
| Edgewalk | Jane | 240 | | W. | 72 |
| Edins | John | 145 | | William | 72 |
| Edleman | Catherine | 42 | | William F. | 72 |
| Edminson | John P. | 315 | Eisenhour | Martin | 198 |
| Edmonds | Samuel | 239 | | Michael P. | 198 |
| Edmondson | James H. | 46 | Eisler | Mary H. | 192 |
| Edmson | Thos. | 148 | | Michael | 191 |
| Edmundson | Thos. | 148 | | William | 192 |
| Edson | Edward | 47 | Eiter | Mae Marguerite | 7 |
| | Susan | 43 | Ekerd | Joseph | 98 |
| Edwards | ----(Judge) | 16 | | Philip | 98 |
| | Alice Shirk | 315 | Ekins | Lizzie A. | 208 |
| | Allen | 88 | Elden | John | 60 |
| | Benjamin R. | 40 | Elderkin | Lathrop | 34 |
| | Casheus | 101 | Eldige | Joseph | 109 |
| | Cassius | 109 | Eldon | John | 60 |
| | Catharine | 170 | Eldridge | John | 20 |
| | Daniel | 86 | Eleman | Jordan | 85 |
| | David | 174 | Elgin | Margaret | 57 |
| | Elizabeth | 42 | Eliot | Isaac | 38 |
| | Granville P. | 198 | Eliott | James | 96 |
| | Henry | 38,43 | Elkins | Eph. | 141 |
| | Isaac | 45 | | Lewis | 173 |
| | Isom M. | 232 | | Martha Ann | 196 |
| | Katharine | 220 | Ellage | Joseph | 99 |
| | Margaret | 33 | Ellas | Athanasious B. | 215 |
| | Morris F. | 118 | Ellenwood | Clara | 9 |
| | Nathaniel G. | 209 | Eller | Adam | 152 |
| | Orvill W. | 208 | | Andrew | 151 |
| | Phoebe | 169 | | David | 160 |
| | Richard A. | 315 | | Leonard | 159 |
| | Rufus | 41 | Elles | Andrew | 104 |
| | Samuel | 169 | | James | 151 |
| | Sarah | 36 | Elliot | James | 98 |
| | Stephen | 40 | | Thos. | 103 |
| | Thomas | 33 | Elliott | George B. | 315 |
| | Walter | 9 | | George Tayl. | 176 |
| Egbert | George | 89,92 | | Harry | 118,315 |
| Eggans | Nancy | 56 | | Isaac | 38,93 |

| | | | | | | |
|---|---|---|---|---|---|---|
| Elliott | John | 129 | Eltzroth | Nicholas | 90 |
| | Lewis | 88 | Elvey | Sarah | 122 |
| | Martha | 34 | Elwell | Rebecca | 60 |
| | Mary Sewall | 315 | Elwood | T.G. | 87,90 |
| | Nannie Gregory | 118 | Ely | Henry | 208 |
| | Paul | 118 | Embree | Amos | 113 |
| | Phoebe Stoker | 315 | Embry | Ella N. | 2 |
| | Thomas | 29,167 | | Virginia N. | 2 |
| Ellis | Abraham | 147 | Emely | Isaac | 99 |
| | Amanda J. | 215 | Emerson | Edward | 167 |
| | Andrew | 95 | Emery | J. | 86 |
| | Ann Louisa | 174 | Emhardt | Adolph G. | 315 |
| | Elvin | 200 | Emich | Jacob | 198 |
| | H.C. | 67 | Emig | Jacob | 202 |
| | James | 151 | Emigh | Barbara A. | 207 |
| | Jehu | 109 | | Barbara Ann B. | 227 |
| | John | 88,101 | | Christian | 222 |
| | John W. | 40 | | Eliza | 200 |
| | Jonathan | 87 | | Grant | 228 |
| | Joseph | 108 | | Izore | 210 |
| | Maransa | 201 | | Liman F. | 222 |
| | Margaret | 169 | | Mary | 202,224 |
| | Martha | 201 | | Mary E. | 205 |
| | Mary | 44 | | William H. | 222 |
| | Miles | 302 | Emmert | Philip J. | 315 |
| | Peter | 160 | Emmons | Thomas F. | 230 |
| | Rebecca | 20 | Emory | John | 151 |
| | Rolbert | 85 | Emrich | Joel | 89 |
| | Roy C. | 302 | | M.W.(Mrs.) | 10 |
| | Runion | 43 | Emrick | E.V.(Mrs.) | 6 |
| | Ruth | 301 | | Granville | 227 |
| | Sallie A. | 67 | Emry | Ann | 169 |
| | Samantha C. | 199 | | John | 151 |
| | Theodore W. | 315 | Emswick | Elias(Mrs.) | 193 |
| | W.H. | 88,90 | Endsley | Elihu | 88 |
| | William | 20 | Endsly | A. | 88 |
| Ellison | Chas. | 157 | | John | 88 |
| | John | 41,151 | Enfield | Jacob | 103 |
| | Richard | 96 | Engleman | Jefferson | 41 |
| Ellmaker | Sarah E. | 324 | | William | 108 |
| Ellman | Wm. W. | 85 | English | Catharine | 175 |
| Ellsberry | Fred H. | 232 | | Henry King | 315 |
| | Frederich H. | 232 | | R.(Mrs.) | 247 |
| | Frederick H. | 232 | | Sarah | 44 |
| Ellwood | Willard M. | 315 | | Stephen | 98 |
| Ellzroth | Frederick | 86 | | Steven | 96 |
| Elmendorf | Emma | 204 | | William | 46 |
| Elmendorff | Wm. | 199 | Enlow | David | 100 |
| Elrod | J.J. | 247 | | Henry | 98 |
| Elston | Eliza | 198 | Enslen | Willard(Mrs.) | 15 |
| | Isaac C., Sr. | 315 | Ensminger | Leonard A. | 315 |
| | Sarah | 203 | Enstminger | John | 85 |

**385**

| | | | | | | |
|---|---|---|---|---|---|---|
| Fischer | Otto E. | 77 | Fiske | William P. | 302 |
| | Pearl L. | 73 | Fislar | ---- | 29 |
| | U. | 69 | | John | 27 |
| | Ursila | 69 | | Sophia | 27 |
| | Ursilla | 68 | Fisler | James | 23 |
| | William | 69 | | John | 20 |
| Fish | Elizabeth | 167 | | William | 20 |
| | Grace S. | 316 | Fissel | Gertrude | 7 |
| | Minerva C. | 171 | Fitch | Alice May | 7 |
| Fisher | ---- | 279,280 | | Mason C. | 34 |
| | Alfred | 166 | Fitchpatrick | Ann | 57 |
| | Alice | 334 | Fitchpattrick | Ann | 57 |
| | Attie | 334 | Fite | Emma H. | 217 |
| | Barbara | 333 | | Fredrick | 217 |
| | Benjamin | 169 | | Joseph | 218 |
| | Bernard | 187 | Fithian | Ada | 119 |
| | Charles | 334 | | Adah | 119 |
| | Charlotte | 333 | | Frank | 118 |
| | Cynthia | 333 | Fitzgerald | James J. | 316 |
| | Daniel | 82 | | Margaret | 226 |
| | David | 82,142 | Fix | Anna | 58 |
| | Dolly B. | 334 | Flack | David | 55 |
| | E.J. | 82 | Flagg | Polly | 173 |
| | Elizabeth | 187 | Flanagan | Erastus | 195 |
| | Frederick | 333 | | John | 101 |
| | Henry | 333 | | Patric | 109 |
| | Jacob | 333 | | Patrick | 101 |
| | Jemima | 57 | | Samuel | 103 |
| | John | 187,227,333,334 | Flanagin | John | 104 |
| | Jonathan | 82 | Flanigan | A. | 16 |
| | Joseph | 172 | | Malinda | 16 |
| | Josephine | 334 | | Patrick | 95 |
| | Leonard | 334 | Flanigin | P. | 104 |
| | Lydia | 169 | Flaningam | Sallie Clark | 316 |
| | Margaretta | 187 | Flaningan | Samuel | 103 |
| | Mary | 7,174 | Flecher | Clvin | 161 |
| | Mary Ann | 166 | Fleehart | Sarah | 22 |
| | Mary M. | 186 | Fleming | ----(Mrs.) | 283 |
| | Mathias | 187 | | Augusta | 224 |
| | Max(Mrs.) | 4 | | Darold T. | 316 |
| | Melissa | 333 | | Elizabeth | 45 |
| | Nicholas | 186 | | Ezekiel | 121 |
| | Olive | 333 | | John | 51 |
| | Orange | 172 | | Joseph | 47 |
| | Polly | 170 | | Lydia A. | 204 |
| | Samuel | 166 | | Rachel | 280 |
| | Sarah | 333 | | Susana M. | 206 |
| | Susanah | 187 | Flemming | Elizabeth | 45 |
| | Willard | 334 | | Elmus | 82 |
| | Wm. A. | 187 | | John | 51 |
| Fisk | Dru | 262 | Flener | Oliver | 87 |
| Fiske | Peleg | 302 | Flesher | Grove K. | 298 |

| | | | | | | |
|---|---|---|---|---|---|---|
| Fleshman | Ephraim | 109 | Flynn | Patrick | 205 | |
| | Jacob | 99,109 | Fodery | J.W. | 158 | |
| | William | 110 | Fogerty | Elizabeth | 169 | |
| Fletcher | Albert B. | 224 | Foley | Celia | 8 | |
| | Anna | 228 | | Cornelius S. | 175 | |
| | Anna L. | 205 | Follett | Nelle K.M. | 316 | |
| | Calvin | 129,161 | Foltz | Herbert W. | 316 | |
| | Charles B. | 227 | | Joannah | 216 | |
| | Charles R. | 223 | Fontain | Matilda | 45 | |
| | Elizabeth | 218 | Fontaine | Cincinnatus | 45 | |
| | Francis M. | 198,209 | Foot | Obed | 161 | |
| | Isaac | 209 | Foote | Adrian V.H. | 198 | |
| | Jane D. | 42 | | Anna | 225 | |
| | Jessee | 198 | | Elmer E. | 227 | |
| | Margaret | 43 | | Obed | 161 | |
| | Martha E. | 211,217 | Forbs | W. | 247 | |
| | Martha Jane | 196 | Forceman | Aaron H. | 36 | |
| | Mary Ann | 196 | Ford | Delia | 217 | |
| | Media | 211 | | Ella E. | 220 | |
| | Nancy | 171 | | Eveline | 202 | |
| | Phebe Jane | 196 | | George | 166 | |
| | Sarah Hill | 329 | | Harland V. | 316 | |
| | Sarah J. | 218 | | Idora A. | 211 | |
| | Schulyer | 225 | | Lambert M. | 208 | |
| | Telitha | 199 | | M.V.(Mrs.) | 7 | |
| | Thomas J. | 208,210 | Fordyce | James | 23 | |
| | Wayland | 199 | Forgason | James | 148 | |
| | Willard | 195 | Fornash | James | 175 | |
| | William H. | 196 | Fornshell | Robert P. | 82 | |
| | William L. | 218 | Forrey | George C. | 316 | |
| | William P. | 222 | Forsee | James | 162 | |
| Flickner | Sarah | 41 | Forsett | David | 152 | |
| Flies | Rosa | 242 | Forsyth | Edgar T. | 316 | |
| Flinn | James | 110 | | Margaret | 38 | |
| | John W. | 87 | | William | 316 | |
| Flint | Benjamin J. | 49 | Fortner | Elizabeth | 55 | |
| | Elizabeth | 51 | Fortrede | Lorena | 9 | |
| | Maria | 49 | Fortune | William | 316 | |
| | Minerva | 54 | Foryth | Charles | 218 | |
| Flock | Anna Barbara | 43 | Fos | John | 89 | |
| Flood | Catharine | 61 | Fosburg | ---- Glenn | 118 | |
| | Noah | 146 | Fosett | Sarah | 35 | |
| Flook | Isaac | 82 | Fosher | Jacob | 58 | |
| Floran | Joseph | 209 | Foss | Cordelia E. | 210 | |
| Florian | Solamon | 203 | | N.H.K. | 195 | |
| Flotron | Justine E. | 43 | Fossette | Mary Ann | 33 | |
| Flowers | Flora | 217 | Fossler | Ben G. | 77 | |
| | Josephene | 219 | | Hannah | 73 | |
| Floyd | Davis | 17,18,19,100 | | John | 73 | |
| | John | 105 | | Minnie M. | 77 | |
| | Polly L. | 18 | | William V. | 73 | |
| | Suanne | 18 | Foster | Bassil | 87 | |

| | | | | | | |
|---|---|---|---|---|---|---|
| Framan | Benj. | 150 | Freet | Mary E. | 211 |
| Framer | Samuel | 96 | | Michael J. | 206 |
| France | J.E.K.(Mrs.) | 3 | | Samuel | 202 |
| | Michael | 82 | Freiday | Wilhelmena | 199 |
| Francis | Joseph | 223 | | Ruth | 306 |
| Franck | Georgianna | 317 | French | Alice Moore | 317 |
| Frane | Thomas B. | 210 | | Amos | 229 |
| Frank | Barney | 186,188 | | Barzilla | 143 |
| | George | 105 | | Charles M. | 226 |
| | Joseph | 218 | | Danel | 104 |
| Franklin | Mary | 214 | | Daniel | 96,98,104,107 |
| | Solomon | 56 | | Daniel Jr. | 102,109 |
| Frantz | Michael | 89 | | Elizabeth | 36,208 |
| Frary | James | 129 | | Henry Jr. | 35 |
| Fray | E.W. | 146 | | Jeff.(Mrs.) | 289 |
| Frazee | Frances | 318 | | Lillian D. | 4 |
| | John | 160 | | Mason | 97,101,103 |
| | Joseph W. | 171 | | Paul | 95,97,105 |
| | Mary T. | 51 | | Rebecca | 55 |
| | Moses Jr. | 141 | | Richard | 96,103,104 |
| | Moses | 153 | Fretageot | Achilles H. | 303 |
| Frazier | Alexander | 161 | | Arthur E. | 303 |
| | Hugh L. | 147 | | Nora C. | 317 |
| | John | 25 | Fretzsha | August | 198 |
| | Mary | 174 | Frey | Israel | 170 |
| | Minerva J. | 168,175 | Frich | Sarah | 218 |
| Frazir | Saml. | 152 | Friday | Betsy | 43 |
| Frazy | Mary Ann | 167 | Friedley | Harmon H. | 317 |
| Fred | Jacob | 44 | | Roy M. | 317 |
| Fredd | Samuel | 54 | | Susanna | 40 |
| Frederick | Chrisian | 86 | Friermood | George | 90 |
| | Mary | 36 | | Jacob | 90,92 |
| | Michael | 37 | Friesner | Ray C. | 317 |
| Fredrick | Louvina | 212 | Frisby | Roger(Mrs.) | 7 |
| | Martha I. | 179 | Fritts | David | 89 |
| | Mary | 179 | Fritz | Augustus | 197 |
| | Michel | 179 | | Bessie M. | 73 |
| Free | O. | 86 | | Ermel L. | 73 |
| Freeman | Benj. | 150 | | Ernest H. | 73 |
| | Blanche | 118 | | Mary K. | 73 |
| | Catherine | 3 | | Minnie | 77 |
| | Mary E. | 3 | | Valentine | 89 |
| | Moses | 130 | Fronefield | Edith E. | 4 |
| | Richard | 51 | Fry | Amos | 195 |
| | Scott | 87 | | Catharine M. | 223 |
| | William | 60,130 | | Charlatie | 228 |
| Frees | Israel | 222 | | Hiram | 81 |
| | John | 82 | | Jacob | 168 |
| Freestone | Amos | 84 | | James B. | 225 |
| | Jacob | 175 | | James Calvin | 166 |
| | Zachariah | 84 | | James P. | 197 |
| Freet | Jerusha M. | 209 | | Lewis | 90 |

| | | | | | | |
|---|---|---|---|---|---|---|
| Fry | Mary | 213 | Galbreth | John | 89 |
| | Mary E. | 221 | Galer | Jacob A. | 82 |
| | Matilda | 198 | Galesby | Thomas | 110 |
| | Sarah Ann | 196 | Gall | Albert | 317 |
| | Simon | 52 | Gallahan | Fanny | 167 |
| | Soloman | 81 | | Mary | 321 |
| | Solomon | 88,90 | | Mary Ann | 166 |
| | Susanah Mar. | 195 | Gallaher | Florence | 317 |
| Fryar | Margaret E. | 308 | Gallaspy | Robert | 130 |
| Frzier | Alexander | 161 | Gallimore | Arthur | 33 |
| Fuchs | Charles F. | 299,303 | Gallion | Matilda | 34 |
| | Frederick L. | 303 | Gallmeier | Anna M. | 8 |
| Fulland | Sam. | 150 | Gamache | Eulallie | 301 |
| Fullen | Sam. | 150 | Gamble | Eliza | 46 |
| Fuller | Harriet | 59 | Ganes | George | 90 |
| | Isaac | 53 | | Oliver | 88,90 |
| | John | 130 | Ganson | Mary | 336 |
| Fulton | Elizabeth | 336 | | William M. | 336 |
| | John | 46 | Gant | Hannah | 49 |
| Fults | Caitty B. | 221 | | James C. | 62 |
| | Ralph | 152 | | Mary | 57 |
| Fulwiler | ---- | 165 | | Nancy | 59 |
| | J.B. | 164 | Gappert | Samina M. | 220 |
| | Jas. B. | 163 | Garard | Nathaniel M. | 195 |
| Funk | Isaac | 102 | Garber | Catharine | 176 |
| | Kate D. | 317 | | Demas | 168 |
| | William | 102,108 | | Michael C. | 303 |
| Funkhouser | Elmer | 317 | | William S. | 317 |
| Furbee | Ellen G. K. | 317 | Garberson | Mary S. | 206 |
| Furgison | James | 148 | Garbinson | George W. | 228 |
| | John | 148 | | Joseph | 212 |
| Furguson | William | 47 | Garbison | Daniel | 203 |
| Furnace | Grace M. | 118 | Gard | Philander | 119 |
| | Roy | 118,119 | | Ross | 119 |
| Furnish | B.F. | 83 | | Sarah | 119 |
| Furry | Henry | 83 | | Serena | 119 |
| Fuston | Elizabeth | 211 | Gardner | Alonzo M. | 317 |
| | Nancy A. | 210 | | Cummins | 56 |
| | | | | G.W. | 90 |
| Gaar | Julia Meek | 317 | | George | 88 |
| Gable | N.H. | 122 | | John | 56 |
| Gabriel | J. | 86 | | Julia | 205 |
| Gaesser | Theobald T. | 317 | | Margaretta | 205 |
| Gage | Henry | 82,83 | | Stonewall J. | 303 |
| | Mark | 82 | | William | 303 |
| Gahn | Ephraim | 86 | Garison | Cornealious | 212 |
| Gailey | Mildred E. | 14 | Garman | Georgianna | 317 |
| Gains | Benjamin | 88 | | Harry Otto | 317 |
| | Edmund | 88 | Garn | Martin | 204 |
| Gaither | John W. | 95 | Garnart | Jacob | 200 |
| | Westley | 110 | Garner | Alfred A. | 220 |
| Galbreath | Robert | 51 | | Henry W. | 217 |

| | | | | | | |
|---|---|---|---|---|---|---|
| Gerhart | Alvin R. | 299 | Gillespie | James | 82 |
| Geringer | Joseph J. | 317 | | Matilda Ann | 59 |
| Gerken | Carl A. | 317 | Gillespy | Leroy S. | 218 |
| German | Charles T. | 215 | Gilley | George B. | 230 |
| German | Elizabeth R. | 206 | Gillham | Alfred | 303 |
| | Harriet | 200 | | Robert Pat. | 303 |
| | Henrietta C. | 198 | Gillie | George W. | 317 |
| | James R. | 227 | Gilliland | Hugh | 102 |
| | Joshua N. | 199 | Gillis | Robert | 6 |
| | Lewis | 218 | Gillmore | Alexander | 130 |
| | Lucretia J. | 198 | | Allexander | 104 |
| | Mathias J. | 197 | Gillson | Lydia M. | 205 |
| | Sarah Adaline | 196 | Gillum | Eliza | 183 |
| Gesaman | Carrie B. | 5 | Gilmore | ----(Rev.) | 288 |
| Getz | Carl(Mrs.) | 9 | | Abijah | 224 |
| | Esther | 3 | | Alexander | 98,130 |
| Gibbons | George Lee | 317 | | Alexandr | 109 |
| | Melinda | 115 | | Ida M. | 224 |
| | Susannah | 115 | | Samuel | 99 |
| Gibbs | Ida A. | 221 | | Thomas | 99 |
| | James | 103 | Gilpin | James | 90 |
| | Maggie J. | 218 | | Levi Lambdin | 317 |
| | Martha | 207 | | Nancy | 123 |
| Gibson | Andrew S. | 102 | | Samuel | 88 |
| | Esther | 62 | | Wm. | 86 |
| | George | 91 | Gingerich | Mary | 211 |
| | Jesse | 114 | Gingery | Martin | 81,88 |
| | John | 20 | Gingrich | Abraham J. | 199 |
| | Rachel | 116 | | Nancy | 210 |
| | Thomas | 20 | | Sarah | 217 |
| | Walter | 317 | Gingrick | Jeremiah | 204 |
| Gifford | Jesse | 130 | Givan | James | 157 |
| | Peleg | 130 | | John | 160 |
| Gilbert | Anna | 173 | Given | John S. | 201 |
| | Charles | 166 | | Josiah | 38 |
| | Jno. A. | 164 | Givens | Frances | 172 |
| | Robert | 247 | | Harry J. | 111 |
| Gildersleeve | W.H. | 317 | Gladden | Claude M. | 317 |
| Giles | James A. | 208 | | Elijah A. | 317 |
| | John | 210 | Glass | Anna M. | 9 |
| | Ralph | 168 | Glaze | William | 88 |
| Gileson | John | 102 | Glazebrook | Harietta | 221 |
| Gill | Spencer | 58 | | Minnie | 218 |
| | William | 121 | Glendennin | Daisy | 119 |
| Gillaspy | George | 130 | Glenn | Archibald | 130 |
| | James | 130 | | Henry | 130 |
| | Robert | 130 | | Nell S. | 118,119 |
| | William | 130 | Glimpse | Emanael | 144 |
| Gillchrees | Stephen K. | 33 | Glisten | Joseph | 155 |
| Gillcrees | Robert | 130 | Glistener | Benjamin | 84 |
| Gilleland | Lydia | 168 | Glossbrenner | Alfred M. | 317 |
| | Wilson | 168 | | Harry W. | 317 |

| | | | | | | |
|---|---|---|---|---|---|---|
| Glover | Beatrice E. | 14 | Goodthunder | Daniel | 239 | |
| | Joseph | 130 | Goodwin | ---- | 29 | |
| | Joshua | 156 | | Amos H. | 22 | |
| Glympse | Amuel | 144 | | Anna E. | 303 | |
| Goble | L.E.(Mrs.) | 13 | | Clarence L. | 317 | |
| | Miranda | 49 | | Daniel | 53 | |
| Goda | Peter(Mrs.) | 6 | | Elias | 108 | |
| Godchaux | Leon | 317 | | George | 20 | |
| Godfrey | Benjamin | 40 | | Judiah | 53 | |
| | Elijah | 85 | | Julia | 242 | |
| | W.L. | 123 | | Lydia | 177 | |
| Godfroy | Chief | 165 | | Mary | 27 | |
| | Clarence | 317 | | Thomas | 41 | |
| | Louis | 16 | | William | 17,20,22,27,28 | |
| Godley | A.L. | 295 | | Willis W. | 18,19,20 | |
| | Albert | 294,297 | Goodykoontz | A.B. | 82 | |
| Goen | Ruben | 229 | | Abram | 83 | |
| Goff | Esther Ann | 42 | | Jacob | 81,82,83 | |
| | John | 204 | | Simon | 81,82,83 | |
| Goforth | Mary | 42 | Gooley | Howard(Mrs.) | 14 | |
| Goin | Edmund | 45,46 | Goon | Eve C. | 198 | |
| | Elizabeth | 37 | | Leah Eliza. | 201 | |
| Going | Jane | 171 | | Mary | 205 | |
| | Ruben | 229 | | Saloma | 199 | |
| Goings | Elnora | 309 | Gooschorn | Polly | 56 | |
| Goldberger | Rose | 14 | Goossens | Emile J. | 317 | |
| Golding | Jane | 51 | Goowin | Elias | 98 | |
| | Oscar | 218 | Goppert | Barbara | 206 | |
| | Sylvester | 52 | | George | 226 | |
| | William | 61 | Gorden | Emma H. | 227 | |
| Goldsberry | Mary J. | 199 | | Selinda | 54 | |
| | Samuel | 157 | Gordon | Achsah | 37 | |
| Goldsmith | Mary | 47 | | Jonathan W. | 231 | |
| | Samuel | 105 | | Joseph | 233 | |
| | William | 100,109 | | Joseph R.T. | 231 | |
| Goldstein | Elisabeth | 218 | | Leander | 299 | |
| Goldthalt | Simon | 86 | | Selinda | 54 | |
| Goldthiat | Oliver | 87 | | Thos. | 247 | |
| Goldthwaite | E.L. | 91 | Gore | Frederick | 25 | |
| Golladay | ---- | 291 | Gorman | Robert | 317 | |
| Good | Emma O'Niel | 166 | Gorsuch | James A. | 303 | |
| | Harvy J. | 201 | | James A. Jr. | 303 | |
| | John W. | 221 | Gortney | Anthony | 105 | |
| | Mary | 195 | | Ephraim | 108 | |
| | Samuel A. | 222 | | Thomas | 108 | |
| | Tobias | 207 | | William | 109 | |
| | William J. | 202 | Gortny | Thomas | 96 | |
| Goode | Blanche | 303 | Goshorn | Laura | 4 | |
| Goodman | Timothy S. | 130 | | Maggie L. | 5 | |
| | William | 98 | Goslee | Sallie | 304 | |
| Goodrich | David | 82 | Gosnell | Charles J. | 299 | |
| | James Putman | 317 | Gossette | John W. | 246 | |

| | | | | | | |
|---|---|---|---|---|---|---|
| Gossom | John | 89 | Gray | Axom | 83 |
| Gossoom | John | 92 | | Daniel | 89,90 |
| Goster | George | 186 | | John | 86 |
| Gott | Richd. | 150 | | Mark Roy | 317 |
| Goudie | Rob't. | 159 | | Tacy | 333 |
| Goudy | Abigail | 165 | | William | 86 |
| | Jacob | 169 | Graydon | Katherine M. | 317 |
| | Rob't. | 159 | Greely | Horace | 243 |
| | Robert S. | 247 | Green | Adam | 99,105 |
| Gouin | Felicia | 164 | | Alpheus | 119 |
| Gould | John H. | 212 | | Clary B. | 222 |
| | Leona | 200 | | Elias W. | 224 |
| | Lucy Candace | 4 | | Eliza Ann | 45 |
| | Rosanna | 200 | | Estor | 215 |
| | Rosetta A. | 202 | | Harvey C. | 198 |
| | Sarah Jane | 209 | | Irvin | 87 |
| | Wallace L. | 202 | | Jesse | 87,89 |
| Goulette | Louise | 242,244 | | John | 60,88 |
| Gowing | Robert | 39 | | Joseph W. | 32 |
| Grace | Jesse | 151 | | Lot | 88,318 |
| Graebner | Susanna | 173 | | Louisa | 46 |
| Gragg | James | 38 | | Orlow | 196 |
| Graghill | Elias | 90 | | Polly W. | 41 |
| Graham | Andrew J. | 201 | | Rufus | 119 |
| | Clara | 239 | | Ruth | 199 |
| | Elizabeth | 37 | | Samuel | 82 |
| | Everett E. | 303 | Greene | Fancisca | 7 |
| | George | 195 | | Katie M. | 212 |
| | John K. | 19,37 | Greenly | Albert H. | 318 |
| | Mary J. | 194 | Greff | William Sr. | 87 |
| | Robert T. | 303 | Gregary | James | 100 |
| | Sarah Jane | 173 | Gregg | Harvey | 130,158 |
| Graner | Elizabeth | 186 | | Hervey | 158 |
| Grant | Margaret | 45 | | Maria | 57 |
| | Thomas | 107 | | Sally | 55 |
| | William | 96,97,104,110 | | Thomas | 87 |
| Graper | Alvina L. | 70 | | Zella | 6 |
| | August D. | 70 | Gregory | Harriett | 115 |
| | Maude | 70 | | John | 98,105 |
| | Susan Kaye | 70 | | Perrin B. | 303 |
| Grary | William | 205 | | Sally | 38 |
| Grass | Daniel | 97 | | Whitney I. | 303 |
| | Danniel | 95 | | William | 96,102,108, |
| | Henrey | 105 | | | 144 |
| | Henry | 95,97 | Greider | Hattie | 10 |
| Grau | Lydia | 317 | Greiner | Samuel | 210 |
| Grave | George W. | 227 | Greist | Oliver H. | 318 |
| Graves | Calvin | 34,127 | Grenart | Franklin | 227 |
| | Elizabeth | 130 | Grenert | Harriett | 224 |
| | George | 130 | Gresham | Carrington | 100 |
| | Milton P. | 210 | | Dudly | 98 |
| | Sarah | 44 | | John | 45 |

394

| | | | | | | |
|---|---|---|---|---|---|---|
| Gresham | Philip | 100 | Grissom | Lawraence | 110 |
| Gresim | Dudley | 104 | | Levi | 182 |
| Gressom | Dudley | 105 | Grist | Ebenzer | 49 |
| | Philip | 109 | | Margaret | 50 |
| | Thomas | 108 | | Mary | 171 |
| Grey | Carl | 243 | Griswold | Amelia | 168 |
| Greyham | Wm. | 104 | | James | 148 |
| Grice | E.C. | 90 | | Letitia | 166 |
| Gridley | Mary Ann | 168 | Groceclose | Andrew | 130 |
| Grier | Eliza | 170 | | John | 130 |
| Griffen | Wesley P. | 215 | Groff | James W. | 303 |
| Griffeth | Azel | 169 | | Sophia | 303 |
| Griffin | Ann | 179 | | William A. | 299,303 |
| | Ida | 312 | Gros | Flora | 312 |
| | Immanuel | 205 | Groshands | Edward | 218 |
| | Martin | 86 | | Conrad | 209 |
| | Mary Jane | 318 | | Elizabeth | 209 |
| | Robert | 86 | Groshaus | Adie R. | 221 |
| Griffith | Albert H. | 318 | | Andrew | 202 |
| | Humphry | 149 | | Ida | 228 |
| | Jane | 114 | | Luety M. | 222 |
| | Joseph | 150 | | Phillip | 201 |
| | Rebecca | 23 | Groshause | Conrad | 196 |
| | Roderick | 25 | Groshouts | Elizabeth | 201 |
| | Samuel | 130 | Grosjean | Ray(Mrs.) | 7 |
| | Sophia C. | 164 | Gross | Gertrude | 10 |
| | Thomas | 130,206 | | Loraine C. | 10 |
| | William N. | 21 | Grosshart | John | 34 |
| Griggs | Anna | 194 | Grossman | -tena | 70 |
| Grigsby | Elizabeth | 40 | | C. | 70 |
| Grills | Merton W. | 318 | | R. | 70 |
| Grimes | Ann Eliza | 168 | Grounds | Margaret E. | 209 |
| | Eleanor | 265 | Grout | David | 130 |
| | Elenor Pearl | 265 | Grove | Clayton | 211 |
| | Ervin | 265 | | Hester A. | 203 |
| | Harrison | 167 | | Sarah | 201 |
| | Lura L. | 265 | | Simon | 100 |
| | Margie M. | 318 | Grover | Emily Monroe | 318 |
| | Nancy W. | 265 | Groves | Catherine | 32 |
| | Sarah R. | 265 | | Daniel | 148 |
| | Thomes | 265 | | David | 146 |
| | William | 87 | | John | 143 |
| Grimm | Walter C. | 298 | | Mary | 37 |
| Grims | Lura | 265 | | Wm. Henry | 147 |
| Grinard | Rachel | 333 | Groyls | George W. | 274 |
| Grindle | J.W. | 89 | Grrett | Wm. | 144 |
| | Jacob | 89 | Grubbs | Samuel Bates | 318 |
| | John W. | 204,226 | Gruber | Leonard | 10 |
| | Samuel | 90 | Grur | Wm. N. | 282 |
| Grinelle | John | 205 | Gudgel | A. | 64 |
| Griner | Benjamin | 57 | | E. | 64 |
| Grisham | Thomas | 99 | | Lucy F. | 64 |

| | | | | | | |
|---|---|---|---|---|---|---|
| Gudgel | Martha | 64 | | Gwartney | William | 98 |
| Guenin | Edward | 86 | | Gwathmey | Samuel | 17,18,23 |
| Guernsey | Henry | 218 | | Gwin | George | 96,99 |
| Guest | Anne | 19 | | | Thomas | 96 |
| | Bazel | 19 | | Gwinn | Mary | 42 |
| | Hannah | 34 | | Gwinnup | George | 57 |
| | Job | 17 | | Gwynn | Margaret | 115 |
| | Martha | 43 | | | | |
| | Mary | 34 | | Haaff | George H. | 193 |
| | Rachel | 19 | | | J.A. | 193 |
| | Sarah | 331 | | | William | 193 |
| Guffey | James | 37 | | Habbard | Tamsey | 51 |
| Guier | Mary Ann | 172 | | Habbe | John F. | 318 |
| Guild | J.W. | 276 | | Habbell | John | 167 |
| Guin | George | 105 | | Habecker | Alice M. | 4 |
| Guiselman | John | 225 | | Haberkorn | Augusta | 6 |
| Guke | John | 223 | | | Emma | 6 |
| Gulick | Charrity | 53 | | Habough | Geo. W. | 88 |
| | William | 23 | | Hack | Elizabeth M. | 318 |
| Gulley | Elsey | 60 | | Hacked | John D. | 227 |
| Gumpper | Adah K. | 14 | | Hackelrode | Sarah | 198 |
| Gunckle | Philip | 165 | | Hackelroth | Sarah | 198 |
| Gunkle | Elizabeth | 175 | | Hacker | Mary E. | 226 |
| | Maria | 172 | | Hacket | Mary | 18 |
| Gunn | Ira W. | 40 | | Hackett | John | 35 |
| | Mathew | 47 | | Hackhaus | Rose | 304 |
| | Nancy Glass | 41 | | Hackley | Frederick | 170 |
| Gurley | Anna | 329 | | | George | 169 |
| Gurnsey | A. Alincoln | 221 | | Hacklman | A. | 188 |
| Gurnsey | Martha A. | 204 | | Hacks | Lydia | 177 |
| | Martha J. | 225 | | Haddon | David | 245 |
| | N.L. | 225 | | | John | 243 |
| | Sarah E. | 207 | | Hadley | Chalmers | 318 |
| Gurnsy | Susannah | 201 | | | Martha | 115 |
| Gurthside | Hannah | 40 | | Haerle | Elisabeth L. | 318 |
| Guse | Ottilie | 224 | | | George C. | 318 |
| Gushorn | Polly | 56 | | Haggerty | Emma J. | 202 |
| Gusmer | August | 211 | | Hagland | James | 149 |
| Gust | William W. | 224 | | Hagle | Alonzo G. | 208 |
| Guthrie | William A. | 318 | | | Angeline | 197 |
| Guy | James | 169 | | | Elias C. | 199 |
| | John Jr. | 170 | | | Laura J. | 206 |
| Guyer | Eleanor | 175 | | | Martha Ann | 216 |
| | Joseph F. | 168 | | | Susanah | 208 |
| | Margaret | 175 | | | William | 200,226 |
| | Rebecca | 172 | | Hague | John | 82 |
| Guynn | Eppy | 113 | | Hail | Wm. | 89 |
| Gwaltney | J.J. | 188 | | Haines | James | 81,83 |
| Gwartney | Anthony | 98 | | | John | 206 |
| | Ephraim | 98 | | | John Michael | 217 |
| | Micajah | 98 | | | Mary Ann | 204 |
| | Thomas | 98 | | | Mary E. | 276 |

| | | | | | | |
|---|---|---|---|---|---|---|
| Haines | Matthias L. | 318 | Hall | Mary | 111 |
| | Myrtle | 6 | | Mary B. | 303 |
| | Nathan | 82,83 | | Mary R. | 226 |
| | Samuel | 92 | | N.C. | 166 |
| | William | 197 | | Olive M. | 65 |
| Hainman | Luther | 57 | | Robert | 211 |
| Hains | Franklin | 217 | | Stephen Sr. | 86 |
| | George | 143 | | Stephen | 49 |
| | John | 82 | | William | 84 |
| Hair | ---- 285,286,288,289, | | Hallam | William | 130 |
| | | 290 | Haller | Edward | 15 |
| | Cynthia | 288 | | Mary R. | 14 |
| | Saml. | 281 | Hallingsworth | Enos | 85 |
| | W. | 288 | | Wm. F. | 85 |
| | Wm. | 281 | Hallowell | Mary | 35 |
| Haire | ---- | 280 | | William | 55 |
| | C. | 280 | Hallowvill | William | 55 |
| Halberstadt | Loring C. | 318 | Halsey | Abagail | 59 |
| Hale | Betsey | 114 | | Catherine | 53 |
| | Desdamona | 7 | | Senca | 60 |
| | Hannah | 37 | Halstead | Abagail | 59 |
| | Virgil | 87 | | Elizabeth | 59 |
| Haley | Daisy L. | 71 | | Josiah P. | 56 |
| | Virgil J. | 71 | | Lillian S. | 302 |
| Hall | A.A. | 144 | Halstedd | Wm. F. | 91 |
| | Abraham A. | 144 | Haltz | Christ. | 247 |
| | Ada | 324 | Halwes | Adelia | 72 |
| | Alfred | 172 | | Henry | 72 |
| | Amos | 97 | Ham | Eli E. | 201 |
| | Anna J. | 216 | Hamaker | A.J. | 90 |
| | Beverly | 65 | | Benjamin | 89 |
| | Edgar Price | 303 | | James | 91 |
| | Elizabeth | 58,169 | | Jefferson A. | 88 |
| | Elmer | 119 | | John | 89 |
| | Emmett M. | 299 | Hamar | Solomon | 38 |
| | Esther | 57 | Hamblen | Daniel G. | 45 |
| | Fred | 119 | Hamelton | Alex. | 146 |
| | George G. | 303 | Hamilton | ---- | 294 |
| | Henry | 174 | | Alex. | 146 |
| | Hiram A. | 198 | | Archibald | 25 |
| | Isaac | 86 | | Dora Miller | 318 |
| | J.F. | 87 | | Emma L. | 4 |
| | James W. | 228 | | Frances F. | 318 |
| | John S. | 161 | | Frank | 1 |
| | Joseph | 169 | | Frank A. | 318 |
| | Joseph Emmett | 318 | | Harry A. | 299 |
| | Julia | 207 | | Hiram | 55 |
| | Leaven E. | 42 | | Hugh | 89 |
| | Lida | 3 | | Isaac | 89 |
| | Lillian M. | 65 | | James | 147,200 |
| | Mable O. | 65 | | Jeremiah | 130 |
| | Malinda | 171 | | Jesse | 24 |

| Hamilton | John | 219 | Haney | Stella C. | 119 |
|----------|------|-----|-------|-----------|-----|
| | Margret | 60 | Hanger | Nancy | 37 |
| | May | 184 | Hani | Amelia D. | 210 |
| | Robert | 54,155 | Hankey | August | 212 |
| | Thos. | 247 | | Gotleib | 208 |
| | William | 25 | Hankins | Stephen | 151 |
| | William W. | 187 | Hann | Elender | 199 |
| Hammack | Isaiah | 37 | | George | 201,219 |
| Hammer | Jeremiah | 87 | | Margaret | 197 |
| | John | 87 | | Martha | 197 |
| | Joseph | 89 | | Melissa A. | 198 |
| Hammitt | George | 334 | Hanna | Ezekiel L. | 62 |
| | Harriet | 334 | | Geo. | 141 |
| Hammon | Davis M. | 191 | | J.N. | 51 |
| | Davis W. | 191 | | J.W. | 156 |
| | John S. | 191 | | James P. | 155 |
| Hammond | Davis M. | 190 | | Jenny | 50 |
| | George W. | 61 | | R.J.H. | 154 |
| | Lola | 179 | | Susan | 52 |
| | William S. | 57 | Hannah | Geo. | 141 |
| Hammons | R.T. | 124 | | James P. | 155 |
| Hamner | James | 130 | | John | 156 |
| | Jemima | 130 | | Phebe | 58 |
| | Joseph | 130 | | R.G.H. | 154 |
| | William | 130 | | Robt. | 150 |
| Hamon | Ransom | 46 | Hannaman | Wm. | 141 |
| Hampton | Sarah S. | 116 | Hannan | Peter W. | 211 |
| Hanaker | John B. | 88 | Hannaway | Amos | 161 |
| Hanan | John W. | 318 | Hannon | J. Walter | 318 |
| Hanaway | Amos | 161 | Hannons | James | 171 |
| Hanby | Maggie | 217 | Hansel | Anna | 58 |
| Hancel | Clarrie | 212 | | Catharine | 57 |
| Hancock | Clarissa | 33 | | John | 57 |
| | James | 41,50 | | Nancy | 52 |
| | Lydia | 190 | Hanselman | Katie A. | 222 |
| | Maggie W. | 119 | | Rosa | 227 |
| | Milton | 180 | Hansleman | Matthew | 41 |
| | Nancy | 38 | Hansley | Nancy | 52 |
| Hand | C.J. | 145 | Hantz | Louisa | 220 |
| | Elizabeth | 206 | Haolloway | William | 201 |
| | Jacob | 44 | Hapeman | Edgar | 221 |
| | James | 39 | Happes | Bartha | 223 |
| | Libia | 42 | Harbaugh | George | 208 |
| | Martha E. | 204 | | John | 102 |
| | Priscilla | 47 | Harberman | Charles | 209 |
| Hanes | Artemius | 201 | Harberson | John | 100 |
| | Charles W. | 222 | | Jonathan | 108 |
| | George | 143 | Harbert | William H. | 168 |
| | Mary | 210 | Harden | George W. | 225 |
| | William | 103,222 | | Henry | 142,158 |
| Haney | Charles | 119 | | Hubert | 267 |
| | John | 104 | | Isom | 107 |

| | | | | | | |
|---|---|---|---|---|---|---|
| Harden | Louise | 239 | Harlin | William | 87 |
| | Mary | 39 | Harman | Charles | 217 |
| | Melinda E. | 181 | | Clarinda E. | 274 |
| | Wm. | 153,160 | | Edmund F. | 274 |
| Hardenbrook | Cornelius | 141 | | James S. | 274 |
| Hardesty | Hamlin | 225 | | John Allen | 275 |
| Hardin | Flora | 323 | | Leverett | 34 |
| | Franklin | 150 | | Nancy M. | 274 |
| | Henry | 142,158 | | Sarah C. | 274 |
| | Isaac | 153 | | Sinai Jane | 274 |
| | Rob't. | 159 | | Thomas L | 274 |
| | Sam'l. | 160 | | Wm. | 274 |
| | Sarah | 290 | Harmiken | John | 230 |
| | Wm. | 160 | Harmon | Abraham | 97 |
| Harding | Abagail | 59 | | Amelia Polk | 274 |
| | Ead | 161 | | Clarinda E. | 274 |
| | Ed | 161 | | Edmund F. | 274 |
| | Isaac | 153 | | Eliza M. | 274 |
| | Israel | 161 | | Elizabeth | 37 |
| | Laban | 161 | | George | 274 |
| | Philip | 150 | | George L. | 274 |
| | Rob't. | 159 | | Henry | 274 |
| | Sam'l. | 160 | | J.B. | 146 |
| | Walter B. | 318 | | Jacob | 99,106 |
| | Wm. | 153 | | James | 146 |
| Hardsock | Isaac | 219 | | James S. | 274 |
| | Mary L. | 203 | | John Allen | 274 |
| Hardwick | Lou | 295 | | Joseph | 97,107 |
| Hardy | George W. | 194 | | Lydia Ann | 165 |
| | John | 201 | | Martha Eliza. | 274 |
| | Rosa L. | 218 | | Martissa S. | 274 |
| Harens | Wm. | 86 | | Mary B. | 275 |
| Hares | Mary | 60 | | Mary Eliza | 274 |
| Harger | Andrew | 181 | | Moses Dooley | 274 |
| Hargrave | Frank F. | 318 | | Nancy Melvina | 274 |
| | Homer P. | 318 | | Nicholas | 18 |
| | James | 101 | | Ruth Senoria | 274 |
| Hargrove | ----(Col.) | 80 | | Samuel | 25 |
| Harison | Alfred | 142 | | Sarah C. | 274 |
| | Issabella | 27 | | Sinah Jane | 274 |
| | Tobitha | 215 | | Steven | 17 |
| Harker | Abram D. | 228 | | Thomas L. | 274 |
| | Clary | 228 | | Wm. | 157 |
| | Mark H. | 318 | | Wiliam Henry | 274 |
| Harkey | Josephing | 191 | | William H. | 275 |
| Harkins | Mary E. | 217 | | William P. | 275 |
| | Matilda C. | 226 | | William Polk | 274 |
| Harless | Calvin G. | 223 | Harmonson | Peter | 130 |
| Harley | Elwen | 88 | Harness | James D. | 215 |
| | Harrison | 88 | | Matthias D. | 208,213 |
| Harlin | A.J. | 87 | Harp | Keziah | 171 |
| | J.W. | 86 | Harper | Bilip | 143 |

399

| | | | | | | |
|---|---|---|---|---|---|---|
| Hartloff | Frederick | 185 | Hatfield | Malinda | 33 |
| Hartman | Charles | 175 | | Mary Wright | 318 |
| | Daniel | 82,144 | | William | 58 |
| | Elizabeth | 175 | Hathaway | Almira A. | 283 |
| | George | 114 | | George M. | 221 |
| | Louis | 231 | | Joseph C. | 221 |
| | Nancy | 60 | | Ollie M. | 207 |
| Hartseiff | Wm.(Mrs.) | 2 | Hatter | Catharine | 195 |
| Hartsell | Fred | 149 | | Hannah | 202 |
| Hartsock | Calesta C. | 202 | | Julius C. | 204 |
| | Cyntha Jane | 207 | Hatton | Melvina | 111 |
| | Nelson | 146 | Hauck | Carrie | 6 |
| Hartsook | John | 86 | Hauffman | Aaron | 84 |
| Hartsough | Mary M. | 318 | | Hart | 84 |
| Harttley | Anna | 228 | Haugh | May Blake | 318 |
| Hartz | Ida M. | 228 | Haun | David | 167 |
| | Jacob | 206 | Havens | Benjamin | 84,91 |
| | Peter | 221 | | Bruce(Mrs.) | 6 |
| Hartzell | Ellen | 122 | | Charles H. | 250 |
| Harvey | George W. | 91,163 | | Chloe J. | 9 |
| | Isaac | 130 | | D.F. | 276 |
| | Jame | 54 | | Daniel Frame | 250 |
| | Jesse | 84 | | Eli | 61 |
| | Thomas | 84 | | Georgia | 250 |
| Harwood | John | 49 | | Howard | 251 |
| Haseltine | Haynes | 62 | | James | 85,124 |
| Hasker | George F. | 225 | | Katherine M.. | 251 |
| Haskinds | Alpha | 33 | | Lola T. | 250 |
| Haskins | John P. | 204 | | Mabel | 250 |
| | Lusebra | 180 | | Mable | 250 |
| | Matthias J. | 210 | | Madalene | 250 |
| | William H. | 211 | | Nellie | 8 |
| Hasley | Sarah | 56 | | Peter | 83 |
| Hasselman | Ida Blood | 318 | | Virginia | 251 |
| Hassheider | ---- | 72 | Hawblitzel | Henry C. | 225 |
| | Emma L. | 72 | Hawerton | John | 96 |
| | J. | 72 | Hawes | Milnor | 169 |
| | J.H. | 70 | Hawk | Abel M. | 172 |
| | M. | 72 | | Rebecah | 51 |
| | Matilda L. | 70 | Hawkins | Eleanor | 34 |
| | N. | 72 | | Elizabeth | 57 |
| Hassler | Fannie S. | 2 | | Emely M. | 200 |
| Hassmer | Joseph A. | 318 | | George | 59 |
| Hasten | Samuel S. | 167 | | Jemison | 145 |
| Hastings | Carter | 83 | | Jesse | 116 |
| | Hugh | 57 | | John | 151 |
| Hasty | Barnhart | 201 | | John R. | 218 |
| Hatch | Mabel | 6 | | Louisa J. | 218 |
| Hatfield | Elizabeth | 47 | | Rachel E. | 226 |
| | George C. | 82 | | Samuel | 88 |
| | Isaac | 82 | | Sarah | 60,204 |
| | Jefferson | 170 | | Thomas | 54 |

| | | | | | | |
|---|---|---|---|---|---|---|
| Heberhart | William G. | 318 | Hemminger | George W. | 197 |
| Hebert | Elizabeth | 6 | | James C. | 228 |
| Heck | Jacob | 109 | | Joseph | 198 |
| Heckard | David | 88 | Hemp | Jacob | 108 |
| Heckman | Geo.(Mrs.) | 6 | Hendelider | Caroline | 37 |
| Hecock | ---- | 183 | Henderson | Albridge | 247 |
| Hecox | Cyrus W. | 216 | | Alexander H. | 228 |
| Hedden | Anna Marietta | 37 | | Ann | 23 |
| Heddy | L.W. | 142 | | Dvid | 81 |
| Hedges | Caleb | 146 | | Elijah | 151 |
| | Henry | 183 | | Isaac | 168 |
| | Jane | 111 | | J. | 67 |
| | Sarah L. | 3 | | Juilette C. | 228 |
| Hedglen | Alexander M. | 197 | | Leven | 58 |
| Hedrick | John | 46 | | Lora L. | 67 |
| | Phebe | 42 | | Lyda E. | 67 |
| Heely | Jabez | 84 | | Mary | 48 |
| Heflick | Samuel | 207 | | Samuel | 161 |
| Hegan | Harmon | 103 | | Susan | 62 |
| Heistand | Abraham | 98,106 | | Thomas | 130 |
| | Christian | 103 | Hendran | Oliver | 131 |
| Heitger | Louis C. | 318 | Hendren | Gilbert R. | 319 |
| Helm | Bailis D. | 88 | Hendrick | Abraham | 159 |
| | Bates | 91 | Hendricks | ---- | 289 |
| | Francis | 88,91 | | Abraham | 159 |
| | James M. | 88 | | Allan | 319 |
| | Thos. | 87 | | David | 131 |
| | Wm. | 149 | | E. | 86 |
| Helmer | Estella K. | 7 | | Geo. W. | 86 |
| Helsey | D.S. | 67 | | I. | 286 |
| | H.J. | 67 | | J. | 282 |
| | Herchel | 67 | | James | 131 |
| Helsley | Eliza J. | 67 | | Jamison | 283 |
| | Franklin R. | 67 | | Lewis | 131 |
| Heltner | A.J. | 89 | | Martisha | 304 |
| Heltzer | George | 218 | | Separate | 131 |
| Hemel | Vermilla F. | 5 | | Squire | 131 |
| Heminger | John | 202,215 | | Thomas A. | 319 |
| | Joseph | 196 | Hendrickson | Edmonia D. | 319 |
| | Mary | 203 | | James | 131 |
| | Susan | 196 | | John | 49 |
| Hemmer | Albert E. | 69 | Hendrix | Walter W. | 304 |
| | Amanda | 69 | Hendrix | William | 304 |
| | Augustus | 69 | Heneld | John | 84 |
| | Daniel S. | 69 | Henesly | John W. | 146 |
| | H.F. | 69 | Henley | Eunice D. | 319 |
| | Heney F. | 69 | | Howard E. | 319 |
| | L.C. | 69 | | John | 84 |
| | Lawrence | 69 | | Lillian E. | 319 |
| | Louise C. | 69 | | Phineas | 84 |
| | Sarah E. | 69 | Henly | Phineas | 91 |
| Hemminger | David | 197 | Henman | Abigail | 57 |

| | | | | | | |
|---|---|---|---|---|---|---|
| Henman | Luther | 57 | Herrod | William | 23,334 |
| Hennessy | Edmond | 247 | Herron | Joseph | 115 |
| Henning | Jacob | 56 | | Josephine | 319 |
| | Thom. | 182 | Hersch | Jennie Rae | 319 |
| Henry | Catharine | 49 | Hershberger | Moses | 194 |
| Henseil | L. Adelia | 4 | Hershey | Lilus | 208 |
| Hensel | Emma | 302 | Hersing | Mira | 217 |
| Henselman | Florence | 225 | Hervey | C.M. | 201 |
| Henshaw | Jacob | 142 | Hess | Charles(Mrs.) | 13 |
| | John W. | 203 | | Elizabeth | 34 |
| Hensley | Ben | 119 | | Marin | 190 |
| | Jeptha | 131 | Hessey | John | 108 |
| | Polly | 131 | Hessong | Sarah | 166 |
| | William R. | 131 | Hester | Craven P. | 131 |
| Hensly | Nancy | 52 | | Pearson Sr. | 85 |
| Henson | Michael | 167 | Heth | H.W. | 110 |
| | William | 111 | Hether | Margaret | 117 |
| Henton | Harriet | 167 | | Sealy | 114 |
| | Thomas | 170 | | Thomas | 131 |
| Hentz | Polina | 216 | | William Jr. | 131 |
| Henz | Amelia | 216 | Hetzel | Conrad | 192 |
| Hepburn | William M. | 319 | Heubschenan | John | 192 |
| Hepner | Caroline | 198 | Heusler | Basil | 319 |
| | Ettie M. | 217 | Hewes | Margaret A. | 2 |
| | Mattie M. | 217 | Hey | Aaron | 35 |
| Hepshire | James | 203 | | Maria | 41 |
| Herath | George | 186 | | Martha | 37 |
| Herbaugh | John | 103 | | Rose | 36 |
| Hergerreader | Sophia | 53 | Heyman | Anna | 8 |
| Herld | Henry | 90 | Heywood | Henry B. | 319 |
| Herndon | Nancy | 57 | Hiatt | Daniel | 85,93 |
| Herod | Henry L. | 319 | | David | 93 |
| | Mapel Clare | 264 | | Elihu | 85 |
| | Margaret | 262,263 | | Jared | 85 |
| | Ralph T. | 264 | | John | 114 |
| | Strather | 262,263 | | John H. | 213 |
| | Strather E. | 264 | | Joseph | 85 |
| | W. | 131 | | Levi | 87 |
| Heron | Katherine | 319 | | Rebecca E. | 218 |
| Herr | Ben | 319 | | Wm. Jr. | 85 |
| | Shirl | 319 | | William A. | 218 |
| | Theodore | 205 | | Wilson | 85 |
| Herrel | Elijah | 84 | Hiatte | Lorenzo | 220 |
| Herring | Fremont(Mrs.) | 14 | Hibben | Evadne H. | 319 |
| Herriott | Samuel | 131 | | George | 319 |
| Herrod | ---- | 28 | | Mae B. | 319 |
| | Ailcy | 334 | Hichcock | Emma | 218 |
| | Elizabeth | 334 | Hickerson | Joseph | 131 |
| | Ellen | 203 | Hickman | Anna | 37 |
| | James | 22 | | Elizabeth | 33 |
| | Saml | 131 | | Enoch | 39 |
| | Sarah | 22 | | James | 38 |

| | | | | | | |
|---|---|---|---|---|---|---|
| Hineman | John | 80 | Hobbs | Noah R. | 52 |
| Hiner | Harmon | 165 | | Robert | 49 |
| Hines | Henry | 131 | | Roderick | 267 |
| | James | 152 | Hobert | John | 162 |
| | Mary | 336 | | Otis | 148 |
| Hinesely | John W. | 146 | Hobson | Wm. | 146 |
| Hinesly | Joshua | 147 | Hochgesang | Robert C. | 319 |
| Hinich | Mary | 336 | Hochstetler | Jacob | 173 |
| Hinkle | Samuel | 167 | Hochstettler | Katharine | 175 |
| Hinkley | Jacob | 83 | Hocket | Eliza | 87 |
| Hinkson | Eliza | 51 | Hockett | Daniel | 87 |
| Hinman | Henry S. | 154 | | Isaac | 111 |
| Hinman | Titus H. | 53 | Hockiday | Alexander | 47 |
| Hinshaw | J.H. | 119 | Hockman | Benjamin F. | 304 |
| Hinton | George | 145 | | Carson | 299 |
| | John R. | 113 | | John | 101 |
| | Verna C. | 9 | | Robert Carson | 304 |
| Hires | Eliza Jane | 60 | Hodge | John | 87 |
| Hirsh | S.F.(Mrs.) | 7 | Hodgson | David | 83 |
| Hisey | Alice | 226 | | Samuel | 83 |
| | Ettie T. | 223 | Hodson | Alfred | 85 |
| Hissong | Annah E. | 225 | | F.O. | 276 |
| Histand | Henry | 98 | | Gertrude B. | 276 |
| Hitch | Othniel | 319 | | Sarah Ann | 252 |
| Hitchcock | David | 227 | | William | 85 |
| | Mary A. | 210 | Hoff | Susannah | 209 |
| | Oscar D. | 223 | Hoffacker | Daniel | 208 |
| Hite | Willis(Mrs.) | 13 | Hoffman | Ambrose | 82 |
| Hitt | Thomas S. | 162 | | Aurelius W. | 199 |
| Hitz | Benjamin D. | 319 | | Catherine | 168 |
| Hizer | Geo. | 87 | | Daniel | 166 |
| | Mary | 209 | | Frederick | 198 |
| Hoadley | C. Vergil | 319 | | John | 174 |
| Hoag | Ann J. | 212 | | N. | 296 |
| | Henrieta | 201 | Hogate | Jessie | 319 |
| | Joseph B. | 210 | Hogget | Alfred | 84 |
| Hoagland | George | 54 | Hoglan | James | 149 |
| | Margaret | 57 | Hoit | Francis M. | 231 |
| Hoaglin | Margaret | 57 | Hoke | Maria | 41 |
| Hobart | Otis | 148 | Holaday | James | 97 |
| Hobaugh | Elias | 177 | Holcom | George | 170 |
| | Elvira | 169 | Holcomb | James Irving | 319 |
| | George | 81 | | Mary | 251 |
| | John H. | 81 | | Nathaniel | 105 |
| | John R. | 88 | Holdcraft | Nathanel | 104 |
| | Mary Jane | 169 | | Seley | 105 |
| | V.D. | 90 | Holder | John W. | 189 |
| | Van D. | 81,88 | Holderman | James | 199 |
| Hobbs | ---- | 28 | | Samuel W. | 208 |
| | Hynson | 28 | Holdesaph | Nathanel | 98 |
| | John | 59 | Holeman | Levi | 87 |
| | Martha Sayles | 319 | | William | 131 |

| Surname | Given Name | Page(s) |
|---|---|---|
| Hoyt | F.M. | 231 |
| Hubart | Erreley | 49 |
| Hubbard | Elijah | 109 |
| | Elisha | 99 |
| | Ella Hurst | 319 |
| | James | 96,103,109 |
| | Walter John | 319 |
| Hubbartt | John A. | 216 |
| Hubbel | Ruth | 59 |
| Hubbell | Joseph W. | 207 |
| Hubble | Ruth | 59 |
| Hubert | John | 82 |
| Huckleberry | Abraham | 22 |
| | Barbara | 22 |
| | David | 22 |
| | Elizabeth | 22 |
| | George | 22 |
| | George Sr. | 17 |
| | Henry | 21,22 |
| | Jacob | 22 |
| | John | 22 |
| | Martin | 22 |
| | Mary | 29 |
| | Susanna | 22 |
| Hucklebery | Mary | 27 |
| Hudale | Conrad | 106 |
| Huddle | Conrad | 100 |
| Huddleston | Elizabeth | 57 |
| | Fred R. | 320 |
| Hudelson | Emory | 119 |
| | Lynn | 119 |
| Hudgell | Mary Ann | 49 |
| Hudleston | Elizabeth | 57 |
| Hudson | Edward | 141 |
| | Gabriel | 170 |
| | Harrison | 89 |
| | John | 60 |
| | Lavina | 176 |
| | Thos. | 154 |
| Huestis | Bertha | 6 |
| Huey | Cyrus | 199 |
| | Cyrus A. | 212 |
| | James F. | 210 |
| | Mary | 123 |
| | Robert | 124 |
| Huff | ---- | 29 |
| | Asenith | 34 |
| | Edmund | 60 |
| | Fannie W, | 320 |
| | Henry | 87 |
| | Hiram | 88,90 |
| | John | 90 |
| Huff | John Sen. | 88 |
| | John Jr. | 88 |
| | John F. | 202 |
| | Mary | 37 |
| | Sarah | 27,28,335 |
| | Tamer | 59 |
| Huffe | Parnenas B. | 45 |
| Huffman | Ann | 21 |
| | Benjamin | 21 |
| | Burk | 34 |
| | Catherine | 21 |
| | Elizabeth | 208 |
| | Isaac | 21 |
| | John | 21 |
| | John H. | 191 |
| | Jonas | 146 |
| | Lewis | 149 |
| | Mary | 21 |
| | Peter | 21 |
| | Rachel | 21 |
| | Rebecca | 21 |
| | Sampson | 143 |
| | Simeon | 121 |
| | Simoson | 143 |
| | Winifred | 21 |
| Hufford | Eliza Ann | 334 |
| | George | 334 |
| | Gideon | 115 |
| | Julian | 117 |
| Huffstutter | John | 39,41 |
| Hugenard | Edna M. | 9 |
| Hugg | Martin M. | 320 |
| Huggins | Edward | 159 |
| Hugh | Alice | 210 |
| | Westly | 89 |
| Hughell | Julian | 54 |
| | Mary Ann | 49 |
| | Pethena | 57 |
| Hughes | ---- | 67 |
| | Edward | 96,103 |
| | Evin | 104 |
| | Hester | 119 |
| | I.H. | 67 |
| | Isaac | 67 |
| | John | 50,102 |
| | M.E. | 67 |
| | Mariah | 55 |
| | Mary E. | 67 |
| | Matthew | 49 |
| | Nathan | 103 |
| | Samuel | 85 |
| | Stephen T. | 35 |

| | | | | | | |
|---|---|---|---|---|---|---|
| Hughey | Wm. | 155 | Hunt | Cantley W. | 111 |
| Hughs | Edward | 104,107 | | Catharine | 43 |
| | Nathan | 105 | | Elizabeth | 50 |
| Hugins | Edward | 159 | | Margaret | 131 |
| | Thos. | 145 | | Timothy | 131 |
| Hulbart | Tamsey | 51 | | William | 131 |
| Hulburt | Anna M. | 9 | | Zachriah P. | 215 |
| Hulick | Mary | 60 | Hunter | Anna | 308 |
| Hull | Celestien A. | 226 | | Augustus | 173 |
| | Ida | 224 | | Benjamin F. | 171 |
| | James | 232 | | Harry | 239 |
| | Joseph | 47 | | Harry | 239 |
| | Mary | 225 | | Joseph | 88 |
| | Wm. | 158 | | Patrick | 95,97,105 |
| Hullinger | Joseph | 86 | Huntington | Benj. F. | 233 |
| | Wm. | 86 | | James N. | 155 |
| Huls | Faima | 227 | Hup | Elizabeth | 175 |
| Hults | G.W. | 81 | | George | 100 |
| | George W. | 82,83 | Hupp | August | 211 |
| | James | 83 | | Augusta | 226 |
| Humbarger | S. | 88 | | George | 106 |
| Humbert | ----(Col.) | 163 | Hurd | Charles S. | 44 |
| | Nancy | 163 | | Harrison | 166 |
| | Russell J. | 320 | Huret | Henry W. | 220 |
| Hume | David H. | 175 | Hurlbert | Tolcott L. | 166 |
| | Joseph B. | 149 | Hurley | Rhoda | 36 |
| Humm | John | 38 | | Samantha | 332 |
| Hummel | Jackson | 88 | Huron | Phebe | 115 |
| | John | 88,90 | Hurshey | Louisa A. | 212 |
| | Levi | 88 | | Mary M. | 215 |
| | Levi B. | 220 | Hurst | Abraham | 96,102 |
| | Wm. H. | 88 | | Benjamin | 96,104 |
| | Zennia M. | 320 | | Beverly | 96 |
| Hummell | John | 81 | | Brittania | 175 |
| Humphreis | John | 109 | | Dorothy | 169 |
| Humphrey | James | 2 | | Elijah | 96,100,106 |
| | James(Mrs.) | 2 | | Elizabeth A. | 212 |
| | Jessie L. | 3 | | Ella | 319 |
| | Mary A. | 2 | | Elzira | 180 |
| Humphreys | Alfred | 195 | | Helen | 53 |
| | Allen | 195 | | Henry | 103 |
| | Charles | 194 | | Jesse | 193 |
| | Eliza | 201 | | John | 103,106,109 |
| | Emma | 210 | | John Sr. | 99,108 |
| | Harriet | 195 | | John Nelson | 174 |
| | Martha | 196 | | Letitia | 193 |
| | Orin | 202 | | Nancy | 55 |
| | Orrin | 212 | | Sarah S. | 193 |
| Humphries | John | 101 | | William | 96,101 |
| Humphryes | Eva | 215 | Husher | Elijah | 173 |
| Humrickhouse | Ebenezar | 176 | Hussey | Mary Bradshaw | 320 |
| Hunley | William | 84 | Huston | Arabe | 210 |

| | | | | | | |
|---|---|---|---|---|---|---|
| Huston | Robt. | 149 | Ingram | Joseph | 45 | |
| | Samuel | 145 | | Mitchell | 45 | |
| Hutchen | Susan | 58 | | Sally | 38 | |
| Hutchens | Getty | 52 | Ingrum | Clem E. | 76 | |
| | Joseph | 19 | | Rose P. | 76 | |
| | Laura E. | 179 | Inks | Joel | 90 | |
| Hutchens | Stephen | 19 | | John D. | 218,225 | |
| Hutcheson | John | 20 | | John Dizon | 221 | |
| | Susan Jane | 204 | | Mary E. | 216 | |
| | Thomas | 20,22 | | Susan C. | 221 | |
| | William L. | 320 | | William C. | 209 | |
| Hutchings | Joseph | 19 | Inman | Elida M. | 220 | |
| | Stephen | 19 | | John S. | 195 | |
| Hutchins | David | 85 | Innfield | Thos. | 108 | |
| Hutchinson | Elizabeth | 43 | Insley | J.J.(Mrs.) | 3 | |
| | Francis | 42 | | William H. | 320 | |
| | John W. | 207 | Ipe | Mary E. | 216 | |
| | Mahala | 46 | Ireland | Adam | 213 | |
| | Sarah | 34,334 | | Dunice M. | 69 | |
| | William | 86 | | Edwin | 69 | |
| | Zachariah | 334 | Irick | Andrew | 121 | |
| Hutinger | Joseph | 90 | Iron Teeth | Mary | 244 | |
| Hutson | Eward | 141 | Irvin | John | 33 | |
| | T.B.S. | 154 | Irwin | Abel | 121 | |
| Hutt | Louisa C. | 220 | | David | 21 | |
| Hutto | William | 131 | | Grace C. | 8 | |
| | William sr. | 131 | | James | 121 | |
| Hutton | Mary | 33 | | Jesse P. | 304 | |
| Hyatt | Margaret | 55 | | John | 33 | |
| Hyde | James H. | 320 | | Jonathan | 121 | |
| Hyler | Abram | 54 | | Mary E. | 4 | |
| Hyne | William J. | 216 | | Nettie | 320 | |
| | | | | Robert | 121 | |
| Igert | Louis Henry | 304 | | Samuel | 121 | |
| | Peter | 304 | | Stephen | 43 | |
| Iglehart | John Eugene | 320 | | Susan | 172 | |
| Iine | Wm. | 90 | | William G. | 320 | |
| Imel | Catherine | 122 | | William J. | 304 | |
| | Ezra | 122 | Isaac | Lee | 147 | |
| | John | 122 | Isenhart | Elizabeth | 122 | |
| | Nathaniel | 122 | Isley | Daniel | 171 | |
| | Samuel | 122 | Isom | John M. | 232 | |
| | Thomas | 122 | Israel | Eliza | 45 | |
| Imrie | Elizabeth I. | 2 | | Isom | 131 | |
| Infield | Thos. | 101 | Iten | Frank | 216 | |
| Ingham | Helen A. | 8 | Ivans | Abraham | 105 | |
| Ingle | William | 177 | | | | |
| Ingleman | Jacob | 101 | Jackman | William | 54 | |
| | William | 101 | Jacks | Green | 82 | |
| Ingold | Jonathan | 161 | | Green B. | 81,83 | |
| Ingram | Andrew | 42 | Jackson | ---- | 88 | |
| | Dinidy | 45 | | Amy | 45 | |

| Jackson | Anderson | 51 | Jacobs | Mary | 305 |
|---|---|---|---|---|---|
| | Andrew | 51 | | Nancy | 55 |
| | Andrew J. | 216 | Jacobson | Addie | 4 |
| | Ann | 116,168 | James | Arvilia | 225 |
| | Armenia P. | 197 | | Henley | 164 |
| | Armsted | 115 | | Mary | 221 |
| | Arvilla | 193 | | Prissilla | 226 |
| | Bessie | 8 | | Reuben | 279 |
| | Catharine | 200 | Jameson | Alexander | 168 |
| | Catherine | 193 | | J.T. | 104 |
| | Corbin | 89 | | John T. | 97 |
| | Eleanora E. | 176 | Jamieson | Gardner | 69 |
| | Elizabeth J. | 196 | | Janet | 287 |
| | Elsey | 147 | | Louise D. S. | 69 |
| | Ephraim | 37 | | Walter A. | 320 |
| | Ethelbert | 179 | Jamison | Francis | 160 |
| | Frances A. | 195 | | John | 147 |
| | Griffin | 81 | Jamisson | James | 107 |
| | Griffith | 82 | | John T. | 109 |
| | Henry A. | 216 | Jammeson | John T. | 98 |
| | Hiram | 85,91 | Jana | James | 222 |
| | Idell | 87 | Jane | Robert | 247 |
| | Isaac | 36,85,145 | Jankoenski | Andrew | 221 |
| | J. | 86 | Jankoske | Kate | 221 |
| | Jacob | 81 | Jankowski | Augusta | 214 |
| | Jesse | 210 | January | Henry S. | 299 |
| | Jobe | 85 | Jarnegan | Benjamin | 170 |
| | Joel | 90 | Jarrel | William | 113 |
| | John | 33,87,90,100, | Jarrett | Anna | 205 |
| | | 145,193 | | Mary E. | 200 |
| | Joshua | 169 | | Nathan M. | 216 |
| | Louisa | 115 | | Sarah W. | 203 |
| | Mansy | 173 | Jaucht | Mary | 305 |
| | Mary | 58,193 | Jay | Allen | 87 |
| | Mary Ann | 173 | | David | 85,91 |
| | McKinney | 56 | | Denny | 85 |
| | Milton | 229 | | Denny Jr. | 85 |
| | Missouri | 193 | | Joseph | 85 |
| | Nancy A. | 181 | | Samuel | 85 |
| | Noah | 150 | Jebeau | Harriet | 173 |
| | Phyllis Wynn | 320 | Jefferes | Elias | 96,108 |
| | Richard M. | 203 | Jefferies | E.J.(Mrs.) | 6 |
| | Richard W. | 167 | Jeffers | Elias | 99,104 |
| | Sarah | 61 | | Nancy | 51 |
| | Stephen W. | 195 | Jeffery | Sarah F. | 165 |
| | Thomas | 145,193 | | Willis | 93 |
| | William | 54,81,193 | Jeffrey | Wm. | 85 |
| | William H. | 195 | Jemmison | James | 103 |
| | Wm. R. | 88 | Jenckes | Ray Greene | 304 |
| Jacobs | Esther | 9 | | Virginia E.S. | 304 |
| | Highland | 53 | Jenison | Rufus | 150 |
| | L.D. | 89 | Jenkins | Bellefield | 86 |

**413**

| | | | | | | |
|---|---|---|---|---|---|---|
| Kapely | Isabella | 39 | Kegebine | Anna | 222 |
| Karaho | John | 239 | Keim | Leah | 174 |
| | Service | 241 | Keister | Edna Mattox | 320 |
| Karnes | Aaron | 32 | Keith | Jacob | 103 |
| | Tabitha | 43 | Kell | Carolyn | 15 |
| Karns | John | 205 | | Robt.(Mrs.) | 7 |
| Karr | James | 50 | Keller | Anthony | 100,110 |
| Karrer | Marie | 320 | | Caroline M. | 227 |
| Karrk | John T. | 189 | | Daniel | 37 |
| Kash | Henry | 218 | | Ezekiel | 214 |
| Kaston | Anna | 227 | | Isaac | 100,108 |
| Katterjohn | Monte M. | 320 | | Jennie | 223 |
| Kauble | Caleb | 141 | | John | 105 |
| Kauffman | Matilda L. | 2 | | John B. | 99,105 |
| | Simon | 84 | | Jonathan | 100 |
| Kaufman | B.H.(Mrs.) | 9 | | Jonathen | 95 |
| | Mary | 18 | | Katherine A. | 308 |
| | Samuel | 18 | | Lewis | 203 |
| Kautz | Frederick R, | 320 | | Lillian | 323 |
| Kays | Katie | 227 | | Rebecca | 175 |
| | Mary Ellen | 205 | | William | 202 |
| | Mathew | 223 | Kelley | Cornelius | 20 |
| Kean | Henrey P. | 105 | | David | 84 |
| | Henry P. | 95 | | Elias | 20 |
| Kearby | Delbert Oscar | 320 | | Elizabeth S. | 320 |
| Kearnes | Elizabeth | 38 | | Francis | 51 |
| | Harrison | 46 | | Hugh | 18 |
| | Silas | 40 | | James | 20 |
| Keaton | William | 132 | | John | 23 |
| Keefauver | Allen | 335 | | Jonathan | 87,108 |
| | Elizabeth | 335 | | Luther E. | 320 |
| | Jessie | 335 | | Margaret | 187 |
| | John | 335 | | Martha | 187 |
| | Mary | 335 | | Michael | 210 |
| Keefe | Catharine | 199 | | Milley | 217 |
| Keefer | ---- | 247 | | Samuel | 87,89 |
| | Wm. B. | 247 | | Thomas F. | 23 |
| Keegan | Abbie C. | 5 | | William | 187 |
| | Helen | 14 | Kellian | Adam | 99 |
| Keeland | William | 132 | | Eli | 99 |
| Keeler | Seth | 145 | Kellmus | Samuel | 229 |
| | Thomas | 141 | Kellogg | Alonzo S. | 39 |
| | Thos. G. | 147 | | Julia Ann | 41 |
| Keen | Henry P. | 97 | Kelly | Adaline | 200 |
| Keenan | Sarah | 34 | | Alfred | 83,85 |
| Keener | Thomas I. | 82 | | Andrew | 96 |
| Keeny | Jonathan | 132 | | Irene | 333 |
| Keep | Henry | 24 | | Isaac | 154 |
| Keeran | Edith L. | 10 | | John | 18 |
| Keesy | Christopher | 175 | | John F. | 179 |
| Keeton | Gabriel | 85 | | John H. | 333 |
| Keever | Daniel G. | 82 | | Margaret | 201 |

**416**

| | | | | | | |
|---|---|---|---|---|---|---|
| Kelly | Nancy | 333,334 | Kent | Arthur S. | 320 | |
| | Rasumen R. | 55 | | Catharine | 336 | |
| | Samuel | 18,187 | | Celesta | 336 | |
| | Sarah E. | 200 | | Jabe | 336 | |
| | T.J. | 334 | Kenworthy | Irinda | 176 | |
| | Thomas | 187 | | John | 116 | |
| | Timothy | 83,85 | Kenzer | Jacob | 115 | |
| | William | 200 | Keokuk | Frank | 239 | |
| Kelmes | Samuel | 229 | Kephart | Elizabeth C. | 197 | |
| Kelser | Daniel | 107 | | George | 132 | |
| Kelsey | Elizabeth | 58 | Kepler | Jacob | 85 | |
| Kelver | Catharine | 199 | | Prudence | 40 | |
| Ken | Mary | 199 | Kepley | George | 44 | |
| Kenada | Ezkial | 106 | Kepner | Matthias T.H. | 198 | |
| Kenard | George L. | 159 | Kepperlin | Axa Ann | 197 | |
| Kenary | Michael | 132 | Kepperling | Mary E. | 216 | |
| Kendal | William | 98 | | Rhoda C. | 209 | |
| Kendall | Allen | 34 | Kepsinger | George W. | 82 | |
| | Anna | 34 | Kerchival | ---- | 293 | |
| | Ben | 270 | Kerkham | Betsey | 116 | |
| | Experience | 36 | Kerlin | Joseph B. | 84 | |
| | James | 107 | Kern | Flora Work | 320 | |
| | Lavinia | 46 | Kerr | James | 50,248 | |
| | Thompson | 97 | Kersey | John | 91,263 | |
| | Thomson | 105 | | Maude | 263 | |
| | William | 106,107 | Kershner | Bruce Lesher | 320 | |
| | Yelly | 108 | Kerwood | W.R. | 119 | |
| Kendrick | Charlotte P. | 320 | | Wayne | 119 | |
| Keneday | James | 41 | Kesner | Jacob | 109 | |
| Kenedy | Martin | 165 | | John | 106 | |
| Kenefick | Michael J. | 217 | Kessinger | G.W. | 81 | |
| Kennady | John | 99 | Kessler | Christopher | 174 | |
| Kennard | Charles | 119 | | Lucinda | 174 | |
| | Frank | 118,119 | | William | 175 | |
| | Levia Hittle | 119 | Ketcham | Flora M. | 320 | |
| Kenneday | Morgan | 43 | Ketchum | Essex B. | 216 | |
| Kennedy | Aaron | 83 | Kethecirt | William | 103 | |
| | Elizabeth | 55 | Ketterman | John | 109 | |
| | James | 41 | Kettleborough | Charles | 320 | |
| | Mary E. | 308 | Kettleman | James | 158 | |
| | Morgan | 43 | Kever | Wm. | 87 | |
| | Nancy | 33 | Kevis | John | 132 | |
| | Patsy | 33 | Key | Zachariah | 82 | |
| | William | 34 | Keyt | Gertude G. | 119 | |
| Kennelly | Mary C. | 9 | Kibler | Anna | 195 | |
| Kenoyer | George | 105 | | Catherine | 194 | |
| | Jacob | 105 | | Elizabeth | 195 | |
| | Lewis | 106 | Kidd | Ellen | 170 | |
| | Louis | 96 | | Nath'l. | 152 | |
| | Micheal | 106 | Kidder | J. | 124 | |
| | Valentine | 108 | | John | 124 | |
| Kenoyorer | Fredric | 105 | | Sarah | 124 | |

**418**

| Kirkam | Robert | 99 |
|---|---|---|
| Kirkham | Michael | 96 |
| Kirkpatrick | James | 96,103,108 |
| | Jennie | 324 |
| | William | 81 |
| Kirtch | Andrew | 214 |
| Kirtley | Wm. | 87 |
| Kise | —— | 230 |
| | Elisha | 230 |
| Kiser | Bertha | 227 |
| | James | 169 |
| | John | 246 |
| | Samuel | 87 |
| Kist | Marian | 240 |
| Kitch | Elijah | 92 |
| Kitchel | Lydia L. | 201 |
| Kitchen | W.C. | 166 |
| Kitley | Francis | 147 |
| Kitly | John | 149 |
| Kittleton | James | 158 |
| Kitts | —— | 285 |
| Kizer | James H. | 173 |
| Kleckner | Jacob | 212 |
| Kline | Amanda | 228 |
| | Manerva | 220 |
| | Mary | 207 |
| | Samuel G. | 206,228 |
| Klingelsmith | Philip | 170 |
| Klingensmith | —— | 174 |
| Klinquensmith | Delia | 300 |
| Klittick | Johannie | 208 |
| Klooz | Edith | 305 |
| Knab | Carl | 232 |
| | Charles | 232 |
| Knachall | George | 206 |
| Knachel | Ettie | 217 |
| Knacht | Theressa | 228 |
| Knapp | Adda M. | 1 |
| | Alfred | 132 |
| | Carl | 232 |
| | Laura | 281 |
| | Marian | 281 |
| | Nancy J. | 213 |
| | William | 211 |
| | William H. | 216 |
| Knight | Adele C. | 323 |
| | Benjamin | 87 |
| | Charles A. | 298 |
| | David | 149 |
| | Martha Richee | 51 |
| | Matilda E. | 5 |
| | Sebborn G. | 83 |
| Knight | Solomon | 85 |
| | Thomas | 84 |
| | William | 132 |
| Knighton | Gertrude | 301 |
| Knisely | Alexander | 321 |
| Kniss | Eliza | 220 |
| Knobloch | Henry | 305 |
| | Mary E. | 305 |
| | Thomas C. | 305 |
| Knoblock | Otto M. | 321 |
| Knoke | Dorthea | 221 |
| Knosman | Augustus H. | 217 |
| Knotts | Della J. | 334 |
| | N.C. | 334 |
| Knowles | Jennie | 306 |
| | Perry | 233 |
| Knowlton | Ellen G. | 317 |
| | Emma Louise | 315 |
| | Fannie | 310 |
| | James(Mrs.) | 14 |
| | Lovina | 321 |
| Koch | Edward W. | 321 |
| Kocks | Herbert(Mrs.) | 14 |
| Koenig | Albert W. | 305 |
| | Bert | 305 |
| Koeppel | Anna B. | 207 |
| Koerner | Caroline | 69 |
| | John G. | 69 |
| | Josephene | 69 |
| Kohler | Nicholas | 192 |
| Kohlmeier | Albert L. | 321 |
| | C. | 70 |
| | Christian | 70 |
| | Christine | 72 |
| | Clarence F. | 70 |
| | Daisy M. | 70 |
| | Edward D. | 71 |
| | Elias | 70 |
| | Emma | 77 |
| | Emory F. | 70 |
| | Fred L. | 70 |
| | Freiderich | 70 |
| | Friderike | 70 |
| | H. | 70 |
| | H.F. | 74,77 |
| | Harry | 77 |
| | Henrietta | 70 |
| | John F. | 77 |
| | L. | 70 |
| | Louie M. | 77 |
| | Louis | 70 |
| | Lucy L. | 71 |

| | | | | | | |
|---|---|---|---|---|---|---|
| Lackey | James | 61 | Lamb | Eli | 86 |
| Lacky | Elizabeth | 49 | | Elizabeth | 40 |
| | Mary | 52 | | Isaac | 23,335 |
| Lacy | J.W. | 115 | | Isiah | 35 |
| Ladach | Leuis | 219 | | John | 93 |
| Ladd | Constantine | 54 | | Jonathan | 93 |
| | Samuel | 85 | | Joseph | 39 |
| Ladley | Nancy | 54 | | Josiah | 35 |
| Laferty | Samuel | 47 | | Lydia | 46 |
| Lafevour | Joseph | 162 | | Mary Ann | 39 |
| Lafollet | Robert | 108 | | Miriam | 34 |
| | Susan | 47 | | Moses P. | 50 |
| Lafollette | Harvey Marion | 321 | | Nancy | 41,335 |
| Lagle | Mary | 45 | | Prentice L. | 40 |
| | Nancy Ann | 44 | | Sarah | 45,46 |
| Laguett | Shadrck | 155 | | Susan | 41 |
| Lahmon | Lewis | 204 | | Thomas | 39 |
| Lahue | Cornelius | 109 | | William | 37 |
| | John | 109 | Lambert | Adam | 175,194 |
| | William | 110 | | Eli M. | 198 |
| Lain | Hannah W. | 202 | Lamey | Bessie | 78 |
| | James P. | 208 | | Henry | 78 |
| | John C. | 197 | Lamma | Isaiah | 88 |
| | John W. | 206 | | Washington | 88 |
| | Mary | 197 | | William | 88 |
| | Mary L. | 226 | Lampson | Rebecca J. | 207 |
| | Matilda C. | 202 | Lancaster | Archillis | 153 |
| | Nancy Ann | 206 | | Joseph | 221 |
| | Sarah | 197 | | Prest. | 143 |
| Laing | Harriett | 50 | | Prestin | 147 |
| Lair | David | 89 | Lance | Ollie | 64 |
| Lake | Elisha W. | 156 | Land | William J.G. | 321 |
| | Isaac | 161 | Landam | George | 144 |
| | Josep | 142 | Landers | Harvey | 227 |
| | Sarah E. | 123 | | John | 43 |
| | Z. | 140 | | Lewis | 87,90 |
| | Zenas | 140 | | Margaret | 41 |
| Lakey | G. | 9 | Landes | Daniel | 169 |
| | Keziah | 116 | Landes | Martin | 168 |
| | Omah | 11 | | William | 165 |
| | Ruth | 115 | Landgrave | Caroline | 170 |
| Lamar | Ann Mariah | 60 | Landis | Daniel | 90 |
| | David R. | 190 | | Jacob | 148 |
| | Edwinia C. | 190 | | Maria | 168 |
| | James S. | 190 | Landon | Hugh McK. | 321 |
| Lamarr | Ann Mariah | 60 | | William T. | 196 |
| Lamaste⁻ | Arch. | 159 | Landram | George | 144 |
| | Zach. | 152 | Lane | Abraham | 132 |
| Lamb | Benjamin | 37,335 | | Benton | 174 |
| | Daniel | 102 | | Charles F. | 249 |
| | David | 87 | | Charles H. | 224 |
| | Edmond | 87 | | Danel C. | 99 |

421

| Surname | Given name | Page |
|---|---|---|
| Lane | Daniel C. | 96,108 |
| | Dora Evaline | 249 |
| | Edward | 105,149 |
| | Elbert | 250 |
| | Franz Delaven | 250 |
| | George G. | 47 |
| | Hannah | 335 |
| | Harriett | 50 |
| | Isabel E. | 214 |
| | James Marlin | 250 |
| | Joab | 335 |
| | Joan | 64 |
| | John | 105 |
| | John M. | 223 |
| | Joseph M. | 250 |
| | Letitia | 250 |
| | Lucile | 325 |
| | Luis Edward | 249,250 |
| | Margaret Ann | 250 |
| | Mary | 196 |
| | Nancy | 46,194 |
| | Noah | 249,250 |
| | Noah Sherman | 249 |
| | Pauline | 243 |
| | Samuel W. | 204 |
| | Sarah | 114 |
| | Susan | 335 |
| | Thomas | 97,105 |
| | Thomas B. | 212 |
| | Valentine | 132 |
| | William A. | 220 |
| | William M. | 249,250 |
| | William W. | 82 |
| | Willis F. | 250 |
| Lang | Francis | 33,34,35 |
| | J. | 65 |
| | John Walter | 305 |
| | Levi | 40 |
| | Nancy | 38 |
| | Olley | 65 |
| | Stangsberry | 42 |
| | Walter John | 305 |
| Langdon | Susanna | 40 |
| Lange | ---- | 65 |
| | Harry A. | 65 |
| | Joanna | 65 |
| | John W. | 65 |
| | Olley L. | 65 |
| Langenbahn | George | 222 |
| Langford | Rob't. | 158 |
| | Steven | 96 |
| Langford | Thos. | 146 |
| Langwell | William | 36 |
| Lanham | Jennette | 301 |
| | Lorinda | 305 |
| Lank | ---- | 124 |
| Lankford | Herber | 227 |
| | Rob't. | 158 |
| | Thos. | 146 |
| Lanney | John M. | 86 |
| Lansdown | Agnes | 6 |
| Lany | William | 195 |
| Lapenta | Vincent A. | 321 |
| LaPlant | Alex | 239 |
| | Charles | 239 |
| | Julia | 239 |
| Lapping | Mary | 44 |
| Laramore | Amos | 207 |
| | Andrew J. | 205 |
| | Charles | 205 |
| | Hannah J. | 212 |
| | Hariet E. | 206 |
| | Martha B. | 224 |
| | Sarah C. | 220 |
| Larch | Mattie L. | 225 |
| Larew | Lavanna C. | 202 |
| | Martha J. | 199 |
| | Martha Jane | 199 |
| | Sarah S. | 199 |
| Large | Rob't. | 153 |
| Largent | Rachael Ann | 172 |
| Larimar | Mary A. | 200 |
| Larimer | Sarah | 68 |
| Lark | Sarah E. | 220 |
| | Stephen C. | 199 |
| Larowe | Lambert | 54 |
| | Rachel | 59 |
| Larrabee | Mary Emma | 4 |
| Larren | Ida L. | 226 |
| | William C. | 225 |
| Larreq | John C. | 200 |
| Larue | Abraham | 54 |
| | Beriann H. | 52 |
| | Briton | 87 |
| | Brittain | 206 |
| | Edward | 97 |
| | Josiah | 45 |
| | Loretta | 52 |
| | Mary | 60 |
| | Rachel | 59 |
| | Thomas | 97 |
| Lash | Adam | 132 |
| | James | 132 |
| | Nancy | 132 |

**423**

| Legg | Frank | 274 | Lenhart | Margaret | 336 |
|------|-------|-----|---------|----------|-----|
| Leggit | William | 132 | Leningpetler | Wm. | 160 |
| Legrand | Wm. | 232 | Lenkins | Lewis | 86 |
| Legros | | 246 | Lenlen | Daniel | 211 |
| Lehman | Amanda | 212 | Lennington | Peggy | 167 |
| | Isaac | 170 | Lenox | H.J. | 86 |
| Lehr | Kittie J. | 5 | | James | 33 |
| Lehue | Cornelius | 102 | Lentz | Isaac R. | 169 |
| | John | 102 | Leonard | Abner | 58,121 |
| | William | 99 | | Charlotte | 44 |
| Leiber | Carl H. | 321 | | George W. | 81,82,83 |
| | Richard | 321 | | Hattie M. | 3 |
| Leiby | May M. | 213 | | James | 146 |
| | Rosa E. | 223 | | John Jr. | 121 |
| Leighty | Lanora | 220 | | Leonard | 198 |
| Leihtz | William H. | 221 | | Sarah | 36 |
| Leisure | Fred | 119 | | William | 132 |
| | Gertrude | 119 | Lepard | Samuel | 203 |
| | John | 119 | Lepper | Benjamin C. | 305 |
| | Ruby | 119 | | Irene E. | 10 |
| | Watson | 119 | | William C. | 305 |
| Lellen | James M. | 144 | Lerch | James M. | 217 |
| Lells | Sarah | 336 | Lesh | Levin S. | 175 |
| Leman | John | 54 | | Ora Wilkens | 321 |
| Lemaster | Peter | 157 | Leska | Henrietta | 205 |
| Lemasters | Arch. | 159 | Leslie | Frank M. | 228 |
| | Lucinda | 337 | Lesly | Christopher | 173 |
| | Zach. | 152 | Lessley | Levi | 108 |
| Leming | Elias | 160 | Lester | James | 158 |
| Lemler | Amanda | 209 | | Martha | 303 |
| | Selena | 209 | Lettell | Reubin | 109 |
| Lemme | Alma May | 70 | | Samuel | 103 |
| | Clinton E. | 70 | Lettill | Saml. | 96 |
| Lemmon | Elias | 160 | Letus | George | 132 |
| | John | 53 | Levan | Minnie | 307 |
| | Walter S. | 321 | Level | Henry | 84 |
| Lemon | Charles | 89 | Leverton | James | 152 |
| | Elias | 33 | | Joel | 161 |
| | Elizabeth | 53 | Levett | Wallace | 154 |
| | James | 20,21,23,24,25 | Levey | Meta C. | 321 |
| | John | 22 | Levi | M. | 247 |
| | John F. | 45 | Levinworth | Seth M. | 34 |
| | John H. | 35 | Lewis | ---- | 66,283 |
| | Rebecca | 201 | | Abner | 60 |
| Lenard | James | 146 | | Abraham | 117 |
| Lenfesty | Charles | 91 | | Andrew | 132 |
| | Robert | 91 | | Celia | 57 |
| | Robert H. | 88 | | David | 50 |
| | Thos. | 89 | | Elizabeth | 39 |
| | W.L. | 91 | | Ella Mogul | 119 |
| | William S. | 86 | | Emaly | 196 |
| Lenfesty | Wm. F. | 88 | | Fannie | 307 |

| | | |
|---|---|---|
| Lewis | George | 84 |
| | Hannah | 39 |
| | Harry | 119 |
| | Henry | 41 |
| | Isiah | 132 |
| | James | 82 |
| | Jane | 34 |
| | John | 84 |
| | Jonathan | 23 |
| | M.E. | 66 |
| | Marietta M. | 3 |
| | Mary | 49 |
| | Mary E. | 66 |
| | Minerva | 176 |
| | Montgomery S. | 321 |
| | Nimrod | 87 |
| | Richard | 33 |
| | Ruthe | 165 |
| | S.M. | 66 |
| | Sarah | 117 |
| | Severe | 132 |
| | Susan | 40 |
| | T.I. | 82 |
| | Thomas | 82,99,104,142 |
| | Walter | 119 |
| | William | 225 |
| Leyhe | Louise H. | 306 |
| Lguat | Shadrck | 155 |
| Liby | Dalbert | 228 |
| Liggett | Blanche | 7 |
| Light | Abner | 102 |
| Lightcap | Frances | 209 |
| | George | 203 |
| | Henry | 210 |
| | Walter | 203 |
| Likens | Carter | 97,102,109 |
| Lillard | Oliver | 90 |
| Lilley | William H. | 95,104 |
| Lilly | Ioisah Kirby | 321 |
| | William H. | 106 |
| Lime | William A. | 298 |
| Lincas | Rebecca | 41 |
| Linch | Elizabeth | 50 |
| Lincoln | Josiah | 103 |
| Linder | Erne E. | 201 |
| Lindley | George T. | 227 |
| Lindsay | Caleb | 185 |
| | David T. | 84 |
| | Rhoda A.E. | 185 |
| Lindsey | Daniel T. | 83 |
| | Elijah | 180 |
| | J.(Mrs.) | 16 |

| | | |
|---|---|---|
| Lindsey | Jesse | 203 |
| | John | 16 |
| | Mary | 16 |
| | Rollin | 115 |
| Lindville | Jeremiah | 55 |
| Line | Charity | 276 |
| | Easton M. | 88 |
| | Jacob | 88 |
| | S.R. | 90 |
| Lines | Delila | 61 |
| | Henry | 276 |
| | Jedidah | 56 |
| | Levi | 87 |
| | Margaret | 276 |
| Lingenfelter | Archibald | 157 |
| | Wm. | 160 |
| Lingle | ——— | 277,278,283 |
| | Mary | 289,290 |
| Linling | Augusta | 225 |
| Linn | Isabella | 58 |
| Linscott | Elizabeth | 304 |
| Linsey | Christopher | 101,108 |
| | Jesse | 99 |
| Linton | Nora Wagoner | 119 |
| Linzey | Jessee | 96 |
| Lipps | George | 122 |
| Lipsett | W.E.(Mrs.) | 4 |
| Lisch | John | 188 |
| Lish | Jennie | 215 |
| | Sarah L. | 208 |
| Listen | Ebenezar | 105 |
| Liston | J.T.(Dr.) | 16 |
| | William M. | 16 |
| Litky | Carolina | 211 |
| Littell | Clarence G. | 321 |
| | Josiah | 98 |
| | Lydia | 20 |
| | Samuel | 98 |
| Little | Albert | 87 |
| | Geo. W. | 87 |
| | J. | 247 |
| | Lindley P. | 321 |
| | Lydia | 20 |
| | Thos. | 162 |
| Little Chief | Elmore | 242,244 |
| Littlejohn | Agnes T. | 7 |
| Littrel | Nathaniel W. | 224 |
| Livengood | Anna R. | 189 |
| | J.B. | 189 |
| | Jesse | 83 |
| | P.E. | 189 |
| | Wm. H. | 189 |

| | | | | | | |
|---|---|---|---|---|---|---|
| Lopp | John | 98 | Lower | George W. | 208 | |
| Lore | Calvin S. | 170 | | Lemuel E. | 204 | |
| Loring | Angelia E. | 222 | | Levi | 206 | |
| | Hester | 216 | | Rebecca | 206 | |
| | Huldah | 218 | | Samuel | 210 | |
| | Ida M. | 211 | | Sarah | 208 | |
| | John | 82 | Lowery | A. Elizabeth | 15 | |
| | Lois J. | 213 | | Philander | 208,219 | |
| | Mary P. | 217 | | Sarah J. | 212 | |
| | Sarah E. | 208 | Lowks | Cornelius | 158 | |
| | Sarah Jane | 203 | | Jacob | 158 | |
| | Wilson T. | 210 | Lowrance | ---- | 296 | |
| Lose | C.J.(Mrs.) | 4 | Lowring | Hudson | 89 | |
| Loser | Edward G. | 223 | Lowry | Benedict W. | 247 | |
| Lothen | Jannett Tho. | 170 | | H.D. | 247 | |
| Lott | Juliane Anna | 49 | Loy | Clarence O. | 321 | |
| Lotz | Abraham | 124 | | Maggie | 221 | |
| Loucks | Cornelius | 158 | Loyd | Sarah | 43 | |
| | Jacob | 158 | Luallen | Wm. G. | 87 | |
| Loudenback | Richard | 51 | Luark | Eli | 61 | |
| Louder | Samuel | 114 | Lucas | Alexander | 88 | |
| Louderback | Bradford A. | 213 | | David | 83 | |
| | Richard | 51 | | Edward | 227 | |
| Loudermilk | Philip | 121 | | Elijah | 83 | |
| Loudy | Rachael | 170 | | F.J. | 90 | |
| Lough | Thomas | 50 | | Frederick P. | 89 | |
| Lougin | William | 81 | | Isaac | 86 | |
| Louis | John | 96 | | Marcellus | 222 | |
| Lounders | Louis | 81 | | Martin | 91 | |
| Love | Ellen | 170 | | Nancy Ann | 197 | |
| | Elvira | 165 | | Thos. | 142 | |
| | Frame | 81,88 | | William | 84 | |
| | Frederick | 86 | Luce | F.T. | 141 | |
| | George R. | 43 | | Matthias | 59 | |
| | James | 88,91 | Luck | Kate | 308 | |
| | Oliver | 87 | Luckey | Wm. | 157 | |
| | William | 169 | Lucky | Elizabeth | 34,115 | |
| Loveall | Nancy | 175 | | Mary | 34 | |
| Loveless | ---- | 183 | | Rebecca | 42 | |
| | Mary | 183 | Luddington | Annanais | 54 | |
| Lovet | Edmund | 147 | Ludlow | Hannah Eliza. | 200 | |
| Lovett | David | 142 | | James | 95,100 | |
| | Edward | 147 | Luecke | Christ.(Mrs.) | 13 | |
| Lovin | Walter | 87 | | E.(Mrs.) | 8 | |
| Low | Anna | 55 | Luehring | D. | 70 | |
| | John F. | 97 | | Diderich | 70 | |
| Lowe | Abraham | 132 | | Ellen L. | 70 | |
| | Anna | 55 | | Minna | 70 | |
| | Jefferson | 132 | | W. | 70 | |
| | Thomas | 132 | Lugar | Barney | 83 | |
| Lowell | Jacob | 25 | | George | 82,83 | |
| Lowell | Sarah | 25 | | John | 82,83 | |

**427**

| | | | | | | |
|---|---|---|---|---|---|---|
| Malcom | George W. | 172 | Mans | Henry | 64 |
| | Jackson | 90 | Mansfield | John | 152 |
| | Joseph | 81 | | Robert | 82 |
| | Samuel | 81,87 | Manson | John | 103 |
| | William | 81,88,90 | Manwaren | C.H. | 104 |
| Malcum | John | 85 | Manwaring | Mary | 49 |
| | Samuel | 85 | Manwarren | Charles | 97 |
| Malin | Eli | 124 | Manwarring | Anna | 53 |
| | Joe | 124 | Manwell | Hannah | 195 |
| | May B. | 123 | Maple | Amos | 119 |
| Mallet | Mary | 115,116 | | Florence | 119 |
| Mallett | Maria | 35 | | John D. | 119 |
| Malone | ---- | 64 | | M.H. | 82 |
| | ----(Mrs.) | 247 | Marcus | Gor. | 143 |
| | A. | 64 | Mardis | Joseph K. | 322 |
| | A.J. | 64 | Marford | John | 96 |
| | Benjamin | 35 | Margan | Jno. | 98 |
| | J. | 64 | Margeson | Rebeca | 51 |
| | L.A. | 64 | Marion | John W. | 210 |
| | Logan | 64 | Mark | James B. | 90 |
| | Lydia | 64 | | Moses | 85 |
| | Nicklas | 64 | Markey | Flora A. | 3 |
| | Sarah | 39 | | Georgene | 6 |
| | Smith Miller | 64 | Marklin | Eliza | 59 |
| Malott | Catherine | 19 | Marks | Benjamin | 88 |
| | Daniel | 86 | | Elisha | 89 |
| | Joseph | 19 | | Oliver P. | 218 |
| | Robert | 87 | | Thomas J. | 87 |
| | Thomas | 87 | Marlow | John | 98 |
| Malsbery | Jacob | 82 | Marlowe | Fred Marion | 322 |
| Malson | Francis | 61 | Marmon | Elizabeth C. | 322 |
| | James | 59 | Marquess | Cyranus | 170 |
| | Matilda | 61 | | Eliza Jane | 175 |
| Man | Andrew C. | 141 | | Israel | 166 |
| Manan | Elizabeth | 60 | Marquis | James | 124 |
| Mane | Grant | 89 | Mars | David | 155 |
| Manis | Poindexter | 124 | Marsh | Ben | 81 |
| Mann | Albert Preston | 306 | | Benjamin | 88 |
| | Andrew C. | 141 | | Caroline | 206 |
| | Henry H. | 306 | | Catharine Ann | 40 |
| | Lucinda | 217 | | Elias | 21 |
| | Mary Abegail | 322 | | Elkin | 21 |
| | Robert P. | 299 | | Enoch | 81,89 |
| | Robert Preston | 306 | | Ephriam | 81 |
| | Rosa | 216 | | Frederick | 223 |
| | Thomas J. | 306 | | Harriet | 43 |
| | Willard | 208 | | Isaac | 81,88,90 |
| Mannah | David | 89 | | J.(Mrs.) | 3 |
| Mans | ---- | 64 | | James | 90 |
| | E. | 64 | | Jersey | 104 |
| | Elizabeth | 64 | | Jesse | 81,95 |
| | H. | 64 | | John | 90 |

**428**

| | | | | | | | |
|---|---|---|---|---|---|---|---|
| Masterson | Mary A. | 191 | | May | ---- | 69,72 |
| | Sylvester | 191 | | | Amos | 88 |
| | Sylvester J. | 186 | | | Blanche Allen | 322 |
| | Wealthy | 171 | | | C. | 72 |
| | William | 165 | | | Charles | 72,74 |
| Matchet | Daniel | 89 | | | Edward H. | 73 |
| Mathena | B. | 90 | | | Elfrieda | 73 |
| Matheny | B. | 88 | | | Eli C. | 73 |
| Matheny | William | 103 | | | Ella | 74 |
| Mathers | Caroline | 3 | | | Emma | 72 |
| Matheson | Esther | 34 | | | Freddie W. | 72 |
| Mathies | Paul | 109 | | | H. | 72 |
| Matlock | Margaret | 116 | | | Hannah | 72 |
| | Nancy | 116 | | | Irvin | 69 |
| | Rosannah | 115 | | | Irvin O. | 69 |
| | Sally | 115 | | | Julia Ann | 33 |
| | Stephen N. | 201 | | | Katherine V. | 73 |
| | Susanna | 114 | | | Louella | 69 |
| | William T. | 113 | | | Louella V. | 69 |
| Matsch | Emma Marie | 8 | | | Lydia Ann | 181 |
| Matter | Milton | 322 | | | M. | 72 |
| Mattern | William E. | 225 | | | Martha | 72,74 |
| Matteson | Elcany S. | 225 | | | Mary Eva | 72 |
| Matthew | William H. | 322 | | | Matilda | 72 |
| Matthews | Alexander | 100 | | | Robert Lee | 73 |
| | James | 133 | | | Roy W. | 73 |
| | John S. | 133 | | | Ruth N. | 73 |
| | Martha | 36 | | | Victor | 73 |
| | Paul | 98 | | | William | 22,72 |
| | William | 172 | | | William C. | 72 |
| Mattingly | Erza | 322 | | | William J. | 72 |
| Mattison | ---- | 181 | | | Willie | 72 |
| Mattocks | Edward | 109 | | Mayall | Affa V. | 335 |
| | Edward Jr. | 98 | | | Alla | 335 |
| Mattox | Edna | 320 | | | Arta M. | 335 |
| | Edward | 98 | | | Daniel | 45 |
| Mauck | Jacob | 96 | | | Dessa S. | 335 |
| Maudlin | Benjamin | 177 | | | Eliza | 335 |
| Maul | Josiah | 53 | | | Emanuel R. | 335 |
| Maurer | Edward | 306 | | | Emues C. | 335 |
| | John J. | 306 | | | James | 335 |
| | Joseph | 306 | | | Joseph | 335 |
| Mawler | Aaron | 87 | | | Lima | 335 |
| | Seth | 87 | | | Margaret | 40 |
| Maxey | Martha Jane | 197 | | | Nancy | 43 |
| Maxwell | Howard | 322 | | | Sada E. | 335 |
| | Ina | 8 | | | Willard L. | 335 |
| | John | 23 | | Mayberry | Joel | 106 |
| | Melissa | 333 | | Mayden | Stephen | 90 |
| | Moses | 55 | | Mayer | Daniel | 207 |
| | Ninrod | 103 | | | Josephine K. | 322 |
| Maxy | Matilda Ann | 196 | | Mayers | Mary | 173 |

430

**431**

433

| Surname | Name | Page | Surname | Name | Page |
|---|---|---|---|---|---|
| McGuire | Martha | 18 | McKenan | James | 38 |
| | Nelson | 90 | McKennon | Isabella | 302 |
| | Oliver | 90 | McKenzie | William | 42 |
| | William | 18 | McKey | Mathias | 185 |
| McHarry | Francis | 47 | McKinley | John | 25 |
| McHatton | Jesse L. | 295 | | Wesley | 114 |
| McHenry | John A. | 173 | | William | 25 |
| | Sarah | 168 | McKinly | Jane | 37 |
| McHurin | Susannah | 47 | McKinney | ----(Rev.) | 277 |
| McIlvain | J.G. | 144 | | E. Kirk | 322 |
| | James | 146,151 | | Elias | 81 |
| | John G. | 144 | | Elias W. | 82 |
| | Louisa | 198 | | George | 41 |
| | Samuel | 142 | | Hezekiah | 133 |
| | Wm. | 142 | | Joseph | 133 |
| McIlwain | Thomas | 121 | | P.S. | 86 |
| McInally | Niel | 157 | | Samuel | 133 |
| McIntere | John | 105 | | William | 82 |
| McIntire | Frances | 326 | McKinsey | Mary | 227 |
| | John | 95,97 | McKlane | Bernard | 19 |
| | Robert | 97,105 | McKlehoe | John | 99 |
| McIntosh | Betsey | 116 | McKnight | David | 50 |
| | George | 95,97 | | George | 133 |
| | Peter | 97 | McKown | Isaac | 46 |
| | William | 103 | | Nancy | 45 |
| | Wm. J. | 151 | McKracken | Harriet | 5 |
| McIvain | Wm. | 142 | McLain | Emeline | 241 |
| McKay | Arthur | 305 | | J.B. | 142 |
| | Frances M. | 305 | | James | 142,152 |
| | James(Mrs.) | 4 | | John | 89 |
| | Norma | 322 | | Moses | 142 |
| | Thomas R. | 233 | | Peter | 241 |
| McKeag | Ellen | 2 | | Zerniah E. | 2 |
| McKean | Jno.(Mrs.) | 4 | McLaine | Conrad | 148 |
| | Sarah E. | 3 | | George | 155 |
| McKedy | ---- | 66 | | James | 152 |
| | Daniel S. | 66 | | John | 143 |
| | George | 65 | | Wm. | 155 |
| | J. | 66 | McLaughlen | John J. | 141 |
| | J.N. | 66 | McLaughlin | Adaline | 217 |
| | M. | 66 | | Anna | 215 |
| | M.A. | 66 | | Catherine M. | 15 |
| | Mary | 66 | | Francis | 156 |
| | R.H. | 65 | | Geor. | 153 |
| | R.S. | 65 | | James | 151,153 |
| McKee | Celine Lodge | 322 | | Sarah E. | 172 |
| | Edward Lodge | 322 | | Stephen | 204 |
| | Elmira | 169 | | Wm. | 141 |
| | James | 169 | | Wm.Jr. | 142 |
| | Rebeccah | 58 | | Wm. T. | 151 |
| | Sam(Mrs.) | 119 | McLean | John | 88 |
| McKeever | A.C. | 296 | | Thomas | 35 |

| | | | | | | |
|---|---|---|---|---|---|---|
| McLellan | James | 192 | McPhail | Margaret A. | 2 |
| | James O. | 192 | McPheron | Casie Ann | 207 |
| | Serilda | 192 | | Malinda | 202 |
| McLoghlir | Catharine | 40 | McPherson | Jacob | 121 |
| | Elizabeth | 40 | | R.E. | 231 |
| | John | 44 | | Wm. | 158 |
| | William | 41 | McQueston | W.H.(Mrs.) | 11 |
| McLure | John E. | 143 | McQuiston | W.H.(Mrs.) | 1 |
| McMacker | Deborah | 2 | McQuoid | John | 49 |
| McMahan | John | 97,103,108 | McRae | Calvin R. | 88 |
| | Joseph | 96,104,106 | | Harrison C. | 91 |
| | Martha | 203 | McRay | Alexander | 97 |
| | Samuel | 103 | | Alexander Jr. | 96 |
| | William N. | 322 | | Daniel | 151 |
| Mcmahon | Joseph | 98 | | Duncan | 96 |
| McManes | Malita | 175 | | William | 96 |
| McManis | Rachel | 166 | McRea | Alexander | 98,106 |
| McMannis | Patrick | 207 | | Alexander Jr. | 101,109 |
| McManoman | William | 58 | | Alexander Sr. | 101 |
| McMean | William | 18 | | Alexander F. | 101,108 |
| McMechile | Jno. | 97 | | Daniel A. | 102 |
| McMertery | James N. | 182 | | Duncan | 101,108 |
| Mcmertry | John | 98 | | John B. | 98 |
| McMickal | John Jr. | 103 | | Mordica | 98 |
| McMillan | Grace M. | 8 | | William | 101,107 |
| McMullen | Marie | 9,15 | MCune | Andrew | 107 |
| McMurray | Arthur G. | 322 | | James | 107 |
| Mcmurtry | James | 100 | | Thos. | 107 |
| McMyrtry | James | 109 | McVay | Wm. | 147 |
| McMytry | John | 105 | McVey | Bert | 228 |
| McNabb | Abner | 157 | | Jennie R. | 224 |
| | Mary Ann | 47 | McVicker | John | 208 |
| McNair | Cassie | 4 | McWhorter | Elizabeth | 54 |
| McNally | Edwin M. | 322 | | Kesiah | 56 |
| McNamee | Wilbur A. | 322 | Meade | John S. | 65 |
| McNary | Samuel | 81,88,91 | | Mary A. | 65 |
| McNealy | Robert | 85 | | Minerva | 65 |
| McNeff | Thomas W. | 38 | Meak | Isack | 105 |
| McNeill | David | 335 | Means | Edward | 169 |
| | Mary | 335 | Mears | Elizabeth G. | 308 |
| | Parker | 335 | Mechal | Peter | 151 |
| | Sarah | 335 | Medley | David | 89 |
| McNew | Anna | 33 | Meece | J.D. | 195 |
| McNitt | Esther Uhl | 322 | Meek | Clara | 216 |
| | James D. | 322 | | George W. | 168 |
| McNown | Hugh | 247 | | Isaac | 98 |
| McNutt | Charles | 299,306 | | John A. | 85 |
| | Charles R. | 306 | | Julia | 317 |
| | Harry F. | 322 | | Mary | 206 |
| | James Roy | 322 | | Sarah | 166 |
| McOwen | William | 111 | | Sylvester | 98 |
| MCown | Edward | 106 | Meeks | John | 187,193 |

| | | | | | |
|---|---|---|---|---|---|
| Michael | Elizabeth | 165 | Miller | Ann | 55 |
| | Franklin | 176 | | Anna Pearl | 324 |
| | Frederick | 82 | | Anna Theresa | 38 |
| | Manual | 143 | | Anthony | 184 |
| | Peter | 87,151 | | Barbary | 52 |
| Michalski | Julius | 224 | | Catharine | 42 |
| Micheaaelscn | Mikel | 202 | | Caty Ann | 33 |
| Michel | Catherine | 236 | | Charlotte | 308 |
| Mick | Jacob | 86 | | Daniel | 184,186 |
| Middelkauff | Ann Maria | 172 | | David | 21,222 |
| Middleton | B. | 86 | | Docey | 36 |
| | Wm. | 86 | | Dora | 318 |
| Middlkauff | Eli S. | 174 | | Earl E. | 75 |
| Miese | Wm. | 89 | | Edith | 323 |
| Miesse | Harry | 323 | | Edward E. | 76 |
| | Lulu M. | 323 | | Elias | 89 |
| Migh | Katey | 166 | | Elizabeth | 21,39,318 |
| Milbourn | David | 80 | | Enfield | 190 |
| | Garry | 80 | | Esther M. | 15 |
| Milburn | Felix | 80 | | Fary B. | 228 |
| | Irene Rose | 80 | | Frank | 306 |
| | Jonathan | 80 | | Frank M. | 306 |
| | Robert | 79 | | Franklin | 199 |
| | Sally | 80 | | Frederick A. | 323 |
| | Sarah | 80 | | Freelove | 174 |
| | William | 80 | | George A. | 76 |
| Miles | Delilah | 34 | | George W. | 222 |
| | Isaac | 95,101,108 | | Gilbert | 76 |
| | Isaac Sr. | 98 | | Grace Moore | 323 |
| | John | 98,100,103,167 | | Harry G. | 76 |
| | John Sr. | 103 | | Hazel | 9 |
| | Joseph | 96,98,104,107 | | Henry | 98,108,219 |
| | Lydia C. | 5 | | Hermena | 76 |
| | Martha | 52 | | Hiram L. | 39 |
| | William C. | 86 | | Hugh Th. | 323 |
| Miley | David | 181 | | Isaac | 35,167 |
| | Jeremiah | 181 | | Isabel E. | 164 |
| | Wilsey | 181 | | Isiah | 83 |
| Milholland | Margaret | 53 | | J. Don | 323 |
| | Stella | 312 | | Jacob | 34,97,105 |
| Millar | Volluntene | 96 | | Jacob C. | 166 |
| Millen | Jacob | 38 | | Jacob L. | 185 |
| Miller | —— | 182 | | Jacob S. | 185 |
| | A.J. | 90 | | James | 52,146 |
| | A.S. | 90 | | James F. | 199 |
| | A.W. | 89 | | James T. | 164 |
| | Abraham | 44 | | Jane | 167 |
| | Adam | 185 | | John | 19,23,47,88,186, |
| | Alexander | 133 | | | 197,198,206 |
| | Alice E. | 15 | | John L. | 225 |
| | Andrew | 87 | | John Robert | 323 |
| | Andrew J. | 199 | | Jonas | 205 |

| Miller | Jonathan | 185 | Mills | Agnes | 133 |
|---|---|---|---|---|---|
| | Joseph | 43,174,211 | | Alanson | 211 |
| | Joseph Medford | 306 | | Edward | 133 |
| | Josephine | 174 | | Elisabeth | 133 |
| | Knox Emerson | 306 | | Hezekiah | 83 |
| | Laura Jane | 200 | | James | 133,287 |
| | Lavona M. | 75 | | Jobe | 84 |
| | Lola C. | 9 | | John E. | 203 |
| | Lucretia | 203 | | Joseph | 81,82 |
| | Margaret L. | 76 | | Maon H. | 212 |
| | Margarett | 186 | | Martha | 133 |
| | Margret | 186 | | Mary | 133 |
| | Marion Clinton | 323 | | Michael N. | 213 |
| | Martha A. | 201 | | Richard | 133 |
| | Mary | 34,46,197,309 | | Robt. | 287,291 |
| | Mary L. | 37 | | Willis | 133 |
| | Mary M. | 70 | | Willis S. | 133 |
| | Maud | 76 | Millspaugh | Flora Hardin | 323 |
| | Michael | 198 | Millus | Mahala | 59 |
| | Minnie A. | 224 | Milner | Charles | 217 |
| | Nancy | 44 | | Jean S. | 323 |
| | Nettie Sweeney | 323 | | Kate | 325 |
| | Owen Lambe | 323 | Milor | Mary | 60 |
| | Paul | 90 | Milroy | —— | 233 |
| | Perry A. | 70 | Milton | John | 183 |
| | Peter | 98,110,196,306 | Minard | Kate | 295 |
| | Peter | 98 | Minebury | Fredrick | 216 |
| | Phebe | 38 | Miner | Ida Jane | 212 |
| | Robert | 190 | | Mary A. | 225 |
| | Robert G. | 323 | | Viena | 176 |
| | Robert V. | 306 | | W.D.(Mrs.) | 4 |
| | Samuel | 86 | Mings | George | 103 |
| | Samuel H. | 185 | Minich | Fanny | 44 |
| | Sarah | 170 | | Jane | 42 |
| | Sarah L. | 3 | Minick | Nancy | 39 |
| | Susan | 41 | Minie | Samuel C. | 85 |
| | Susanna | 57 | Minnear | Minnie | 227 |
| | Thomas | 58,323 | Minnich | Martha | 167 |
| | Vinton | 90 | Minnis | Calvin | 79 |
| | Volentine | 98 | | Polly | 79 |
| | William | 40,90,96,98, | Minor | Henry L. | 22,24 |
| | | 107,195,204 | | James | 89 |
| | William H. | 306 | Minser | Caroline | 208 |
| | William J. | 188 | Minton | John | 83 |
| | Winfield | 323 | Minturn | Joseph Allen | 323 |
| | Zeb | 150 | Mires | Sally | 116 |
| Milligan | W. | 247 | | William | 211 |
| Millikan | Mabel Warner | 323 | | Wm. | 143 |
| Millinger | Jacob | 111 | Miser | George | 89 |
| Millis | Fred Clark | 323 | Mishler | Daniel | 197 |
| | Mahala | 59 | | Elizabeth | 195 |
| Mills | —— | 285 | | Margaret | 197 |

| | | | | | | |
|---|---|---|---|---|---|---|
| Mishler | Sarah | 195 | Moffett | Joseph A. | 46 |
| Misselhorn | Adele C. K. | 323 | | Paul G. | 323 |
| Mitcham | Harriet | 46 | Moffitt | Emma | 119 |
| | Nelson | 47 | Mohahan | Bernadette | 7 |
| | Winney | 47 | Mohler | Catharine | 212 |
| Mitchel | Aaron | 133 | Mohr | Anna | 300 |
| | Catharine | 236 | Moler | Abram | 88 |
| | Robert | 103 | Moll | Theophilus J. | 323 |
| | Thomas J. | 227 | Monahan | Edith | 8 |
| | William A. | 81,218 | | Jane | 36 |
| Mitchell | Eli | 121 | Monday | Eliza | 35 |
| | Flemming | 121 | | Henry | 154 |
| | James | 37 | | John | 157 |
| | Jane | 51 | | Larkin | 159 |
| | John | 119 | Mondy | Henry | 154 |
| | Lam. G. | 156 | Monforth | I.G. | 286 |
| | Moses | 119 | Monohan | Mary Magdalene | 307 |
| | Pinkney | 119 | Monroe | Aaron | 197 |
| | Sarah Ann | 53 | | Abel G. | 197 |
| | Sibella | 302 | | Amelia A. | 65 |
| | William | 119 | | Charles A. | 298 |
| | William C. | 323 | | Cynthia Jane | 197 |
| Mitchum | Jesse | 35 | | Edward | 221 |
| | Mahala | 42 | | Frederick K. | 65 |
| | Nancy | 47 | | George A. | 298,306 |
| | Violet | 35 | | George W. | 306 |
| Mitten | Arthur G. | 323 | | Isabella | 287 |
| Miulle | Henry S. | 205 | | Janie | 239 |
| Mize | Nancy | 35 | | Lydie | 239 |
| | Sarah | 35 | | Lydie | 239 |
| Mocassin | James | 240 | | Marie L. | 10 |
| | Maggie | 240 | | Mary E. | 197 |
| Moccasin | James | 240 | | Nancy | 33 |
| | Maggie | 240 | | Pearl | 65 |
| Moch | Jacob | 104 | | Phebe Ann | 204 |
| Mock | Abraham | 101,107 | Monroz | Alvira | 198 |
| | David | 107 | Montague | Wm. | 155 |
| | Issabella | 227 | Montgomery | America B. | 189 |
| | Jacob | 99,107 | | Anna E. | 189 |
| | Jonathan | 102,104,109 | | John | 22,50 |
| | Joseph | 100,107 | | Joseph G. | 45 |
| | Katie A. | 228 | | Mary | 274 |
| Moderwell | Jay(Mrs.) | 1 | | Matilda | 189 |
| Modlin | Dilton | 85 | | Nelson W. | 189 |
| | Reuben | 84 | | Samuel | 52 |
| Modoc | Elwood N. | 240 | | W. | 247 |
| Moeller | Velma W. | 323 | | Walter H. | 323 |
| Moellering | E.C.(Mrs.) | 13 | | Wayne | 189 |
| Moeres | Henry | 103 | | William | 53 |
| Moffat | James E. | 323 | | William H. | 189 |
| Moffet | Mary | 35 | Moody | Fred E. | 306 |
| Moffett | Dorothy Dell | 323 | | George W. | 306 |

| | | | | | | |
|---|---|---|---|---|---|---|
| Moody | James | 51 | | Moore | Sarah | 167 |
| | Jane | 49 | | | Thos. C. | 87 |
| | Pruella | 58 | | | Volley | 60 |
| Moon | Elihu | 87 | | | William | 114 |
| Mooney | Isaac | 171 | | | William H. | 277 |
| | Jennie J. | 7 | | Moores | Charles(Mrs.) | 323 |
| | Nannie | 330 | | | Charles W. | 323 |
| Moor | Benjamin | 90 | | Moorhead | Ruth | 314 |
| | Calvin | 53 | | Moorman | Benjamin | 219 |
| | James | 278 | | | John | 85 |
| | John | 84 | | | Levi | 92 |
| | Meredith | 219 | | | Thomas | 122 |
| | William | 114 | | | W.A. | 122 |
| Moore | Aaron H. | 86 | | Moran | Thomas Francis | 323 |
| | Alice | 317 | | More | Edward | 169 |
| | Anna F. | 205 | | | Haben H. | 104 |
| | Betsey | 114 | | | Robert | 133 |
| | Calvin | 53 | | Moreland | Jones | 85 |
| | Catharine P. | 18 | | | Richard | 105 |
| | Chandler C. | 167 | | Morely | John | 60 |
| | Daniel | 56 | | Morgain | John | 84 |
| | David | 58 | | Morgan | Amanda | 191 |
| | Deborah Duane | 323 | | | Beverly M. | 32 |
| | Edmund | 50 | | | Charles | 295 |
| | Edward | 85 | | | Charles F. | 295 |
| | Elizabeth | 114,175 | | | Daniel | 59 |
| | Emily Eliz. | 176 | | | David | 95,99,106 |
| | Enoch W. | 88 | | | David H. | 191 |
| | Ethel M. | 323 | | | Elijah | 104,106 |
| | F.A. | 85 | | | Elizabeth | 191 |
| | Harbin H. | 103 | | | Evan | 96,106 |
| | Henry A. | 42 | | | George F. | 218 |
| | Henry D. | 175 | | | James T. | 191 |
| | Isaac | 81 | | | John | 96,106,191 |
| | Jalez | 83 | | | Joseph | 91 |
| | James W. | 85 | | | Lulu | 191 |
| | Jesse | 88 | | | Mary | 57,235,236 |
| | Jesse C. | 323 | | | Mary Jane | 171 |
| | John | 40 | | | Perry J. | 83 |
| | John W. | 87 | | | Raymond C. | 323 |
| | Julia Harrison | 323 | | | Robert L. | 191 |
| | Levi | 133 | | | Thomas | 43 |
| | Lucinda | 176 | | | William | 96,99 |
| | Lucretia | 302 | | | Wm. S. | 191 |
| | Patterson | 89 | | Morie | Jonas | 143 |
| | Perry G. | 323 | | Morine | George | 89 |
| | Philip | 133 | | | Jefferson A. | 89 |
| | Rebecca B. | 279 | | | Thomas | 89 |
| | Robert | 133 | | Moritz | Peter | 88 |
| | Robert K. | 18 | | Morman | Lewis | 83 |
| | Samuel | 124 | | Morphew | Robert | 111 |
| | Samuel C. | 85 | | | Sarah | 111 |

**440**

| | | | | | | |
|---|---|---|---|---|---|---|
| Mowrey | Valentine | 56 | Murphey | Callie J. | 214 |
| Mowry | Jacob | 107 | | Dorothy Isabel | 207 |
| Mowser | Anthony | 143 | | John | 133 |
| | Maria | 34 | | Pierson | 133 |
| Moyer | Barbara Mar. | 174 | | Thomas | 48 |
| | Frank C. | 221 | Murphy | —— | 247 |
| Mozingo | John | 133 | | ——(widow) | 247 |
| Muck | George | 103,107 | | Alfred | 172 |
| Mudd | Austin | 36 | | Barton W. | 228 |
| Mull | Joseph | 166 | | Francis | 164 |
| Mullan | —— | 284 | | Henry | 89 |
| | F. | 282,285 | | Isaac | 38 |
| | Francis | 283 | | J.B.(Mrs.) | 297 |
| | I. Sr. | 284 | | Jacob | 51 |
| | John | 183 | | John | 90 |
| | Sarah | 284 | | Jno. K. | 247 |
| Mullen | Henry | 280 | | Maranda | 189 |
| | John | 280 | | Maurice | 324 |
| | Nancy | 280 | | Sprig | 247 |
| Mullendore | Catherine | 263,264 | | Thomas | 86 |
| | Jessie U. | 263 | | William | 204 |
| | Maude M. | 264 | Murray | Andrew | 85 |
| | Maxy | 264 | | Harriet | 337 |
| | Mazy | 263 | | St. Clair | 337 |
| | Wilda | 262 | | William | 93 |
| | Wilda W. | 264 | Murrell | Henry | 16 |
| | William | 263 | Murry | Amos | 228 |
| | William E. | 264 | | Henry | 87 |
| | Wilma | 262 | Musselman | Aggie L. | 213 |
| Mullenneax | Permenter | 133 | | Daniel | 133 |
| Muller | Mary K. | 7 | | Henry | 133 |
| Mullikin | Frank(Mrs.) | 264 | | Hiram | 167 |
| | Thirza | 47 | Mussgrave | John | 155 |
| Mullinex | Permenter | 133 | Mussleman | Danel | 97 |
| Mulvain | Alice C. | 203 | Mussleman | Daniel | 109 |
| | Luisa J. | 224 | Myer | H.M. | 72 |
| Mulvane | William O. | 218 | | Henry | 72 |
| Mulvin | Minerva V. | 204 | | Jacob | 82 |
| Mumford | Eugene Bishop | 324 | | John | 90 |
| Munden | Elisha | 25 | | Mary | 72 |
| | Nancy | 25 | | Matilda | 72 |
| Munger | Mariar Ann | 169 | Myers | Abraham | 83 |
| Munn | Peter F. | 207 | | Alfred | 207,222 |
| Munroe | Lydia A. | 222 | | Archibald | 44 |
| | Martin M. | 204 | | Betsy | 114 |
| Munsonburgh | Emley | 215 | | Burton D. | 324 |
| Murden | Elizabeth | 166 | | Elizabeth | 205 |
| | Naomi | 164 | | George W. | 198 |
| | Orpah Ann | 175 | | Hannah M. | 202 |
| | Thomas | 166 | | Henry | 159 |
| Murdock | Thomas | 97 | | Jacob | 204 |
| Murgotten | Wm. | 247 | | John | 162 |

| Surname | Given name | Page |
|---|---|---|
| Nixon | Lydia Ellen | 305 |
|  | N.T | 119 |
|  | Sophia Parker | 120 |
| Noble | Catharine | 59 |
|  | James | 90 |
|  | Rebecca Maria | 60 |
|  | Thomas B. | 324 |
| Noblitt | Quentin | 324 |
| Noe | Alex. | 148 |
|  | Aquilla W. | 161 |
|  | Lysander | 82 |
| Noel | James W. | 324 |
| Noflesh | Carrie | 244 |
|  | Mable | 242 |
| Nolan | Jas. | 247 |
|  | Maria | 206 |
|  | Val | 324 |
| Noland | Joel J. | 180 |
|  | Math. T. | 153 |
| Noland | Stephen C. | 324 |
| Noll | Irene M. | 9 |
| Nollen | Mariah | 207 |
| Nolting | Emma | 73 |
| Nones | Celestine | 3 |
| Noonan | Matilda | 219 |
| Nordstrum | L.D.(Mrs.) | 12 |
| Nordyke | Mary | 322 |
| Norman | Henry | 86 |
|  | Polly | 114 |
| Norres | Ephraim | 105 |
|  | Garey | 105 |
| Norrice | Schyler C. | 211 |
|  | Wm. H. | 158 |
| Norris | Daniel W. | 47 |
|  | Joe L. | 324 |
|  | William | 134 |
| North | Gabriel | 99,107 |
|  | James | 161 |
|  | John | 144 |
|  | Joseph | 157 |
| Northrop | Caroline W. | 58 |
| Northrup | Caroline W. | 58 |
| Norton | Alfred | 85 |
|  | Archilli C. | 335 |
|  | Arthur | 87 |
|  | Daniel F. | 324 |
|  | Drury | 39 |
|  | Eugene | 86 |
|  | George C. | 335 |
|  | George H. | 335 |
|  | Matilda E. | 5 |
| Norton | Stephen | 90 |
|  | Tamar | 335 |
|  | William | 335 |
| Norvell | Mary Ann | 60 |
| Norvelle | Mary Ann | 60 |
| Norwood | Geo. | 141 |
|  | Lydia | 305 |
| Nose | George | 83 |
| Note | Peter | 87 |
| Notingham | O.P. | 90 |
| Nott | Amy | 335 |
|  | Celesta | 336 |
|  | Samuel | 335 |
|  | Stephen H. | 336 |
|  | Thomas | 335,336 |
| Nouls | Perry | 233 |
| Novark | Albert | 221 |
| Nowlin | Ambrose E. | 324 |
| Nox | John F. | 188 |
| Noyer | Betsey | 167 |
| Nuby | Ed. | 159 |
| Nugent | Benedick | 22 |
|  | Ignatius | 22 |
|  | John Ross | 22 |
|  | Levi Augustus | 22 |
|  | Polly | 22 |
|  | Walter C. | 324 |
|  | Willoughby | 22 |
| Numan | Darethee | 182 |
| Nunley | A. | 66 |
|  | E. | 66 |
|  | Thomas H. | 66 |
| Nunn | Joseph | 153 |
| Nutall | William | 41 |
| Nutter | Andrew J. | 201 |
| Nye | James | 210 |
|  | Mariann | 52 |
| Oakes | Lucretia | 59 |
|  | Lydia | 51 |
|  | Mansur B. | 324 |
| Oatman | J. Harvey | 306 |
|  | Margaret | 308 |
|  | Rachel | 46 |
|  | Simeon | 116 |
|  | Thomas J. | 306,307 |
| O'Bannon | Lew M. | 324 |
|  | Lillian Keller | 324 |
| Obenauer | Hattie S. | 324 |
| O'Brien | Cornelius | 324 |
|  | Dennie | 224 |
|  | James J. | 298 |
|  | Moses | 51 |

| | | | | | | |
|---|---|---|---|---|---|---|
| O'Brien | William H. | 324 | O'Neil | Kitty | 226 |
| O'Bryan | Anna | 35 | O'Neill | Margaret | 324 |
| O'Connell | Charlotte R. | 15 | O'Niel | Lewis | 144 |
| O'Conner | William | 222 | Onstott | Andrew | 172 |
| O'Connor | Agnes J. | 2 | | Catherine | 168 |
| | Cornelia F. | 2 | | George W. | 173 |
| Odam | Silas | 47 | Opord | William | 151 |
| Odeor | William | 48 | Oppear | William | 151 |
| Odle | Esther | 123 | Oppy | William E. | 222 |
| Oehlmann | Edith H. | 303 | Orbison | Henry(Mrs.) | 2 |
| Ogden | Agnes | 4 | Orcutt | Wm. | 246 |
| | John | 336 | Oren | Alexander | 85 |
| | Joseph | 336 | | Hazel E. | 15 |
| | Mary | 336 | | Helen | 10 |
| | Mary W. | 50 | Orff | John(Mrs.) | 2 |
| | Nancy P. | 58 | | Julia E. | 3 |
| Ogle | Elisha | 87 | | Mary Ella | 2 |
| | John | 134,155 | Orme | Chas. | 147 |
| Ohl | Conrad Lawren. | 307 | O'Rourke | Elizabeth | 8 |
| | John William | 307 | Orr | Flora E. | 3 |
| O'Kain | Margaret | 57 | | Kate C. | 4 |
| Oldeor | William | 48 | Orris | Lovena | 202 |
| Oldham | Charles M. | 164 | Orsborn | Thomas | 91 |
| | Elizabeth | 135 | | Henry | 84 |
| Olds | F.(Mrs.) | 5 | Orth | Albert A. | 324 |
| Oliar | Arthur L. | 324 | Ortman | Lillian | 6 |
| Olin | Frank W. | 324 | Orum | Siger Carol. | 174 |
| Olinger | Henry | 147 | Orvis | Robina | 1 |
| Olive | George S. Sr. | 324 | Osbon | Milley | 59 |
| Oliver | Chester D. | 77 | Osborn | Alice | 188 |
| | David | 82,83 | | Betsey | 113 |
| | H. | 92 | | Chase Salmon | 324 |
| | John | 82 | | Daniel | 188 |
| | Joseph Doty | 324 | | Edy | 48 |
| | Margaret | 167 | | Eliza | 195 |
| | Mary | 304 | | Emery J. | 188 |
| | Matilda S. | 77 | | George W. | 163,220 |
| | O. Delmar | 77 | | Isaac D. | 219 |
| | Thomas | 336 | | John E. | 217 |
| Olson | August J. | 219 | | John W. | 195 |
| O'Mara | Catharine | 167 | | Lane B. | 188 |
| | Joe(Mrs.) | 8 | | Mary A. | 215 |
| Omeara | Sylvester | 174 | | Mary Ellen | 199 |
| O'Morrow | Patrick | 169 | | Milley | 59 |
| | Rogers | 171 | | Polly | 115 |
| O'Neal | Catharine | 195 | | Redden | 52 |
| | Chas. | 144 | | Richard | 336 |
| | Eliza | 61 | | Ruth | 123 |
| | Laughlin | 89 | | Samuel | 199 |
| | Lewis | 144 | | Susan | 216 |
| | Thos. | 156 | | William | 59 |
| O'Neel | Chas. | 144 | | William S. | 188 |

446

| | | | | | | |
|---|---|---|---|---|---|---|
| Osborne | Amos | 210 | Paddox | Joseph | 110 |
| | Charles | 64 | Padget | William | 98 |
| | Clarence W. | 325 | Padon | Mary | 50 |
| | Ruth | 64 | Pagani | Humber P. | 325 |
| Osbourne | Samuel M. | 44 | Page | Anne T. | 208 |
| Ostrander | Sarah Ann | 40 | | Egbert E. | 217 |
| Otis | Frederick B. | 325 | | Martha J. | 221 |
| Otiss | Josiah | 90 | | Tilley | 195 |
| Ott | Mary | 211 | Pagett | William | 107 |
| | Paulina | 205 | Pain | Alexander | 212 |
| Otwell | Stith M. | 46 | | Morgan | 83 |
| Overbay | Arthur S. | 325 | | Morgan L. | 83 |
| Overby | Absalem | 40 | | Morris | 84 |
| | Elizabeth F. | 41 | | William | 57 |
| | Thirza | 41 | Paisley | John | 109 |
| Overholtz | Orten | 84 | Pallard | Jesse | 98 |
| Overman | E.C. | 86 | Palmer | Horace | 189 |
| | Eli | 93 | | Jacob | 88 |
| | Ephraim | 93 | | John | 83 |
| | J. | 86 | | John R. | 82 |
| | Joel | 86 | | Joshua | 134 |
| | John | 87 | | Reuben J. | 41 |
| | Nathan | 54,92,120 | | Robt. C. | 181 |
| | Sarah | 120,166 | | Sanford | 189 |
| | Stephen | 86 | | Sarah | 38,189 |
| Overmeyer | Judd(Mrs.) | 7 | | Sarah A. | 215 |
| Overton | Garland | 105 | Palmore | Edith E. | 202 |
| | Garlin | 97 | | John A. | 213 |
| Owen | Charity | 115 | Pancake | Mary | 182 |
| | Clara Eaton | 7 | Pangborn | Anne Porter | 325 |
| | Harris | 49 | | Walter H. | 233 |
| Owens | —— | 27,28 | Pangle | Clarinda | 203 |
| | Alonzo C. | 325 | Paper | H. | 278,286 |
| | Christopher | 204 | Papet | ——(Mrs.) | 280 |
| | Frances | 324 | Parcels | Philip | 176 |
| | Henry | 22 | Parduien | Mena | 223 |
| | John | 22,235 | Parham | Edna | 7 |
| | Mary L. | 220 | Paring | Maria | 62 |
| Owings | Isiah | 89 | | Ranna | 62 |
| | Lemon | 89 | Paris | Emma | 260 |
| Owins | John | 155 | | Florence Jean | 258 |
| Owl | Sally | 58 | | Marie | 260 |
| Owsley | Nancy | 54 | | Richard | 258 |
| Ozenbaugh | Elizabeth | 168 | | Rusell | 260 |
| | | | | Russel A. | 259 |
| Pace | Davie | 229 | | Russell | 260 |
| Packwood | Samuel | 25 | | Ruth | 258 |
| Padax | John | 98 | Parish | George | 222 |
| Paddax | Jonathan | 101 | | Sophronia | 228 |
| Paddoc | David | 34 | Park | ——(Rev.) | 270 |
| Paddox | John | 108 | | Isaac | 46 |
| | Jonathan | 108 | Parke | Silas | 82 |

| | | | | | |
|---|---|---|---|---|---|
| Pierson | William | 209 | | Thomas | 159 |
| | William G. | 202 | Pohlmeyer | Helen L. | 15 |
| Pike | Edna Jones | 325 | Poland | Jennie K. | 325 |
| | Samuel | 163 | | William | 162 |
| | Sarah L. | 197 | Polhamus | Helen J. | 11 |
| Pilcher | Amaziah | 86 | Poling | William | 162 |
| | Charles | 82 | Polk | Amelia | 274 |
| Pile | Rebecca | 23 | Polley | Frederick | 325 |
| | Richard | 23 | Pollock | Thomas | 18 |
| | Thomas | 22 | Polson | William | 101 |
| Pilebs | James | 103 | Polston | John | 102,192 |
| Pilgraim | Micheal | 107 | Pond | Ephraim | 262 |
| Pilgrim | Michael | 102 | | Hiram | 55 |
| Pilkinton | Abraham | 38 | | Mary | 61 |
| Pinnick | Rufus E. | 325 | | Warren | 58 |
| Pitcher | Joshua | 83 | Pool | Charlotte | 336 |
| | Thomas | 134 | | Elizabeth | 336 |
| Pitman | David | 42 | | Jas. | 147 |
| | Laurence | 102 | | John | 336 |
| Pitsenberger | George | 165 | | Joseph | 332,336 |
| | William | 175 | | Nancy | 332 |
| Pittenger | Lemuel A. | 325 | | Thomas | 336 |
| Pittman | James | 98,104,107 | Poole | Frank(Mrs.) | 3 |
| | John | 107,199 | Pooler | David | 239 |
| | John Sen. | 108 | Poor | Abraham | 134 |
| | John B. | 20 | | Anna | 175 |
| | Lawrence | 107 | | Daniel | 199 |
| Pitts | Step. | 150 | | Matthew | 134 |
| Pixler | Abram | 82 | | Washington | 175 |
| | Robert | 82 | Poore | David | 112 |
| Plaess | John | 43 | | Robert | 35 |
| Plasket | William | 24 | Poorman | Alfred P. | 325 |
| Platter | Amelia Waring | 325 | | Sarah E.E. | 325 |
| Platts | Leopold | 176 | Pope | Gaspar | 19 |
| Platz | Phebe | 169 | | Gasper | 25 |
| Pleasant | John | 93 | | George W. | 114 |
| Plew | Elizabeth | 46 | | James | 113 |
| Ploch | Carl A. | 325 | | Katie | 205 |
| Plume | John | 99 | | Nannie E. | 228 |
| Plumer | N.C. | 156 | | Phebe | 115 |
| Plummer | Ira | 148 | | Robert M. | 90 |
| | Norman | 156 | | Worden | 18 |
| Ply | Jerusha | 166 | Porter | Andrew W. | 194,196 |
| Podach | Mary | 221 | | Barney B. | 45 |
| Poe | Gabriel P. | 84 | | Elizabeth | 207 |
| | Jacob | 47 | | Ezra | 89 |
| | John J. | 84 | | Henry | 157 |
| | Patrck J. | 84 | | James Sr. | 148 |
| | Pleasant P | 84 | | James Jr. | 162 |
| Pogue | Bennett | 152 | | Nicholas | 152 |
| | John | 144 | | Sarah | 206 |
| Pogue | Joseph | 145 | Portlock | David L. | 51 |

| | | | | | | |
|---|---|---|---|---|---|---|
| Portteus | David | 53 | Powel | Susanah | 257 |
| | Thomas | 51 | | Thomas | 84 |
| Posey | Emily | 53 | Powell | Albert(Mrs.) | 6 |
| | Mary | 182 | | Amy Susannah | 257 |
| | Thos. | 103,104 | | Asher Townsend | 257 |
| Post | Swain | 222 | | Daniel | 87 |
| Poston | Clement L. | 325 | | George Lott | 257 |
| Poter | John B. | 197 | | J.F. | 87 |
| | Ruthan | 222 | | James | 88 |
| Pothoff | Fred(Mrs.) | 13 | | John | 58 |
| Potmen | Edward | 173 | | John Carson | 257 |
| Potter | —— | 283,284,288,289 | | Joseph | 256,257 |
| | Allis | 211 | | Joseph Milton | 257 |
| | Daniel | 163 | | Lewis | 88 |
| | Earl | 82 | | Margaret Anna | 257 |
| | Emily Alice A. | 203 | | Mary | 169 |
| | Harriet Sophia | 163 | | Mary Catharine | 257 |
| | I.S. | 287 | | Rebeca | 257 |
| | James C. | 215 | | Rebecca Jane | 257 |
| | Joseph | 37 | | Richard | 257 |
| | Mahala | 43 | | Susannah | 256 |
| | Martha | 44 | | Thomas | 169 |
| | Mary E. | 3 | Power | Eva Belle | 304 |
| | S.S. | 280,282 | | Joseph | 83 |
| | Samuel | 42 | | Richard L. | 325 |
| | Susan | 37 | Powers | James S. | 51 |
| | William | 98,104 | | Jane | 55 |
| | William H. | 106 | | John | 134 |
| Potterf | Margarite | 171 | | John K. | 134 |
| Pottorff | John | 18 | | John S. | 60 |
| Potts | Andrew | 102,104,106 | Pownall | Horace | 209 |
| | Jacob | 101,103 | Poynter | John | 117 |
| | John | 102,107 | Prather | Basel | 23 |
| | John B. | 97,104 | | Bazil R. | 18 |
| | Joseph | 108 | | Jeremiah | 39 |
| | Katharine | 117 | | Julia | 305 |
| Pouge | John | 144 | | Samuel | 23 |
| Poulson | Frances | 42 | | Thomas | 18 |
| Pound | Joseph | 18,19 | | William | 17 |
| Powel | Anna | 256 | Prathor | Isaac | 116 |
| | Anne | 256,257 | Pratt | Coburn | 298 |
| | Any | 257 | | Mary A. | 325 |
| | Charles | 256,257 | | Sarah Smith | 325 |
| | Elizabeth Ann | 257 | Prechett | Sally | 117 |
| | George | 256,257 | Presley | Thomas | 134 |
| | Harrison H. | 82 | Presnall | Elihu | 85 |
| | Isaac Jame | 257 | Pressnell | Abraham | 85 |
| | John | 82 | Preston | Abraham L. | 325 |
| | John B. | 256,257 | Pretty Back | Oscar | 242 |
| | Joseph | 256,257 | Prettyman | Aaron N. | 202 |
| | Richard | 256,257 | | Alice S. | 215 |
| | Samuel | 256,257 | Prettyman | Charles | 204 |

| | | | | | | |
|---|---|---|---|---|---|---|
| Rank | Rena | 223 | Readen | Spencer | 91 | |
| | Samuel David | 166 | Reader | Jonathan F. | 83 | |
| Rankin | Rachael | 175 | | Wm. H.H. | 83 | |
| Ranking | Robert | 45 | Ready | Matthew | 43 | |
| Ransburg | Harper J. | 326 | Reagan | Daniel | 159 | |
| Ransom | Francis | 34 | | John | 143,147 | |
| | Hiram | 38 | | Wilks | 159 | |
| | Nellie P. | 5 | | Wm. | 147 | |
| Ranstead | Susana | 198 | Reagin | John | 147 | |
| Rappaport | Leo M. | 326 | | Timothy | 247 | |
| Rarden | Amanda | 51 | Ream | Noah | 88 | |
| | Ann | 57 | Reasor | Eunice | 41 | |
| | Moses | 53 | | Sarah | 45 | |
| Rarick | George M. | 216 | Reavis | Isaac | 87 | |
| Rariden | Ann | 57 | Rebstock | Alice T. | 221 | |
| | James | 49 | | Mary E. | 227 | |
| Rathburn | Mary Ann | 204 | | Nathaniel | 200 | |
| Ratliff | Joseph | 93 | Record | Charity | 61 | |
| Rauh | Louise | 12 | Records | Frances M. | 218 | |
| | Samuel Elias | 326 | Rector | Benjamin | 176 | |
| Raush | Wm. | 85 | | Ida M. | 228 | |
| Raver | Abigail | 168 | | Louisa | 170 | |
| Rawalt | Benjamin | 336 | | Samuel C. | 218 | |
| | Elizabeth | 336 | Recy | ---- | 28 | |
| | Enoch | 336 | Red Horse | Vina | 242 | |
| | Henry | 336 | Redd | John B. | 175 | |
| | James | 336 | Reddick | Earl | 120 | |
| | John | 336 | | Elishah | 154 | |
| | Jonas | 336 | Redfield | Ovanda | 38 | |
| | Jonas R. | 336 | | Richard Jr. | 36 | |
| | Mary | 336 | Redman | Charles K. | 46 | |
| | Seth | 336 | | Henry | 216 | |
| Ray | Cary T. | 326 | | Joshua W. | 25 | |
| | Edith | 116 | | Nancy | 34 | |
| | James M. | 160 | Redugh | Samuel | 95,100 | |
| | John | 160 | Reece | ---- | 116 | |
| | Rhoda | 334 | Reed | A.W. | 86 | |
| | Samuel | 152,160 | | Ann | 59 | |
| Rayburn | J.L. | 165 | | Archibald C. | 147 | |
| Raymer | Elizabeth | 174 | | Armareta | 200 | |
| Raynelds | Robert | 219 | | Bazel | 61 | |
| Raypholty | John | 89 | | Charlotte | 33 | |
| Raypholtz | Anthony | 89 | | Della Shoup | 326 | |
| Razor | James | 191 | | Dorothy | 197 | |
| Rea | Emory Lee | 71 | | Eliza | 211 | |
| | Lot | 87 | | Elizabeth C. | 42 | |
| | Naomi Lee K. | 71 | | Hannah | 168 | |
| | Virginia Eva | 250 | | Isaac | 153,201 | |
| Read | A.C. | 147 | | Jacob | 199 | |
| | James | 97 | | Jed. | 151 | |
| | William | 146 | | John | 25,201,202, 204,223 | |
| Reade | Anna Ruth | 326 | | | | |

456

| | | | | | | |
|---|---|---|---|---|---|---|
| Reed | Joseph | 23 | Renbarger | Charles | 89 |
| | Joseph B. | 56 | | Isaac | 82 |
| | Joseph H. | 169 | Renberger | G.W. | 89 |
| | Levi | 86 | | Henry L. | 89 |
| | Lucy May | 220 | | Isaac | 89 |
| | Lyde A. | 219 | | James | 89 |
| | Mary | 209 | Renck | William | 140 |
| | Matilda | 43 | Rendsbaugher | Caroline | 209 |
| | Olive J. | 218 | Rengland | Joseph | 134 |
| | Otheniel | 58 | Reniker | David | 209 |
| | Rebecca | 55 | Rennaker | James | 90 |
| | Sarah | 23 | | John | 89 |
| | Thomas | 206 | | Michael | 89 |
| | Thurza | 208 | | Samuel | 89 |
| | Waldo | 241 | | Wm. | 89 |
| | William | 19,23,54,206 | Rennals | Isaac | 157 |
| Reede | Ellen | 196 | Rennick | Percival G. | 326 |
| Reeds | Nancy | 52 | | William | 140 |
| Reedy | David | 134 | Reno | Thomas | 82 |
| Reeg | Jacob B. | 222 | Replogle | Angeline | 204 |
| Reehling | Ruth H. | 15 | Reprogal | Nettie D. | 226 |
| Reel | Henry J. | 84 | Reprogle | Charles C. | 226 |
| Reep | Henry | 24 | Requa | Florence | 2 |
| Rees | Gabriel | 82 | Reselka | John | 199 |
| | Lewis | 170 | Reser | William M. | 326 |
| Reese | Joseph | 23 | Restow | Michael | 215 |
| | Paula C. | 9 | Retherford | David | 182 |
| Reeves | Calvin | 232 | Rettig | Nellie S. | 326 |
| | Jacob F. | 176 | Reuber | Charles | 232 |
| | N.W.C. | 118 | Reuter | Charles | 232 |
| | Rufus | 172 | | Christopher | 232 |
| | Sampson | 87 | Reveles | Mary | 236 |
| Reffer | Samantha | 211 | Revels | Edmon | 236 |
| Rehard | John H. | 220 | | Esther | 235 |
| Reich | Mary S. | 222 | Reyburn | J.L. | 164 |
| Reichart | H.(Mrs.) | 5 | | James M. | 167 |
| Reid | Caroline W. | 78 | | Margaret | 173 |
| | Hazel | 317 | | W.M. | 164 |
| Reilly | Peter C. | 326 | Reymer | John | 34 |
| Reins | Samuel | 165 | Reynolds | Berien | 53 |
| Reitze | Augusta G. | 4 | | Blanche | 307 |
| | Helen | 6 | | James | 36,113 |
| Remick | William | 39 | | Lucretia | 114 |
| Remmel | Ada E. | 2 | | Martin | 258 |
| Remy | Benjamin W. | 57 | | Michael T. | 258 |
| | Charles F. | 326 | | Patricia Ann | 258 |
| | Delilah | 49 | | Ruth Parris | 258 |
| | John T. | 61 | | Samuel | 21 |
| | Joseph | 48 | | Scarlett M. | 86 |
| Renaker | Wm. | 85 | | Susanah | 218 |
| Renard | Benjamin | 272 | | Thomas | 83 |
| Renard | Francis P. | 24 | Rhea | John W. | 82 |

457

| | | | | | | |
|---|---|---|---|---|---|---|
| Riley | Abagail E. | 209 | Roberts | Andrew | 115 |
| | Alexus | 148 | | Benjamine | 141 |
| | James | 101 | | Bertha A. | 224 |
| | John H. | 101 | | Edna Carroll | 120 |
| | William | 100 | | Edward | 160 |
| Rin | Lewis | 116 | | Elizabeth | 47 |
| Rinebolt | Laovina , | 215 | | Frances | 42 |
| Rinehard | Seward | 227 | | Hardin | 42 |
| Rinehart | Orville(Mrs.) | 7 | | Hiram S. | 43 |
| Ring | ----(widow) | 247 | | Isaac | 84,149 |
| | Jacob | 86 | | Jacob | 157 |
| Ringer | Conrod | 142 | | James | 33,85 |
| | David | 157 | | Jesse | 148 |
| | Jacob Jr. | 141 | | John | 87 |
| | Jacob Sr. | 141 | | Joseph | 22 |
| Ringland | Joseph | 134 | | Leonard | 120 |
| Ringleber. | Adam | 211 | | Margaret A. | 66 |
| | Elizabeth | 209 | | Mary | 40 |
| Ripley | William C. | 227 | | Mary A. | 220 |
| Risk | Polly | 52 | | Michael B. | 82 |
| Risley | Mary | 182 | | Minor | 145 |
| Ristine | Theodore H. | 326 | | Nancy | 39 |
| Ritchey | Margaret | 175 | | Phineas | 82 |
| Ritchie | John | 159 | | Raul | 81 |
| Rite | Thomas | 96 | | Robat R. | 224 |
| Ritter | John | 85 | | Robert R. | 221 |
| | Mary | 311 | | Sarah | 41 |
| | Michael | 85 | | Susan | 43 |
| | Owen | 216 | | Thomas | 43 |
| Ritterhouse | Anthony | 124 | | William | 25,33,82,85, |
| | Geo. | 124 | | | 121,149 |
| Rivers | John | 134 | | Wm. J. | 181 |
| Roach | Hugh | 58 | Robertson | Alexander | 230 |
| | Jos. | 247 | | Deborah | 2 |
| Roache | Oleanda | 243 | | Eleanor M. | 326 |
| | Steven | 245 | | Isaac | 46 |
| Road | G.H.D. | 87,88,90 | | James | 18 |
| | George H. D. | 81 | | James T. | 97,106 |
| Roadearmel | ---- | 182 | | Robt. | 146 |
| Roads | Abram | 83 | Robeson | Philip W. | 134 |
| | Andrew F. | 134 | Robins | Lemuel | 35 |
| | J.R. | 159 | | Lisha | 224 |
| | Sam'l. B. | 149 | Robinson | Arthur | 135 |
| Robb | James | 239 | | Gamaliel W. | 209 |
| Robberts | Joab | 87 | | George H. | 53 |
| | Joseph | 85 | | Henry | 168 |
| Robbin | Sarah E. | 226 | | James | 39 |
| Robbins | Elizabeth | 177 | | James A.D. | 205 |
| | Emmer D. | 172 | | Jennie D. | 218 |
| Robbinson | George H. | 53 | | John P. | 173 |
| Robers | Dorothy E. | 112 | | Mary Yandes | 326 |
| Roberts | Abigail | 36 | | Orpha A. | 7 |

| Surname | Given | Page |
|---|---|---|
| Robinson | Russell | 40 |
|  | Thomas | 135 |
|  | William | 135 |
|  | William W. | 135 |
| Robison | Frank | 216 |
|  | Jesse | 135 |
|  | Martha | 22 |
|  | Richard | 135 |
|  | William | 22 |
|  | William C. | 135 |
| Roblins | John | 97 |
| Robston | Mathew | 104 |
| Roby | Betsy | 23 |
|  | Emily | 225 |
|  | Henry | 23 |
|  | Leonard | 23 |
|  | Lucy | 23 |
|  | Townley | 20 |
| Roche | Maria | 39 |
| Rock | Cornelius J. | 220 |
|  | John W. | 224 |
|  | Mariah | 219 |
|  | Samuel F. | 204 |
| Rockafellar | Anna | 52 |
|  | Rebecca | 54 |
| Rocker | Benjamin | 54 |
| Rockey | Frank | 271 |
|  | Franklin | 266 |
|  | Franklin J. | 267 |
|  | Joe | 267 |
|  | Sara | 271 |
| Rocks | Elizabeth | 202 |
| Rockwell | George S. | 205 |
|  | Grant R. | 225 |
| Rockwood | William M. | 326 |
| Rodarmel | Amanda | 180 |
| Rodd | Josie | 242 |
| Roden | Allen | 100 |
|  | Thomas | 98 |
|  | William | 100,104 |
| Rodes | Lewis | 101 |
|  | Michael | 103 |
|  | William | 100 |
| Rodgers | Elizabeth | 39 |
|  | Emma | 205 |
|  | Henry | 37 |
|  | Jas. | 142 |
|  | Joseph | 86 |
|  | Kirk | 224,227 |
|  | Robert | 208 |
| Rodin | Allen | 106 |
|  | Thos. | 106 |

| Surname | Given | Page |
|---|---|---|
| Rodin | William | 110 |
| Rodman | Joseph | 87 |
| Roe | Amos | 135 |
|  | John | 135 |
|  | Richard | 135 |
| Roebel | Helen R. | 15 |
| Roebuck | Wesley S. | 326 |
| Rogers | Aaron Grigsby | 326 |
|  | Ada C. A. | 326 |
|  | Aquilla | 18 |
|  | Benjamin | 265 |
|  | Clement L. | 224 |
|  | Elisabeth A. | 265 |
|  | Henry C. | 207 |
|  | J.W. | 89 |
|  | James | 56 |
|  | Mary M. | 337 |
|  | Rupert | 112 |
|  | Sarah | 265 |
|  | Thomas | 103,110 |
|  | Walter G. | 199 |
| Rogier | Elizabeth L. | 15 |
| Rohrer | S.B.(Mrs.) | 7 |
| Rohsenberger | Elizabeth M. | 307 |
| Rohyans | Helen M. | 11 |
|  | Mildred C. | 8 |
| Roland | Perlu | 286 |
| Role | Benjamin | 96 |
|  | George | 84 |
| Roll | Isaac | 155 |
|  | Joseph | 144 |
| Roller | Anna B. | 204 |
|  | Annie M. | 221 |
|  | Catharine E. | 206 |
|  | Jacob B. | 204 |
| Rollins | Enoch | 95 |
|  | Enock | 105 |
|  | John | 95 |
|  | Joseph | 82 |
| Roman | Hattie F. | 249 |
| Romig | Elias | 197 |
|  | Isaac | 195 |
|  | Joseph | 196 |
|  | Mary E. | 225 |
|  | Sarey | 195 |
|  | Soloman | 215 |
|  | Susannah A. | 219 |
| Romine | Noah | 86 |
|  | Samuel B. | 207 |
| Rook | Frederick | 135 |
| Rooker | Samuel | 155 |
|  | Wm. D. | 159 |

| Surname | Given | Page | Surname | Given | Page |
|---|---|---|---|---|---|
| Rooker | William M. | 199 | Rouk | Sally | 58 |
| Rooks | Rosanna | 242 | Rouls | Alice | 270 |
| | Susie | 240 | | Alice Ann | 266,267 |
| Roose | Isaac | 200 | | D.S. | 270 |
| | Jesse | 199 | Roup | John | 200 |
| | Mary C. | 215 | Roupe | Anna | 223 |
| | William E. | 223 | Rouse | Fred. A.A.O. | 222 |
| Rorick | Schuyler | 227 | | Mary | 49 |
| Rose | Ebon | 243 | | Thomas | 40 |
| | Eleanor | 37 | Roush | Emma J. | 122 |
| | Eleazer | 60 | | Isaac | 85 |
| | Frederick D. | 326 | | Michael | 81,88,90 |
| | Gladys W. | 326 | Rouze | Mary | 49 |
| | Jane Eliza | 41 | Rovenstine | John A. | 202 |
| | Jappa | 121 | Row | Daniel | 102,105 |
| | Samuel | 82 | | Ella Yater | 326 |
| | Stiles | 199 | Rowan | Jacob | 105 |
| Roseberry | Alexander | 60 | | M. | 247 |
| | James | 56 | | Margaret B. | 326 |
| Rosenberger | William | 205 | | Mary E. | 2 |
| Rosendale | Samuel | 169 | | Wm. | 247 |
| Rosenthal | Hattie | 5 | Rowbottom | Anna | 307 |
| | Henry | 176 | | Harry E. | 307 |
| Roskie | Julius | 206 | | James | 307 |
| Ross | Adellia V. | 4 | Rowe | Bessie W. | 10 |
| Ross | Albert E. | 182 | | Clara | 4 |
| | Anna | 207 | | Lou M. | 308 |
| | Augusta | 210 | | William | 207 |
| | Betsy | 308 | Rowell | Byron D. | 210 |
| | Caroline | 211 | | Daniel | 208 |
| | Frances Mc. | 326 | Rowen | Jacob | 97 |
| | Franklin | 216 | Rowland | ---- | 277,279,285, 286,287 |
| | George | 20,21,25 | Rowland | Cathrine | 196 |
| | Jane | 53 | | I. | 280 |
| | John | 2,45 | | John | 286 |
| | John B. | 171 | | John P. | 278 |
| | John Graham | 307 | | P. | 287 |
| | John Isom | 307 | | Perlu | 287 |
| | Katie A. | 5 | | Peter | 282,283 |
| | Laura E. | 9 | Rowlands | Phil | 288 |
| | Lavenia | 51 | Rowley | Alpheus B. | 37 |
| | Peter | 37 | Royce | ---- | 28 |
| | Reason | 85 | | John | 30 |
| | Samuel | 53 | | Lewis(Mrs.) | 264 |
| | William | 135 | Royse | John | 27 |
| Rost | Carrie | 214 | | Sarah | 27 |
| Rothermel | Elizabeth | 197 | Ruby | Charles E. | 326 |
| | Margaret | 196 | Rucker | Benjamin | 54 |
| Rottmayer | Carrie C. | 308 | | Jonathan | 85 |
| Rotunge | Joseph | 18 | | Reuben | 23 |
| Rough | George A. | 225 | Rudman | Easter | 49 |
| Roughf | Michael | 163 | | | |

| | | | | | | |
|---|---|---|---|---|---|---|
| Saltkeld | Caroline M. | 46 | Saunders | Sarah | 56 |
| Sample | Joseph | 87,147 | Savage | ---- | 285 |
| | Sallie S. | 326 | | Rosa | 274 |
| Sampley | Adelia K. | 70 | Savery | Alfred A. | 221 |
| Sampson | Melinda | 42 | | Emma L. | 210 |
| Samuel | Christopher | 44 | | Willis | 219 |
| | Lucinda | 114 | Saviers | Dorothy E. | 15 |
| Samuels | Joseph | 239 | Savilla | Hannah Ann | 171 |
| | Robt. F. | 158 | Sawder | Polly | 114 |
| Sanderlin | Mary E. | 206 | Sawyer | William | 211 |
| Sanders | Allen | 213 | Saxe | ---- | 231 |
| | Elizabeth | 46 | Sayer | John | 213 |
| | Elizabeth Ann | 61 | Sayers | James Harvey | 175 |
| | Everett | 326 | Sayler | Henry B. | 91 |
| | Hannah | 53 | Saylor | Margaret | 8 |
| | I.N. | 149 | Scales | John | 182 |
| | Isaac N. | 149 | Scamore | Thomas | 207 |
| | John S. | 135 | Scantlan | Sarah | 37 |
| | Sarah | 56 | Scarlet | J.T. | 246 |
| | Ura | 326 | | William | 232 |
| | William | 135,161 | Schaad | Christ Jr. | 299 |
| | Wm. T. | 143 | Schaaf | A.H.(Mrs.) | 8 |
| Sanderson | John | 40 | Schaeffer | Susan E. | 1 |
| | William C. | 299 | Schau | P. | 70 |
| Sandford | Hattie L. | 199 | Schebart | Chathrine | 218 |
| Sandman | Anna P. | 266,267 | Schell | Ellen | 303 |
| Sands | James | 96,102 | | Mary M. | 3 |
| | John | 97 | Schenck | Corinne | 314 |
| | Leah | 242 | | Eugenia | 315 |
| | Mary | 33 | Scherer | W.W.(Mrs.) | 7 |
| Sandusky | Elizabeth | 35 | Scherginger | Geor. W. | 190 |
| Sanford | Deliah | 204 | Scherrer | Anton | 327 |
| | Jonathan | 198 | Scherzer | Jobst | 192 |
| Sansberry | Charles T. | 326 | Schessler | Christopher | 211 |
| | Maud Mahorney | 326 | Scheumann | Emma | 7 |
| Santarelli | Laura Morton | 327 | Schiemann | Ernest | 232 |
| Sapenfield | David | 106 | Schiffbauer | Minnie | 240 |
| | Jocab | 109 | Schiltges | William B. | 327 |
| Sapingfield | George | 180 | Schimann | Ernest | 232 |
| Sappenfield | Louis | 110 | Schinosliksi | Emma | 218 |
| Sarver | John | 103 | Schipper | Alfred Andrew | 307 |
| | Peter | 103 | | Frank Anthony | 307 |
| Sater | Hannah | 50 | Schlatter | Caroline | 3 |
| Sattenfield | James | 101 | | Emmeline | 3 |
| Sauer | Adele P. | 7 | Schmidt | Antona | 220 |
| | Emma | 6 | Schmidt | August | 224 |
| | Martha | 6 | | Clara C. | 7 |
| Saunders | George | 171 | | Daniel | 232 |
| | John | 122 | | Theodore | 232 |
| | Pertina | 115 | | Tim | 232 |
| | Rhoda | 116 | Schmiedt | Carl | 69 |
| | Sally | 116 | Schmiedt | Caroline | 69 |

| | | | | | | |
|---|---|---|---|---|---|---|
| Seabrook | John Wesley | 307 | Selby | Joshua B. | 192 |
| | Paul | 307 | | Malinda A. | 180 |
| Seagraves | Elizabeth | 211 | | Otto | 83 |
| | Jefferson | 199 | | William | 180 |
| | John W. | 210 | Self | Sarah | 39 |
| | Lemuel | 207 | Selgrove | Jacob | 145 |
| | Mary A. | 215 | | James | 158 |
| | Silas | 210 | | Joseph | 156 |
| | William | 205 | Sellears | Amelia | 228 |
| Seagrist | Elizabeth | 208 | Sellers | Abraham | 149 |
| Seal | Benjamin | 55 | | Alfred Perry | 176 |
| | Caleb | 56 | | Catharine J. | 171 |
| | John | 84 | | Joseph | 220 |
| | Martha | 61 | Sells | Abraham | 135 |
| | William | 40 | | David | 135 |
| Seals | Benjamin | 55 | | John | 135 |
| Seamore | Amanda | 211 | | Vivian | 267 |
| Searles | Ebenezer | 24 | | William | 135 |
| | Henry | 32 | Selock | Mary B. | 220 |
| Sears | Catharine | 44 | Seltenright | Daniel | 175 |
| | Christena | 42 | Seltzer | Jacob | 72 |
| | Christopher | 90 | | Victoria | 72 |
| | Jacob | 44 | Selwell | Recard | 105 |
| | Louis M. | 327 | Selwyn | John | 239 |
| Seaton | James | 22 | Senache | Anna | 239,242 |
| | Mary | 6 | Sensner | Peter G. | 103 |
| Seay | Mary Ellen | 306 | Sergeant | Abel M. Jr. | 36 |
| Sebens | Seben | 218 | Serles | Ebenezer | 24 |
| Sebridge | Leverndon | 212 | | Rosanna | 50 |
| Sebring | Geo. | 124 | Serls | S.R. | 90 |
| Seburn | Saml. S. | 144 | Sero | Vincent | 43 |
| Secrest | Buck | 112 | Seton | Jno. | 100 |
| | Mary Ann | 199 | Setter | John | 151 |
| | Sarah | 200 | Setters | John | 151 |
| Secrist | Henry | 207 | | Samuel P. | 160 |
| | Jacob | 88 | Seveney | James | 20,25 |
| | Susan | 208 | Seward | Abel | 152 |
| Secust | John | 88 | | Amos D. | 164 |
| Sedgewick | Scipio | 160 | | Jonathan | 154 |
| Sedwick | Scipio | 160 | | Stephen | 82 |
| Seeger | D.R. | 89 | Sewell | Mary | 315 |
| Seely | Benjamin | 49 | Seybold | Mahlon | 135 |
| | Sophia | 49 | Seymour | Eliza J. | 209 |
| Sees | John Vincent | 327 | | Mary Angel. | 202 |
| Segraves | Jefferson | 200 | | Sarah A. | 203 |
| | Stephen | 174 | Shackelford | I.M. | 83 |
| Segrist | Rebecca | 213 | | J.T. | 82 |
| Segur | Margaret B. | 327 | | John | 82 |
| Seifert | Augusta | 218 | Shackleford | John G. | 189 |
| Seiles | Rosanna | 50 | Shaddinger | Sarah | 167 |
| Seiter | Blasey | 85 | Shadinger | Mary | 171 |
| Selby | James | 135 | | Sarah | 164 |

| Shafer | Benjamin F. | 211 | Sharpe | Henry | 172 |
| | Clara Alice | 223 | | James | 170 |
| | David | 85 | | Julia Ann | 171 |
| | Elizabeth | 135,200 | Sharrar | Andrew | 150 |
| | John B. | 215,225 | | George | 146 |
| | John C. | 121 | | John | 146 |
| | John H. | 223 | | Michael | 143 |
| | Margaret J. | 68 | Shatto | Alma H. | 215 |
| | S. | 68 | Shatzer | Wm. | 90 |
| | S.E. | 68 | Shaver | Charles | 108 |
| | Tabitha L. | 223 | Shaw | Archibald | 327 |
| | William H. | 204 | | Elenor | 53 |
| | William Henry | 135 | | Elizabeth | 62,195 |
| Shaffer | Amos A. | 224 | | Elvira Jane | 203 |
| | John C. | 327 | | Hamilton | 55 |
| | Mary | 171 | | Henry V. | 212 |
| | Phillip | 247 | | James W. | 38 |
| | Polly | 55 | | Jerusia | 56 |
| | Simon | 135 | | Jonathan | 58 |
| | William | 135 | | Joseph | 22 |
| Shahan | James | 176 | | Josephine | 219 |
| Shainhuber | Henry | 81 | | Mahala | 54 |
| Shake | George | 19 | | Margret J. | 214 |
| Shank | Daniel | 89,90 | | Merrit W. | 226 |
| | James | 57 | | Orpheus | 222 |
| Shanklin | Lon(Mrs.) | 120 | | Peter | 196 |
| | Long(Mrs.) | 119 | | Walter C. | 175 |
| | William | 168 | Shaws | Young | 86 |
| Shanks | Daton | 221 | Shawver | Alexander | 115 |
| | Ida | 221 | | Matilda | 333 |
| | Rosetta | 207 | Shay | Timothy | 181 |
| | William Carey | 327 | Shearer | Sally | 32 |
| Shannon | Isaac | 229 | Shearry | Jane | 54 |
| | J.F. | 89 | Shearwood | Mary | 56 |
| | John | 116 | Sheehy | Mary E. | 168 |
| | L.W. | 89 | Sheely | Emma J. | 222 |
| | Lydia Ann | 43 | Sheet | John | 147 |
| Sharewood | Anna | 61 | Sheets | Anne | 256 |
| Sharp | Abbie J. | 1 | | Fredrick | 152 |
| | Alonzo | 226 | | George | 256 |
| | Armilda | 208 | Shefer | David S. | 207 |
| | Daniel E. | 224 | Sheib | Ferdinand | 188 |
| | David | 155 | | Peter | 188 |
| | Lanora | 224 | Shelby | Evan | 24,25,26 |
| | Loranzo D. | 182 | | Isaac | 24,25 |
| | Mary A. | 205 | Shelden | Julia Ann | 222 |
| | Mellissa | 209 | Sheldon | ---- | 278,279 |
| | Thomas H. | 161 | | Rose A. | 328 |
| | William | 98,105 | Shelds | Joshua | 98 |
| Sharpe | Alonzo | 207 | Shell | Andrew J. | 225 |
| | Elizabeth | 173 | Shelly | Sarah A. | 208 |
| | Francis R. | 214 | Shelner | George | 165 |

| | | | | | | |
|---|---|---|---|---|---|---|
| Shelton | Susannah | 116 | Shields | Susanna | 43 |
| | Thos. | 153 | | Wm. | 16 |
| Shepard | Mary | 172 | Shies | Xavier | 46 |
| Shepard | Wm. | 124 | Shiffert | Tilara | 176 |
| Shepherd | Allen | 37 | Shilling | Edgar W. | 224 |
| | Elcy | 59 | | Hiram G. | 215 |
| | Humphrey | 39 | | Sarah | 219 |
| | John | 98,104,108 | | Schuyler C. | 222 |
| | Sarah | 56 | Shilts | John H. | 327 |
| | William | 102,105 | Shindelar | Frank | 211 |
| Sheppard | Sarah | 56 | Shindler | William | 39 |
| Sher | Sampson | 174 | Shingles | John | 155 |
| Sherbody | Estella | 15 | Shinhulser | Henry | 88 |
| Sherck | Catharine | 199 | Ship | —— | 28 |
| | Matilda | 198 | | John | 135 |
| | Sarah Ann | 198 | Shipley | Maggie | 120 |
| Sherer | Andrew | 150 | Shipman | Elizabeth | 27 |
| | George | 146 | | Margaret | 27,28 |
| | Jacob | 145 | | Mary | 27 |
| | John | 146 | | Stephen | 27,28 |
| | Michael | 143 | Shipp | John | 135 |
| | Valentine | 145 | | Margaret M. | 327 |
| Sheridan | Carroll | 8 | Shira | Philip | 86 |
| Sherley | Martha E. | 203 | Shireman | Elizabeth | 177 |
| Sherly | John | 147 | Shirk | Alice | 315 |
| Sherman | Clara D. | 227 | | Joseph Henry | 327 |
| | Ennie E. | 221 | | Mactiline | 196 |
| | S.M. | 89 | Shirley | Elizabeth | 37 |
| Sherow | Levi | 201 | | John | 44,195 |
| Sherry | M. Evan | 327 | | Joseph | 176 |
| Sherwin | Wm. K. | 172 | | Mary | 171 |
| Sherwood | Anna | 61 | | Phil. | 143 |
| Shetler | Elizabeth | 173 | | Philamon | 143 |
| Sheton | Thos. | 153 | | William C. | 327 |
| Shewey | Daniel | 166 | Shirtleff | Oliver | 149 |
| Shibe | Casper | 33 | Shivels | Louis B. | 189 |
| Shideler | Aaron | 85 | Shively | Mausuria | 228 |
| | Lewis | 52 | | Sarah F. | 223 |
| Shields | ——(Mrs.) | 16 | | Susan | 199 |
| | David | 96,98,104,107 | Shivley | Samuel | 197 |
| | Eliza | 335 | Shoaff | Martha | 268 |
| | Elizabeth | 135 | Shoaft | —— | 183 |
| | Henry B. | 39 | Shobert | Elizabeth | 175 |
| | James R. | 37 | Shock | Nancy | 216 |
| | Jesse | 102 | Shockly | Polly | 116 |
| | Jesse Leroy | 327 | Shoeles | John | 84 |
| | Jessee | 106 | Shoemaker | Bargil | 82 |
| | Joel H. | 45 | | Elizabeth | 166 |
| | John | 230 | | Henry | 44 |
| | Joshua | 96,105 | | James | 44 |
| | Robert | 96,98,104,106, | | John | 176 |
| | | 135 | | Lucretia E. | 210 |

| | | | | | | |
|---|---|---|---|---|---|---|
| Sillings | David | 38 | Simson | Abram | 82 |
| | Malinda | 40 | Sinclair | Anna | 6 |
| Silman | Somers B. | 39 | | Elizabeth | 39 |
| Simcox | Wilson | 199 | | James | 82 |
| Simler | John | 98 | | John P. | 82 |
| Simmons | Abram | 327 | | Orlinda S. | 1 |
| | Charlotte | 54 | | Robert S. | 327 |
| | Emily | 217 | | Susan S. | 2 |
| | Emma | 213 | Sinclier | Sarah | 203 |
| | Gertie | 239,245 | Singer | James Harvey | 307 |
| | Jacob | 218,220 | | Jesse | 298 |
| | Jane | 53 | | Jesse George | 307 |
| | Mary J. | 226 | Singleton | Albert F. | 225 |
| | Nancy Ann | 207 | | Frances E. | 216 |
| | Rebecca | 200 | | George | 307 |
| | William | 201 | | George S. | 214 |
| Simms | Daniel W. | 327 | | James | 219 |
| Simon | Sophia | 327 | | Jesse A. | 298,307 |
| Simons | George W. | 83 | | Margaret | 117 |
| | H. | 93 | | Thomas | 117 |
| | Henry | 83 | | William | 116 |
| | J. | 87 | Sinks | Noah | 159,173 |
| | Martin | 83 | Sirit | Rachel | 9 |
| | Nathan | 93 | Sisson | Winfield E. | 327 |
| Simonson | Mariah | 50 | Six | James | 89 |
| | Minah | 54 | Sizelove | Catharine | 61 |
| Simpkins | Elias D. | 144 | | Charity | 60 |
| | Isaac | 154 | | Joseph | 61 |
| Simpson | ---- | 193 | Skelton | Charlie | 74 |
| | Emma | 207 | | Charlotte C. | 74 |
| | Gracie M.D. | 259 | | Festus | 74 |
| | J.T. | 89 | | Flora | 75 |
| | John | 58 | | John | 80 |
| | Josephene | 223 | | Malinda | 74 |
| | Lizzie D. | 70 | | Robert J. | 192 |
| | Martha | 209 | | Vaughn Wade | 74 |
| | Mary | 53 | | William N. | 75 |
| | Mary J. Lang | 65 | | Zacharia | 192 |
| | Milton A. | 70 | Skillman | Thomas | 172 |
| | Minah | 54 | Skilman | Court V. | 51 |
| | Oliver | 59 | Skiner | Smith | 83 |
| | Peter | 80 | Skinner | Ellen | 54 |
| | Polly | 60 | | Indiana | 38 |
| | Richard | 80 | | Wm. H. | 182 |
| | Robert | 88 | Slack | Clarissa | 61 |
| | Sally | 61 | Slagel | Lydia | 168 |
| | Sarah A.F. | 207 | Slagle | Elizabeth E. | 166 |
| | W. | 65 | | Joseph | 82 |
| | W.J. | 65 | Slater | John | 181 |
| Sims | Frederick A. | 327 | | Malinda | 182 |
| | Lester P. | 327 | | Mary D. | 180 |
| Sims | William | 51 | | Nancy Love | 306 |

| | | | | | | |
|---|---|---|---|---|---|---|
| Slaughter | David | 60 | Small | Reuben | 85,86 | |
| | James | 58 | | Ruben | 93 | |
| | James B. | 96,105 | | William | 185 | |
| | Margaret | 56 | Smalley | Elijah | 59 | |
| | Mary S. | 50 | | John | 53 | |
| | Moses | 135 | | Sarah | 198 | |
| | Rebecca | 176 | | Sarah Anna | 210 | |
| Sleeth | James K. | 162 | Smally | Catharine | 50 | |
| Sleight | Harriet M. | 200 | | John | 53 | |
| Slider | Anna L. | 308 | Smart | Hez. | 148 | |
| | Chester C. | 308 | | John P. | 202 | |
| | E.R. | 308 | | Joseph | 60 | |
| | James | 39 | | Thomas W. | 62 | |
| | Margaret | 27,30 | Smeltzly | Eleanor | 327 | |
| Slight | Jesse | 198 | Smiley | Eliza | 39 | |
| | Thomas | 195 | | John | 136 | |
| Sloan | Andrew | 151 | | Samuel | 136 | |
| | James | 148 | | William | 136 | |
| | Menda | 115 | Smith | ---- | 296 | |
| | Ruth Ann | 209 | | A.K. | 296 | |
| Slocum | Cornelius | 25 | | Abel | 115 | |
| | Jacob | 204 | | Abraham | 101 | |
| | Mary | 196 | | Abraham G. | 308 | |
| Slone | Andrew | 151 | | Adam | 35,40,43 | |
| | Davis | 154 | | Albert | 298 | |
| | James | 148 | | Albert P. | 327 | |
| Sloos | Peter | 135 | | Alice | 136 | |
| Slouterback | Daniel | 84 | | Andrew | 98,106,143 | |
| Slover | Abraham | 89 | | Andrew M. | 154,204 | |
| | John | 89 | | Ann | 39 | |
| Sluyter | May | 262 | | Asa Jr. | 40 | |
| Slythe | Jonathan | 37 | | Bettie Dufour | 327 | |
| | Robert | 33 | | Butler | 159 | |
| Small | Albert G. | 327 | | C.M.(Mrs.) | 123 | |
| | Amos | 84 | | C.W.M. | 89 | |
| | Archibald | 157 | | Carissa | 179 | |
| | Benjamin | 87 | | Cary | 158 | |
| | David | 149 | | Catharine | 24 | |
| | Elenor | 176 | | Charles | 102,105,160 | |
| | Elihu | 87 | | Charlotte | 207 | |
| | Gideon | 87 | | Chauncy P. | 41 | |
| | Henrietta | 185 | | Constantine | 87 | |
| | J. | 86 | | Dan | 151 | |
| | Jabez | 84 | | Daniel | 60 | |
| | Jesse | 93 | | David | 20,121 | |
| | John F. | 185 | | David Ernest | 308 | |
| | John W. | 185 | | Delilah | 46 | |
| | Joseph | 85 | | Della V. | 226 | |
| | Joshua | 93 | | E.R. | 154 | |
| | Josiah | 85 | | Eldridge And. | 308 | |
| | Josiah Jr. | 84 | | Eli | 228 | |
| | Nathan | 84 | | Eliza | 228 | |

**471**

| | | | | | | |
|---|---|---|---|---|---|---|
| Spacht | Elenor | 167 | Spicer | Alexander | 241 |
| Spalding | John A. | 37 | | Almina A. | 224 |
| Spanger | David | 22 | | Christena | 210 |
| Sparks | Amos | 61 | | Daniel | 244 |
| | Euphresine | 288 | | Fannie | 241 |
| | Frank Hugh | 327 | | George W. | 173,210 |
| | J. | 87 | | Jacob | 244 |
| | Mary | 48 | | Louis R.L. | 222 |
| | Moses | 121 | | Lucy | 243,245 |
| | Nappy | 52 | | Mary | 244 |
| | Rebecca | 117 | | Mary Ann | 206 |
| | Zachariah | 136 | | Mary Jane | 220 |
| Spaulding | George W. | 230 | | Minnie | 244 |
| | John | 230 | Spiker | Flora M. | 224 |
| Speakman | Phebe | 25 | Spinner | Augusta | 208 |
| Speaks | William | 44 | | Eliza | 227 |
| Spear | John | 89 | Spletstover | Anna | 200 |
| Spears | Andrew | 18 | Splitlog | Alex | 244 |
| | John | 82 | | Ida | 243 |
| | William | 136 | | Inez | 244 |
| Spease | Elizabeth | 320 | | Jacob | 244 |
| Specklemier | Mary | 117 | Spoor | Clara | 215 |
| Speelman | Aaron | 211 | | Della May | 210 |
| | Almira | 207 | | Filmore T. | 207 |
| | Hannah | 218 | | Helen H. | 210 |
| | Jacob | 89 | | Louisa B. | 198 |
| | Maggie | 223 | | Sarah M. | 215 |
| | Martha A. | 200 | | William C. | 198,213 |
| | Retta | 222 | Spore | Belle | 2 |
| | Richard | 89 | Spradlin | John | 55 |
| | Sarah E. | 225 | | Sarah | 54 |
| | Solomon | 200 | Sprague | George M. | 224 |
| | William | 202 | | Otis | 151 |
| | William V. | 228 | | Rosetty | 227 |
| Spell | Spencer | 87,89 | Sprall | Benjamin | 24 |
| Spellman | George F. | 298 | Spray | Sarah | 176 |
| | Mary C. | 200 | Spredgins | F.H. | 182 |
| Spence | W.F. | 85 | Springer | Albert N. | 266 |
| Spencer | Charles | 166 | | Albert(Mrs.) | 270 |
| | Charlotte | 57 | | Alfred Newton | 267 |
| | Elijah | 103 | | Edward | 136 |
| | Emily | 57 | | Ella | 270,271 |
| | Jacob | 87 | | Margaret | 51 |
| | Jenny | 303 | | Peggy | 51 |
| | John | 40,59 | | Sarah Ellen | 267 |
| | Lawrence | 120 | | William | 136 |
| | Stella | 303 | | William G. | 136 |
| | Thomas C. | 105 | Springhorn | Sophia Simon | 327 |
| | William | 98,104,106 | Sproatt | Emily | 40 |
| Spensor | George | 96 | | Isaac | 33 |
| | William | 96 | Sproule | James V. | 299 |
| Sphung | Alfred A. | 215 | Sproull | Margaret | 36 |

| | | | | | | |
|---|---|---|---|---|---|---|
| Stephenson | Andrew | 229 | Steward | Susanna | | 115 |
| | Catharine | 195 | Stewart | —— | | 80,182 |
| | Ciddie V. | 221 | | Amanda E. | | 203 |
| | J.W. | 247 | | Catharine | | 200 |
| | James C. | 216 | | Charles | | 82 |
| | John | 51 | | Cynthia Ann | | 44 |
| | John W. | 224 | | David | | 22,90 |
| | Joseph A. | 274 | | Eleazer | | 136 |
| | Laura C. | 227 | | Eli | | 136 |
| | Laura O. | 225 | | Elihu | | 82 |
| | Levi | 205 | | Eliza Jane | | 203 |
| | Mariah | 223 | | Elizabeth | | 22,42 |
| | Martha E. | 275 | | Elizabeth E. | | 308 |
| | Robert | 59 | | Hudson | | 85 |
| | Sarah E. | 222 | | Ida | | 270,271 |
| Steutsmar | Lewis M. | 220 | | Ida May | | 267 |
| Stevans | Benj. | 105 | | Isaac | | 22 |
| Stevens | Andrew J. | 220 | | James | | 17,21,27 |
| | Chancy | 52 | | James W. | | 43 |
| | Charles E. | 299 | | Jennie | | 213 |
| | David | 136 | | John | | 136 |
| | Isaac | 159 | | John Edward | | 266,267 |
| | James | 105 | | John W. | | 221 |
| | James M. | 52 | | Lementa | | 136 |
| | John | 101,105 | | Lewis | | 27,174 |
| | Joshua | 141 | | Mary | | 217 |
| | Mary E. | 1,225 | | Merchant | | 21,22 |
| | Nellie | 325 | | Minnie E. | | 331 |
| | Thomas | 107 | | Nancy Ann | | 200 |
| | Wash. C. | 246 | | Nella | | 27 |
| Stevenson | Albert | 200 | | Nelly | | 28 |
| | Albert C. | 215 | | Rebecca | | 22 |
| | Anderson | 229 | | Rebecca An | | 43 |
| | Cornelius | 197,203 | | Samuel | | 21 |
| | Geneva | 223 | | Samuel A. | | 79 |
| | Ida | 240 | | Sarah | | 57 |
| | James R. | 328 | | Sarah C. | | 182 |
| | Jane | 115 | | Stephen | | 22 |
| | Joanna C. | 313 | | William | | 37,38,57 |
| | Kenyon | 328 | | Wm. N. | | 231 |
| | Levi | 200,201,216 | | Zillah M. | | 10 |
| | Margaretta | 204 | Stibole | Joseph | | 88 |
| | Mary J. | 171 | Stickler | Elizabeth | | 225 |
| | Nancy | 116,209 | Stifel | Mary | | 120 |
| | Robert | 59 | Stigleman | Jemima | | 217 |
| | Rosanna | 201 | Stik | Samuel | | 169 |
| | Sarah J. | 205 | Stiles | Ellen | | 307 |
| | Stephen | 205 | | Robin B. | | 224 |
| | William | 226 | Stillwell | C. Darvin | | 75 |
| | William H. | 203 | | Charles E. | | 75 |
| Steward | Eliza | 42 | | Ethel | | 75 |
| | Nancy A. | 222 | | J. | | 89 |

| | | | | | | |
|---|---|---|---|---|---|---|
| Streete | William | 84 | Stuart | James | 28 |
| Streib | George | 89,90 | | Mary | 42 |
| | Jacob | 90 | | Mary Howell | 328 |
| | Jacob Sr. | 89 | | Rebeckah | 27,30 |
| | Jacob Jr. | 89 | Stubbs | Abisha | 58 |
| Stretch | James A. | 86 | | Abishar | 52 |
| Strew | Charles | 225 | | Elias | 55 |
| Strickland | Albert Eugean | 73 | | Felix | 57 |
| | Alice B. | 74 | Stubs | Abisha | 58 |
| | Alice M. | 77 | Stuck | Bartha | 224 |
| | Earl | 76 | | Daniel | 156 |
| | Elisha Sen. | 79 | Stucker | James | 44 |
| | Ethel | 76 | | John | 43 |
| | Irma | 77 | Studabaker | Hattie | 323 |
| | Karl | 75 | Studebaker | Ada L. | 328 |
| | L.J. | 74 | | Anne | 313 |
| | Larry Lynn | 77 | | Clement W. | 328 |
| | Larry W. | 76 | | Grace | 316 |
| | Lillian M. | 75 | Studyvin | Stephen | 81,82 |
| | Marvin | 77 | Stukenberg | August | 328 |
| | Samuel C. | 117 | Stull | Reginald B. | 328 |
| | Thelma G. | 74 | Stump | Florence A. | 10 |
| | William E. | 77 | Stunkel | Fridrich | 71 |
| Strickler | George | 82 | | Louis | 73 |
| | Jenet | 239 | | Maria | 70 |
| | Jeremiah | 82 | | Sarah L. | 71 |
| Striker | Nancy M. | 176 | Sturdavant | Maria | 51 |
| Strimback | Hannah | 216 | Sturdevant | Fear | 51 |
| Stringback | Menervia J. | 201 | | Maria | 51 |
| Stringer | John | 61 | Sturgeon | Margaret | 262 |
| | Thomas | 59 | Sturges | Amelia | 36 |
| Stringfield | William | 103 | Sturgis | Charles E. | 328 |
| | William R. | 109 | Stutesman | Jonathan | 176 |
| Strong | Josephine | 1 | Stuteville | Antoinette | 306 |
| | S.M. | 182 | | John G. | 190 |
| Strope | Mary R. | 207 | Stutsman | Daniel | 22 |
| Stroube | George | 308 | | David | 113 |
| | Owen L. | 308 | | George | 247 |
| Stroud | Joseph | 19 | | Jacob | 22 |
| Stroup | Daniel | 121 | | Lucy J. | 208 |
| | Jacob | 81 | | Mary | 22 |
| | John | 85,90 | | Samuel | 22 |
| | Joseph | 121 | Stutz | Joseph | 170 |
| Stryker | ---- | 279,284 | Stutzman | Elizabeth | 205 |
| | Charles S. | 172 | Suan | Syrus A. | 87 |
| Stuart | Benjamin | 114 | Sulgrove | Eli | 159 |
| | Charles | 118 | | James | 158 |
| | David | 27,29 | | James Sr. | 141 |
| | Eliza | 42 | Sulivan | Jeremiah | 89 |
| | Hol. I. | 120 | Sullender | Wallace | 24 |
| | I. | 283 | Sullivan | Charles | 299 |
| | Ithamer | 119 | | George W. | 328 |

477

478

| | | | | | | |
|---|---|---|---|---|---|---|
| Swearings | Christein | 103 | Tague | Mary E. | 306 | |
| | Christian | 100 | Tailor | Isaac | 44 | |
| Sweat | Frank | 112 | Talbee | Mary | 115 | |
| Sweateon | John | 114 | Talbert | George A. | 221 | |
| Sweeney | Nettie | 323 | | Sarah | 202 | |
| Sweet | Warren(Mrs.) | 9 | Talbot | Juliet M. | 44 | |
| Sweetland | A.T.(Mrs). | 13 | Talbott | Charles | 175 | |
| Sweetman | Martin | 247 | Talkington | Edgar | 328 | |
| Sweetser | James | 87 | Talor | Isaac | 114 | |
| | Philip | 60 | Talsier | Clar | 241 | |
| | Phillip | 137 | | Katie May | 242 | |
| Sweney | James | 20 | | Rosa | 243 | |
| Swick | Samuel | 43 | | Senia | 243 | |
| Swift | Ann | 59 | Talyor | Etta E. | 219 | |
| | Charley | 243 | Tanier | Chas.(Mrs.) | 5 | |
| | Ella Lyon | 328 | Tann | Mary Ann | 167 | |
| | Frank(Mrs.) | 13 | Tannen | Briant | 33 | |
| | S.A. | 81,82 | Tanner | Cornelius | 201 | |
| Swiggett | Thomas | 59 | | George W. | 213 | |
| Swinehart | Elizabeth | 166 | Tapp | Erna | 10 | |
| Swinn | Sylvester | 268 | Tarmon | Mary Alice | 12 | |
| Swisher | Anthony | 85 | Tarter | Enos | 336 | |
| | David W. | 85 | | Frederick M. | 336 | |
| | Isaac | 88 | | Peter | 336 | |
| | James | 91 | | Peter S. Sr. | 336 | |
| | Malinda | 168 | Tayler | Mariah | 169 | |
| | Matilda | 170 | Tayllor | Elizabeth | 33 | |
| | Thomas B. | 175 | Taylor | Addie | 307 | |
| Switzer | Andrew J. | 217 | | Albert H. | 198 | |
| | George W. | 328 | | Alex | 247 | |
| Swope | George | 86 | | Alfred | 201 | |
| | Joseph | 89 | | Anna | 37 | |
| | Marinda | 45 | | Artillis R. | 224 | |
| Swosick | Richard | 104 | | Chas.(Mrs.) | 2 | |
| Swoverland | Sarah | 173 | | Daniel | 54 | |
| Sybert | John | 107 | | Edward | 38 | |
| Sycloaff | Catharine | 38 | | Eliza A. | 200,205 | |
| Sylva | Carrie E. | 302 | | Elizabeth A. | 220 | |
| Symbler | John | 108 | | Elizabeth M. | 40 | |
| Symons | James | 83 | | Ellen | 195,203 | |
| | Jesse | 253,254 | | Ellen D. | 207 | |
| | Lydia | 253,254 | | Emeline | 226 | |
| | Sarah | 253,254 | | Florence | 225 | |
| Syron | Rose A.S. | 328 | | Frank Bursley | 328 | |
| | | | | George | 168 | |
| Taber | Ruth | 240 | | Grayson B. | 39 | |
| Tabler | Jacob | 107 | | Harriet | 32 | |
| Tacket | Delany G. | 170 | | Helen Ruth | 77 | |
| Taeller | Elizabeth | 33 | | Herbert C. | 328ʼ | |
| Taff | James | 156 | | Isaac | 44 | |
| Taffe | George | 153 | | Isaac S. | 230 | |
| | James | 156 | | Isabelle H. | 328 | |

| Surname | Given name | Pages | Surname | Given name | Pages |
|---|---|---|---|---|---|
| Thomas | Henson | 40 | Thompson | J.J. | 297 |
| | Hily | 55 | | James | 81,89,90,137,206 |
| | Isaac | 83,84,197 | | James B. | 299 |
| | Jeremiah | 87 | | James J. | 197 |
| | Jesse | 93 | | James S. | 223 |
| | John | 84,93 | | Jane | 137 |
| | John W. | 176 | | Jesse | 117 |
| | Joseph | 54 | | John | 18,20,137,144,152, 281 |
| | Julian | 200 | | John L. | 86 |
| | Lucy Adams | 329 | | John Lewis | 308 |
| | Mary E. | 220 | | John W. | 208 |
| | Milton | 85 | | Joshua | 26 |
| | Nelson | 83 | | Lawrence | 99,108 |
| | Noah | 86 | | Margaret | 167 |
| | Nora E. | 329 | | Margaret A.C. | 303 |
| | Oliver | 68 | | Maria | 208 |
| | Rachael | 173 | | Martha J. | 219 |
| | Rebecca | 171 | | Mary | 206 |
| | Robert | 137 | | Mary A. | 297 |
| | Rosetta | 68 | | Millie | 8 |
| | Samuel J.S. | 222 | | Nancy | 44,176 |
| | Sarah E. | 122 | | Nathan | 88 |
| | Simeon | 86 | | Pleasant M. | 220 |
| | T.E.(Mrs.) | 13 | | Rebecca J. | 329 |
| | Thomas | 42 | | Robert | 97,105 |
| | William | 87,172 | | Samuel | 23,41 |
| Thomason | Absalon | 82 | | Samuel Albert | 308 |
| | Absolem | 83 | | Samuel R. | 82 |
| Thommason | William P. | 44 | | Sarah A. | 212 |
| Thompson | ---- | 23 | | Sarah F. | 201 |
| | Adam | 156 | | Susan | 23 |
| | Alexander | 137 | | T.A. | 297 |
| | Alfred | 137 | | T.J. | 206 |
| | Andrew J. | 220 | | Thomas sr. | 137 |
| | Ann | 137 | | Thomas jr. | 137 |
| | Barnabas | 35 | | Vesta O. | 10 |
| | Blanche | 297 | | W.D. | 87 |
| | Celia | 137 | | Will(Mrs.) | 7 |
| | Charles N. | 329 | | William | 97,105,190 |
| | Clark | 64 | | William H. | 329 |
| | Cora Bell | 217 | | William P. | 105 |
| | Cynthia | 113 | Thorn | Henry S. | 49 |
| | Ebenezer | 121 | Thornburg | Fred | 120 |
| | Elijah | 115 | | Mary | 45 |
| | Elizabeth | 23,172,206 | | Mary C. | 212 |
| | Ezra C. | 121 | | Rebecca J. | 209 |
| | Fannie K. | 294 | | Shadrack | 83 |
| | Franklin | 88,90 | | Shadract | 81 |
| | George H. | 121 | | Shedrick | 82 |
| | Helen | 10 | | William H. | 220 |
| | Henrey | 105 | Thorne | S.S. | 85 |
| | Henry | 97 | | | |

| | | | | | | |
|---|---|---|---|---|---|---|
| Volkamer | William J. | 219 | Walden | John | 155 |
| Volker | —— | 71 | | Joseph | 37 |
| | Alma N.C. | 71 | | Rufus | 82 |
| | J. | 71 | | William | 45 |
| | L. | 71 | Waldenmaier | Benjamin C. | 329 |
| | Roy J. | 71 | Walder | Jacob | 198 |
| Vonnegut | Anton | 329 | Waldo | Wanda Lou | 251 |
| | Emma Schnull | 329 | Waldron | Lemon | 86 |
| Voorhees | Maria M. | 61 | Walk | Carl F. | 329 |
| Voorhis | James | 154 | | Julia E.F. | 329 |
| Vories | George W. | 207 | Walker | —— | 180 |
| Voris | Carlton W. | 218 | | Alfred | 336 |
| | James | 154 | | Ann | 336 |
| | Myrtillus J. | 329 | | Arthur | 336 |
| | Wm. | 89 | | Charlotte | 34 |
| Vornholt | Alms | 304 | | Christiana | 137 |
| Vosburgh | John H. | 202 | | Daniel | 137 |
| Voshall | Daniel W. | 41 | | David | 37,137 |
| Vreland | George W. | 46 | | Delilah | 38 |
| Vrooman | Henry W. | 329 | | Elizabeth H. | 329 |
| Vurpillat | Constance | 197 | | Emily | 336 |
| | | | | Fanny | 43 |
| Wabaugh | George | 88 | | George | 114 |
| Waddington | Augusta | 222 | | Harriet | 336 |
| | Ralph B. | 329 | | Henry | 336 |
| Waddle | John | 137 | | Jacob | 137 |
| Wade | Catharine | 173 | | Jefferson | 336 |
| | John | 96,102,108 | | Job | 336 |
| | Margaret A. | 3,329 | | John | 43,137 |
| | Sadie E. | 306 | | John M. | 329 |
| | Thomas B. | 203 | | Leonidas | 336 |
| Wadell | Eliza | 172 | | Lewis | 229 |
| | Rebecca Ann | 169 | | Margrett | 113 |
| Wadkins | Joel | 144 | | Mary | 336 |
| Waggoner | Alfred | 117 | | Matilda J. | 211 |
| | David | 51 | | Meredith | 336 |
| Wagner | David | 92 | | Nancy | 114,165 |
| | Fred(Mrs.) | 14 | | Thomas L. | 113 |
| | J.M. | 89 | | William | 239 |
| | Joseph M. | 329 | Walks | Samauel | 98 |
| | Sarah Hill F. | 329 | Wall | B. | 86 |
| | J.B. (Mrs.) | 5 | | David | 81,82 |
| Wailey | Sarah R. | 163 | | J.S. | 90 |
| Wainman | John Frederick | 309 | | James | 299 |
| | John Nelson | 309 | Wallace | Andrew(Mrs.) | 4 |
| Wainright | Vincent | 57 | | B.P. | 85 |
| Wainwright | Guy A. | 329 | | David | 49 |
| | Lucius M. | 329 | | George W. | 58 |
| | W.W. | 329 | | H.F. | 86 |
| Wait | Clarissa | 166 | | J.T. | 63 |
| Walcott | Benjamin D. | 329 | | John W. | 87 |
| Walcott | Gladys | 326 | | Joseph | 53 |

| Weathers | Thomas | 22 | | Weiberle | H.E. | 74 |
|---|---|---|---|---|---|---|
| Weaver | C.W.(Mrs.) | 5 | | | Henry E. | 77 |
| | David | 86 | | | Paul E. | 77 |
| | Elizabeth | 39 | | | Setta | 77 |
| | Franklin | 89 | | Weiche | Beatha | 211 |
| | Helen E. | 9 | | Weil | Tilla | 219 |
| | Martin | 175 | | Weir | John | 50 |
| | Mildred A. | 15 | | | John A.J. | 87 |
| | Nancy | 39 | | | Robert | 23 |
| | Thomas | 138 | | | Sophia A. | 297 |
| Webb | A. Marion | 6 | | Weisenburger | Lewis | 330 |
| | Abel | 58 | | Welborn | Anne Acton | 330 |
| | Daniel A. | 156 | | | George W. | 309 |
| | David | 138 | | | James Y. | 309 |
| | George | 86 | | | W.J. | 118,119 |
| | H. | 90 | | Welch | A. | 90 |
| | James A. | 86 | | | Abraham | 194 |
| | Jemima | 60 | | | Almeda | 337 |
| | Otto P. | 175 | | | Christopher | 52 |
| | William | 93 | | | David | 90 |
| | Zelia K. | 330 | | | Elizabeth | 224 |
| Webster | A.J. | 225 | | | Jacob R. | 337 |
| | Allen | 37 | | | James | 337 |
| | Elizabeth | 171 | | | Michael J. | 222 |
| | Geo. W. | 86 | | | Nancy Jane | 196 |
| | W.H. | 86 | | | Nina E. | 15 |
| | William M. | 82 | | | Patrick | 19 |
| | Wm. R. | 89 | | | Sally | 51 |
| Weckler | William | 168 | | | Sarah Melinda | 337 |
| Weddell | Dee | 298 | | Weldon | Benj. D. | 180 |
| Weddington | Thersia | 204 | | Well | Frederick | 219 |
| Wedington | Thursy | 202 | | Welleck | Michael | 169 |
| Weed | Eli B. | 225 | | Weller | Margaret | 335 |
| | Franklin D. | 224 | | | Phillip | 198 |
| | Sarah M. | 226 | | Wellington | William | 84,91 |
| Weeks | H.P. | 86 | | Wells | Ed. | 144 |
| | Minerva | 205 | | | Eli | 148 |
| Weer | Marjorie S. | 330 | | | Elizabeth | 42 |
| | Paul Wiley | 330 | | | Harriet M. | 4 |
| Weesner | Micajah | 92 | | | James | 204 |
| Wegner | Paul | 208 | | | Jesse | 138 |
| Wehe | Richard | 232 | | | Joseph V. | 36 |
| Wehrling | Celeste | 303 | | | Mary Wheeler | 330 |
| Wehs | Richard | 232 | | | Rebecca | 39 |
| Weiberle | A.M. | 74 | | | Sarah S. | 210 |
| | Albert C. | 74 | | | William | 47 |
| | Alice M. | 77 | | Welman | Orris | 276 |
| | Alma | 77 | | | Samuel | 98 |
| | Caroline | 74 | | Welsh | Alva | 212 |
| | Christian C. | 77 | | | Benjamin | 220 |
| | Ellen F. | 77 | | | Daniel | 86 |
| | Ernest | 74 | | | David | 88 |

| Welsh | Frank | 215 |
| | James | 56,172 |
| | James B. | 225 |
| | John | 34,220 |
| | Jonah | 87 |
| | Mahala | 213 |
| | Mary A. | 211 |
| | Mary C. | 213 |
| | Morgan | 216 |
| | Sarah Francis | 196 |
| | Vine | 204 |
| Wendell | Ephraim | 108 |
| Wennegar | Eliza | 226 |
| Wentrote | Sarah | 175 |
| Wentworth | Edward N. | 330 |
| | Hannah | 117 |
| Wentz | Abner R. | 217 |
| | Merideth | 213 |
| Werbalow | Mine | 212 |
| Werner | Ellie May | 212 |
| | Isaac | 207 |
| | Mary R. | 216 |
| | Peter | 202 |
| Werts | Henry | 109 |
| Wertsbaugher | Rebecca A. | 215 |
| Wertz | John J. | 174 |
| Weseman | Olga K. | 9 |
| Wesner | Jacob | 103 |
| West | Benjamin | 206 |
| | Chalista C. | 42 |
| | Eliza M. | 37 |
| | Hannah E. | 205 |
| | Harriett | 116 |
| | Henry F. | 122 |
| | Huldah | 33 |
| | Jesse | 98,104 |
| | Jessee | 107 |
| | John | 145 |
| | Mary | 197 |
| | William H. | 199 |
| Westbey | Harriet | 35 |
| Westfall | Albert | 88,90 |
| | Stephen | 98,107 |
| | Thomas | 88 |
| Westhaver | Cristena | 200 |
| | Mary | 201 |
| | Phebe | 208 |
| Weston | James | 62 |
| | Joseph | 53 |
| | William | 60 |
| Wetherhclt | Peter | 222 |
| Wetherill | Richard B. | 330 |

| Wetherow | W.B. | 90 |
| Wetzel | Julian S. | 330 |
| Whaley | Gendron M. | 330 |
| | Goodlet | 180 |
| | Nancy Jane | 172 |
| Wharton | —— | 138 |
| | Joseph | 138 |
| | Mary E. | 207 |
| Whartoner | Elizabeth | 55 |
| Whatener | Elizabeth | 55 |
| Wheat | Joseph | 97,101,104,110 |
| Wheatley | Elias | 232 |
| | Ella Cockrum | 330 |
| Wheaton | Charles | 69 |
| | Flora C. | 69 |
| | Madline | 51 |
| | Mavis | 78 |
| | Peter Winston | 70 |
| | Rebecca Ann | 281 |
| | Warren | 78 |
| Wheeler | Charles | 35 |
| | Ellen | 54 |
| | G. Bradley | 246 |
| | George | 38 |
| | Homer H. | 330 |
| | Isabel 'Hebe' | 138 |
| | Lawrence M. | 330 |
| | Margaret J. | 333 |
| | Mary | 330 |
| | Mary Ann | 208 |
| | Nathan | 138 |
| | Thos. | 99 |
| | Timothy | 103,109 |
| | Walton M. | 330 |
| | Walton Mark | 330 |
| Whenden | Thomas | 52 |
| Wherrott | Nancy | 334 |
| Wherry | David | 92 |
| Whett | Mary E.J. | 201 |
| Whimsey | Phelix | 101 |
| Whinnery | Joseph | 88 |
| | Mills | 81,88,90 |
| Whiper | Henry | 229 |
| Whipker | Henry | 229 |
| Whipple | Arta M. | 98 |
| | Peter | 241 |
| | R.T. | 105 |
| Whisler | Henry | 86 |
| | Jacob | 86 |
| Whistler | Jacob | 81 |
| | Jacob Sr. | 86 |
| | Samuel | 86 |

| | | | | | | |
|---|---|---|---|---|---|---|
| Wind | Hugh | 241 | Winters | Edmond | 89 |
| Windel | Amelia C. | 226 | | Josiah | 35 |
| Windell | Anthony | 108 | | Seth A. | 123 |
| Windisch | Frank | 219 | | Terrel | 144 |
| Windish | Clarra A. | 225 | | Thomas S. | 103 |
| | Rosa | 215 | | William | 101 |
| Windle | John | 102,109 | Winton | Gendron M.W. | 330 |
| Windsor | Rebecca | 278 | Wintworth | Daniel | 87 |
| Wine | Benjamin | 88 | | Wm. | 87 |
| | George | 88 | Wintzell | —— | 285 |
| | George W. | 88 | Wipperman | Franklin H. | 330 |
| Winegar | Mary | 213 | Wire | Peter | 121 |
| Wineger | Henry | 201 | Wise | Charles | 61 |
| Wines | Mahlon | 85 | | Conrad | 106 |
| Wingate | Joseph | 159 | | George | 99 |
| Winger | Otho | 330 | | Jacob | 98,107 |
| Wingfield | Cecil | 299 | | John | 98 |
| Wingon | Joseph | 89 | | John S. | 85 |
| Wink | Lewis Sr. | 120 | | Mahalia S. | 201 |
| Wink | Solomon | 120 | | Peter | 98,107 |
| Winkels | Edward | 155 | | Sarah Ann | 60 |
| Winkle | Jermiah | 109 | | Urias J. | 202 |
| Winn | Elizabeth | 56 | Wiseman | Andrew | 103,110 |
| Winney | Mary Jane | 240,243 | | James | 96,98,106 |
| | Reid | 239 | | John | 164 |
| | Thomas | 244 | | Melinda | 337 |
| Winnfield | Julia M. | 167 | | Philip | 96,99,109 |
| Winscott | Thomas | 57 | | Phillip | 104 |
| Winsell | George | 207 | | William | 101,104 |
| Winship | —— | 336 | Wishard | Elizabeth M. | 331 |
| | Elizabeth | 336 | | Frances S. | 331 |
| | Francis E. | 50 | | John | 139 |
| | Jabez L. | 59 | | Robert | 139 |
| | Julian | 59 | Wisner | David F. | 205 |
| Winslow | Althea | 327 | | Jacob | 108 |
| | Henry | 83 | Wispler | Jacob | 88 |
| | Hugh W. | 83 | Wistler | Jacob | 90 |
| | Jepe | 83 | Wiswell | Wm. Wallace | 283 |
| | Jesse | 83,95 | Witehead | Permelia | 195 |
| | Jesse W. | 84 | Witham | James | 174 |
| | John | 84 | | William H. | 217 |
| | Margret | 59 | Withers | Vivian | 10 |
| | Milton | 83,84 | Witherspoon | E.A. | 65 |
| | Nixon | 84 | | J.T. | 65 |
| | Seth | 84 | | Namie Lucelia | 65 |
| | Thomas | 84 | | Violet Ann | 64 |
| | William | 84 | Wixson | Willard W. | 331 |
| Winson | Wm. | 154 | Wolary | William | 90 |
| Winter | Henry | 168 | Wolcott | Adellia V. | 4 |
| | John | 101,108 | | Eben H. | 331 |
| | Thos. S. | 101 | | Lida Brown | 331 |
| Winters | Ann | 171 | | Roger | 331 |

| | | | | | | |
|---|---|---|---|---|---|---|
| Woolley | Ann | 172 | Wright | David | 91 |
| | William S. | 43 | | Edmund | 337 |
| Woolly | Samuel | 161 | | Edward | 153 |
| | Zachariah | 139 | | Eli | 97,102,106 |
| Woolman | Benjamin | 81 | | Ella M. | 225 |
| | Burl | 91 | | Ellis W. | 184 |
| | Burr | 88 | | Elmer | 337 |
| | S.H. | 81 | | Esther | 37 |
| | S.N. | 91 | | Fannie | 320 |
| | Samuel | 88 | | Frederick | 207 |
| | Woodson | 90 | | George | 146 |
| Woolpert | Andrew | 164 | | George W. | 309 |
| | Araminta | 171 | | Grant F. | 331 |
| | Hosea | 174 | | Harriet | 337 |
| | Mamine | 172 | | Harvy | 152 |
| Woolsey | Celia | 64 | | Henry | 61 |
| | G. | 63 | | James | 35,36,91,175 |
| | J.J. | 63 | | James A. | 84 |
| | Martha | 3 | | James W. | 185 |
| | Sarah A. | 63 | | Jesse | 161 |
| Wooton | Andrew | 85 | | Joel | 101,106 |
| Word | U.W.(Mrs.) | 12 | | John | 145 |
| Worden | Charles J. | 331 | | John E. | 184,185 |
| Work | Flora | 320 | | John H. | 206 |
| | John Jr. | 21 | | John S. | 331 |
| | Joseph | 87 | | John W. | 337 |
| Working | Caroline | 203 | | Jonathan | 96,98 |
| | Christina | 206 | | Jordon | 154 |
| | Magdalena | 209 | | Joseph | 106 |
| | Margaret | 198 | | Lavina | 170 |
| Worley | Willis W. | 205 | | Lewis P. | 337 |
| Worlow | Peter | 98 | | Lucretia N. | 331 |
| Worrall | Rachel | 30 | | Margaret | 184 |
| Worthington | D.(Mrs.) | 2 | | Mark E. | 223 |
| Wortman | Gertrude | 6 | | Mary | 318 |
| Wotson | Henry | 108 | | Mary R. | 206 |
| Wought | Jonathan | 109 | | Melinda | 337 |
| Wright | A.T. | 92 | | Nancy | 40 |
| | Aaron | 154 | | Nancy E. | 168 |
| | Admiral W. | 309 | | Nathan | 85 |
| | Alfred R. | 184 | | Noah | 151 |
| | Alice | 247 | | Reuben | 103 |
| | Burrell | 331 | | Robert | 83 |
| | Catherine | 179 | | Ruebin | 110 |
| | Chancy M. | 215 | | Ruel | 121 |
| | Charles | 83 | | Samuel S. | 214 |
| | Charles W. | 224 | | Sarah | 335,337 |
| | Charley | 337 | | Sarah Jane | 120 |
| | Christena | 212 | | Sarah Margaret | 265 |
| | Christopher C. | 184 | | Sidney A.M. | 171 |
| | Clabourn | 82 | | Thomas | 37 |
| | Dan. | 154 | | W.W.(Mrs.) | 3 |